Home-Work: Postcolonialism, Pedagogy, and Canadian Literature

28

REAPPRAISALS:
CANADIAN
WRITERS

Home-Work: Postcolonialism, Pedagogy, and Canadian Literature

Edited by
Cynthia Sugars

University of Ottawa Press

2004

REAPPRAISALS:
Canadian Writers

Gerald Lynch
General Editor

National Library of Canada Cataloguing in Publication

Home-work : postcolonialism, pedagogy and Canadian literature / edited by Cynthia Sugars.

(Reappraisals, Canadian writers ; 28)
Includes bibliographical references.
ISBN 0-7766-0577-1

1. Canadian literature – Study and teaching – Canada. 2. Canadian literature – History and criticism – Theory, etc. 3. Postcolonialism. I. Sugars, Cynthia Conchita, 1963- II. Series.

PS8021.H64 2004 C810'.7'071 C2004-901259-2

University of Ottawa Press gratefully acknowledges the support extended to its publishing program by the Canada Council and the University of Ottawa. We also acknowledge the support of the Faculty of Arts of the University of Ottawa for the publication of this book.

We acknowledge the financial support of the Government of Canada through the Book Publishing Industry Development Program (BPIDP) for our publishing activities.

UNIVERSITY OF OTTAWA
UNIVERSITÉ D'OTTAWA

Cover illustration: Charles Pachter, *Mooseplunge*
Cover design: Laura Brady

ISBN 0-7766-0577-1 ISSN 1189-6787

542 King Edward Street, Ottawa, Ont. Canada K1N 6N5
press@uottawa.ca http://www.uopress.uottawa.ca

Printed and bound in Canada

Contents

Postcolonial Pedagogies

Decolonizing the Classroom

Teaching/Reading Native Writing

Pedagogies in Practice

Historical Imperatives

Acknowledgements

I am grateful to the Social Sciences and Humanities Research Council of Canada for a grant that helped gather these scholars together. I am also indebted to the Faculty of Arts of the University of Ottawa for its financial support of this project, from its contribution to the 2002 conference, to their publication subvention, to its ongoing support of the "Reappraisals" series as a whole. My thanks to my Canadianist colleagues in the Departments of English at the University of Ottawa (especially Gerald Lynch) and Carleton University for their encouragement, advice, and participation at various stages in this project. I am also grateful to the two anonymous readers who responded so enthusiastically to this collection and offered insightful suggestions for its improvement. I would very much like to thank Charles Pachter for generously allowing me to use his *Mooseplunge* image on the cover of this book. And thank you to my two research assistants, Tobi Kozakewich and Amanda Mullen, both doctoral students in Canadian literature at the University of Ottawa, who were in on this project from the beginning. Finally, thank you to the contributors to this volume, for partaking with such commitment to what is surely destined to be an ongoing dialogue about postcolonial pedagogy.

Postcolonial Pedagogy and the Impossibility of Teaching: Outside in the (Canadian Literature) Classroom

CYNTHIA SUGARS

> [E]very true pedagogue is in effect an anti-pedagogue, not just because every pedagogy has historically emerged as a critique of pedagogy . . . but because in one way or another every pedagogy stems from its confrontation with the impossibility of teaching.
>
> — Felman 72

Canadian Literatures in the Classroom

> Writing Canadian literature has been historically a very private act. . . . Teaching it, however, is a political act.
>
> — Atwood, *Survival* 14

IN HIS ACCOUNT of the early years of the academic study and teaching of Canadian literature, Desmond Pacey provides a telling and amusing anecdote about colonial attitudes and Canadian literature in 1952.[1] Founded by A.S.P. Woodhouse at the University of Toronto, the inaugural gathering of ACUTE (Association for Canadian University Teachers of English) was to include a session on Canadian literature, the first conference session ever to be devoted to the subject.

Woodhouse had begrudgingly agreed to include the session on the program, but convinced that it would draw few attendees, he had assigned a tiny room on the second floor of Hart House to the event. Pacey, who with Earle Birney was scheduled to speak at the session, made his way that afternoon little expecting what lay ahead:

> As I reached the foot of the stairway leading to the second floor I was astonished to find that the whole stairway was jammed with people, and as I tried vainly to push my way through the mob I met Woodhouse, similarly struggling to get down.
>
> "Good heavens, Pacey," he said, "Something is very wrong. Two centuries of English literature—and only a handful of people. And on the other hand *Canadian literature* (said in a tone of supreme disdain)—and just look at the mob!"
>
> "I'm terribly sorry, sir," I said. . . . (69)

Pacey's memoir provides a vivid picture of the early struggles for Canadian literature in the Canadian academy, and his ingratiating apology to Woodhouse, while no doubt ironic, highlights the perceived subordinate status of Canadian literary study (and of the scholars involved in that field) at that time. Nor are the martial metaphors of struggle and combat accidental, for in those early days of Canadian literary study, a sense of embattlement was keenly felt. As late as 1973 Pacey was still asking, "We may have won a battle, but have we really won the war?" (69). I can even recall that in the late 1980s, as I was heading off to do graduate study in English, I was advised by a professor at the University of Windsor not to specialize in Canadian literature because, I was told, only inferior scholars embarked on that field.

I am pleased to say that I disregarded this bit of advice. Of course, my experience in the 1980s, and Pacey's in the 50s and 70s, were not isolated occurrences. Similar struggles had been taking place on university campuses for decades before that decisive ACUTE meeting in 1952. In her biography of Roy Daniells, *Professing English*, Sandra Djwa provides a lively account of some of the early struggles Daniells experienced when trying to introduce Canadian literature into the university curriculum at the University of Manitoba. Even his attempt to have Sinclair Ross's *As For Me and My House* introduced onto first-year reading lists in 1941 was met with flat out rejection by the university administration (209). Daniells's trials represent one moment in a long series of similar battles. While Heather Murray notes that the debates around the teaching of English literature in Canada in the late 1880s did not address the question of the teaching of what was still considered to be an immature Canadian literature (33), it wasn't long after that that Canadian texts were beginning to be introduced into university courses. Pacey dates the first university course in English Canadian literature at 1906–07, taught by J.B. Reynolds at an affiliate of the University of Guelph (the MacDonald Institute), followed the next year by Susan E. Vaughan at McGill (68; see also Fee and Monkman 1086). By the early 1920s, courses in Canadian literature were being taught by Alexander MacMechan at Dalhousie University and J.D. Logan at Acadia, with universities across the country following suit shortly after.

Nevertheless, as Lorne Pierce caustically observed in his 1927 foreword to *An Outline of Canadian Literature*, "Until recently, Canada enjoyed the unenviable distinction of being the only civilized country in the world where the study of its own literature was not made compulsory in the schools and colleges. Even now the effort is sporadic" (n.p.). Fee and Monkman echo this tentative note in their observation that many of the Canadian literature courses in the 1920s and 30s were offered only intermittently (1086). Pacey observed that by 1948 only two universities were offering full courses in Canadian literature: the University of Saskatchewan and the University of Guelph (67). Likewise, Malcolm Ross recalls that as a student at Queen's in the early 1950s, Canadian literature was represented as the last two weeks on an American literature course (180). A revolutionizing moment occurred in the summer of 1955, when a conference on Canadian writing organized by Roy Daniells and F.R. Scott in Kingston concluded with a session which proposed a series of "resolutions" to establish "a more prominent place to Canadian literature in school curricula, textbooks, colleges, and universities" (Djwa 311). As Djwa notes, this conference "laid the foundations for the future academic study of English and Canadian literature" (311).

An established curriculum in graduate and undergraduate training in Canadian literature did not become solidly entrenched until the 1960s, and even then it was on a somewhat ad hoc basis.[2] Such programs were dependent on the availability of professionals trained in the field of

Canadian literature as well as anthologies, journals, conferences, and critical studies devoted to Canadian authors, a phenomenon that was in turn dependent on what many, such as Robin Mathews and James Steele at Carleton University, saw to be the necessary "decolonization" of the academic study of English in Canada more generally. Despite the sense in the 1960s that the position of Canadian literature in the Canadian school and university system was secure, A.B. Hodgetts's *What Culture? What Heritage?* sparked a nation-wide controversy in 1968 when he critiqued the inadequacy of Canadian content in Canada's schools (comparable to the uproar provoked more recently by J.L. Granatstein's *Who Killed Canadian History?*). The result was a Royal Commission, launched in 1972 by the Association of Universities and Colleges of Canada under the chairmanship of T.H.B. Symons. Its mandate was "to study, report, and make recommendations upon the state of teaching and research in various fields of study relating to Canada at Canadian universities" (qtd. Cameron 21–22). The publication to emerge from this venture, *To Know Ourselves* (1975), was an extensive account of Canadian content in the university curricula and a series of recommendations to right the imbalance the Commission discovered. According to the Symons report, only 8 per cent of undergraduate courses in Canadian university English departments included on their syllabi any Canadian content (35), while the numbers for graduate-level training were even more meagre (36). A respondent to the Commission stated that "'until very recently, Canadian literature has been denigrated—as a swamp into which a serious scholar ventured at his (economic) peril'"; at the same time, "curriculum and planning committees . . . made it evident that they regarded [Canadian literature] as unworthy of serious study" (37). Symons's conclusion was far from sanguine: "there is no developed country in the world with comparable resources that devotes as little attention [as does Canada] to the support of its own culture and of education relating to itself" (15). Hence Pacey's question in 1973: "We may have won a battle, but have we really won the war?" (69).

Every year that I teach my introductory undergraduate survey of Canadian literature, I tell my students this story to demonstrate how recent, relatively speaking, the presence of Canadian literature is in Canadian university English departments. Each year, the students express surprise. For those students who regard the course as a nuisance, one additional requirement standing in the way of their completion of a university degree in English, this story of embattlement and struggle seems like ancient and irrelevant history. But for a few, it adds a tinge of immediacy and helps to historicize their presence in the CanLit classroom; it makes their participation in the study of Canadian literature meaningful. Indeed, what these various narratives remind one of is just how fraught the struggle for the academic study of literature in Canada was (a struggle which in the early century went hand in hand with the struggle for a Canadian literature more generally). As Stan Fogel has argued, the teaching of Canadian literature began as an "oppositional practice" (155) . . . as well as a postcolonial one.

The intersection between colonization and literary education, and the battles for the introduction of English literature into university curricula, have of course been famously outlined by Terry Eagleton and Gerald Graff. It is Gauri Viswanathan, however, who most explicitly examines the links between imperialism and the teaching of English. In *Masks of Conquest*, Viswanathan outlines the ways English literary study was used to "civilize" colonized subjects—both the British working classes and those "natives" in the imperial colonies, particularly India. Nor are the imperialist foundations of this educational project negligible for those of us teaching and studying into the twenty-first century. As John Willinsky points out, "Given the enormity of imperialism's educational project and its relatively recent demise, it seems only reasonable to expect that this project would live on, for many of us, as an unconscious aspect of our education" (3). This was true, of course, in Canada well into the late twentieth century, not only in terms of how the canon of Canadian literature came to be constituted and disseminated, but also in view of the assumed borderlines of nation-space and the myriad delineations thought to traverse and define the nation's people and the national *zeitgeist*. At the level of the professing of literature, Margaret Atwood and Robin Mathews provide informative accounts of the colonizing nature of English literature teaching in Canada in the late 1960s and 70s, and both were aiming to reach wider audiences in their plea for the decolonization of Canadian cultural education.[3] In various places Atwood describes the colonial educational curriculum in Canadian schools in the 1940s and 50s. In *Survival*, her "CanLit" manifesto of 1972, she describes the teaching of Canadian literature as "a political act. If done badly it can make people even more bored with their country then [*sic*] they already are; if done well, it may suggest to them *why* they have been taught to be bored with their country, and whose interests that boredom serves" (*Survival* 14; see also Atwood, "Nationalism"). Various fictional treatments explore similar terrain. The "Empire Bloomers" section of *Cat's Eye* is perhaps Atwood's most famous fictional account of this kind, while Wayne Johnston provides a memorable account of English literary education in a private college in Newfoundland in the early nineteen-hundreds, when the young Joey Smallwood is mocked by his headmaster for wanting to write the great Newfoundland novel that would teach the people about their culture and history.

Nevertheless, it is easy for those of us engaged in the teaching of Canadian literature to forget its once precarious footing. Like the institutionalization of English literature in the nineteenth century, and later of American literature (and, more recently, postcolonial literatures of various regions and nationalities), the institutionalized study of Canadian literature was a topic that provoked fierce resistance and contestation. At the turn of the twenty-first century, when postcolonial revisionings and pedagogical interrogations of the discipline of English literature have become more readily accepted, it is perhaps too easy to forget the radical, anti-colonial roots of the discipline of Canadian literature. This is doubly true in that much postcolonial criticism today has shifted its focus to the imperialist nature of the Canadian literary canon itself. Arif Dirlik's well-known critique of postcolonialism is a response to this blindness on the part of contemporary postcolonial theorists. His call to historicize the project of postcolonialism represents an attempt to call attention to anti-colonialist and nationalist movements that are often dismissed by contemporary postcolonial discourse, struggles which "did not presuppose an essentialist primordialism, but rather viewed cultural identity as a project that was very much part of the struggle for liberation that it informed" (15).[4]

Critics such as Heather Murray, Patricia Jasen, and Sarah Philips Casteel have undertaken a complementary project in their accounts of the foundations of English Studies in Canadian universities. However, Margery Fee's "Canadian Literature and English Studies in the Canadian University," together with the articles by Jennifer Henderson and Kathleen Marie Connor in this collection, is one of the few extended discussions of the normalizing and colonialist underpinnings of early Canadian literary pedagogy, and her account is illuminating for any discussion of the teaching of Canadian literature today. Fee highlights the integral ambivalence at the core of English-Canadian literary study. On the one hand, Canadian literary scholars defended Canadian literature on an evaluative, "universal" basis—as good writing in and of itself. On the other, they were bound to define Canadian literature as a separate category of study, and hence had to fall back on some notion of national distinctiveness. As a result, their defence of Canadian literature was seen to be tainted by political/national interests, which in turn rendered it suspect (and subordinate) in the eyes of those committed to a transcendent universalism. This is the contradiction that informs the theoretical stance of such a notable critic and professor of Canadian literature as Northrop Frye. However, it is also a contradiction that haunts postcolonial (re)imaginings of Canadian literature—hence today one finds postcolonial debates focusing on the contest between the national and the local in Canadian literary study, or between the national and the global, where the very term *Canadian* is seen to be complicit with either a conflating universalism or a debilitating parochialism (see Sugars, "Can"). The postcolonial, in a sense, allows one to be both of these simultaneously, and therefore also provides a useful meta-pedagogical entry into discussions of the teaching of Canadian literature. As Donna Palmateer Pennee puts it in her contribution to this collection, it enables one to straddle the national and the literary, a crossover that has formed the stumbling point of discussions of Canadian literature pedagogy from its very beginnings.

Postcolonial Pedagogies and the Unthought Known

> [Y]ou ask me if I can teach you, when I tell you there is no such thing as teaching, only remembering. (Socrates to Meno, in Plato, "Meno" 42)

This volume of essays is intended as a "reappraisal" of the field of Canadian literary study from the perspective of recent developments in postcolonial and pedagogical theory. At the outset, my aim was to gather a group of scholars to discuss the influence of the last few decades of postcolonial theorizing on the teaching of Canadian literature. In 1995,

Aruna Srivastava insisted that "postcolonialists must scrutinize the place that pedagogy . . . has in our theorizing of the postcolonial and that we must also *write* about it, talk about it, deprivatize the almost pathological isolation in which we teach" ("Introductory" 13). This collection represents an instance of such self-scrutiny, while also aiming to assess the extent to which this project has been inaugurated. The impetus behind this book, then, was to inquire whether we had, indeed, reached a point of reappraisal of the way we teach and think about Canadian literature. Had the focus of postcolonial perspectives on relations of power, and on the politics of cultural representation, influenced or altered the ways that Canadian literature was being taught? What impact was this having both inside and outside the classroom? Or, as some critics have suggested, was there evidence of a gaping divide between academic theory and pedagogical practice? In other words, despite the radical rhetoric of postcolonial literary theorists, did the approach to teaching Canadian literature, and institutional practice as a whole, remain as traditional as ever?

The articles gathered in this collection would seem to refute the despondent prognostications implicit in the latter questions. Most undertake an interrogation of the colonialist contours of traditional pedagogical paradigms. Many suggest alternative, "de-colonizing" ways to approach the study and teaching of Canadian literature. Many, in turn, wish to effect some intersection between intellectual discourse in the academy and social change in the world beyond. Yet this is not to say that every battle has been won, to echo Pacey once again. John Willinsky's 1998 *Learning to Divide the World* remains an important text for any discussion of the interrelation of postcolonial inquiry and pedagogical concerns. By highlighting the ways imperialism's legacy is at the foundation of Western education and continues to condition our ways of conceptualizing the world, Willinsky seeks to address those issues, namely issues surrounding race and racism, that were buried when they became too uncomfortable in a purportedly postcolonial world. On the one hand, postcolonial theoretical discourse has enabled this self-reflection to occur. Nevertheless, its scope has admittedly been limited: it has not enabled us to supersede engrained habits of defining and dividing the world, nor has it brought with it an adequate decolonization or reassessment of institutional structures and practices. Srivastava notes that despite the seeming entrenchment of postcolonial approaches in the academic study of English, "the often-unquestioned and rarely contested hierarchies and relations of power in the university or college" remain intact ("Introductory" 12–13). "Our analyses . . . of cultural texts," she states, "seem so often not to pertain to our institutional texts, discourses, and processes" (13). Gary Boire, Leslie Monkman, and Stephen Slemon, in this collection, likewise warn against a too ready complacency about the supposed post-colonializing of the Canadian academy. This impasse might suggest that we find ourselves at something of a turning point in the ways many of us, teachers and students, are reappraising the discipline.

Nevertheless, there have been some attempts in recent years to reconceptualize the academic study of literature. Perhaps the most concrete connections between the postcolonial and the pedagogical have been the various "post-colonializings" of the academy in the restructuring of university English departments across the country, such as those at the University of Guelph, Wilfrid Laurier University, the University of British Columbia, and the University of Saskatchewan. Paul Hjartarson's article in this collection, "Culture and the Global State: Postcolonialism, Pedagogy, and the Canadian Literatures," gives a timely account of similar discussions as they concerned the English program at the University of Alberta between 1999 and 2002.

Current considerations of the intersections between postcolonialism and globalization represent another way in which postcolonial theoretical discourse is shifting, although a number of critics, such as Leslie Monkman in this volume, continue to be skeptical about this so-called "reinvention" of the field. In a sense, postcolonial studies have always been "global," notably in their comparatist impetus and in their commitment to revealing the constructed nature of all claims to cultural purity. At the very least, postcolonialism has long been torn between competing pulls towards the global and the national/local. Mariam Pirbhai's and Heike Härting's contributions to this collection explore some of the conflicted dynamics of hybridity and diasporic identity in a global context. At the same time, there has been a concomitant reappraisal of the importance of national constructs within these debates, as, for instance, Donna Palmateer Pennee provides here. The opening section of this collection includes articles that argue both standpoints, while Brenda Carr Vellino's notion of a "Human Rights Pedagogy" offers a pedagogical paradigm that insists on a meeting point between the vectors of national and global citizenship.

In addition to the theory-versus-practice (ivory tower–versus–"real" world) dichotomy that continues to inform so much postcolonial and feminist thought,[5] an historicizing of the work we do as literary scholars might invite yet another set of questions about the implications of these interrogations (and post-colonializings) of a national pedagogy. In light of the struggle for Canadian literature over much of the twentieth century, to what extent could the various post-colonizings and deconstructions of the discipline, and of pedagogy itself, forfeit the victories that were so hard won earlier on? Might Charles Pachter's image of the plunging moose, which appears on the cover of this book, represent both a reappraisal of the field and a hint at its demise, perhaps even a wilful self-destruction on the part of its practitioners? This problematic is perhaps comparable to the dangers associated with the deconstruction of the unified subject for women and colonized subjects more generally: to what extent is Canadian literature, now that it has been secured as an independent field of study, in danger of being rendered obsolete, and is this cause for concern? And if so, how might one engage with what are undoubtedly important postcolonial and poststructuralist critiques of the field without dismissing the advances made by earlier Canadianists as irrelevant, or embracing them as safely beyond reproach? How, as I've asked elsewhere, might one undertake a post-colonializing of the postcolonial ("National"), and what would such a venture look like? It is this latter task—a reappraisal of an institutionalized Canadian literary postcolonialism—that many of the theorists in this volume are undertaking.

A scepticism towards the nationalist underpinnings of the Canadian educational establishment is not new. Even in 1968, when outlining the apparent crisis in Canadian education, A.B. Hodgetts decried the destructive influence of an over-defensive siege mentality when it came to Canadian studies:

> tensions and conflict are necessary and inevitable in democratic countries. . . . civic education in Canada has been too much concerned with consensus. The conflicts within our society have been swept under the classroom desk and grayed out in the textbooks. We have been unfavorably surprised by the number of teachers and administrators who continue to believe . . . in a definitive Canadian history textbook that "emphasizes our common achievements and eliminates controversy." (11)

All of the essays in this collection emphasize the agonistic intersection of Canadian culture and pedagogy. What is new is this volume's attempt to assess the influence of postcolonial theoretical interventions on these dynamics. While these essays range in tone from renewed optimism to outright skepticism, they share a sense of commitment to the task of inquiry, a feeling that what and how we teach matters, and a refusal to let one's "worrying about the consequences of knowing" (Willinsky 16) become consolidated into an active will not to know. While some critics here, such as Pennee and Carr Vellino, are interested in the renewed role of a civic education or "critical citizenship," they are alive to the contradictions and negotiations that such an enterprise necessitates. In fact, this awareness of what Diana Brydon calls the "cross-talk," a mode that is beautifully demonstrated by Danielle Schaub's example of teaching *In Search of April Raintree* in Israel, becomes part of the very pedagogy they propose. Hodgetts's comments, then, are clearly applicable to the field of Canadian literary study—not just to textual content or literary history, but also to the very establishment of the discipline itself. This may be what Gerald Graff intimates in his insistence on teaching the "conflicts" (261), but Smaro Kamboureli, Roy Miki, Diana Brydon, and others represented here are equally committed to interrogating these legacies of consensus in the broader public sphere. Likewise, the essays by Beverley Haun and Linda Radford insist on the importance of introducing a postcolonial pedagogy into the public school system.

These reflections might lead one to consider a series of unsettling questions about the institutionalized study of Canadian literature. What, indeed, has been swept under the carpet in the accepted history of the Canadian academy, such as I have outlined it above? Who remained on neither the winning nor the losing side of the battle, but in some invisible space in between? Do these figures represent the "unthought known" of a nominally postcolonial cultural history? The sort of micro-historical approach proposed by Heather Murray in these pages might be the very thing to mitigate against the "learned forgetfulness" that Willinsky identifies as integral to the Western educational project (263). It is for this reason that Willinsky proposes a self-critical "educational accountability" that would examine "how our own imaginations were educated" (239) and what our imperial-based education "has underwritten and who [*sic*] it has denied" (16).

For me, these and other pedagogical questions were sparked after years spent discussing such concerns with fellow teachers, students, and professors of Canadian literature. Whether between classes, at university functions, on examination committees, or even on social occasions, conversation always seemed to return to questions of pedagogy. How do you approach such-and-such in the classroom? What practical methods do you use? What do you do when . . . ? Even today, I still find myself exchanging teaching ideas, course outlines, and in-class exercises with colleagues—sometimes within my department, sometimes across the country via e-mail. The enthusiasm that keeps us asking these questions is reflected more broadly in the popularity of the pedagogy and professional concerns sessions at the annual meeting of the Association for Canadian College and University Teachers of English (ACCUTE) as well as the steadily growing "Approaches to Teaching" series published by the Modern Language Association—and not just on the part of Canadian literature specialists.[6] The energy and enthusiasm (and sheer numbers!) of those who attended the University of Ottawa's May 2002 "Postcolonialism and Pedagogy" symposium were a further indication of just how seriously Canadian literature professionals take their role as teachers, despite what we know is a too heavily weighted accounting of research and publication on the part of university administrations, not to mention the fact that so few PhD programs in English provide pedagogical training for their students.

In formulating this topic, I also wanted to see how recent developments in pedagogical theory were influencing Canadian literature teaching. How far had we moved from the original version of "professing" literature as a reference to, as Djwa describes it, "an individual who professed" (7). Was a critical pedagogy, such as has been outlined by Henry Giroux and others, having an impact on the teaching of Canadian literature? And could one even speak of "teaching" in the same ways any longer? Giroux discusses the "radical pedagogy" movement of the 1970s, and notes its flaws—namely that it persisted in being reactive rather than productive, failing to see schools "as sites of contestation, negotiation, and conflict" ("Schooling" 130). The essays gathered in this volume contribute to the growing body of theory in this revised wave of decolonizing pedagogical theory. Indeed, Giroux's articulation of a more accountable "critical pedagogy," or his sense of the role of "border pedagogy" in "developing a democratic public philosophy" (*Border* 28), has been taken up by any number of scholars and professors of postcolonial theory, in Canada and elsewhere. Spivak's call for "un-learning our privilege as our loss" is perhaps the most well-known example (*Post-Colonial* 9). Many of these critics have been influenced by Paulo Freire's oppositional pedagogy described in his 1968 *Pedagogy of the Oppressed*, and one can see the influence of Freire's and Spivak's work in a number of the essays in this collection.

In effect, what many of these theorists of a postcolonial or decolonized pedagogy are responding to is the disciplinary aspect of traditional pedagogy and the lack of self-awareness on the part of the professor/teacher/institution. As Freire puts it (citing Marcio Moereira Alves), the central problem in such knowledge-imparting contexts is "an absence of doubt" (23), which is echoed by Giroux's notion of critical pedagogy as a mode of "uncertainty" ("Popular" 252). Helen Hoy's work is an exemplar of some of these pedagogical arguments; in her account/performance of teaching Canadian Native women's writing in *How Should I Read These?*, Hoy insists on a kind of "methodological humility" in relation to her students and to the texts she/they read, a stance that is echoed in Laurie Kruk's and Margaret Steffler's contributions to this volume, and which in turn foregrounds aspects of the texts and classroom learning experience that are unanticipated.

Sherene Razack outlines some of the problems with a traditional disciplinary approach to teaching in *Looking White People in the Eye*, and has more recently spoken about the way the teacher aims to police or keep the peace in the classroom ("Bodies"). This can occur in an obvious way, in terms of the various ways students are "silenced" in the classroom, but also in terms of the ways certain patterns of thought are structured and imposed, the ways we are schooled in "borderlines and boundaries" (Willinsky 1; Giroux, *Border* 28–29), and the ways "our theories and practices are involved in a particular libidnal economy and social imaginary" (Todd 2). The linear, progressive teacher-to-student notion of knowledge transfer (the student as blank slate or empty receptacle; the teacher as holder and transmitter of information) has been challenged by numerous critics in recent decades who argue that the potential for critical self-reflection is belied by the very nature of this process. In *Revolutionary Pedagogies*, Peter Trifonas argues against this approach to teaching, describing it as a form of "pointless pedagogy": "A pointless pedagogy is not aimless, that is, without purpose or direction. It is, however, conceptually and performatively unquestioned . . . offering no opening toward a recognition of what it might exclude as being unlike itself" (xii). Sharon Todd's collection, *Learning Desire: Perspectives on Pedagogy, Culture, and the Unsaid*, likewise looks at the paradoxical nature of pedagogical desire (on the part of both teacher and student), the goal of which is to teach "the limits of knowability" (1). "Knowledge holds the promise of fulfillment," she argues, "but only for those who . . . place themselves in a position of 'feeling want,' of longing for that which they feel a lack. . . . [Education] 'creates' desire as it offers the means for its gratification" (2). Similarly, in *Scandalous Bodies* Smaro Kamboureli articulates a notion, taken up via the American deconstructionist Barbara Johnson, of "negative pedagogy." Based in a psychoanalytic questioning of cognitive self-presence, such a stance involves attention to what the teacher/professor/student does not know. The job of teaching brings with it a specific kind of responsibility (or what Razack refers to as a "politics of accountability"), a responsibility that "entails the recognition that what we know may already be contaminated by what we do not know, and vice versa" (25). As Kamboureli states, "negative pedagogy redefines the object of knowledge as nothing other than the process leading towards ignorance" (25).

The lack of self-consciousness exhibited on the part of a disciplinary pedagogy and its practitioners is precisely what theorists of postcolonial approaches to culture and society oppose. Connected to this, however, is the question of whether postcolonialism is always pedagogical, always containing within it some notion of its interventionist—and possibly didactic—potential. And where does one draw the line between this and the will to discipline? This is something that Maria Campbell recognizes only too well in her response to Linda Griffiths's well-intended attempts to "learn" her: "'When the student is ready, the teacher is there, so the teacher can learn'" (Griffiths 89). Eve Kosofsky Sedgwick raises a similar concern in her interrogation of typical constructions of student-teacher transference: "Is it true that we can learn only when we are aware we are being taught? . . . It's so often too late when we finally recognize the 'resistance' . . . of a student/patient as a form of pedagogy" (153–54). These are some of the questions that recent postcolonial theorists have been directing towards the so-called "mission" of postcolonial theory itself. To what extent does the postcolonial need to be post- or de-colonized? This interrogation has been especially forceful among anti-racist and anti-classist critics, such as

Aruna Srivastava, Arun Mukherjee, Roy Miki, Terry Goldie, Gary Boire, and Roxanne Rimstead, who see in current mainstream Canadian critical discourse a universalizing, obfuscating, and co-opting tendency.

The notion of a postcolonial pedagogy also entails an accountability beyond the confines of the classroom. Some critics have written about this in terms of a critical citizenship (see the essays by Pennee and Carr Vellino in this collection). Giroux, for instance, outlines his conception of border pedagogy as a means of linking "the notions of schooling and the broader category of education to a more substantive struggle for a radical democratic society" (*Border* 28), while Willinsky sees his inquiry into the imperialist legacy of education as a means to "renew connections between education and the arts as an intellectual enterprise of consequence in the world" (240). Others, following Spivak's recent work, speak in the context of increasing globalization and the necessity of a form of responsive and responsible "transnational literacy." These interrelated understandings of a critical postcolonial pedagogy extend Homi Bhabha's notion of the pedagogical versus the performative as he outlines it in "DissemiNation." Bhabha defines the pedagogical in terms of a sense of authority and teleology (the linear, rationalist narrative highlighted by many of the theorists noted above). The normalizing nature of the pedagogical, he argues, is what characterizes a traditional "nationalist pedagogy" (145), and is likewise what informs the "pedagogies of patriotism" identified by Eva Mackey in *The House of Difference* (59). The performative, by contrast, refers to the ways people are subject to the process of signification, and how the pedagogue is interpellated by the very texts/concepts he/she is intent on disseminating. Many contemporary theorists of a postcolonial pedagogy are interested in the various ways one might "perform" the pedagogical, as well as how one might "teach" the performative. In effect, this is what I mean by a post-colonializing of the postcolonial. It represents an attempt at an awareness of one's positioning vis-à-vis the national (and possibly even postcolonial) pedagogical imperative, and a further attempt to interrogate it in various ways. This might occur on a practical level in terms of one's approach to a text in the literature classroom, or as a reassessment of historical and cultural metanarratives, or as a re-evaluation of critical responsibility within national and global contexts, or even as a sense of the ways Canadian culture is interpellated by intranational and international communities more broadly. The latter is in part what Len

Findlay intends in his call to "always indigenize!" in relation to the intellectual pursuit and transmission of knowledge. This process of "indigenization"—very different from Terry Goldie's and others' notions of the settler-invader's indigenization attempts as a means of becoming "Indian"—would represent one way of bringing the repressed contents of Canadian history and culture to the fore in individual performances of Canadian pedagogy.

The emphasis on what we do not know, as cultural commentators and students, can have another inflection. The critical pedagogue might want to keep in mind that there are some things that she does not know that she knows. British psychoanalyst Christopher Bollas refers to this as the "unthought known," and there are certainly various levels of "unthought knowns," especially in view of the transferential teaching situation, that impinge upon and enrich the learning experience for both teacher and student. Connected to this are theories of location and agency, particularly those which view the classroom as a site of production. As Richard Cavell argues, the teaching context is "not a unified space but a number of transvestic sites that are *produced* by and through the agendas of those who participate in it, including the instructor" (101). Socrates put this into words well before psychoanalysis tried to theorize it. In the excerpt from his dialogue about knowledge and teaching that forms the epigraph to this section, Socrates insists on teaching as "remembering."[7] This has overlaps with bell hooks's conception of an "engaged pedagogy" in *Teaching to Transgress* (15), in the sense that what these critics emphasize are the intangibles of pedagogical transference. I mean *transference* here in the psychoanalytic sense, in terms of the multi-directional psychic exchange, on various unconscious levels, between two or more people, not in terms of an overt "transfer" of information from teacher to student. This is certainly related to the approach that Arun Mukherjee is advocating in her contribution to this collection when she stresses the imperative of acknowledging psychic exchange within the classroom and addressing the reality of pedagogical trauma; Gerry Turcotte invokes a similar approach in his notion of a pedagogy of the uncanny. Shoshana Felman speaks of this in terms of the "pedagogical revolution" sparked by the discovery of the unconscious: "As a process that gives access to new knowledge previously denied to consciousness, it affords what might be called a lesson in cognition (and in miscognition), an epistemological instruction" (76).

Lawrence Grossberg describes the pedagogical process in similar terms, stressing the importance of "listen[ing] for the 'stutterings,' the unexpected dialects and misspeakings, the unpredicted articulations" (20). Forfeiting one's control over the pedagogical transference might be one way of allowing unconscious contents—subjective, historical, cultural—to speak . . . which might in turn be one way of understanding how a pedagogy might be on its way to becoming *post*-colonial.

"Mooseplunge": From Risky Stories to Fragile Texts

> Imperialism afforded lessons in how to divide the world. . . . Its themes of conquering, civilizing, converting, collecting, and classifying inspired educational metaphors equally concerned with taking possession of the world—metaphors that we now have to give an account of, beginning with our own education. (Willinsky 3)

Perhaps my greatest surprise when I started to edit the submissions for this volume was the number of contributors who chose to discuss the encounter between national pedagogy and globalization—and further, to define where a postcolonial approach would fit in this discourse, if at all. This redirection has been initiated in part by Spivak's shift in focus from a decolonizing of traditional pedagogy toward a pedagogy of transnational literacy, a project begun in "Teaching for the Times" and in *Outside in the Teaching Machine*, and later extended in *A Critique of Postcolonial Reason*. However, in the context of discussions of Canadian literature pedagogy, this shift in focus represents a relatively new direction in Canadian theoretical discourse. The section of this volume entitled "National Pedagogy and Globalization" gathers six essays that approach this topic from different perspectives.

Smaro Kamboureli's discussion of the culture of celebrity in Canada takes as its impetus the notorious "Canada Reads" contest launched on CBC Radio in 2002. Her essay explores the ways professional postcolonialism and the culture of celebrity have become implicated in the service of a national pedagogy. This culture of celebrity is committed to a particular kind of "global" national ideal, figured euphorically as a "nation of plenitude" (52), an ideal which is belied by the very tentative nature of

Canada's postcolonial status. The supposed harmonization of cultural differences embodied by this ideal is epitomized in the reception of Michael Ondaatje's *In the Skin of a Lion*, the book that won the Canada Reads contest in 2002. This celebration of Ondaatje is based on an erasure of certain parts of history, which in turn supports the nation's role as pedagogue and reproducer of a sanitized, if globalized, cultural memory.

Wishing "to forge international connections beyond those associated with older notions of 'universalism' and newer notions of 'globalization,'" Diana Brydon invokes "Zygmunt Bauman's definition of globalization as not about what 'we wish or hope *to do*' but rather 'about *what is happening to us all*'" (60). Given the reality of this global context, Brydon argues, we "need some way to signify the reclamation of agency, a reclamation that can no longer be claimed at the national level alone." In this way, she undertakes a shift from a nation-based "postcolonial" vision of cultural-historical relationships, and substitutes Spivak's call for a "transnational literacy." As Brydon argues, "Transnational literacy expands critical literacy into a more empathetic mode of reading that Spivak calls 'critical intimacy,' which must then be directed to the task of understanding new modes of globalizing power and the ways in which they have easily co-opted certain forms of now-established postcolonialism . . . to their agenda" (62). It is such a mode of reading that Brydon aims to explore in her classroom teaching by emphasizing the "cross-talk," the "contrasting assumptions, expectations, and understandings of the terms of classroom engagement, the object of study, and the function of education within the nation" (57–58). Ultimately, Brydon is asking, "How may these cross-currents be negotiated so that genuine learning can occur?" (58).

Donna Palmateer Pennee's article, "Literary Citizenship: Culture (Un)Bounded, Culture (*Re*)Distributed," in part offers a direct response to Brydon. Concerned that the focus on the current era of globalization as a "post-cultural moment" (in the sense that cultures are no longer considered to be local or "bounded") risks an emptying out of the significance of the local, Pennee aims to resuscitate the vector of the national for strategic means. Primarily, she is interested in the potential of the national as a forum for "literary citizenship." In this way, she focuses on what she considers to be the realm of the "*not negligible*" in her teaching of Canadian cultural studies. "For the time being," she argues, "there is no question of doing without the national; it is rather a matter of doing the national differently" (83).

Roy Miki's "Globalization, (Canadian) Culture, and Critical Pedagogy: A Primer" explores the ways the social implications of pedagogy must be moved to the forefront of our work as professors and academics. As Miki argues, "Attention to the pedagogical scene of our practices would help us account for the contingencies of our own location(s)—whether in the classroom, or in our research and writing, or in our social and cultural relations with each other" (97). This critical engagement, he hopes, will enable us to address the changes affecting all of us as we negotiate the accumulating indeterminacies prompted within an era of increased globalization. In the process, critics might be able to rearticulate those limits of the nation that have been brought to light by the global.

Paul Hjartarson opens his essay by inquiring into the very usefulness of the term *postcolonialism* at this historical juncture. How, he asks, "do we meaningfully separate postcolonialism from the many other developments, such as postmodernism, cultural studies, critical race and critical legal studies, and globalization, that have transformed both the discipline of English and our teaching in the past several decades?" (102). Postcolonialism, he argues, has not adequately addressed its relation to the nation-state, which renders its relation to a category titled "Canadian literatures" problematic, especially in an era of "globalized literary studies" (104). Hjartarson explores these questions by focusing on a particular case in point: the revision of the University of Alberta's English curriculum from 1999–2002. Even as postcolonial critics and theorists increasingly find themselves addressing the interrelations of postcolonialism and globalization, it is finally impossible, Hjartarson argues, "to theorize either the postcolonial or the global adequately without taking nation-states and their cultures fully into account" (113).

Leslie Monkman takes as his focus the anthologization of Alice Munro in *The Norton Anthology of English Literature* in order to demonstrate the conflicted relationship of national and global perspectives. In his view, "the study of Canadian literature has not been a 'very powerful force' in our discipline over the past 25 years," and as a result, the "failure to acknowledge the *actual* status of Canadian writing in English in our curricular structures leaves us badly positioned to define appropriate local strategies for addressing . . . 'globalizing literary studies'" (122–23). The negotiations involved in the restructuring of the *Norton*, Monkman argues, have ultimately been disappointing. This process has not moved us towards a more equal representation of English literatures in their pluralities, but has instead moved us into the realm of a "containing" Global Lit (126), with all of the negative connotations that epithet implies. What gets forgotten in the various critiques of nationalist discourses is "an acknowledgement of existing curricular power relations" (129). In agreement with Pennee, Monkman is arguing for a form of "strategic nationalism" (and not, of course, merely Canadian nationalism), which will enable continued attention to individual locations of context and production (129), while nevertheless remaining cognizant of the disabling nature of nationalist configurations.

The second section of this volume, "Postcolonial Pedagogies," gathers essays which in some way delineate a project for a postcolonial pedagogical approach. In "Everything I Know About Human Rights I Learned from Literature: Human Rights Literacy in the Canadian Literature Classroom," Brenda Carr Vellino outlines her project for a human rights pedagogy in her Canadian literature classes. In her view, the absence of substantive education in the fundamental instruments, institutions, processes, and consequences of democracy in even the most obvious disciplinary contexts is a significant omission in light of the critical role the UN envisions for human rights literacy. Making the case that literature participates in international human rights culture because of its special ability to evoke ethical empathy, Carr Vellino works from the assumption that the classroom is an arena of advocacy work. Human rights pedagogy, she contends, moves analysis out of the abstract and into the realm of direct intervention in public-sphere deliberation.

In "Compr(om)ising Post/colonialisms: Postcolonial Pedagogy and the Uncanny Space of Possibility," Gerry Turcotte offers a provocative proposal for a pedagogy of the uncanny. Beginning with a personal account of his experience organizing a conference on postcolonial theory at the University of Wollongong, and notwithstanding the numerous pitfalls in any idealistic postcolonial endeavour, Turcotte reiterates the ways unsought-for moments of uncanny disruption and slippage can be used for productive ends. This is what Turcotte identifies as a means to "gothicize" literary institutions (163). A postcolonial pedagogy, he proposes, will enact a "moment of unsettlement: this moment where our own solid ground is shown to be both substantial and insubstantial, simultaneously" (158). Turcotte thereby echoes a number of other theorists, including Brydon and Mukherjee in this collection, vis-à-vis the importance of making use of those moments of ambivalence and tension in the literature classroom: "To negotiate these tensions," he argues, "is not only an intellectually necessary critical response, but a sound pedagogical practice, producing at best an uncanny space of possibility" (159).

Beverley Haun moves the discussion in an important direction by shifting from the university context to the sphere of public education, taking as her focus the introduction of a postcolonial pedagogy in public-school teaching. Her goal is to transform the ways teachers and students engage with issues of public memory and literary texts by refocusing teacher training and curricula through a postcolonial lens. Haun's paper is at once a theoretical discourse and a practical initiative, for she concludes her discussion by providing a detailed outline of concrete suggestions for implementing a postcolonial supplement into school curricula. In so doing, Haun hopes to find a means of enabling "the participants to transform any Western pedagogical experience into a postcolonial one" (178).

The section entitled "Decolonizing the Classroom" gathers essays that focus on the various silencings and oppressions that can take place in institutional classroom settings, especially with regard to race and class. Arun Mukherjee shifts the emphasis from the student to the teacher, focusing on racism in the classroom and the effect it has on women professors of colour. Noting the more usual emphasis on the abstract, theoretical aspects of critical pedagogy, Mukherjee examines the psychodrama and pain that occur in classroom situations where "fragile texts" are being discussed (195). By turning "the searchlight of hindsight" (200), as she beautifully phrases it, Mukherjee focuses on her personal struggles to navigate "the tangled emotions and thoughts that reading and teaching these texts have evoked" (196).

According to Terry Goldie, postcolonialism is in danger of becoming "post-ideological" (223) in the sense that everything to some degree can be said to have become postcolonial. Goldie is particularly concerned with the confusion of race with "postcolonial," and the ways this fusion effects an erasure of the class aspects of the subaltern. If many postcolonial theorists and professors construct the literature of the postcolonial subject out of a need to locate the subaltern, the Canadian devotion to multiculturalism has led to a "mis-recognized subaltern" (227). In the university English course, a place devoted to bourgeois professors and bourgeois students, those working in postcolonial approaches to Canadian literature, Goldie argues, must trace ethnicity and race in ways that attempt to disrupt Whiteness while also disrupting our comfortable class(room) locations.

Gary Boire continues this emphasis on "the uncanny presence of social class" (229) in the teaching of Canadian literature and in the functioning of the institution as a whole. In this respect, Boire's essay, with Monkman's, Goldie/Meer's, and Mukherjee's (and, in the afterword to this volume, Slemon's), stands as an important document of institutional critique. In his view, "radical pedagogy cannot exist within the precincts of the university" because of the pernicious effects of "endowed privilege," which works "to maintain a conservative agenda" in the university (230). Boire's account functions as a sobering wake-up call, particularly for those who might be tempted to feel complacent about the emancipatory and democratizing effects of the introduction of postcolonial theory into the academy. Boire highlights the ways the supposedly enabling and ennobling rhetoric of postcolonialism has itself been co-opted by other, often economically driven, agendas, and proposes three areas for reconsideration: outreach, administration, and careerism.

If Mukherjee, Goldie, and Boire explore the vestiges of Empire in our pedagogical practices, Rob Budde highlights the ways the discourses of Eurocentrism and racism are all too present in the contemporary Canadian cultural landscape. Budde makes use of selected examples of such materials in his classroom teaching. In "Codes of Canadian Racism: Anglocentric and Assimilationist Cultural Rhetoric in the Classroom," he demonstrates how the rhetorical devices used in media, letters, literature, government policy, and cultural theory buttress and substantiate continually evolving racist ideologies. Through a creative adaptation of these texts as pedagogical tools, he argues, teachers and students can confront and reassess personal and cultural assumptions about race.

Heike Härting continues the focus on globalization and postcolonial studies in the fourth section of this volume, "Reading/Teaching Native Literatures." Focusing on Jeannette Armstrong's novel *Whispering in Shadows,* Härting explores the ways the novel repositions concepts of cultural hybridity in the context of recent theories of globalization. By dramatizing cultural hybridity through the perspective of indigenous resistance movements, Armstrong contests typical understandings of hybridity as a metaphor for cultural ambivalence or global biodiversity. In both cases, questions of social justice are reduced to symbolic forms of representation. The struggle against neo-colonial globalization outlined in Armstrong's novel through the metaphor of "cell memory" involves a shaping of the global present through interrelationships of the land, the body, and the community. By considering the cultural and eco-biological effects of global restructuring, Härting demonstrates how the study and teaching of Canadian literature might be situated within the field of globalization studies.

The remaining essays in this section focus very closely on practical instances of teaching Native literatures in the university classroom. Susan Gingell's "Teaching the Talk That Walks on Paper" discusses the problems of teaching Native orature and suggests some strategies for doing so. Gingell notes the recent call to include the teaching of Aboriginal oral traditions in university curricula; however, teaching this material is not without its attendant difficulties. Providing a lively and exemplary account of some of the problems incurred in attempting to "translate" this material from page to voice, Gingell takes as a case study her experience teaching the versions of Aua's songs reproduced in Goldie and Moses's *Anthology of Native Literature*. Among the pedagogical challenges, she argues, is communicating that the aesthetics of orature are not identical to those of literature but are directly related to the demands and contexts of particular oral performances.

Laurie Kruk's account of her experience setting up a Native literature course at Nipissing University engages with various strategies for sharing classroom power. Kruk is particularly interested in what happens when non-Native professors and/or readers "speak for" writers whose experience has traditionally been colonized and misunderstood by the dominant White majority. She speaks from her experience as a non-Native instructor developing such a course intended primarily for non-Native students. How, she asks, does one do so without re-colonizing?: "Is the purpose to engage honestly and fully with [Native literature's] differences or difficulties? Or, to seek out a reflection of our own needs, questions, concerns?" (304).

Danielle Schaub presents a fascinating case study of her experience teaching Beatrice Culleton Mosionier's *In Search of April Raintree* to university students in Israel. By analyzing the strategies used in Canadian texts of resistance, students in other geopolitical contexts can examine how minority groups elsewhere in the world manage to express antagonism and establish agency. *In Search of April Raintree* becomes a useful text for Israeli students of different backgrounds—Muslim, Christian, Jewish, Druze, Beduin, or atheist—for the very reason that it does not allow easy resolutions surrounding questions of colonialism and identity. From her reading of students' responses to this novel, Schaub shows the often wrong-headed assumptions we make about ourselves and others, often in the name of "postcolonial" enlightenment, and she demonstrates how these assumptions can be used as a positive lesson in conflict resolution. The "real-world," pedagogical impact of Schaub's approach is insightful.

The section entitled "Pedagogies in Practice" contains essays that focus on a particular pedagogical moment or practical approach in the teaching of Canadian literature, and offers an important complement to the more theoretically focused pieces that comprise the opening sections of this volume. A focus on practical experience and strategies was evident in the essays by Gingell, Kruk, and Schaub in the previous section, and this emphasis continues here. Misao Dean's evocative and poignant account of her father's canoe paddle offers an important discussion of the profundity of objects in our conception of ourselves as individuals and as Canadians. Dean uses her personal experience to discuss the ways material "things" can function as a focus of analysis in the postcolonial classroom. Because they endure over time, objects serve to naturalize and reproduce particular cultural and national traditions. The essay suggests ways that objects might be interrogated in the classroom in terms of how they contribute to myths of individual and national identity, and how in contexts such as museum displays and collections, they work by "stabilizing the shifting and changing self-representations of cultural collectivities" (348).

Margaret Steffler delineates a postcolonial approach for teaching postcolonial texts, focusing on the ways language collisions can be used constructively in the teaching of such Canadian works as Alistair MacLeod's *As Birds Bring Forth the Sun*, Rohinton Mistry's *Tales from Firozsha Baag*, Michael Ondaatje's *Running in the Family*, Thomas King's *Green Grass, Running Water*, and Rudy Wiebe's *The Blue Mountains of China*. Her interest is in the ways languages exist in a state of collision in these texts rather than reaching some kind of resolved hybrid form. This state of tension, she argues, is often at the centre of the text in question, and remains that which teachers and students alike are drawn to confront. Such moments in these works help to break down assumptions about ownership of language, and serve to position the reader as Other in relation to the text. Experiencing the inaccessibility of words on the page, she argues, can be a powerful teaching moment when students suddenly "feel" their exclusion through their position as reader.

Lisa Grekul's contribution examines the marginalization of Ukrainian Canadian literature in Canadian literary studies and suggests new approaches for incorporating it into the pedagogical canon. Despite the increasingly heterogeneous nature of the Canadian literary canon, Grekul argues, Ukrainian Canadian writing continues to be under-represented. She lays the responsibility, in part, on Canada's multicultural policy, which segregated isolated groups from the Canadian mainstream. Many of the texts that she considers openly criticize multicultural ideology and its repercussions; however, as long as these authors continue to be read through an ethnographic lens, they will fail to have their voices heard beyond the local Ukrainian Canadian community.

Mariam Pirbhai's "To Canada from 'My Many Selves'" appraises the impact of South Asian diasporic writing in English on pedagogical and theoretical approaches to Canadian literature. Her study highlights the diversity of "South Asianness" in Canada, thereby providing a more culturally and historically grounded understanding of writers who otherwise get subsumed as "representatives" of South Asian populations. Pirbhai brings us back to the global dimensions of literary study, emphasizing the transcultural over the multicultural by focusing on the global reach of South Asian diasporic populations. The consideration of a shared diasporic experience necessitates an interdisciplinary approach to literature that neither erases difference nor maintains a binary and hierarchical view of culture and identity politics. Pirbhai thus suggests that the teaching of diasporic writing in Canada requires an approach that moves more fluidly within and beyond the borders of Canadian literature rather than by repeating conceptual models—such as minority discourse, immigrant writing, ethnic writing, and postcolonial literature—which continue to maintain notions of the cultural, literary, and discursive "periphery."

The section entitled "Historical Imperatives" gathers a number of articles that insist on an historical approach to the connections between pedagogy and colonialism in English Canada. In "Literary History as

Microhistory," Heather Murray argues that while critical work on Canadian literature is often "historical in its orientation," this work "has not been accompanied by a parallel dialogue on historical method" (405). To make up for this absence, Murray offers an extensive account of a new model for literary historiography in Canada, one that departs from more traditional models of national or regional histories and which combines two interrelated meanings of microhistory (microhistory as method and microhistory as scope). As she states, "Construction of a national literary history is rendered impossible by the simple fact that 'state' and 'nation' are in such a complex correspondence" (412), hence her emphasis on the local community formation. As an example of her approach, Murray focuses on a murder that took place in the debating society for Fugitive men run by Mary Ann Shadd in 1853. By emphasizing the synchronic value of particular "case studies," Murray's approach provides a model for a nonnationalist literary history, while also offering possibilities for a new pedagogical method.

Carole Gerson extends Murray's interest in Canadian literary history. Her account of the material history of Pauline Johnson's published work provides an illuminating lesson for those attempting to historicize their readings of Canadian literature, and Canadian book history, in the classroom. Focusing on the layout and design of Johnson's key works, and the ways these material factors contributed to the exoticization of Johnson in England, Gerson demonstrates how Johnson's personal identity and public reception subsequently became overdetermined. Speaking in particular of Johnson's first volume of poetry, *The White Wampum*, Gerson notes how the book strengthened Johnson's position as a First Nations advocate while also fostering her identification as an artificial "Iroquois Poetess" (432), consequently excluding her from other literary historical categories. Using these insights when teaching Johnson's work can help illuminate the vicissitudes of literary reputation-making and the impetus towards a containing national pedagogy at work in what Kamboureli terms "the culture of celebrity."

Renée Hulan's "Margaret Atwood's Historical Lives in Context: Notes on a Postcolonial Pedagogy for Historical Fiction" discusses the usefulness of postcolonial theory for the teaching of Canadian historical fiction. While acknowledging that "postcolonial critique can have its own exchange value if it is treated only as a standpoint and not as both a methodology and a form of knowledge" (443), Hulan affirms the potentially enabling and transformative value of a postcolonial pedagogy. Soon after it was published, Atwood's *Alias Grace* prompted a flurry of critical discussion about historical fiction, though few responses truly engaged with the imperialist contexts of the novel's premise. By reading *Alias Grace* in conjunction with Atwood's Clarendon lecture on Sir John Franklin in *Strange Things*, Hulan brings into conjunction two interrelated narratives that deal with the historiography of convict women. By complicating the novel in this way, Hulan offers a reading of the novel that stresses "the colonial period as imperial rather than proto-national" and thereby prompts students to "'think postcolonial'" (456).

Jennifer Henderson provides a fascinating account of the historical interconnection between nationalism and literary pedagogy in her examination of early twentieth-century debates about the creation and education of future Canadian citizens. Focusing on the writings of Ernest Thompson Seton and Lucy Maud Montgomery, Henderson examines the ways a discourse of national pedagogy was already contemporary with these writers: "At the turn of the century, these projects of socialization often took the form of compromises between romantic educational philosophy and more utilitarian educational schemes to prepare pupils for work in rural and urban Canada" (463). The new pedagogical theory espoused by liberal education reformers of the time, including the emphasis on the pedagogical value of "personality" and "play," is present in the "'nation-tinged'" (463) fiction of Seton and Montgomery. Paradoxically, this emphasis on individuality and constructive ungovernability was in turn related to the broader pedagogical project of educating the reader according to the emergent normative scheme of good citizenship. Henderson's essay thus contributes to ongoing postcolonial investigations into the relationship between literature and the making of national selves.

Kathleen Marie Connor's contribution shares Henderson's focus on the intersections of early twentieth-century writing and the formulation of a national pedagogy. Connor's account of the "dominion-itive" role of Ernest Thompson Seton's realistic animal tales in the constitution of a national Canadian literary pedagogy underscores the interconnections of cultural representation and colonialist discourse, and highlights their mutual implication in private and public discourses about citizenship and identity. Connor's focus on children's literature utilizes a form of critical "border pedagogy" (499) and argues for a postcolonial interrogation of the ways these texts continue to be disseminated in Canada. "If a study of post-colonialism in education is to be something more than an autopsy of worlds that collided," she concludes, "a decision needs to be made about how to extend theory into pedagogical practice" (499).

Linda Radford shifts the focus to the university teacher-education classroom. Like Haun, Radford is advocating the introduction of a postcolonial pedagogy in secondary schools (and in the training of secondary-school teachers). Arguing that teachers are usually taught to read historical fiction uncritically, Radford examines the ways pre-service teachers engage with texts that depict a problematic history. As Radford notes, "Between the teachers' own refusal to discuss a text and the teacher education program's limitations, the 'I am teacher' (all knowing) and 'you are student' (empty vessel) model remains entrenched despite all of the well-intended talk about student-centred learning and critical thinking skills" (510). The genre of juvenile historical fiction presents particular obstacles to classroom literature teachers because it forces teachers and students to engage with "'risky stories'" (507). Radford takes as her case study Canadian writer Karleen Bradford's 1992 novel *There Will Be Wolves*, and asks how teachers' engagements with this text can be used as a site for postcolonial education. This applies to their revised approach to this difficult text as well as to the ways their initial responses might be used to reflect upon and "post-colonize" current reading and teaching practices.

Finally, Stephen Slemon offers an afterword that performs a reappraisal of the notion of a postcolonial pedagogy. Slemon is somewhat less sanguine than many of the contributors to this collection, and hence, perhaps, provides a fittingly inconclusive conclusion to a volume concerned with impossible necessity. In his view, the period of the last two decades of pedagogical optimism has not borne fruit: "We are now in the aftershock of a decade of indifferent achievement in the practice of postcolonial literary pedagogy" (519). Writing of the inherent incommensurability of postcolonialism and pedagogy, Slemon argues that the two "do *not* easily come together in the study and teaching of the Canadian literatures in Canadian universities" (519). Because literary pedagogy has its foundation in a form of "social engineering" (520), its pairing with an emancipatory postcolonial approach is rendered inherently problematic.

How does one teach the postcolonial? If it is this incompatibility that is at the core of this collection of papers, it may nevertheless be true that one can turn this problematic into a productive pedagogical lesson. If the pedagogical, in Canada, was from the very outset both compromised and postcolonial, it may also be true that the postcolonial is always, necessarily pedagogical. As Slemon concludes, "A postcolonial pedagogy . . . cannot do other than seek out the genuine difficulty inherent in the material it finds before itself" (523). At this particular historical, pedagogical moment, perhaps that is no small endeavour.

NOTES

1. Pacey limits his discussion to an English-Canadian context. Because debates about the teaching of a national literature have tended to consider anglophone and francophone contexts separately, this volume is likewise focused on the teaching of Canadian literature in anglophone Canada (which is not the same as saying that these critics do not sometimes teach and/or study francophone texts). Fee and Monkman's entry on "Teaching Canadian Literature" in the *Encyclopedia of Literature in Canada* includes a brief history of the teaching of French-Canadian literature in Québec.
2. Of course, coterminous with the institutionalization of Canadian literature within Canadian English departments was the advent of Commonwealth Studies. According to Stephen Slemon, Commonwealth Literary Studies came into existence in response to "the maniacal Anglocentrism that dominated English department curricula and canons in their home countries" ("Post-Colonial" 185). See also Brydon, "Introduction," and Tiffin, "'Lie Back'" and "Plato's Cave," for articles that discuss this connection.
3. In linking Atwood and Mathews in this way I do not mean to suggest that they were always in agreement. Mathews's stinging review of *Survival* appeared in the 1972/73 issue of *This Magazine* and Atwood was invited to respond to it (see her "Mathews and Misrepresentation" reprinted in *Second Words*; Mathews's review is reprinted in his *Canadian Literature: Surrender or Revolution*). In Mathews's view, Atwood's account focused too exclusively on surrender and survival, and not enough on moments of overt struggle and active anti-Americanism. The subtitle of Mathews's 1978 study, "Surrender or Revolution," invokes what he saw to be their differing perspectives.
4. For an historical account of the beginnings of postcolonial literary discourse in Canada, see Brydon, "Introduction." See also my anthology of early and contemporary essays of Canadian postcolonial theory, *Unhomely States.*

5. See Cavell for an account of the occlusive nature of this "inside/outside" dichotomy in pedagogical and postcolonial theory (105).
6. As of June 2003, the MLA series is up to 82 volumes.
7. I am indebted to Felman's chapter on education in *Jacques Lacan and the Adventure of Insight* for calling my attention to this evocative passage from Plato's *Meno* (69).

WORKS CITED

Atwood, Margaret. *Cat's Eye*. Toronto: McClelland, 1988.

———. "Mathews and Misrepresentation." *This Magazine* 7.1 (1973): 29–33. Rpt. in *Second Words* 129–50.

———. "Nationalism, Limbo and the Canadian Club." 1971. *Second Words: Selected Critical Prose*. Toronto: Anansi, 1982. 83–89.

———. *Survival: A Thematic Guide to Canadian Literature*. Toronto: Anansi, 1972.

Bhabha, Homi K. "DissemiNation: Time, Narrative and the Margins of the Modern Nation." *The Location of Culture*. London: Routledge, 1994. 139–70.

Brydon, Diana. "Introduction: Reading Postcoloniality, Reading Canada." *Testing the Limits: Postcolonial Theories and Canadian Literatures*. Ed. Diana Brydon. Spec. issue of *Essays on Canadian Writing* 56 (1995): 1–19.

Cameron, David. *Taking Stock: Canadian Studies in the Nineties*. Montreal: ACS, 1996.

Casteel, Sarah Philips. "The Dream of Empire: The Scottish Roots of English Studies in Canada." *ARIEL* 31.1–2 (2000): 127–52.

Cavell, Richard. "Transvestic Sites: Postcolonialism, Pedagogy, and Politics." *Dangerous Territories: Struggles for Difference and Equality in Education*. Ed. Leslie G. Roman and Linda Eyre. New York: Routledge, 1997. 99–112.

Dirlik, Arif. *The Postcolonial Aura: Third World Criticism in the Age of Global Capitalism*. Boulder: Westview, 1997.

Djwa, Sandra. *Professing English: A Life of Roy Daniells*. Toronto: U of Toronto P, 2002.

Eagleton, Terry. *Literary Theory: An Introduction*. Oxford: Blackwell, 1983.

Fee, Margery. "Canadian Literature and English Studies in the Canadian University." *Essays on Canadian Writing* 48 (1992–93): 20–40.

Fee, Margery, and Leslie Monkman. "Teaching Canadian Literature." *Encyclopedia of Literature in Canada*. Ed. William H. New. Toronto: U of Toronto P, 2002. 1084–89.

Felman, Shoshana. "Psychoanalysis and Education: Teaching Terminable and Interminable." *Jacques Lacan and the Adventure of Insight: Psychoanalysis in Contemporary Culture*. Cambridge: Harvard UP, 1987. 69–97.

Findlay, Len. "Always Indigenize!: The Radical Humanities in the Postcolonial Canadian University." *ARIEL* 31.1–2 (2000): 307–26.

Fogel, Stan. "CanLit and Class(room) Struggle." *Studies in Canadian Literature* 25.2 (2000): 145–58.

Freire, Paulo. *Pedagogy of the Oppressed*. Trans. Myra Bergman Ramos. New York: Seabury, 1970.

Giroux, Henry A. *Border Crossings: Cultural Workers and the Politics of Education*. New York: Routledge, 1992.

———. "Schooling as a Form of Cultural Politics: Toward a Pedagogy of and for Difference." *Critical Pedagogy, the State, and Cultural Struggle*. Ed. Henry Giroux and Peter L. McLaren. Albany: State U of New York P, 1989. 125–51.

Giroux, Henry A., and Roger Simon. "Popular Culture and Critical Pedagogy: Everyday Life as a Basis for Curriculum Knowledge." *Critical Pedagogy, the State, and Cultural Struggle*. Ed. Henry Giroux and Peter L. McLaren. Albany: State U of New York P, 1989. 236–52.

Goldie, Terry. *Fear and Temptation: The Image of the Indigene in Canadian, Australian, and New Zealand Literatures*. Montreal: McGill-Queen's UP, 1989.

Graff, Gerald. *Professing Literature: An Institutional History*. Chicago: U of Chicago P, 1987.

Granatstein, J.L. *Who Killed Canadian History?* Toronto: HarperCollins, 1998.

Griffiths, Linda, and Maria Campbell. *The Book of Jessica: A Theatrical Transformation*. Toronto: Coach House, 1989.

Grossberg, Lawrence. "Introduction: Bringin' It All Back Home—Pedagogy and Cultural Studies." *Between Borders: Pedagogy and the Politics of Cultural Studies*. Ed. Henry A. Giroux and Peter McLaren. New York: Routledge, 1994. 1–25.

Hodgetts, A.B. *What Culture? What Heritage?: A Study of Civic Education in Canada*. Curriculum Series 5. Toronto: OISE, 1968.

hooks, bell. *Teaching to Transgress: Education as the Practice of Freedom*. New York: Routledge, 1994.

Hoy, Helen. *How Should I Read These?: Native Women Writers in Canada*. Toronto: U of Toronto P, 2001.

Jasen, Patricia. "Arnoldian Humanism, English Studies, and the Canadian University." *Queen's Quarterly* 95.3 (1988): 550–66.

Johnston, Wayne. *The Colony of Unrequited Dreams*. 1998. Toronto: Vintage Canada, 1999.

Kamboureli, Smaro. *Scandalous Bodies: Diasporic Literature in English Canada.* Don Mills: Oxford UP, 2000.

Mackey, Eva. *The House of Difference: Cultural Politics and National Identity in Canada.* Toronto: U of Toronto P, 2002.

Mathews, Robin. *Canadian Literature: Surrender or Revolution.* Ed. Gail Dexter. Toronto: Steel Rail, 1978.

———. "Survival and Struggle in Canadian Literature." *This Magazine* 6.4 (1972/73): 109–24.

Mathews, Robin, and James Steele. *The Struggle for Canadian Universities.* Toronto: New Press, 1969.

Mukherjee, Arun. *Postcolonialism: My Living.* Toronto: TSAR, 1998.

Murray, Heather. *Working in English: History, Institution, Resources.* Toronto: U of Toronto P, 1996.

Pacey, Desmond. "The Study of Canadian Literature." *Journal of Canadian Fiction* 2.2 (1973): 67–72.

Pierce, Lorne. *An Outline of Canadian Literature (French and English).* Montreal: Louis Carrier, 1927.

Plato. "Meno." *Great Dialogues of Plato.* Trans. W.H.D. Rouse. Ed. Eric H. Warmington and Philip G. Rouse. New York: New American Library, 1956. 28–68.

Razack, Sherene. "Bodies That Make Canada White." Body Talk/Parler du Corps conference. University of Ottawa, 23 Nov. 2002.

———. *Looking White People in the Eye: Gender, Race, and Culture in Courtrooms and Classrooms.* Toronto: U of Toronto P, 1998.

Ross, Malcolm. "Canadian Culture and the Colonial Question." *The Impossible Sum of Our Traditions: Reflections on Canadian Literature.* Intro. David Staines. Toronto: McClelland, 1986. 163–83.

Sedgwick, Eve Kosofsky. *Touching Feeling: Affect, Pedagogy, Performativity.* Durham: Duke UP, 2003.

Slemon, Stephen. "Post-Colonial Critical Theories." *New National and Post-Colonial Literatures: An Introduction.* Ed. Bruce King. Oxford: Clarendon, 1996. 178–97.

Spivak, Gayatri Chakravorty. *A Critique of Postcolonial Reason: Toward a History of the Vanishing Present.* Cambridge: Harvard UP, 1999.

———. *Outside in the Teaching Machine.* New York: Routledge, 1993.

———. *The Post-Colonial Critic: Interviews, Strategies, Dialogues.* Ed. Sarah Harasym. New York: Routledge, 1990.

———. "Teaching for the Times." *Dangerous Liaisons: Gender, Nation, and Postcolonial Perspectives.* Ed. Anne McClintock, Aamir Mufti, and Ella Shohat. Cultural Politics 11. Minneapolis: U of Minnesota P, 1997. 468–90.

Srivastava, Aruna. "Anti-Racism Inside and Outside the Classroom." *Dangerous Territories: Struggles for Difference and Equality in Education.* Ed. Leslie G. Roman and Linda Eyre. New York: Routledge, 1997. 113–26.

———. "Introductory Notes: Postcolonialism and Its Discontents." *ARIEL* 26.1 (1995): 12–17.

Sugars, Cynthia. "Can the Canadian Speak?: Lost in Postcolonial Space." *ARIEL* 32.3 (2001): 115–52.

———. "National Posts: Theorizing Canadian Postcolonialism." *International Journal of Canadian Studies* 25 (2002): 41–67.

———. *Unhomely States: Theorizing English-Canadian Postcolonialism.* Peterborough: Broadview, 2004.

Symons, T.H.B. *The Symons Report.* Toronto: Book and Periodical Development Council, 1978.

Tiffin, Helen. "'Lie Back and Think of England': Post-Colonial Literatures and the Academy." *A Shaping of Connections: Commonwealth Literature Studies—Then and Now.* Ed. Hena Maes-Jelinek, Kirsten Holst Petersen, and Anna Rutherford. Sydney: Dangaroo, 1989. 116–26.

———. "Plato's Cave: Educational and Critical Practices." *New National and Post-Colonial Literatures: An Introduction.* Ed. Bruce King. Oxford: Clarendon, 1996. 143–63.

Todd, Sharon. "Desiring Desire in Rethinking Pedagogy." *Learning Desire: Perspectives on Pedagogy, Culture, and the Unsaid.* Ed. Sharon Todd. New York: Routledge, 1997. 1–13.

Trifonas, Peter Pericles. Introduction. *Revolutionary Pedagogies: Cultural Politics, Instituting Education, and the Discourse of Theory.* Ed. Peter Trifonas. New York: Routledge, 2000. xi–xxi.

Viswanathan, Gauri. *Masks of Conquest: Literary Study and British Rule in India.* London: Faber, 1989.

Willinsky, John. *Learning to Divide the World: Education at Empire's End.* Minneapolis: U of Minnesota P, 1998.

The Culture of Celebrity and National Pedagogy

SMARO KAMBOURELI

I

I'M ON PAT BAY HIGHWAY, Wednesday morning, the twentieth anniversary of the Charter of Rights and Freedoms, driving home after dropping a friend at the Swartz Bay ferry terminal. Naturally, I'm listening to CBC. Mary Walsh is hosting the most recent "do" about Canadian literature. "The Battle of the Books," an ad in the *Globe and Mail* calls it, a literary competition imaged as warfare in keeping with the times. The panel, consisting of the novelists Leon Rooke and Nalo Hopkinson; lead singer of the Barenaked Ladies, Steven Page; actor Megan Follows; and the former prime minister Kim Campbell, is to decide on the book that the entire nation ought to read. As Campbell puts it, the winning book should have the capacity to engage the whole nation in conversation. The contenders are Margaret Atwood's *The Handmaid's Tale,* George Elliott Clarke's *Whylah Falls,* Margaret Laurence's *The Stone Angel,* Rohinton Mistry's *A Fine Balance,* and Michael Ondaatje's *In the Skin of a Lion.*

After the usual CBC repartee, Mary Walsh discloses the contents of the ballots. This is the first morning of The Battle, and it's *The Stone Angel* that is eliminated. Listening to the panelists explain why they voted as they did, some of them admitting that they have not read all of the selected titles, I find their process of elimination to be as whimsical and arbitrary as the rules of Ondaatje's *Elimination Dance*. As I'm switching off the engine in the carport at home, I'm listening to Rooke's husky voice. He explains why he voted against *In the Skin of a Lion*. It's "stunningly written," he declares, "Ondaatje's blue-collar novel." A very apt phrase, it seems to me: "Ondaatje's blue-collar novel," with the emphasis placed on the author's name, ironizes what Ondaatje in scare quotes—"Ondaatje" as signator, to echo one of Frank Davey's reading tropes—stands for: the internationalization of Canadian literature, a writers' writer become a writer of the world, avant-gardism subsumed by commodification. *In the Skin of a Lion* is not the kind of "blue-collar novel" that aspires to be read either as an indictment against industrialism or as an inspiration for readers to rally against the exploitation of poorly waged immigrants. After all, its protagonist declares that "I don't believe the language of politics, but I'll protect the friends I have" (122). His loyalty to friends gets him involved in events that could be seen as instances of political activism, but they are not marked by the kind of altruism and political idealism blue-collar heroes are likely to be imbued with.[1] But this is not the reason why this "blue-collar novel" fails for Rooke; he finds it too romantic, the love relationships too "gooey." "Yes," Mary Walsh joins in enthusiastically, "Ondaatje cannot write dialogue." How Canadian, I think to myself, to affirm, while knocking down a peg or two, the celebrated status of a national author.

This snippet of panel talk is symptomatic of the state of cultural affairs in Canada today. Twenty-five years ago or so, the Writers' Union and writers' guilds, among other groups across the country, were still lobbying the mass media and ministries of education for wider representation of Canadian books. Today, first-novel authors are offered large advances; many novels are simultaneously released in Canada and in foreign editions; writers like George Elliott Clarke and Rohinton Mistry, who would have had a difficult time finding a publisher not too long ago, are virtually household names; and authors like Russell Smith have regular columns in national newspapers. Never mind that the average number of homegrown novels a Canadian high-school student has read by graduation time is a mere five ("School's Out"). After all, the local has not only undergone multiple fragmentations; it is already subsumed by what Arif Dirlik calls "global localism" (34), and we inhabit as much real as virtual space—not to mention that reality, if we agree with Baudrillard, is a matter of competing simulacra.

But this is no reason to plunge into melancholy. Canadian literature has indeed reached new heights of prominence. Consider the many literary festivals and prize-giving occasions, gala events that get full and extensive media coverage. The fact that prizes like the Giller award for fiction, the Griffin for poetry, and the Charles Taylor for literary non-fiction have substantial capital value may be one of the reasons for the attention garnered by literature today. Even poetry, whose marketing value has always been low if not non-existent, has become a weekly feature of the *Globe and Mail.* And if, in this post-Gzowski period of media-CanLit romance, we fly on Air Canada, we can read the winners of CBC's poetry competition in *En Route,* or experience momentary surprise upon coming across, in the same magazine, the glamorous photo-portrait of a Canadian poet known, among other things, for her activism against racism. No, Marlene Nourbese Philip has not become a fashion model; she is the artist-of-the-month feature.

To put this otherwise: we've reached that point of modernity when the binaries of cultural logic are dissolved, without their tensions necessarily being resolved or erased, when the materialization of the dream of progress has been fulfilled or indefinitely deferred, depending on whether we are, say, on Richard Rorty's, David Hollinger's, or Jürgen Habermas's side,[2] or look at world affairs today through a Derridean, Foucauldian, or Jamesonian lens. Modernity may or may not have run its course, but its progressivist and positivistic logic is certainly re-figured as the telos of global culture, a telos that grants teleology a new meaning, for it recognizes no borders or destinations since its goals are those of profit-making and of converting everything, including human genes, into commodities.

Lest we university professors feel left out of this effortless circulation of culture, let's admit that academics, including humanists, are no longer simply the object of irony or derision for their indulgence in arcane knowledge or their use of theory. As I'm reminded by the *Globe and Mail,* "Canada's universities are anything but aloof ivory towers" (Valpy A1). Indeed, philosophers like Mark Kingwell expound on the virtues of cultural studies in newspapers; words like postmodernism and deconstruction have become naturalized in the lexicon of media discourses; what I still call the Learneds receives its own modicum of media exposure;[3] and the brain drain or gain in the domain of the Canadian academe often warrants front page news.

It is not, then, only Canadian literature that seems to have reached its apotheosis at the dawn of the twenty-first century. Canadian academics themselves—at least post–September 11, as a recent study declares—have "garner[ed] newspaper, TV and radio exposure worth almost $25-million in advertising" (Valpy A10). The synecdochic relation of academic discourse to actual capital not only shows that corporatism has infiltrated university culture today—one of the reasons why universities are no longer the intellectual ivory towers they used to be but are, instead, becoming the new colonies of capitalist logic—but also illustrates that intellectual discourse has lost its critical distance from marketing fields and the global economy. This is the case not only because, as Masao Miyoshi says, "[t]he technical complexity of the TNC [transnational] mechanism requires academic expertise in sophisticated research, explanation, and management of immense information data" (96), but also because humanists, too, including postcolonial critics, are susceptible to the same powerful, opaque as well as transparent, sensible as well as nefarious, forces that drive globalization. The efficacy of humanist discourse is already curtailed before it is launched, the result being that humanists are put in the position of playing the role of "explicators" at best, or "apologists" at worst (Miyoshi 96). Still, undoubtedly, one of the effects of the globalization of culture, in the context of my argument here, is that both literature and the humanities have achieved a visibility and circulation they never enjoyed before.[4]

Ours has become a culture of celebrity—yet another naturalized phrase in today's popular as well as academic discourse. In an ironic reversal of the tropes that mark the Canadian pastime of deriding our neighbours in the south for their fetishization of success in the realm of popular culture, it would seem we have followed suit, yet once again. But if this is really the case, if Canadian culture has reached, if not exceeded, the visibility we wanted it to attain, at what cost, if any, has Canadian literature achieved this status of celebrity? What are the implications of this shift from, what Henry Giroux calls, "the spectacle of politics" to "the politics of the spectacle" (63)? How does the Canadian culture of celebrity relate to what Stephen Slemon identifies as "professional postcolonialism" (27), namely our persistent attempt to introduce cultural differences into our discipline, and translate them (both cultural differences and the discipline of English) into the classroom? And how are both the culture of celebrity and professional postcolonialism imbricated, if they are, in the machinations of national pedagogy?

I'm not going to volunteer answers to all these questions—they are too loaded, too complex in their discursivity to deal with in a single essay. Instead, I have opted to tease out only a few of their implications, albeit in my usual circuitous fashion.

II

That there is a tight relationship—structural, ideological, and material—between cultural production and the representation of the nation, between institutions producing and disseminating literature (e.g., publishing houses, newspapers, think tanks, and universities) and the apparatus of the state (e.g., ministries of education, the Canada Council, provincial arts councils, and the SSHRC), is a given. The entire corpus of Canadian criticism today, together with the debates that take place in institutional contexts, especially in the Humanities, in critical journals and public fora, testifies to that. Irrespective of whether we wish to adopt, revise, or refute, say, Robert Lecker's neo-humanistic view of the Canadian literary canon; Frank Davey's culturalist semiotics of that same tradition; Jon Kertzer's liberal humanist nostalgia for a renewed nation; Linda Hutcheon's postmodern interpretation of the contradictions inherent in Canadian literature; Roy Miki's rigorous critique of racialization; Diana Brydon's postcolonial analysis of literature and institutions; or Barbara Godard's poststructuralist account of what informs and distorts the formation of literary history in Canada—literature has irrefutably emerged as a major player in the transformation the Canadian state has been undergoing in this era of global market economies.

"Literature," Barbara Godard wrote recently, "works no longer in the service of the nation's identity . . . but to further its economic security in an era of global capitalism. 'Culture,' first disembedded from precapitalist traditional life ways and positioned as a countervailing force to industry . . . is now an autonomous and self-regulating field of social reproduction and domain of value positioned asymmetrically as a counterforce to democracy within an all-encompassing 'economy' to whose ends it is subordinate" (221). The contradiction in Godard's argument that literature is autonomous and self-regulating yet subordinate to economy is a telling instance of the paradoxes that inform, on one hand, the location of culture in Canadian society today and, on the other, the complicity that marks the relationship between the institutions that facilitate and disseminate the production of literature and the state itself. And yet, this may not be a contradiction at all, but the effect of an undeclared differentiation that she skips over.

Culture has never been autonomous and self-regulating. Even when, for example, Arif Dirlik traces the "'cultural turn' of the last two decades . . . to a new awareness of culture not just as a function of material structures but as an autonomous force itself in the making of modernity" (22), a change he links to the operations of global capitalism, the autonomy he has in mind is decidedly gauged by various contingencies. Culture has always been a multivocal sign implicated in the making of national narratives, if not of nations themselves. This becomes apparent in the ways in which culture has been defined at least by one major postcolonial critic, Edward Said. The various definitions of culture Said provides to frame his argument in *Culture and Imperialism* do not cancel each other out. If anything, the more he attempts to elaborate on their differences, the more the distinctions he makes collapse into each other.

Said begins with a definition that we could, in turn, define as disciplinary: culture encompasses "all those practices, like the art of description, . . . that have relative autonomy from the economic, social and political realms" (xii). A view of culture that shares the same ideological tradition as humanism, it is what has shaped, too, the tradition of our profession. English has undergone dramatic changes, especially in the last part of the twentieth century, and it would be more accurately defined today as English Studies, but the notion that literature has somehow intrinsic value, a principle crucial to this view of culture, continues to be inscribed, directly or subliminally, in our discipline.

The second definition of culture Said attempts to offer is the Arnoldian one: culture as "a concept that includes a refining and elevating element, each society's reservoir of the best that has been known and thought" (xiii). Still maintaining its autonomy from society, as far as Said is concerned, this notion of culture is granted instrumentality, the ability to play a significant role in the pedagogy of citizens. Significantly, this definition, too, is humanistic in origin. Despite its presumed ability to school society, it preserves its autonomy but also claims for itself a utility whose directionality speaks of a one-way influence, a monologic form of instruction. This hegemonic role of culture that underlines Arnold's "demand for an intellectual deliverance" of the public (20) becomes apparent when we examine it in the context of Kant. In *Conflict of the Faculties*, he writes:

> Enlightenment of the masses is the public instruction of the people in its duties and rights vis-à-vis the state to which they belong. Since only natural rights and rights arising out of the common human understanding are concerned here, then the natural heralds and expositors of these among the people are not officially appointed by the state but are free professors of law, that is philosophers who, precisely because this freedom is allowed to them, are objectionable to the state, which always desires to rule alone; and they are decried, under the name of enlighteners, as persons dangerous to the state. (153)

The philosophers of law, in this context, are the producers and custodians of culture. The affiliation of culture with law is, then, a double symptom of its universality and of the hegemonic function of its pedagogical role. Thus, in keeping with the Enlightenment logic, culture, in Said's second definition, renders the state a panopticon inhabited by "subjected sovereignties." For Foucault,

> [h]umanism invented a whole series of subjected sovereignties: the soul (ruling the body, but subjected to God), consciousness (sovereign in a context of judgment, but subjected to the necessities of truth), the individual (a titular control of personal rights subjected to the laws of nature and society), basic freedom (sovereign within, but accepting the demands of an outside world and "aligned with destiny"). In short, humanism is everything in Western civilization that restricts *the desire for power*: it prohibits the desire for power and excludes the possibility of power being seized. The theory of the subject (in the double sense of the word) is at the heart of humanism and this is why our culture has tenaciously rejected anything that could weaken its hold upon us. (221–22)

If the utility of this view of culture lies in its imperative to restrict the power of the people, the knowledge to which they are exposed is by default constrained, and pedagogy, in turn, is shown to be the practice that facilitates this process. Thus the benevolence that underscores the humanistic goal of edifying people is synonymous, to borrow William Spanos's words, with the imperial intention "to annul the force of desire of a colonized or territorialized otherness" (*End* 60). The pedagogy that disseminates, while being produced by, this view of culture is not, then, a pedagogy that liberates the citizen; rather, its aim is to fashion the political unconscious of people in terms that serve the raison d'être of the state. It is not surprising, then, that Said sees this second definition of culture as gradually becoming "associated, often aggressively, with the nation or the state." This kind of culture "is a source of identity," he argues, a "sort of theater where various political and ideological causes engage one another" (xiii). It is this notion of culture that is affiliated with national narration and canonization, that, for example, John Guillory problematizes in *Cultural Capital*, and that, eventually, gave rise to the culture wars and debates in the humanities departments of American and Canadian universities. This culture erects borders, while simultaneously preserving its universal and imperial signature. Interestingly, as Said points out, this idea of culture, despite its alignment with the nation, is "somehow divorced from, because transcending, the everyday world" (xiii).

But if this is the case, if indeed this kind of culture is as politically neutral as Said seems to think it is, how different is his second definition of culture from the first one? Said's elucidation of this point doesn't help much; it may disclose his persistent commitment to developing an oppositional critical practice, but it also reveals one of the contradictions in his work. He refers to the "difficult truth" (xiv) he, like "[m]ost professional humanists" (xiii), "discovered," namely, that many of his favourite French and British artists take no "issue with the notion of 'subject' or inferior races so prevailing among officials who practiced those ideas as a matter of course" (xiv). These are the artists who have created the very classics that occupy the privileged centre of, in Spanos's apt phrase, "the panopticism of post-Enlightenment literary discourse" (*End* 48). Far from lacking a politics, these texts embody the knowledge humanistic pedagogy circulates; theirs is a politics that can be both visible and invisible, the politics of cultural orthodoxies, the doxa of the state, in other words, what is constituted as normative. It is this body of works—we can call them classics, masterpieces, Western literature—that comprises as much the cultural capital of the nation as the object of critique for the postcolonial projects of some critics like Said.

Said's attempt at defining culture is intended to suggest the complicity that stains the postcolonial critical enterprise, an important thing to keep in mind in view of the righteousness that characterizes, at least in my view, certain kinds of postcolonial criticism and practices today. It is also a gesture toward apologia for his dealing precisely with the kind of works that are the reservoir of the very Enlightenment values he sets out to deconstruct. We might agree, then, along with Rosalind O'Hanlon, Benita Parry, Jonathan Arac, and Aijaz Ahmad, among others, that Said's own critical enterprise "commutes between" the recognition that the subject is decentred and culture is hybrid *and* the desire—a diasporic desire at that—to insist on the need of "conserving specific structures of communal subjectivity invented by dominated peoples" (Parry 30).[5] This ambivalent ethos, together with the fact that, at the same time Said bemoans the perils of nationalism, he argues for what Gregory Jusdanis calls "the necessary nation,"[6] demonstrates the irreducible paradox that marks his project: namely, that it stands at the crossroads of postmodernity and modernity.

Rather than positing this ideological, and methodological, quandary as the Achilles heel of Said's work, as some critics have already done, I would like, instead, to look at it as a paradigmatic instance exemplifying the genealogy of what I believe haunts the culture of celebrity in Canada. Despite its varied domains of performance and production, what I call the culture of celebrity here participates in the same syntax of national pedagogy, thus sharing, in a fashion, a similar ethos and ideology with respect to its relation to the nation.

III

Though primarily seen as a product of modernity, national pedagogy does not come into being in that phase of Western thought that was shaped by the Enlightenment. In the same way that the construction of what Martin Bernal has called the "Aryan model" in *Black Athena* originates with the ethnographic and romantic movements in Germany, the humanist period of the Enlightenment that gave rise to the civilizing project of Eurocentric colonialism is itself the product of Roman imperialism. As Spanos, among a few others, has shown via Heidegger's *Parmenides*, the colonization and appropriation of Greek thinking by the Romans was applied to their intention to "'win the hearts and minds' of extraterritorial Others to the essential principles informing [the Roman] way of life" (*America's* 65). It is significant for my purposes here that this colonization project, according to Spanos, employed as its fundamental instrument *eruditio et institutio in bonas artes,* that is, "scholarship and training in good conduct" (xix–xx). This not only demonstrates the validity of "Said's claim that humanist culture is complicitous with imperialism" (65), but also bears historical, philosophical, and philological witness—something I do not have the space to go into—to the fact that the genealogy of modernity points not to the *aletheia* of Greek thought but, rather, to the reductive Roman translation of *aletheia* into *veritas.* To put it simply: the unconcealment signified by *aletheia,* namely an "open" and "errant" inquiry, a play of differences, what Spanos calls an "agonistic Greek *paideia,*" is rendered as a "correctness," a matter of "the True and the false" (121), implemented through "the production of a dependable manly citizenry" whose sole goal is to "establish," "legitimate," and perpetuate the hegemonic values of the state (xix–xx).[7]

In light of this genealogical context, we cannot afford to see national pedagogy as a means in the service of the Enlightenment project, a discursive practice that leads people to maturity in the Kantian sense of producing modern subjects, or, as Margery Fee has put it, the "organic process" through which "national cultures develop . . . beginning with infancy and moving toward maturity" (21). In the Enlightenment, national pedagogy is emancipatory, synonymous with *Bildung.* As Holland and Lambropoulos say, it is "the principal social technology that has supported and (re)produced the individual as autonomous self in modernity" (5). In her dissertation, "Subjectivity, *Bildung,* Pedagogy: 'Coming of Age' in Modernity," Jackie Heslop traces the genealogy of *Bildung* as the "spectre" that "haunts the expertise of pedagogical science" which "grounds and legitimizes the discourses—as well as many counterdiscourses—of contemporary education" (Chapter 7, 1). It is through this master narrative that national pedagogy figures, to echo Arnold, as a "mighty agency of deliverance." What is elided, though, when we see national pedagogy solely as an Enlightenment project, is its role as a power instrument of, to quote Spanos again, "cultivation . . . intended to inscribe in the 'young' a relay of colonialisms extending from" the private sphere the subject inhabits, "through consciousness, language, gender, and race, to civil, political, and international society" (*America's* 121).

Understood not merely as a "cultivation" project that has gone awry, but as a mission consonant with colonialism, national pedagogy loses any semblance it may have of benevolence, and, instead, is shown to be a pedagogy of coercion. In this context, national pedagogy seems to be akin to the concept of empire as articulated by Michael Hardt and Antonio Negri. Empire, in their joint study of the same title, is "an order that effectively suspends history and thereby fixes the existing state of affairs for eternity. . . . It is a regime with no formal boundaries that operates on all registers of the social order. Empire not only manages a territory and a population but also creates the very world it inhabits" (xiv–xv). Considered in this light, national pedagogy has a permeating power that does not recognize boundaries. It gathers into its domain everything, including those discourses it seeks to cancel out, a strategic gesture in Michel de Certeau's sense of it. It is my contention that only if we approach national pedagogy from this double genealogical perspective, and acknowledge its ghostly ability to seep into and absorb the totality of what constitutes it, will we be able, on one hand, to appreciate fully its symbolic violence and, on the other, to re-inscribe, if not reinvent, our subjected subjectivities in a posthumanist context. This is essential as a tactic—again in de Certeau's definition of the word[8]—that may enable us to make sense of national pedagogy as an "imperium of affect."

The "imperium of affect"—Emily Apter's expression—encapsulates what I have been trying to articulate so far: that is, national pedagogy as an imperial project with at once a decidedly imperialist lineage and a globalizing intent. I would like to quote Apter at some length:

> The world of affect seems to take up where the critique of performativity leaves off: that is, at the point where antiessentialism has become a given and the market in identity-production is oversaturated. The imperium of affect marks a return to "easy"; to feelings washing about in a depoliticized space of the transnational commodity. . . . Affect is about ethnic and racial particularisms that have lost their hard edges and become substitutable formulas or caricatures of nation, race, and gender. . . . [It is] about the indiscriminate, loving embrace of "others." . . . Affect stages political

> events with realist expectations; that is, with perfect foreknowledge of the basic immunity of "the system" to its viral attacks. . . . [Affect] alludes to what happens to oppositional discourse when it turns into "happy" multiculturalism. (19)

It is within the domain of this imperium of affect that the culture of celebrity operates. The product of similar political and material economies, the culture of celebrity is imbricated ideologically and materially in its operations.

Invariably triumphalist in its representation, the culture of celebrity is the avatar of national pedagogy. It is what translates the panopticism of national pedagogy into public spectacle. In that, it depends for its affect on Jeremy Bentham's principles of supervision, "axial visibility" and "lateral invisibility" (Foucault 200–01): that is, it is at once manifest and unverifiable. This doubleness is what guarantees its hegemony. And its hegemony, like most hegemonies, is at once disciplinary and laudatory. Produced as much through the collaboration of different institutional structures as through various subliminal processes, it promotes formative narratives that hijack dissention and appropriate differences. Though it doesn't foster a unified aesthetics as such, it nevertheless advances a discourse of values which, more often than not, materialize the uneasy coexistence of modernity and postmodernity. Thus, though it is highly visible, and unabashedly posits itself as the self-evident best of what the nation has to offer, it remains loudly mute about the ideology of the knowledge it transmits, and strategically shies away from adopting a monologic aesthetic. It is through all these, and other, traits that the culture of celebrity executes what I take to be its fundamental function: the manufacturing of public memory.

Public memory, according to Roger Simon, "is grounded in a shared pedagogy of 'rememory' [Toni Morrison's concept], a decidedly social repetition or, better, a rearticulation of past events suffused with demands of remembrance and learning across generations, across boundaries of time, space and identification" (62). Cultural memory has already become a major trope through which we address some of the more pressing concerns of our time. However, despite the fact that, as Michael Roth writes, memory "is the key to personal and collective identity," memory is also what "makes it extremely difficult for people to share the past . . . [and thus] have confidence that they have a collective connection to what has gone before" (qtd. in Simon 62). The culture of celebrity is maximally equipped to reconcile the disjuncture caused by this twofold role of memory. The public memory it engineers reconstructs the nation in the political unconscious of the citizens by eliding certain parts of its history while foregrounding others.

IV

Let me return to "The Battle of the Books." The battle is over, and, though not every Canadian, as Campbell predicted, may be reading the winner, the faithful listeners of CBC will have already heard it read on the air. The winner, or, as one journalist put it ironically, "the survivor" of the battle, is *In the Skin of a Lion*. If my reading of the tropes that inform the culture of celebrity is right, then *In the Skin of a Lion* deserves the distinction.

Though located within a clearly defined historical time and place, it fabricates a spatial economy of knowledge and power which, despite its historiographic structure, reproduces the nation's symbolic violence. Ondaatje touches history with a gentle hand. He doesn't want, at least in this novel, to disturb too much history as national artifact, nor does he keep the effects of history in the closet. Nevertheless, he is certainly masterful at translating effect into affect. What has been celebrated about the Ondaatje oeuvre—and the culture of celebrity, I should say, always works toward the construction of oeuvres; witness the examples of such literary celebrities as Robertson Davies, Mavis Gallant, Margaret Atwood, Carol Shields, and Timothy Findley—that is, his poetics of violence and characters who thrive on the edge, relies on his romantic aestheticization of failure and the eroticization of politics. More specifically in terms of my overall argument, the great success and appeal his work enjoys is, at least in part, contingent on the fact that Ondaatje writes postmodern novels that reproduce, and continue, the project of modernity. The ambivalent coexistence of postmodernity and modernity is, I think, an important element of the culture of celebrity. Take as an example Carol Shields's *The Stone Diaries*. Structured like a *Bildung*, it is a novel in which the maturity its protagonist reaches is crowned by depression. Postmodern in its formal and narrative aspects, it embraces, thematically, the tenets of modernity. Ironically, though, most critics do not recognize this novel's contradictory impulses; they assume that there is unity between its aesthetics and its themes.[9] We find a similar tension between postmodernity and modernity in most novels that become part of the culture of celebrity. Richard B. Wright's recent novel, *Clara Callan*, too, which won virtually all prizes given to fiction in the year of its release, exemplifies this phenomenon.

Ondaatje's work is a case in point, too. From Buddy Bolden to Caravaggio, if not the English patient, from Billy the Kid to Anil, his characters surface from the margins of history to claim a place for themselves in the surplus of history. As Davey has argued, "[o]ne general ahistorical model of Canadian society—rich and poor, exploiter and exploited—yields to an even more general but implicitly patriarchal one in which all men appear to have some access to sensuous visionary experience which can link them with a universal human fabric" (155). Thus the novel showcases differences only to harmonize them (Davey 156).

How this harmonization of differences is practised and what it signifies become apparent in *In the Skin of a Lion*. Aligned with the *Bildung* tradition, the novel opens with a section entitled "Little Seeds." In it, the protagonist, Patrick, a young boy at the time, has his first intimations of what the world is about. He is the son of Hazen Lewis, a single father. Hazen Lewis is a logger, "an abashed man, withdrawn from the world around him, uninterested in the habits of civilization outside his own focus" (15). Though Patrick does not grow to be as solipsistic as his father, he inherits his father's isolationist character. Heredity, together with the ways in which Patrick both embodies and supersedes it, can be seen as an allegory of the incestuous relationship of modernity and postmodernity, of the former's presumed disinterestedness and the latter's self-reflexiveness, of the nation as family and as an assembly of differences. Patrick, we read, "has clung like moss to strangers, to the nooks and fissures of their situations. He has always been alien, the third person in the picture. He is the one born in this country who knows nothing of the place" (156–57). Canada, to echo Homi Bhabha, as an unhomely house, and the house of fiction as an uncanningly familiar site. Still, in the novel's exploration of Patrick's self-formation, these "strangers" occupy a parasitic location both emotionally and historically, for they inhabit, as Dennis Duffy has shown, the Toronto slums. Like Arthur S. Goss's photographs that document the modernization taking place in that period by "employ[ing] the rhetoric of artistic nationalism" (Duffy 14), photographs that served as an inspiration for the novel, Ondaatje's narrative remains nourished by the same legacy of modernity and the colonial logic of Westernization.

The novel as a record of Patrick's coming of age may memorialize, as so many critics hasten to notice, the as yet unnarrated story of Macedonian immigrants, but it falls short, I believe, of "redress[ing] the imbalance of official history" (Barbour 179). Still, though Barbour begins his study of the novel by claiming that Ondaatje "joins a large group of contemporary postcolonial writers" who seek to "inscrib[e] the 'unhistorical' memories of immigrant populations" (179), he states that the "liberal sympathies of the text often clash with its leftist political agenda" (200), and concludes by asserting that, though the "stories are there, [and] the ordinary people whose effort has built the country have been named," the novel "refuses to pretend that this naming can replace the official histories; at best it can supplement them and demonstrate the contingency of their truths" (205). Irrespective of the intentionality that drives the narrative, it is precisely the attempt to engage with some of the immigrants in Toronto at the time while reiterating the imperial power that contributes to the formation of official culture that puts this novel in the service of national pedagogy, that accounts, at least in part, for why it emerged as the winner of "The Battle of the Books."

The immigrants' representation in the novel is a clear manifestation of the imperium of affect. "The southeastern section of the city where [Patrick] now lived was made up mostly of immigrants and he walked everywhere not hearing any language he knew, deliriously anonymous. The people on the street, the Macedonians and Bulgarians, were his only mirror" (112). This self-reflexive occasion is not so much an instance of desiring or fetishizing otherness, as it is a lesson in how efficacious the imperium of affect can be. Patrick, confident in his white skin (even though he may not be aware of it because of its normativity) and nationality, can afford to delight in his anonymity. But if it is his anonymity that he sees reflected in these immigrants, theirs does not necessarily signify the same thing. Their anonymity is the kind that points to the opposite of liberation, for they remain subjected to the material and political effects of the hegemonic society they inhabit. A synonym of their parasitic presence in Toronto, their anonymity remains largely unthematized. Instead, it is adopted as a trope that fulfills Patrick's own need for invisibility.

If invisibility has a certain allure for Patrick, it is not only because someone else's vanishing act provides him with employment or sends him on the way to what is going to be the big love of his life, but precisely because he occupies a spectatorial position, a position that coincides with the novel's narrative perspective: it is his story that also narrates the story of those immigrants. And it is his gaze, a gaze similar to that constituting the culture of celebrity, that constructs their image. Interestingly, the politics that characterizes this gaze, a politics that constantly shifts from being that of the spectral to being that of the spectacle, is what aligns the culture of celebrity to national pedagogy. Thus only as long as these immigrants are represented as spectres of themselves can they become a mirror of Patrick's image. Patrick's self-image needs their otherness, an otherness whose representation evokes the same "pictorialist values" that Duffy argues characterize Goss's images (115):

> That is how Patrick would remember [the immigrants he works with] later. . . . If he were an artist he would have painted them. . . . What did it mean in the end to look aesthetically plumaged on this October day in the east of the city five hundred yards from Front Street? What would the painting tell? That they were . . . Macedonians mostly. . . . That during the day they ate standing up. That they had consumed the most evil smell in history, they were consuming it now, flesh death which lies in the vacuum between flesh and skin, and even if they never stepped into this pit again—a year from now they would burp up that odour. . . .
>
> They were the dyers. They were paid one dollar a day. . . . All of these professions arrived in morning darkness and worked till six in the evening, the labour agent giving them all English names. . . .
>
> For the dyers the one moment of superiority came in the showers at the end of the day. They stood under the hot pipes, not noticeably changing for two or three minutes—as if, like an actress unable to return to the real world from a role, they would be forever contained in that livid colour, only their brains free of it. And then the blue suddenly dropped off, the colour disrobed itself from the body, fell in one piece to their ankles, and they stepped out, in the erotica of being made free.
>
> What remained in the dyers' skin was the odour that no woman in bed would ever lean towards. Alice lay beside Patrick's exhausted body, her tongue on his neck. . . . (130–32)

This is vintage Ondaatje, the best evidence why this book materializes the intentions of national pedagogy. Present in their redolent flesh, none of these immigrants is named in these three pages that I have quoted from here. And the shifts from the dire conditions of their living to the erotics of taking a shower are so subtly executed that it takes a second read to notice that what has started as a critical exposition of immigrant labour has been used as a prop to stage an intimate erotic moment between Patrick and his lover. The "erotica of being made free," then, is a luxury that only Patrick has the privilege to experience. The anonymous Macedonians remain just that, anonymous, smelly, and emasculated, therefore undesirable.

With the exception of a couple of immigrants—notably, Nicholas and Caravaggio—the Macedonians, whose history this novel is supposed to have made known, are represented collectively. We read of Macedonian cake, of a Macedonian-style moustache (113), of Macedonian pantaloons, of a Macedonian night, yet we would be hard pressed to define what constitutes Macedonian culture. It is precisely this undifferentiated particularity, this levelling of differences, that fulfills the project of national pedagogy. Their difference is named but only insofar as it can be imag(in)ed by someone who occupies a dominant spectatorial position—yet another example of how public memory works.

It becomes apparent, then, that the historicization that the culture of celebrity acknowledges operates according to the requirements of modernity. It offers an amnesiac representation of history, the kind that is articulated "in the negative: Why could [they] not achieve that which [others] have achieved? Ironically, the answer to this question," Dirlik argues, "more often than not, has been . . . translated into the vocabulary of tradition as 'because tradition held [them] back'" (Dirlik 27). Ondaatje enables the Macedonians' entry into dominant discourse, but he does so by representing history in drag. From Caravaggio dressed as a woman or taking on the persona of a rich man, to Patrick pretending to be a guerrilla, to the cloaking of unsavoury labour practices in erotically charged language, this novel's narrative is marked by the "vested interests" of official historical discourse.

V

The public memory engineered by national pedagogy through the culture of celebrity is not necessarily the kind mobilized by a nostalgia for the past. Memory, in this context, is not ana-historic; rather, it has a proleptic function. It engages the past but it does so in order to restructure the present and remember the future. The cohesiveness of the national imaginary that emerges from it is not the same as the cohesive nation of that past. While that cohesiveness depended on constructing an imaginary homogeneity, the cohesive nation of the present has moved beyond a genetic sense of national kinship; instead, it depends on—in fact it celebrates—the politics of difference. It is, technically, a transcultural nation, a nation at once of "heritage groups," indigenous peoples, and many diasporas, but one that sees "the affirmation of difference as an end in itself" (Dirlik 41). The premise prevailing in Canadian criticism that Canada is a postcolonial state is just that: a premise. As Diana Brydon writes, "the post does not refer to the end of colonialism, but rather to what was formed under colonialism and remains after official colonialism is abandoned and colonialism begins to be recognized as a major component of modernity" (5). If in its earlier configuration the nation was self-defined by the very limits it set, by its various technologies of inclusion and exclusion, today it posits itself as a nation of plenitude, hence the euphoria induced by the culture of celebrity.

NOTES

1. Douglas Malcolm also talks about Patrick's political activism, but our readings are diametrically opposite. See his article, "Solos and Chorus: Michael Ondaatje's Jazz Politics/Poetics."
2. See, for example, their essays in the recent volume, *What's Left of Enlightenment?: A Postmodern Question* (Baker and Reill). *Enlightenment, Passion, Modernity: Historical Essays in European Thought and Culture* (Micale and Dietle) also addresses similar issues.
3. This year's Congress of the Social Sciences and Humanities (formerly known as the "Learneds") was announced (advertised?) by its own five-page "partnership marketing supplement" in the *Globe and Mail*.
4. As with some other aspects and manifestations of cultural and academic life, there is a belatedness that characterizes the presence of the academe in the Canadian mass media when compared to that in the United States.
5. See also Arac, Ahmad, and O'Hanlon.
6. For Jusdanis, the nation is "necessary" in that it "allow[s] peoples to look for collective inner strength, to preserve their identities in the face of perennial change, and to strive for justice." Though his defense of the nation, which he presents as a long-overdue and necessary "apology" (3) for the many ways in

which the nation has been vilified, does not lose sight of the fact that nationalism "continue[s] to agitate . . . as a twin-headed force, releasing chaos into the world and leading to internecine strife" (15), it is fraught with problems, as becomes apparent, at least to this reader, in his brief section on Canada which concludes with the facile statement that "[i]t is instructive that Atwood [in *Survival*] connected the essence of Canadian literature with cultural survival. . . . The anxious questions posed by Atwood over the existence of an autochthonous literature have to do with the very essence of being Canadian" (148). If there is anything that allows him to reach this unproblematized, and obsolete, conclusion it is that his Canadian research material is limited to the late 1960s and early 70s (Richard Gwyn's 1995 *Nationalism without Walls: The Unbearable Lightness of Being Canadian* being the only recent reference).

7. See also Spanos's "Heidegger's *Parmenides*."

8. While strategy, for de Certeau, "transform[s] the uncertainties of history into readable spaces" (36) and contributes to "an economy of the proper place" (55), tactic is "a calculated action determined by the absence of a proper locus" (37). Rey Chow is one postcolonial critic who has employed de Certeau's distinction with constructive results. As she says, strategy is appropriated by "those who are committed to the building, growth, and fortification of a 'field.' A text, for instance, would become in this economy 'a cultural weapon . . .'" (16). While "a *strategic* attitude . . . repeats what [it] seek[s] to overthrow," her critique engages "the tactics of those who do not have claims to territorial propriety or cultural centrality" (25). She never loses sight of the fact that "as intellectuals the battles we fight are battles of words" (17).

9. See, for example, Mellor, "'The Simple Container of Our Existence.'"

WORKS CITED

Ahmad, Aijaz. "Orientalism and After: Ambivalence and Metropolitan Location in the Work of Edward Said." *In Theory: Classes, Nations, Literatures.* Bombay: Oxford UP, 1992. 159–219.

Apter, Emily. *Continental Drift: From National Characters to Virtual Subjects.* Chicago: U of Chicago P, 1999.

Arac, Jonathan. "Criticism between Opposition and Counterpoint." *Edward Said.* Ed. Paul A. Bové. Spec. issue of *boundary 2* 25.2 (1998): 55–69.

Arnold, Matthew. "On the Modern Element in Literature." *The Complete Prose Works.* Vol. 1. Ed. R.H. Super. Ann Arbor: U of Michigan P, 1960. 18–37.

Baker, Keith Michael, and Peter Hanns Reill, eds. *What's Left of Enlightenment? A Postmodern Question.* Stanford: Stanford UP, 2001.

Barbour, Douglas. *Michael Ondaatje.* New York: Twayne, 1993.

Bernal, Martin. *Black Athena: The Afroasiatic Roots of Classical Civilization. Vol. I.–The Fabrication of Ancient Greece 1785–1985*. New Brunswick, NJ: Rutgers UP, 1987.

Bhabha, Homi K. "The World and the Home." *Dangerous Liaisons: Gender, Nation, and Postcolonial Perspectives*. Ed. Anne McClintock, Aamir Mufti, and Ella Shohat. Minneapolis: U of Minnesota P, 1997. 445–55.

Brydon, Diana. "It's Time For a New Set of Questions." *Essays on Canadian Writing* 71 (2000): 14–25.

Chow, Rey. *Writing Diaspora: Tactics of Intervention in Contemporary Cultural Studies*. Bloomington: Indiana UP, 1993.

Davey, Frank. *Post-National Arguments: The Politics of the Anglophone-Canadian Novel Since 1967*. Toronto: U of Toronto P, 1993.

de Certeau, Michel. *The Practice of Everyday Life*. Trans. Steven Rendall. Berkeley: U of California P, 1984.

Dirlik, Arif. "Postmodernism and Chinese History." *boundary 2* 28.3 (2001): 19–60.

Duffy, Dennis. "Furnishing the Pictures: Arthur S. Goss, Michael Ondaatje and the Imag(in)ing of Toronto." *Journal of Canadian Studies* 36.2 (2001): 106–29.

Fee, Marjorie. "Canadian Literature and English Studies in the Canadian University." *Essays on Canadian Writing* 48 (1992–93): 20–40.

Foucault, Michel. *Discipline and Punish: The Birth of the Prison*. Trans. Alan Sheridan. New York: Vintage, 1979.

Giroux, Henry. "Mis/Education and Zero Tolerance: Disposable Youth and the Politics of Domestic Militarization." *boundary 2* 28.3 (2001): 61–94.

Globe and Mail. 24 May 2002: section T.

Godard, Barbara. "Notes from the Cultural Field: Canadian Literature from Identity to Hybridity." *Essays on Canadian Writing* 72 (2000): 209–47.

Guillory, John. *Cultural Capital: The Problem of Literary Canon Formation*. Chicago: U of Chicago P, 1993.

Hardt, Michael, and Antonio Negri. *Empire*. Cambridge: Harvard UP, 2000.

Heslop, Jackie. "Subjectivity, *Bildung*, Pedagogy: 'Coming of Age' in Modernity." PhD Diss. U of Victoria, 2001.

Holland, Eugene W., and Vassilis Lambropoulos. "Introduction." *The Humanities as Social Technology*. Spec. issue of *October* 53 (1990): 3–10.

Jusdanis, Gregory. *The Necessary Nation*. Princeton: Princeton UP, 2001.

Kant, Immanuel. *Conflict of the Faculties*. Trans. Mary J. Gregor. New York: Abaris, 1979.

Malcolm, Douglas. "Solos and Chorus: Michael Ondaatje's Jazz Politics/Poetics." *Mosaic* 32.3 (1999): 131–49.

Mellor, Winifred M. "'The Simple Container of Our Existence': Narrative Ambiguity in Carol Shields's *The Stone Diaries*." *Studies in Canadian Literature* 20.2 (1995): 96–110.
Micale, Mark S., and Robert L. Dietle, eds. *Enlightenment, Passion, Modernity: Historical Essays in European Thought and Culture*. Stanford: Stanford UP, 2000.
Miyoshi, Masao. "A Borderless World? From Colonialism to Transnationalism and the Decline of the Nation-State." *Cultural Production and the Transnational Imaginary*. Ed. Rob Wilson and Wimal Dissanayake. Durham: Duke UP, 1996. 78–106.
O'Hanlon, Rosalind. "Cultures of Rule, Communities of Resistance: Gender, Discourse and Tradition in Recent South Asian Historiographies." *Social Analysis* 25 (1989): 94–114.
Ondaatje, Michael. *Elimination Dance*. Ilderton, ON: Nairn Publishing House, 1978.
———. *In the Skin of a Lion*. 1987. Toronto: Penguin, 1988.
Parry, Benita. "Overlapping Territories and Intertwined Histories: Edward Said's Postcolonial Cosmopolitanism." *Edward Said: A Critical Reader*. Ed. Michael Sprinker. Oxford: Blackwell, 1992. 19–47.
Said, Edward W. *Culture and Imperialism*. New York: Knopf, 1993.
"School's Out for Many Canadian Books." *Globe and Mail* 17 Apr. 2002: R2.
Simon, Roger I. "The Touch of the Past: The Pedagogical Significance of a Transactional Sphere of Public Memory." *Revolutionary Pedagogies: Cultural Politics, Instituting Education, and the Discourse of Theory*. Ed. Peter Pericles Trifonas. New York: Routledge, 2000. 61–80.
Slemon, Stephen. "Climbing Mount Everest: Postcolonialism in the Culture of Ascent." *Canadian Literature* 158 (1998): 15–42.
Spanos, William V. *America's Shadow: An Anatomy of Empire*. Minneapolis: U of Minnesota P, 2000.
———. *The End of Education: Toward Posthumanism*. Minneapolis: U of Minnesota P, 1993.
———. "Heidegger's *Parmenides*: Greek Modernity and the Classical Legacy." *Journal of Modern Greek Studies* 19 (2001): 89–115.
Valpy, Michael. "Universities Fear Attention Deficit: Media Exposure Highly Coveted, Study Finds." *Globe and Mail* 13 Apr. 2002: A1, A10.

Cross-Talk, Postcolonial Pedagogy, and Transnational Literacy

DIANA BRYDON

MY TITLE, "CROSS-TALK," EVOKES the ambivalence of the conflictual classroom where dialogue is engaged about issues that matter enough to get people angry. Postcolonial questions in Canadian contexts can function like lightning rods for channelling complex and inarticulate anxieties about the changing shape of the nation. This paper was first inspired by my surprise at the anger that Dionne Brand's perspective on the Writing Thru Race conference, held in 1994 after significant media controversy, can still inspire, several years after its enactment. It arises from my attempts in the classroom, together with my students, to work through that anger to create a more productive dialogue around how to situate Writing Thru Race, what it signified, and how it continues to signify today.[1] More recently, I have been again surprised by continuing hostility toward casting Canadian literature in postcolonial contexts and dismissals, both passive and active, of anything postcolonial, either literature or theory. The ability to arouse emotional as well as intellectual reactions may be one of literary study's greatest strengths but how to negotiate strong opposing emotions is not easily managed. To bring postcolonialism into the Canadian literature classroom is to ignite controversies seldom generated by a focus on generic conventions or prosody. Cross-talk may arise, then, from unacknowledged emotional investments in certain contexts, but it may also come from contrasting assumptions, expectations, and understandings of the terms of classroom engagement, the object of study, and the function of education within the nation. How may these cross-currents be negotiated so that genuine learning can occur?

I cannot provide pedagogical solutions in this paper because there is no quick fix, and if there were, a postcolonial approach, by definition, would be suspicious of it. If you find my evasiveness here frustrating, then you understand how many students who are seeking answers feel when they are confronted instead with the proliferating questions that come with any postcolonial approach to learning. There is no mastery here. Because postcolonial pedagogy must question so much of what is taken for granted within and beyond the classroom, its practice can be profoundly destabilizing for all concerned.

An elaboration of the goals of such work can help to reorient the discussion. I take as axiomatic three starting points elaborated by Kathleen McCormick in *The Culture of Reading and the Teaching of English*: "First, students must become able to analyse how they themselves are culturally constructed as subjects-in-history. . . . Second, they must learn to analyse how texts are likewise culturally constructed, how they are produced in particular sets of social circumstances and reproduced differently in different circumstances. Third, they can then use such cultural and historical analysis to develop and defend critical positions of their own" (9). This is a mandate attentive to what Homi K. Bhabha terms "the politics of location." If Canadian students (and I include teachers within this category) are to undertake such a program, then we will need to come to terms with Canada's history of colonialism and its current position within the global order as it has affected our lives and shaped our thinking, recognizing, of course, that our individual experiences of this process will not be homogeneous. Many will find it an uncomfortable process, invoking different kinds of unease, but it may also prove energizing. McCormick concludes: "What we need to learn is that theorizing, not just theory, is what our curricula need" (191). And I would add, more specifically, that postcolonial theorizing is what Canadian literature in the classroom needs if Canadian students are to understand why Himani Bannerji describes Canada as "a liberal democracy with a colonial heart" (75).

I cannot provide answers but I can provide a preliminary charting of the issues at stake when postcolonialism meets Canadian literature in the classroom. The unspoken mediating term in this encounter is multiculturalism, which complicates understandings of Canada and the postcolonial in very different ways. I avoid this term here because it invokes a different agenda and its employment carries a host of new problems in its wake. I deplore the conflation of multiculturalism and postcolonialism that is currently taking place in predominantly US contexts. It is important to distinguish those US usages of the term from the Canadian debates, but even in the Canadian context many analyses of multiculturalism tend to assume as starting points many of the things that postcolonial thinking questions: the nature and function of citizenship, community, ethnicity, historicism, and home, for example. Canadian discussions of multiculturalism usually situate their discussions within national historical contexts, paying little attention to the legacies of imperialism. While sophisticated work is being done on multiculturalism in dialogue with postcolonial theories, I must bracket those discussions today.[2]

Monika Kin Gagnon's definition of multiculturalism in her "Primer for Xenophilic Beginners" provides a succinct definition of a key point of tension built into the term: "Canadian policy supporting cultural diversity, passed as an official act in 1988. So Canada's got culture and multiculture" (86). It is that double standard that postcolonial theorizing can both expose and move beyond, while also recognizing the equal sting in Gagnon's even pithier definition of "post-colonial" as "Deeply offensive to First Peoples" (86). This second definition, which assumes that "post" means simply "after," points to the fact that postcolonialism means many different things to different people. If, as Sneja Gunew notes, multiculturalism "is a term with global resonances but very different national inflections" (46), then postcolonial theorizing, in its many current manifestations, is an even more complex matter. Postcolonial theorizing in the Canadian literature classroom must attend to these histories of contestation, to the various disciplinary, national, and global configurations of its usage, while also recognizing that these various national inflections are themselves never singular but also multiply constituted. What matters most, finally, is how work identifying itself as postcolonial is employed and the results that it achieves. As Roy Miki notes, "Unreflective liberal gestures toward 'cultural' and 'post-colonial' studies . . . can all too easily become a vehicle for disciplinary management . . ." (174). Graham Huggan's *The Postcolonial Exotic* provides several revealing examples of the rerouting and defusing processes that can divert a postcolonial agenda into just another curricular choice within an unchanged disciplinary structure. In other words, the same dangers that attend the practice of postcolonial theory can also threaten the effectiveness of postcolonial pedagogy.

To understand current contexts for introducing postcolonial pedagogies into the Canadian literature classroom, it is useful to review their intertwined histories in Canadian university contexts, where postcolonial studies derive largely from earlier work within Commonwealth literary studies. Often many of the same people involved in introducing Canadian literature into the classroom were also involved in the early stages of developing Commonwealth literature as a recognized field of study: people such as John Matthews, John Moss, Bill New, Bob Robertson, Clara Thomas, and many others.[3] Under the editorship of Bill New (1977–1995), the journal *Canadian Literature* regularly situated its vision of Canada within larger Commonwealth contexts, while also recognizing Canada's bilingual status within that primarily anglophone disciplinary configuration.[4] Canadian and Commonwealth literatures began to infiltrate English departments in Canada during roughly the same period and were often seen as complementary enterprises, but there is an implicit tension between the transnationalism of contemporary postcolonial studies and the nationalism that has traditionally attended the study of a national literature, whether that be in a relatively disguised form, as with English literature, or more openly, as with American and Canadian literatures. By bringing postcolonial theories and Canadian literature into the same classroom, we can usefully test the assumptions of each.

I realize that the term "transnational" is controversial and may set certain alarm bells ringing within nationalist circles. I use it here to indicate my desire to forge international connections beyond those associated with older notions of "universalism" and newer notions of "globalization." If we accept Zygmunt Bauman's definition of globalization as not about what "we wish or hope *to do*" but rather "about *what is happening to us all*," that is, as referring "primarily to the global *effects*, notoriously unintended and unanticipated, rather than to global *initiatives* and *undertakings*" (60), then we need some way to signify the reclamation of agency, a reclamation that can no longer be claimed at the national level alone. We cannot ignore globalization but we can ask how to restore the agency once exercised through the state under changing global conditions. This is especially important now when to adhere to old ideas of nationalism may act to reinforce, rather than challenge, globalizing tendencies. As Bauman points out, "there is neither logical nor pragmatic contradiction between the extraterritoriality of capital" and "the renewed emphasis on the 'territorial principle'" amongst proliferating feeble sovereign states (67). Under these changed conditions, holding too closely to older notions of national identity may not prove the most effective way to preserve the ability of Canadians to shape the decisions that affect their daily lives, which I take to be the ultimate goal of pedagogy and decolonization alike.

Like Smaro Kamboureli in *Scandalous Bodies*, I employ pedagogy to indicate not only teaching and learning practices within the classroom but also the ways in which those practices are themselves constrained within a national pedagogy, which Kamboureli describes as "the subtle and not so subtle ways in which the desire-machine of the state socializes us" (3). Eva Mackey, in *The House of Difference,* provides illuminating analysis of certain "pedagogies of patriotism" in official Canadian narrations of the nation, which have their subtler counterparts within Canadian literary criticism and history. Contemporary dialogues about theory, literature, and pedagogy address this double context. They have a history roughly contemporaneous with the rise of postcolonial and feminist liberation movements mid-century. Robert Con Davis argues that the "impetus for an oppositional pedagogy comes from two sources—third world attempts to reject foreign domination in education and radical attempts to rethink the nature of social change in France after the May 1968 student/worker uprisings" (250). I would add feminism to this list. Since then, canon wars, culture wars, and controversies over political correctness have come and gone. Arguments have been advanced promoting a "cultural literacy" that polices entrance into the status quo. The founding of the Dominion Institute in 1997 with the aim of enabling Canadians to "rediscover the links that exist between our history, civic traditions and common identity" (Gray R3) is a Canadian offshoot of this cultural literacy movement and a conscious effort to intervene within a national (and nationalist) pedagogy. These initiatives have in turn been countered by calls for a "critical literacy," dedicated to the analysis of the connections between "knowledge and power" (Con Davis 254). Postcolonial pedagogy derives from oppositional pedagogy's belief that teaching is "a social practice and a cultural construct, a dynamic and unfinished (hence 'impossible' to fix) activity"

(264). It aligns itself with oppositional pedagogies and the promotion of critical literacy yet it also seeks to go beyond these movements in significant ways.

Gayatri Chakravorty Spivak, in her "charting of a practitioner's progress from colonial discourse studies to transnational cultural studies" (*Critique* ix–x), suggests the need to develop a "transnational literacy." Transnational literacy expands critical literacy into a more empathetic mode of reading that Spivak calls "critical intimacy," which must then be directed to the task of understanding new modes of globalizing power and the ways in which they have easily co-opted certain forms of now-established postcolonialism, including celebrations of hybridity and resistance, to their agenda. I would like to experiment in developing such a mode of reading within my classrooms.[5] Spivak's focus on "a productive acknowledgement of complicity" within metropolitan postcolonialism (xii) and her strategy of attempting "to persuade through the discontinuity of odd connections or reconstellation" (65) strike me as particularly appropriate for re-situating Canadian texts beyond the confines of an outmoded nationalist discourse without giving up on the nation entirely. This latter point is crucial, as Donna Pennee and others stress throughout this volume. Canada is reinvented through its literature and through its encounters with postcolonialism in the classroom, but a postcolonial future does not necessarily imply a postnational state of affairs.

While the old academic ideals of disinterested inquiry seem more and more remote from actuality, the new ideals of democratizing the classroom and opening it out into the world are difficult to implement. It is impossible to think about decolonizing the classroom without attending to the larger institutional structures that shape and contain our classes: the discipline, the university, and the nation are enmeshed in world systems that we need to understand if we are to change them. Gerald Graff explains: "A university is a curious accretion of historical conflicts that it has systematically forgotten" (257). We could say the same of a nation. I am moved by John Willinsky's statement, in *Learning to Divide the World: Education at Empire's End*: "This book has been written against the learned forgetfulness and complacency displayed in the face of history. How far we can go in seeing the world other than as we have inherited it, I do not yet know. The educational project always lies ahead" (263). Postcolonial pedagogy looks ahead through looking critically and intimately at the learned forgetfulness and complacency built into the educational project as we know it and its complicities with both imperialist and nationalist projects.

"The best of postcolonialism," according to Spivak, "is autocritical" ("Foreword" xv). The goal of autocritique is to create new forms of agency but also, I think, to aspire toward that old ideal of Truth even as we remain aware of the interferences that will always arise from personal investments brought to the classroom by students and teacher alike, each with their own truths that require respect. Like feminism, postcolonialism has always had an activist agenda: to decolonize the mind, as Ngugi memorably put it, but also to create a more equitable world than imperialism offered. Now that neo-liberal globalization appears to have replaced both colonialism and neo-colonialism with its own particular versions of inequity, the goal remains the same although the methods may differ. According to Spivak: "The necessary collective efforts are to change laws, relations of production, systems of education, and health care" (*Critique* 383). In Canada, but not everywhere, most of these remain matters largely within the control of the nation although that autonomy is eroding in each domain.

Spivak is careful not to label this the "real" work, as if the work in the classroom were secondary. These collective efforts may be necessary to create the goal of a just society, but the work of teaching can both seek to perform that goal and create the conditions to make it happen within the world outside the classroom. Spivak continues: "But without the mind-changing one-on-one responsible contact, nothing will stick" (383). Such a statement needs careful elaboration. Postcolonial pedagogy does aim to change minds and change the world, yet it cannot fall into the pedagogical assumptions that once made conversion such a potent ally of imperialism. Gauri Viswanathan's insistence on "the need to historicize conversion not only as a spiritual but also a political activity" has helped me to see the sources of my unease with this term in its dual historical role of embodying "assimilation and dissent" (xvii) as well as in "modernity's invention of religious fundamentalism as its necessary antithesis," a subject little addressed in anti-orientalist and postcolonial critiques (xiv). I am persuaded by Viswanathan's argument that we currently lack "an adequate vocabulary" to deal with the worldliness of conversion as a border-crossing process, despite the "many instances of conversion movements accompanying the fight against racism, sexism, and colonialism" (xvi). Education is about responsible mind-changing yet has so often been imbricated in pedagogies of coercion and irresponsible persuasion that it is still difficult to write about how the process envisioned by Spivak might proceed.

Through postcolonial pedagogy, the teacher will be changed along with her students, and the commitment to changing cannot end with the end of the school year. Ultimately, postcolonial pedagogy aims to encourage citizens desirous and capable of creating a better world, one founded on a respect for all humanity and for the natural world we inhabit. But the ultimate effect of the "one-on-one responsible contact" that Spivak calls for, and that can take place in the literature classroom, between teacher and student, between student and student, and between text and student, cannot be predicted or controlled. Postcolonial pedagogy should not be in the business of producing converts to a cause, however worthy, because all causes can be perverted. The goal of postcolonial work can never be allowed to congeal into a fixed program because there is an inherent tendency in any form of fixity to become oppressive and because all movements toward liberation can be co-opted. A department with too coherent a vision of its mission, however progressive that vision may be, can therefore feel constraining in a way that a department riven by genuine disagreements will not, as long as there is respect and students are not enlisted to take sides.

This is why Spivak insists that the mind-changing must happen on both sides, and remain a constant process, with no clear end in sight other than that "impossible, undivided world of which one must dream, in view of the impossibility of which one must work, obsessively" (*Critique* 382). Her analogy here is to Jacques Derrida's definition of ethics as "the experience of the impossible" (*Critique* 427) and his insistence that "Justice cannot pass in a direct line to law; that line is a non-passage, an aporia. Yet justice is disclosed in law, even as its own effacement" (427). Spivak's book is itself a teacherly demonstration of how such a "concept-metaphor of the 'experience of the impossible'" (426) works. *A Critique of Postcolonial Reason* seeks to effect that "one-on-one mind-changing" through calling into being a new kind of reader, one who reads with "critical intimacy" to develop "transnational literacy."

Mieke Bal argues that "reading is what the book is about, what it does, and what it teaches." It "teaches how to read, *otherwise*." This "otherwise" is a "form of readerliness based on multiplicity" (2) that "deploys aesthetics to fight aesthetics" and to oppose "the rift between aesthetic and political literary work" (11). I see critical intimacy as consonant with the goals that John Mowitt sets for teaching literature: "to make people better able to comprehend the conditions and limits of their lives, and better able to translate this comprehension into the practical structuring of daily life at both the local and global levels" (55). It is a mode of reading that rejects "the tendency to equate thinking with problem solving, where reflection is subordinated to the requirements of efficacy" (Adorno and Horkheimer, cited in Mowitt 56). Therefore, as Ian Baucom notes, Spivak enacts "obliquity (the indirect route) as a form of reason" (419). Mark Sanders provides a more extended description of this process: "If putting oneself in the place of another is indispensable to ethics, it is inevitable for a reader; if there is an opening for the ethical in reading, and for the ethical to open from reading, it is this. Spivak's point of intervention is to teach the reader to experience that place as (im)possible . . . and in so doing, to acknowledge complicity in actuating the texts and systemic geopolitical textuality that make it so" (7).

How does such a mode of reading serve the development of transnational literacy? Spivak claims: "It is my belief that a training in a literary habit of reading the world can attempt to put a curb on . . . superpower triumphalism only if it does not perceive acknowledgement of complicity as an inconvenience" (*Critique* xii). Transnational literacy means more than reading widely and doing one's homework, and it is not consonant with older notions of world literature or with surveying the territory through imperial eyes. Once again, I find John Mowitt suggestive here. He urges: "Let us drop the traditional obsession with being 'well-rounded,' and replace it with the aim of being 'well-grounded'" (63). Our conference logo, the plunging moose, may appear to have failed this test.[6] But sometimes leaps into the unknown must precede grounding and the panoptical view must be abandoned to read with critical intimacy. To be grounded in the critically intimate recognition of the complicities of the local may be a student's best defence from the "postcolonial exotic" so ably analyzed by Graham Huggan, if the trap of misperceiving "postcolonial teaching as an autoethnographic exercise in cultural translation" can be avoided (247).

Yet groundedness and its defences against exotification are themselves threatened. Bauman believes that "localities are losing their meaning-generating and meaning-negotiating capacity and are increasingly dependent on sense-giving and interpreting actions which they do not control" (2–3). This is why groundedness now must imply not only embeddedness in a specific locality but also an awareness of how that embeddedness is itself embedded within transnational structures. Huggan argues in *The Postcolonial Exotic* that "postcolonial studies is situated within the context of a utopian pedagogic imaginary that simultaneously recognizes that the institutional constraints placed upon its political effectiveness may in fact form part of the field's attractiveness—and its wider commercial appeal" (261). To get out of this double bind, the teacher will need to develop what Mark Sanders terms "an itinerary of agency in complicity" (1).

My own teaching has been influenced by pedagogical developments of the last two decades in which Gerald Graff's notions of "teaching the conflicts" and metaphors of the conversation have assumed greater prominence, but my understanding of postcolonial theory insists that such innovations in themselves are insufficient. Classroom work must be more than a conversation; it must become collaborative work dedicated to concentrated learning and unlearning, and to engagement with the issues of the times as they present themselves. My ideal classroom would provide a space where learning and unlearning could happen through dialogue based on mutual respect. (This paper addresses the reality of the classrooms I know and what happens within them, but questions around access remain crucial for postcolonial pedagogy. Who populates these classrooms and who is excluded from them? How can transnationally literate work move beyond the classroom walls? Now that I have written this paper, these other questions strike me as possibly more urgent.)

The majority of students I teach are self-selecting: they are looking for ways to challenge the constructions of their own privilege and the institutional structures that both benefit and thwart them, but they also need to practise negotiating challenge and working with uncertainties. Such questing can begin to form a common ground for postcolonial inquiry, but that ground needs to be established by each new group in its own way. It is hard to write about teaching. Each classroom dynamic is different; each class creates its own community. What works with one group fails with another. What works one day may fail another. The teacher must always be prepared to shift strategies, reconsider goals, adapt to the demands of an ever-changing present. Yet while the particular mix of classroom dynamics, expectations, and privileges to be unlearned (for teacher and for student) may differ from group to group, some generalizations may be ventured about the contexts in which we teach. These include contexts of privilege, the forms of sanctioned ignorance that official cultural literacy and the discipline promote, and the classroom as a workplace, in which teachers and students "are always gendered, raced, and classed workers" (Briskin and Coulter 254).

My provisional title for this paper named "(mis)understandings in the classroom" as its focus because I wanted to destabilize accepted binaries between understanding and misunderstanding, learning and unlearning, what is taken and what is mis-taken, not just to underline the ways in which uses of theory may be creatively deployed in what Spivak terms "reconstellative or scrupulously mistaken" ways (*Critique* 128), but also to highlight the productive potential within those very moments we are taught to fear and to avoid: moments when we might be caught out not knowing; asking a stupid question; making a mistake. In the postcolonial classroom these can be the sources of productive play that might lead eventually to decolonizing the classroom. I encourage what might seem to be obvious or redundant questions in the classroom because I believe that there is no such thing as an unproductive question. If one student is uncertain or confused, then that feeling is likely to be shared. The questions that surprise us, give us pause, momentarily silence us as we wonder where to begin in trying to formulate an answer, are exactly the kind of questions that we need, as we re-craft our beginnings to match where our students begin. Working against the self-censorship that silences what might be construed as the stupid question is not an easy task, as the story of the emperor's new clothes reminds us. Progressive pedagogies have encouraged us to work with what each student brings to the classroom setting, but they have tended to stress the positive value of what students already know but do not realize they know. While that is important, what they really do not know is also crucial as a starting point for discussion. We need to find ways of eliciting and sharing ignorance that remedy that failing without stigmatizing the person who dares to ask what might appear to be a stupid question. We need to be able to turn such questions toward examination of how ignorance is itself actively produced and how certain forms of ignorance actually receive social sanction. Increasingly, more and more areas of ignorance are losing their stigma as anti-intellectualism receives official sanction from many sources of traditional authority, such as the presidency of the United States. I have become intrigued by the forms of "sanctioned ignorance" that we bring to the classroom, those forms of ignorance we feel no need to remedy, and indeed may wish to protect.

I speculate that much of the cross-talk in my classrooms may come from such sources. I find great value in Spivak's notion of "un-learning our privilege as our loss" (*Post-Colonial Critic* 9). But that privilege feeds on forms of sanctioned ignorance that are so close to our sense of who we are that they are very hard to address through logical analysis alone. In such situations, trying to read through "critical intimacy" may help break blockages. Some forms of sanctioned ignorance are tied up with our national identity as Canadians: the interplay of pride in multiculturalism and denial of structural racism, analyzed so well by Smaro Kamboureli, Roy Miki, and Sherene Razack, is a particularly sensitive area, as are the issues of indigenous land claims, rights, and creativity. In a tangential comment, Spivak suggests that "those who have stayed in place for more than thirty thousand years" present a "radical limit" that is "the name of the other of the question of diaspora" (*Critique* 402). Similarly, Arif Dirlik suggests that "indigenism may be of paradigmatic significance in contemporary politics globally" (237). Such comments set an agenda still to be worked through, one that will be particularly important for expanding Canadian postcolonial dialogues in future.

Working through the cross-talk, those moments when the normal circuits of give-and-take discussion get broken, is part of the task of postcolonial pedagogy as I understand it. But prompting that cross-talk in the first place, so that it can be worked through, is essential. Too often misguided notions of politeness prevent these debates from emerging. We must constantly seek strategies to bring such muted disagreements to the fore and in ways that allow them to do their productive work. One tactic that has worked for me some of the time is the assignment of short response pieces or position papers that students may choose to deliver on the first day that a new set of readings are assigned. Several of these replace the traditional seminar presentation. By having a group of students present their responses in sequence before opening discussion to the class, it is possible to stage contradictory readings in such a way as to open further discussion rather than forcing the premature taking of sides. With four radically different readings of a single text unfolding in sequence, it becomes easier for the presenters and their listeners to entertain alternative possibilities to their own earlier certainties without getting caught up in the kind of competitive rivalries that a formal debate or paired seminar and previously assigned seminar response encourage.

George Elliott Clarke's play, *Whylah Falls* (an adaptation of his award-winning long poem), proved a lightning rod for hotly contested ideological differences among my students that might have led to a hardening of positions without the blessing of this strategy. Instead, our understanding of the play itself and of the disagreements that separated us became enriched by this exercise in collaborative listening and the discussion to which it eventually gave rise. The play's positioning between black Atlantic and black Canadian discourses further enabled our discussions of what was at stake in this staging of multiple forms of belonging to move beyond the binary of racist/anti-racist that had sometimes stymied earlier class discussions.

Our responses to *Whylah Falls* coalesced in an astonishing range of differences that together enriched our appreciation of Clarke's achievement, of the text's dialogues with intersecting local and global discourses, and of our combined strength as a collaborative group. I am experiencing similar moments of wonder, illumination, and excitement as the interdisciplinary Major Collaborative Research Initiative group with which I am currently working on globalization and autonomy continues to identify and negotiate our genuine differences in approach. For its full development, "transnational literacy" will require such cross- and inter-disciplinary collaboration. In the meantime, as Spivak suggests, the individual teacher "can break rules" (*Critique* xiii). What does she mean by this? I think that she is warning against the arrogant notion that any single person may practise interdisciplinarity on her own with the erudition that it demands. At the same time, she is also insisting that it is still possible to question the unspoken division of labour that accompanies disciplinary expertise by breaking the rules that divide disciplines, obscuring our ability to draw connections across them. For Spivak, however, it is important to earn the right to break rules by first doing one's homework, without ever assuming that such homework will be sufficient. *A Critique of Postcolonial Reason* enacts this kind of rule-breaking cross-talk, thinking through and across the disciplines of philosophy, literature, history, and cultural studies.

Many of the formal pedagogical strategies entrenched within the university and the student expectations that they create about what learning entails discourage this kind of rule-breaking and the questions that it raises. Richard Cavell has written compellingly about his own postcolonial pedagogical strategies in working against the "queen for a day" model for organizing the graduate seminar, a model in which each student takes a turn to be the authority on a topic, without fundamentally challenging the authoritarian structure of the arrangement. If teachers seeking to introduce postcolonial pedagogies into the classroom think that this model does not go far enough in democratizing the classroom, some students are now asking for even this seminar model to be replaced by graduate lecture courses. Such requests are fuelled by the belief that education can be comprehensive, that students have gaps to fill, and that lectures are the quickest way to fill them. They also assume that mastery of a topic is still possible. The coverage model, the canon, and even notions of opening up the canon have each worked against the teaching of postcolonial literatures in an equitable fashion within the English department. Such models also work against integrating postcolonial pedagogies across the curriculum.

In insisting that learning involves unlearning, a process that is slow, unending, and dependent on the give and take of a classroom where questions are encouraged, postcolonial pedagogies swim against the currents of the times. If traditional teaching addresses forms of ignorance deemed unacceptable, then postcolonial pedagogy addresses those forms of "sanctioned ignorance" that are often rewarded and may exist everywhere, including among "the theoretical elite" (Spivak, *Critique* x).

What are the particular forms of sanctioned ignorance encouraged by Canadian literature and postcolonial study in the classroom? Sherene Razack has identified an agenda for critique in three "organizing constructs that most often enabled students to deny that oppression existed: rights thinking, essential woman, and the culturalization of differences" (17). Each of these may be confused with postcolonial agendas, which are also generating their own forms of sanctioned ignorance. We must continue asking Spivak's question: "in what interest are differences defined?" (357). And Razack's question: "Where am I in this picture?" (170). Transnational literacy involves thinking against the grain of what we think we know and don't know; it demands alertness to the changing function of what it means to take certain positions within local and global contexts.

Spivak's book enacts the difficulty of negotiating this changing terrain and unhinging "the clashing machinery" (397) of the ideological interferences that distort understanding of it, and hence our access to agency within it. For Spivak, transnational literacy means rethinking "globality away from the US melting pot" (402). Part of the task before those of us engaged in bringing postcolonial pedagogies into Canadian literature classrooms will be to specify what transnational literacy might mean for Canadians. How can we begin to rethink globality away from our own forms of sanctioned ignorance and re-ground it through postcolonial pedagogies that address our here and now? As I have suggested in this paper, comparative postcolonial contexts as well as pedagogical strategies may be employed to begin engaging in such work, but the task of elaborating the many dimensions of this challenge remains before us.

ACKNOWLEDGEMENTS

I am grateful to all the students in the class with whom I worked through the angry reaction to Dionne Brand's perspective on the "Writing Thru Race" conference, who generously shared the explorations on which this paper is based with me, and to the three groups of students in classes in postcolonial theory who helped me to grapple with the complexities of Spivak's text. Much of the discussion in this paper is based on their insights. I also owe a debt of gratitude to the Social Sciences and Humanities Research Council of Canada, who funded my standard research grant, "Postcolonialism: The Critical Heritage," from which much of this work initially derived, and who more recently have funded two complementary research projects, "The Ends of Postcolonialism" and "Globalization and Autonomy," which are enabling me to develop this work further with a dedicated group of graduate and undergraduate students.

NOTES

1. The Brand essay we discussed was "Notes for Writing Thru Race." "Writing Thru Race," a writers' conference limiting enrolment to "First Nations writers and writers of colour," attracted the attention of the media from February to May

1994, focusing debates on competing understandings of Canadian national identity, multiculturalism, and race. For a fuller analysis, see Miki 144–59; Gagnon 66–71; and Kanaganayakam. Also, for a briefer contextualization of this issue within larger debates, see Coleman and Goellnicht 1–29.

2. See Padolsky for a useful account of multiculturalism and its current debates that is attentive to postcolonial questions. For more extended analysis, see Bannerji and Mackey.

3. For more of this history, see Maes-Jelinek, et al.

4. This paper is written from within my own placement within a university English department, where the question of Quebec is acknowledged but often bracketed. Quebec has its own history of engagements with postcolonial theory and Quebec literature has its own history of development within university French departments that I cannot elaborate here. Nonetheless, engagement with the issues raised by Quebec remains important, although they are configured quite differently within Canadian and postcolonial studies. Given institutional constraints, however, these questions seldom arise in significant ways within the pedagogical practices I am considering here. Perhaps they should. Reconfiguring issues and re-constellating fields is part of what I take this collection of essays to be about. I am grateful to colleagues at Guelph and Western for guidance in thinking through issues of curricular as well as pedagogical reform.

5. Jennifer Wenzel writes of trying to apply these principles, as articulated earlier in Spivak's *Imaginary Maps*, to her reading of this text.

6. [Editor's note: The plunging moose conference logo was a detail from Charles Pachter's aluminum sculpture entitled *Mooseplunge* (1996), which Pachter kindly gave me permission to use for the conference brochures and posters. Pachter's 1976 painting, *Mooseplunge*, is reproduced on the cover of this volume.]

WORKS CITED

Bal, Mieke. "Three-Way Misreading." *Diacritics* 30.1 (2000): 2–24.

Bannerji, Himani. *The Dark Side of the Nation: Essays on Multiculturalism, Nationalism and Gender*. Toronto: Canadian Scholars' P, 2000.

Baucom, Ian. "Cryptic, Withheld, Singular." *Nepantla: Views from South* 1.2 (2000): 413–29.

Bauman, Zygmunt. *Globalization: The Human Consequences*. New York: Columbia UP, 1998.

Bhabha, Homi K. *The Location of Culture*. London: Routledge, 1994.

Brand, Dionne. "Notes for Writing Thru Race." *Bread Out of Stone*. Toronto: Coach House, 1994.

Briskin, Linda, and Rebecca Priegert Coulter. "Introduction: Feminist Pedagogy: Challenging the Normative." *Canadian Journal of Education* 17.3 (1992): 247–63.

Cavell, Richard. "Transvestic Sites: Postcolonialism, Pedagogy, and Politics." *Dangerous Territories: Struggles for Difference and Equality in Education*. Ed. Leslie G. Roman and Linda Eyre. New York: Routledge, 1997. 99–112.

Coleman, Daniel, and Donald Goellnicht. "Introduction: 'Race' into the Twenty-First Century." *Essays on Canadian Writing* 75 (2002): 1–29.

Con Davis, Robert. "A Manifesto for Oppositional Pedagogy: Freire, Bourdieu, Merod, and Graff." Henricksen and Morgan 248–67.

Dirlik, Arif. *The Postcolonial Aura: Third World Criticism in the Age of Global Capitalism*. Boulder: Westview, 1997.

Gagnon, Monika Kin. *Other Conundrums: Race, Culture, and Canadian Art*. Vancouver: Arsenal Pulp, Artspeak Gallery, Kamloops Art Gallery, 2000.

Graff, Gerald. *Professing Literature: An Institutional History*. Chicago: U of Chicago P, 1987.

Gray, Charlotte. "And the Rest Is History." *Globe and Mail* 23 Apr. 2002: R3.

Gunew, Sneja. *Framing Marginality: Multicultural Literary Studies*. Melbourne: Melbourne UP, 1994.

Henricksen, Bruce, and Thais E. Morgan, eds. *Reorientations: Critical Theories and Pedagogies*. Urbana: U of Illinois P, 1990.

Huggan, Graham. *The Postcolonial Exotic: Marketing the Margins*. London: Routledge, 2001.

Kamboureli, Smaro. *Scandalous Bodies: Diasporic Literature in Canada*. Toronto: Oxford UP, 2000.

Kanaganayakam, Chelva. "Writing Beyond Race: The Politics of Otherness." *Toronto Review* 12.3 (1994): 7–16.

Mackey, Eva. *The House of Difference: Cultural Politics and National Identity in Canada*. Toronto: U of Toronto P, 2002.

Maes-Jelinek, Hena, Kirsten Holst Petersen, and Anna Rutherford, eds. *A Shaping of Connections: Commonwealth Literature Studies—Then and Now*. Sydney: Dangaroo, 1989.

McCormick, Kathleen. *The Culture of Reading and the Teaching of English*. Manchester: Manchester UP, 1994.

Miki, Roy. *Broken Entries: Race, Subjectivity, Writing*. Toronto: Mercury, 1998.

Mowitt, John. "Survey and Discipline: Literary Pedagogy in the Context of Cultural Studies." *Class Issues: Pedagogy, Cultural Studies, and the Public Sphere*. Ed. Amitava Kumar. New York: New York UP, 1997. 48–64.

Padolsky, Enoch. "Multiculturalism at the Millennium." *Journal of Canadian Studies* 35.1 (2000): 138–60.

Razack, Sherene H. *Looking White People in the Eye: Gender, Race and Culture in Courtrooms and Classrooms*. Toronto: U of Toronto P, 1998.

Sanders, Mark. "Postcolonial Reading." Rev. of Gayatri Chakravorty Spivak *A Critique of Postcolonial Reason: Toward a History of the Vanishing Present. Postmodern Culture*. Online. 18 Oct. 1999. 14 Jan. 2004. <http://www.iath.virginia.edu/pmc/text-only/issue.999/10/1.r_sanders.html>.

Schwarz, Henry, and Sangeeta Ray, eds. *A Companion to Postcolonial Studies*. Oxford: Blackwell, 2000.

Spivak, Gayatri Chakravorty. *A Critique of Postcolonial Reason: Toward a History of the Vanishing Present*. Cambridge: Harvard UP, 1999.

———. "Foreword: Upon Reading the *Companion to Postcolonial Studies*." Schwarz and Ray xv–xxii.

———. *The Post-Colonial Critic: Interviews, Strategies, Dialogues*. Ed. Sarah Harasym. New York: Routledge, 1990.

Viswanathan, Gauri. *Outside the Fold: Conversion, Modernity, and Belief*. Princeton: Princeton UP, 1998.

Wenzel, Jennifer. "Grim Fairy Tales: Taking a Risk, Reading *Imaginary Maps*." *Going Global: The Transnational Reception of Third World Women Writers*. Ed. Amal Amireh and Lisa Suhair Maja. New York: Garland, 2000. 229–51.

Willinsky, John. *Learning to Divide the World: Education at Empire's End*. Minneapolis: U of Minnesota P, 1998.

Literary Citizenship: Culture (Un)Bounded, Culture (*Re*)Distributed

DONNA PALMATEER PENNEE

THIS PAPER OFFERS THEORETICAL considerations of the ways in which literary postcoloniality in the teaching of Canadian literatures constitutes both a continuation of and a departure from the institutionalized history of literature as a key mode of delivery in civic education. To say that postcolonial pedagogy continues and departs from the institutionalization of literary studies is to say something of such obviousness that it would seem not to bear repeating, yet it is precisely to "the obvious" that pedagogy must attend insofar as both pedagogy and the obvious perform so much social—and so much complex—work. An equal obviousness that underwrites my thoughts about the past and the potential of literary citizenship is that literary studies are being conducted in an era of globalization: the very categories on which the dominant curricular edifice has stood—the categories of territorial sovereignty and cultural sovereignty as mutually constitutive—can no longer (pretend to) bear the weight of cumulative geo-temporal changes and the concomitant diversification of culture. The fact that literary studies can no longer operate as a vehicle for expressing and organizing a would-be homogeneous social structure is not, however, an argument *not* to use the literary for a heterogeneous but nevertheless shared social structure.

The present moment of globalization implies also a post-cultural moment in the anthropological sense that "cultures" are no longer produced, experienced, or distributed as bounded, or, as localized and particularized to *a* "people," or to "peoples" who can then be compared. This post-cultural moment implies that culture is no longer susceptible to analysis in bounded ways (see, for example, Howes; Appadurai). But the present moment of globalization also harbours the historical impetus of postcolonial responses to those much earlier moments of globalization, known as imperial and colonial territorial expansion: invasion settlement that was both armed by and in the midst of producing the apparatuses of state. This historical precedent of postcolonial responses to globalization remains grounded in geo-temporal, social, national, and state specificities. To put together the terms *postcolonial* and *Canadian literatures*, as this volume has done, and as many of us do in our places of critical and creative work, is to keep on the table for discussion how the *literary* and the *national* remain categories and modes of productivity and reproductivity. Together, they constitute both historically developed (and therefore immanent) and temporally imminent sites for arguing that culture represents not only the bounds and parameters of identity but also the less bounded but equally crucial processes of identification. National literary cultural expression has been both a source of and a response to colonization: as such, postcolonial literary studies are necessarily a methodological hinge between what is possibly the end of a malign cultural nationalism and the beginning of perhaps a more benign globalization. This methodological hinge opens a door onto the possibility that citizenship can be critically acculturated in a university literature classroom.

Such ruminations arise directly out of questions raised by my teaching, research, and curriculum administration over the past five or so years. At the undergraduate level, I have been teaching (primarily) Canadian literatures, along with methodology courses (critical practice and theory); at the graduate level and in my research, I have been examining and asking questions of cultural nationalisms in the context of globalization studies. I have also worked on major curricular revisions during this same period, revisions that were in part designed to begin to move away from the more traditional structuring of the literature degree by categories of national literatures. This particular confluence of activities has required an almost daily engagement with questions about the future of the discipline of literary studies: what is the social and political function of literary studies at the present time and in the immediate future; what is the object of literary studies? what knowledges and effects do literary studies produce? whose work are we or should we be asking our students to read, why, and by what methods, with what assumptions in mind? These are, of course, not new questions: what is new, as Foucault might have said, is "the event of [their] return" (58), the temporal opportunities for altered dispensations and dispositions (opportunities deftly pursued by such postcolonialists as Homi Bhabha [e.g., "DissemiNation"] and R. Radhakrishnan [e.g., "Ethnic"]).

I work in a university that is fairly representative of Canada's white anglophone mainstream: though my campus is less than 100 kilometres from Toronto, one of the world's most multiracial and multi-classed cities, the student and faculty population, though changing, is still predominantly white, middle class, Anglo-Celtic, Protestant (especially the faculty). So my ruminations arise from working in this location, among this demographic, and from what I see as the need to capitalize on two things in particular: one, that most undergraduate literature majors love literature; they love reading, they love form, and they love language (even though they may not always use it with the precision that they or I might like); they love and honour creative writers; and they understand themselves to be of a social minority for that love, not least of all because it seems to imply a forfeiting of any chance of well-paid employment; and two, that most undergraduate majors are both very fond of Canada and not unfamiliar with its shortcomings even if they occupy spaces of racial, linguistic, and economic privilege. These two things, a love of literature and an analytical fondness for Canada, strike me as *not negligible* opportunities with which to work.

They suggest that the category of the national and the category of the literary continue to be important heuristics with which to proceed. As a major vector of historical processes as well as a major vector of analysis, the national remains useful in our attempts to cross the major divide of globalized life—the divide between increasing social fragmentation on the one hand, and an increasing need for alternative methods of social integration, on the other. Literary studies that continue to work in methodologically specific ways with the category of the national offer forms of political and historical knowledge as forms of civic education; they offer a means of developing what several postcolonial literary scholars, among them Smaro Kamboureli and Len Findlay, have been calling *critical citizenship*, produced through a critical comparative approach to both minoritized and majoritized discourses within the Canadian nation-state (see Findlay's call to "Always [i]ndigenize" and Kamboureli's strategy of "negative pedagogy" [25]).

Minoritized literatures remind us that nations are made, not born, and are thus open to refashioning. Majoritized literatures, if studied historically and comparatively, also remind us that nations are made, not born. It does not follow, however, that the nation is a category to be dispensed with; rather, the category of the national remains necessary to think with at the present juncture of *inter*-national and *intra*-national relations. The national is a category that, while it produces structures of majority and minority, nevertheless is operating at its historical limit, as Stuart Hall and others might put it, using the deconstructive language of Jacques Derrida: globalization, particularly in its economic forms, has put the nation as a category and a structure "under erasure"; the nation is "no longer serviceable" in its "originary and unreconstructed form," and yet it is necessary to go on thinking with the nation, seeking legal recourse through the nation, doing business through (though not for) the nation, and performing cultural critique with the nation in its "detotalized or deconstructed" but nevertheless still operative "forms" (Hall 1).

This space and moment of the nation at its limit is also the space and moment signalled by those inaudible parentheses in my paper's subtitle: binding and/as unbinding, distributing and/as redistributing, but doing so within a methodologically bounded space that is also, perhaps, operating at its historical limit, the *category* of a national literature. What I want to suggest here is that it might be necessary to invest a little longer in the ongoing power of the nation as a referent and a concept in the literary domain, even as we may disagree with the term's uses, or may be wary of practices in its name. Literary citizenship entails communicative acts that function to the degree that they do precisely because we perform (in part) as subjects in our production and recognition of the attributes of Canada as a nation and of literatures as modes of identification, even though and even as we are differentially positioned to do so. While it is true that such terms as *nation*, *nationalism*, and *culture* do not have singular or stable meanings, they are terms that nevertheless circulate in day-to-day power relations, inside and outside of the geographic entity of Canada with sometimes pernicious but always sufficient stability to make a difference.

The terms *nation*, *nationalism*, and *national culture* circulate widely; they have explanatory and other kinds of power; they have a high though not homogeneous recognition factor; they are key to certain actions and affects in the world despite their ambiguity, and despite their relative diminishment by certain processes of globalization; and they are contentious terms precisely because people differentially located and empowered cannot agree on their contents and are differentially on the receiving end of the meanings and practices of these terms. All of which, again, makes the category of the national *not negligible* for literary analysis and the cultivation of critical citizenship. And if you're troubled by that formulation "not negligible" as a negative statement, then that makes at least two of us, but I cannot say in advance what the category might be positively, because I'm not thinking about the category as content but as method, as a set of relations, as potential.

Just as the category of the nation remains important, so too the category of the literary remains crucial to think with as a specifically *cultural* practice. In both the aesthetic and anthropological senses of cultural practice, the literary can perform work that cannot be performed elsewhere in the social with the same degree and kind of affect and freedom. The fact that the literary is less powerful in neo-realist political terms than, say, the International Monetary Fund, does not mean that we should give up on the literary as a form of knowledge or intervention. Homi Bhabha, among others, defends precisely this "specific value of a politics of cultural production; because it makes . . . [the cultural text] the grounds of political intervention, it . . . extends the domain of 'politics' in a direction that will not be entirely dominated by the forces of economic or social control. Forms of popular rebellion and mobilization are often most subversive and transgressive when they are created through oppositional *cultural* practices" ("Commitment" 20). I want to argue for the continued value of literary culture as a form of interventionist diplomacy, not as a form of bridge-building or "wilful illiteracy" so carefully excoriated by George Elliott Clarke (183, n.14; 168); rather, interventionist diplomacy might be a practice of acquiring wilful literacy to produce forms of communal knowledge of people different from yet similar to "ourselves," whomever we are.

But I want also to relocate this interventionist diplomacy within the notion that culture, and literary culture in particular, represents ourselves to ourselves: this inter-articulation, this coming together of both inter-national and intra-national representations, is crucial to arguments for the political productivity of the postcolonial literary, whether those arguments are made by creative practitioners or critical practitioners, from majority or minority positions, because inter-national and intra-national representations *are* the substance of today's multi-faceted practices of both speaking for and speaking to the people with whom we live, even when such speech may be unintended altogether. If you'll permit such a paradoxical phrase here, it is simply of the nature of social life in the present that creative literatures constitute both inter- and intra-national speech. "Canadian" literatures are written by and read by people who are not the same but who are similar, who share species similarity (see Gilroy), who live in interlocking geopolitical public spheres, and whose repertoires include mass communications media. In this present temporality and spatiality of the nation, I think literary studies speak to and speak for, to quote Adrienne Rich on the political problem of the pronoun, "We who are not the same. We who are many and do not want to be the same" (225).

This kind of willingness, even necessity, to risk the first person plural under certain circumstances parallels a willingness to risk a new form of cultural nationalism in the present. As R. Radhakrishnan has asked, "Is nationalism . . . 'always already' corrupt and defective in its agency? Whatever the answer may be in the long run, . . . it is crucial for the postcolonial subject to produce a critical and deconstructive knowledge about nationalism" ("Nationalism" 86). It is also crucial for *majority* subjects to produce a critical and deconstructive knowledge about nationalism. As William Connolly suggests, "it is necessary to practice the arts of experimental detachment of the self from the identity installed within it, even though these are slippery, ambiguous arts hardly susceptible to full realization. For it is probably impossible and surely undesirable to be human without some sort of implication in a particular identity, yet it is how an identity is experienced and how it defines itself with respect to different identities that is crucial . . ." (9). In other words, it's how we get from *identity* to *identifying with* that is crucial, from a state of being to a process of being and of becoming, a process that includes the processes of being citizens, of being interventionist diplomats.

My pedagogical and/as civic objective is to read, study, teach, and learn Canadian literatures as a place in which to practise the arts of experimental detachment of the self from the identity installed within it. I am trying to practise literary studies as a space of what Simon During refers to as "the civil Imaginary," a space that facilitated a public sphere apart from the state and the nation as those structures were being conceived in the eighteenth century: that space is open again to be occupied as the public sphere of the nation-state negotiates with other public spheres in response to globalization ("Literature" 142). Indeed, global civil society cannot be negotiated without, as Gerard Delanty argues, "the internal transformation of public spheres at national and subnational levels. . . . [C]osmopolitanism can succeed only if it is connected to civic communities from which it draws the strength to resist globalization" (1). During's more recent argument for "literary subjectivity" is also not negligible at the present time ("Literary"). Literary studies organized methodologically (but not "categorically") by the name of the national can offer a space of a "political imaginary" in which to practise what Connolly calls "'agonistic democracy,' a practice that affirms the indispensability of identity to life, disturbs the dogmatization of identity, and folds care for the protean diversity of human life into the strife and interdependence of identity\difference [*sic*]" (x). In other words, and in reference to what I said above vis-à-vis the historically developed and temporally imminent sites of the national literary, we may be occupying a temporality in which national literary studies can defamiliarize both majoritized and minoritized notions and experiences of citizenship and identification: national literary studies, understood as a process, provide for a kind of literary citizenship as a form of cultural and civic participation and cultural and civic legitimation in the social imaginary. Literary studies organized under the rubric of the national create a space to ask civic questions of state policies and inherited notions of nationalism.

Pollyanna Pennee, you say, or worse, that I speak from the security—or is that insecurity—of a multiply majoritized position, which is fine for me but not for everyone. I am aware that this argument for the national literary runs exactly counter to the statement that minorities are kept out of the national canon, that a national literary canon represents an exclusionary production of majoritized, normative values. I am not denying that statement nor am I suggesting that there are no real differences of power in access to the materials for literary production and reception, nor do I think that long histories of practices of minoritization are at an end.

Rather, I am taking that statement not only as a historically accurate one, but also as a temporal one, in the sense that there is agency in changing times, in the sense that that statement—that national literary studies are exclusionary—may be operating at its historical limit. In other words, the work that everyone in this volume is engaged in is *not negligible*. I am also trying to work in the spirit of Chandra Talpade Mohanty's interventions in cross-cultural feminist communities: in other words, I am not arguing *for* or *against* generalizations when I ask us to think about retaining for purposes of critical citizenship the categories of the national and the literary. Rather, I am arguing for the pertinence and timeliness of what Mohanty calls "careful, historically specific [and] complex generalizations" (349). I am also taking heart from Jürgen Habermas's statement that "There are no laws of history in the strict sense, and human beings, even whole societies, are capable of learning" (123).

A case can be made for the continued, though differentiated, relevance of imagining community at the national level for strategic purposes. In practice, this works out (in what I attempt in my classrooms at any rate) as a pedagogy based on mobilizing different kinds of representations of Canada (from literary to literary critical to state policy to sociology, law, and newspaper coverage, for example) in order to analyze how minoritization and majoritization occur in relation to each other, in relation to a bounded political but unbounded cultural sphere, and in relation to the specificities of the literary as a form that is and is not real. Retaining the category of national literatures requires us to make that correlational move over and over again, to traffic between the material and the ideational, and to teach and to learn differentiation while also teaching and learning similarities that are not reducible to sameness. The category permits the double and doubling action of generalizing and/as particularizing, heterogenizing and/as homogenizing. In this double and doubling move, a move that Len Findlay also advocates in his essay "Always Indigenize!," we can both continue and depart from literary studies as a form of civic education, as a form of teaching citizenship in flexible, historical, and imminent ways. But it is imperative that this pedagogy be also literary, not merely sociological, as George Elliott Clarke, among others, reminds us; it is imperative that we are acculturated *by* the literature and not the other way around, that the formal properties of the literature are understood to be as significant as and approached with the same care as the issues about which writers write, or about which some of their critics insist they write.

*

The pressure exerted by globalization on the structures and functions of literary studies might be understood as not unlike the pressure formerly exerted on the field by structuralism and post-structuralism: these movements pressured, by interrogating and historicizing, the categories of the author, the subject, and the boundaries of literary works. As a result, a lot of people jumped to the conclusion that these categories, especially the category of the subject, had been made to disappear in ways that precluded certain kinds of interventions of historical and political importance (such as some kinds of feminisms and some kinds of postcolonialisms). Most of us have recovered from that particular and pervasive non sequitur: to paraphrase Derrida speaking about the relation of deconstruction to metaphysics (i.e., "There is no sense in doing without the concepts of metaphysics in order to shake metaphysics" [280]), there is no question of doing without the author, the subject, or the boundaries of literary works. It is rather a matter of doing the author, the subject, and the boundaries of literary works differently. For the time being, there is no question of doing without the national; it is rather a matter of doing the national differently. For diasporas do not come from nor do they travel through and exist in thin air, nor do citizenships. They *are* grounded even if not always landed. This, too, is not negligible.

ACKNOWLEDGEMENTS

This paper was produced during the tenure of a Standard Research Grant from SSHRC. Thanks to Professor Sugars and her team for bringing together such a splendid group of teachers, writers, and scholars, and putting together such a productive conference program. Thanks to interlocutors in Ottawa as well as at conferences in Toronto (NEMLA) and Ustron, Poland (Canadian Studies, University of Silesia and the Civic Education Project) in spring 2002, where I delivered papers that attempted to work out versions of this paper's theoretical considerations through the case of a particular course, "ENGL 2640 Culture, Location, Identity: Minoritized Literatures in Canada and Beyond." Thanks especially to students in 2640 as well as to students in my graduate courses on cultural nationalisms in the context of globalization for always fruitful discussions.

WORKS CITED

Appadurai, Arjun. "Disjuncture and Difference in the Global Economy." *Modernity at Large: Cultural Dimensions of Globalization*. Public Worlds I. Minneapolis: U of Minnesota P, 1996. 27–47.

Bhabha, Homi K. "The Commitment to Theory." *The Location of Culture*. London: Routledge, 1994. 19–39.

———. "DissemiNation: Time, Narrative, and the Margins of the Modern Nation." *Nation and Narration*. Ed. Bhabha. London: Routledge, 1990. 291–322.

Clarke, George Elliott. "Harris, Philip, Brand: Three Authors in Search of Literate Criticism." *Journal of Canadian Studies/Revue d'études canadiennes* 35.1 (2001): 161–89.

Connolly, William E. *Identity/Difference: Democratic Negotiations of Political Paradox*. Ithaca: Cornell UP, 1991.

Delanty, Gerard. *Citizenship in a Global Age: Society, Culture, Politics*. Issues in Society. Buckingham: Open UP, 2000.

Derrida, Jacques. "Structure, Sign, and Play in the Discourses of the Human Sciences." Trans. Alan Bass. *Writing and Difference*. Chicago: U of Chicago P, 1978. 278–93.

During, Simon. "Literary Subjectivity." *ARIEL* 31.1–2 (2000): 33–50.

———. "Literature—Nationalism's Other?: The Case for Revision." *Nation and Narration*. Ed. Homi Bhabha. London: Routledge, 1990. 138–53.

Findlay, Len. "Always Indigenize!: The Radical Humanities in the Postcolonial Canadian University." *ARIEL* 31.1–2 (2000): 307–26.

Foucault, Michel. "The Order of Discourse." Trans. Ian McLeod. *Untying the Text: A Post-Structuralist Reader*. Ed. Robert Young. London: Routledge & Kegan Paul, 1981. 51–78.

Gilroy, Paul. *Against Race: Imagining Political Culture Beyond the Color Line*. Cambridge: Belknap/Harvard UP, 2000.

Habermas, Jürgen. *The Inclusion of the Other: Studies in Political Theory*. Ed. Ciaran Cronin and Pablo De Greiff. Studies in Contemporary German Social Thought. Cambridge: MIT P, 1998.

Hall, Stuart. "Introduction: Who Needs 'Identity'?" *Questions of Cultural Identity.* Ed. Stuart Hall and Paul Du Gay. London: SAGE, 1996. 1–17.

Howes, David, ed. *Cross-Cultural Consumption: Global Markets, Local Realities.* London: Routledge, 1996.

Kamboureli, Smaro. *Scandalous Bodies: Diasporic Literature in English Canada.* Don Mills: Oxford UP, 2000.

Mohanty, Chandra Talpade. "Under Western Eyes: Feminist Scholarship and Colonial Discourses." *boundary 2* 12.3/13.1 (1984): 333–58.

Radhakrishnan, R. "Ethnic Identity and Post-Structuralist Differance." *The Nature and Context of Minority Discourse.* Ed. Abdul R. Jan Mohamed and David Lloyd. New York: Oxford UP, 1990. 50–71.

———. "Nationalism, Gender, and the Narrative of Identity." *Nationalisms and Sexualities.* Ed. Andrew Parker, Mary Russo, Doris Sommer, and Patricia Yaeger. New York: Routledge, 1992. 77–95.

Rich, Adrienne. "Notes towards a Politics of Location." 1984. *Blood, Bread, and Poetry: Selected Prose 1979–1985.* New York: Norton, 1986. 210–31.

Globalization, (Canadian) Culture, and Critical Pedagogy: A Primer

ROY MIKI

We always have to apprehend ourselves in the fullness of the historical moment in which we live.

— Dionne Brand, cited by Paulo da Costa 9

*

Prime the engine
my father used to say

and sure enough
it started

But primed too much
it would flood

the smell of gasoline
in a stalled time

And by the way
he would add

don't forget the primer
or the paint won't bind

He knew about machines
and about relationships

*

LET'S START WITH a few selected definitions, drawn from *The New Penguin English Dictionary*:

"Prime": from the Latin, *primus* (first):

1. noun: the most active, thriving, or successful state
2. adjective: first in importance
3. verb: to put (something, especially a pump) into working order by filling or charging it with something; to apply a first coat, e.g., of paint or oil, to (a surface), especially in preparation for painting.

Hence, "Primer":

1. noun: a book that provides a basic introduction to a subject
2. noun: material used in priming a surface, especially a type of paint used as a first coat.

Three qualifications then follow:

1. Other meanings have been left in the dictionary as the unsaid.
2. I wouldn't deny the play of all the meanings cited.
3. But in this talk I'm interested primarily in "primer" as the first coat that prepares a surface for painting, and "prime" as an act of putting something into working order.

So this will be a speculative approach to what might form the methodological and conceptual parameters of a critical postcolonial pedagogy for the urgencies that motivate our practices as scholars and teachers at this moment.

*

I feel very privileged to be sharing space in this volume with critical thinkers whose work I have drawn from in my own efforts to figure out "where we're at" these turbulent globalizing days. Figuring out "where we're at," of course, invokes a time-space complex, and for academics who may imagine themselves inhabiting a kind of trans-conditional sphere of neutrality, such efforts bring risks and perhaps even threaten to awaken the demons that always hover on the edges of ratiocination. Yet, for those of us who have chosen to take on the pleasures and the burdens of critical and literary thought, the search for full meaning—once the gold nugget of literary interpretation—has become all too familiarly slippery in these unruly post-post times (in the plural) of global drifts. In these drifts—and this is what makes them so shifting and shifty—the conditions of globalization are both referenced and produced, thus giving off a doubleness of effect and affect that is making the work of critical reflection much more fraught with the uncertainty of purpose and agency. At which points, we are asking ourselves more frequently than ever before, do the products of our labour—in the classroom, in our relations with colleagues, and in our social interactions—compromise the integrity of a critical relationship to systems of dominance and privilege? In other words, when the knowledge we produce loses the stability of referenced certainties, then the "truth" value of our work translates itself into discourses that can no longer be trusted to carry out the effects of our intentions. When every word, or at least the "primed" words in our academic language—the medium of our articulations—begins to be seen and heard in scare quotes, we quickly sense that it has taken on what I have referred to in a previous talk as the quality of counterfeit bills ("Living"). I'm drawing on Leslie Hall Pinder's essay in which she posits the incommensurability of applying, in the time-space territorial demarcations of a Canadian courtroom, the colonial discourse of laws based on property rights to the "land" as imagined by First Nations subjects who had been displaced. The language, in this instance, takes on the aura of fakeness and therefore becomes untrustworthy as a medium for equitable social transactions and intersubjective exchanges.

I would speculate, then, that the current conditions of postcolonial studies—if, indeed, we want to retain and advance this disciplinary framework[1]—cannot avoid the pervasive social "ache" of indeterminacy and anxiety that has infiltrated the everyday in the wake of 9.11, the primary trauma that brought the violence of global forces into the immediacy of our local lives. Instead of dwelling on this event, however, I want to address some critical consequences that were drastically intensified by 9.11

but which are consistent, I think, with the intensity of the phenomenon of "globalization" that has become so pervasive in our recent history.

The implications of globalization are vast, as witnessed in the proliferation of research and publications on the subject. Here, in its Canadian contexts, I want to approach the phenomenon as both the medium and the product of the dramatic transformations that have occurred in the post–Cold War era (late 1980s on). Its forces are manifest, in the broadest strokes, in an unstable complex of interlocking trajectories: the undermining and/or unravelling of the social, political, and cultural machinations and mandates of the nation-state; the ascendance of transnational corporate values that are obsessed with market-driven agendas, along with an anti-inflationary mental state that thrives on social policies primarily hurting the poorest and most vulnerable of social subjects; the devaluation of citizenship as the most legitimate means affecting state policies and directions, transforming politics into a public relations affair; and a frenzied and idolatrous relationship to the proliferation of commodities which sparked a social splurge of desires for an ever more fantasized—and fantastic—technologized future.

For those of us who struggle to retain a critical perspective on all the hyped up speed of changes that globalization appears to be generating, there are other signs—yet to be articulated perhaps—that cultural formations are in the midst of contradictory tensions. This horizon has brought some new and increasingly familiar patterns:

- Even in the loss of more locally controlled means of production, in the demise of small literary presses for instance, some cultural figures have come into the flow of enormous capital expansion.
- Even while a silence has descended on the so-called "politics of identity," corporate interests have embraced the commodification of difference as good for business.
- And even while the benefits of technology and finance capitalism have made it possible for everyone to become his or her own capitalist, social initiatives and policies that measure principles of equity have given way to class hierarchies deprivileging subjects outside the Information Technology (IT) monetary loops.

The cultural crisis marking the present is constituted on an ensemble of formations through which the politics of identity finds itself re-articulated in the discourse of more mobile subjectivities. Our current interrogation of the limits of various critical frameworks, including the postcolonial, have brought into play questions that implicate the cultural effects of cross-border exchanges, diasporic processes, and hybrid relations. In part, these are terms that now expose what has been termed by Nestor Garcia Canclini, John Tomlinson, and others a "deterritorialization" of the nation-state in the Cold War era—particularly the compromising of its power to manage (though obviously without complete success) hierarchies of raced, gendered, and classed identities.[2] Cultural processes were then mediated through the constant making of policies and administrative support for dominant institutions that maintained the hegemony of a coherent national culture. In that construct the signs of incoherence and chaos were embodied in those "visible minorities" (in the state-produced discourse) who were both incorporated and identified simultaneously. The liberalism of the post-war period that underwrote the drive to produce a Canadian national culture was thus inherently riven by the riddle of "difference" that constituted its liberalism and, in this formation, called forth the struggle of "minority subjects" to transgress and transform its borders. This is why, I think, the demise of identity politics in the wake of globalization brought with it a silence that was not filled by a return to the good old days of the nation. That narrative of the nation had already moved elsewhere, i.e., had unravelled, and as a consequence the links between place (as territory) and identity (as a stable Canadianness) were also disarticulated in the process. All of the specific sites of the urban local, in turn, opened to the influx of the global—symptomatically so, as one minor instance within a plethora of instances, in the arrival say of Starbucks coffee houses all over Vancouver.

The activism of the social movements that characterized the Cold War era has been replaced by an omnipresent neo-liberalism that thrives on the consumerist values of commodity culture. As Masao Miyoshi writes, a "pervasive acceptance of consumerism is . . . both a cause and effect of neoliberalism. Without vast and rapid consumption, the capitalist economy would just collapse" (292). It is in this now familiar field of consumption and reception that cultural production and critical reflection must necessarily operate.

Is the nation as such then gone? Is the way now open for the unfettered magnification of the neo-liberal agenda of an ever engulfing capitalism? I don't think so.

The catastrophic impact of the World Trade Center attacks on 9.11 in provoking the immediacy of a pervasive social and economic trauma in the United States, with its ripple effects in Canada, England, and Europe, exposed a strong and unpredictable undercurrent of resistance to—and even a hatred of—the capitalist commodity culture of which the United States is both the symbolic and material sign, and of which the twin towers of the World Trade Center were seen as that nation's synecdoche. The vast infrastructures that constitute the economic and financial networks of transnational corporations, including the nation-states woven into their operations, are not monolithic and immune to oppositional forces. Moreover, the mass protests against the World Trade Organization, the most powerful instrument for global free trade agreements, give further evidence that strategically positioned social activism through global coalitions has the potential to pressure corporate interests not to sidestep questions of social justice and the uneven distribution of material benefits. Massive disbelief and outright hostility towards neo-liberal capitalist agendas can threaten the microstructures of markets and cause unpredictable elements of chaos. Witness, for instance, the economic crisis of so-called "consumer confidence" in the wake of 9.11, and President Bush's injunction to spend as a sign of loyal citizenship.

But I am straying from the focus of this primer. What remains compelling, for those of us engaged in literary scholarship, is the recognition that globalization is far from being uniform, but is instead a multi-dimensional and multi-layered process of interactions in which local and national sites are inflected by global determinants. These determinants are heavily, but not wholly, driven by the agenda of corporate capitalism with its neo-liberal values that privilege the self-interested "individuals" who form the nexus of a social system of consumerism with its valorization of commodities. In other words, while the disseminating forces of globalization appear indomitable—i.e., have the air of inevitability—they can never be totalizing precisely because they are dependent on the continuing expansion of capital for sustenance, and this contingency makes their own processes vulnerable to unexpected events, such as 9.11, and the interventionist tactics by anti-capitalist activists. The flows that thus embody the uncertain and uneven interactions between the near and the far, the immediate and the distant—hence the local and the global—are themselves implicated in conditions of compromise that make positioning, for critical thought, less the arrival at stability and much more a dynamic process of negotiations with subject formations that vary in relation to specific conditions.

The temptation, in these obviously challenging circumstances, is to succumb to the normative drive of self-interested individualism and to adopt the language of investment as a game in which the goal is to maximize profits. This has had, I think, a significant impact on younger writers and artists whose work has signified as cultural commodities in global economic terms. The pressure to provide more transparency of form and subject positionings that ride the crest of consumer-based dominants has undermined the critical power of cultural work, particularly its power to resist and oppose normative assumptions, offering in their place alternative approaches to the real. On the other hand, in institutional frameworks, such as in the university, the temptation to follow the routes of maximum self-advancement and privilege is also strong. What David Li has termed the "gospel of privatization"—the favoured tactic of governments that are intent on finding a niche in the global economy—has been evident in the now normalized corporatization of the so-called "knowledge industry" that the university has become, and this "gospel," he says in a provocative speculation, can have the "effect not only of polarizing the haves and have-nots of the world, but also of infiltrating the psychic makeup of the individual who is now likely to regard predatory 'self-interest' and 'optimal waste' as the rational norm of life" (277).

The atomization of the "individual" who acts at a distance from sociality, protected by the institutional borders of the university, is of course the antithesis of critical discourses concerned with emancipatory goals and the transformation of social norms. But let's not kid ourselves; the attraction of such a positioning is enormous in an academic culture that valorizes the holy grail of the appropriately weighty CV. In saying this, however, I do not intend to project an air of cynicism; rather, by reminding us of the corporate values that now pervade the terminology of academic research, I want to suggest—to recall what Pierre Bourdieu said some years back—that "there are no longer any innocent words" (40). Language is invested with the networks of production and consumption that mark the broader formations of global forces. This awareness, in turn, helps us comprehend how crucial positioning, and thus our response-ability, has become in shaping the intellectual sites of our research and writing. Here the assumption is that no "point" in the trajectories of our scholarship is free from, or otherwise untouched by, the complicated ensemble of forces and conditions that function, in specific ways, to condition our formations as social subjects.

Given all this—and here I want to draw on Canadian contexts, the area of my own preoccupations over the past decade and more—it would seem imperative that we begin by acknowledging the limits of knowledge production in Canadian academic spheres. Just as we function without seeing ourselves from behind, so now we have become more acutely aware than ever before that we cannot anticipate and comprehend, at all times, the backside of its effects. In other words, in a situation similar to creative writers and artists, we cannot control the contexts of its reception and the uses to which it might be put, far beyond the limits of our intent. What we might read as a socially progressive act may, in certain contexts of elsewhere, be mobilized for contrary purposes. In the constraints of the corporatization of our knowledge, this threat is more dramatically visible for scientists and social scientists who rely on corporate funding to undertake their projects, but even literary scholars cannot be sure whether the critical approaches and methods they practise on any given text will lead to a questioning of dominant social relations or to their solidification. At what point, in other words, can we be certain that the products of our labour are enabling progressive change and not maintaining the very power relations we think we're undoing? I would suggest that the implications of this question are woven into the uncertainties that have entered our work to generate the "ache" that will not go away.

The crisis in CanLit studies, and the crisis in Canadian studies as a whole, has to do with a substantial disruption of purpose and direction, a disruption that has disabled its narrative formation. I am reminded of a passage from Néstor García Canclini's *Consumers and Citizens* on the effects of globalization on nation-state formations, which I think is uncanny for recent Canadian cultural history, given that he is talking about Latin American conditions:

> Now we see vanish, once and for all, those identities conceived of as the expression of a collective being, of an idiosyncrasy, or of an imagined community secured by bonds of territory and blood. National culture is not extinguished, but it is converted into a formula that designates the

> continuity of an unstable historical memory, continually reconstructed in interaction with transnational cultural referents. (29–30)

The "unstable historical memory" that arrives in the vanishing of a constructed national identity is then a present condition, but one that reconfigures all the elements that gave that identity the coherence of narrative origins. In the midst of global shifts, such an arrival becomes the occasion for an intense engagement with critically reflexive models of interpretation. For instance, in terms of the cultural theory of those such as Stuart Hall who have addressed the exclusionary discourses of the nation-state, the crisis opens up the potential for a process of re-articulation[3] through which the nation as such is re-membered; that is, reconceived as a difference-producing formation enabled by a complex of discourses, including a pervasive language of racialization, that took as its normative core the white male heterosexual subject as its typical citizen.

This could, for instance, involve research that examines various constituting events in the narrative history of CanLit, its production and modes of reception, its institutional discourses, its complicit interactions with the shifting contours of the nation-state, its political and social affiliations with its enabling genealogies, and its function in the effects of racialization, ethnocentrisms, gender and class relations, and representational schemata. Such work would not only reveal that globalization is not a movement "beyond" the problems of the nation-state, but a mode of translation in which previous hierarchies undergo reconstruction in their "interaction with transnational cultural referents."[4]

In this light, the concept of the "local" may be reinvented, no longer as the point of reference in a centralizing nation-state formation, but as itself the prime site where the uneven flows of the near and the distant, the immediate and the far, are both consumed and performed in our daily interactions. The local, then, is a geographical location, but it may also encompass all the specific events that condition our interactions with the vastly layered spaces of contemporary cultural formations that fan outward. The partiality (in both definitions of the word) of the local is obviously a limit, but then again the biological exigencies of daily life necessarily situate us in quotidian relations with material specifics. It may also be a vantage point in that the local, as a model of the intersection of contradictory forces, can provide the impetus for critical—and perhaps postcolonial—studies that are attentive to points of intersection between cultures, creative texts, theories, discourses, and transnational movements.[5]

With such an ethics in mind, it is interesting to ask: what then lies beyond the unravelling of the nation-state? Do we progress to more inclusive cultural conditions, perhaps in something resembling a renewed multiculturalism? Or do we reclaim or simply let go of cultural sovereignty as our collective right? If we do reclaim, what will that sovereignty look like? Can there be viable identity formations that are both collective and not limited by the exclusivity of nation-state formations (with their need for an other to constitute the self)? But maybe, on fourth or fifth thought, is the CEO language of the boardroom starting to make sense, and is there a happy future in neo-liberal capitalism that will bring on ever new cultural commodities in a feast of rare treats? But then again, perhaps social conditions can be likened to psychological states, and we have entered into the phase of the manic-depressive: on the one side a vision of eternal abundance made possible by the proliferation of capital but depressing because of the emptiness at the core of acquisition for its own sake; on the other side, the loss of hope in collectivities that can produce a sociality attentive to the democratic aims of social justice, cultural creativity, and economic security.

All of this speculation gets us to the slippery nitty-grits of agency in the face of all the complexities that are making our work as critical scholars both difficult and more necessary than ever before. We can no longer continue with our work as "business as usual." Here I want us to consider the potential for a critical pedagogy in the historical juncture invoked in this primer. In doing so I suggest that the term pedagogy be approached as broader than the institutional confines of our teaching and research, and that it encompass a movement back and forth between their confines and the social and cultural variables of multiply formed subjects who are embedded in local/global networks—or the elements of a "glocalization"[6]—that cannot be grasped in their totality. It is out of an inability to totalize without, in effect, closing off variables that would make our knowledge contingent, that we need more than ever to understand the specific limits making possible what we know and therefore to leave open the spaces of what we don't know. So the question for a critical pedagogy becomes "what are we doing when we do what we do?" The *what* in turn implicates the *how*, the *why*, and the *where*. These are basic frames of a reflexive methodology that will make our agency more attentive to the ethical dimensions of knowledge production and consumption in which the issue of "benefit" comes sharply into focus; that is, who ultimately benefits from the intellectual work we perform as teachers and scholars in highly invested institutions that are themselves nodes in the flows of transnational capital? The event of reading cultural texts, in the classroom and in our studies, brings into play a vast complex of interrelationships that incorporate, close by, the biological and social semiology of our living bodies in specific time and space, but fan out to interact with the local, national, and global conditions of all the material and symbolic values attached to the reception, containment, and interpretation of the diverse range of cultural productions.

In the midst of the structures producing indeterminacy, uncertainty, and ambivalence in our positioning vis-à-vis a desire to engage in progressive scholarship, the epistemological and social implications of pedagogy have moved directly into the foreground of our work as academics (who are themselves social subjects). Disciplinary positioning, and declarations of neutrality and objectivity, are no longer—and never really were—a guarantee that the effects of our research will not feed into hierarchic relations of power. Attention to the pedagogical scene of our practices would help us account for the contingencies of our own location(s)—whether in the classroom, or in our research and writing, or in our social and cultural relations with each other. It is at this location that we might be able to envision more malleable methods to negotiate the intellectual and social shifts occurring all around us and, at the same time, to prompt us to re-articulate the nation-based formations whose very limits have become the disturbances brought to prominence by the influx of global flows.

*

Coda:

At the academy awards
she wears $3 million diamonds
around her bare neck and $3 million

diamond studded shoes
on her bare feet

and she is surrounded
by body guards —
the ultimate right guards

As the voice announces
"Reach out and globalize someone"

NOTES

1. While acknowledging the contested status of the term *postcolonial*, it nevertheless seems important not to blame the term but to critically question and qualify the always invested contexts of its referential deployments. Its potentially liberating powers are dependent on the critical modes through which it is performed. As a fixed and predetermining frame, it can easily fall prey to normalizing discourses that reproduce cultural hegemonies. For a cogent defense of postcolonial readings of literary texts, especially apropos those involved in CanLit studies, see Diana Brydon's "Compromising Postcolonialisms: Tomson Highway's *Kiss of the Fur Queen* and Contemporary Postcolonial Debates" where she argues for "acceptance of postcolonial literary critique as a partial, provisional, and imperfect approach that nonetheless allows pressing questions to be asked about the relations of text and world, the limits of disciplinarity and interdisciplinarity; and the multiple contexts in which postcolonial critics conduct their work" (16).
2. Tomlinson adopts the term *deterritorialization* to describe "the weakening or dissolution of the connection between everyday lived culture and territorial location. However, this is not typically experienced as simply cultural loss or estrangement but as a complex and ambiguous blend: of familiarity and difference, expansion of cultural horizons and increased perceptions of vulnerability, access to the 'world out there' accompanied by penetration of our own private worlds, new opportunities and new levels" (128).
3. My understanding of the term "re-articulation" is informed by various discussions with Jeff Derksen. See especially his exceptional mobilization of the term as the basis for critical theory in his dissertation, "Globalism and the Role of the Cultural." Hall explains the concept of articulation in "On Postmodernism and Articulation: An Interview with Stuart Hall."
4. Or another critical method, akin to the practice of re-articulation, could

involve, in Roland Bleiker's terms, "Nietzsche's method of genealogy, expanded and popularized through the work of Michel Foucault. . . . Genealogies focus on the process by which we have constructed origins and given meaning to particular representations of the past, representations that continuously guide our daily lives and set clear limits to political and social options" (25). And of course to cultural options as well. For Bleiker, the genealogical method is especially appropriate for constructing modes of dissent vis-à-vis the uneven and multi-dimensional effects of globalization. Drawing on the work of David Campbell and social theorists, he proposes the term "transversal" as a means of negotiating the complicit and contradictory flows that constitute the effects of global formations. My thanks to Heike Härting for pointing me towards Bleiker's book.

5. As Ien Ang reminds us, such studies enact a practice that "depends *par excellence* on the ethics (and a politics) of the encounter: on the claimed productivity of dialogue across disciplinary, geographical and cultural boundaries, on a committed desire to reach out to the 'other,' and on a refusal to homogenize plurality and heterogeneity as a way to resist, subvert or evade hegemonic forms of power" (163).

6. Tomlinson references Roland Robertson's use of this term to insist that "the local and the global . . . do not exist as cultural polarities but as mutually 'interpenetrating' principles." Robertson, he says, appropriated the term "from (originally Japanese) business discourse where essentially it refers to a 'micro-marketing' strategy—'the tailoring and advertising of goods and services on a global or near-global basis to increasingly differentiated local and particular markets'" (195–96).

WORKS CITED

Ang, Ien. *On Not Speaking Chinese: Living between Asia and the West.* London: Routledge, 2001.

Bleiker, Roland. *Popular Dissent, Human Agency and Global Politics.* Cambridge: Cambridge UP, 2000.

Bourdieu, Pierre. *Language and Symbolic Power.* Ed. John B. Thompson. Trans. Gino Raymond and Matthew Adamson. Cambridge: Harvard UP, 1991.

Brydon, Diana. "Compromising Postcolonialisms: Tomson Highway's *Kiss of the Fur Queen* and Contemporary Postcolonial Debates." *Compr(om)ising Post/Colonialism(s): Challenging Narratives and Practices.* Ed. Greg Ratcliffe and Gerry Turcotte. Sydney: Dangaroo, 2001. 15–29.

Canclini, Néstor García. *Consumers and Citizens: Globalization and Multicultural Conflicts.* Trans. George Yudice. Minneapolis: U of Minnesota P, 2001.

da Costa, Paulo. "An Interview with Dionne Brand." *Filling Station* 23 (2001): 8–11.

Derksen, Jeff. "Globalism and the Role of the Cultural." PhD Diss. U of Calgary, 2000.

Hall, Stuart. "On Postmodernism and Articulation: An Interview with Stuart Hall." *Stuart Hall: Critical Dialogues in Cultural Studies*. Ed. David Morley and Kuan-Hsing Chen. London: Routledge, 1996. 131–50.

Li, David Leiwei. "Globalization and the Humanities." *Comparative Literature* 53.4 (2001): 275–82.

Miki, Roy. "Living in Global Drift: Thinking the Beyond of Identity Politics." Paper presented at the "Transculturalisms Canada Symposium: Cultural Mingling: Between, Among, Within Cultures." 21–24 February 2002, Green College, UBC; ICCS, Transculturalisms Project. Online. <http://www.webct.ubc.ca/SCRIPT/Transculturalisms/scripts/serve_home> (enter through <http://transculturalisms.arts.ubc.ca/>, 2002 Symposium).

Miyoshi, Masao. "Turn to the Planet: Literature, Diversity, and Totality." *Comparative Literature* 53.4 (2001): 283–97.

Pinder, Leslie Hall. "To the Fourth Wall." *Vancouver Forum: Old Powers, New Forces*. Ed. Max Wyman. Vancouver: Douglas and McIntyre, 1992. 19–51.

Tomlinson, John. *Globalization and Culture*. Chicago: U of Chicago P, 1999.

Culture and the Global State: Postcolonialism, Pedagogy, and the Canadian Literatures

PAUL HJARTARSON

> The last several decades have witnessed an extraordinary expansion of the scope of literary studies. Often associated with methodological and interpretive narratives such as deconstruction; the new historicism; cultural studies; ethnic, race, gender and sexuality criticism; and the rapid formation of the subfield of postcolonial studies, this widening of the field imaginary goes well beyond such developments to encompass a reconfiguration of the object of literary study and something like a revolution in the kinds of questions we put to it.
>
> — Giles Gunn, "Introduction: Globalizing Literary Studies"

> What are we going to do with those older categories—nation, culture, and English—which function as the absent structure that shapes and yet haunts global culture and the idea of literature itself?
>
> — Simon Gikandi, "Globalization and the Claims of Postcoloniality"

I

THIS BOOK BRINGS INTO critical relation two fields of study, postcolonialism and pedagogy, and proposes to examine the Canadian literatures within that context. While I welcome the foregrounding of pedagogical concerns, configuring the topic as *Postcolonialism and Pedagogy* raises three significant issues for me. In raising these issues, my desire is not to call into question either the topic itself or postcolonialism as a critique but to underscore the incredible change sweeping through the discipline of English—indeed, through the humanities and social sciences generally—the fluidity of the situation at present, and the confused nature of the debates those changes have engendered. I would, however, like to reconfigure and refocus our discussions.

The first two issues are inextricably related. The first concerns what, for want of a better term, I shall call the "big picture," that is, whether it is possible, in this context, meaningfully to separate postcolonialism either from the historical formations of colonialism and modernity it critiques or from the theoretical developments such as postmodernism and global studies it seeks to displace in the classroom. Postcolonialism, like postmodernism, stages a rupture with the past—with colonialism and the nation—but it is haunted by that past and by those historical formations. "The postcolonial condition," Simon Gikandi observes in "Globalization and the Claims of Postcoloniality," "is embedded, through colonialism and nationalism, in the politics of modernity"; thus, he argues, "postcolonial theorists may have sought to forget the nation in order to become global, but the nation has not forgotten them" (641, 639). These issues are themselves embedded in larger debates regarding our shifting understanding of the university and the repositioning of the humanities in relation to the social sciences, debates that shape both curriculum and pedagogy. If the focus of this book is postcolonialism and pedagogy, how do we meaningfully separate postcolonialism from the many other developments, such as postmodernism, cultural studies, critical race and critical legal studies, and globalization, that have transformed both the discipline of English and our teaching in the past several decades?—At a time when the humanities themselves are undergoing fundamental changes? How do we discuss the postcolonial from a pedagogical perspective without either reducing it to one or two issues—indigeneity, hybridity, or race, for example—or making it stand in for all of these other developments? Given these questions, it is misleading to speak either of postcolonialism *and* pedagogy or of something termed "postcolonial pedagogy": to gather all of these other developments under the catchphrase "postcolonial" would, it seems to me, render that term meaningless.

The second, related issue is that the postcolonial itself is a highly contested and conflicted field of study.[1] There is little agreement, for example, regarding either the meaning of the term or the scope of the field. What Diana Brydon wrote seven years ago, in the Introduction to *Testing the Limits: Postcolonial Theories and Canadian Literature*, still in many ways characterizes the situation:

> Postcolonial theory is currently proliferating at a bewildering rate, so that it now seems preferable to substitute the plural form for the singular. To write of postcolonial theories is to recognize the multiplicity and fundamental incompatibility of much that now passes under the rubric of postcolonial. Debates about the proper definition of the field and its appropriate mission are charged with excitement and sometimes acrimony. A strong shared sense that these things matter and are worth contesting has resulted in little agreement as yet about the history, scope, and boundaries of the field. (2)

Nor was—or is—she alone in that assessment. In "Post-Colonial Critical Theories," Stephen Slemon describes *postcolonialism* as "a portmanteau word—an umbrella thrown up over many heads against a great deal of rain. Confusion," he observes, "necessarily abounds in the area" (183). Much of that questioning comes from people within the emerging field. The confusion may be a sign of postcolonialism's vigour, an indication that "it is still a field very much in the making," or it may suggest, as Gaurav Desai fears, "that the 'global' is fast replacing the 'postcolonial' as a category of analysis" (536). (The issue of postcolonialism's relation to globalization has come into the foreground in the years following publication of *Testing the Limits.*) In either event, the confusion makes meaningful discussion of postcolonialism and pedagogy difficult.

The final issue the configuration of this book's topic raises for me is the positioning of the Canadian literatures in the issues at stake here. In linking the postcolonial and pedagogy, the book pushes into the background the issue of postcolonialism's relation to the national literature. I do not want to be misunderstood on this issue: I have no interest in debating whether the Canadian literatures are postcolonial. That question, it seems to me, is both wrong-headed and unproductive. Postcolonialism and the Canadian literatures are two very different projects. What *is* productive is the tension between them. Postcolonialism has been so intent on announcing "the end of the nation-state and the proliferation of cultural relationships characterized by difference and hybridity" (O'Brien and Szeman 612) that it has not adequately addressed its relation to the nation-state or its culture. In this paper I explore these three issues and focus my analysis on the place of the Canadian literatures in globalized literary studies. My argument is that postcolonial critique is not well served by its disavowal of the nation-state.

II

The first issue regarding the configuration of the topic is postcolonialism's problematic relation to modernity, on the one hand, and to competing critiques of it, such as postmodernism and global studies, on the other. In a discussion of classroom practices, is it possible meaningfully to separate postcolonialism from the many other movements that have shaped the discipline and our teaching in the past two decades? The problematic relationship of postcolonialism to modernity, postmodernism, and globalization has been analyzed by a number of theorists and critics, some of them postcolonialists who are interrogating the issues from within. Since this book is concerned with pedagogy I want to develop this issue not by addressing these debates here—though I shall take up some of them later in the essay—but by reporting upon the way those debates have helped to shape the curriculum where I teach. For the past three years (1999–2002), the Department of English at the University of Alberta has been engaged in a comprehensive review of its undergraduate curriculum, a review which I organized and led. The review was not conducted by a small committee working in isolation but by the department as a whole via panels, area group meetings, surveys, workshops, e-mail, and retreats. Last spring the department voted by an overwhelming majority to adopt new program requirements and a new slate of courses we developed as a result of that process. Postcolonialism had a significant role to play in those changes but it was neither the only nor the dominant force shaping the new curriculum. The dominant forces were the repositioning of the humanities in relation to the social sciences; related to that repositioning, the emergence of theory generally as a structuring force in English; the move to cultural studies; and, in keeping with the above, a significant re-conceptualization of the object of study itself.[2] I do not have time here to discuss the new curriculum in detail but I want briefly to comment on two developments.

The first involves the department's desire to move beyond national literatures and periodization as the structuring forces of the discipline and, balanced with that, the recognition that both nations and the use of national categories to organize literary studies were unlikely to disappear any time soon.[3] The new curriculum creates space for faculty and students to engage texts outside the constraints of national categories and periods. Although we have attempted to create this space throughout the curriculum, it emerges most clearly in the 200-level courses and these were unquestionably the focus of the most intense debates regarding curricular change. The organizing committee for the review developed the following rationale for these courses, all of which are single-term:

> Courses at the 200 level are intended to do two things: introduce students to methods and paradigms central to the discipline, and provide them with "windows" onto literary study (with perspectives, that is, on how specific methodologies ask questions of texts, why such questions have come to be asked, and what their asking can achieve and/or foreclose). These courses will perform two equally important functions: to prepare honours and majors students for further study in English; and to serve students from outside the department who desire to read and discuss literary texts. Each course presents a set of key texts from a particular critical methodology or paradigm, and a selection of literary, cultural, and/or social texts on which to put the strategies or moves from the critical material into practice. This second selection of texts might be tightly focussed (historically, geographically, generically, thematically) or more diverse in its scope. Expect a 200-level course to offer a dynamic interplay between these two groups of texts. (Hjartarson, et al. 3)

The paradigm courses at this level are organized into three broad categories titled, respectively, "Histories," "Textualities," and "Politics." Under "Histories," we developed three variable-content courses: "Making Books," "Making Readers," and "Histories in Texts." Under "Textualities," we also developed three variable-content courses: "Signs and Texts," "Reading and

Interpretation," and "Narrative Theory and Poetics." Under "Politics," we developed four variable-content courses: "Class and Ideology," "Gender and Sexuality," "Race and Ethnicity," and "Empire and the Postcolonial." The courses in the Politics category undoubtedly generated the most debate. There is no denying either the interplay of these categories—that is, of the three larger categories and of the paradigms organized within them—or the exclusions that any one configuration of them might imply. Ultimately, the department accepted the organizing committee's view that each course should be seen as foregrounding one or more categories without treating them in isolation from the others. We also developed a course titled "The Literary Institution." Because that course examines the discourse that produces, among other things, the paradigms structuring our 200-level offerings, we placed it outside those categories. The titles of these courses, we believe, reflect the paradigms shaping the discipline and informing our teaching in the classroom. Instructors assigned to any of the "Politics" courses might well approach them under the banner of the postcolonial but they might also teach them as, for example, feminists or historical materialists.

The second point about the new curriculum concerns the Canadian literature courses. The Canadianists made two significant, structuring decisions. One was to move away from genre/period/nation survey to a concern with the concepts and issues involved in reading Canadian cultures (the title of one of the new courses), a decision that led rather than simply followed the path eventually taken by the department as a whole. The other was strongly to support the development of courses in Aboriginal literature—including one at the first-year level—and to have the department offer these courses independently of either Canadian or American literature, on the one hand, or of the postcolonial, on the other. The reason for this relative positioning of Canadian, Aboriginal, and postcolonial literatures is, I hope, clear: the more immediate issue for Aboriginal liter-ature courses is perhaps less their relation to the national and postcolonial literatures than whether they should be developed within English or elsewhere within the university—in Native Studies, for example—or by English and Native Studies working together. (That is how our first-year Aboriginal Literature and Culture course was developed.)

III

The second issue concerns the definition and scope of postcolonialism as a field. In Alan Lawson's view, postcolonialism is a conflicted field. In "Postcolonial Theory and the 'Settler' Subject" he writes:

> As I see it, postcolonial theory manifests two quite different impulses that remain in perpetual tension within its strategies and its trajectories. As, "essentially," a theory of difference, postcolonialism articulates itself through an insistence on the representation, inscription, and interpretation of the particular, the local, that which is not the same. It resists universals. But as a mode of analysis and historicocultural [sic] explanation, as a heuristic polemic, postcolonialism forever desires to become another grand narrative, another of the Great Explanations. (20)

It is at the level of "grand narrative" and "Great Explanation" that postcolonialism has generated most debate. I personally am more interested in postcolonialism as a reading strategy and critique rather than as narrative and Great Explanation. Although many postcolonial theorists argue that the term names not only a reading strategy but literatures and critical practices that highlight certain kinds of commitments, politics, and identities, the term itself serves, in the first instance, as a spatiotemporal marker (O'Brien and Szeman 610). In "Post-Colonial Critical Theories" Slemon observes that "One of the most vexed areas of debate within the field of post-colonial theory has to do with the term 'post-colonial' itself" (179), and, as he notes, the problem involves the meaning of both "post" and "colonial." "The term 'post-colonial' or 'post-colonialism,'" he writes,

> has to be seen as problematized at the outset by lack of consensus on what it is that makes the term "colonial" meaningful—that is, by a lack of consensus . . . over what it might mean to be "post" the "colonial" moment. If neo-colonial relations still prevail between and within modern nations, if the "practices, theories and attitudes of dominating metropolitan centres" (to re-employ Said's words) remain in place after European colonialism has formally ended, then at some level contemporary "post-

> colonialisms," however they are conceived, must take place within a structure of contemporary and continuing imperial relations. (183)

Others have advanced similar arguments. I will not rehearse here Anne McClintock's argument that the term postcolonial "is haunted by the very figure of linear development that it sets out to dismantle" (*Imperial Leather* 10–11), but what she says about colonialism "return[ing] at the moment of its disappearance" might well also be said about the nation.[4]

Another vexed area of debate within the postcolonial is the scope of the field. The authors of *The Empire Writes Back* define the postcolonial as "cover[ing] all the culture affected by the imperial process from the moment of colonization to the present day" (2). A recently published issue of *South Atlantic Quarterly* entitled *The Globalization of Fiction/The Fiction of Globalization* advances a similar view, arguing that "from the high point of European imperialism to the end of the Cold War, *all literature was postcolonial literature*" (611; emphasis in original). Interestingly, the editors of that volume, Susie O'Brien and Imre Szeman, also argue that "*all literature is now global, all literature is a literature of globalization*" (611; emphasis in original). As Vijay Mishra and Bob Hodge pointed out over ten years ago, the problem with defining the postcolonial with the breathtaking spatial and temporal sweep advanced in *The Empire Writes Back* and in the *South Atlantic Quarterly* volume is that it erases difference. This is postcolonialism as totalizing narrative and Great Explanation. In their critique of *The Empire Writes Back,* Mishra and Hodge recall Edward Said's "well-known warning that even with the best of intentions one might, and sometimes does, give the impression that through one's own discourses the Other is now representable without due regard to its bewildering complexity" (402). Other theorists have defined postcolonialism narrowly to designate the decolonization following World War II—often focused on South Asia—and tend to conceive *postcolonial* as a replacement for the now infrequently used term *Third World.* This use is historically more defensible—though not without its own homogenizing tendencies—but it problematizes Canada's participation in the postcolonialism thus defined. Another reaction to the problems with the postcolonial as a spatiotemporal marker is to focus on postcolonialism as a reading strategy and as a political movement and to push the historical issues into the background. The problem with that response, ultimately, is the need to historicize the critique itself.

IV

The final issue I raised concerning the configuration of the topic is the way it seems to finesse postcolonialism's relation to the national literatures. Responding to what he perceives as the growing tendency in postcolonialism to frame issues in terms of a First World/Third World, the-West-and-the-rest binary, Lawson seeks in "Postcolonial Theory and the 'Settler' Subject" to theorize the settler-invader subject. He recently redeveloped those ideas for a sixteen-page entry on "Settler Colonies" he co-authored with Anna Johnston and published in *The Companion to Postcolonial Studies*. According to Johnston and Lawson,

> The crucial theoretical move . . . is to see the "settler" as uneasily occupying a place caught between two First Worlds, two origins of authority and authenticity. One of these is the originating world of Europe, the Imperium—the source of its principal cultural authority. Its "other" First World is that of the First Nations whose authority they not only replaced and effaced but also desired. . . . To each of these First Worlds, the settlers are secondary—indeed, supplementary. That secondariness makes it clear that the settler was also the "go-between" for the European First World with that which it has strategically named the Third. The "settler" acted as a mediator rather than as a simple transmitter of Imperialism's uncomfortable mirroring of itself. (370)

In the earlier essay Lawson spoke of Canada as part of the "Second World," a concept he and Slemon had developed in other contexts. In the *Companion* entry all references to the "Second World" disappear.[5] There is, however, another, more perplexing change. Although Johnston and Lawson critique the cultural politics of the representation of settlement and argue that the displacement of First Nations people is cultural and symbolic as well as physical, they choose to designate the European colonists as "settlers" rather than as "settler-invaders" or simply as "invaders," a strategy favoured by some of my students. Here is the rationale they offer:

> In the 1980s, analysts of colonialism and postcolonialism began to reexamine the implications of "settler colonies," often starting by reinstating the more historically accurate term "settler-invader" to emphasize the

> violence that the single, ostensibly benign, term "settler" concealed. This essay uses the term "settler" for reasons of brevity, but the "invader" rider should always be kept in mind, as it is in the theory. (362)

You can see the problem here: if the displacement of First Nations peoples is cultural and symbolic as well as physical, the continued use of the "ostensibly benign" term *settler* is, at best, problematic.

There are other problems as well.[6] Although I am drawn to the idea of colonialism as negotiation, this model, with the settler-invader at its centre, grants interiority and psychological complexity to the invader-colonizer rather than to the colonized. The more basic issue for me is this: what is at stake for the Canadian literatures in being named postcolonial? The literatures within Canada that could most legitimately claim postcolonial status in the post–World War II era are arguably the First Nations literatures and the literatures of Canada's minority cultures, *not* the national literature itself—and I'm not at all convinced that proponents of either literature seek recognition as postcolonial in the way proponents of English-Canadian literature sometimes do. In any event, as I indicated at the outset, the Canadian literatures and postcolonialism are very different projects. Both, however, are caught up in globalization and have a role to play in it.[7] That the national and global are opposed is just one of the many fallacies of the globalization debate. As a number of theorists have argued, globalization is not opposed to nation-states but works through them and, in some ways, increases their power (Panitch, et al. 12–13). "Theorizing globalization without the state," Martin Shaw argues, "is like playing Hamlet without the Prince." Yet, that is precisely what many postcolonial theorists attempt. Now, more than ever, cultural critics and theorists need to understand not only culture's relation to the nation-state or how nation-states are transforming themselves in the global era, but the changing place of national cultures and literatures in those developments. Some will argue that, in the contemporary world, culture is no longer tied to the nation, that, as a result of globalization, culture is a transnational phenomenon. But, as Gikandi points out in "Globalization and the Claims of Postcoloniality," "the argument that culture is the symptom of a new global order has to contend with a difficult question," a question "embedded" in what Gikandi terms the "Leavis project": "How could culture, an idea so powerfully embedded in national traditions, be transformed into a transnational category?" (653). Gikandi's question is one of many that needs to be addressed.

In "Beyond Discipline: Globalization and the Future of English," Paul Jay argues that English departments should

> mov[e] away from a traditional division of discrete national literatures into ossified literary-historical periods and giv[e] the history of global expansion, trade, and intercultural exchange precedence in our curriculum over the mapping of an essentially aestheticized national character. In this model the older paradigm for literary study would cease to stand at the center of the discipline and would become an object of study among others in a field that spent more time teaching its students about the history of the discipline, which after all has shifted remarkably since the late nineteenth century in ways that until recently we kept hidden from our students. (43)

While the nation/period paradigm may, at some point, cease to structure the discipline—a prospect that would not bother me—it is no more likely to disappear than the nation-state itself. To say that the nation-state is unlikely to disappear is not to endorse or celebrate the state: it is to acknowledge its material existence and the power it exerts, including its considerable resources in the cultural and literary fields of production (including funding for the conference that led to this book and for the research of many of its participants).

Will globalization mean the end of national cultures? My own premonition is that national cultures may take on more importance in a globalized world. Paradoxical as it may seem, the organizational categories of nation and period may be reinvigorated by the globalization of literary studies. Consider, for example, Jay's own proposals regarding the study of literature organized in national categories. Arguing that English departments need to move beyond "the outmoded nationalist paradigm," he adds:

> This does not mean we should abandon the study of literary texts and cultural practices in relation to the modern nation-state. That study, however, ought to concentrate on the relation in historical and materialist terms. We ought to focus less on identifying what seems inherently English

> or American [or Canadian] in the literatures we teach and write about and more on understanding the functional relation between literature and the nation-state, how literary writing has been theorized and politicized in efforts to define and empower nation-states, especially from the Enlightenment onward. This kind of approach must give primary attention to the historical role literature has had in global systems of cultural exchange and recognize that this exchange has always been multidirectional. With the understanding that globalization is a long historical process, we can usefully complicate our nation-based approach to the study of English, not by dropping the nation-state paradigm but by foregrounding its history and its function *for* the nation-state, insisting that our students come to understand the instrumental role literature has played in the complicated world of transnational and cultural relations. (42)

Jay seems caught in a contradiction here: whereas throughout most of the essay he seems intent on decentring the nation/period paradigm, here he is apparently content simply to "complicate" it. Nevertheless, in the short term, the direction he sketches out for the study of literary and cultural texts and practices in relation to the state seems promising; it enables an understanding both of literature's relation to the state and of its role in the transnational mediation of culture. In the long term, however, we need to theorize the changing relation between culture and the "global state."

V

What is the place of postcolonialism in all of this? As Slemon points out in "Post-Colonial Critical Theories," the many projects arrayed under the umbrella of postcolonialism

> assume no common object of description, let alone a common theoretical or critical methodology. And just as obviously, these descriptive enterprises will not be grounded in a common political goal—indeed, much post-colonial critical work carries no political commitment whatsoever. (184)

Postcolonial critics and theorists with and without political commitments will, in the near future at least, increasingly find themselves negotiating postcolonialism's relation to globalization. As this essay undoubtedly suggests, I am drawn to Gikandi's analysis. As he notes, "the discourse of globalization seems to be perpetually caught between two competing narratives, one of celebration, the other of crisis" (629), with postcolonialism tending toward the celebratory narrative. Whatever its shortcomings, Gikandi rightly argues, "the postcolonial perspective on globalization has been the most salient attempt to question older forms of globalization based on the centrality of the nation and theories of modernity" (636). Like Gikandi, however, I am not convinced that postcolonial critique has achieved the break with colonialism or the nation it announces. Unlike Michael Hardt and Antonio Negri, however, I am not prepared to dismiss the postcolonial altogether.

According to Kalpana Seshadri-Crooks, "postcolonial studies is at present beset by a melancholia induced paradoxically by its new-found authority and incorporation into institutions of higher learning" (3). Its melancholia, it has been said, "derives from a growing sense of the *limits* of its politics and its thorough incorporation into the Western academy – both arguably symptomatic of postcolonialism's failure to address the conditions of globalization that simultaneously enable its production and erode its political purchase" (O'Brien and Szeman 607). With its focus on pedagogy this book is itself, in part, yet another sign of postcolonialism's incorporation into the Western academy. Is it a sign of the waning of both postcolonial studies and the national literatures? I think not. Postcolonial studies are inextricably bound up in contemporary studies of the global and have much to offer as a critique of earlier, social sciences–based theories of globalization. At the same time, both postcolonial and global studies are inextricably bound up in the nation-state and its cultures. For more than a century now, theorists of various persuasions have predicted the imminent demise of the nation-state. While the nation-state is undeniably an historical formation that arose in a particular time and place and that will just as undeniably give way, at some future date, to some other political formation, it has proved remarkably resilient over the past century and more. It has proved resilient because it has changed over time and, if Panitch, Shaw, and others are right, it continues to change. In the final analysis, it is impossible to theorize either the postcolonial or the global adequately without taking nation-states and their cultures fully into account.

ACKNOWLEDGEMENTS

This essay developed out of the interplay of several activities: my teaching of English-Canadian literature; my work on the University of Alberta Department of English curriculum review (discussed, in part, in this essay), including my participation in the Canadian literature discussion group; and my ongoing research. My debt to colleagues and students is profound and wide-ranging. I should particularly like to acknowledge the debt I owe to three groups of thinkers: the members of the 2001–02 curriculum committee, Katherine Binhammer, Kris Calhoun, David Gay, Kathryn Laurie, Mark Simpson, Sherryl Vint, and Maisaa Youssef; the members of the Canadian literature discussion group, including Douglas Barbour, Christopher Bracken, Cecily Devereux, Chris Gittings, Lisa Laframboise, Ian MacLaren, Julie Rak, Cheryl Suzack, and Janice Williamson; and to my students, old and new, particularly Vinny Kurata and Tracy Kulba.

NOTES

1. My own analysis focuses on several moments in that ongoing debate, most notably Mishra and Hodge's review of *The Empire Writes Back*; Hall's reply to Shohat, McClintock, and Dirlik, in "When Was 'the Post-Colonial'?"; Slemon's "Post-Colonial Critical Theories"; and Brydon's *Testing the Limits* and "It's Time for a New Set of Questions."
2. Compare Gunn's analysis of the changing field of literary studies, particularly the passage quoted as an epigraph to this essay. In the English Department at the University of Alberta, as elsewhere, feminist analysis has played a significant role in rethinking the discipline.
3. This is, of course, a debatable issue. On the relevance of nation and period as categories in the organization of English studies and the analysis of literary texts, see Gikandi and Jay. On the impact of globalization on nation-states, see Panitch, "Globalisation and the State," and Shaw.
4. McClintock first advanced these arguments in "The Angel of Progress: Pitfalls of the Term 'Postcolonialism.'" For a critique of McClintock, see Hall.
5. See Lawson, "A Cultural Paradigm for the Second World," and Slemon, "Unsettling the Empire: Resistance Theory for the Second World." For a critique of Three Worlds theory, see Ahmad.
6. In the Introduction to *Testing the Limits,* Brydon defends the use of

postcolonial to describe the literatures of Canada. For a recent critique of writing regarding settler-invader colonies, see O'Neill.

7. For a brief overview of the large and growing body of work on globalization, see Jay 34 ff. Although Jay rightly argues that globalization has a long history, my concern here, and the concern of many of the critics I cite, is with globalization in the post–World War II era and, particularly, the intersection of global studies, understood as a social sciences–based project, with literary studies, most notably postcolonialism. (The intersection of postcolonialism and globalization is one more manifestation of the changing relations—at once stimulating and troubled—between the humanities and social sciences.) For a very different view of globalization and postcolonialism, see Hardt and Negri.

WORKS CITED

Ahmad, Aijaz. "Three Worlds Theory: End of a Debate." *In Theory: Classes, Nations, Literatures*. London: Verso, 1992.

Ashcroft, Bill, Gareth Griffiths, and Helen Tiffin. *The Empire Writes Back: Theory and Practice in Post-Colonial Literatures*. London: Routledge, 1989.

Brydon, Diana. "Introduction: Reading Postcoloniality, Reading Canada." *Testing the Limits: Postcolonial Theories and Canadian Literature.* Ed. Diana Brydon. Spec. issue of *Essays on Canadian Writing* 56 (1995): 1–19.

———. "It's Time for a New Set of Questions." *Essays on Canadian Writing* 71 (2000): 14–25.

Desai, Gaurav. "Rethinking English: Postcolonial English Studies." *A Companion to Postcolonial Studies*. Ed. Henry Schwarz and Sangeeta Ray. Oxford: Blackwell, 2000. 523–39.

Gikandi, Simon. "Globalization and the Claims of Postcoloniality." *The Globalization of Fiction/The Fiction of Globalization*. Ed. Susie O'Brien and Imre Szeman. Spec. issue of *South Atlantic Quarterly* 100.3 (2001): 627–58.

Gunn, Giles. "Introduction: Globalizing Literary Studies." *Globalizing Literary Studies*. Ed. Giles Gunn. Spec. issue of *PMLA* 116 (2001): 16–31.

Hall, Stuart. "When Was 'the Post-Colonial'?: Thinking at the Limit." *The Post-Colonial Question: Common Skies, Divided Horizons.* Ed. Iain Chambers and Lidia Curti. London: Routledge, 1996. 242–60.

Hardt, Michael, and Antonio Negri. *Empire.* Cambridge: Harvard UP, 2000.

Hjartarson, Paul, and the members of the committee. *Report of the Curriculum/Organizing Committee*. April 2002. Department of English, University of Alberta. 1–19.

Jay, Paul. "Beyond Discipline?: Globalization and the Future of English." *Global-*

izing Literary Studies. Ed. Giles Gunn. Spec. issue of *PMLA* 116 (2001): 32–47.

Johnston, Anna, and Alan Lawson. "Settler Colonies." *A Companion to Postcolonial Studies.* Ed. Henry Schwarz and Sangeeta Ray. Oxford: Blackwell, 2000. 360–76.

Lawson, Alan. "A Cultural Paradigm for the Second World." *Australian-Canadian Studies* 9.1–2 (1991): 67–78.

———. "Postcolonial Theory and the 'Settler' Subject." *Testing the Limits: Postcolonial Theories and Canadian Literature.* Ed. Diana Brydon. Spec. issue of *Essays on Canadian Writing* 56 (1995): 20–36.

McClintock, Anne. "The Angel of Progress: Pitfalls of the Term 'Postcolonialism.'" *Colonial Discourse/Postcolonial Theory.* Ed. Francis Barker, Peter Hulme, and Margaret Iverson. Manchester: Manchester UP, 1994. 253–66.

———. *Imperial Leather: Race, Gender and Sexuality in the Colonial Context.* New York: Routledge, 1995.

Mishra, Vijay, and Bob Hodge. "What is Post(-)Colonialism?" *Textual Practice* 5.3 (1991): 399–414.

O'Brien, Susie, and Imre Szeman. "Introduction: The Globalization of Fiction/The Fiction of Globalization." *The Globalization of Fiction/The Fiction of Globalization.* Ed. Susie O'Brien and Imre Szeman. Spec. issue of *South Atlantic Quarterly* 100.3 (2001): 603–27.

O'Neill, Phillip R. "Settler Colony." *Encyclopedia of Postcolonial Studies.* Ed. John C. Hawley. Westport: Greenwood, 2001. 402–05.

Panitch, Leo. "Globalisation and the State." *Between Globalism and Nationalism: The Socialist Register.* Ed. Leo Panitch and Ralph Miliband. London: Merlin, 1994. 60–93.

Panitch, Leo, Peter Gowan, and Martin Shaw. "The State, Globalisation and the New Imperialism: A Roundtable Discussion." *Historical Materialism* 9 (2001): 3–38.

Seshadri-Crooks, Kalpana. "At the Margins of Postcolonial Studies: Part I." *The Pre-Occupation of Postcolonial Studies.* Ed. Fawzia Afzal-Khan and Kalpana Seshadri-Crooks. Durham: Duke UP, 2000. 3–23.

Shaw, Martin. *Theory of the Global State: Globality as Unfinished Revolution.* Cambridge: Cambridge UP, 2000.

Slemon, Stephen. "Post-Colonial Critical Theories." *New National and Post-Colonial Literatures: An Introduction.* Ed. Bruce King. Oxford: Clarendon, 1996. 178–97.

———. "Unsettling the Empire: Resistance Theory for the Second World." *World Literature Written in English* 30.2 (1990): 30–41.

Canadian Literature in English "Among Worlds"

LESLIE MONKMAN

In the immediate aftermath of the events of September 11, 2001, at the Pentagon and the World Trade Center, assertions that "the world" had irrevocably changed dominated American media coverage of the attacks. Early counter-reactions from voices such as Susan Sontag and Noam Chomsky met with intense resistance as tantamount to treason. Within a fortnight, Slavoj Žižek was pointing out that Peter Weir's film, *The Truman Show,* offered an appropriate gloss on the dominant American reaction to the events of the 11th as a radical disruption of "the world":

> The ultimate American paranoiac fantasy is that of an individual living in a small idyllic Californian city, a consumerist paradise, who suddenly starts to suspect that the world he lives in is a fake, a spectacle staged to convince him that he lives in a real world, while all people around him are effectively actors and extras in a gigantic show. The most recent example of this is Peter Weir's *The Truman Show* (1998) with Jim Carrey playing the small-town clerk who gradually discovers the truth that he is the hero of a 24-hours permanent TV show. (1)

Canadians subject to what Glenn Willmott has anatomized as a national proclivity for "ressentiment" would want to add to Žižek's observation that both Peter Weir as Australian director and Jim Carrey as Canadian star of *The Truman Show* are products, in part, of national discourses at least once removed from the continuing isolationist predilections of late twentieth-century United States.

Indeed, in the days following the 11th, Australians were watching their prime minister, who happened to be in Washington at the time of the attacks, being pointedly ignored as he offered feverish statements of support. Simultaneously, Canadians were protesting the failure of President Bush even to mention Canada in the long list of allies included in his initial address to Congress. Meanwhile, the immediately affirmed bond between the British prime minister and the American president as each other's best ally in both peace and war served as a reminder of the powerful partnership in the new millennium of the dominant national and imperial discourses of the two preceding centuries. For Australians and Canadians subject to neo-colonial *ressentiment*, it could also spur memories of Peter Weir's *Gallipoli* if not Jim Carrey's *Dumb and Dumber*.[1]

In addressing this alliance of British and American power in the limited sphere of Canadian literary study in English, this paper uses as a focus the addition of Alice Munro to the most recent edition of *The Norton Anthology of English Literature*, the first and only Canadian writer to be represented there. Interested neither in British canon-bashing nor in knee-jerk nationalist reactions to the power of American publishing, I nevertheless want to argue that even in an age of instant Web anthologies and individualized course packs, *The Norton* and its imitators function as both reflections and reinforcers of powerful and continuing neo-colonial assumptions underlying literary study in Canada. That anthologies are designed in relation to their perceived primary market and that they function as conservative instruments of interpellation is hardly new news. But in looking at the doubled imperialism of *The Norton* in a Canadian pedagogical context, I want to suggest that amid the daunting array of post-colonial[2] pedagogies advanced inside our classrooms, this strong national alliance should breed reflection on the curricular and departmental structures and contexts surrounding classes on Canadian writing.

At the same cultural moment as we rigorously contest constructions of the national inside our classrooms in order to address issues related to First Nations, multiculturalism, and globalization, "nations continue to exist because the major players have a vested interest in their continuing"

(Brennan 673). Those national vested interests are clearly evident in the union of canonical and publishing power in London and New York. While not unaware of potential charges of being both reactionary and reductive, I want to suggest, first, that dismissal of the national at the level of our institutional negotiations may be premature, and secondly, that one measure of our commitment to post-colonial pedagogies addressing Canadian writing could be how much attention we give to the national literatures in English of India or Nigeria, Australia or New Zealand. As Stephen Slemon observes, "an inculcation of local and nationalist knowledges goes nowhere as a post-colonial pedagogy unless it enters into specific negotiations with the practices of an anti- or counter-colonialist theoretical critique" (157). The opportunity for an encounter with those knowledges at a more than superficial level seems, however, to be a necessary element in an informed post-colonial pedagogy.

In the context of last year's special *PMLA* issue, "Globalizing Literary Studies," and the powerfully transitive participle in that title, Canadian literature, along with those of Australia and New Zealand, may be particularly vulnerable to the forces of globalization given its position within the various disciplinary and interdisciplinary structures associated with post-colonial studies. As Graham Huggan observes, within this field,

> the putatively "non-hegemonic" literatures and cultures of Africa, Asia and the Caribbean are welcomed for the insights they provide on diasporic patterns of identity, history and self-empowerment, [but] the more ostensibly privileged, predominantly white literatures and cultures of former settler colonies like Canada, Australia or New Zealand are quite likely to disappear from view. (241)

Suffering the usual dilemmas of those dealing with the problematic status of invader-settler literatures, I want, on the one hand, to celebrate the long overdue advertising in the 2001–02 academic year of tenure-track positions in "African Literatures in English" and "Anglophone Literature of Africa and/or the Caribbean" at the University of Alberta and the University of Toronto respectively. Concurrently, I want to suggest that a failure to expand the limited profile in our curricula of other national and regional literatures, including those of other invader-settler cultures, limits our capacity to situate Canadian writing effectively not only in relation to

British canonical and American publishing power but also in relation to many of the issues associated with post-colonial pedagogy.

I

First published in 1962, *The Norton Anthology of English Literature*, through its first four editions, represented writing of the British Isles under a title untroubled by its homogenizing of the literature of England and literature in English. Acceptance of this conflation of the national and the linguistic rests on what Jonathan Culler identifies as

> a special structure of exemplarity at work in literature. . . . The structure of literary works is such that it is easier to take them as telling us about "the human condition" in general than to specify what narrower categories they describe or illuminate. . . .
>
> But the combination of offering universality and addressing all those who can read the language has had a powerful *national* function. . . . To present the characters, speakers, plots, and themes of English literature as potentially universal is to promote an open yet bounded imagined community to which subjects in the British colonies, for instance, are invited to aspire. In fact, the more the universality of literature is stressed, the more it may have a national function. (36–37)

As the multiple discussions of the impact of Wordsworth's "daffodils" on colonial children suggest,[3] the implications of the powerful link between the national and the universal in relation to the British canon have been the subject of intense analysis since the 1960s. What has received less attention in Canada is the actual representation in our curricula of the multiple national literatures in English beyond those of Canada, Britain, and the United States.

The elision in "English literature" of "literature in English" and "the literature of England" aroused no resistance in *The Norton*'s primary market in the United States at its inception because the study of American language and literature had already established a parallel political and linguistic legitimacy dating from Noah Webster's *A Grammatical Institute of the English Language (1783–85)* and the subsequent publication of his *American Dictionary of the English Language* (1828) and the related school "speller" that had sold more than sixty million copies by 1890 (Hart 902).[4] In the United States by 1962, *The Norton*'s market was already marked for both curricular and publishing purposes by the organization of the study of English around the literary histories of both the British Isles and the United States, a structure subsequently reflected in W.W. Norton's publication of *The Norton Anthology of American Literature* (1979) as a companion to *The Norton Anthology of English Literature.* Even as Prime Minister Blair and President Bush reaffirm a parallel political partnership leading to a joint nomination for the Nobel Peace Prize, Harvard continues to name its department "The Department of English and American Literature and Language."

In the wake of the canon controversies of the 1980s and 90s, Robert Scholes makes the obvious point that within such curricular and publishing structures, "other Anglophone literatures—even Canadian—have held a peripheral place" (145).[5] What I want to recall, of course, is that in the Canadian market for the early editions of *The Norton* in the 1960s and 70s, Canadian literature was as peripheral as it was, and is, in the United States. Indeed, in a pattern notably contrasting with that of the United States, that status in Canada was often justified by arguments noting that American literature was also peripheral in Canadian curricula and program requirements dominated by the literature of the British Isles. Even the great expansion of courses in English-Canadian literature in the 1970s left those courses viewed as "add-ons" rather than as announcements of a fundamental realignment in departmental curricula. Indeed, departmental curricular battles over required undergraduate course groupings usually found Canadian literature competing with American literature, but rarely threatening principles of coverage governing requirements for the study of British literature. Instead, when the number of Canadian courses approached or matched the number of American courses, nationalist aspirations were satisfied.

Canadian nationalism, even at its peak, could never sustain the presumption of a "Department of English and Canadian Literature and Language" to parallel Harvard's. Instead, Alice Munro could satirize the limited horizons of American provincialism in *Lives of Girls and Women* with the arrival in Jubilee of Aunt Nile, the new American wife of Del Jordan's Uncle Bill, and the bearer of a perspective much noted in the current president of the United States.

> Nile meanwhile looked amazed and unhappy as someone who had never even heard of foreign countries, and who is suddenly whisked away and deposited in one, with everybody around speaking an undreamt-of language. Adaptability could not be one of her strong points. Why should it be? It would put in question her own perfection. (92)

Thus, as nationalist Canadians of the 1960s and 70s looked to the United States for threats to our national culture, *The Norton* reflected and reinforced the continuing canonical power of British colonialism.

For its first four editions, then, *The Norton* ignored literature from outside the British Isles but, in doing so, conveyed quite different messages to American and Canadian students. By 1972, Tom Symons' report for the Commission on Canadian Studies, *To Know Ourselves*, tempered earlier nationalist enthusiasm with the finding that only 8 percent of undergraduate courses in Canadian departments of English dealt in any way with Canadian literature. David Cameron's 1996 successor to the Symons report, *Taking Stock*, found this number rising to 12 percent, and Cameron expresses surprise that English departments report the smallest proportion of Canadian content among the nine disciplines surveyed (53). An indication of the institutional ambivalence and ambiguity underlying this figure emerges when it is placed beside a report received by Cameron from the Association of Canadian College and University Teachers of English proclaiming Canadian studies "a very powerful force in the discipline" (142).

What I want to suggest is that the study of Canadian literature has not been a "very powerful force" in our discipline over the past 25 years, whether one judges by the naming of our departments, the program requirements for our undergraduate and graduate students, or the construction of "area" classifications for appointments, graduate comprehensive examinations, or graduate and undergraduate program reviews. I am, however, less interested in belatedly repeating nationalist arguments of the 70s than in stressing that a failure to acknowledge the *actual* status of Canadian writing in English in our curricular structures leaves us badly positioned to define appropriate local strategies for addressing a world in which "globalizing literary studies" becomes a *PMLA* mantra.

II

The status of American literature in the United States as the one invader-settler literature to function as a significant other to British literature has the potential, then, to reinforce the link between nation and literature in London and New York while other post-colonial national literatures continue to be marginalized. Nationalists of the 1960s and 70s fought to gain a status for English-Canadian literature equal to that of American literature *in Canada*, but rather than seeking the ideological parity with British literature achieved by American literature in the United States, some proponents of Canadian literary study adopted a strategy more attuned to a different national culture by allying themselves with teachers and critics of "Commonwealth" literatures in English.

As a glance at just his early work reveals, no one has offered a better "Commonwealth" model of how it is possible to move between Canadian and other post-colonial literatures in English than W.H. New. Writing an introduction to George Woodcock's first collection of essays on Canadian literature, *Odysseus Ever Returning*, New observes that for Woodcock, "the literature of Europe provides the touchstones by which to estimate the worth of the new" (xii); for New, those touchstones are in post-colonial discourse. In the Introduction to his 1971 anthology of "English stories from around the world," *Four Hemispheres*, New acknowledges that most of the writers included in the anthology

> are not well known, and the few who are—Mansfield, Lessing, Naipaul, Spark, White—perhaps for that reason seem the oddities. One of the things this collection does, however, is to put them back into the context from which they emerged as major world writers, and to place beside their stories the interesting work of some of their compatriots. (v)

What interests New in these stories is "the distinctive use of the English language" (ix) and "the resilience of English as a literary language around the world" (viii).

In 1975, the Foreword to New's *Critical Writings on Commonwealth Literatures: A Selective Bibliography to 1970* (the first book-length bibliography available to students of those literatures) identifies the book as "neither more nor less than a guide and aid to research in a field of literary study that is only just recently attracting serious international attention" (1); the adjective "Commonwealth" is a "bibliographer's term of convenience for those countries still devising an English-language literary culture" (1). In that same year, New published *Among Worlds: An Introduction to Modern Commonwealth and South African Fiction*, with seven chapters (The West Indies, South Africa, East and West Africa, Canada, New Zealand, Australia, South Asia) attempting to outline "thematic parallels that mark the literary contemporaneity of each Commonwealth culture and examine some of the ways in which writers have used their cultures' preoccupations to construct separate and multiple worlds" (1).

Now often derided for promulgating national "false consciousness," homogenizing anglophilia, and other sins often more evident to their attackers than to those subject to their pedagogical practices, "Commonwealth" critics nevertheless challenged the overwhelming dominance of the British canon in Canada by beginning the process of introducing courses in writing from outside of Great Britain, the United States, and Canada. Although the comparative courses have been the primary objects of attack, both for being under-theorized and for appropriative combinations of texts and cultures, they have survived as "Commonwealth" or "post-colonial" courses under various theoretical rubrics, usually focused exclusively on contemporary writing and, despite their critics, usually more concerned with facilitating distinctions than with conflating disparate cultures. For the purposes of curricular categories related to "coverage" requirements, these courses have been treated as "add-ons" to existing categories, leaving core geographic and temporal assumptions and biases in the curriculum intact.

The courses more rigorously focused on national or regional literatures in English outside of Canada, Britain, or the United States presented a stronger challenge to existing curricular structures by insisting on other literary histories predating 1960 and on imagined communities outside of Europe and continental North America. These courses, however, are now threatened by the dismissal of such geographic categories as nationalist or racialist essentialisms even as other areas of the curriculum remain unaltered. As early as 1994, in his much-cited "Postcolonial Culture, Postimperial Criticism," W.J.T. Mitchell could observe that just as writers in English outside of England and the United States were gaining unprecedented public recognition in the late decades of the twentieth century, the attention of the literary academy shifted from introducing them into classrooms and curricula to focus instead on literary theory emanating from those imperial centres. In Canada, a related shift towards "postcolonial" as framed by Said, Spivak, and Bhabha, but under-inflected by the work of those such as W.H. New on literature outside of the Anglo-American axis, arrested a development now frequently seen as obsolescent in the face of both globalization and the issues associated with post-colonial studies.

Approaching its fifth edition in 1986, *The Norton* offered ample canonical resources for exploring the concerns of interest to Euro-American theorists and so could largely continue to ignore that the literatures in English of Africa, the Caribbean, Canada, or Australia now claimed national and regional space. Derek Walcott was the only writer to be added to *The Norton* from any of these literatures, with any impact of this inclusion on the anthology's editorial principles occluded by grouping Walcott with other "contemporary" poets, the others of course all working in Great Britain and Ireland. The inclusion of Walcott, nevertheless, marks the beginning of the breakdown of the strategic blurring of language and nation underlying *The Norton*'s editorial principles of selection. St. Lucia–born and a resident of Trinidad and the United States, Walcott, identified succinctly as "the Black Caribbean poet," is the first writer not significantly associated with the British Isles to be included in *The Norton*.[6]

The sixth edition in 1993 could note that Walcott had won the Nobel Prize for Literature in the preceding year, and the Preface tersely stated that "the writer of prose fiction Nadine Gordimer and the poet Fleur Adcock are now included" (xxxviii). The introductory essay for Gordimer cites her Nobel Prize in 1991, and the bio-critical introduction to Adcock notes that she is New Zealand–born but has been resident in London since 1963: "One of a growing number of Commonwealth poets whose work is enriching English literature, Adcock simultaneously reflects the decorum and distanced violence of life in the predominantly white former dominions" (2387). Although this comment invites further analysis on various fronts, my own immediate interest is two-fold. First, the "white former dominions" enter the literary economy of *The Norton* through the work of a New Zealand–born poet who published her first volume a year after moving permanently to London. Secondly, despite the influence of Salman Rushdie's "The Empire Writes Back with a Vengeance" in 1982 and his announcement a year later that "'Commonwealth Literature' Does Not Exist," the centripetal assumptions underlying *The Norton* remained undisturbed a decade later. Similarly, when Terry Eagleton proclaims that "the days when any half-decent verse or prose emanating from the former Empire could be recruited as 'Commonwealth literature,' ascribed a sort of country rather than town membership of the literary club, have vanished forever" and that "the Home Counties view of literature has now been decisively despatched" (19), I remain unpersuaded. Although one homogenizing version of "Commonwealth literature" has been justifiably rejected by Rushdie and, more recently, by Amitav Ghosh, fulfillment of Rushdie's call for "all English literatures" ("'Commonwealth'" 70) to be studied together is scarcely evident. Instead, I see the most recent edition of *The Norton* as a better indicator of the changes at work in the move from "English language and literature" towards Pico Iyer's migrant "global soul" and singular "Global Lit" (Foran 64).

III

Amidst such shifts and debates, the most significant influence on the changes in the most recent edition of *The Norton* published in 2000 would seem to be the appearance of a competing anthology in 1999, *The Longman Anthology of British Literature*. *The Longman* explicitly announces a geographic principle of selection encompassing the whole of the British Isles but acknowledges that "most speakers of English live in countries that are not the focus of this anthology" (xxix–xxx). In response, after 38 years of avoiding or eliding such questions, the seventh edition of *The Norton* (2000) acknowledges nervously that "the *national* conception of literary history, the conception by which English Literature meant the literature of England or at most of Great Britain, has begun to give way to something else" (xix). That "something else" beyond the national quickly evaporates, however, in the continuing acknowledgment that "we have separated off, for purposes of this anthology, English literature from American literature" (xviii). And the spectre of the MLA's Division 33 oft-cited but unchanged title, "Literatures in English other than British and American," reappears as this sentence continues: "but in the selections for the latter half of the twentieth century we have incorporated a substantial number of texts by authors from other countries" (xviii).

At last, then, joining earlier Nobel winners, Walcott and Gordimer, and London resident, Adcock, are single figures from Australia, Nigeria, and Canada (Les Murray, Chinua Achebe, and Alice Munro), as well as V.S. Naipaul, Jean Rhys, Anita Desai, Salman Rushdie, and J.M. Coetzee. In addition, for the first time, a long essay titled "The Persistence of English" traces "the emergence and spread of the English language" (jacket copy). Not surprisingly, when the "Major Authors" edition of *The Norton* appeared last year, Les Murray, Alice Munro, and even that London–New Zealand hybrid, Fleur Adcock, disappeared as completely as John Howard, Jean Chrétien, or Helen Clark do in Washington or London. A millennial discourse of globalization blindly frames *The Norton*'s Year 2000 changes: "English literature, like so many collective enterprises in our century, has ceased to be principally the product of the identity of a single nation; it is a global phenomenon" (xix).

Increasingly pushed to acknowledge the slippages inherent in their constructions of the national and the global, American users of *The Norton* now look for broader principles of recognition and representation. Robert Scholes, recently elected incoming president of the MLA for 2003, observing that "we have been thoroughly indoctrinated by 'coverage' as the organizational basis of our field" (148), argues for a curriculum that would allow us to get out from under the weight of a curriculum "oriented to English literary history" (153). For Scholes, the "old curriculum" can only see the introduction of new writers "as a drain on the basic mission of covering the masterpieces of British and American literature" while "a curriculum oriented to English textuality," for which Scholes has been arguing for more than three decades, would see courses from a broader spectrum of contemporary writing in English as serving "a vital function" (153).

Michael Bérubé, acknowledging his indebtedness to Reed Way Dasenbrock's work a decade ago, makes "a modest proposal" in *The Employment of English* for a focus on contemporary world literatures in English as a vehicle for, first, bridging literary and post-colonial cultural studies, and secondly, making it "possible for English departments to expand their concern with the English language while becoming less . . . well, *English*, in the process" (28) by moving away from a "centripetal" canon focused on the British Isles:

> This canon contains many of the greatest writers ever to inhabit and expand the English language, of course, but it also does double duty as an agent of Anglo-American national affiliation: just as the New Right likes to pretend that the United States has some deep genetic connection with Periclean Athens, so too do the Anglophile supporters of the centripetal canon like to pretend that you cannot understand "literatures in English" unless you have first completed the "coverage" requirements that will acquaint you with Gawain, the Miller's tale, and MacFlecknoe—not to mention the three nineteenth-century British novelists who will secure your employment by Milton Rosenberg at WGN in Chicago. Yet it is not entirely clear, at the very least, that the British canon before 1790 (exclusive of Shakespeare, of course, who is not only our language's greatest writer but also cannot be challenged in the slightest without provoking a national scandal) is quite as deserving of the place it now occupies in the United States; and it is not entirely clear why, if we now spend so much disciplinary time on British literature, we could not just as well (in some future incarnation) devote more of our time and energies to African, Indian, Caribbean, Australian and Canadian writing in English. (29)

Bérubé's "modest proposal" stresses a radical increase in the inclusion of contemporary world literature in English but praises Dasenbrock's complementary argument for shifting the existing canon from a centripetal focus "oriented toward the England of Pope, Fielding, Richardson, and Johnson, [to] a centrifugal canon [that] might focus on Swift, Defoe, Smollett, and Boswell" (cited by Bérubé 29).

Bérubé recognizes that his proposal will meet fierce resistance from colleagues who will see their own areas of specialization marginalized still further, and he acknowledges that "it's one (relatively easy) thing to shuffle the canon; . . . it's quite another (much harder) thing to shuffle the professoriate" (30). Like John Guillory, he sees canonical revision as "shifting the weight of the syllabus from older works to *modern* works, since what is in question for us are *new* social identities and new writers" (Guillory, cited by Bérubé 30). What is missing here is an acknowledgement of literary histories predating the contemporary in world literatures in English other than those of Britain and the United States. Our classrooms and *The Norton* now reflect the dramatic impact of colonial discourse theory and analysis on the study of every period of British and American literatures over the past two decades, but the pre-contemporary texts examined remain relentlessly linked to those two national literatures. Reflection on hiring committee discussions of temporally identified tenure-track positions in fields such as eighteenth- or nineteenth-century literature reveals the pervasiveness of this cultural myopia. As Tracy Ware notes in relation to Canadian literature, the insistent restriction of post-colonial literatures to the contemporary consigns earlier writing to "a pre-natal limbo" (87).

As an alternative to Scholes's and Bérubé's respective emphases on an ungeographically marked textuality and on contemporary texts outside the Anglo-American axis, I want to argue for what Donna Palmateer Pennee labels "a strategic nationalism or a least a strategic particularity in a so-called borderless world" (191). The arguments against any appeal to the concept of "national literatures" are well known. We now explicitly challenge nationalist discourses by arguing that "no distinct national character or essence exists that literature can express, even if we disguise the obsoleteness of the concept by rechristening it 'cultural practices'" (Clausen 48) or by exploring the limits of any discourse constructing an imagined community at the cost of effacing some members of that community. What is missing in such arguments, however, is an acknowledgement of existing curricular power relations. Thus, when Christopher Clausen argues that "literary nationalism . . . ought to be a transitional rather than a final position" (48), we could acquiesce if the curricular playing field were level. But in the absence of such a tabula rasa, to assume that we have reached a point to celebrate "the study of a collective literary achievement that offers extraordinary rewards if explored as a multiethnic, multicultural whole" (48) seems utopian if not just naive. Until the assumptions associated with literary study outside the Anglo-American axis approach those of their curricular rivals, the adoption of some form of strategic nationalism in debates outside the classroom seems crucial to informed post-colonial study inside those classrooms.

Although a shift in emphasis is possible at every institution, larger universities with comprehensive graduate programs in English have unique opportunities (and responsibilities) to assign tenure-track positions not just to specialists in "postcolonial theory" or omnibus "post-colonial literature(s)" but to specialists in national literatures other than those of Great Britain, Canada, or the United States. Bérubé argues that

> if literary study wants to become more cultural and cultural study needs to become more literary, it is hard to imagine a more fitting institutional negotiation of these desires than an English department whose curriculum centers not on the British Isles but on the global ramifications of the world travels of the language first spoken in the British Isles. (32)

He continues by suggesting that in the absence of our demoralized profession having "much of a public rationale for itself," the study of world literatures in English offers the public a rationale it can understand. More specifically, I would argue that amidst the multiply inflected rhetorics of "internationalization" and "globalization" at the senior administrative levels of our universities, both deans and provosts are likely to be more responsive to arguments based on strategic nationalism than to those resting on the assertion that "before postcolonial studies, Western scholarship was an embarrassment" (O'Brien and Szeman 606).

In the continuing and impossible project of "provincializing Europe" (Chakrabarty) and internationalizing the United States, postcolonial strategic nationalism may seem an outdated response to the macro-narratives of globalization. But "the world" may have changed less after September 11th than we are encouraged to assume, and the effects of thinking about our curricula and appointments in terms of strategic nationalism may not only help us situate Canadian writing more appropriately but also help us address the consequences of Canadian political and academic complicity with colonialism by reducing our own provincialism.

NOTES

1. Jim Carrey's announcement of his intention to seek American citizenship within a week of the presentation of the conference version of this paper and Celine Dion's emergence from temporary retirement to sing "God Bless America"

("my home sweet home") within a week of September 11, 2001, should suggest an appropriately ironic perspective on these introductory distinctions.

2. See Ashcroft for a useful comment on the post-colonial/postcolonial debate: "A simple hyphen has come to represent an increasingly diverging set of assumptions, emphases, strategies and practices in post-colonial reading and writing. The hyphen puts an emphasis on the discursive and material effects of the historical 'fact' of colonialism, while the term 'postcolonialism' has come to represent an increasingly indiscriminate attention to cultural difference and marginality of all kinds, whether a consequence of the historical experience of colonialism or not. . . . Admittedly the hyphen can be misleading, particularly if it suggests that post-colonialism refers to the situation in a society 'after colonialism', an assumption which remains tediously persistent despite constant rebuttals by post-colonialists. . . . Undoubtedly the 'post' in 'post-colonialism' must always contend with the spectre of linearity and the kind of teleological development it sets out to dismantle. But rather than being disabling, this radical instability of meaning gives the term a vibrancy, energy and plasticity which have become part of its strength, as post-colonial analysis rises to engage issues and experiences which have been out of the purview of metropolitan theory and, indeed, comes to critique the assumptions of that theory" (10–11). Following Ashcroft's arguments, and particularly resistant to the tendency of many proponents of "postcolonial" to exclude invader-settler literatures, I have retained the hyphen in this paper.

3. See Karen Welberry.

4. In his review of Jill Lepore's *A Is For American* (New York: Knopf, 2002), Hugh Kenner notes: "Americans still say 'Look it up in *Webster*,' alluding to a man who devoted his long life (1758–1843) to reorganizing the 'English' people spoke and wrote in a country that had just severed its ties with England. There had been other proposals for a national language, for instance Hebrew, both to distance Yanks from Britain and to signal them as a chosen people. French and Greek were also considered. But what Noah Webster proposed was simply to teach all Americans to spell and speak alike, yet differently in detail from the people of England. The result would be an 'American language, to become over the years as different from the future language of England, as the modern Dutch, Danish and Swedish are from German, or from one another'" (12).

5. Peter Hitchcock notes the power of the word *anglophone* in this peripheralization: "What could be more harmless than the OED definition of *Anglophone* as a person who speaks English? As soon as one begins to specify this person, and this English . . . , the innocence of the word dissolves into a history of colonial and postcolonial import. Anglophone is always somebody else's English just as Anglophone literature is somehow not American or English" (758).

6. Salah Hassan cites Jonathan Arac's invocation of "hypercanonization" in

discussing the prevalence of single authors or texts being asked to assume "a singular representative function" (298) as post-colonial texts are slowly admitted to the pedagogical canon: "In fact, the critical opening of the canon attributed to postcolonial theory and its related pedagogical practices has meant only a slight revision to canonical practices in literary studies . . ." (303).

WORKS CITED

Abrams, M.H., et al., eds. *The Norton Anthology of English Literature*. Seven editions. New York: Norton, 1962–2000.

Ashcroft, Bill. *Post-Colonial Transformation*. London: Routledge, 2001.

Bérubé, Michael. *The Employment of English*. New York: New York UP, 1998.

Brennan, Timothy. "Cosmo-Theory." *South Atlantic Quarterly* 100.3 (2001): 658–91.

Cameron, David. *Taking Stock: Canadian Studies in the Nineties*. Montreal: Association for Canadian Studies, 1996.

Chakrabarty, Dipesh. *Provincializing Europe: Postcolonial Thought and Historical Difference*. Princeton: Princeton UP, 2000.

Clausen, Christopher. "'National Literatures' in English: Toward a New Paradigm." *New Literary History* 25 (1994): 61–72.

Culler, Jonathan. *Literary Theory: A Very Short Introduction*. Oxford: Oxford UP, 1997.

Damrosch, David, ed. *The Longman Anthology of British Literature*. New York: Longman, 1999.

Dasenbrock, Reed Way. "What to Teach When the Canon Closes Down: Toward a New Essentialism." *Reorientations: Critical Theories and Pedagogies*. Ed. Bruce Henricksen and Thaïs E. Morgan. Urbana: U of Illinois P, 1990. 63–76.

Eagleton, Terry. "A Spot of Firm Government." Rev. of *God, Gulliver and Genocide*, by Claude Rawson. *London Review of Books* 23 Aug. 2001: 19–20.

Foran, Charles. "Books without Borders." *Enroute* Dec. 2001: 63–66.

Ghosh, Amitav. "Amitav Ghosh & the 2001 Commonwealth Writers Prize." Ghosh Home Page. 15 Feb. 2002 <http://www.amitavghosh.com>.

Globalizing Literary Studies. Spec. issue of *PMLA* 116.1 (2001).

Guillory, John. *Cultural Capital: The Problem of Literary Canon Formation*. Chicago: U of Chicago P, 1993.

Hart, James D. *The Oxford Companion to American Literature*. New York: Oxford UP, 1965.

Hassan, Salah. "Canons after 'Postcolonial Studies.'" *Pedagogy* 1.2 (2001): 297–304.

Hitchcock, Peter. "Decolonizing (the) English." *South Atlantic Quarterly* 100.3 (2001): 749–71.
Huggan, Graham. *The Postcolonial Exotic.* London: Routledge, 2001.
Iyer, Pico. *The Global Soul.* New York: Knopf, 2000.
Kenner, Hugh. "The Republic of Letters." *Times Literary Supplement* 26 Apr. 2002: 12.
Mitchell, W.J.T. "Postcolonial Culture, Postimperial Criticism." *Transition* 56 (1992): 11–19.
Munro, Alice. *Lives of Girls and Women.* 1971. Toronto: Penguin, 1997.
New, W.H. *Among Worlds: An Introduction to Modern Commonwealth and South African Fiction.* Erin: Press Porcepic, 1975.
———, comp. *Critical Writings on Commonwealth Literatures: A Selective Bibliography to 1970.* University Park: Pennsylvania State UP, 1975.
———. *Four Hemispheres.* Toronto: Copp Clark, 1971.
———. Introduction. *Odysseus Ever Returning.* By George Woodcock. Toronto: McClelland, 1970. ix–xv.
O'Brien, Susie, and Imre Szeman. "Introduction: The Globalization of Fiction/ The Fiction of Globalization." *South Atlantic Quarterly* 100.3 (2001): 603–26.
Pennee, Donna Palmateer. "Culture as Security: Canadian Foreign Policy and International Relations from the Cold War to the Market Wars." *International Journal of Canadian Studies* 20 (1999): 191–213.
Rushdie, Salman. "'Commonwealth Literature' Does Not Exist." 1983. *Imaginary Homelands: Essays and Criticism 1981–1991.* London: Granta, 1991. 61–70.
———. "The Empire Writes Back with a Vengeance." *Times* [London] 3 July 1982: 8.
Scholes, Robert. *The Rise and Fall of English.* New Haven: Yale UP, 1998.
Slemon, Stephen. "Teaching at the End of Empire." *College Literature* 19.3 and 20.1 (1992–93): 152–61.
Symons, Thomas H.B. *To Know Ourselves: The Report of the Commission on Canadian Studies.* Ottawa: Association of Universities and Colleges of Canada, 1972.
Ware, Tracy. "Canadian Literary Culture." *PMLA* 115 (2000): 89–90.
Welberry, Karen. "Colonial and Postcolonial Deployment of 'Daffodils.'" *Kunapipi* 19.1 (1997): 32–44.
Willmott, Glenn. "Canadian Ressentiment." *New Literary History* 32.1 (2001): 133–56.
Žižek, Slavoj. "Welcome to the Desert of the Real." Zizek Official Home Page. 17 Sept. 2001. 22 Sept. 2001 <http://alt.venus.co.uk/weed/current/zizek.htm>.

Everything I Know about Human Rights I Learned from Literature: Human Rights Literacy in the Canadian Literature Classroom

BRENDA CARR VELLINO

> We who live in fortunate lands where we have inherited good things . . . are prone to accept freedom, the most important of these good things, with an indifference which is the greatest threat to its continuance.
>
> — Lester B. Pearson

"This universal declaration of Human Rights as a common standard of achievement for all peoples and all nations, to the end that every individual and every organ of society, keeping this declaration constantly in mind, shall strive by teaching and education to promote respect for these rights and freedoms. . . ." So proclaimed the UN General Assembly in 1948. Today, when I introduce a copy of the Declaration to my Canadian Literature students, a majority have never held one in their hands much less studied it. When asked which human rights are important, the majority emphasize freedom of expression. For most, this is itself a symptom of privilege. Civil wars, famines, diasporas, and daily threats to bodily and community integrity happen elsewhere. The absence of substantive exposure to the fundamental instruments, institutions, histories, promises, and limitations of human rights in even the most obvious educational contexts is a significant omission in light of the critical role the United Nations envisions for human rights literacy.[1]

The 1993 Vienna Convention on Human Rights, which devotes a portion of its proceedings to the role of education, and the United Nations proclamation of a Decade of Human Rights Education from 1995–2005 point to the enduring relevance of what must be at once a local, national, and transnational endeavour. Indeed, after September 11, 2001, and the ensuing "war on terror," being informed about the international culture of human rights and justice is essential in a world where mutually entwined consequences of east/west and north/south histories are playing themselves out at all times both globally and locally. Further, Madame Justice Louise Arbour's critical role in bringing Slobodan Milosovic to trial at The Hague and her initiative in establishing the International Criminal Court indicate that commitment to justice within an international human rights culture is a Canadian commitment (if not always upheld in practice).

My paper seeks to explore the ways in which a human rights pedagogy might enrich readings of Canadian literature and, reciprocally, to discover what a postcolonial contextualized approach to Canadian literature might offer human rights pedagogy. The majority of human rights courses at present overlook consideration of literature, while most Canadian higher-education courses, including literature courses from a postcolonial perspective, overlook human rights as an essential thought category.[2] In my classroom experience, I have found that bringing together Canadian literature, postcolonial theory, and human rights pedagogy enriches each category. Most productively, it pushes the possibilities of literary citizenship for Canadian student readers toward greater critical engagement with the public and social spaces of their lives and those addressed by the writers and their contexts. This notion of the "reader as citizen" first came to me via Margaret Atwood's *Survival*. While I do not share her 1972 vision of seeking a cultural map for a unitary Canada, her juxtaposition of reader with citizen is immensely provocative (15). Literary citizenship beckons the reader to consider the politics of her own locations in body, community, nation, and world from the perspectives of the politics of others' locations invoked through the imaginative transference of the literary encounter. When human rights literacy is part of the reader's cultural knapsack, she learns to read the diversity of social experience in the Canadian context in both a local and global way.

Some critics may wish to counter my enthusiasm for an international culture of human rights by referring to the weakening role of the

United Nations in tandem with the decline of nation-states under pressure from global trade alliances, increasing heterogeneity, and political fragmentation. While the United Nations by its very name seems to be a constellation of bounded entities, dependent on the old notion of the sovereign nation, its covenants and charters historically challenge and constrain the notion of national autonomy as an alibi against prosecution for violation of citizens' rights (Weeramantry 160). The culture of human rights is historically a transnational, non-governmental civil society phenomenon as evidenced by international anti-slavery and women's suffrage organizations in the nineteenth century and by NGOs like Amnesty International, Human Rights Watch, and Doctors Without Borders in the twentieth and twenty-first centuries, some of which have played a major part in introducing and/or drafting covenants in an evolving human rights culture (Florini 185). Critics may also wish to take issue with the very assumption of universal rights and argue that the notion is largely a Western invention, the suspect offspring of liberalism, which is misplaced and oppressive if mapped onto non-Western contexts. Justice Weeramantry of The Hague argues in *Justice Without Frontiers* for the ancient intercultural roots of two central propositions of human rights culture—dignity and equality with their responsive codes of justice—in all of the major world wisdom and spiritual traditions, including Islam, Judaism, Christianity, and Buddhism (6–8).[3] Further, the liberation movements of the twentieth century, including civil rights, indigenous, women's, and gay movements, as well as the independence struggles of the formerly (and arguably still) colonized world, all invoke the norms, language, and aspirations of human rights culture.

I do not wish to suggest that we ignore the lessons of critical anthropology, among others, about the need to honour the complexity of local knowledges and contexts, but I contend that it is essential to uphold a provisional and particularized universal in the interest of an international culture of human rights.[4] By this I mean a generalizable notion that is nuanced by attention to complexities of history, context, and body. Such a strategy is part of what I term "critical humanism," one which interrogates and situates those inherited Enlightenment notions which are problematic, but which we cannot live without.[5] I am here coming out of the closet as a "critical humanist" to suggest that humanism, like literature and nation, is an intellectual and ideological category which requires reconstructive renovation rather than flat out dismissal.[6] Seyla Benhabib also relevantly urges such reconstructive work: "Among the legacies of modernity which today need reconstructing but not wholesale dismantling are moral and political universalism, committed to the now seemingly 'old fashioned' and suspect ideals of universal respect for each person in virtue of their humanity; the moral autonomy of the individual; economic and social justice and equality; democratic participation; the most extensive civil and political liberties compatible with principles of justice; and the formation of solidaristic human associations" (*Situating* 2). A context-accountable, but generalizable notion of a common humanity also opens the door to getting past sit-on-your-hands privilege, guilt, or apathy, which I encounter regularly with students (most of whom are from the privileged majority), without collapsing into sentimental or paternalistic constructions of a decontextualized suffering other.[7] Such a notion enables a sense of connection with others who are not like me but like me, as well as responsive civil society action based on shared vocabularies of democracy, rights, and justice.

What does all of this have to do with Canadian literature in a postcolonial framework? A 1994 article from the *Association for Canadian Studies Bulletin*, titled "Education on Human Rights and Democracy in Canada" (Gibbs and Seydegart), provoked one of those "eureka" shifts in me; quite suddenly, the connections between national literature studies, minority ethnic and diaspora studies, postcolonial criticism (all of which I was currently engaged in), and human rights/democracy studies came sharply into focus. My 12 years of experience as a member of CACLALS (Canadian Association for Commonwealth Language and Literary Studies) and ACQL (Association for Canadian and Quebec Literatures) bears out that most of us who entered the profession as Canadianists from the 1980s onward began to tilt toward postcolonial analysis as a significant conceptual framework for thinking through the literature of a nation emerging from its former colonial status, while still vexed by asymmetrical power relations between itself, First Nations, and diverse ethnic communities within its geopolitical boundaries. Postcolonial criticism, because of its relationship to national liberation struggles and the enduring historical consequences of colonization, is directly implicated in the international culture of human rights and democracy, yet it is rarely discussed in these terms. Ajay Heble is the rare exception when he suggests that human rights questions are one of the "new contexts" for Canadian criticism (92). A postcolonial approach already mandates that we do not teach Canadian literature in isolation from intercultural and interdisciplinary contexts of world literature, history, and politics. Take the period of exploration, conquest, slavery, and settlement by way of example. Anti-slavery societies are among the earliest transnational manifestations of human rights civil society. Susanna Moodie, as most of us now know, participated in one of these as scribe for the slave narrative of Mary Prince, before her marriage and immigration to Canada (Ferguson 33). I offer this as a context for her progressive debate with another settler wife about "allowing" Black people to sit at her dinner table, as well as destabilizes her objection to working-class people doing the same in *Roughing It in the Bush* (213–21). I also consider the early Black presence in Canada in relation to the slave trade and the American Civil War through discussion of slave narratives and freedom songs from the first volume of George Elliott Clarke's anthology of Black Nova Scotian writing, *Fire on the Water.*

Most Canadian literature criticism takes the form of an interrogation of cultural nationalism from a "postnational" perspective focused on heterogeneities of region, gender, sexuality, race, and ethnicity. What is missing in this conversation is an engagement with the interdependence of nation and citizenship.[8] If, as postcolonial studies advocate, nation is a powerful force in constructing social identity, so then is citizenship within states that variously adhere to and/or violate the norms of individual and collective human rights. Critical citizenship calls for a similar intensity of work to that being done on other aspects of identity formation such as gender and race (Strong-Boag 236). As an American-Canadian, I bring to my encounter with the Canadian nation a profound scepticism about patriotic nationalism and the failures of a democratic state in which all citizens were not created equal from its inception; at the same time, I share a persistent idealism with those who seek to use the aims of democracy to make the state more accountable for its failures. Further, just as literature has been variously doing the cultural work of nation, it has also often been doing the cultural work of official and unofficial citizenship. What carries over from my American roots into my Canadian literature classroom, then, is an ardent belief in the pursuit of democratic culture which is often manifest through citizens forming civil society alliances.[9]

By situating my approach to my Canadian literature teaching within a human rights/postcolonial framework, I seek to open up sustained reflection on the ways that the literary imagination contributes to the democratic experiment in Canada, the ways writers and readers are part of that conversation. Briefly, I want to suggest what a human rights pedagogy looks like, a subject to which a rich array of studies have been devoted, particularly since the UN Decade of Human Rights Education was declared from 1995–2005.[10] Human rights pedagogy promotes human rights literacy, that is, engagement with the history, values, concepts, key documents, and organizations integral to democratic values and aspirations, especially the norms of human dignity, equality, inalienability, and justice (Weeramantry 162). Canadian human rights pedagogy explores the possibilities, limitations, and the particular applications of these within our national context. Precisely because my Canadian Literature course is organized around representations of nation, and because our nation, like all nations, is part of the vexed history of conquest, empire building, slave trade, immigration, settlement, displacement, relocation, and subsequent cultural criss-crossings, a postcolonial framework is highly compatible with the aims of a "critical human rights consciousness" (Flowers, *Handbook* 8). This involves a critical understanding of the conditions that interfere with rights, the ability to recognize the human rights dimensions of particular situations in history, narrative, and everyday life, to debate the relevance or necessity of particular human rights interventions, and, ideally, to recognize the possibility of one's own agency in taking responsibility for acting to influence human rights solutions, promotion, and protection (Tibbitts n.p.).

I open the year, as many do, with some discussion of what counts as Canadian identity, but re-framed in the context of the writer and reader as citizen. I suggest that active and critical Canadian citizenship not only requires familiarity with and pride in our cultures, histories, and values, but also requires democracy and human rights literacy. This involves familiarity with the major documents, aspirations, violations, and protections of human rights as these are played out in the Canadian context, including provincial, national, and global manifestations. I hand out a "human rights tool box" which includes copies of the UN Declaration, the Canadian Charter, the Multiculturalism Act, and an international human rights time-line. We spend a class studying the United Nations Declaration, brainstorming a Canadian human rights timeline, and developing a framework within which to pursue discussion of human rights questions relevant to the developing values of the democratic experiment in Canada.[11] From our first contemplation of the reader as a citizen within a human rights culture, I set forth some questions about the cultural work literature may do on behalf of nation, citizenship, and human rights. Does the text imply or more directly call forth citizen writers or readers? How do we experience our own citizenship through questions, narrative situations, and character dilemmas posed by the literature? What kind of cultural work is the text doing on behalf of nation building, maintaining, or renovating? What representational strategies, character situations, historical moments call up questions of belonging and non-belonging, country as home-place and alien space? How central are human rights values to the citizenship structures of the text? A human rights framework provides a unifying matrix for issue-based teaching that derives from a critical rainbows approach combining insights from feminisms, queer theory, critical race theory, critical multiculturalism, and postcolonial and ecological theory. Students sometimes feel that they are asked to jump through many politically correct hoops when they are asked to engage with these assorted frameworks as they are evoked by the different course readings, but what they all share is a common rights heritage, whether it be experience of violations or an evolving rights culture that seeks to protect and redress violations. "Learning to see through a human rights lens" re-frames many postcolonial and other issues as significant rights-focused categories (Flowers, *Handbook* 38).

A non-inclusive list of human rights related categories which are manifested through the contexts, narratives, conflicts, and diverse representational strategies of Canadian literatures in English include the following: forced migration, slave trade, immigration, displacement, diaspora, and transculturation; settler-invader societies; racial, ethnic, linguistic, and religious minorities' histories, cultures, and experience of discrimination; war and suspension of civil liberties; gender and sexuality discrimination; and the relationship of the nation to all of the above. Further, I link human rights questions to three conceptual categories: social identity, body, and agency. Because the body is freedom's limit, the site where violations are scored, marked, amplified, endured, and resisted, reading for the body is an essential strategy for a human rights pedagogy. Twenty years of gender, queer, race, and postcolonial theory have variously foregrounded the body as a central category to each. As an abstract category, it is highly theorized and necessarily so, but as an experiential entity, it is the locus where social suffering registers daily as close as one's own skin and bones, within situations of insidious domestic abuse and catastrophic political events on a global scale.[12] Late twentieth-century body studies have tended to focus on the pleasures of the desiring body, which is a refreshing break from centuries of anti-body religion and philosophy; however, day-to-day embodiment questions are most acute when the body is in a state of deprivation—hungry, shelterless, subject to extremes of weather, and the limitations of disease, age, and pain. Ethical representations of the vulnerable and suffering body in literature join with Amnesty International appeals in a collective endeavour to bring an end to suffering (Scarry 9). The body in literary representation as itself, as metaphor, as voice or refusal of voice, as subjugated and/or resisting is a primary strategy of witness. As Albert Camus notes, the artist is "freedom's witness" in that he or she testifies "not to the law, but to the body" (Felman and Laub 108). While specificities of the social body must be carefully attended to, the body is also a primary node of connection across the different locations of writers, narrative situations, characters, and readers. Feeling, sentience, embodiment, and affect all do critical work in fostering human rights consciousness in citizen readers.[13]

Literature as a context for human rights education addresses several problems in human rights legal and philosophical culture—decontextualizaton and abstraction—which tend to flatten local cultures and erase particular subjectivities.[14] Postcolonial approaches to literature have urged the restoration of historical, political, economic, and geographical contexts to our readings. Literature, being of its time and place, always calls forth such an approach either implicitly or explicitly. Literature also calls forth attention to subjective complexity, the inner world of writers, characters, protagonists, and readers, giving particular attention to the struggles for agency of ordinary people in everyday life. The affective powers of the imagination cultivate compassion for those dissimilar from me, "an ethics of reciprocity," without which a culture of human rights and democratic futures would be impossible (Nussbaum xvi; Ricoeur 186). Literature is distinguished from other human rights discourses by its ability to evoke subjective contexts to the readerly imagination and, in so doing, awaken empathy and solidarity with the character/protagonist situations which the reader is called into relationship with. Literature, as Paul Ricoeur suggests, becomes a kind of "ethical laboratory" for thought experiments in which we wrestle with ethical dilemmas through imaginative suture with characters, speakers, and identity locations in ways not available to us in newspaper, television, historical, and perhaps even Amnesty International reports (163–64, 170). Rather than seek to disrupt the phenomenon of character identification so common in first readings of texts, I use it as a leverage point where students may venture toward intersubjective regard for "the other as myself" (Ricoeur 193). In a human rights framework, this could take the form of trying out positions of participant, bystander, witness, or intervener in a situation of rights violation (Flowers, *Teaching* 1–2). Here is where the audacious claims of my title—"Everything I know about human rights I learned from literature"—begins to make sense. While this is something of an exaggeration, students frequently respond to such works as *Obasan* or *Disappearing Moon Cafe* or *Not Wanted on the Voyage* or *Whylah Falls* with "I never knew" or "I'd never thought about this" or, more dramatically, "I will never think about Canada in the same way." One of the goals of human rights pedagogy is "connected learning," a capacity to make meaningful links between learning and everyday life.[15] For example, what do the immigration policies that contextualize *Disappearing Moon Cafe* have to do with immigration policy after the American September 11th?

Throughout the year, we consider the ways that the creation of overarching myths, narratives, and symbols of nation involve selective forgetting of the unsavoury elements of a nation's history. As Edward Said asserts in "Nationalism, Human Rights, and Interpretation," "For the intellectual to be 'for' human rights means, in effect, to be willing to venture interpretations of those rights in the same place and with the same language employed by the dominant power, to dispute its hierarchy and methods, to elucidate what it has hidden, to pronounce what it has silenced or rendered unpronounceable" (198). Former BC Chief Justice Thomas Berger makes explicit the link between Canadian democratic ideals, citizenship, and a less than ideal human rights history in *Fragile Freedoms*. In the "Cultural Collisions" section of my CanLit course, the narratives arising from the fateful encounters between explorers, settlers, and First Peoples are students' first opportunity to reflect on the contradictory representations which betray clashing early rights and cultural domination values in such writers as Susanna Moodie or David Thompson. Notions of essential human dignity collide with pseudo-anthropological notions of racial superiority and inferiority. George Copway, the Ojibway Methodist missionary, in his autobiography, appeals to Christian justice discourse and liberal natural rights discourse, both of which were at the time heavily linked with the anti-slavery movement (22–23). Surprisingly, most human rights curricula, including the few I could find offered in literature, overlook indigenous peoples' rights and earth rights as essential to a rights culture, just as the early documents do (Flowers, *Handbook* 6). Postcolonial theory can make an essential intervention into human rights pedagogy and curricula by redressing these omissions.

Joy Kogawa's *Obasan* is a twentieth-century human rights literary cornerstone.[16] In counterpoint to this novel's testimony to the personal, family, community, and national consequences of concentration-camp internment of Japanese-Canadians during World War II, I hand out copies of the Multiculturalism Act and the Charter. While the novel was written before these essential Canadian human rights documents, it comments on the emerging official discourse of multiculturalism and is itself part of the challenge minority rights advocates pose to the democratic experiment in the wake of a history scarred with rights violations. Just as the United Nations Charter of Rights is a response to the pressures of history, particularly the Jewish Holocaust, so the Canadian Charter may be seen, in part, as a response to the pressures of Canada's postcolonial history. Further, we look at how these central Canadian documents explicitly embed themselves in a genealogy of international human rights documents and culture by invoking them directly in their preambles. Human rights culture is a continuous work in progress within and between nations. I disagree with Roy Miki's reading of the novel's liberal humanist agenda which, he argues, privileges the private inner discourse of Naomi over the politically engaged discourse of Aunt Emily, so that the novel's radical possibility collapses into quietism (115, 140).[17] Perhaps one reason for this (mis)reading is that the Buddhist values central to the spiritual thread of the novel are not carefully attended to by Miki and most critics. He notes only the Anglican Christianity, which he takes as a sign of Western colonization, but it is also important to consider how the community minister Nakayama-sensei alters Christian values in a hybrid Anglican-Buddhist spirituality. There are competing registers and urgencies in the novel of spiritual life, imaginative life, embodied life, and social being which, taken together, comprise the whole person experience. It is precisely this novel's intimate negotiation of the impact of public racism and state policy on inner life, bodily integrity, family, and community which is so persuasive.[18] Again and again, I have witnessed the kind of critical thinking this novel has stimulated in student journals, papers, group work, and classroom debates. While some critics may see these as classic liberal moments, marked by passing White guilt, I see tentative shifts in thinking about self, others, and belonging or disenfranchisement within Canada as promising steps toward critical citizenship. If I risk sacrificing theoretical and critical complexity in my second-year courses for pragmatism, so be it. For students, Joy Kogawa is one literary citizen who makes a difference; she shows the possibility of literary agency at the intersection of literature with civil society advocacy. [19]

Teaching Canadian Literature offers an opportunity to promote and interrogate values intrinsic to Canadian democracy. Chief among them is respect for and commitment to a culture of human rights here and internationally. Postcolonial pedagogy is, by its investments, implicitly bound up with human rights awareness, violations, and protection. Making a postcolonial human rights pedagogy explicit in Canadian literature teaching may make a modest contribution to decreasing student apathy and increasing future civil society participation, which is our best hope for keeping governments responsible and responsive to the democratic ideals they espouse. In Canada, where our fragile freedoms are often taken for granted, where democracy suffers from lack of rigorous citizen participation, awakening the citizen in student readers is critical to democratic futures both here and globally. I wish to close by echoing Ajay Heble: "is it utopian of me to suggest that Canadian critics and teachers have a responsibility, however modest, to initiate and nurture forms of solidarity which will help bring about progress, help facilitate change both in the current distribution of social relations and in the popular understanding?" (92).

ACKNOWLEDGEMENTS

This article reflects a ten-year internal conversation on pedagogy, deeply informed by a number of Canadian colleagues and mentors (sometimes unbeknownst to them) who have an equal passion for teaching, literature, and social justice, most especially Barbara Leckie, Robin (Edwards Davies)

Buyers, Dorothy Nielsen, Larry McDonald, Parker Duchemin, Paul Keen, Ashok Mathur, Aruna Srivastava, and Terry Goldie. I owe especial thanks to my mother, Barbara Carolyn Heil Bishop, and my grandfather, Frederick Lebeis Heil, who awakened in me a love for responsible citizenship, to Andre Vellino for being a companion on the journey, and to my two beautiful daughters, Karuna and Sarah, from whom I borrowed precious time to work on this essay and for whom I yearn for a more just and peaceful world.

NOTES

1. A 1997 American Human Rights survey found that 93 per cent of Americans cannot even name the UN Declaration of Human Rights, or much less have ever held it in their hands and read it (Flowers, *Handbook* 16). One can only guess that similar statistics would result from a similar survey in Canada. Such absence of even the most basic human rights literacy suggests that democracy is bereft of substance in North America.

2. Most human rights courses are offered in the obvious disciplines of law, political science, philosophy, sociology, and anthropology. Flowers' *Human Rights Here and Now* has a helpful "Lit and Human Rights" unit; Amnesty International has published a resource notebook, *Teaching Human Rights through Literature*; and I found several human rights and literature syllabi on the Web: Julie de Sherbinin's "Human Rights and World Literature," Colby College, and J.S. Peters' "Literature and Human Rights," Columbia University.

3. For a rich history of the early, diverse roots of twentieth-century human rights culture, see Paul Lauren's "My Brother's and Sister's Keeper: Visions and the Birth of Human Rights" in *The Evolution of International Human Rights*.

4. I adapt this notion of the concrete and therefore partialized universal from Seyla Benhabib in "The Generalized and Concrete Other" in *Situating the Self*. Other critics such as Cornel West and Edward Said have called for a similarly strategic universalism in the service of justice.

5. In an interview with Howard Winant, Gayatri Spivak speaks of "collective agency" as a category "one cannot not want," but which we must subject to persistent critique (93). She speaks in another interview of acknowledging "the dangerousness of what one must use," in this case strategic essentialism (129). It seems appropriate to extend her method to work with a strategic universal for human rights culture.

6. Susan Stanford Friedman argues for the necessity of reforming a number

of relevant categories to thinking about human rights—agency, identity, self, author, experience, meaning, and authority (187).

7. I am increasingly uncomfortable with the trend in radical pedagogies to read student crisis moments such as anger, guilt, tears, and resistance as a sign of effective teaching. I once received an angry e-mail from a White male student who dropped my Canadian literature course, asserting, "You came to destroy everything I ever thought." This "teachable moment" made me aware of my need to be responsible for my unfair advantage in being a senior learner with ten or more years of post-secondary learning behind me. In my experience, meeting students where they are and unfolding critical consciousness gradually is more effective than overwhelming them with critique.

8. For a helpful overview of citizenship and civil society theory, see Kymlicka and Norman.

9. In *A Place for Us*, democracy theorist Benjamin Barber defines *civil society* as the third space between the state and commerce.

10. Of the myriad resources available, I have found Ishay's *The Human Rights Reader*; Flowers' *Human Rights Here and Now* and *The Human Rights Education Handbook*; Lauren's *The Evolution of International Human Rights*; Berger's *Fragile Freedoms*; and Kleinman's *Social Suffering* particularly useful. Useful Web resources include: Human Rights Resource and Education Centre, University of Ottawa <http://www.uottawa.ca/hrrec>; Human Rights Internet <http://www.hri.ca>; and Human Rights Resource Center, University of Minnesota <http://www1.umn.edu/humanrts/hrcenter.htm>.

11. The pedagogical scenario that I outline in this paragraph is a composite of several different approaches I have taken over a number of years in my Canadian Literature survey course. Human rights questions are clearly not the only angle of inquiry around which the course is organized. Currently, I divide the course into four thematic clusters: "Cultural Crossings and Collisions," "Land Claims," "Reinventing the Nation," and "Heritage-Community-Identity." See Flowers' *The Human Rights Education Handbook* for an excellent group-work activity section which includes human rights timeline brainstorming (84).

12. Body theory that has been helpful to my linkage of human rights, representation, and literature includes Elaine Scarry's *The Body in Pain*, which argues that the body and culture are simultaneously unmade through the inhumanities of torture and war, while conversely, the act of creation is laden with "ethical consequence," bound up with ending crimes against human bodily integrity (22–23); and Thomas Csordas' *Embodiment and Experience*, in which he cautions against an objectified bodiless body which is discussed primarily as a cultural phenomenon that has little relationship to the lived body, the "threatened vehicle of human being and dignity" in situations of political violence. He calls for

attention to the "multiple body"—experienced in a variety of lived, social, cultural, and consumer contexts, and regulated through institutional practices and discourses (3–6). Csordas helpfully articulates the overlapping interactions between sentience, representation, subjugation, and agency.

13. A weekly reading-commentary assignment works well as a venue for students to informally express their affective, subjective responses to the readings.

14. Richard Wilson argues that abstract liberal conceptions of justice and rights result in decontexualization that discounts and underreads subjective agency (23, 134–60). For human rights courses that problematize context and human rights, see Jody Ranck's "Power, Culture, and Human Rights" and Eric Stover/Jody Ranck's "The Politics of Human Rights and Humanitarian Interventions" on the Web at University of California at Berkeley <http://www.medanthro.net/academic/syllabi/humanrights.html>.

15. For two inspiring resources on connected learning, see Brownlee and Schneider, and Gabelnick.

16. Kogawa's *Obasan* and Atwood's *The Handmaid's Tale* are the only Canadian texts I found on American or world literature bibliographies of literature and human rights.

17. I apologize if I have oversimplified Roy Miki's admirably subtle analysis of *Obasan*.

18. An important contribution of the liberation movements of the twentieth century to human rights culture has been to shift the emphasis from the liberal focus on the individual to collective or peoples' rights. See Felice for attention to this problem. *Obasan* negotiates both the individual child-protagonist's rights violations and that of her family and community. However, Miki expresses concern that the novel becomes an icon of "groupness," one writer's representation standing in for the experience of all Japanese Canadians (173).

19. In a similar vein, we look at the consequences of the Chinese Exclusion Act and Head Tax on three generations of women and men in Sky Lee's *Disappearing Moon Cafe*. First Nations, Jewish, Québécois, and gay or lesbian Canadian writers all invoke human rights questions and culture either implicitly or explicitly.

WORKS CITED

Atwood, Margaret. *Survival: A Thematic Guide to Canadian Literature*. Toronto: Anansi, 1972.

Barber, Benjamin. *A Place for Us: How to Make Society Civil and Democracy Strong*. New York: Hill and Wang, 1998.

Benhabib, Seyla. *Democracy and Difference: Contesting the Boundaries of the Political*. Princeton: Princeton UP, 1996.

———. *Situating the Self: Gender, Community and Postmodernism in Contemporary Ethics*. New York: Routledge, 1992.

Berger, Thomas R. *Fragile Freedoms: Human Rights and Dissent in Canada*. Toronto: Clarke, Irwin, 1982.

Brownlee, Paula P., and Carol G. Schneider. "The Challenge of Connected Learning." *Liberal Learning and the Arts and Sciences Major*. Vol. 1. Washington, DC: Association of American Colleges, 1991.

Clarke, George Elliott, ed. *Fire on the Water: An Anthology of Black Nova Scotian Writing*. Vol. 1. Lawrencetown Beach, NS: Pottersfield, 1991.

Copway, George. "The Life of Kah-Ge-Ga-Gah-Bowh." *The Oxford Anthology of Native Literature*. Ed. Daniel David Moses and Terry Goldie. Toronto: Oxford UP, 1992. 17–25.

Csordas, Thomas J., ed. *Embodiment and Experience: The Existential Ground of Culture and Self*. Cambridge: Cambridge UP, 1994.

Felice, William. *Taking Suffering Seriously: The Importance of Collective Human Rights*. Albany: SUNY P, 1996.

Felman, Shoshana, and Dori Laub. *Testimony: Crises of Witnessing in Literature, Psychoanalysis, and History*. New York: Routledge, 1992.

Ferguson, Moira, ed. *The History of Mary Prince*. Ann Arbor: U of Michigan P, 1987.

Florini, Ann M. "Transnational Civil Society and Human Rights." *The Third Force: The Rise of Transnational Civil Society*. Tokyo: Japan Center for International Exchange, 2000. 177–209.

Flowers, Nancy, et al. *The Human Rights Education Handbook*. Minneapolis: Human Rights Resource Center, 2000.

Flowers, Nancy, ed. *Human Rights Here and Now*. Minneapolis: Human Rights Resource Center, 1998.

Flowers, Nancy, et al. *Teaching Human Rights through Literature*. Human Rights Education Resource Notebooks. New York: Amnesty International USA, 1997.

Friedman, Susan Stanford. "Negotiating the Transatlantic Divide: Feminism after Poststructuralism." *Mappings: Feminism and the Cultural Geographies of Encounter*. Princeton: Princeton UP, 1998. 181–98.

Gabelnick, Faith, et al. *Learning Communities: Creating Connections among Students, Faculty, and Disciplines*. San Francisco: Jossey-Bass, 1990.

Gibbs, Heather, and Magda Seydegart. "Education on Human Rights and Democracy in Canada." *Association for Canadian Studies Bulletin* (Winter 1994): 1, 12–15.

Heble, Ajay. "New Contexts of Canadian Criticism: Democracy, Counterpoint, Responsibility." *New Contexts of Canadian Criticism*. Ed. Heble, et al. Peterborough: Broadview, 1997. 78–97.

Ishay, Micheline, ed. *The Human Rights Reader*. New York: Routledge, 1997.

Kleinman, Arthur, et al., eds. *Social Suffering*. Berkeley: U of California P, 1997.

Kogawa, Joy. *Obasan*. Markham: Penguin, 1981.

Kymlicka, Will, and Wayne Norman. "Return of the Citizen: A Survey of Recent Work on Citizenship Theory." *Ethics* 104 (Jan. 1994): 352–81.

Lauren, Paul. *The Evolution of International Human Rights*. Philadelphia: U of Pennsylvania P, 1998.

Lee, Sky. *Disappearing Moon Cafe*. Vancouver: Douglas & McIntyre, 1990.

Miki, Roy. *Broken Entries: Race, Subjectivity, Writing*. Toronto: Mercury P, 1998.

Moodie, Susanna. *Roughing It in the Bush*. 1852. Toronto: McClelland, 1989.

Nettleton, Sarah, and Jonathon Watson, eds. *The Body in Everyday Life*. London: Routledge, 1998.

Nussbaum, Martha. *Poetic Justice: The Literary Imagination in Public Life*. Boston: Beacon, 1995.

Ricoeur, Paul. *Oneself as Another*. Trans. Kathleen Blamey. Chicago: U of Chicago P, 1992.

Said, Edward. "Nationalism, Human Rights, and Interpretation." *Freedom and Interpretation*. Ed. Barbara Johnson. New York: Basic Books, 1993. 175–205.

Scarry, Elaine. *The Body in Pain: The Making and Unmaking of the World*. New York: Oxford UP, 1985.

Spivak, Gayatri. Interview with Ellen Rooney. *differences* 1.2 (1989): 124–56.

———. Interview with Howard Winant. *Socialist Review* 3 (1990): 81–97.

Strong-Boag, Veronica, et al., eds. *Painting the Maple: Essays on Race, Gender, and the Construction of Canada*. Vancouver: UBC P, 1998.

Tibbitts, Felisa. "Emerging Models for Human Rights Education." *Issues of Democracy* 7.1 (Mar. 2002). Online. US Department of State, Human Rights Education <http://usinfo.state.gov./journals/itdhr/0302/ijde/tibbitts.htm>.

Weeramantry, Christopher. *Justice Without Frontiers: Furthering Human Rights*. The Hague: Kluwer Law International, 1997.

West, Cornel. "The New Cultural Politics of Difference." *Out There: Marginalization and Contemporary Cultures*. Ed. Russell Ferguson, et al. New York: New Museum of Contemporary Art, 1990. 19–36.

Wilson, Richard A. "Introduction." *Human Rights, Culture and Contexts: Anthropological Perspectives*. Ed. Richard Wilson. London: Pluto, 1997. 1–27.

———. "Representing Human Rights Violations: Social Contexts and Subjectivities." *Human Rights, Culture and Contexts* 134–60.

Compr(om)ising Post/colonialisms: Postcolonial Pedagogy and the Uncanny Space of Possibility

GERRY TURCOTTE

> Fear of freedom, of which its possessor is not necessarily aware, makes him see ghosts. Such an individual is actually taking refuge in an attempt to achieve security, which he prefers to the risks of liberty.
>
> — Freire 16

THE TITLE OF THIS PAPER is drawn from a conference of the same name that I co-organized in 1999 at the University of Wollongong in Australia (see Ratcliffe and Turcotte). Although the general aim of the conference was to interrogate the notions of the postcolonial, it originally began as a wider discussion about the way postcolonialism had developed as a worldwide industry, and the growing sense that the pioneering efforts of Canadian and Australian scholars in shaping this field had been marginalized. My fear with this juggernaut of an academic industry was that the so-called fringe or peripheral celebration of the field was being recolonized by the familiar empires. The United States and Britain, somehow, were buying up this potentially radical, interrogative area of academic studies, so that it began not only to speak a centralist agenda, but more alarmingly, the modes of its production were once again made to reside in, and so shape more than ever the interests of, the traditional centres. Routledge, for example, in setting itself up as a monolith, and Carfax, by buying up the key journals in the field and then insisting that scholars sign away their authorial rights in order to be published in these strategic sites, were in a sense, it seemed to me, returning us to the paradigms of old. So that while arguments about the flaws, and even exclusions, of what some critics termed the "failures" of postcolonialism were undeniable, the ex-centric force that allowed for an often profound radicalism to take place was diminished.[1]

This, as I say, was a starting point for the conference. It rapidly became something else, in part because of a sense both in the classroom and in the theoretical arena that the way the conference was shaped to speak about such concerns might control the discussion—might reproduce a range of systemic occlusions and keep out a range of voices that were routinely elided: in particular Indigenous and minority voices. As I discussed the imminent conference with my students in a range of subjects, the issue of institutional control was ever present.

If we accept, as I think we must, the now commonplace assertion that, as Stephen Slemon puts it, "colonialist literary learning is at the primal scene of colonialist cultural control, and that a pedagogy of the book plays a necessary and material role in the strategic production of willing subjects of Empire" (153), it remains for us to decide what sorts of strategies we are willing to put in place to militate against such structures, while also recognizing the implacable power of the totalizing educational system we operate within. As Aruna Srivastava has argued, "the academy is based on relationships that are identical to and indeed a consequence of the imperialistic impulse" (17), and it is precisely this cluster of academic imperatives and practices that we need to dismantle, or at the very least highlight, in the interrogative function of a postcolonial pedagogy.

This, of course, is easier said than done when our funding, job security, teaching surveys, and peer review processes may depend on silence on such issues. But this can't be the full reason that, as Ajay Heble has noted, "attention to the specific material conditions of teaching . . . is absent from so much writing on critical pedagogy" (148). Maureen McNeil has argued that "much critical theory is rather vague about specific pedagogic activities" (qtd. in Heble 148), and this is certainly because many of us find it difficult, not just to strike a balance between the need to "tak[e] sides on heated issues" (Heble 151) and the more traditional demands of a humanistic learning environment that insists on a democratized field of discussion, but also to find ways in which to enact what can be extremely threatening, highly disempowering re/views of traditional power structures and the way so many of us are implicated in them. These politicized interventions can be threatening to us: to the way our job is secured, to the way we've been trained to proceed, to the manner in which we take umbrage in a series of collective rights accrued over centuries—all of which can be difficult to surrender.

And for students who just want to read a good book, having their entire ethico-political point of view held up for scrutiny tends to take the shine off a favourite novel. There's no question that even with the most successful strategies for discussing these issues, for examining "how we privilege and institutionalize certain knowledges" (Srivastava 13), inevitable resistance arises, expressed via attacks on political correctness and over-sensitivity, through charges of reverse racism, and so forth.

With this in mind, when I sat down, as coordinating organizer of "Compr(om)ising Post/colonialisms," I decided to try a different approach to the process of structuring a conference, and in particular to the way Indigenous participants are often invited to be involved. I contacted many colleagues, artists, writers, politicians, and elders in Indigenous communities, and, together with a cultural adviser, asked these Indigenous figures both *if* they would be involved in the project, and if so, *how* they wished to participate. Slowly, through a lengthy process of consultation, we put together a provisional program of Aboriginal involvement. Some chose to do keynote addresses, others to organize panels, and still others insisted that they wished to stay peripheral to the project, to set up storytelling, basket-weaving, video and Web installations on the margins of the conference venue, where people could "drop by" and participate, or ignore their efforts altogether, without these initiatives being contained by the conference. Once this was in place, I began to plan the non-Indigenous components of the conference.

Many who were there seemed to revel in both the academic rigour, but also the innovative and dynamic cross-cultural participation that the conference produced, despite its location in an academic setting. What it also meant was that many rules of conference protocols were constantly being redefined by different cultural and intellectual paradigms. Starting times, participants, subject matter, abstracts—all of these operated, at times, provisionally rather than prescriptively. As word spread of the spirit of the organizational strategy for the conference, Indigenous participants from all over Australia sent word to say that they might drop by. And when they did, the more senior people took their places on a panel or workshop instead of the scheduled speakers. A now-famous Aboriginal dance group arrived to inform me that they'd added six members to the company, so that twelve rather than six performers would be present. Unbeknownst to all but a few, our conference program was a moveable feast, driving our printery to distraction until the very last moment.

One of the ideas, of course, was to interlink this conference with previous course topics, and to use this as a lead-in to upcoming academic subjects. To do this I wrote to or telephoned scores of my undergraduate students who had studied particular subjects, and who I knew were enrolled in courses that would be connected to the subject matter, to alert them to the conference, and to signal that it could be used in their forthcoming academic work. Postgraduates working in the specific areas of postcolonialism were heavily involved, and not just as gophers, but as participants, chairs, advisers, so that, to this day at least two of my PhD students still communicate regularly with writers and theorists they first met there. Another international student chose to study in the English Studies Program because of the conference.

The idea was to create a living project that both involved and yet existed independently of the academic enterprise, and that somehow shifted some of the traditional paradigms that govern so many of our gatherings. It's important to say that I'm not claiming here that I and my colleagues were necessarily successful at this. I'm sure we fell far short. Rather I'm signalling what we hoped for, while being entirely aware that the institutional frame probably made our utopic hope nonsensical. But it was a way, for me at least, to begin to think about a postcolonial pedagogy that did not resist, or merely gesture towards, a community activism. It was a way to take the university out into the community and to compromise, in the best sense, our rather rigid borders.

In doing this we were aware of Spivak's caution that, as Slemon phrases it, "The moment in which we infiltrate Third World 'knowledges' into Western literary education . . . we become complicitous with the information-retrieval systems of imperialist custodianship, and thus we become complicitous in the founding of a 'new orientalism' on the site we had hoped would function as an agent of resistance" (Slemon 154). We saw many Indigenous participants, schooled by years of participation in

European projects, opting to do formal conference papers; many proposed these projects because they expected it to be what we wanted.

When I invited a renowned Aboriginal chef to prepare the food for an historic exhibition of Indigenous art works, bringing Tasmanian fibre works and their artists to the mainland for the first time, I was both surprised and nervous about the choice to produce a traditional bush meal. Not because I was worried about disenfranchising European palates, but because I feared being accused of buying into cultural stereotypes. Ironically, when I announced to the two octogenarian matriarchs from the Tasmanian group that the food we'd be serving might include witchety grubs and kangaroo balls, one of them turned to the other and said, "Looks like we're having McDonald's again tonight."

That night, a strange mixture of euphoria and nervous breakdown took hold. The entire conference, for me, was an exercise in pragmatic, rather than merely theoretical, cross-culturality. It sought to balance a range of interests and forms of (self)representation, attempting (though failing as I've shown) to steer clear of a type of cultural tourism that can sometimes be produced in such events, while also surrendering and reproducing a series of representational gestures (such as the traditional dancing and bush food) insisted on by the cultural activists themselves. I think it's fair to say that this was both one of the most energizing and yet simultaneously terrifying experiences of my life.

I invoke this idea of simultaneity and terror deliberately, to begin to play with the idea of the uncanny. For some ten years now I have written on and studied the idea of the uncanny, the gothic, and the ghostly in postcolonial literatures.[2] My focus has been in particular on the way Canadian and Australian writing have turned to the gothic to articulate a particularly colonial, and then post-colonial, poetics. And in the last few years I have been especially interested in the way minority writers have re-appropriated uncanny discourses in order to interrogate and either escape or reply to dominant paradigms.

Throughout this work, what has always struck me is the way this uncanny, dare I say this gothic, rupture has infiltrated or indeed characterized the classroom—the experience and space of teaching itself. As well as my research work, I have been involved in core university activities circulating around the issue of pedagogy and teaching skills. This first conference, in fact, emerged because one of my postgraduates lamented that we were always going elsewhere for conferences (in what was a strange echo of early CanLit debates). It was given shape in part by my efforts, over ten years, to teach Canadian literature, and comparative Canadian and Australian literatures, in regional Australia. And it developed because of my keenness to reproduce a number of experiments that I had acted out in the classroom to try to overcome the many difficulties that constantly impeded the way Canadian literature (among other things) was presented to my students.

In one of Freud's most famous essays, "The 'Uncanny,'" he argues that a definition of the uncanny hinges on two (inter)related and putatively oppositional terms: the *heimlich* and the *unheimlich*—the homely and the unhomely. Freud meditates on the way place and experience may be rendered unhomely or unfamiliar precisely by the simultaneity of overlapping or competing moments—particularly where the familiar is made unfamiliar and both conditions exist simultaneously. As I've argued elsewhere, it is precisely this quality of belonging and alienation that marks the colonial condition as uncanny—and which sees the postcolonial function similarly. In one of its myriad definitions, the "post" in postcolonial suggests the after of something that has not yet passed, a semantic piece of sophistry, which produces an uncanny terror in both those peoples who accept and who reject its parameters.[3] It would certainly be true to say that many of my Aboriginal students have been driven to exasperation by the premise that their (neo)colonial state has passed. And definitions that play with the notion of "post" as other than a temporal signifier frequently signal what one of my students referred to as the "having-it-both-ways language of the oppressor."

Critics such as Gelder and Jacobs use the notion of the uncanny to discuss "the usual binary structure upon which commentary on Aboriginal and non-Aboriginal relations is based" (24). They speak of the way the "'uncanny' can remind us that a condition of unsettledness folds into this taken-for-granted mode of occupation." And they go on to speculate on the way a "(future) condition of 'reconciliation'" is imagined and how the uncanny "remind[s] us of just how irreconcilable this image is with itself" (24). I am taken here with a possible connection between this sense of the uncanny and the way it characterizes a politicized though contradictory field (reconciliation politics) and a comparably fraught field like postcolonial pedagogy, in which so often the desires of the field—counter-hegemonic play, anti-canonical gestures, recognition of material realities, and so forth—run up against its uncanny impossibilities, reproducing hegemonic power structures through its institutional frame, its language, the setting up of "canons of the non-canonical," and eliding the material realities through its theoretical preoccupations and economic barriers. As Srivastava has put it, "postcolonialism is rife with contradictions that reside in the often-unquestioned and rarely contested hierarchies and relations of power in the university or college" (17).

Not surprisingly given its preoccupations, postcolonialist work is frequently enacted in a comparative dimension. Needless to say, comparative study is always in a sense an uncanny exercise. It is both a presentation of the familiar and of the unfamiliar, and its purpose is often the stress on the idea of fraught simultaneity. The most fruitful exercise of the comparativist is often a type of cross-cultural experimentation, where a familiar text is read against, or beside, or at the same time as, an unfamiliar text. And as anyone who has taught comparatively will attest, the similarities can be fascinating, may even have initially suggested the comparative dimension, but they are often the least interesting part of the process. The fascination derives from the uncanny moment—the moment of rupture where one's own political stance, one's own secure racialized position, one's faith in a system of language, or law, is irrevocably shaken by a type of analogy that the comparative dimension makes manifest. The challenge is in not sanitizing this moment—refusing to make it safe and contained. This, I know, is the hardest part of the process, especially as it is enacted in an overdetermined space like the classroom.

Teaching is almost always, at its best, about elucidation. It is about the opening up of texts to understanding; it is about revealing an unseen dimension of a text, and in turn, of allowing a text to open an unseen truth about ourselves. Teaching, through the tools it uses, should allow for what Jonathan Culler identifies as the unsettling sense of theory:

> The nature of theory is to undo, through a contesting of premises and postulates, what you thought you knew, so the effects of theory are not predictable. You have not become master, but neither are you where you were before. You reflect on your reading in new ways. You have different questions to ask and a better sense of the implications of the question you put to works you read. (Culler 17; see also Huggan 260)

This, too, is a utopic definition, particularly as it emerges about a post-structuralist discourse that is so often attacked for its "language games" and for moving away from actual "political struggles of real people, outside such discursive frontiers" (Tapping, qtd. in Huggan 260). But the principle is important, and part of the way that a pedagogical practice can escape the same sort of charges so often levelled at post-structuralist and postcolonial methods is by finding ways to enact precisely this moment of unsettlement: this moment where our own solid ground is shown to be both substantial and insubstantial, simultaneously. How this is done is difficult to say. My own suggestions thus far have, often, involved repudiating the very environment I am paid to function in, by dis/locating classes, by creating significant alternative events and urging students to interact with them. But I am conscious, too, that these oppositional events do not replace the academy. They do not obliterate my syllabus. They do not divest me of my power as an academic, or my power to compel, though often they recontextualize that power by introducing me into arenas where I am at best a facilitator, and often not even that.

Ajay Heble, in commenting on the way we can attempt to unlearn privilege, discusses a number of critical arguments, which I believe in, concerning the importance of teaching texts that invite us to "identify sympathetically with individual members of marginalized or oppressed groups," and of the way such interactions can produce a "kind of sympathetic engagement with the Other [which] is, in fact, often seen as central to the purpose of postcolonial pedagogy" (Nussbaum and Aegerter respectively, qtd. in Heble 154). But I very much share Heble's concern with the implication that somehow "sympathetic engagement with fictional characters who are epistemologically or ontologically remote from our own areas of experience, may simply function as a kind of surrogate for actual encounters with real-life 'others' in the daily world of our lived experience" (154). Just as dangerous is what Heble refers to as "academic (and often elitist) expressions of affiliation with marginalized and oppressed peoples" (154).

My own strategies for what Heble calls "ethicizing the classroom" have no doubt only partially been effective. Certainly they are not "practical" and they are far from cost-effective (from both a personal and a financial viewpoint). Running a major international conference, or running a series of public parallel events on issues being covered in the classroom (usually six or more a year), or even inviting experts as well as students from marginalized or oppressed peoples to participate on a regular basis in the teaching of my subjects (and remunerating them for this role), only goes so far. It may well produce a range of uncanny effects, but again it doesn't unsettle/dismantle the entrenched institutionalized hierarchies of power that are marked by the academy. But it does begin to tug at the boundaries that separate the academy from the community. As Slemon has argued,

> if, in Gramscian terms, an oppositional or counter-hegemonic practice can be seen to *secure* a politics of oppression simply by *recognizing* that its dominant binaries remain in place, a processive pedagogy of thinking *through* methodological contradiction can also be redirected towards real social *change* at the level of the local. And it can begin that redirection by opening within English Studies itself—the *place* of colonialist management—a cognitive space in which the subject-to-be-educated reads the effects of ideology in *both* personal and political dimensions, and finds within that space . . . something that functions as a "room for manoeuvre." (159)

In many ways the notoriously self-reflexive and apologetic dimension of postcolonial criticism, which is markedly expressed in response to what Huggan calls the "constitutive tension" within the field "between 'revisionary forces' and 'institutional containment'" (261), is probably its most energizing dimension. To negotiate these tensions is not only an intellectually necessary critical response, but a sound pedagogical practice, producing at best an uncanny space of possibility. That it is always open to self-serving postulating and to formulaic citational gestures is a given, but this fact does not discredit the method—just the practitioner.

Postcolonial methodologies have more than ever helped us as teachers to be critically aware of how we bring prejudices, values, and preconceptions to the way we interpret and see things. And it is up to us to press this interrogative space. At times that glimpse of ourselves produces only mundane revelations. More often than not, though, the insights can be ground breaking. For me, this has often occurred at the level of Aboriginal or minority works, where the effort not simply to teach or introduce non-canonical texts into the equation but also to re-structure the traditional spaces in which these texts are read, has been key. Whatever success I may have had in this has in part been enabled by my migrant status in Australia. If it is true that comparativist study produces an uncanny effect, it is similarly true that migration is an uncanny gesture, especially when one moves into a culture as putatively similar to Canada as Australia.

For me the border crossing, which I signal above in terms of classroom or pedagogical dynamics, was mirrored by the move I made to Australia, and contributed to the ways I thought about postcolonialism and pedagogy—about hybridity and transitionality. Such an understanding does not guarantee a practical or even ground-breaking approach to ethicizing the classroom, or to unsettling the institutionalized knowledges that contain and perhaps even curtail our best energies as teachers. But it did make me aware of the need to insist on and champion those uncanny moments where the postcolonial can produce a ruptured, fraught space, in which the possibility for change is visible and, more importantly, possible.

For a French Canadian such as myself, who learned to camouflage his Québécois accent to escape a range of prejudices and violence in the English school system in Canada, it's true to say that I arrived in Australia thinking I'd mastered the system: that I was fluently bilingual, linguistically inconspicuous, and hence feeling overly confident that I would easily fit into a system that used the same language. How could I know that it would be more difficult to live in a culture with subtle linguistic differences than in glaringly different ones? I certainly never expected the sheer volume of gaffes I produced in my early years, fuelled by my misguided expectation that everything should be comprehensible. I made no such simplistic assumptions about Aboriginal culture. I approached it with caution and respect because I expected it to be different. Indeed, I made few assumptions about the many Aboriginal cultures I encountered. As a result, I think I insulted fewer Indigenous colleagues than non-Indigenous ones; and I realized that the differences were more substantive and might take a lifetime to come to know, however imperfectly. I realized too that many dimensions of this life were not mine for the taking or for the knowing.

Nevertheless, because of my migrant status I was allowed into places I wouldn't otherwise have been permitted to enter. I remember well sitting in a house during the bicentennial protests in 1988 with the renowned poet and activist Kath Walker/Oodgeroo, and being told, "You're here because you're not Australian."[4] That scenario was repeated countless times. And as I learned a bit more about indigenous cultures in Australia, I learned, too, to my shame, of my inadequate knowledge of indigenous cultures in Canada. It reminded me that the learning process is never complete. As a result, I returned to Canada time and again, and met with elders throughout the country. I sat in learning circles and tried at last to find ways to teach about cultures that were so different from mine—even to discover if I should presume to do this in the first place. When I asked Maria Campbell, "Should I not teach Métis texts since I'm not Métis?" she told me, "That would be worse than not knowing about the texts. Learn, instead, to teach with humility, and seek advice. Leave the picture always a bit incomplete and acknowledge that." I'm sure Maria Campbell won't remember my visit with her—but it certainly changed me. I took that message to heart.

When I was asked to teach a comparative Canadian Studies course, and to create an Introduction to Canadian Literature subject soon after my appointment at the University of Wollongong, I made what I think are valiant efforts not to reproduce the much-criticized traditional CanLit syllabus. I had read critiques of what Arun Mukherjee calls the "eurocentric curricular diet" (87), and I was determined not to be guilty of such constructions. To my shock, though, I found that the world of publishing worked against such departures. As I've argued elsewhere,

> Canada's greatest folly, and that which most adversely affects the teaching discipline in Australia, is the refusal of major Canadian publishers to meet the demand for books. There are a variety of reasons for this, and they range from failing to take adequate account of the "implications of geography," as one critic has argued, to the pressures of American and British copyright restrictions which mean that book prices can be more than doubled by distribution and freight costs. Susanna Moodie's *Roughing It in the Bush*, published by the New Canadian Library for approximately $6.00, was for a time available only through British Virago press—for $28.00! This is a strong deterrent to students who must contemplate the purchase of some eight to ten Canadian titles.[5]

When I wrote this in 1995, I thought we'd reached extremes. But these prices correspond to those books most readily accessible in Australia. All those texts that I selected because they were stunning or challenging works, but that were published by minority presses, were often even more expensive, if obtainable at all. Again, a few years back I wrote that,

> If there's a glitch in the ordering, for example, and the books are air-freighted, a copy of *One Good Story, That One* suddenly sells for $30.00, or *Looking for Livingstone* for $28.95. It is a grim reality of student life that students will count the number of pages and divide it by the price before making up their minds to buy a book. *One Good Story* and *Livingstone* remained unbought until I successfully pleaded with the bookstore to absorb some of the cost, and brought the price down (and then urged them to process my orders when they arrived, rather than wait until it was too late to get the books by sea mail). (8)[6]

The year after I wrote this, *Looking for Livingstone* arrived in the bookstore with a $44 price-tag! *Ana Historic* retailed for $46. Atwood, Ondaatje, and Munro for approximately $20 each. More insidious were the e-mails we received from a number of distributors to tell us that books were out of print. Jack Hodgins' *The Invention of the World*, for example, was "out of print." When we later checked with the authors themselves about these putatively unavailable books we discovered that this wasn't the case. Even when efforts were made to go directly to the small presses, it was often impossible to secure copies for one reason or another.

The effect of this was to conservatize my reading lists; to force me to work with more canonical writers, simply because their books were available in Australia. What it meant was that more effective strategies to contextualize this list needed to be put into place. With Indigenous studies subjects I made a point always of working with Aboriginal teachers, writers, and artists—of consulting widely, of opening the classroom to these guest speakers, of organizing parallel public events, and just as importantly, of insisting that the university find ways of remunerating these speakers for their time and knowledge. The effect, as with the postcolonialism conference I first mentioned, has at times been terrifying. Doing this means that I surrender the sorts of control that, as a student, I watched my professors wield. It means that the idea of rigid plans is often an impossibility precisely at a time when government watchdogs most require them. It also pretty much guarantees that debate will be plentiful, that no one point of view will dominate. And this necessitates developing a great deal of support material for students, who often arrive, in the early years at least, expecting answers, and who get very stressed when they're offered questions instead. I think that this, too, is a systemic thing—a type of control mechanism that has frequently served dominant institutions. And dismantling such expectations is a crucial first step in attempting to shift the paradigms, even in the midst of an undeniable and concrete structure like a university that always already qualifies most of our more radical efforts.

The comparative exercise produces rich and often unexpected texturing of our knowledge base—and sometimes it produces ruptures that are nearly impossible to resolve. Similarly, imposing a critical methodology—even one as contested and multifaceted as postcolonialism—or refusing an expected and accepted pedagogical practice, can be profoundly unsettling. My point in this paper has been to highlight the power of spaces of slippage and uncertainty—a way to make the *heimlich unheimlich*, to problematize if not eliminate racist views, and to "gothicize" the putatively shadowless body of institutions we engage with, be they nations, novels, conferences, or classrooms.

ACKNOWLEDGEMENTS

I would like to thank the Government of Canada and the International Council for Canadian Studies for a Faculty Enrichment Grant, which allowed me to participate in the "Postcolonialism and Pedagogy" symposium at the University of Ottawa where this paper was first delivered, and which allowed me to work with and consult numerous scholars and writers working in related fields. My thanks too to the University of Ottawa, which offered me a Visiting Research Fellow position for the time of the conference.

NOTES

1. For an extended discussion of these issues, and the way they circulated around and through the conference, see Ratcliffe and Turcotte.

2. See Turcotte "Australian Gothic," "English-Canadian Gothic," "Footnotes," "How Dark," and "Sexual Gothic."
3. Although there are many expressions of this view, see Johnston in particular.
4. For a transcript of the interview that resulted from this meeting, see Oodgeroo.
5. This paper, "True North Down Under: Cross-Cultural Approaches to the Teaching of Canadian Studies in Australia," was presented at the "Cross-Cultural and Comparative Approaches to Canadian Studies" conference, U of Birmingham, 19 May 1995. Although it was accepted for publication by an unrelated press, the volume never appeared.
6. Originally presented as "Teaching Canadian Literature: An International Perspective," panel discussion with Christl Verduyn, Robert Thacker, and Donna Palmateer Pennee, "A Visionary Tradition: Canadian Literature & Culture at the Turn of the Millennium" conference, U of Guelph, 10–14 Nov. 1999. See Turcotte, "Hitting Home," for the published version of this paper.

WORKS CITED

Culler, Jonathan. *Literary Theory: A Very Short Introduction*. New York: Oxford UP, 1988.

Freire, Paulo. *Pedagogy of the Oppressed*. Trans. Myra Bergman Ramos. London: Penguin, 1975.

Freud, Sigmund. "The 'Uncanny.'" *Collected Papers: Papers on Metapsychology, Papers on Applied Psycho-analysis*. Trans. Joan Rivière. Vol. 4. London: Hogarth, 1956. 368–407.

Gelder, Ken, and Jane M. Jacobs. *Uncanny Australia: Sacredness and Identity in a Postcolonial Nation*. Melbourne: Melbourne UP, 1998.

Heble, Ajay. "Re-ethicizing the Classroom: Pedagogy, the Public Sphere, and the Postcolonial Condition." *College Literature* 29.1 (2002): 143–60.

Huggan, Graham. *The Postcolonial Exotic: Marketing the Margins*. London: Routledge, 2001.

Johnston, Pam. "Reality Collisions: Social Justice vs. Post-Colonialism." Ratcliffe and Turcotte 97–104.

Mukherjee, Arun. *Postcolonialism: My Living*. Toronto: TSAR, 1998.

Oodgeroo Noonuccal [Kath Walker]. "'Recording the Cries of the People': An Interview with Oodgeroo Noonuccal (Kath Walker)." With Gerry Turcotte. *Aboriginal Culture Today*. Ed. Anna Rutherford. Aarhus: Dangaroo, 1988. 18–30.

Ratcliffe, Greg, and Gerry Turcotte, eds. *Compr(om)ising Post/colonialism(s): Challenging Narratives and Practices*. Sydney: Dangaroo, 2001.

Slemon, Stephen. "Teaching at the End of Empire." *College Literature* 20.1 (1993): 152–61.

Spivak, Gayatri Chakravorty. "Can the Subaltern Speak? Speculations on Widow-Sacrifice." *Wedge* 7/8 (Winter/Spring 1985).

Srivastava, Aruna. "Postcolonialism and Its Discontents." *ARIEL* 26.1 (1995): 12–17.

Turcotte, Gerry. "Australian Gothic." *The Handbook of Gothic Literature*. Ed. Marie Mulvey Roberts. London: Macmillan, 1998. 10–19.

———. "English-Canadian Gothic." *The Handbook of Gothic Literature*. Ed. Marie Mulvey Roberts. London: Macmillan, 1998. 49–53.

———. "Footnotes to an Australian Gothic Script: The Gothic in Australia." *Antipodes* 7.2 (1993): 127–34.

———. "Hitting Home: (Mis)re/presenting Canada Abroad." *Littcrit* 28.1 (2002): 5–9.

———. "How Dark Is My Valley?: Canadian and Australian Gothic." *Scarp* 22 (1993): 26–32.

———. "Sexual Gothic: Marian Engel's *Bear* and Elizabeth Jolley's *The Well*." *ARIEL* 26.2 (1995): 65–91.

———. "True North Down Under: Cross-Cultural Approaches to the Teaching of Canadian Studies in Australia." Cross-Cultural and Comparative Approaches to Canadian Studies Conference. U of Birmingham. 19 May 1995.

From Praxis to Practice: Prospects for Postcolonial Pedagogy in Canadian Public Education

BEVERLEY HAUN

THIS PAPER IS DIVIDED into two parts. It begins by reviewing current postcolonial pedagogical theory, both focusing on its interests and identifying its omissions in relation to public education in Canada. It ends with an appendix of practical suggestions for implementing a postcolonial pedagogical supplement designed to transform teachers' and students' understanding, public memory, and reading of curricular texts.

Postcolonialism in the academy gives voice to an expression of resistance that is born out of a Western discourse of exclusion. It is an inevitable construction of the Western academy at the end of Empire as students and teachers from many cultures seek to find space in scholarly discourses—ironically, discourses established largely through an imperial education project. Postcolonial theorizing seeks to understand the way the imperial frame of mind has shaped Western culture, history, politics, economics, and education by examining the relations of power within the imperial project, the textual basis of that power, and the subject positions we each inhabit in relation to it. Understanding the imperial project, examining the various forms of resistance to it, imagining a dismantling of the unequal power structures it has generated, and envisioning a subsequent restructuring to achieve global harmony in diversity are central to postcolonial discourse.

Postcolonial studies largely developed as a reformative discourse within the field of English literature. In this literary context it can be defined as a study of colonial discursive practices and the various kinds of resistances and evasions engaged in by writers working to decolonize the imagination. At the same time, as emphasized by Leela Gandhi, it creates a space in the academy for non-Western critics to present their "cultural inheritance as knowledge" (ix), and it also serves to reveal the invisible codings of the dominant ideology under which the Western world lives.

Much current educational theorizing in the West focuses on the extent to which postcolonial theory might inform and reshape pedagogy, and Canada, as a diverse collective of peoples, sharing space as a result of colonialism, has a vested interest in this examination. A review of many of the points and counterpoints in this discussion may yield useful insights for envisioning the best model for Canadian pedagogical practices across the education system. What follows weighs key points in this debate and offers a postcolonial supplement to current curricula that would help shift its emphasis from the centre.

In her Red Deer College address, "Postcolonial Pedagogy and Curricular Reform," Diana Brydon outlines the pedagogical aspects of the postcolonial discourse she identifies, creating a useful framework from which to open up a discussion of the broad implications and possibilities for a Canadian postcolonial pedagogy. While Brydon emphasizes postcolonialism's function in trying to make sense of literary work in the world, she also enumerates the spaces constituted within it that serve to draw it away from the exclusive domain of literary studies, prompting us to "rethink how knowledge is constructed" and "how it can be decolonized." Postcolonialism also enables a "rethinking of national belongings and multicultural interactions," helping to expose the binary of centre and other that still shapes the Canadian national model. It prompts a rethinking of how, as Brydon says, "first world countries interact with countries internationally" (4)—the "placement of [a country] within global systems of power" (5)—and it exposes the imposition of neo-colonialism over the vestiges of nineteenth-century colonialism. It prompts us to recognize the need to respect each other's alterity rather than yearn toward a coercive blending of diversity. With such a focus, postcolonial discourse enjoins a move from theorizing and articulating goals, to developing ways of achieving goals "through transgression" (4).

Brydon also outlines limits to postcolonial discourse and points out that one form of postcoloniality is not appropriate to all locations. A colonial settler society like Canada, formed on the indigenous lands of the First Nations, cannot work from the same postcolonial model as a country that had a limited interlude of colonial administration within a much longer recorded cultural history like India. For this reason, a country's definition of its postcoloniality will determine the focus of its postcolonial pedagogy (5).

As well as taking into consideration the nature of a location's postcoloniality, Brydon identifies the "placement of a country within the current global system of power" as needing to be considered in defining what form postcolonial pedagogy will take. As Gayatri Spivak has pointed out, the United States, with its own revolutionary end to colonial rule, has seen itself as an international saviour, particularly since the end of the Second World War (275). This self-staging is being played out now in the simplistic "*you're either for us or against us*" militaristic stance of the United States against terrorism. Articulating a postcoloniality within this neo-colonial location presents a daunting task. While our interest here is particularly Canadian, the increased shared security between Canada and the United States will need to be examined for its implications in shaping Canadian policy and postcolonial pedagogy.

With such vastly different locations as Canada, India, and the United States as sites for postcolonial pedagogy, it is evident why Brydon emphasizes that each location must "test its goals against the needs" of its students and its local communities. While postcolonial pedagogy is developing a complexity that allows it to articulate discrete formations for each location where it is invested, Brydon sees it as still an incompletely formed entity. Postcolonialists are still "articulating its goals" which are "still being defined" (5). At the same time it is growing from a satellite English literature theory to a central academic position where it shapes the whole curriculum "from classroom interaction and curricular change to the role of the university in the world" (1). Through this process it is moving outside its original literary mandate to discover "more fully nuanced understandings of what has happened and is happening in our world as the relations of the local and the global are being reconfigured" (5).

Leela Gandhi, in her introduction to *Postcolonial Theory*, also speaks to postcolonialism's need for diversification in its academic "mode of address." She is concerned that it "learn to speak adequately to the world that it speaks for." Gandhi sees postcolonialism as needing "to acquire the capacity to facilitate a democratic colloquium between the antagonistic inheritors of the colonial aftermath" (x). She sees the "way out of our shared past" as being achieved by "thinking rigorously about our pasts" (9). For her, history is the discourse "through which the West has asserted its hegemony over the rest of the world" (170), and "Western philosophy, at least since Hegel, has used the category of 'history' more or less synonymously with 'civilization'—only to claim both of these categories for the West, or more specifically for Europe." Gandhi points out that "Western Imperialist expansion has all too often been defended as a pedagogical project of bringing the 'underdeveloped' world into the edifying condition of history." History, in this project, becomes the "grand narrative on which Eurocentrism is 'totalized' as the proper account of all humanity" (170–71). For Gandhi, a postcolonial engagement with the discipline of history takes as strong a place as its literary counterpart in the academy. For other postcolonial theorists, the postcolonial needs to be as all-encompassing as the imperial project against which it directs its voice.

Much of the focus of postcolonial pedagogy is in the university and there is an understandable desire to continue shaping this significant discourse at that level as it increasingly exposes the imperial web that spins us. However, there must be recognition of the fact that postcolonial study, kept as an academic discipline, cannot help but comfortably maintain, create a space for, and reproduce, its own middle-class sensibilities. The academy tends to draw upon and produce participants in the middle class. Postcolonial study, for such students, may either appease ancestral guilt for colonial practices and privileges, or may justify claiming a place in the same power base created and maintained by colonial privilege. As long as postcolonialism is kept as a discourse of the academy, whether exclusive to English literature or appropriated by other discourses, it will maintain and reproduce for itself middle-class privilege at the level of theory. It is by developing a postcolonial pedagogy, moving from a theory of *praxis* to actual practice at the level of action for social change in primary and secondary public education, that students from all socio-economic levels will have an opportunity to be exposed to, and participate in, cultural awareness and transformation.

Mapping the Imperial Enterprises of the West

Edward Said, in *Culture and Imperialism,* and John Willinsky, in *Learning to Divide the World*, have mapped out major aspects of the relationship of imperialism to the development of Western thought in a way that implicates more than literature and history in the imperial enterprises of the West. Said has demonstrated that "many of the most prominent characteristics of modernist culture, which we have tended to derive from purely internal dynamics in Western society and culture, include a response to the external pressures on culture from the *imperium*" (188). Willinsky has detailed just how Western culture developed in tandem with the European explorers and "discoverers," from the first crisis of realizing that the world existed in a form different from that depicted by the thirteenth-century *mappa mundi*, to the "studying, classifying, and ordering" of land, flora, fauna, and humanity "within an imperial context," giving "rise to peculiar and powerful ideas of race, culture, and nation" (2–3). Willinsky's work is of particular interest to a mapping of postcolonial pedagogical issues because he goes on to explain how the West used their new-found knowledge to "divide up" and "educate the world" according to the version of it that they had constructed (3).

Willinsky demonstrates the consequences of how "a few of the cognitively adventuresome scholars" of the fifteenth century recognized that in the exploits and booty of the explorers and discoverers was "such an amassing of new evidence" that it afforded "an opportunity for rethinking what this earth was and could now be" (24). Postcolonialists today, having recognized the extent to which scholarship itself has been constituted within Western ideology, once again recognize the opportunity for rethinking how we see the world and how the world could be. For this reason there is an urgency to develop postcolonial discourse as widely as possible to articulate the reforms needed in Western scholarship as well as to reform the Western vision of the world. Postcolonial scholars are grappling with the place for, and the scope of, postcolonial discourse within the academy and beyond.

Brydon has questioned whether postcolonialism should continue to be located in English departments and urges its connection with issues of global capitalism and post-structuralism (5). Spivak calls for its yoking to the social sciences and the idea of making postcolonialism a core of a transnational study of culture (277). Because of the capacity of postcolonial discourse to articulate dominant Western ideology and to mesh with other cultural discourses, it is in flux, moving from its place as a discrete subset of academic literary studies to providing a context and a vocabulary for a rethinking of all tertiary as well as primary and secondary education. But in spite of its capacity to encompass the pedagogical whole, postcolonial discourse is itself a contested site as its theorists strive to contain its energies while they continue to refine their insights and deconstructive techniques.

Theorizing a Postcolonial Project for the Public Education System

According to Brydon, intervening in the world too quickly replaces trying to make sense of the world and of literary work and may glamorize transgression over first fully understanding what deconstructive work still needs to be done. She is concerned that there "is still work to do in the shaping of a new knowledge formation, conducted in the full recognition that, as Stuart Hall puts it, 'we are irrevocably within a power-knowledge field of force'" (5). Specifically, Brydon expresses a discomfort with postcolonial pedagogy as education for social change (3). She is most concerned with the kind and degree of authority such approaches invest in the teacher, and rightly so. Teacher education and curricular preparation for such work would need to address issues of authority as part of the key theorizing and development of a postcolonial pedagogy for social change. Chandra Mohanty focuses on one aspect of teacher authority when she prescribes that teachers must speak *about* third world experience, not speak *for* it (148). At the same time, teachers must be immersed in postcolonial discourse themselves in order to examine the extent to which their own understanding of the world and sense of authority about knowledge is implicated in and a reflection of the imperial project. Teacher training as well as student curricula need to be refocused through a postcolonial lens.

Another issue that concerns several postcolonial theorists working to articulate a postcolonial pedagogy is the way in which postcolonialism can be misinterpreted as part of a multicultural discourse. Brydon is concerned that postcolonialism will be "invoked only to serve multicultural ends in the first world" (4), but that the very reasons for cultural diasporas will remain unproblematized. Sharing a similar concern, Spivak cautions against a postcolonial canon of third-world literature leading to a new orientalism (277). Spivak is also concerned that through postcolonial discourse the indigenous elite from other countries will claim marginality (277), distorting the social-cultural understanding that the discourse is striving to articulate. Arun Mukherjee's concerns are quite the opposite, pointing out that not all English language writing produced in former colonies is written back to the imperial centre (9). Nor are all levels of society from such countries represented in the literature of those countries (21). She advocates regional studies in addition to postcolonial studies to avoid homogeneous essentializing of non-Western cultures to the West, and to avoid centring the West in all studies about former colonies. While regional studies certainly have their place, it is too soon to turn our backs on the Western imperial project and its aftermath. There is still much work to do to raise awareness of the imperial ideology that has shaped so much of the world, and to caution against the neo-imperialism currently manifesting itself through globalization and the fight against terrorism.

Just as one can create a symbiotic teaching relationship between two texts by juxtaposing them to speak to each other, so, as Spivak says, "the relationship between academic and 'revolutionary' practices" can work symbiotically "in the interest of social change" (53). Postcolonial literary criticism has "vigorous investments in cultural critique"; and by combining the critical vocabulary of the postcolonial literary discourse with revolutionary practices, the two should be able to bring each other to "productive crisis" (53). In order to achieve this crisis, Henry Giroux recognizes the need for a new vocabulary, one that exposes and replaces the language of the old paradigm that often produces knowledge and social relations serving to legitimate specific entrenched relations of power. New language can help challenge and destabilize currently dominant relations of power to make way for rethinking and restructuring social relations (*Border* 21). At the same time as the vocabulary of literary postcolonialism is needed to recognize the binary power constructions that currently shape "knowledge, social, cultural, economic, and subject positions," Giroux cautions that we must avoid the "trap of reversing the old colonial legacy of the oppressed and the oppressor" (20).

This framework so far has been focused on curricular discourse and method; it also needs to address the students, since all students need to have a positive way of positioning and investing themselves in an educational project that lays bare the myriad permutations of colonialism. All students need to understand how their subject positions are constituted through the discourses in which they participate, and from which they enter and engage postcolonial issues. Otherwise they may only have available to them discourses through which to constitute essentialized identities, both for themselves and each other, that hinder rather than enhance the educational process. Giroux cites Antonio Gramsci in relation to the need for students to be able to "locate themselves in history while simultaneously shaping the present" to allow "people to imagine and desire beyond society's existing limitations and practices" (*Border* 22). Gramsci, however, was not considering the multicultural complexity of the contemporary world. How do we, with our understanding of Western hegemony, enable students to locate themselves without falling into old binaries? The deeply embedded Western constructions of race that created privileged space for those of European descent and subjugated space for all Others entrenched a dichotomy so deep that it is difficult to bring into focus and difficult to deconstruct in its most subtle manifestations. One of Giroux's suggestions for shifting from this construct is to "make whiteness visible as an ethnic category" so that it can be seen as no more than a "cultural difference" and no longer as a "group marker" ("Living" 51). As long as people of European descent do not see their own colour as part of the hegemony of the centre, but speak of being colour-blind as if all colours are invisible (as they see their own Whiteness), they will continue to be constituted by an ideology that helps them avoid the issue of racial inequality while they simultaneously benefit from it (McLaren, "Unthinking" 145). While important elements of education for social change, these steps still do not offer a strategy for diffusing the guilt and self-loathing that can accompany the process of becoming visible for these students.

White guilt can silence White students or can result in some students resisting the personal and social transformation afforded by a postcolonial curriculum for social change. According to Peter McLaren, a consequence of non-White students fully recognizing Eurocentric privilege and the "tyranny of the whole" can be a "dictatorship of the fragment" ("Multiculturalism" 207): the silencing of the White students, overridden by voices of the formerly colonized. For this reason another aspect of postcolonial pedagogy for social change must be the development of strategies that focus on the importance of learning to listen to, speak to, and be taken seriously by each other (Giroux, *Border* 27). One way McLaren thinks this can be accomplished is by affirming "the 'local' knowledge of students within particular socio-political and ethnic locations" ("Multiculturalism" 207). This need to suit postcolonial discourse to the specific location of the students echoes Brydon's advocacy of tailored, or historically personalized, postcolonial studies. A positive shared vision of "totality," which McLaren defines as politics working at the micro as well as the macro levels, needs to be established as a goal for students to counterbalance the possibility of White silencing or denial and the current "emphasis on difference and discontinuity" ("Multiculturalism" 207).

Roger I. Simon has proposed two practical strategies adaptable to specific postcolonial locations. The first requires engaging historical representations, the "social memories constructed by one culture . . . that form a false basis of communal existence" ("Forms" 131). A focus on historical representations can take place at all levels, from contesting the terrain of national identities and "the public legitimacy of institutions" based on Eurocentric "social truths," to considering the representation of specific episodes in local history (132). As well as proposing specific strategies for students to engage large-scale social and historical constructions, Simon offers a strategy for individuals to listen to their interior responses when they hear the testimony of displaced others, such as peoples of the First Nations of Canada. Settler Canadians and more recent immigrants who have internalized colonial rhetoric and think of Canada as a new land, for example, can listen to Aboriginal testimony to find the space between their "Canadian public memory" and the testimony they witness. Through an attentive listening, or "summoned sensibility"—a willingness to listen openly, to respond, and to "accept co-ownership of the testimony witness"—Canadians can reconstruct their own understanding of history ("Touch" 70–75), moving from an unconscious colonial mindset to a postcolonial one. Simon has gone beyond theorizing the need for reconstructing public memory as part of a postcolonial pedagogy to offering listening strategies for implementing this practice as an important part of the individual's unlearning and relearning.

Michael Apple emphasizes the need for theorists to combine the practical with the theoretical, and he calls for strategies such as Simon's to be made available in existing mainstream educational publications, providing critical answers to the teacher's question of "What to teach on Monday" (246). He points out that

> many teachers have socially and pedagogically critical intuitions. However, they often do not have ways of putting these intuitions into practice because they cannot picture them in daily situations. Due to this, critical theoretical and political insights have nowhere to go as embodied concrete pedagogy where the politics of curriculum and teaching must be enacted. Thus we need to use and expand the spaces in which critical pedagogical stories are made available so that these positions do not remain only on the theoretical or rhetorical level. (246–47)

The development of postcolonial discourse needs to continue. The development of postcolonial pedagogy needs to continue, particularly in theorizing the authority of the teacher and the subject position and agency of the student, and if social and cultural change is to be as important as understanding, we need to engage all levels and ages of students as participants in the process.

From Theory to Practice: The Need for a Postcolonial Educational Supplement

Three initial steps come into play when considering a move from an imperial pedagogical model to a postcolonial one. They consist of identifying the subject positions of the teachers and students involved in any specific educational endeavour, recognizing the power dynamics at play in the teacher/student relationship largely as a consequence of those subject positions, and only then moving into postcolonial course work by identifying the overtly imperial or more subtly Eurocentric assumptions underlying the curriculum in question. By establishing the internally and externally persuasive discourses that constitute us, and by acknowledging the power dynamics and performance positions of all involved in the educational process before beginning to actually focus on course content, it should be possible to lay the groundwork for enacting ethical student/

teacher relationships and then directing our mutual energies to the work of re-educating our imaginations and public memories.

What we need to teach our students and ourselves to aim for in this process is the creation of, and conscious holding open of, an imaginary space where we maintain a meta-cognitive awareness of the exclusionary discourses we are constituted by. We can each hold open a space for the difference of every Other to coexist. Such is a necessary part of a postcolonial classroom, both to be aware of a Eurocentric imperial curriculum that has been informing our educated imaginations and also to create the space for standing separate from that narrative as we respond ethically to others through and during our studies.

Jacques Derrida's version of the "supplement," described in *Of Grammatology*, can be called on here to help envision an idea of the "between" space the postcolonial student must inhabit. The supplement, as its name implies, is an addition, a surplus to something already existing that creates the fullest measure of presence by being added on (144). The supplement adds onto, but only with the intention of replacing or intervening, it insinuates itself in-the-place-of (145). We cannot wait for a wholesale rewriting of the existing educational system before we begin to teach from a postcolonial point of view, and so Willinsky, in *Learning to Divide the World*, has proposed a way to convert any existing curriculum, no matter how imperially oriented or Eurocentric, through the addition of such a postcolonial supplement.

The inflection of the postcolonial supplement would vary from moment to moment, creating a space of double signification. This inflection would take two main forms in the postcolonial classroom. In the first, the signification of the students and teachers shaped through the Western education system, and the space they hold open for responding to the curriculum from a postcolonial point of view, would come into play. In the second, the double signification would be composed of the students and teachers retaining conscious hold of how their understanding of their various Others has been constructed. Each inflection in these pairings "is by turns effaced or becomes discreetly vague in the presence of the other." "[Whether] it adds or substitutes itself, the supplement is exterior," outside that to which it is super-added, alien, and other to the main discursive space it joins (145), but stitched to it, combining with it to form a new between-space. It is through its difference, in this case, from the main educational discourse that it supplements, that it is able to change the shape of or alter the intent of the main. Creating a space at the start of a course for students and teachers alike to engage in meta-cognitive reflexivity and then adding to that space a postcolonial supplement that can be inflected to encompass students and teachers, as well as the curriculum itself, will enable the participants to transform any Western pedagogical experience into a postcolonial one.

APPENDIX

Mapping Postcolonial Pedagogy: Displacing the Effects of the Imperial Education Project While We Are Still under Its Thrall

The following information, in summary form, is divided into six sections, each intended to be useful in itself or in conjunction with other sections depending on the starting point of the postcolonial pedagogy project in question. The first three sections are concerned with changing awareness of teachers and students, and "unpacking" existing curricula. The fourth section is intended to facilitate an understanding of the constructed nature of reality both inside and outside the classroom in the West. The fifth and sixth sections are concerned with transforming curricula and teaching into a postcolonial pedagogy, and envisioning a new Canada.

1. Teacher Awareness

> We need fearlessly to . . . teach the generations of young people how the world has been constructed and in whose interest. We need the theoretical and practical tools to help [ourselves and] them "un-do" and "un-learn" the oppressive lessons of the hegemonic discourse to which [we] have all been exposed. (Kohli 74)

- Recognize what comes of having one's comprehension of the world so closely tied to one's conquest of it (Willinsky 3).
- Understand that knowledge draws its boundaries almost exclusively from a European model of culture and civilization and

connects learning to the mastery of autonomous and specialized bodies of knowledge (Giroux, "Postmodern" 177).

- Recognize that education represents a struggle for meaning and control over power relations (Mohanty 147).
- Recognize the domination of ideology which is invisible when you are inside of it.
- Understand the need to protest the meta-narrative of the dominant ideology, to reform it, and to envision a new teaching practice.
- Understand our location in the education process and the institutions through which we are constituted (Mohanty 148).
- Recognize that the questions we ask within our discipline are shaped by the assumptions we bring to it.
- Understand the process by which some groups get known in and as history, and other groups and events are ignored by "colonial" history (Gandhi 7).
- Understand how difference (concepts of identity, ethnicity, and race) has been formed and represented historically.
- Recognize how concepts of race and identity relate to privileges of power and knowledge.
- Understand that academic institutions produce paradigms, canons, and voices that embody and transcribe race and gender (Mohanty 147).
- Understand how educational practices assist in the construction of hegemony; how particular forms of authority are secured through the organization of the curriculum at all levels of schooling.
- Recognize the need to question who has the authority to interpret the identity of subject positions.
- Recognize that the content taught makes assumptions about the learner and that teachers must be aware of those assumptions.
- Understand the need to create a dialogue with rather than a speaking for others (McLaren, "Multiculturalism" 215).
- Understand how the relationship of the reader and the text is organized; how the reader enters into the symbolic flow of capital from the world of the text.
- Develop an awareness of the space from which we speak as teachers (Brydon 2).

- Recognize that teachers of European heritage need to examine their White ethnic history to avoid judging their own cultural norms as neutral and universal.
- Understand what it means in practice to produce and disseminate knowledges in culture (Brydon 3).
- Recognize how the questions we ask of literature are shaped by the assumptions we bring to it (Brydon 3).

2. Student Awareness

> Students and teachers are all actors in narrative configurations and employments that they did not develop but that are the products of historical and discursive struggles that have been folded back into the unconscious. (McLaren, "Multiculturalism" 212)

- Students need to understand the concept of meta-cognition and the need to stand back from their own learning experiences.
- Students need to develop a critical distance from their own education.
- Recognize that the Western comprehension of the world is tied to having conquered so much of it (Willinsky 3).
- Understand how concepts of identity, ethnicity, and race have been formed and represented through history.
- Understand the process by which some groups get known in and as history, and other groups and events are ignored by "colonial" history (Gandhi 4).
- Recognize how concepts of race and identity relate to privileges of power and knowledge.
- Understand that we "view our own images" and "stereotypes as embodied qualities that exist in the world and we act upon them" (Gilman in McLaren, "Multiculturalism" 217).
- Recognize how particular ways of presenting the past might be implicated within our understanding of current unjust social relations (Simon, "Forms" 137).
- Recognize the way that the authority of a discipline invites com-

plicity with the historic point of view it offers on events (Simon, "Forms" 137).

- Recognize the possibility for the renewal of the educational, media, and cultural structures influencing our everyday lives.

3. *Unpacking Existing Curricula*

> Teachers [need] to be prepared to examine together with their students how a particular configuration of pedagogic forms, group and institutional structures, and personal histories and capabilities may be forming a dynamic of threat and exclusion. (Simon, *Teaching* 96)

- Determine the dominant ideology informing a subject, text, or unit.
- What cultural work does this subject, text, or unit do, and in what contexts (Brydon 2)?
- How does this text mean, to whom, situated where (Brydon 2)?
- How are anthologies themselves actively involved in the production of knowledge (Brydon 4)?
- How do the different sets of questions we might ask of a text reveal different dimensions in the work under study (Brydon 3)?
- How is difference policed as much through the neglect of certain questions as through the advancing of others (Brydon 5)?
- Examine the content of the text or unit to see what it assumes about the subject:
  - Does it display interpretive biases (Simon, "Forms" 136)?
  - Is culturally specific knowledge presented in texts as if it is universal (136)?
- Determine if the authorial voices embody and transcribe a particular paradigm of race and gender (Mohanty 147).
- Determine if the text or unit supports a heterogeneous or a homogeneous community or larger society.
- Determine if White ethnic history is being presented as the cultural norm—as neutral and universal (McLaren, "Multiculturalism" 215):

  - Is Whiteness being used as a cultural marker against which the Other is defined (215)?
  - Is multiculturalism being presented as Others joining the centre?
- Examine the content of the text/unit to see what it assumes about the identity of the learner.
- Determine why specific texts are used, who authorized them, what and whose interests are served by their continued use (Simon, "Forms" 136).

4. *Understanding the Constructed Nature of Reality Both Inside and Outside the Classroom in the West*

> Imperialism consolidated the mixture of cultures and identities on a global scale. But its worst and most paradoxical gift was to allow people to believe that they were only, mainly, exclusively, white or black, or Western, or Oriental. Yet just as human beings make their own history, they also make their cultures and ethnic identities. No one can deny the persisting continuities of long traditions, sustained habitations, national languages, and cultural geographies, but there seems no reason except fear and prejudice to keep insisting on their separation and distinctiveness, as if that was all human life was about. Survival in fact is about the connections between things; in Eliot's phrase, reality cannot be deprived of the "other echoes [that] inhabit the garden." It is more rewarding—and more difficult—to think concretely and sympathetically, contrapuntally, about others rather than only about "us." (Said 336)

- Recognize that the classroom is a site of instruction, a political site, and a cultural site (Mohanty 147).
- Recognize that the media, inside and outside the classroom, are also sites of instruction, political sites, and cultural sites.
- Determine whose interests are being served by the representations in the classroom and in the media.
- Recognize that our experience of each other must be seen as historically based, contingent, and the result of interpretation (Mohanty 154).
- Recognize our own complicity with historically constituted forms (Simon, "Forms" 132).

- Understand how our own actions reflect our relation to the past (132).
- Understand that we produce, reinforce, recreate, resist, and can transform ideas about race, gender, and difference (Mohanty 147).
- Determine the origins of our current values and beliefs (Simon, "Forms" 132).
- Recognize that we can knowingly continue with, reject, or modify our current values and beliefs (132).
- Recognize that our differences of race, gender, and nation are merely the starting points of new solidarities and new alliances, not terminal stations for depositing our agency and identity (McCarthy and Dimitriadis 58).
- Understand the need to adopt another subject position from which to critique and distance oneself from one's "own" subject position (Janmohamed 246).
- Learn to dis-identify with our own subject positions (246).
- Understand the need to keep the best of one's own identity while critiquing larger cultural values (246).

5. Transforming Curriculum and Teaching into a Postcolonial Pedagogy

> Thus the task at hand is to decolonize our disciplinary and pedagogical practices. The crucial question is how we teach about the West and its Others so that education becomes the practice of liberation. (Mohanty 151)

5a) Questions to ask of curriculum content:

- How does this text write or study the Other? In what institutional or discursive setting? For what audience? And with what end in mind (Giroux, *Border* 25)?
- What does the content of this text or unit, which we teach, assume about the learner?
- How can our curriculum and our teaching strategies facilitate the production, rather than the reproduction, of knowledge (Brydon 3)?

- How should curriculum, viewed through a postcolonial lens, be highlighted or altered to convey a non-hegemonic view?
- What are the pedagogical implications of reading a text *across* cultural and historical differences?
- What would a literary anthology look like that was shaped by postcolonial pedagogy (Brydon 4)?

5b) Questions to ask of teaching practices:

- How do we move from received messages and meanings to having students make their own meaning, in their own contexts, from materials they have appropriated to a postcolonial point of view?
- Who speaks (text, teacher, student), under what conditions, and for whom (Giroux, *Border* 26)?
- How do we make transparent the prejudices in the relationship of the reader to the text through the way we value it, critique it, place it ideologically, or subscribe to it?
- When teaching a "problematic" text, what other text can be juxtaposed with it to highlight or speak to its problematic nature?
- How do we avoid teaching in such a way that students of European origin do not further define others as distant?
- How do we avoid teaching in such a way that students of European origin do not appropriate the pain of others to appease their own historical guilt?
- How do we convey that there are a variety of ways of understanding the world; that there is not just one norm (Mohanty 152)?

5c) Suggestions for teaching practice:

- Work with students to define for your classroom purposes a narrative space from which postcolonial conditions may be created.
- Following a critique of hegemony, have students consider their identity formation by mapping their subject positions in relation to multiculturalism (McLaren, "Multiculturalism" 217).
- Have students identify the various modes of authority that would

need to be transformed in order to move towards a just world where one does not domesticate the Other (218).

- Have students envision how the various modes of authority would need to be transformed in order to move towards a just world where one does not domesticate the Other (218).
- Address questions of audience, voice, power, and evaluation while maintaining a focus on material to highlight any embedded biases or points of view (Mohanty 153).

5d) Instructions for students (giving students a critical distance from their education):

- Ask whose voice speaks in the text.
- What is the subject position of the speaker?
- What agency does the speaker have?
- Is the speaker misrepresented in the text?
- Are all "kinds" of speakers who should be included found in the text?
- Are some speakers erased?
- Is there a gap between the intention of the text and its execution?
- Is there a gap between the overt radical surface of a text and its covert bourgeois nationalist unconscious (Mukherjee 141)?
- Recognize, when you read a narrative, where you are situating yourself in relation to others in the narrative (Simon, "Forms" 139).
  - Actively, consciously step outside that relationship to initiate the reconstruction of the relationship, to foster a mutually respectful, mutually curious, non-subordinating interdependency (139).
  - Actively listen/read the testimonies of others, accepting co-ownership of their experiences. Through co-ownership shift your personal world view (Simon, "Touch" 66).
- Recognize the value of engaging in the lives of others through their cultural production as if they matter—not as tourists, but as fellow travellers on the planet.

6. Envisioning a New Canada

> The major task, then, is to match the new economic and socio-political dislocations and configurations of our time with the startling realities of human interdependence on a world scale. . . . a new critical consciousness is needed, and this can be achieved only by revising attitudes to education. Merely to urge students to insist on one's own identity, history, tradition, uniqueness may initially get them to name their basic requirements for democracy and for the right to an assured, decently humane existence. But we need to go on and to situate these in a geography of other identities, peoples, cultures, and then to study how, despite their differences, they have always overlapped one another, through unhierarchical influence, crossing, incorporation, recollection, deliberate forgetfulness, and, of course, conflict. We are nowhere near "the end of history," but we are still far from free from monopolizing attitudes toward it. These have not been much good in the past—notwithstanding the rallying cries of the politics of separatist identity, multiculturalism, minority discourse—and the quicker we teach ourselves to find alternatives, the better and safer. The fact is we are mixed in with one another in ways that most national systems of education have not dreamed of. To match knowledge in the arts and sciences with these integrative realities is, I believe, the intellectual and cultural challenge of moment. (Said 330–31)

- Articulate alliance-building strategies that move across and within differences (Kohli 74).
- Focus plans for social justice around resource distribution not identity (McLaren, "Unthinking" 159–60).
- View identities as unstable and historically situated (McLaren, "Unthinking" 164).
- Develop a sense of shared responsibility without a sense of shared identity.
- Create a decentred unity in the classroom that addresses environmental degradation, multiple feminist voices, undifferentiated gender roles, postcolonialism, and anti-racism (Apple 245).
- Articulate counter-narratives of emancipation in which new visions, spaces, desires, and discourses can be developed that offer everyone the opportunity for rewriting their own histories differently (Giroux, "Living" 51).

- Regard experiences as if they were about to disappear (Said 336).
  - Identify what it is about experiences that anchors them or roots them in reality (336).
  - Decide what you would save of them, what you would give up, what you would recover (336).
- Articulate Canada as a cultural palimpsest: a layering of cultures, that we can move within, across, and through in multiple dimensions and with multiple identifications.
- Set aside notions of "nation" to join in the creation of a counter-space, ultimately so finely imagined that others desire to join us there. For the way we envision ourselves and the way we live in the world are established first in our imaginings and then in our actions to make them so.

WORKS CITED

Apple, Michael W. "The Shock of the Real: Critical Pedagogies and Rightist Reconstructions." *Revolutionary Pedagogies: Cultural Politics, Instituting Education, and the Discourse of Theory*. Ed. Peter Pericles Trifonas. New York: Routledge, 2000. 225–50.

Brydon, Diana. "Curricular Reform and Postcolonial Studies." 22 March 1997. Keynote Address. Red Deer College, Alberta. April 2001. <http://publish.uwo.ca/~dbrydon/red_deer.html>.

Derrida, Jacques. *Of Grammatology*. Trans. Gayatri Chakravorty Spivak. Baltimore: John Hopkins UP, 1974.

Gandhi, Leela. *Postcolonial Theory: A Critical Introduction*. New York: Columbia UP, 1998.

Giroux, Henry. *Border Crossings: Cultural Workers and the Politics of Education*. New York: Routledge, 1992.

———. "Living Dangerously: Identity Politics and the New Cultural Racism." *Between Borders: Pedagogy and Politics of Cultural Studies*. Ed. Henry Giroux and Peter McLaren. New York: Routledge, 1994. 29–55.

———. "Postmodern Education and Disposable Youth." *Revolutionary Pedagogies: Cultural Politics, Instituting Education, and the Discourse of Theory*. Ed. Peter Pericles Trifonas. New York: Routledge, 2000. 174–95.

Janmohamed, Abdul R. "Some Implications of Paul Freire's Border Pedagogy." *Between Borders: Pedagogy and Politics of Cultural Studies*. Ed. Henry Giroux and Peter McLaren. New York: Routledge, 1994. 242–52.

Kellner, Douglas. "Multiple Literacies and Critical Pedagogies." *Revolutionary*

Pedagogies: Cultural Politics, Instituting Education, and the Discourse of Theory. Ed. Peter Pericles Trifonas. New York: Routledge, 2000. 196–221.

Kohli, Wendy. "Postmodernism, Critical Theory and the New Pedagogies." *Postmodernism, Postcolonialism and Pedagogy*. Ed. Peter McLaren. Albert Park, AU: James Nicholas, 1995. 65–76.

McCarthy, Cameron, and Greg Dimitriadis. "All-Consuming Identities: Race and the Pedagogy of Resentment in the Age of Difference." *Revolutionary Pedagogies: Cultural Politics, Instituting Education, and the Discourse of Theory*. Ed. Peter Pericles Trifonas. New York: Routledge, 2000. 47–60.

McLaren, Peter. "Multiculturalism and Pedagogy of Resistance and Transformation." *Between Borders: Pedagogy and Politics of Cultural Studies*. Ed. Henry Giroux and Peter McLaren. New York: Routledge, 1994. 192–222.

———. "Unthinking Whiteness: Rearticulating Diasporic Practice." *Revolutionary Pedagogies: Cultural Politics, Instituting Education, and the Discourse of Theory*. Ed. Peter Pericles Trifonas. New York: Routledge, 2000. 140–73.

Mohanty, Chandra Talpade. "On Race and Voice: Challenges for Liberal Education in the 1990s." *Between Borders: Pedagogy and Politics of Cultural Studies*. Ed. Henry Giroux and Peter McLaren. New York: Routledge, 1994. 145–66.

Mukherjee, Arun. *Postcolonialism: My Living*. Toronto: TSAR, 1998.

Said, Edward. *Culture and Imperialism*. 1993. New York: Vintage, 1994.

Simon, Roger I. "Forms of Insurgency in the Production of Popular Memories: The Columbus Quincentenary and the Pedagogy of Counter-Commemoration." *Between Borders: Pedagogy and Politics of Cultural Studies*. Ed. Henry Giroux and Peter McLaren. New York: Routledge, 1994. 127–42.

———. *Teaching against the Grain: Texts for a Pedagogy of Possibility*. Critical Studies in Education and Culture series. Toronto: OISE, 1992.

———. "The Touch of the Past: The Pedagogical Significance of a Transactional Sphere of Public Memory." *Revolutionary Pedagogies: Cultural Politics, Instituting Education, and the Discourse of Theory*. Ed. Peter Pericles Trifonas. New York: Routledge, 2000. 61–80.

Spivak, Gayatri Chakravorty. *Outside in the Teaching Machine*. New York: Routledge, 1993.

Willinsky, John. *Learning to Divide the World: Education at Empire's End*. Minnesota: Minnesota UP, 1998.

"You Don't Even Want to Go There": Race, Text, and Identities in the Classroom

ARUN P. MUKHERJEE

> [O]ne cannot predict the amount of crisis a class can contain until the crisis becomes too much. But neither can one predict what will become a crisis, and so we must return to the question of anxiety in learning.
>
> — Deborah Britzman 87

TEACHERS OF ENGLISH, postcolonialists or others, have not paid much attention to pedagogical matters. Classroom teaching is the major part of what we do, and we undergo several levels of evaluation of our teaching practices. Yet, as Heather Murray suggests, we do it in the context of the "intense privatization and isolation of the classroom" and "the lack of written record of its practices" (161). In a special issue of *PMLA*, devoted to "The Teaching of Literature," Biddy Martin expresses surprise about the lack of material on pedagogy:

> Given the vast attention now paid to the performativity of gender, sexuality, race, ethnicity, nation, literature, it is surprising that there is not more writing about pedagogy and the construction of knowledge in our classrooms and in our daily interactions with one another and with undergraduate and graduate students. (23)

Murray and Martin draw our attention to a very serious gap in the research about university teaching of literature. In a field such as postcolonial studies, which is so fraught, given the many challenges that confront it, there is, I believe, a particular need to record, examine, and share the successes and failures of our teaching strategies and practices. It is curious that this need remains neglected in the burgeoning body of critical and theoretical writing on postcolonial studies. Gayatri Spivak's "How to Teach a 'Culturally Different' Book," and Richard Allen and Harish Trivedi's *Literature and Nation: Britain and India, 1800–1990,* while ostensibly about teaching, are exercises in providing "background information" to cultural outsiders who can then go on to teach these texts with greater understanding. Neither Spivak nor Allen and Trivedi consider the fact that texts have both cognitive and affective dimensions. No attention is paid in studies such as these to the classroom dynamics where students and teachers with heterogeneous identities, marked by differences of race, gender, class, and sexuality, study texts that are called "multicultural" and/or "postcolonial."

This paper is a partial attempt to address these questions through an exploration of subjects and subjectivities as they are negotiated and articulated within the parameters of a course called "Postcolonial Writing in Canada" that I have taught off and on for the last ten years. My approach is based on Martin's suggestion that "Analyses of teaching require both the objectification of subjectivity and the use of anecdote and autobiographical experience" (23). I will be looking at some significant moments between me, a South Asian female academic, and my very heterogeneous students as we engaged with the texts of Canadian writers of racialized hyphenated identities.

The classrooms in which I teach today are profoundly different from the ones I sat in as a student in the early seventies at the University of Toronto, and entered as a teacher in the mid-seventies, first as a teaching assistant, then as an itinerant contract instructor in places as disparate as Toronto, Regina, and London, Ontario, and finally, 12 years ago, as a tenured professor at York University. Sometimes, in my moments of despair, I feel that not much really seems to have changed in terms of institutional culture and its White supremacist structures that I encountered as a student and teacher in classrooms where I would be the only person of colour. However, I do know that profound changes have occurred, mainly—though not only—because the communities in which we live and work have changed so greatly. I now live in one of the most ethnically diverse cities in the world, and work on a campus whose student body is as varied as the city in which it is situated. I presume Gayatri Spivak has a point when she claims: "Whatever our view of what we do, we are made by the forces of people moving about the world" (*Death* 2).

The multi-ethnic, multiracial, and multicultural classroom that this change in the demography of Canada has produced is, for me, a postcolonial space, with all its contradictions. It is a microcosm of the outside world where people of various ethnic and racial backgrounds find themselves, in John Porter's famous words, in a "vertical mosaic." In the particular classroom that I am going to talk about here, 35 men and women, most of them in their twenties, and their teacher, negotiate their identities as they read a body of texts that I brought together under the pragmatically chosen course title, "Postcolonial Writing in Canada."

The choice of the course title was a Trojan horse operation, and not a declaration of the postcoloniality of the writers included in it. In fact, one of them, Thomas King, in his well-known essay, "Godzilla vs. Postcolonial," argued forcefully how inappropriate this theoretical and temporal category was for discussing Native Canadian literature and life. And it is quite possible that the other writers on my course list may have similar reservations about being called postcolonial.

However, my decision to go with this title rather than the one I really wanted, that is, "Racial Minority Writing in Canada," was based on my hard-nosed assessment of what a new, untenured faculty member could or could not get past a curriculum committee in 1992. I may have been wrong about what I thought of the curriculum committee. However, I believe that my anxiety is in itself instructive.

In fact, as my colleague, Terry Goldie, has shown in a recent work on this course's title, my fears and anxieties were not simply neurotic but produced by an accurate internalization of the discipline's proprieties. In his interchange with Goldie, our department chair, Kim Michasiw, who I suppose has to be guided by such ground realities as enrolment numbers and the curriculum committees higher up, replied that "The term 'postcolonial' is a brand name and a brand name that has market cachet." Michasiw also argued that *visible minority* was "somewhat less safe" than *postcolonial,* which he saw as "post-ideological" (306–07).

I believe Michasiw is quite astute in his reading of postcolonial as "post-ideological." I take it to mean that the postcolonial is now safely ensconced in the academy and does not give the establishment any bad dreams. Insofar as no sit-ins were carried out in postcolonialism's name and insofar as its meaning is infinitely stretchable, being all at once a methodology, a temporal marker, and an identity for some (I remember the book of Spivak's interviews called *The Postcolonial Critic*), it is no threat to anybody.

Postcolonialism, then, is an academic discourse, or jargon, that I do not fully control but must negotiate with. It has been both an enabling and a disabling category for me. When it becomes too predictable a theoretical grid, always ending up with "subversion" or "resistance," it becomes disabling. Let me give you an example: A graduate student, writing on Arundhati Roy's *The God of Small Things,* commented that Sophie Mol's death symbolized the failure of Chacko and Margaret's marriage which, of course, was symbolic of a colonized/colonizer relationship. Ergo, all interracial and intercultural marriages will end up in divorce and death. Far too often, students want to read a text to uncover "What's postcolonial about it." I have written about this phenomenon, which I call "the postcolonial anxiety," elsewhere ("Postcolonial").

I find it enabling to think of postcolonial as a temporal category characterizing the era in which we live, a time after colonization, to be sure, but a time when we are recovering from, or trying to recover from, the material effects and mindsets of colonization. The US invasion of Iraq shows that this recovery follows the classic Marxian recipe of "one step forward two steps back." But as someone who marched in the anti-war rallies in Toronto, I view this attempted recovery as a global process, going on in many parts of the world, including Canada, of confronting the structures of oppression and transforming human consciousness.

My classroom, I believe, is one of the arenas where this process is enacted and participated in by way of struggle against the status quo as well as resistance to change. My students and I, endowed with personal subjectivity and forms of consciousness developed in various locations within Canada's raced, gendered, classed, and sexist/heterosexist social spaces, come together in this classroom for various reasons. The 26 weeks we spend together reading and responding to Canadian writers with racialized, hyphenated identities—Native, African-Caribbean, Indo-

Caribbean, Chinese, Japanese, and South-Asian—are, for me and my students, fraught with conflicting emotions and outcomes. Based on what they write in their journals and essays, and what I think and feel about my interactions with them, I believe this journey together is exciting, liberating, and empowering on the one hand, and explosive, enraging, and excruciatingly painful on the other.

We do not ask, perhaps cannot ask, our students to write what "really" happened in the classroom. Their journals sometimes provide a glimpse into the abyss, as when a student writes about other students rolling their eyes during her presentation or another one writes about overhearing some White students in the hallway criticizing their teacher, a behaviour that he, as a person of colour, believes to be an example of lack of respect for a woman professor of colour. Some of the opinions expressed in some of my students' journals, and the tone in which they are expressed, make me feel terribly upset, sad, pained. I feel personally hurt when a student writes, as well as states in the classroom, that he is surprised to see such "poor writing" as Maria Campbell's in a "university literature course." I literally feel kicked in the stomach when I read or hear that Dionne Brand or Kerrie Charnley are practising reverse racism.

I have been poring over tons of books on critical pedagogy, feminist pedagogy, and anti-racist pedagogy to find out how teachers deal with these emotions of pain and hurt. However, while there is a lot of talk in these books on methods, theories, and visions, there is very little writing that deals with the psychodrama of the classroom where people give and receive pain. Among the theoretical works that *do* deal with affect, I found Deborah Britzman's and Alice Pitt's work very useful, even though they construct a universal teacher, presumably gendered and sexualized, but unmarked by race. It is a handful of works—such as bell hooks' *Teaching to Transgress: Education as the Practice of Freedom*, John A. Williams' *Classroom in Conflict: Teaching Controversial Subjects in a Diverse Society*, and Bonnie Tusmith and Maureen T. Reddy's collection, *Race in the College Classroom: Pedagogy and Politics*—that spoke about the classroom conflicts in terms of race and made me realize that I was not the only one having these problems. However, these works are about the American academy and hence not always relevant to my situation in Canada. In Canada, while Himani Bannerji's work addressed, perhaps for the first time, the issue of the racialized teacher's body, only Patricia Monture-Angus and

Aruna Srivastava have provided accounts of classroom realities for racialized teachers.

John A. Williams suggests that conflict in the classroom has something to do with "the student body [becoming] increasingly diverse":

> Related to this new diversity is an intense and potentially explosive political atmosphere. When controversial subjects enter the class—whether these are international conflicts, hotly debated political or social questions, or the clash of deeply held moral orientations or group identities—someone is likely to be offended, someone is likely to complain. The very possibility of discussing such matters in an atmosphere conducive to learning cannot be taken for granted. A class can break down, and the teacher is vulnerable to accusations that he or she has been insensitive or biased—serious charges in today's climate. (1)

Williams' subject is South African and American history and so his book, although extremely useful in many ways, still does not help a teacher of literature. Our dominant ideologies and our methodologies are quite different from those of history, although both disciplines do deal with texts. Secondly, he speaks as a White American male and faces challenges different from mine which have to do with my being a Canadian woman of colour.

As I said earlier, this problem of a "different" response to history or literature based on one's "complexion," to use Terry Goldie's term (300), has not been theorized much, let alone articulated. One of the earliest hints that "complexion," or bodies, or race, does matter in how we will read texts comes in Kenneth Burke's work. Although he did not go far enough with it, reading these words of his for the first time remains one of my light-bulb moments:

> As . . . [an] instance of how the correctness of form depends upon the ideology, we may consider a piece of juvenile fiction for Catholic boys. The hero will be consistently a hero: he will show bravery, honesty, kindness to the oppressed, strength in sports, gentleness to women—in every way, by the tenets of repetitive form, he will repeat the fact that he is a hero. And among these repetitions will be his converting of Indians to Catholicism. To a Catholic boy, this will be one more repetition of his identity as an

> ideal hero; but to the Protestant boy, approaching the work from a slightly different ideology, repetitive form will be endangered at this point. (147)

I have wondered why Burke did not even consider what the Indian boy reading this fiction might feel. Nevertheless, he is perhaps one of the first to speculate about the aesthetic effects of literary texts being differently felt based on one's identity. White feminists went on to write about their differential readings of women's writings, but did not record classroom battles about these texts.

Perhaps literary critics and theorists have harboured a naive assumption that new, radical readings of texts filter unproblematically into the classroom. Education theorists such as Alice Pitt, who write on "resistance," do record moments of students resisting both dominant and radical agendas of their teachers, but much of this research has been highly philosophical or declamatory, unenlivened by actual classroom situations.

Authorizing Readers: Resistance and Respect in the Teaching of Literature, by Peter J. Rabinowitz and Michael W. Smith, touches on the volatility associated with the teaching of what they interchangeably call "multicultural literature" and/or "fragile texts" in the last chapter of their book. In the very last paragraph of the book Rabinowitz and Smith make the following remarks:

> In the end, there are no risk-free courses of action for teachers and critics, no way to guarantee that any discussion of a text, even if it begins with an authorial reading, will be bruise-free. I'm not even sure that avoiding bruises should be a goal. Some feelings ought to be bruised, ought to be challenged. But weighing what I take to be a positive discomfort like that of Nancy's student upon reading Wilde against the bruising a gay student might feel at yet another assertion of heterosexual privilege and power is an enormously complicated task. If we take seriously the possibility that art can improve us, we have to take seriously the possibility that our reading will maim us. But even if we can never eliminate the risks involved—in fact, especially if we can never eliminate the risk involved—it is still worth discussing how to articulate them and how to confront them responsibly. And the more we raise culturally charged questions in the classroom—the more we talk about issues of sexuality, ethnicity, and global politics—the more urgent the need for such discussion becomes. (152)

I found it ironic that the book ended just when they had begun to talk about my problem, albeit in a highly roundabout way, without delving any further into why some people may feel "bruised" when being taught (once again, as in most pedagogical literature, the focus is on the students and not on the teacher) texts by "multicultural"—their term—writers, and where one goes from there. Nonetheless, I am thankful to them for the metaphors of "bruising" and "maiming." Reading certain texts, these metaphors point out, can be a truly hurtful business.

I have not found any road map (revising my paper one year after the University of Ottawa's "Postcolonialism and Pedagogy" conference and too soon after the Iraq "war," I am struck by that phrase) that would help me grasp the chaotic feelings of being bruised all over that I experience when teaching these racialized Canadian writers or make sense of how they affect me as a person and a teacher, in turn affecting my students. I believe that these racialized texts have such a visceral effect on me and my students because they are about Canada and not some far away place. They cannot be othered, although they do meet denials and disavowals. Here, in this paper, I would like to articulate, and perhaps to sort out, the tangled emotions and thoughts that reading and teaching these texts have evoked in me. As to how my teaching from the standpoint of "being bruised all over" may have affected my students, I can only make speculations based on their comments and written work.

Himani Bannerji helps me begin:

> It has been difficult to write about being a student and a teacher in Canada. I would rather not have learnt or taught all the lessons that I did in these classrooms which mirror our everyday world. But there is no better point of entry into a critique or a reflection than one's own experience. It is not the end point, but the beginning of an exploration of the relationship between the personal and the social and therefore the political. And this connecting process, which is also a discovery, *is* the real pedagogic process, the "science" of social science. (*Thinking* 55)

The problems, the tangled emotions that I face in my "Postcolonial Writing in Canada" course, are of a different order from the ones I faced, for example, when, as a teaching assistant and, later, as a contract instructor, I had to teach against the celebratory narratives of White feminists in praise of writers I found exclusionary and racist (Mukherjee, "Reading"; "Right"). They are yet again different from the gamut of thoughts and emotions I experience when teaching my course on South Asian Literature. Nonetheless, the experiences I have had in those other classrooms do impinge on what I do and how I react in this particular classroom.

Earlier, I alluded to the little jabs of pain when reading some of my students' journals and finding out their views on Native Canadian writing. I would now like to talk about some interactions around the teaching and learning about texts in my/our classroom that have stayed in my memory, evoking and provoking a lot of questions that I am still trying to work through.

The first encounter I would like to talk about has to do with Shani Mootoo's *Cereus Blooms at Night*. After a wonderful seminar presentation by two students who had evidently worked very hard on it, the class discussion focused on Chandin Ramchandin and what may have turned him into a monster who repeatedly brutalized and raped his own daughters. Some students felt that it was the emasculation and rage he experienced when his wife eloped with her White lesbian lover who had earlier rejected his offerings of love. However, another student—a woman of colour—insisted that it was because of Chandin's experiences of colonization, that is, the migration of his family from early twentieth-century India as indentured workers, his adoption by the missionaries who wanted to convert indentured workers to Christianity, and finally, their prohibition of his desire for their daughter on the pretext that she was his sister.

This student's insistence that colonization can turn human beings into raging monsters capable of violating the ultimate taboo was passionately opposed by those who had tried to explain it by his reaction to his wife's and her lover's lesbian affair and elopement. I stepped in at this point, suggesting that both points of view had merit and perhaps Chandin's loss of control and falling apart were caused by his experiences as a colonized subject as well as his inability to come to terms with, on the one hand, Lavinia's rejection of his proffered love and, on the other, her elopement with Sarah, Chandin's wife. Feeling that the discussion was stuck in this one groove, I veered it towards other aspects of the text.

So, imagine my surprise when, after the class ended, three students, all of them White, approached me and told me, in voices that I read as reproachful, that I should not have let the view that colonization had made

Chandin a rapist go unchallenged. They insisted that colonization could not be blamed for everything people did. And they demanded that I return to this issue in the next class.

While I agreed to revisit the issue at the beginning of the next class, I found it difficult to understand why they were so upset. As far as I was concerned, I had responded to the heated argument in the class by putting the matter in terms of nature versus nurture theories, and suggesting that the ones who did not want to "excuse" Chandin's behaviour belonged to the former camp while the others who "explained" his behaviour by shifting the blame to colonization belonged to the latter.

Was this a "race" issue, I wondered. I remembered that one of the students who had insisted that I raise the issue again and deal with it had, in an earlier class, said that she had felt stigmatized in some classes as a blond-haired, White woman. Her remark was in response to a student of colour who had referred to a new field of study called "White Studies." Her remark about feeling stigmatized remained unanswered. Neither I nor the class picked up on it. I have thought a lot about it since and have wondered why I had not had the courage to ask, "So, why do you feel that way?"

When I look back on my connecting the student's earlier comment about her feeling of stigmatization because of her body with her insistence that I revisit the debate on the cause of Chandin's behaviour, I must connect the dots in my own psyche. I now think I felt that this student and her fellow students wanted to disavow the havoc of colonization, for otherwise, as Whites (White privilege is never an easy topic to discuss), they might have to shoulder the blame for the suffering of the Indo-Caribbeans shown in Mootoo's text. By insisting that no one but Chandin was responsible for his monstrous behaviour, they could distance themselves from the text.

But when I opened the next week's class by referring to the controversy and restated my points about nature versus nurture, I had not yet figured out my own feelings. The passions that had flared a week ago were no longer in evidence either. And yet, the student, who had insisted on the devastating effect of colonialism on people's psyches, reiterated her views on the matter in her journal that week:

> Last week's class ended with my trying to argue the possibility of a link between incest and abuse and colonialism. What I wanted to say but chose

> not to, in the light of the growing sense of irrationality among my fellow students is as follows. . . . I don't see where my logic has failed me as far as the last class' discussion is concerned. Colonization has meant a doubly difficult existence for those whom it has left in its wake.

This passionate exchange (where obviously students on both sides felt that I had not handled the situation satisfactorily) reminded me of another exchange I had witnessed in 1993, not in my class, thankfully, but at a panel of students discussing Black women's autobiography. The White student had felt angry at the Black women writers' textual anger. She had felt that they were scapegoating her. Her words remain etched on my memory years after they were uttered: "I didn't put shackles around their ankles, so why are they blaming me?"

Writers of colour, particularly Black writers, are routinely deemed to be angry. On numerous occasions after the publication of my book, *Towards an Aesthetic of Opposition: Essays on Literature, Criticism and Cultural Imperialism,* I was told by disciplinary gatekeepers that my book was "too angry." Dionne Brand, in her interview with Dagmar Novak, underlines how endemic the problem is:

> White critics tend to describe black emotion as either angry or sad, no matter what else is going on in the text, no matter how many other emotions they are confronted by in the characters in that text. . . . [T]he cultural codes which the critic uses to identify black characters are white cultural codes which see blacks in general as either angry in general or sad in general! (276–77)

I find that students either love Brand's writing or they hate it. The haters found *Land to Light On* "too extreme" and "anti-Canadian." In my class, these conflicted responses to Brand's poetry were certainly based on race.

If texts make readers angry and uncomfortable, why is it, I wonder, that we seldom see those emotions expressed, or analyzed, in literary criticism? If critics, the vast majority of whom are also teachers, documented and dealt with these moments of anger and discomfort, we might be able to negotiate these explosive moments in our classrooms a bit more successfully.

Because of the episode related to Black women's autobiographies that I have just recounted, I was somewhat prepared to respond to a White student who commented that Himani Bannerji's article, "The Sound Barrier: Translating Ourselves in Language and Experience," had made her very angry. My prior experiences, and reflection on those experiences, gave me the courage to ask her to explain why Bannerji had made her angry rather than respond through an awkward silence. The student had many things to say. It was, she felt, the whole tone of the essay, as though Bannerji was blaming Canadians for her difficulties with writing in English. Why, she asked, did Bannerji have to write in English if she found it so hard? She felt that Bannerji had no right to portray the bank teller as she did: "How can a Toronto white bank teller's silent but eloquent look of contempt from a pair of eyes lurking in her quasi-Madonna (is that it?) hairdo be conveyed to a Bengali speaking, Bengali audience of Calcutta?" ("Sound" 33). She also felt that Bannerji had an insulting tone towards Canadians, calling them "they."

Several students of colour responded to her, saying Bannerji had a right to her experience. As for me, I realized that up to that moment, I had never read the article from any other point of view except the writer's, perhaps because I, too, have experienced similar put downs in public places. However, I did understand the anger and hurt this young person, innocent and ignorant about the past, felt while reading Bannerji. Bannerji's portrayal of the bank teller, particularly the word "lurking," is unsettling. I should have perhaps detoured into a reading of Fanon and talked about how Fanon shows that even the most casual interracial encounter can become traumatizing. Perhaps next time such a situation occurs in my class, I will do that. But this time around, all I said to the student and to the class was that her reading showed how texts trigger very different responses for different readers, based on things such as race, gender, class, and sexual orientation. And then I went back to the point I was making, that according to Bannerji, her text, in drawing from the signifying systems of a non-Western culture, leaves "gaps" and "holes" for a reader from outside her culture.

Thus far I have been talking about student comments and emotions, and my responses—sometimes inadequate—to them. Now I want to turn the searchlight of hindsight towards myself and revisit my comments and my behaviours towards students.

This memory has to do with a seminar on Wayson Choy's *Paper Shadows*. The student, well versed in postmodernism, talks about the fragmented self and the constructedness of memory. He gives examples from the text where Choy's memories of childhood events differ from those of his aunt's or his friend's. Exhaustive as the seminar was, it perturbs me that the student has not looked at Choy's memories that document Chinese Canadian experience of racism: like his grandfather's burial in a Chinese-only cemetery, his excursions with various bachelor uncles, the brutal assault on his friend, or his father's stories about how he got back at his racist employer. Outwardly, I speak about the problems with applying a postmodernist reading to Choy's memoir. I suggest that postmodernism's emphasis on the unreliability of memory inadvertently suggests that his memories about the suffering of Chinatown bachelors or his father's anger with his racist employer are unreliable and, therefore, not true.

The student, who was one of the quiet ones, did not respond. I later wondered why I did not pursue my *ex cathedra* comments as questions to him and chose, instead, to engage in a diatribe against postmodernism in general. Why did I not come out in the open, so to speak, and ask him why he had ignored all the memories that document the community's suffering and Choy's own lingering pain? Why did I not ask how he would apply the postmodern destabilizing of memory to their historical truth? I also wondered whether I had not sounded too disapproving.

Although I remained dissatisfied with my tone, I could not let go, for days afterwards, of the student's ignoring of Choy's memories that document the Canadian state's and White Canadians' racism against Chinese Canadians at the time when Choy was growing up. Did the student not pay attention to these aspects of Choy's memory because we are so used to thinking about memory as an extremely private thing? Or, I wonder, is this another case of disawoval?

The next incident I want to talk about has to do with a seminar presentation on Shyam Selvadurai's *Cinnamon Gardens*. I began to feel deeply restless when the presenters opened the seminar with the statement that they felt disappointed that both the main characters in the text were defeated by their society's traditions, and that they did not have the strength to break loose of the constraints of their society. What I read as Balendran's choice to not leave his family for his lover Richard when Richard comes to Ceylon, and Annalukshmi's decision to wait until she really felt sure about which of the three alternatives available to her she liked best, were read as defeats by the students.

What disturbed me about their presentation was their laying all the blame on the "traditions" of Ceylonese/Sri Lankan society, disregarding the evidence in the novel that Balendran's father had threatened Richard by brandishing the power of the British law of the time that criminalized homosexuality. Similarly, while Annalukshmi, for me, had choices and was shown to be acting on them, for my students, she was yet another case of defeat through "tradition's" stranglehold. I can now say that if I felt disturbed and angry, it is because I come across this "victims of tradition" paradigm, that Chandra Mohanty has written so eloquently about in her well-known essay "Under Western Eyes: Feminist Scholarship and Critical Discourses," far too frequently for my liking.

When thinking afterwards about my interaction with the presenters, I felt that I had upset and intimidated the students by my questioning of their interpretation. I had tried to point out passages in the text that challenged their reading. In return, they had pulled out some lines that I felt were being lifted out of context. As a teacher who does not want to be dictatorial regarding the authority of her reading, I felt deeply conflicted. I felt a sort of despair, which I have felt many times before when my students found South Asian women characters to be too passive or too oppressed, especially when they went on to compare their own freedoms and rights as Canadian women with the constraints and oppressions experienced by South Asian women, no matter what time period, class, caste, or place involved. (The flip side of my own experience is that of South Asian students who have sometimes complained to me and other South Asian teachers, about the negative picture of India that Dalit[1] and/or feminist texts paint. They complain that such texts only further confirm the stereotypes that White Canadians harbour about South Asia.)

The students, feeling my negative vibes, spoke to me after the class. They told me that they had worked very hard on their presentation and I was being unduly hard on them. Although I won the game—if an unequal contest between students and teachers can be so called—by sitting down with them and pointing out all the passages that validated my points and proved them wrong, I did not feel good about my win. The students wanted to know their grades for the presentation and felt relieved that they hadn't done as badly as they thought they had done, or, that I wasn't coming down as hard on them as they had feared.

Luckily for me, Selvadurai was coming to our class the week after.

Among the many questions he was asked that day was one of mine: "Some of the students felt that Annalukshmi and Balendran are defeated by their society. They felt disappointed that characters who had started with so much promise had come to accept defeat by the end. Could you comment on that?" Selvadurai told us that Annalukshmi had not given up at all, that she was waiting before she decided on her next step. And that waiting rather than jumping into something headlong was itself an act of great courage. And as far as Balendran was concerned, he, too, had made a choice out of options available to him at a particular time and place in history. He said it in such a convincing way that the students' journals, essays, and even exam answers echoed him!

But how often do we have the luxury to call upon an author for clarifications? And how much weight do these authorial interventions have when the author has been declared dead, anyway?

Besides reading the characters in terms of Western liberal humanist notions of motivation and action, class discussion indicated that students had also misread some crucial scenes. A scene describes an artists' gathering where the men and women, belonging to the Ceylonese elite, are dressed "unusually": "Instead of suits and ties, most of the men wore sarongs or vertis, clothes that were usually worn at home" (376). One student felt the gathering was suspect because "they were all inappropriately dressed." So a scene that portrayed colonized Ceylonese elite re-appropriating the indigenous modes of dressing had been read as denoting impropriety and decadence. Selvadurai's eloquent reflection on the passage, provoked by my question, I think, got across to many a student.

I am aware that texts cannot be policed and I, too, misread many texts, as an ESL student in my teenage years in India. That inevitable fact of life stood in my face when I read a student's paper, in which she read Balendran's marriage to his cousin as incestuous and as proof of his and his family's—that word again—colonized mind. Never mind that the text does say that cousin marriages, albeit among maternal cousins, among Tamils are the norm, not the exception (Balendran and Sonia's marriage is disapproved of in some quarters because they are paternal cousins).

Why did the above (mis)reading just amuse me as opposed to the one about Annalukshmi's character which so bothered me? I believe it happened because of the baggage I had carried from many misreadings of South Asian women in the media, in the classroom, and in scholarly writings. I need to learn to not respond viscerally when students carry out the interpretive operations that make non-Western women, in Chandra Mohanty's well-known words, "a unified 'powerless' group," "generally dependent and oppressed," prior to an analysis, "archetypal victims" (58). Instead, I need to learn to challenge them, but in a non-threatening, cheerful sort of way.

The final incident, or non-incident, as it may be construed, that I wish to talk about is a student comment when we were discussing M.G. Vassanji's *Amriika*. We read the text less than a week after the riots, in early March 2002, in the western Indian state of Gujarat in which, according to unofficial estimates, at least 2000 Muslims were killed by Hindu mobs. I was telling the class what a radical gesture it was on Vassanji's part to give his Muslim hero a surname like Ramji, after the Hindu god Ram. This is the only name he goes by, and does not tell anyone what his first name is.

Predictably, the students had not heard about the destruction of the 400-year-old Babri Mosque in Ayodhya in 1992, the subsequent nation-wide riots in India, the orchestrated attempts of Hindu fundamentalist groups to build a temple to Ram on the site of the demolished mosque, and how these events of the last ten years had now led to yet more violence. As I was giving this background, a White student commented about his reading about the "holocaust" Muslims had carried out in the past. I felt stunned and speechless at this moment. I did not know how to respond. I asked him where he had heard about it. He said he had read about it in many places, including the Internet.

Since the rest of the class wasn't joining in, either to confirm or to disagree, I decided not to go any further into it, except to say that it was a very complex matter, or some such thing. I did not want to have a one-on-one dialogue on a very sensitive and personally painful topic. A lot of revisionist accounts are currently being produced in India and abroad, both by historians and lay persons, that present Muslims as "invaders" and "colonizers," and hold Muslims responsible for all the ills of modern-day Hinduism and Indian society. My decision not to delve into these controversies was influenced by a previous experience. Some years ago, I was tripped up when, while studying Arundhati Roy's *The God of Small Things*, a South Asian student and I got caught up in a rather heated exchange about the justness of the caste system and the glory of the Aryans. I find that while most non–South Asian students know little or next to nothing of the complexities of social relations in South Asia, some South Asian students come in with what I would call a "mythic" narrative of South Asian history and culture, which they may have absorbed from their parents or other sources of information. And, of course, there isn't only one such mythic account, since South Asian identies, both in South Asia and in Canada, are so heterogeneous. In a classroom situation, these perspectives present huge challenges to the teacher. And yet writers like Rohinton Mistry, Michael Ondaatje, Anita Rau Badami, and M.G. Vassanji are taught and written about in Canada with scant regard for things like South Asian history, culture, and politics.

Every year, some of my students tell me via their course evaluations that they felt my course shouldn't have been called a literature course, that it was more like a social science or a history or a religion course. Or that there was too much attention paid to racism. Some admonish me for not treating "texts as texts." While I cannot do much about the opinions expressed in course evaluations, I felt disturbed enough to answer a student who had decided to write her entire paper on how Shani Mootoo's novel, like any other literary text, focused on aesthetic matters rather than on issues such as racism and gender oppression. I have attached my response to this student here as an Appendix.

The arrogance and authority with which these students express this New Critical orthodoxy about literature in criticizing my reading and pedagogical practices indicate to me how powerful the hold of formalist criticism continues to be. The message these students are sending me is that my approach to literature is abnormal or incorrect, or worse, ignorant. I wonder which classrooms these students have passed through and what makes them so sure about how literature ought and ought not to be read.

When I come across such comments in my evaluations, I wonder whether it was these students who wrote in their essays and journals that Maria Campbell's *Halfbreed* was not literature, that it didn't meet their "literary standards." What is the relationship, I wonder, between those evaluations that criticize me for "doing" social science and this response to Native Canadian writers in a student's journal: "The works of literature of First Nations writers often seems [*sic*] to me to be one-dimensional, as it is almost always about oppression, racism, and the results that follow."

Should I place any importance on the fact that the above response is that of a White, male student? The thoughts and emotions that go through me when I read comments like these are at once contradictory and painful. I cannot articulate them adequately.

"You see such shocking pictures on TV, you don't even want to go there," a South Asian student had said, with a shudder, on the first day of the tutorial in my course on South Asian literature. She was responding to a CTV docudrama on arranged marriage, dowry, and bride-burning in India that had been aired that week. There are things happening in many parts of the world, shown live on my TV screen, that remind me of her comment and the unsaid volumes behind it. It seems to me that in my classroom speech, there are all kinds of silences and inhibitions that I, too, have refused to deal with. I have left too much unsaid. Like my student, I, too, don't even want to go there.

When I wrote those words a year ago, I did not know the following comment of Freud: "*Whatever may happen, it is imperative to go there*" (qtd. in Pitt 54). I truly had a sense of the uncanny when, recently, I came upon these words in Alice J. Pitt's *The Play of the Personal: Psychoanalytic Narratives of Feminist Education*. Quoting Shoshana Felman quoting Lacan, Pitt is talking about the researcher's need to bring painful memories to the surface and confront them head on: "Pedagogy uses the creative play between prior prohibitions and their suspension. When learning is conceptualized as a linear process based on rational judgment, too easily forgotten are the traumas of confronting, losing, and refinding psychic investments that accrue to the learner. However, also forgotten are the Ego's tendencies to lay down new prohibitions at the very site of these creative acts" (79).

I, then, must give heed to Freud's injunction: "*Whatever may happen, it is imperative to go there.*" In this paper I have attempted that difficult task. The following words of Aruna Srivastava, in a paper entitled "Anti-Racism Inside and Outside the Classroom," strike a chord in me: "I am keenly aware that one of my strongest shortcomings is my desire to avoid conflict and confrontation in the classroom; like many, I have used the concept of safety as a kind of refuge (and in so doing, have been tyrannized by it)" (120). I have found solace in the words of teachers like John A. Williams who have written honestly about their moments of distress, avoidance, and loss of control: "I make no claim that I handled these incidents in an exemplary manner. I was unprepared for them, and my main reaction was probably embarrassment, my main motivation to avoid risk for myself" (5).

Going there, or revisiting those moments of crisis management, certainly helps a little bit, although not entirely, when a new crisis erupts, either for the teacher or for the students. This year, when once again I heard about the liberated Western norms and oppressive South Asian traditions, I asked the students whether the "pro-life" assassins of doctors who performed abortions were also a part of the liberated Western tradition. I do believe I succeeded in creating some dissonance as evidenced by one student paper's reference to my comment as she discussed the tendency to create binary oppositions.

I don't think I have been able to do more than scratch the surface here. Not all experience can be narrativized. But what I have tried to articulate here is that pedagogy is not only about learning the right theory or methodology. Pedagogy is also about the colour and sex of the teacher's body. And pedagogy is as often about pain as it is about joy and freedom. I am afraid that the questions I have tried to deal with here are not the ones that are discussed in the voluminous materials being written on radical pedagogies, postcolonial or otherwise. The race of the teacher is seldom problematized in these accounts, the assumption being that the teacher is a raceless, genderless, classless figure of authority, and not a raced, gendered, classed participant in the political economy of the classroom. Through this anecdotal and autobiographical exploration, I have tried to remind my readers that our classrooms are very much a microcosm of the world, "chaotic, confusing, and disordered, a place of pain, denial, anger, and anxiety" (Srivastava 121). For me, the classroom has never been, and perhaps never will be, a "safe space." To pretend otherwise in a world where curricula for Afghanistan and Iraq are being produced on contract by the US Faculties of Education is to delude oneself.

I believe articulating our problems is the first step towards a more open, more honest pedagogy, a pedagogy that does not fear to utter discomfiting truths. And there is no other effective method of articulating them than telling our own stories. My paper, then, is a modest step in that direction, towards lessening that "intense privatization and isolation of the classroom," as Heather Murray enjoins us to do.

NOTE

1. Dalit is a self-chosen identity of people formerly known as "untouchables." The word Dalit comes from Marathi and means "ground down" or "crushed."

WORKS CITED

Allen, Richard, and Harish Trivedi, eds. *Literature and Nation: Britain and India, 1800–1990*. London: Routledge, 2000.

Bannerji, Himani. "The Sound Barrier: Translating Ourselves in Language and Experience." *Language in Her Eye: Views on Writing and Gender by Canadian Women Writing in English*. Ed. Libby Scheier, Sarah Sheard, and Eleanor Wachtel. Toronto: Coach House, 1990. 26–40.

———. *Thinking Through: Essays on Feminism, Marxism, and Anti-Racism*. Toronto: Women's Press, 1995.

Brand, Dionne. Interview with Dagmar Novak. *Other Solitudes: Canadian Multicultural Fictions*. Ed. Linda Hutcheon and Marion Richmond. Toronto: Oxford UP, 1990. 271–77.

Britzman, Deborah P. *After Education: Anna Freud, Melanie Klein, and Psychoanalytic Histories of Learning*. Albany: State U of New York P, 2003.

Burke, Kenneth. *The Philosophy of Literary Form: Studies in Symbolic Action*. Baton Rouge: Louisiana State UP, 1967.

Campbell, Maria. *Halfbreed*. Toronto: McClelland, 1973.

Charnley, Kerrie. "Concepts of Anger, Identity, Power, and Vision in the Writings and Voices of First Nations Women." *Fireweed* 32 (1991): 32–43.

Choy, Wayson. *Paper Shadows: A Chinatown Childhood*. Toronto: Penguin, 1999.

Goldie, Terry. "Answering the Questions." *Is Canada Postcolonial?: Unsettling Canadian Literature*. Ed. Laura Moss. Waterloo: Wilfrid Laurier UP, 2003. 300–11.

hooks, bell. *Teaching to Transgress: Education as the Practice of Freedom*. New York: Routledge, 1994.

King, Thomas. "Godzilla vs. Post-Colonial." *World Literature Written in English* 30.2 (1990): 10–16. Rpt. in *New Contexts of Canadian Criticism*. Ed. Ajay Heble, Donna Palmateer Pennee, and J.R. Struthers. Peterborough: Broadview, 1997. 241–48.

Martin, Biddy. "Introduction: Teaching Literature, Changing Cultures." *PMLA* 112.1 (1997): 7–25.

Mohanty, Chandra Talpade. "Under Western Eyes: Feminist Scholarship and Critical Discourses." *Third World Women and the Politics of Feminism*. Ed. Chandra Talpade Mohanty, et al. Bloomington: Indiana UP, 1991. 51–80.

Monture-Angus, Patricia. "Flint Woman: Surviving the Contradictions in Academia." *Thunder in My Soul: A Mohawk Woman Speaks*. Halifax: Fernwood Publishing, 1995. 53–73.

Mootoo, Shani. *Cereus Blooms at Night.* Vancouver: Press Gang, 1996.

Mukherjee, Arun P. "Postcolonial Theory, Postcolonial Literatures and Postcolonial Anxiety." *The Politics of Literary Theory & Representation: Writings on Activism and Aesthetics.* Ed. Pankaj K. Singh. New Delhi: Manohar, 2003. 177–92.

———. "Reading Race in Women's Writing." *Postcolonialism: My Living.* Toronto: TSAR, 1998. 107–16. Orig. published in *Changing Methods: Feminists Transforming Practice.* Ed. Sandra Burt and Lorraine Code. Peterborough: Broadview, 1995. 127–35.

———. "Right Out of Herstory: Racism in Charlotte Perkins Gilman's *Herland* and Feminist Literary Theory." *Postcolonialism: My Living.* Toronto: TSAR, 1998. 117–29. Orig. published in *Returning the Gaze.* Ed. Himani Bannerji. Toronto: Sister Vision, 1993. 159–75.

———. *Towards an Aesthetic of Opposition: Essays on Literature, Criticism and Cultural Imperialism.* Toronto: Williams-Wallace, 1988.

Murray, Heather. *Working in English: History, Institution, Resources.* Toronto: U of Toronto P, 1996.

Pitt, Alice J. *The Play of the Personal: Psychoanalytic Narratives of Feminist Education.* New York: Peter Lang, 2003.

Porter, John. *The Vertical Mosaic: An Analysis of Social Class and Power in Canada.* Toronto: U of Toronto P, 1965.

Rabinowitz, Peter J., and Michael W. Smith. *Authorizing Readers: Resistance and Respect in the Teaching of Literature.* New York: Teachers College Press, 1998.

Roy, Arundhati. *The God of Small Things.* New York: Random House, 1997.

Selvadurai, Shyam. *Cinnamon Gardens.* London: Anchor, 1999.

Spivak, Gayatri Chakravorty. *Death of a Discipline.* New York: Columbia UP, 2003.

———. "How to Teach a 'Culturally Different' Book." 1991. *The Spivak Reader: Selected Works of Gayatri Chakravorty Spivak.* Ed. Donna Landry and Gerald Maclean. New York: Routledge, 1996. 237–66.

Srivastava, Aruna. "Anti-Racism Inside and Outside the Classroom." *Dangerous Territories: Struggles for Difference and Equality in Education.* Ed. Leslie G. Roman and Linda Eyre. New York: Routledge, 1997. 113–26.

Tusmith, Bonnie, and Maureen T. Reddy, eds. *Race in the College Classroom: Pedagogy and Politics.* New Brunswick: Rutgers UP, 2002.

Vassanji, M.G. *Amriika.* Toronto: McClelland, 1999.

Williams, John A. *Classroom in Conflict: Teaching Controversial Subjects in a Diverse Society.* Albany: State U of New York P, 1994.

APPENDIX

My Comments on X's Paper

Your essay grapples with some large issues, like how literature should be studied, but fails to apply your own criteria to the two texts you say have had a profound impact on you. I would now like to itemize my observations on the various problems in your essay:

(1) The most serious problem in your essay has to do with your inadequate attention to the basic tools of writing: grammar, syntax, punctuation, spelling, structure of the argument, paragraphing and transitions between paragraphs. Battling with your syntax, spellings and punctuation on the one hand, and with the lack of a clear progression in your argument on the other, I found it rather difficult to understand what you were trying to say.

(2) I am distressed to hear that "racism is a preconceived notion." Racism is not a notion but a fact. You seem to suggest that the "class," i.e., I, "twisted" the texts to "conform to the thesis of the course, that racism in Canada exists." Racism, and colonialism, were the major determinants of the experience of the writers studied in this course. It was, therefore, imperative to pay attention to them. However, I fail to see how paying attention to these important historical and contemporary realities faced by the writers and the communities they come from "twisted" the texts. I am truly perturbed to learn that the "context of the course and the way the books were read" created "distractions and barriers to an understanding of the work itself" for you. I fail to understand why attention to racism, colonialism and other important issues such as sexism and heterosexism created "barriers" and "distractions" rather than enhanced your understanding of the texts. I wonder if your discomfort with historical realities, such as racism, prevents you from fully engaging with texts that come out of those realities.

(3) You make categorical statements about literature: "Literature should not be used to defend or uphold social politics." That seems to be a rather narrow and intolerant view of what literature is or should be. Writers as

ancient and canonical as Aristophanes, Shakespeare, Milton, Voltaire, Emile Zola and Yeats have written on social politics of their time, and it would be impossible to decipher their texts without paying attention to the "temporary social needs" they were writing about. When Faulkner in his Nobel Prize acceptance speech says, "Man will prevail," he is making a social comment. Only some literature fits concepts such as "art for art's sake" or "Poetry should not mean but be." For the most part, these concepts are false. Indeed, the idea that a literary text is "a well wrought urn," to be enjoyed, appreciated and admired for its own sake is a product of the 1950s and 1960s and reflects the assumptions and politics of that time. It has no pedigree.

(4) As I have already noted on your journal entries, your categorical statements assume that there is only one way of reading literature. In this paper too, you make this argument. In fact, there are many approaches to reading literature as any basic "Introduction to Literature" will enumerate. The postcolonial approach rejects this formalist methodology, opting for one that, without disregarding formal aspects, infuses them with historical, cultural, political contexts in its analysis of texts. Since the course was on Postcolonial writing, the theoretical and critical approach was also postcolonial. The theoretical essays read in the beginning of the course should have alerted you to the "thesis" of the course.

(5) You claim that you as a reader responded to the "beauty of the language, use of motif, metaphor, descriptions of characters and place." However, your comments fail completely to demonstrate your ability to look for them in the texts of your choice. You got sidetracked from your topic when you went into meta issues such as what literature is and how it should be read. Instead of focusing on the writers' "use of motif, metaphor, descriptions of characters and place," you wasted precious space in dealing with things that were irrelevant to your topic. As a result, your essay does not indicate whether or not you can speak about motifs and metaphors etc. competently. There are many handbooks, written with the undergraduate student in mind, that give detailed instructions on how to write on above-mentioned topics that you feel are the core of literary appreciation. I recommend that you start with Raman Selden's *Practicing Theory and Reading Literature: An Introduction.*

Afterthought: As I reread my comments to the student today, I am reminded of my desperate desire to re-establish authority that I felt had been put in jeopardy by this student. I did that by using the language of scholarly authority to communicate with her, fully conscious of the contradictions of my position.

The following words of Patricia Monture-Angus help me cope with my feelings when I have to mark essays that trouble me, be it because of their tone or the ideas expressed in them:

> The examination papers were unlike any I have every [sic] seen before. Some were openly hostile. The hostility did not manifest itself so much in overt racist comments (such that I could show them to the Dean and be certain he would understand the problem). They were subtly hostile in the way in which the students used the law. The air of European superiority found in the early cases seeped off the pages of some of the examinations. The examinations were very difficult for me to mark. I had a physical reaction, a constant nausea, to the marking of those papers. I am still angry about the racism I was forced to inflict upon myself. I am still angry because there are no current mechanisms or structures within the university that would protect me from such hostility. (62)

Monture-Angus goes on to talk about the difficulty of dealing with what we call "sensitive issues" in a large class, the challenges to her authority as a racialized professor, and, finally, the course evaluations which said that she was "not objective and that the course was about political opinions and propaganda, not law" (62). It helps to know that the problems I face are not mine alone and have a deeper cause than my own individual competence or interpersonal skills.

Is There a Subaltern in This Class(room)?

TERRY GOLDIE with ZUBIN MEER

FOR THE LAST 20 YEARS, Gayatri Chakravorty Spivak has been my guru. I could explain what I mean by that word, but I think I'll just let it resonate. Take it as used by a White Canadian who does not specialize in South Asian studies, who came of age at a time when *guru* was a bit of wild exotica which meant—something or other that was very cool. Since then I have learned a bit more about what *guru* might mean, but still only a bit.

I should also mention, however, that my co-writer, Zubin Meer, is a much younger man, a Parsi, and a doctoral candidate at York University, who works on Marxism and Indian historiography. He says,

> I was born after the North American era of the "guru": I am not particularly interested in the latest phase of Western Indophilia, embodied in the 1960s, American counter-cultural movement's exoticized celebration of all things Indian, from yogic spiritualism to Goa's beaches. And what's more, that world is largely alien to me. I am interested, however, in the manner in which the idea of a guru connects to a certain Eastern, especially but by no means exclusively Indian, conception of textuality. In the Western conception of textuality, largely bequeathed to us by Christian hermeneutics and exegesis, the text is a treasure trove, an autonomous, self-sufficient, closed, finished entity, from which meaning is a nugget to be extracted. In various

> Eastern conceptions, Sikh, Hindu, but also Islamic and Zoroastrian, the text is fundamentally open, in the sense that it self-consciously acknowledges its own ontological status as only one half of a dialectic, as a dancer without her partner. Such conceptions of textuality, then, include some recognition that the text requires a human partner, quite literally, to activate it.

I take these words as yet another guide, to the text in performance. Still, Zubin's participation in this version of the paper is limited. I wrote the paper, building on his suggestions offered by e-mail.

I have been teaching at universities for 25 years and Zubin is a new PhD candidate, but we both see this problem of the Canadian postcolonial within the shape of our present institution. At York, *postcolonial* is a collective term for the literatures of the former British Commonwealth, a usage common elsewhere. This does not deny that many other literatures come from countries that evolved out of the tentacles of the European empires, but most don't appear in an English department. Thus, this label is not precise but pragmatic. No such label would be needed for these courses except for our acceptance of a market in which national literatures such as Indian and Jamaican are unlikely to get individual courses, at least before the specialized honours seminars, and postcolonial is a better grab-bag than the alternatives, which have run the gamut from *commonwealth* to *third world*, *world*, *emergent*, and many others.

Many of the arguments over the meaning of *postcolonial* react to the definition in *The Empire Writes Back*: "We use the term 'post-colonial,' however, to cover all the culture affected by the imperial process from the moment of colonization to the present day" (2). Some oppose the use of any word. Anne McClintock states:

> Asking what *single* term might adequately replace "post-colonialism," for example, begs the question of rethinking the global situation as a *multiplicity* of powers and histories, which cannot be marshalled obediently under the flag of a single theoretical term, be that feminism, marxism or post-colonialism. (302–03)

Presumably, McClintock would see the York label as a troublesome obedience. We might better give these courses some less loaded connective term, such as *various*. Harish Trivedi provides a specifically Indian response through the word *uttar-upniveshvad*: "To evoke the Hindi word for post-colonialism is at once to begin to perceive post-colonialism differently. Except that post-colonialism would not let us do that" (238). His sad summary is that "the post-colonial double-bind seems to be that not to participate in what is a globally hegemonic discourse would be to dig oneself into a bottomless hole, while to participate at all in this discourse as now constituted would be at once to be compliant and complicit, however radically oppositional one may claim one's agenda to be" (245). In other words, the central difficulty is the foreignness of the theoretical model. One might argue that in its attempt to cover such varied ground, *postcolonial* is never likely to be at home.

I still find the discussion by Vijay Mishra and Bob Hodge to be the most compelling excursion through the vicissitudes of the term. They begin with *The Empire Writes Back* and confront what they see as its "postmodern resonance":

> Meaning resides in the "slippage" of language; meaning is constantly deferred; meaning grows out of a dialectical process of a relationship between the margins and the centre (meaning arises out of a discourse of marginality); meanings are not culture-specific and in postcolonial texts are constructed metononymically, not metaphorically. Since metonomy defers meaning, it is repetitive, and returns to haunt us in a replay of a version of the Gothic. (286)

The theoretical interpretation offered here is not an easy one. I think the spectre the writers offer in the last sentence is a reference to the hidden psychology that we now see to be at the core of the gothic. The meaning is metonymic because it is a response to placing, rather than offering either an inherent referentiality, in which a subject represents the object, or a metaphor, in which meaning is represented figuratively, as the subject uses a self-conscious association to suggest the character of the object. It appears that at least part of the problematic that they see in *Empire* is an inadequate view of the power of the specific subject within her specific culture.

My own partial contribution to this argument was an article titled "Queerly Postcolonial," which calls for a recognition that most of the theorizing on the "postcolonial" pays very little attention to what could be called postcolonial literature: "In many ways this is the pain of the difference between the Leavisite discovery of the human within the postcolonial text and the poststructuralist search for fragmentation." I said of Edward Said: "It must seem at least somewhat paradoxical that this most famous scholar of the textual oppression of the colonial subject should seem so unable to respond to the textual expression of the postcolonial subject" (12–13). Still, as Zubin notes, that subject, no matter how expressed, remains key to the postcolonial:

> But it is highly unlikely that Ashcroft, Griffiths and Tiffin are interested in dealing with "all" culture affected by colonialism, but rather, only those cultures receiving the raw end of the colonial deal (i.e., victimized cultures). For example, I would like to argue that it is precisely because of, and not despite, its hegemony, that the USA should be considered postcolonial.

As I write, the United States has conquered Iraq. Few would see this as a symptom of the postcolonial status of the United States, yet as I observed elsewhere, it certainly fits Zubin's model:

> Many see this as a prime example of the continuity of colonialism. Even the family business narrative of the process fits the colonial paradigm. The father, the originator of most postcolonial discussion in English, Great Britain, is supportive although he has largely retired from the enterprise, after centuries of imperialist busyness, starting before the first factory of the East India Company in 1611. His strongest son, the United States, has taken over and actually runs the shop much like old Dad, a bit of trade monopoly here, a bit of religious moralizing there, and a use of the military when a spoiled child has need of the rod. ("Where is Queer?")

As I understand it, the School of Literature and Performance Studies at the University of Guelph has at least in some sense agreed with this broad model and has decided to foreground issues of imperialism and colonialism in all its literature courses, not just those texts receiving Zubin's "raw end." Thus all the works of Shakespeare, beyond the usual tokens such as *The Tempest*, become objects of postcolonial studies, very much according to the rubric offered by *The Empire Writes Back*, but does this make

Shakespeare a postcolonial subject? Presumably not. In this guise, *postcolonial* is useful as a method of reading but not as a taxonomy.

Robert Young, in his almost encyclopedic *Postcolonialism: An Historical Introduction*, looks at the broad range of imperialism and states: "Postcolonial cultural critique involves the reconsideration of this history, particularly from the perspectives of those who suffered its effects, together with the defining of its contemporary social and cultural impact" (4). Suffering seems to be in some sense key. He goes on: "Postcolonial theory is distinguished from orthodox European Marxism by combining its critique of objective material conditions with detailed analysis of their subjective effects" (7). Young is no doubt too narrow in suggesting that there is no recognition of anything beyond the "objective material" in European Marxism, but his phrasing is resonant. Young moves from suffering "effects" to subjective "effects." Thus the postcolonial might be the suffering subject.

Spivak's *A Critique of Postcolonial Reason* states that her purpose was "to track the figure of the Native Informant" (ix), but the trail is faint in many places. Zubin refers to "the sin that Said's *Orientalism* commits: namely, letting the din and cacophony of the empire, quite literally, drown out, or silence, the voice of the Other. . . . The notion of the native informant is fundamentally a positivity, while that of the colonial subject is fundamentally a question of negation and alterity." Spivak states, "After 1989, I began to sense that a certain postcolonial subject had, in turn, been recoding the colonial subject and appropriating the Native Informant's position" (ix). Spivak seems primarily interested in the postcolonial as recent migrant, as in her own example as an Indian-born academic in the United States, but it might have various other designations, such as creolization, as in the Jamaican motto, "Out of many, one people."

In Canada, "out of many, one people" has been enshrined as *multiculturalism*. That word shows no consideration of race, and the various government programs that have been promulgated under this rubric rather consider ethnicities. In the minds of most Canadians today, however, multiculturalism specifically refers to that euphemism, *visible minorities*. The phrase designates *other-than-white* without mentioning nasty words such as race. At least one race group has carefully excluded itself. Native persons often assert the importance of the difference between the *visible minorities* category and the Inuit and First Nations, particularly in terms of indigeneity. A Native person is no doubt the object of racism and oppressed by a White hegemony, but a Native person defines identity rather from a specific relation to the land. Len Findlay has said that our call in Canada should be "Always indigenize." As a person who has critiqued the indigenization through which the European invaders have naturalized themselves to become us Canadians, I am wary of this. In far too many conferences—rather in the vast majority—indigenous peoples are much more often a topic than a present voice. Perhaps a better call might be, "Where are the indigenous?" I think that should resonate in all academic gatherings—in all gatherings—in Canada.

Canada provides an unusual case, met by few others, in being hegemonically postcolonial yet with an indigenous postcolonial minority and an increasingly large postcolonial minority from relatively recent immigration. The first is postcolonial in that Canada continues to be shaped by its colonial heritage with Great Britain and by its neo-colonial relations with the United States. The second is postcolonial in the sense that all of the fourth world is. *Fourth world* refers to indigenous peoples of nations where independence has been achieved for the state but in which the indigenous peoples are minorities who continue to live as the colonized in relation to my first category who act as colonizers. The First Nations are ostensibly free, but their socio-economic status bears little resemblance to liberation. The third is postcolonial in the sense of having come from countries which are generally recognized as postcolonial, such as Jamaica and India, but also fulfill that primary rubric: they are Black or brown.

It is a typical move to claim that citizenship is what matters and thus all three categories can be equal, as all can be Canadian citizens. Yet, it is constantly recognized that the first group seems little different from other White first-world cultures. It is particularly popular in Canada to observe that the most popular "American" comedians are often Canadians (Jim Carrey, John Candy, Eugene Levy, Martin Short), as are the favourite popular singers in a variety of categories (Alanis Morrissette, Celine Dion, Shania Twain, Avril Lavigne). In other words, we can pass for the big guys. The second group represents "the Indian problem," as First Nations continue, five centuries after the first invasion, to find it difficult to accept the values of the hegemonic order or to gain many of its benefits. On the other hand, while the third postcolonial group often enters the country with little and must face extensive racism, from the first group, from the state, and even from each other, they tend to conform to the immigrant tradition in North America and many rapidly become exemplary achievers in capitalism. As just one example, Michael Lee-Chin, a Jamaican immigrant, recently donated 30 million dollars to the Royal Ontario Museum. The conservative columnist Margaret Wente emphatically observed that he has required no affirmative action in order to become one of Canada's wealthiest men.

While these three categories skirt around hegemony and economic status, they also skirt around "the native." Many years ago I heard someone from my first category introduced as a "native" of Ottawa. He corrected the speaker: "No, I am not a 'native': I was just born there." The common use of *native of* to mean *born in* that place is corrected by the much more ideologically heavy meaning of being of the First Nations. Then for the third category, the problem is reversed. For someone of, say, South Asian ethnicity, it is difficult for the hegemony to ever accept nativity. I have a friend who is fourth-generation Canadian and people constantly ask her, "So where are you from?" The answer is Calgary, regardless of the difficulty some—usually but not always White—Canadians have with accepting a Sikh as a native of Calgary.

So only category two is "Native" but all are "postcolonial." Yet can they be postcolonial in common parlance? Regardless of the careful definition in *The Empire Writes Back*, *postcolonial* seems tied to a racial other. A special issue of *ARIEL*, entitled "Institutionalizing English Studies: The Postcolonial/Postindependence Challenge," provides a variety of takes on such questions, but one example, in its typically American slippages, suggests what the postcolonial is today. The title of "Art and the Postcolonial Imagination: Rethinking the Institutionalization of Third World Aesthetics and Theory" seems quite clear, but its purpose is much less so. It claims that the *post* in postcolonial is "a sign and cultural marker of a spatial challenge and contestation with the occupying powers of the West in the ethical, political, and aesthetic forms of the marginalized" (McCarthy 233). "Marginalized" could mean many things, but when the article assumes, without further qualifications, that Toni Morrison is a "postcolonial artist," it seems *postcolonial* is once again simply Black or brown. They might as well say *subaltern*.

Even Spivak might find this reference dismaying, or perhaps insufferable. The pun seems necessary. Ever since Spivak first used the word *subaltern*, anyone who has in some sense suffered has claimed subalternity. In the late 1990s, a great deal of academic attention was paid to trauma and all too often this trauma was deemed sufficient to produce something looking like a subaltern. Still, Ranajit Guha's original definition for the Subaltern Studies Group is of interest: "the demographic difference between the total Indian population and all those whom we have described as the 'elite'" (Guha 8). This avoids simplistic racial distinctions although, as Spivak notes, it carries with it a connotation of a neglected victim.

My title is a nod towards Stanley Fish's *Is There a Text in This Class?* Like Spivak's non-speaking subaltern, Fish's phrase is constantly parodied. My reworking looks to both the subaltern, I think the unstated target of so much of what is called postcolonial, and also that question of class. In this I am trying to avoid a reductive view that sees class as defined directly by economic status and yet I am recognizing the centrality of economics. Much of postcolonial theorizing could be placed under the heading of cultural studies. While at its best "culturalism" improves the Marxist tradition by adding to the economic base, by treating culture as central to materialism, much of culturalism seems completely to forget economic issues. The tenor of Guha's definition suggests that whatever else the subaltern is, she cannot be a part of the economic hegemony.

One of the great assets of culturalism is the common emphasis on the importance of race, especially in the work of the great definer of culturalism, Stuart Hall. Lest I seem to be going the other way in this comment on class, I still wish to assert that erasing race from the concept of the subaltern is clearly an error, especially in a realm of White hegemony such as Canada. Yet Spivak notes the too easy assumptions of race for "the postcolonial informant on the stage of U.S. English studies" (360). She confronts the tendency by this figure to identify so readily "with the other racial and ethnic minorities in metropolitan space" (360). Given the reasonable assumption that university professors and their students constitute the elite of which Guha wrote, regardless of their racial or class heritage, their analyses of the subaltern do not represent the self but rather the other, although at times an other of the same ethnicity as the self. Their work is in sympathy.

Still, it can be both sympathetic and materialist. Zubin comments on terms such as *postcolonial*:

> I would like to see the terms used less as subjective, pseudo-psychosocial markers and more as indicators of objective determinants of social reality. Why can we not admit that these literatures were shaped by a very long and complex history of capital and labor, colony and empire?

If race is the first unstated assumption of the term *postcolonial*, class is the second. While most of the authors deemed postcolonial in Canada do not exist in an inferior class position but rather, by education and status, constitute more of an elite, many, if not most, represent, in the figurative sense, such classes, in some cases post- and in other cases pre-immigration to Canada.

Fitting Young's description of postcolonial theory as concerned with subjective effects, the members of the Subaltern Studies Group have usually pursued their object as a subject. Her identity is established by difference but once identified they search for her consciousness in a rather romantic quest. Zubin suggests that we see this as a quite precise version of "sympathy":

> In *Social Origins of Dictatorship and Democracy*, Barrington Moore, Jr. writes: "For all students of human society, sympathy with the victims of historical processes and skepticism about the victors' claims provide essential safeguards against being taken in by the dominant mythology. A scholar who tries to be objective needs these feelings as part of his ordinary working vocabulary" (525). Moore signifies by the term "sympathy," above all, a moment of contact, an encounter, at the level of the mind, and thus, gives pride of place to the emotive lives of historians: like the rudders of a ship, our emotions are, or at least, should be, amongst the chief determinants of a given academic discourse.

Regardless of the emotions Zubin and I are embracing, there seems no question that *postcolonial* will continue to be the term. In a comment which reminds me of Stephen Slemon, Zubin suggests,

> Such definitional debates reveal that postcolonial criticism refuses to take its definitional nomenclature at face value, that it aims to employ its vocabulary cautiously and contextually, conducting its inquiries with a healthy dose of vigilant skepticism. The field of study steadily, if falteringly,

> strives towards ever greater clarity, cogency and explanatory power in the analytic-conceptual arsenal at its disposal.

Perhaps Zubin betrays his youth—or I betray my age in making that remark—when he concludes:

> I believe that the most pressing challenge awaiting us in literary studies lies in this very vein, in writing the great metaphysic of postcolonial literature, or rather, via a theorizing of various national, regional or ethnic archives, in writing the great metaphysics of various postcolonial literatures.

I cannot embrace any endeavour to write "the great metaphysic" of anything, but I agree that the constant debate over words such as *postcolonial* and *subaltern* seems to represent "vigilant skepticism" and a desire for greater power "in the analytic-conceptual arsenal."

Yet I must note that the use of the term "arsenal" clearly moves us all in the direction of war. Are we back with the Americans in Iraq? Or is this just one more example of male figures of combat, which feminist linguists so often admonish? Zubin's phrasing here seems to imply a battle by the postcolonials against some hegemonic order, but perhaps there is a civil war among postcolonial critics, a battle over the arsenal. If so, what is it about? Is it simply a literary war, or a linguistic war? It is obviously not a physical war, unless there have been skirmishes at conferences of which, I am thankful, I am not aware. Perhaps it is in some sense an economic war, about language commodities.

I think the primary reason postcolonial wins, at least in this case, is less than perfectly principled. Rather than some triumphal revision of Derrida's white mythologies, it is a rather more debased coinage. Here I agree with a slightly different Slemon who posited *postcolonialism* as "an object of desire for critical practice: as a shimmering talisman that in itself has the power to confer political legitimacy onto specific forms of institutionalized labour . . ." (45). Kim Michasiw, head of York's English department, in a comment e-mailed to me, takes an understandably sales-oriented approach to these questions:

> The term "postcolonial" is a brand name and a brand name that has market caché. The nearest parallel would be "cultural studies" under which

> act of branding are published and publicized all manner of texts that would have belonged to some other genre a decade ago (theory, for instance). From our point of view retaining "postcolonial" in a title is a marketing advantage.

One might agree that *postcolonial* is an attractive logo but what of alternatives? Kim continued:

> From an administrative point of view "postcolonial" is post-ideological while "visible minority" (especially the "minority" part) is somewhat less safe. I'd not be surprised if one of the upper committees which vet such things were to suggest that "visible minority" might scare off white students. There also might be some twitching about suggesting that anyone at York is a minority.

The term *visible minority* seems typically Canadian. It says *race* without saying race. It of course depends on all kinds of assumptions that go well beyond the bland claims of multiculturalism. Most assume that certain visible characteristics are typical of southern Italians, of certain groups of Jews, of Swedes, of the Irish, but these ethnicities are not now considered visible minorities. Had the term existed in the past, all of these would have been considered such by the English hegemony in Canada, who freely denoted the physical appearances of the non-English through words of far less delicacy. Still, most Canadians would assume that they know what *visible minority* means today. Any careful analysis would demonstrate, however, that *visible minority* lacks the precision it seems to offer and at the same time avoids the necessary import of *subaltern*. Presumably *visible minority*, unlike *subaltern*, is not inherently other than the elite. It implies the inevitability of White hegemony yet it fails to recognize the many ways in which non-White Canadians become part of the hegemonic order, as in the case of Michael Lee-Chin. It is difficult to deem that someone is outside the hegemony if he can donate 30 million dollars to a museum. While we might never agree on an absolute demarcation of who is and who is not subaltern, Guha's definition implies a shape to the figure for which all of our studies seem to yearn.

I suspect that Kim Michasiw's observations about York will hold true for most of Canada. Neither *visible minority* nor *subaltern* is ever likely to appear post-ideological. On the other hand, regardless of so many claims by Arif Dirlik and others, *postcolonial* is not so bereft of meaning as to necessitate its abandonment. I still would claim that postcolonial is viable as a reading strategy, and includes many different ideological problematics, but perhaps as a denotation of people, the postcolonial subjects, the term looks too "post-ideological" to be viable. Not that I actually believe that post-ideological is possible. I hope I don't seem too deconstructive if I suggest that "post-ideological" is, like "post-feminist," one of those dangerous ideologies not unlike Francis Fukuyama's "end of history." Never trust an ideology that denies that it is one.

A last word from Zubin:

> There is a central division between postcolonial as an epistemological marker, a textual analytic or a methodology, and as an ontological/metaphysical marker, what you call the postcolonial subject. The former usage employs a constructivist logic and suggests that postcolonialism is a function of the theoretically self-conscious analyst; the latter usage employs a realist-positivist logic and suggests that postcolonialism is a function of concrete, historical agents, of their ontologies, their epistemologies, their phenomenologies. The big question comes down to: whose being, whose existence, are we talking about?

Zubin's "epistemological marker" seems a bit larger than my "reading strategy," but they inhabit similar territories. As he suggests, in this category postcolonialism, whatever it might be, is used as an analytical tool. The obvious problem is that this process implies that postcolonialism is something which is done by a postcolonialist to a text. The other, Zubin's "ontological/metaphysical marker," seems to be something that is already in the text and which the analyst discovers. The postcolonialism is not in any sense bestowed upon the text but rather is inherent to it. The question Zubin raises is whether there is a "being" in the process. If the text is the primary object but the postcolonialism is in the application, then presumably there is no ontology at stake. One might find a being in the analyst, but rather than a being the analyst is presumably rather more of a diagnostician. I suspect we analysts are less divorced from the subject than this would suggest. If we are "talking about" postcolonial, then no matter how complex our theoretical claims, we are likely looking for the ontology within. So Zubin and I, this *we*, are talking about some "subaltern" ontology. We look for this ontology through a name that broadcasts itself as problematic and multifariously ideological. It offers a combination of discomfiting observations most students and academics are unlikely to enjoy: 1) there are significantly oppressed minorities in Canadian society; and 2) while your parents, your aunts, even your brothers and sisters might be, you are unlikely to be a member of one.

My original intention was to move to a broader representation of race-based writing, but a more useful method might be to follow Spivak's argument. The Native informant in Canada is a special category, which needs to be isolated from the term *postcolonial* or even the *subaltern*. The intertwining of immigration patterns and Canada's particular role in the history of imperialism can hide the specific importance of the First Nations and this must never be allowed. Still, those same patterns have created new implications for the postcolonial in Canada for which many of us seem compelled to search. Guha's definition of subaltern produces a context for this search in our classrooms. As Spivak shows, the capital *s* Subaltern cannot speak, but a literature that could be labelled "postcolonial writing in Canada" might be the representations of the subaltern by authors who might be mis-recognized as subaltern.

It would be possible here to engage in a long discussion of the Lacanian implications of that mis-recognition. There are no doubt deep psychological needs being met by those who pursue the subaltern, regardless of whether or not they believe themselves to be part of the category. Simply the process of mis-recognition, however, is worth consideration. As many theorists have shown, identification is a necessary but difficult process. One might say it is an impossible process because it is dependent on assumptions of sameness that deny obvious difference. It is in identifying the Other that one constitutes the self, but it is also in identifying with at least some "others" that the self is able to constitute herself as a possible identity. We all believe ourselves to be unique individuals but we also recognize the inevitability of patterns and groups. I wish to be an individual but I would never wish to be a stateless individual, so I might be comfortable to identify as a Canadian.

Such processes of identification are particularly interesting in multicultural Canada. Thus to be a Canadian citizen is no doubt more important psychologically to an immigrant from Iraq than it is to me, someone born in Canada more than 50 years ago. Yet if asked for an identity, I will say "Canadian," not without pride. The Iraqi-Canadian is likely to say "Iraqi," with pride in her origins and yet possibly a sadness at what her country has become. This identity, however, in no sense suggests a lack of pride in being a Canadian citizen. All of these identifications are engaged in some sense in mis-recognition, in that none of us is precisely that identity, whatever it might be. In Lacan's mirror stage, the individual recognizes the self in the mirror but this is clearly in a sense wrong. For a start, the image is reversed, opposite to the real self. Even more important, this image is an object whereas the self is a subject. Yet we must engage this process in order to be who we are. We feel ourselves as subjects but we only see ourselves as objects. And we see others as objects. Yet we must learn their possibilities as subjects. This goes beyond recognition to something which Spivak has called "ethical singularity," to deal with the other as though the self.

The subaltern in Canada requires identification, requires mis-recognition. The "outside" critic, the person who feels him or herself to be of the elite, wants to identify a subaltern in order at least to begin to find the consciousness of that victim of the hegemony. Spivak herself recognizes the impossibility of this victim in her title: the reader wishes to hear that identity that in its pure definition cannot speak. The reader yearns to encounter the ultimate victim of imperial history, to embrace a subjectivity at the extreme of the "raw end of the colonial deal." In the present our need is to understand not the Cecil Rhodes of the process but the subaltern. The choice of the reader who is outside, who does not claim to be one with the subaltern's race or ethnicity, might be to accept a slightly subaltern figure, one who does not truly fit the identity but is sufficiently subaltern to be mis-recognized, although sufficiently non-subaltern to speak. Similarly the reader who is "inside," who does make at least some such claim, can find an almost subaltern whom she can mis-recognize as herself. Thus her speaking in itself represents the possibility that at least the slightly subaltern can speak.

As Lacan and his followers have shown so often, mis-recognition is a mistake but also a necessity. We need to mis-recognize in order to create our positions in the world. The yearning for Zubin's "objective determinants" is doomed but perhaps the lack of that yearning is also doomed, doomed in the sense that the necessary energy of the pursuit of a subaltern consciousness would be erased. We need that sympathy to which Moore referred, but still more we need to see and hear that mis-recognized subaltern. Or, in other words, the postcolonial subject.

WORKS CITED

Ashcroft, Bill, Gareth Griffiths, and Helen Tiffin. *The Empire Writes Back.* London: Routledge, 1989.

Dirlik, Arif. "Response to the Responses: Thoughts on the Postcolonial." *Interventions* 1.2 (1999): 286–90.

Findlay, Len. "Always Indigenize!: The Radical Humanities in the Postcolonial Canadian University." *ARIEL* 31.1–2 (2000): 231–53.

Fish, Stanley. *Is There a Text in This Class?: The Authority of Interpretive Communities.* Cambridge: Harvard UP, 1980.

Fukuyama, Francis. *The End of History and the Last Man.* New York: Avon, 1993.

Goldie, Terry. "Introduction: Queerly Postcolonial." *ARIEL* 30.2 (1999): 9–26.

———. "Where is Queer?" Forthcoming in *Postcolonial Studies.*

Guha, Ranajit. *Subaltern Studies.* Delhi: Oxford UP, 1982.

Hall, Stuart. "Cultural Studies: Two Paradigms." *Media, Culture and Society* 2 (1980): 57–72.

Lacan, Jacques. *Écrits.* Paris: Seuil, 1970-71.

McCarthy, Cameron, and Greg Dimitriadis. "Art and the Postcolonial Imagination: Rethinking the Institutionalization of Third World Aesthetics and Theory."*ARIEL* 31.1–2 (2000): 231–53.

McClintock, Anne. "The Angel of Progress: Pitfalls of the Term 'Post-Colonialism.'" *Colonial Discourse and Post-Colonial Theory: A Reader.* Ed. Patrick Williams and Laura Chrisman. New York: Columbia UP, 1994. 291–304.

Mishra, Vijay, and Bob Hodge. "What is Post(-)colonialism?" *Colonial Discourse and Post-Colonial Theory: A Reader.* Ed. Patrick Williams and Laura Chrisman. New York: Columbia UP, 1994. 276–90.

Moore, Barrington, Jr. *Social Origins of Dictatorship and Democracy: Lord and Peasant in the Making of the Modern World.* Boston: Beacon Press, 1966.

Said, Edward. *Orientalism.* London: Routledge & Kegan Paul, 1978.

Slemon, Stephen. "The Scramble for Post-Colonialism." *The Post-Colonial Studies Reader.* Ed. Bill Ashcroft, Gareth Griffiths, and Helen Tiffin. London: Routledge, 1995. 119–25.

Spivak, Gayatri Chakravorty. *A Critique of Postcolonial Reason: Toward a History of the Vanishing Present.* Cambridge: Harvard UP, 1999.

Trivedi, Harish. "India and Post-Colonial Discourse." *Interrogating Post-Colonialism: Theory, Text and Context*. Ed. Harish Trivedi and Meenakshi Mukherjee. Shimla: Indian Institute of Advanced Study, 1996. 231–47.

Wente, Margaret. "Move Over, Old Guard." *Globe and Mail* 5 Apr. 2003: A21.

Young, Robert J.C. *Postcolonialism: An Historical Introduction*. Oxford: Blackwell, 2001.

How Long Is Your Sentence?: Classes, Pedagogies, Canadian Literatures

GARY BOIRE

> But for continental Europe we should go slow and for some areas shut out their people as we would a bubonic plague. For all the Orient the only policy is and must be exclusion. Where we cannot marry, where we cannot worship, where we cannot eat, there we cannot live. The Eastern and Western races cannot unite. Biologists tell us that where they intermarry their progeny is an ill-joined product, two brains rattling in one skull.
>
> — Stephen Leacock, discussing immigration policy in *Our British Empire: Its Structure, Its History, Its Strength* (qtd. in Willinsky 14)

THIS CRANKY ACADEMIC discussion has two aims. One is to explore the uncanny presence of social class (more precisely, working classes) within the Canadian literatures—and how this ghostly revenant conjures in the classroom the related spectres of law, transgression, and power. To teach the reality of social class as both a literary trope and a socio-political category, in other words, raises issues concerning, not solely pedagogy or social hierarchy, but personal agency, identity politics, and subject formation. In this modest proposal I share an understanding with my friend, Alan Lawson, who approaches postcolonialism as "a textual effect, as a reading strategy, as a politically-motivated and historical-analytical movement [that] engages with, resists, and seeks to dismantle the effects of colonialism in the material, cultural-theoretical, pedagogical, discursive and textual domains" (Lawson 156). Lawson's definition demands that any postcolonial activity, especially pedagogy, address both its own discursive and political construction (or determination) as well as the matrix of power relations in our social world. Postcolonial activity—in a manner quite different from Leacock's racist vision—also has two brains rattling around in one skull; but one looks inwards, one looks outwards. And both look critically.

Within these contexts a postcolonial pedagogy is by definition a demystifying activity that dismantles both our many inherited textualities and the very tools we use to read, understand, and teach them. As the platitude puts it, radical pedagogy is a political action that leads to personal and social change for both student and professor. My own timid attempts to explore literary representations of law and social class—and their intersections with race, gender, caste, and sexual orientation within the Canadian literatures—aim to participate in this very process. Simply to mention class awareness in Canada—a nation-state whose official narratives obscure the reality of social classes—heroically revolutionizes student awareness and constitutes a counter-discursive crusade against an axis of imperial and pedagogical evil.

Or does it?

My second aim is decidedly less sanguine than my first. I want to argue that radical pedagogy cannot exist within the precincts of the university—and even if it tries to come into being, it does so within a state of siege. But this siege no longer takes the form of the blunt, union-busting dismissals of the Winnipeg General Strike. It's a struggle, rather, whose Fanonian weaponry takes the form of endowed privilege. I'm thinking specifically here of the educational and economic privileges bestowed on the post-war, pseudo-radical, working- and middle-class students of the late fifties and early sixties: these are the subsidized baby boomers, many of whom have now become the conservative foundational pillars of the academy. I'm thinking most precisely, in short, about how economic and educational privilege is used to maintain a conservative agenda; or, as Fanon illustrates in *The Wretched of the Earth,* how too often the radicals of yesterday internalize the principles of their opposition and become today merely mimic versions of the original enemy at the gates.

Because of institutional conditions, political compromises, and the interpellated ideologies that constitute and sustain a still predominantly

White, male, heterosexist, middle-class academic elite, we have a professoriate that—whatever its claims to the contrary—replicates and perpetuates the class values of a capitalist nation-state. Research is commodified within a celebrity star system (i.e., the Canada Research Chair program; Ontario's Premier's Research Excellence Award; the Polanyi Prizes); many (albeit not all) chairs and deans value multiple notches in the desk-post over one or two long-fermented reflections; and pedagogy is so commercialized that we now celebrate super-classes of thousands, complete with hip-hop soundtracks and infomercials during intermissions.

How can one say with a straight face, not only that one practises a radical resistance, but that it has any material revolutionary effect, within this MuchMore mentality of the contemporary Canadian university?

As Aijaz Ahmad so pointedly observes, "the characteristic feature of contemporary literary [and I would argue, pedagogical] radicalism is that it rarely addresses the question of its own determination by the conditions of its production and the class location of its agents" (6). He continues in a vein that surely must cut many of us to the quick: "in the rare cases where this issue of one's own location—hence of the social determination of one's own practice—is addressed at all, even fleetingly, the stance is characteristically that of a very poststructuralist kind of ironic self-referentiality and self-pleasuring" (6–7). Our knowledge industry, in effect, is grounded in a simple and complex system, one that prioritizes individual egos, individual ambitions; that disavows the reality of social class; and that constructs, through its apparatuses, a professoriate that cannot help but reproduce a hierarchical class structure which, in turn, guarantees their jobs, incomes, and social niches—all possessing vastly more social capital than the national average. It is precisely these jobs, incomes, and social niches—this social capital, I suggest—that should be the target of any truly radical, self-reflexive, and deconstructive pedagogical work.

I hope to elaborate upon these themes in my remaining discussion, which has three protagonists: (1) Marcel Marceau; (2) Julienne; and (3) Mr Chips.

Part 1: Marcel Marceau

In his brilliant book, *White Mythologies*, Robert Young discusses Emmanuel Levinas and his struggle with "ontological imperialism." Levinas addresses the problem that "when knowledge or theory comprehends the other, then the alterity of the latter vanishes as it becomes part of the same" (13). This "ontological imperialism," Levinas argues, "though outwardly directed, remains always centred in an incorporating self . . . [so that] freedom is [always] maintained by a self-possession which extends itself to anything that threatens its identity" (14). According to Young, then, Eurocentric theory (and I would argue pedagogical practice) within the academy thus duplicates Western foreign policy, where democracy at home is maintained through colonial or neo-colonial transformation of the foreign Other (14). John Willinsky puts it more succinctly in *Learning to Divide the World*, when he points out that within Britain's educational project in colonial India, "knowledge operated as a force, with *mastery of the subject* the operative educational metaphor and faith" (44).

Now within the postmodern academy, "theory" has become an integral part of the average career path of most, if not all, Canadian and postcolonial students. And yet theory, according to Levinas, "is constitutively unable to let the other remain outside itself, outside its representation of the panorama which it surveys, in a state of singularity or separation" (14). Our principal tool of deconstruction or de-mystification, in other words, is implicitly complicit with the object of our deconstruction and in need of deconstruction itself. In teaching our students how *not* to divide the world, have we inadvertently taught them how to divide it in ways that suit their own (and our own) personal, professional, and postcolonial ambitions? You are either with us (as postcolonialists) or against us (as fossilized academic detritus). The question, of course, is how to de-totalize this naive binary: how to decolonize the colonizing drive of postcolonial theory itself?

At this point I need to consider a second, perhaps more concrete territory, but one that is no less antagonistic to a radical pedagogy, and that, of course, is the university itself.

For the professoriate, the university was historically, and is now, a place where people are forced to consume our goods and services, thereby providing us with jobs and money. But, more complexly, as a field of capitalist production, one based on principles of competition, commodification of knowledge, hierarchy, historical periodicity, and the purity of disciplinary categories, the academy is, by definition, both ambivalent and internally conflicted. Premised, as it were, on an archeology of disavowal. Let me try to clarify this claim.

Any cultural field, as Bourdieu argues, constitutes a discursive "space of forces in constant tension and systemic interdependence[,] . . . an arena of permanent struggles and conflicts which, ultimately, involve the structure of the field itself" (Wacquant 72). In the case of the university, the various personal investments, the multiple cultural, social, patriarchal, governmental, institutional, and departmental configurations that coalesce to form it, also compete amongst themselves within and against it. In a word, these antagonistic, yet symbiotic, discursive forces coalesce to form an ambivalent, inwardly riven, yet outwardly united field, which, in turn, disavows its own ambivalence and political complicities. Inside the multiple folds of this disavowal, the university (like the law) seeks endlessly to reproduce itself while endlessly facing the constant threat of disintegration. Particularly in Tory Ontario.

Within this system, the pedagogue is constructed as magistrate and places his or her students (and him- or herself) within a syntax or sentence of mis-recognized regulated desires. This is a controlled linearity in which the pedagogue operates within, not so much a middle-passage between an author or information and student, but in what Neil Hertz calls "a dramatic occupation, more or less earned, of the position of authority itself" (qtd. in Murray 193). What interests me most in this relationship is that the method of perpetuation (and perpetration) of pedagogical practices and representations is essentially a semiotic of mis-recognized power relations. That is: although *theoretically* we teach our students to surpass ourselves in a continual re-reading and re-defining of a canon of Canadian literature, I wonder to what extent we, like theory itself, are "constitutively unable to let the [student] other remain outside [ourselves], outside [our] representation of the panorama which [we] survey, in a state of singularity or separation"—particularly separation from the rough and tumble world of the working classes?

The student body, as it were, is approached, not only as a blank and malleable surface, a body whose productivity is to be increased while its potential for subversive resistance is to be minimalized, but essentially as an automatic mechanism, an object meant to mesh with the objects it manipulates until it becomes a replicant of the magisterial pedagogue. This dynamic, in turn, is executed through a conscious erasure of knowledge in the formation of knowledge itself, a kind of imposed "splitting," to use the language of abuse therapy. This disciplinary pedagogy, in other words, as a type of scribal gymnastic and political interpellation, transforms the student-other into the clone recipient of seminal discipline. The student as colony; as "once-Other-but now-almost-self"; the student whose name is always and already that of the infamous and perfectly silent mime: Marcel Marceau.

Picked up with relish and incorporated into modernist principles of a unified subject, progressivist ideals, totality, and mastery, this ancient but still persistent pedagogy winds its reptilian way along the smooth contours of an historical telos, while it paradoxically inculcates an ahistorical sense of oneself. The mystifying signalizations, which Foucault pinpoints as the method of communication between teacher and pupil, not only remove both students and professors from a sense of their own historical and cultural particularity (and by extension, their own relativity, what Ahmad calls their "location"), this process also delusively suggests the transhistorical position of the authoritarian pedagogue. It also then paradoxically inculcates the belief in the possibility of historical mastery: there is one past, which one can master if only by becoming a pedagogue. Within this juridical sense of pedagogical sentencing there is, needless to say, little room for the bad grammar of postcolonial writing. And even less room for the flourishing of a postcolonial avowal—the disruptive de-sentencing of a postcolonial, resistant pedagogy.

As postcolonial pedagogues, how, if at all, can we stop this kind of intellectual "self-pleasuring"? One way, I would like to suggest, is by paying attention to the likes of Julienne.

Part 2: Julienne

One way, I think, to stop this kind of intellectual self-pleasuring is to dig very deep holes when we read and teach the Canadian literatures. By that, I mean we should begin to listen to critics and theorists such as John Willinsky and, to a lesser degree, the early Fredric Jameson. If reading a text is comparable to analyzing the dreams or unspoken desires of a culture, then we can learn and teach much by dismantling and understanding what Willinsky describes as "all that lies buried in this [imperial] body of knowledge" (3)—what lies repressed within the unconscious of the nation-state called Canada. Or, to put on it a very different spin, consider Jameson's notion of literary form as a socio-symbolic message:

> In its emergent strong form a genre [and, I would argue, a pedagogy] is essentially a socio-symbolic message, or, in other terms, that form is immanently and intrinsically an ideology in its own right. When such forms are re-appropriated and refashioned in quite different social and cultural contexts, this message persists and must be functionally reckoned into the new form. . . . the ideology of the form itself, thus sedimented, persists into the latter, more complex structure, as a generic message which coexists—either as a contradiction or, on the other hand, as a mediatory or harmonizing mechanism—with elements from later stages. (140–41)

In one sense we can use Jameson and Willinsky as starting points to unearth the burial of, for example, social class within the Canadian imaginary. Not unlike Derrida's notion of the trace—or Freud's theory of the uncanny—Jameson's "sedimentation" simply and complexly points toward the archeological nature of texts (and people) and champions a sober and meticulous unearthing of the uncanny, a bringing to light of that which has (and, from a ruling-class position, *should have*) remained in darkness. Willinsky, especially, reveals the archeology of racism, homophobia, and sexism embedded in our post-imperial educational practices—how "learning to divide the world" is one way of not recognizing where is here.

I'm thinking here specifically of Hugh MacLennan's excruciating but perennially taught novel, *Two Solitudes* (1945), which every undergraduate knows is a nationalistic parable sedimented upon the story of Ulysses and the quest motif. Now, interestingly, most readers will have no difficulty remembering and identifying Paul (the Ulysses figure) or Heather (his faithful Penelope) or even the irascible Captain Yardley (the Ancient Mariner) or the subtly named Huntley McQueen (the capitalist Cyclops)—all key players in this nationalist odyssey. But who remembers Julienne? Who exactly is this woman with whom Kathleen compares herself when she complains to her husband, "You never want to talk to me about anything any more. I might as well be Julienne?" (88). Who is this woman "so familiar [that] Athanase scarcely noticed her" (82)?

Julienne—the *doppelganger* housekeeper of the Tallard family home—

is a fascinating minor character precisely because she is constructed to be so forgettable, so invisible, so both "here and not here" at the same time. What intrigues me, however, is not so much the fact that a minor working-class female character is marginalized or that her economic and social position is depicted as somehow natural or unquestionably and organically part of the social fabric. Rather, what is crucial is the fact that MacLennan should choose that fascinating word, *familiar*, or what Freud would describe as the *heimlich*, the homely, the very notion Freud found so crucial in theorizing the uncanny or the *unheimlich*. Consider.

On one hand Freud opined that the uncanny describes that peculiar fear that occurs when that which should remain repressed, doesn't: when that which has been disavowed reappears and is terrifying—not because it is strange, but precisely because it is so *familiar*. And within this simple definition we have, I think, what Homi K. Bhabha has popularized as the crucial psychic displacement or cultural *Enstellung* of the colonial subject, what J. Laplanche and J.B. Pontalis describe as "latent thoughts . . . transposed, as it were, into another key [where] they are also distorted in such a fashion that only an effort of interpretation can reconstitute them" (qtd. in Bhabha 183). Is Julienne, in other words, so familiar, so *heimlich*, that she has been over-seen, forgotten, made invisible? Has she—like Marius' very low-profile wife, Emilie (remember her?)—become a crucial part of the historical and cultural amnesia that makes up Athanase Tallard's brave new world of a (male) industrialized Quebec (or, indeed, of Hugh MacLennan's new post-war Canada)?

In one sense Julienne is metonymic: class, more specifically the working classes, have become invisible through disavowal, through what Freud and, in a very different context, Bhabha, both identify as an unconscious splitting of the Self, a disavowal of that Other who allows one to become one's Self, but who, in turn—recalling Levinas—is re-incorporated into the over-seeing self. The working-class character, like the indigene of settler literature or the woman of MacLennan's 1940s imagination, is simply *not supposed to be there.* When they do appear, it is as ghosts, freaks, weird upsurges from the underbelly of the Canadian body politic. Or, in this case, a scarcely noticeable *familiar* housekeeper.

But this is only one tip of the iceberg. What truly fascinated Freud in his linguistic play with the *unheimlich* is that ultimately the two opposites of *heimlich* and *unheimlich* collapse each into the other—ultimately both words mean the same thing. As Freud remarks: "*heimlich* is a word the meaning of which develops towards an ambivalence, until it finally coincides with its opposite, *unheimlich*" (377).[1] That which is familiar is simultaneously alien; the alien is simultaneously familiar. And it is at this point that we can begin a radical deconstruction of MacLennan's representation of the working-class Julienne. She is familiar, quite simply, because of past practice: Athanase doesn't see her because she's part of the furniture. But this familiarity masks or represses or mystifies the truly terrifying legal and historical violence by which the working classes were defined as transgressions by the ruling (and legalized) elite—aberrations to be legislated and confined within an untouchable social category.

At this point we can begin to see Athanase not so much as a tragically progressive, failed industrialist but more as a naive, complicit participant in the varying historical forces that both oppress him (as a francophone) yet sustain his economic superiority to other francophones which in turn oppresses characters such as Julienne and others (as working-class minions). Similarly, Julienne herself may well be alien to Kathleen—a crumpled old housekeeper miles away from Kathleen's glamorous self-image—but Julienne is uncannily (and terrifyingly) familiar to Kathleen precisely because her gender intersects with her class and holds up to Kathleen an unforgiving and relentless mirror of her own gendered and classed existence within both francophone Quebec and patriarchal Canada. Julienne, in other words, is truly familiar and unfamiliar—and it is in this role that she becomes one key into our own analysis of class within the novel.

The point of such erasures, I think, is both obvious and important. They illustrate the kinds of social mystifications that authors can replicate in their literary representations. And to point out this kind of blind spot, this cultural amnesia, is one crucial step in *not* replicating authorial erasures, in developing both a postcolonial pedagogy and an anti-colonial, political awareness in students of Canadian literature. But is it enough simply to point out such erasures, to foreground this treatment of class in a classic Canadian text? What material effect would such classroom performances actually have? What material impact does one actually have with the academic publication of one's observations? How radical is one more essay, one more article, one more book, or (with respect to our superb organizers and a large dollop of self-irony) one more conference paper?[2]

To begin to answer such leading questions I would like now to turn to the third protagonist of my discussion: Mr Chips.

Part 3: Mr Chips

One beginning answer, I think, to the question, "How do we proceed?", is provided in the writings of such postmodernist educational theorists as Stanley Aronowitz, Henry A. Giroux, Nelida Pinon, R. Radhakrishnan, and Heather Murray—all of whom draw, in varying degrees, on the empowering theories of Paulo Freire. We must teach our students to read and write. But more importantly, we must teach them why and how *we* do and why and how *they* should learn to. Nelida Pinon, especially, provides me, at least, with an initial stepping stone. She argues in inimitable fashion that "You must know who is the object and who is the subject of a sentence in order to know if you are the object or subject of history. If you can't control a sentence you don't know how to put yourself into history, to trace your own origin in the country, to vocalize, to use your voice" (qtd. in Giroux and Aronowitz 114).

Syntax. History. Traces. Vocalization. Pinon's aphoristic comment explicitly alludes to these four crucial topoi within the postmodern pedagogical enterprise. These four terms suggest for me how we might begin to evolve an educationally fruitful, politically active, and theoretically rigorous postcolonial pedagogy. This is clearly and elegantly obvious. The aphorism, however, also contains within itself some of the elusive slippages that are so often occluded in our various teachings of the Canadian literatures. There is initially the erasure of class (or origins in the country) within the classed room. There is moreover the seamless linkage of Foucault's famous dyad: power/knowledge. And finally (and for me most interesting), there is the wondrously slippery play of juridical power and forceful discipline that exists in that odd postcolonial word, *sentence.* To understand a sentence truly is to recognize where and why one exists within a legal and legalizing discourse—and this, in turn, is a kind of state violence that sanctions or outlaws specific forms of knowledge.

I think we must address, in the first instance, the fact that the classroom is an interstitial *symbolic field* in which, as Pierre Bourdieu and Jean-Claude Passeron argue, "both teacher and teaching are already 'receivable' by the students precisely because of the legitimation 'already' conferred on every pedagogic transmitter by the traditionally and institutionally guaranteed position *he* occupies in a relation of pedagogic communication" (qtd. in Murray 195). The classroom exists, therefore, as a site of symbolic violence, a field of competing forces. And, as Heather Murray has so persuasively argued, we need to deconstruct this violent institutionalized charisma, to evolve an historicized pedagogy which avows its own forming configurations. "A 'conditional' analysis," Murray argues, "conditional in both senses, as self-reflexive and cognizant of determinants, and as provisional—undertaken by both teachers and students, using the classroom, its situation, and its work as one example of the production of literary discourse is . . . a first step in teaching and learning theory theoretically. Which is to say, to teach and learn politically" (Murray 198).

The result of such a self-reflexive locating could be, not a new and unidirectional, reactive monolithic discourse, but a hybridized critical pedagogy, which incorporates a meta-critical plurality of (1) theoretical positions; (2) pedagogical methods (negotiated marking, for example); and, (3) most crucially, a range of interdisciplinary topics culled from the entire prism of cultural production (film studies, television, journalism, local histories, local arts, music, and political theory, to name but a few).

But I'm aware that hybridization can easily transform into an ineffective plurality: as Terry Eagleton has opined, in our postmodernist celebration of multiplicity, we run the powerful risk of simply reduplicating the dividing, commodifying, and regionalizing tactics of capitalism itself. I'm aware that if we risk a postmodernist strategy, as Arun Mukherjee has warned, we also take the risk to re-homogenize and re-totalize the multiplicities that are the postcolonial worlds. But I'm also aware that we currently run the more invidious liberal gauntlet of a self-imposed liberal silence: we run the risk of not saying anything about anything at all. How then do we tread between such fine lines of nationalism and internationalism, postmodernism and postcolonialism, appropriation and silence?

Consider, if you will, three keywords that guide my own, quasi-Mr Chipsean, thinking about pedagogical practices.[3]

1. Outreach

I strongly disagree with Eagleton and Jameson that the academy is *not* an ivory tower but rather the site of particularized class struggle. Ho ho ho. Simply to be able to make that remark is a signal of privilege and wealth, of middle-class comfort and inertia. On the contrary, the university is most certainly, if not an ivory, then a platinum or silicon-chip or Pepsi-Cola tower reserved for either the rich or the poor-ish who are willing to become poorer by contracting a lifetime of debt through Canada Student Loan; as for being a *site* of anything, it is without doubt a site where people who are not especially hungry *talk* (a lot) *about* particularized class struggle. Whatever the subject taught within the university curriculum, as part of a "curriculum" it remains, if not a form of academic "self-pleasuring," then certainly the source of solid middle-class incomes, superb dental plans, and job security. But thankfully the university is a limited venue; the classroom, as Murray wisely points out, is only one site of educational practice.

My point is that we need also to teach in prisons, in working centres, in public libraries, in interdisciplinary programs off campus, in women's shelters, in hospitals and hospices, in factories, in reading circles, in group homes. ***We need to extend our precincts.*** My nice middle-class students produce superb Marxist analyses of class in *Two Solitudes* or indeed of gender construction in Mootoo or Atwood. But they also crave an *A* in order to get into MBA programs, Law School, or the public sector. I think we delude ourselves if we believe that our university classrooms are anything other than catalysts for the next generation of capitalists (academic or otherwise).

2. *Administration*

I never thought I would say this—especially given my previous point. But finally, to adapt Samuel Johnson, I suggest we participate more in the dull duties, not of an editor, but an administrator—either university administration or administration of our various collective bargaining units. (And I'm aware that either of these choices runs perilously close, not so much to abandoning, but crucifying one's career.) But this acknowledgement/proposal springs from a meditation upon one of John Willinsky's observations about the role of anti-colonial educators:

> The question we face today is how the lessons that were drawn from the centuries of European expansion continue to influence the way we see the world. Even as imperialism's "period of real cultural authority" has been eclipsed by forms of neocolonialism and the new transnationalism of

> science and technology, many of the ideas of the world generated by imperial designs on it "retain their position in education." (25)

The inclusion of a few more courses in Canadian literature, Canadian Studies, Canadian film, or whatever—however desirable—will do little to invigorate and radicalize a Canadian pedagogy. But as administrators who are also Canadianists, we then have the opportunity to perform that necessary excavation envisaged by Jameson, the un-dividing of the world called for by Willinsky. Not that administering a faculty or a union will change the world—but it can change the way we deploy the university and its apparatuses; it can open doors to interdisciplinary programs; it can mentor a saner and more carefully honed idea of what constitutes productivity; it can outreach to communities; it can destroy the institutionalized charisma of the professoriate—a charisma that is not only shamanistic but shameful.

But, most crucially, administrative activity can begin the real political work of reconfiguring *how* our universities are funded by provincial governments, how money—filthy necessary lucre—is directed away from funding chartered jets and golf-course renovations and toward new buildings for badly needed space, new hires to reduce professor-student ratios back to a reasonable number, and more money for books, writing technologies, and the time and space to develop critical thinking within and without the universities. These are the changes that would allow rather than vitiate a postcolonial praxis.

3. Careerism

I'm reminded here of a Zen paradox: that to follow the Way is to commit oneself to a long and arduous journey—all the while knowing that there is no self and that there is no journey. Obviously people need jobs, enjoy and need research, and produce critically important work that enriches the intellectual life of the nation. Writing and publication in many cases *is* a form of radical pedagogy. I don't dispute or carp against this kind of academic praxis. But I do challenge the overblown and ultimately self-absorbed sense of our own importance—the ideology that is responsible, not only for the comic posturings of a star system, but the ridiculously deluded assumption that academic literary pedagogues within the university perform radical political work. This is an ideology that accounted for a situation a few years back where a colleague of mine remarked that I needn't read a particular essay this colleague had written.

"Why not?" I asked nervously.

"Because it isn't very good, it was just a toss-off that I needed to beef up the CV for tenure," my colleague quipped.

This is not learning. This is not the matrix for a radical pedagogy. On the contrary, it is evidence that we who were once Other to the official university Self have been incorporated into the same; and that we who are now the Same are modelling and grooming our students away from their innate alterity. We simply have to stop meaningless publication; senior members need to stop frantic writing and egotistical self-pleasuring and attend to the needs of their students; we need to erase our own academic egos and self-interests; we need to re-valorize the act of pedagogical interaction by agitating and fighting for more hires, more space, and better student-professor ratios. We all need, through our unions and administrations, to re-examine and re-evaluate the primary (fetishistic) role of publication in evaluations for tenure and promotion. And part of this process involves resistance to the pedagogical replications of such capitalist values as commodification, quantification, and fetishism.

*

As Henry Giroux remarks, "we need to combine the modernist emphasis on the capacity of individuals to use critical reason in addressing public life with a critical postmodernist concern with how we might experience agency in a world constituted in differences unsupported by transcendent phenomena or metaphysical guarantees" (117). In short, we need to look closely at the vestiges of Empire within our knowledges and histories and pedagogical practices. Because when we do, we may discover to our chagrin—but also our wisdom—the political reality that exists beneath our sunshine sketches of the educated imagination.

NOTES

1. See Freud's puzzlement in the same essay: "What interests us most . . . is to find that among its different shades of meaning, the word *heimlich* exhibits one

which is identical with its opposite, *unheimlich*. What is *heimlich* thus comes to be *unheimlich*. . . . on the one hand, it means that which is familiar and congenial, and on the other, that which is concealed and kept out of sight" (375).

2. This paper, like the others in this book, was first presented at the "Postcolonialism and Pedagogy" symposium at the University of Ottawa, 3–5 May 2002.

3. Readers interested in an extended portrayal of the beloved pedagogue should consult James Hilton's classic novel, *Goodbye, Mr. Chips* (1935).

WORKS CITED

Ahmad, Aijaz. *In Theory: Classes, Nations, Literatures*. London: Verso, 1992.

Bhabha, Homi. "Signs Taken for Wonders: Questions of Ambivalence and Authority under a Tree Outside Delhi, May 1817." *"Race," Writing and Difference*. Ed. Henry Louis Gates, Jr. Chicago: U of Chicago P, 1985. 163–84.

Bourdieu, Pierre. "The Force of Law: Toward a Sociology of the Juridical Field." Trans. R. Terdiman. *Hastings Law Journal* 38 (1987). 814–53.

Eagleton, Terry. *Literary Theory: An Introduction*. London: Blackwell, 1983.

Fanon, Frantz. *The Wretched of the Earth*. Trans. Constance Farrington. Pref. Jean-Paul Sartre. Harmondsworth: Penguin, 1983.

Foucault, Michel. *Discipline and Punish: The Birth of the Prison*. Trans. Alan Sheridan. New York: Vintage, 1979.

Freud, Sigmund. "The 'Uncanny.'" 1919. *Sigmund Freud: Collected Papers*. Vol. 4. Ed. Ernest Jones. London: Hogarth, 1950. 368–407.

Giroux, Henry, and Stanley Aronowitz. *Postmodern Education: Politics, Culture and Social Criticism*. Minneapolis: U of Minnesota P, 1991.

Jameson, Fredric. *Marxism and Form: Twentieth-Century Dialectical Theories of Literature*. Princeton: Princeton UP, 1974.

Lawson, Alan. "Comparative Studies and Post-Colonial 'Settler' Cultures." *Australian-Canadian Studies* 10.2 (1992): 153–59.

MacLennan, Hugh. *Two Solitudes*. Toronto: Macmillan, 1945.

Mukherjee, Arun. *Oppositional Aesthetics: Readings from a Hyphenated Space*. Toronto: TSAR, 1994.

Murray, Heather. "Charisma and Authority in Literary Study and Theory Study." *Theory/Pedagogy/Politics: Texts for Change*. Ed. Donald Morton and Mas'ud Zavarzadeh. Urbana: U of Illinois P, 1991.

Wacquant, Loic. "Symbolic Violence and the Making of the French Agriculturalist: An Enquiry into Pierre Bourdieu's Sociology." *Australian and New Zealand Journal of Sociology* 23 (1987): 76.

Willinsky, John. *Learning to Divide the World: Education at Empire's End.* Minneapolis: U of Minnesota P, 1998.

Young, Robert. *White Mythologies: Writing History and the West.* London: Routledge, 1990.

Codes of Canadian Racism: Anglocentric and Assimilationist Cultural Rhetoric

ROBERT BUDDE

THE CANADIAN DISCOURSES of power that flow around race and racism infiltrate texts as diverse as a provincial referendum, the Multiculturalism Act, and prominent newspaper ads, and these discourses, both official and popular, are sources for a much wider public perception and sensibility, ones that foster attitudes intolerant of difference. Classroom study of these texts offers an opportunity to unravel the many unquestioned Canadian assumptions regarding ethnicity, visible minorities, and especially, First Nations identity and status. One of the functions of the university environment is to examine ideologies that have been previously accepted and passively consumed, enabling a rejection of these precepts and forging the possibility of radical changes in thinking.

In classroom explorations of things as specific as pronouns or as expansive as national credos, one can revise and transform a Canadian ethos that has, since its inception, been founded on racist principles. Such a view of national foundations may disturb students, but it seems essential to the kind of social justice that Canada purportedly espouses that we address and reconsider this groundwork. The language of postcolonial study, while often mired in the Canadian tradition of looking elsewhere in the world for injustice, and bound by the academic tendency to distance and generalize, does offer a resource with which to describe the intricacies of racist discourses. Alongside such writers and theorists as Smaro Kamboureli, Fred Wah, Roy Miki, Jeannette Armstrong, and Marlene Nourbese Philip, a postcolonial/cultural studies/Canadian studies unit would chart the various rhetorical configurations of nation, citizenship, democracy, us/them binaries, ethnicity, multiculturalism, and colour in Canada.

Addressing racism in the class always seems a risky venture; it involves self-reflection, vulnerability, and an awareness of one's own conditional/conditioned language. While difficult, it is the ethical ground that writers and readers across the country are asking teachers to enter. What we might first recognize are the multiple ways in which issues of social justice are superseded by something else. To put it simply, social justice often gives way to other interests: White psychic security, "progress" as measured by financial stability or privilege, principles of democracy and "good government," abstract notions of nationhood, moral standards, and a tradition of scholarly discourse and theoretical objectivity. The critical distance that is created by theoretical or policy discourse remains a crucial element in a Canadian racist ethos. Since the signs of *multiculturalism* and *postcolonialism* have been misdirected from the outset and so ravaged of their potential for political resistance, might we be forced to re-conceive a theoretical basis? Like the Indian Act and other government and court decisions, issues of efficient management have overshadowed principles of social justice and the adequate recognition of historical violence, so much so that nationhood and citizenship may be too enmeshed in these principles to be disentangled. Might we be led to name a new consciousness of these pervasive ideologies *post-Canadianism*?

The actual reading and analysis of texts in the postcolonial classroom often involves a stalwart refusal to look at the text and its language. This aversion takes on aspects of defensiveness, distancing, and the safety of certain types of knowledge. The immediate tendency is to look away, to fall back on cliché or learned responses:

- "If they want equality, why are they asking for special status."
- "I am not responsible for my ancestor's sins."
- "It just should be settled, once and for all."
- "Canada is the most tolerant nation in the world, why do they complain?"
- "They are feeding off the system."

We have heard these before. That monumental "they" persists even when there are Aboriginal and other students of colour in the class. It is useful to return to these statements as rhetorical strategies alongside more obviously racist statements and texts because this type of defensiveness appears again, even in more official documents. Race as a linguistic or semiotic structure can be a key to opening up the possibilities of other impressions and expressions of difference.

The exaggerated White supremacist attitudes that are displayed in the ad purchased by the Coalition for a Humanistic British Canada (see Appendix A) offer a specific text to explore in terms of language and rhetorical strategies. Once the context of the substantial cost and large distribution of this ad is highlighted (it was run in 30 Canadian newspapers and magazines including the *Toronto Star*, *Vancouver Sun*, *Winnipeg Free Press*, *Edmonton Journal*, and *Globe and Mail*), students become sobered by the implications of what they read. They chuckle at some of the provisions in the ad, especially the bit about "aggressive clothing choices," but when we begin to go through the points, there is a strange combination of recognition and repulsion in the responses. Sections that garner the most attention initially are the "requirement" for "mainstream cultural assimilation" and the call for an "end to Canada's multicultural policies and related affirmative action policies." Other observations that typically emerge are:

- the link between British culture and "morality" or "values"
- the link between an adherence to sexist role models, White supremacy, and a monolithic tradition
- the slippery use of pronouns like "we" ("These are all peoples we share much with"), "all Canadians," and "our" ("our European heritage")
- the calculated effort to make the ad look official and government-related through the use of an emblem at the top and the subtitle "Policy Statement"

The fact that the ad ran in so many newspapers (some unapologetically) reveals one of the ways in which freedom of speech and other democratic rights become a tool for the active management of race relations and cultural hegemony. The "we" becomes a linguistic sign that carries with it the weight of the power of the majority at the expense of justice and, dare I say, humanism. It is this omnipresent and pervasive underpinning of Canadian identity that has guided race relations for hundreds of years. The pronoun reflects a fictional assumption of centrality and community.

The pronoun choice has resonance in that it connects to more official government documents concerning First Nations and multicultural policy. A similar pronoun problem appears in this statement by the Department of Canadian Heritage:

> Through multiculturalism, Canada recognizes the potential of all Canadians, encouraging them to integrate into their society and take an active part in its social, cultural, economic and political affairs. (Department of Canadian Heritage)

The chasm between "them" and "their society" is what stands out. Here, "all Canadians" works in a less threatening way, but there remains an invasive sense of "they" and the assumption of a central (absent?) culture, society, and nation. Roy Miki contends that Canadian "multiculturalism" has "proven to be an efficient means of engineering internal inequities in ways that have protected white neo-colonialist cultural representations" (150). The subtle manoeuvres of mainstream culture and dominant ideology create a Canadian race hegemony that takes as its foundation seemingly indisputable values of inclusion and validation, democracy and progress, harmony and vitality. What is lost is full recognition of historical truths, current inequities, and continuing, hurtful attitudes. The call to "full participation" suggests that this integration into the structures of Canadian culture is the answer to the race "problem." Issues of land claims, redress, institutional racism, police harassment, and immigration discrimination are not on the table as contributing to or hindering a "multicultural" nation. "Full participation" and integration become the whitewashing, the smoothing over, the cultural amnesia that conditions a national consciousness.

The troubled crux of postcolonial thinking in Canada is not so much whether Canada is racist or not, it is how the language of racialized thought can be recognized and translated (as a transformative act) into social justice activism, anti-racist action, and the reformation of colonially-inscribed institutions. Questions that might be asked by a postcolonial Canadian subject/student are:

- what are the ideological foundations of Canadian culture that prevent a healthy self-identification and autonomy for people of colour?
- what racist residue is still laced into Canadian consciousness, left over from the "discovery" and "settlement" of Canada?
- what links are to be made between a traditionally conceived and analyzed "colonial mentality," and a more contemporary and fluidly dominant North American racist ideology?
- how are the Canadian government's policies to be read in terms of their racist overtones/intentions?
- why is theory so disinclined to address specific issues of racism?

This last question has already been asked, but with muted and insufficient answers. Aruna Srivastava discusses this inexplicable exclusion:

> A conference on postcolonial pedagogy, followed by another two months later, on *gender, colonialism, postcolonialism*. A few intrepid souls slither past *race*. I start getting edgy, worried. Angry, even. What about racism? Power? Abuse? And what about pedagogy? We are teachers, students. I ask a colleague if *post-colonialism* has room for *anti-racism*. He's not sure; his take is *anti-colonialism*. I meet silence when I ask others. Discomfort perhaps. Or: *surely it goes without saying, among us postcolonialists*. (46)

Such a lack of real engagement with anti-racist issues raises questions about the function of the whole liberal/multicultural/mosaic conception of a unified Canadian identity.

The call might be for a wholesale rethinking of the Canadian cultural "mosaic" and the "full participation" proclaimed by the Multiculturalism Act. The Ministry of Multiculturalism was established to disperse money rather than to address the endemic racism that haunts this country. Smaro Kamboureli, while exploring Canadian multiculturalism and diasporic literature, describes the nation's drive to define ethnicity through a policy that "reifies minorities as that which the cohesive nation is not" (92). This reification involves the "'preservation' of ethnicity [and] lodges the ethnic subject within a museum case because of a 'heritage' . . . that is presumed to be stable and unambiguous, and therefore easily reproducible" (106). The binary bind of colonial/postcolonial neatly packages central Canadian racist ideologies and, more often than not, places the racialized subject safely in the Third World, in the Orient, back overseas, or on the reserve.

Kamboureli points to another, equally persistent, strategy in Canadian public policy concerning ethnicity; rather than reifying there is a tendency to erase difference. In discussing the Multiculturalism Act, she argues that "this legal document seeks to overcome difference rather than to confront incommensurability. Belying its intent to address systemic inequities, it executes an emancipatory gesture in the name of homogeneity and unity" (101). The claim that "we are all immigrants" (Atwood 62) effectively denies difference and, so, regulates its role in the nation-state. Kamboureli uses Walter Benjamin's sense of *incommensurability* to suggest both the necessary role of difference and the importance of recognizing that these ambivalent identities are continually in flux. Miki identifies this as seeing "race" as a construction, as produced, largely by a dominant anglocentric cultural milieu, and a sign that necessarily calls for troubling ambivalence, a sign under erasure. This indeterminacy would straddle, or better yet, striate, the equally damaging poles of reification and denial. Here and not here. This address of "race" largely comes about through a material/historical recognition of racist acts and rhetoric that both places the racialized subject in a national landscape and displaces him/her from a (fictionalized) national epistemology and ethos.

The various epistemological activities that the Multiculturalism Act initiates are reproduced in the types of rhetorical strategies taken on by the literary theorist. Here is how this apparatus might break down:

- assimilation through denial of systemic racism
- creation of economic dependence on a central and traditionally structured institution
- naming and categorization of difference that "serves to re-repress the already repressed" (Kamboureli 167)
- rendering of the "founding" nations an invisible/absent centre (much in the same way Rushdie sees "Commonwealth" fiction)
- monumentalization of history and "heritage" so as to clearly place

the hyphenated homeland (i.e., Japanese-Canadian, etc.), so you have Brian Mulroney calling to extend condolences to Rajiv Gandhi following the Air India crash even though most of the passengers were Canadian citizens

- claiming of a "multicultural" environment through a "universalizing rhetoric," which erases "ethnicity" and its "differential role" (Kamboureli 100) as a resistance to dominant racist and colonial ideologies

It would be foolish, I think, to separate mainstream academic and centralized government institutions in terms of their functioning ideologies. As such idealism might suggest, the status quo rests firmly in the hands of Canadian academia. A postcolonial pedagogy, in order to address social injustice and racist ideology, has the daunting task of working against its own context and traditions along with those assumptions being carried into the class by instructors and students.

The landmark Nisga'a treaty in 2000 performs a mobility that calls into question citizenship, authority, reliance, and jurisdiction in a way that unsettles the status quo of race politics in this nation. The Nass Valley is now here and not here; it re-articulates colonial contact space. For Gloria Anzaldúa, this kind of motility as "home" is a hazardous yet freeing border space for the *New Mestiza* who occupy the borders of race, nation, and language in the southern United States:

> Borders are set up to define the places that are safe and unsafe, to distinguish *us* from *them*. A border is a dividing line, a narrow strip along a steep edge. A borderland is a vague and undetermined place created by the emotional residue of an unnatural boundary. It is in a constant state of transition. (3)

This unsettled but potentially powerful border existence holds both pain and joy for the trans-border/nomadic/hybrid/racialized subject. This shifting liminal space is a site of deterritorialization, a border existence, outside of traditional jurisdiction divisions, where something as apparently basic as *citizenship* breaks down as a referent and becomes a floating signifier. Without the unhinging of race as a referent, race talk threatens to become a symbolic "reserve" or "internment camp" where difference may be kept at bay.

One of the responses to the Nisga'a agreement has been the Campbell government's controversial referendum on treaty negotiations. The contexts for this referendum are many and complex. British Columbia is unique in Canada because it does not have ratified treaties like the rest of the country. Treaty attempts have been blocked by a series of provincial governments so that most BC First Nations do not have those agreements that are held sacred in other parts of the country. The NDP Clarke government that preceded this Liberal government forged ahead and signed the Nisga'a Treaty that returned to the Nisga'a 19 000 hectares (an area less than at least two ranches in south-central BC), a cash settlement, and an unprecedented amount of autonomy in terms of self-government. Panic ensued and, in part, a change of government was the result.

The referendum itself has some caveats to it. It is clear that a majority *yes* vote would support the already established approach to treaty negotiations as outlined by the government, whereas a *no* vote would not be binding whatsoever and easily ignored. The referendum is designed to manufacture support for a previously articulated position, not, as referenda traditionally do, to gauge public opinion on a particular issue. This is a clear example of the ways in which government can *create* public opinion and further propagate Canadian racist ideals. In the referendum text (see Appendix B), all the questions have been arranged (in some remarkable syntactic twists) so that the "yes" option is the government's desired option. The text of the referendum raises many questions about motivation, impact, and an apparent amplification of alarming trends in race relations and rhetoric. The questions are simplistic and meant to solicit a kind of gut reaction by the voting public. Of course, I want parks maintained. But this is not the whole story. It seems to me that most answers would have to be "it depends." The first five questions (and possibly number 7 depending on what "harmony" means) are intent on defending against possible treaty-land awards in the future, regardless of legitimacy. Question number 6 is to defend against the type of autonomy that the Nisga'a have won, especially in its assertion of the federal and provincial power to "delegate." The last question has been vociferously defended as installing full equality to First Nations by disavowing preferential treatment and reducing a welfare-state dependency. In the "whereas" at the top the principle of the policy is outlined: *workable, affordable, certainty, finality*, and *equality*. All of these terms, except perhaps *equality*, are specifically geared to create economic stability for corporate investment and activity. It is clear here that the issues of justice are taking a back seat to the bottom line of provincial finance and economic growth. History, ethics, and identity are not in the equation. The first question raises a further question about what "private property" entails. In recent Supreme Court decisions there has been a growing recognition of a non-Western definition of *property* and the cultural vibrancy that preceded colonization in Canada. Why could this question not replace "expropriated" with "reclaimed"?

As in the Coalition ad, the phrase "all British Columbians" has curious implications. If, and it is fairly clear this is the case, these provisions are to protect against treaty claims, then it is clear that "all British Columbians" means non-Aboriginal. In this instance, even a *no* answer would buy into a rhetorically charged ethos that reaffirms a colonial premise. This enveloping "hailing" gesture left the voter no choice but to not participate, even at the expense of enabling a *yes* vote. All aboriginal organizations in BC advised disregard for the referendum or an officially spoiled ballot. Not here, not there. This entails an important refusal to acknowledge Canadian White supremacist interpellation even when it is lodged firmly within principles of democracy and free speech. There was less than a 40 per cent response to the referendum, indicating a clear aversion to its founding principles. However, of the participants, 90 to 95 per cent voted *yes* to the government-mandated provisions. How the province uses this dangerously manufactured mandate is yet to be seen.

The politics of land claims, redress, anti-racism, and class equality have been effectively quarantined by government, academia, and media. One of the dictates of any regime is to effectively silence and quarantine any resistance to dominant ideological state apparatuses. This manoeuvre can be accomplished through physical displacement but also through a type of language effect (via parts of speech like pronouns) that symbolically displaces. What a Canadian ethos has failed to address are the complex issues of diaspora, First Nations, and the displaced or racialized experience *that makes up Canada at a basic level.* This is not that same argument that we are all raced and immigrant and different; this is an argument that racial conflict, inequity, toxicity, and systematically damaging discrimination is a foundation of this nation. Race theory is not a fringe issue raised by a special interest group but fundamental, central to Canadian identity.

APPENDIX A

Coalition for a Humanistic British Canada
Policy Statement

The coalition believes it is crucial that the British and French roots of Canada be recognized and respected by all Canadians. We are calling for a recognition of the very special status of Quebec as Canada's French province, and for the recognition of the British system of government, and British institutions for all Canadians not living in the province of Quebec.

British culture must be enhanced, protected and preserved in the same manner as French culture has been protected by recent administrations in the province of Quebec. In this respect, the coalition is calling specifically for:

a) School uniforms for all children attending Canadian schools
b) An emphasis on early teaching of English literature and moral values
c) A massive increase in immigration, most especially from the U.K., France, Italy, Germany and other such countries including The Ukraine, Russia and Kossova. These are all peoples we share much with now.
d) A substantial increase for Arts funding in Canada for traditional British theatre and music
e) A preservation and enhancement of architecture which best reflects our European heritage
f) A requirement that mainstream cultural assimilation be carried as a matter of course, for all Canadians.
g) An end to Canada's multicultural policies and related affirmative action policies and initiatives for all

We are as well calling for a return to traditional values and recognition of the traditional roles provided in the support of families. Specific changes we seek include:

a) An end to equal rights treatment in such areas as war combat, etc. as to men and women
b) A revision of marital awards on divorce to encourage better motivated, longer marriages

We would like to encourage a return to traditional modes of dress as well. We think that women should avoid too much exposure from aggressive clothing choices. Men should wear trousers rather than jean clothing substitutes, while women should likewise return to skirts and dresses. A great example for the children.

Finally, we think the CBC in particular has been quite negligent in carrying out its responsibilities to help raise responsible thinking children by providing too much trash on television rather than the more edifying programs available on Public television. In particular, shows such as Upstairs Downstairs from the BBC provide a much better role model environment for our children we believe, over many of the choices currently being made by the state owned broadcaster.

If you are concerned with the preservation of traditional family values in Canada, we ask that you write your member of parliament. Its postage free when you indicate the letters MP on the envelope addressed to parliament hill. You might also wish to include a copy of this advertisement.

When you write, we hope you will also express your support for FREE TRADE with Britain NOW, as well as a BLANKET PASSPORT offer to British citizens of tenure.

You may reach us at:
Coalition for a Humanistic British Canada
Michael E. Chessman, Founder
255 Wellesley Street east #2 Toronto, M4X 1G8
Toll Free: (800) 961-2678 Fax: (416) 929-4658
Website: www.geocities.com/britishcanada
Email: britishcanada@sprint.ca

APPENDIX B

Whereas the Government of British Columbia is committed to negotiating workable, affordable treaty settlements that will provide certainty, finality and equality;

Do you agree that the Provincial Government should adopt the following principles to guide its participation in treaty negotiations?

1. Private property should not be expropriated for treaty settlements.

2. The terms and conditions of leases and licences should be respected; fair compensation for unavoidable disruption of commercial interests should be ensured.

3. Hunting, fishing and recreational opportunities on Crown land should be ensured for all British Columbians.

4. Parks and protected areas should be maintained for the use and benefit of all British Columbians.

5. Province-wide standards of resource management and environmental protection should continue to apply.

6. Aboriginal self-government should have the characteristics of local government, with powers delegated from Canada and British Columbia.

7. Treaties should include mechanisms for harmonizing land use planning between Aboriginal governments and neighbouring local governments.

8. The existing tax exemptions for Aboriginal people should be phased out.

WORKS CITED

Anzaldúa, Gloria. *Borderlands La Frontera: The New Mestiza*. San Francisco: Anne Lute, 1988.

Atwood, Margaret. *The Journals of Susanna Moodie*. Toronto: Oxford UP, 1970.

Kamboureli, Smaro. *Scandalous Bodies: Diasporic Literature in English Canada*. Toronto: Oxford UP, 2000.

Miki, Roy. *Broken Entries: Race, Subjectivity, Writing*. Toronto: Mercury, 1998.

Ministry of Heritage. "Canadian Multiculturalism: An Inclusive Citizenship." 10 July 2002. <http://www.pch.gc.ca/multi/inclusive_e.shtml>.

Rushdie, Salman. "'Commonwealth Literature' Does Not Exist." *Imaginary Homelands: Essays and Criticism 1981–1991*. New York: Granta/Penguin, 1991. 61–70.

Srivastava, Aruna. "Wielding Words (for craig)." *West Coast Line* 27.1 (1993): 46–51.

Reading against Hybridity?: Postcolonial Pedagogy and the Global Present in Jeannette Armstrong's *Whispering in Shadows*

HEIKE HÄRTING

> The famous "four freedoms" laid out by Franklin Roosevelt were freedom of speech and religion, freedom from want and fear. . . . My candidate for top of the list is freedom of memory.
>
> Most Canadians are lucky enough to enjoy extensive access to their own history, with relatively few restrictions. In far too much of the world, . . . efforts to recapture the history of war, abuse and injustice are met with denial, indifference, scorn or outright terror.
>
> Yet there are people, often survivors of atrocities, who insist on the right to remember . . . Such a man is Mateo Pablo, . . .[a] 43-year-old Chuj Maya Indian, [who witnessed] the slaughter . . . [of] his wife and two children [by the] Guatemalan army. [He] now lives in Montreal.
>
> — Paul Knox, "On the Right to Remember"

> We have to campaign for human rights as a whole. The victims of new incurable diseases, the victims of social injustice, and the victims of war and impunity—all these are equally important. Often when we talk of human rights we get stuck in the particular. I don't think the nations of the world have ever really thought of human rights in global terms. The UN does not always apply its own universal principles consistently.
>
> — Rigoberta Menchú, *Crossing Borders* 137

Epigraphs, Contexts, Positions

Both of these epigraphs serve as a rough itinerary of this essay's conceptual inquiries and multi-generic reading practices. Through their different political perspectives, the two quotations raise questions about, first, indigenous accounts of what Zygmunt Bauman calls the "human" and "social consequences of the globalizing process" (1), and, second, the theoretical and pedagogical value of diverse concepts and metaphors of cultural hybridity in an indigenous context. But they are also a reminder that "epigraph[s]," in Jacques Derrida's words, "will never make a beginning" but comprise an indefinite network of texts (*Dissemination* 43) and conversations. Indeed, to a great extent, the topic of this essay and the selection of my epigraphs are contingent on Jeannette Armstrong's arrangement and choice of epigraphs to her novel *Whispering in Shadows.* Both her epigraphs from Pauline Johnson's (Tekahionwake) poem "Moonset"[1] and Armstrong's poem "frogs singing"[2] draw attention to the physicality of land and the human connections it facilitates. Also, the absence of a clear demarcation between the end of the epigraphs and the beginning of the novel emphasizes cultural continuity and prohibits a clear division between an *hors texte* and the beginning of the novel proper. More specifically, both poems stretch over two pages and "frogs singing," the second epigraph, is printed parallel to the opening of the novel, which is itself a prose fragment written through metaphors of illness, land, and interior and exterior maps of belonging.

But rather than situating Armstrong's novel in a Derridean paradigm of an all-encompassing and consuming textuality, I suggest that the epigraphs foreground the generic hybridity of Armstrong's text and locate it in the heterogeneous but culturally specific traditions of First Nations women's writing and representation. To begin with, thematically Johnson and Armstrong share an interest in the modes of indigenous knowledge production. Like the speaker of Johnson's poem, Armstrong's protagonist, Penny Jackson, an Okanagan visual artist and environmental activist, examines the relationship between colonial and indigenous languages, between the land, community, and the social and individual body, or what she calls "cell memory" (191). Furthermore, by quoting Johnson, Armstrong signals the need to investigate culturally hybrid practices of identity and representation from an indigenous perspective. Such an investigation would displace the term hybridity from its past uses as a means and sign of cultural assimilation and death in, for example, Duncan Campbell Scott's and Catharine Parr Traill's imperial narratives of Canadian nation formation. It is against the imperial desire for, in Veronica Strong-Boag and Carole Gerson's words, "a new 'hybrid' people" that would guarantee the "survival of superior Aboriginal individuals and traits in a population amalgamated under Anglo-Canadian suzerainty" (23), that we must read Armstrong's dramatization of cultural hybridity.

In particular, Johnson's repeated metaphor of the "shadow-land" in "Moonset" recalls her poem "In the Shadows." Both of these poems, we might argue, could be easily misread as nature poems in the tradition of Wordsworthian Romanticism. But it is precisely through their organic construction of theme, rhythm, and sound that these poems foreground what Armstrong sees as the "musical coherence" ("Land Speaking" 189) of indigenous land and language. As Armstrong explains, in the case of her people, the Okanagan language, N'silxchn, "was given to us by the land we live within" and it "recreates sounds of the land in its utterance" (175, 188).[3] These sounds and words of "the Okanagan language carr[y] meanings about a time that is no more. . . . [They] whisper more than the retelling of the world" (181). In a different language context, the "discrepant engagements" and noises (Mackey) that result from the translation of indigenous voices into an imperial language context underlie the indigenous presence in Johnson's poems.[4] The title of *Whispering in Shadows*, then, points to the subjective agency and generic hybridity produced through the interplay of the colonial and indigenous languages in Armstrong's text. Moreover, beyond paying homage to Pauline Johnson as a cultural translator and vanguard of First Nations women's writing, the metaphors of "shadows" and "shadow-land" open up a liminal but never fully transparent space of individual, communal, and spiritual transformation. It is this socially hybrid space that Armstrong's novel inhabits and reinscribes with the ecological effects of global neo-colonialism, with the invisible but perpetual presence of systematized racism, and with acts of anti-colonial resistance. Thus, Armstrong's epigraphs engage in a dialogue between two First Nations women writers, who, across their historical and political divides, recognize cultural hybridity as a contested space, which, in Gayatri Spivak's words, "one cannot not want to inhabit yet must criticize" (*Outside* 64).

It is clear, however, that a reading of cultural hybridity in the context of First Nations writing entails certain risks for a non-indigenous critic, and relative newcomer to Canada, such as myself. First, given my own history of migration from Berlin (Germany) to Canada's West Coast and subsequent settlement on land belonging to First Nations,[5] I bring to mind the figure of the privileged hybrid migrant, who is complicit with rather than resists dominant pluralist identity politics. From this latter perspective, hybridity is easily co-opted by an "unexamined culturalism" (Spivak, *Critique* 377) and employed in the global trafficking of indigenous and other cultures. Indeed, as a hegemonic concept of identity management, cultural hybridity ensures that, under the rules of global capital expansion, "*trading the* [indigenous] *Other*" (89), as Maori theorist Linda Tuhiwai Smith puts it, remains "big business" (90). Smith's comment stands as a reminder of the flexibility of capital and its ability not only to accommodate but to thrive on cultural difference and multiculturalism, with which hybridity is frequently associated. In fact, as San Juan, Jr. recently argued, "capital ethnicizes peoples to promote labor segmentation [, resulting in] hybridity and other differential phenomena" (6).

Smith, however, situates her materialist critique of hybridity in a historically specific understanding of how Western theories of expansion, i.e., "cultural imperialism" and today's "reframed discourse of globalization" (88), have produced the indigenous Other as the "first truly global commercial enterprise" (89) and cultural commodity. Examining the functions and effects of hybridity in an indigenous context, particularly from my privileged, Western perspective, then, has to work through an ethical caveat that acknowledges difference *as* difference and as a sign of uneven power relations. For, as Smith avers, in the past, Western researchers have generally theorized the "'fatal impact' of the West on indigenous societies . . . as a phased progression from: (1) initial discovery and contact, (2) population decline, (3) acculturation, (4) assimilation, (5) 'reinvention' as a hybrid, ethnic culture" (88). This kind of taxonomy confines indigenous subjectivity to a state of perpetual victimization and "hopelessness," while denying "indigenous perspectives" that articulate the same process of colonization in terms of "(1) contact and invasion, (2) genocide and destruction, (3) resistance and survival, (4) recovery as indigenous peoples" (Smith 88). The latter account replaces the colonial practices of "'reinventi[ng]'" indigenous as "hybrid" culture by indigenous practices of self-determination and political autonomy. Thus, to me, dealing with questions of hybridity in an indigenous framework requires that I address the ways in which Western practices of knowing—popular and academic modes of knowledge production—transform the indigenous subject into an object of knowledge and a global commodity fetish. Put differently, reinventing the particularities of indigenous cultures and histories in terms of hybrid identities involves, in the classical Marxist sense of commodity fetishism, erasing the material conditions, namely the history of conquest and imperialism, that produced hybrid identities as commodities of the exotic and erotic in the first place.[6]

Furthermore, as a postcolonial scholar, I work within an institutional and national context of power that is designed to promote a politically sanitized version of cultural hybridity. Indeed, postcolonial studies has often and rightly been charged with homogenizing different histories of colonialism and resistance and with perpetuating the self-consolidating practices of Western modes of knowledge production about the colonial Other. Especially pertinent to a critique of postcolonial studies in the context of this paper is Thomas King's observation that "[p]ostcolonial might be an excellent term to use to describe Canadian literature, but it will not do to describe Native literature" (12). The term *postcolonial*, he insists, relies on a linear understanding of time, takes the arrival of the Europeans as its dominant point of reference, and "remains, in the end, a hostage to nationalism" (12), and thus cannot account for indigenous concepts of time, aesthetic standards, and modes of self-identification. In other words, as an academic discipline, postcolonialism more often than not covers over political and historical differences in the name of a global "hybrid, ethnic culture" (Smith). Yet, if, as Diana Brydon argues, postcolonial thinking is "a locally situated . . . attempt to think through the consequences of colonialism" and "to circumvent imperial . . . habits of mind" (10, 11), postcolonial reading practices still perform an interventive act of cultural critique. Provided they heed Len Findlay's provocative exhortation to "always indigenize" (307), postcolonial reading practices help to trace the particular colonial legacies of our global present. Armstrong's novel, I suggest, mediates the complex relationships between imperialist habits of thought, neo-colonialism as globalization, and indigenous "recovery" (Smith).

According to Smith and Findlay, the challenge is to create the conditions of possibility for strategic alliances between non-indigenous postcolonial and indigenous researchers. But what do such alliances involve? With great vision and theoretical rigour—but perhaps with too much optimism, considering the present conservative political climate of the academy—Findlay suggests that such an alliance would produce "innovative, non-appropriative, ethical cross-cultural research, postcolonial institutional ethnographies, and a more just understanding and achievement of the strategic as such" (313).[7] From my perspective, building such an alliance also requires that we examine what Armstrong's protagonist, Penny, calls "globe plotting" (152) in order to shift such dominant paradigms of postcolonial analysis as the nation-state, hybridity, and cultural difference into the field of transnational studies. The term *globe plotting* seems particularly apposite for developing, in Spivak's words, a pedagogy of "transnational literacy" (*Critique* 315), and an indigenous critique of global neo-colonialism. For, "globe plotting" addresses the dispossession of indigenous land through transnational corporations and the NAFTA. It examines the ecological and social ramifications of the restructuring of indigenous land under the guise of development and progress, as well as indigenous resistance to land theft. Simultaneously, it draws attention to the ways in which globalization connives with or "plots" narratives of deliberate social and economic underdevelopment and reinvents itself as the sign and carrier of the good and just society. Read as a new trope of transnationalism, "globe plotting" urges us to ask: What are the strategies of containment or divide and rule that continuously keep indigeneity from the purview of postcolonial critiques of globalization? "In what interest," to quote Spivak again, "are differences [of indigeneity] defined" or concealed (*Critique* 357)? As a pedagogical task, learning to become transnationally literate entails an active participation in "the production of legitimizing cultural" narratives of globalization (*Critique* 340). By staging the ideological contradictions of hybridity in different cultural, political, and communal contexts, Armstrong's novel generates a critique of the legitimizing practices of globalization while articulating narratives and communities of anti-global resistance.

The remainder of my essay, then, examines some of the contradictions of hybridity in greater detail and argues that, in the context of Armstrong's novel, cultural hybridity functions as a postcolonial *pharmakon*.[8] At no point, however, do I wish to promote hybridity as a normative concept of cultural pluralism or of cosmopolitan agency. On the contrary, my discussion problematizes hybridity as an analytical category that mediates between the local and the global through the practices of a "critical localism" (Dirlik 22)[9] and thereby seeks to contribute to the development of a pedagogy of transnational literacy. In particular, I ask how we can read emerging narratives of globalization. For example, what are the tropes through which these narratives "plot" a global imaginary? Furthermore, given that the notion of cultural hybridity has been instrumental in rethinking the field of Canadian literature in postcolonial terms, I ask what kinds of knowledge does cultural hybridity yield if read through indigenous accounts of Western global expansion? In what follows, I first read cultural hybridity, in Homi Bhabha's terms, as "a problematic of colonial representation" (114) with which to probe the representation of indigenous peoples in Canadian media and academic discourses of globalization. In particular, my reading of Paul Knox's *Globe and Mail* article, "On the Right to Remember: The Petanac Massacre," employs cultural hybridity as a discursive reading practice through which to examine the structure of colonial desire that shapes Canada's dominant imaginary. I will then take a closer look at the rhetoric of hybridity and its ideological functions in discourses of biodiversity and the Human Genome Project as they relate to Armstrong's novel. By way of conclusion I discuss two of the novel's recurring tropes of hybridity, namely the metaphors of cancer and "cell memory," and their transformative effects.

Cultural Hybridity: Public Discourse and Colonial Desire

Knox's article was published in the *Globe and Mail*'s Comment section, "Worldbeat," and thereby, in advance, is associated with the rhetoric of cultural syncretism rather than with a radicalized form of multiculturalism that "performs a critique . . . of the limits of . . . civil society" (Spivak, *Critique* 353). The article tells the story of Mateo Pablo, one of 13 survivors of the Petanac massacre perpetrated against indigenous Mayans by the Guatemalan government on 14 July 1982, and its recent documentation in Montreal filmmaker Mary Ellen Davis's film *Haunted Land* (2002). At first reading, the article appears to support the concerns of the survivors of indigenous genocide in Guatemala's 36-year-long civil war, a war that claimed over 200 000 victims. In fact, when Knox writes that the survivors' "right to remember . . . inscribe[s] in our collective memory inconvenient facts and deeds," he supports the collective lawsuit the Petanac survivors filed against General Efrain Rios Montt in June 2001 and submitted to the International Criminal Court (ICC). General Montt was Guatemala's president at the time of the massacre and is now, as Knox mentions, leader of the government faction in Guatemala's congress. The article echoes what the survivors articulate in their "Public Statement" (*Projet Accompagnement*) as "their right to historic memory and . . . to bring dignity and justice to those who have seen their family members massacred" (Knox). But how does the article translate—as I think it does—a highly political undertaking into a "cultural dominant" (Spivak, *Critique* 313) of Canada's nation-state?

At second glance, the article reveals a number of significant gaps. For one, Knox consistently neglects to mention the involvement of the USA in Guatemala's civil war.[10] This kind of elision suggests a double standard of moral judgment when it comes to assigning blame for indigenous genocide. For, while the USA, and by extension Canada, mobilizes for its own "war on terrorism," it conveniently forgets its support of state terrorism in South America for its economic and political gain in the past. Guatemala is only one of many examples. In a similar vein, Knox's reluctance to address US complicity with Guatemala's military junta inadvertently endorses the US's scandalous demand for "immunity from investigation and prosecution for genocide, crimes against humanity, and war crimes in the ICC" (Amnesty International 2). Furthermore, at closer inspection, the article seems concerned less with the rights of indigenous peoples to social justice and redress, than with what I see as a double disavowal of Canada's practices of "internal colonialism" (Tennant 3). First, Knox's binary narrative constructs Canada in opposition to the despotism and corruption of Guatemala's government as a free and democratic nation, which offers "most Canadians" equal "access to their own history." The words "most Canadians," however, suggest, in Bhabha's terms, an instance of "colonialist disavowal" because they reveal a moment of guilty hesitation and textual instability. Through this textual ambiguity we can glimpse both Knox's denial of Canada's perpetual yet constitutive violence enacted against indigenous peoples—the minus, to paraphrase Bhabha's brilliant phrase, at the origin of the nation (160)—and, as a character of Armstrong's novel observes, a political blindness towards

Canada's secret acceptance of Guatemala's government for the sake of American free trade (164).

Interestingly, Knox's denial or act of willful forgetting of Canada's own history of indigenous genocide goes hand in hand with his defense of Mateo Pablo's "right to remember." Knox's call for the "freedom of memory" designates an instance of colonial hybridity because it functions as the "sign of the productivity of colonial power" (Bhabha 112). More specifically, Knox's advocacy of indigenous peoples' right to remember is premised on the invocation of and adherence to the four founding freedoms of Western democracy as they have been articulated by Franklin Roosevelt. For this reason, the "freedom of memory" Knox calls for is a priori embedded in the Preamble to the Human Rights Charter rather than in the *Draft Declaration on the Rights of Indigenous Peoples*. Thus, Knox's article inserts Mateo Pablo's testimony and his position as an indigenous subject into the dominant grammar of Western democracy. The unwitting ruse of Knox's narrative is twofold. First, it conceals that, in the words of Maria, a Guatemalan activist in Armstrong's novel, democracy functions as an alibi of global development politics and as a means "to further dispossess the desperate" (148). Second, it consists in what Bhabha sees as the "strategic reversal of the process of domination through disavowal," which "secure[s]" "the . . . authority" of Western democracy as globalism's political dominant (112). In Knox's case, championing a global cause of indigenous justice occasions the promotion of Western democracy, regardless of its colonial legacies.

Read through Bhabha's notion of hybridity, Knox's article reveals its own hidden marks of colonial desire. For, in his narrative of indigenous rights, the indigenous subject acts as Canada's moral conscience and serves to establish and legitimize Canada's political claims to global citizenship. It is at this juncture of the national and the global that my reading of Knox's article becomes an exercise in transnational literacy. For, while Knox's article emerges as one of Canada's new and populist narratives of global citizenship, it can do so only by perpetuating what Jack Healy aptly defines as a pervasive colonial "habit of power," a missionary "habit of mind" (73) that Europeans have adopted to legitimize their subjugation of the indigenous peoples of the Americas and Australia since the Renaissance. In the context of Canadian history, this way of enacting power, Healy argues, "established the text of Amerindian-European relations as religious, theological, and ethical. The frame within which an Indian subject would emerge would often be a moral one" (77). Similarly, in Knox's text Pablo Mateo becomes visible as a moral subject. More precisely, as in the history of colonialism, Knox's uncritical humanism works in self-consolidating ways. It seeks out the encounter with the "indigenous Other" as an ethical but not political subject to be saved and reformed in the name of democracy. In this way the article domesticates Mateo Pablo's political struggle, inserts it into a dominant culturalist vision of global justice, and, to adapt Armstrong's term, re-plots Mateo Pablo's story as an "inscape" (Healy 76) into Canada's emerging global imaginary. Read as a lesson in "transnational literacy," then, the article teaches us that in the technologies of colonial desire and disavowal, "[e]very declared rupture is an undeclared repetition" (Spivak, *Critique* 333).[11]

My reading of Knox's text, then, raises the question as to what extent theories of hybridity can produce accounts of "global plotting." In his influential critique of cultural hybridity, Pheng Cheah argues that Bhabha's notion of hybridity is no more than a "closet idealism" (302) and is unable to engender critical explanations of globalization's uneven economic effects. With their "antilocalist" tendencies (297), hybridity theories "reduce" the "material realities" of globalization to "its symbolic dimension" (302). Contrary to Bhabha, Cheah argues that, despite its many problems, the nation-state needs to be acknowledged as "both historically unavoidable and ethically imperative" to counter the polarizing effects of globalization (300). Although Cheah is right to argue that cultural hybridity cannot account for the complexity of postcolonial agency, his wholesale dismissal of the concept also undermines a still urgently needed analysis of the technologies of colonial desire in current political and cultural discourses of globalization. But more importantly, Cheah's renewed faith in the nation-state ignores that, in Spivak's words, the "failure of a civil society" in both the postcolonial and the Western nation-state "is now a global situation" ("Diasporas" 91). To a considerable degree, this failure consists of the exclusion of indigenous concerns and rights from the theoretical discourses of re-imagining the nation through linked global and local social and economic relationships.

In contrast to Cheah, Armstrong invites a reading of hybridity as an analytical frame of colonial desire. At an early stage of both the novel and Penny's developing political consciousness, she and her White friend Julie meet a group of male political science students who, along with their professor, ponder their professional careers as members of the educated

White middle class. Having little sympathy with the self-centred lamentations of her peers, Julie confronts them with a future of global impoverishment, rising local unemployment, and "government deficits" (64), while exposing the sexist behaviour of their professor. But Julie's stance as a feminist with an awareness of global politics is, in part, purchased at the price of Penny's voice. When, in spite of Julie's repeated invitation, Penny refuses to participate in the debate, Julie calls to the male students: "Hey you guys, did you know Penny's an Indian? . . . She's a legend. . . . She's absolutely irreverent to the status-quo. Are you an anarchist Penny?" (67). Like Knox's self-consolidating practice of Othering, Julie's colonial disavowal is expressed in her desire to turn Penny into an exotic subject of cultural difference. In fact, by addressing Penny at once as "an Indian," "a legend," and "an anarchist," she revamps the colonial stereotype of the noble savage to authorize her own political agency. Moreover, Julie's attempt to incorporate Penny into a universalized model of political liberation constructs Penny as a generic "Third World Woman" (Mohanty) and romanticizes her as "woman-native-other" (Trinh). Through Julie's interpellation, Penny emerges as a monolithic subject whose native status becomes the guarantor of truth and authenticity in the service of Julie's "radical" feminist politics. Despite her courage and later solidarity and continued friendship with Penny, Julie unwittingly reduces Penny to an allegory of her own political desire and thereby not only instrumentalizes Penny but signifies what Inderpal Grewal and Caren Kaplan call the "cultural imperialism" of "global feminism" (17).

As I have argued in this section, hybridity needs to be understood as an interventive practice into the operations of White colonial desire if it is to maintain its critical purchase. The next section investigates the instrumental and destabilizing function of indigenous peoples in the production of legitimizing narratives of neo-colonial globalism and proposes a critique of hybridity as a normalizing rhetoric of biodiversity.

"Global Plottings" of the Indigenous: Biodiversity and Genetic Mapping

The second epigraph of this essay is an excerpt from Rigoberta Menchú's *Crossing Borders*, a collection of essays that documents her global campaign for the recognition of indigenous peoples and their rights on an international level. As Penny's partner, David, remarks, "[n]ot a single seat in the United Nations from the western hemisphere is an Indigenous Nation" (*Whispering* 147). In contrast to Cheah, Menchú insists on thinking about human and indigenous rights through a global rather than a national perspective. Because, on the one hand, she maintains that indigenous people "don't appear as specific peoples in the Universal Declaration of Human Rights" and therefore neither occupy a legally enshrined position in most national constitutions nor have any rights in an international court of law (144). On the other hand, she advocates the protection of the social and political autonomy of those who are at the receiving end of globalization, who are, to a large extent but not exclusively, the indigenous peoples of the world. Yet, Menchú's work is frequently hampered by the UN's lack of a serious commitment to social justice for indigenous peoples. For similar reasons, Penny considers The International Year for the World's Indigenous People (1993) as declared by the UN a "damn farce" (184). Despite the seemingly coincidental nature of the thematic contingency between Menchú's and Armstrong's texts, the links between both writers become less arbitrary once we consider how the testimonial writing practices of Menchú's famous autobiographical narrative, *I, Rigoberta Menchú*, inform the generically hybrid narrative form of Armstrong's novel. Moreover, both writers address and condemn the ways in which transnational corporations are indirectly and directly responsible for the recurrence of old diseases and the emergence of new diseases. After all, Penny's cancer and the death of Menchú's friend Maria are caused by pesticide poisoning contracted through spraying apples in Penny's case and spraying cotton in Maria's.[12]

Furthermore, as political activists working on a national and international level, Penny and Menchú participate, however unwillingly, in the structures of oppression they seek to dismantle. For example, as a UN delegate, Menchú must work within the framework of the Human Rights Declaration yet knows that "the issue of human rights—connected with their systematic violation, with cholera, with AIDS, or with political repression—is often used as an excuse for not tackling the global issue of a people's economic, social and political rights" (*Crossing* 138). Here, Menchú insists that the battle against violations of human rights comes at the cost of a deliberate political blindness towards the violation of basic human rights and the systemic poverty suffered by those who live under the rule of multinational capital. Second, her words sound a warning to all political fetishists of authenticity because in order "for the victims of the world's problems to gain entrance" into "the world's main problem-solving body" (*Crossing* 138), they must work within the ideological framework and administrative structures of the UN. Political change, or what, in a different context, Edward Said calls the "*voyage in*" (244), takes place in an at once hybrid and limited framework of cultural negotiations. This perhaps also accounts for Penny's "deep and silent rage . . . [a] rage for all that she is somehow complicit in" (184). Menchú's political critique, then, points to the predicament of the indigenous subject in a transnational world.

After having told her interlocutor, the anthropologist Elisabeth Burgos-Debray, her life-story, Menchú ends her account with a rhetorical flourish, reminding the reader that although she "travelled to many places . . . to talk about [her] people," she is "still keeping [her] Indian identity a secret" (*I, Rigoberta* 247). As a resisting indigenous subject, Menchú situates herself on the cusp of three converging positions: a global and necessarily heterogeneous position; a communal position that refuses absolute transparency to guard against cultural appropriation; and a personal position that makes her both an outsider and insider to her people.[13] A negotiation of these shifting positions through different forms of learning also lies at the heart of Armstrong's novel. Like Menchú, Penny travels around the Americas to talk about the Okanagan people and learn about the plight of other indigenous peoples. She participates in many international conferences on indigenous rights and discovers that "the stories [of speakers from different communities around the globe] mesh and overlap as one story. . . . Millions of brown people, despised, abused, hungry, landless, reduced to slave-like labour. Disease and death" (148). From different perspectives, all of these stories deal with the "plotting" of the globe through, in Armstrong's words, a common experience and "perspective toward colonialism and [its] contemporary issues" (Interview 137). While Armstrong certainly concurs with Spivak's notion of a "kinship in exploitation" (*Critique* 380), she also insists on establishing particular narratives of indigenous exploitation. Through these narratives, she argues, indigenous writers not only establish and communicate different experiences of colonialism to each other, but they also resist the colonizers' identification and representation of indigenous peoples.[14]

In Armstrong's novel, these narratives of exploitation and resistance examine the changes particular indigenous communities experience through the local effects of globalization. On a fact-finding mission to Chiapas, Penny realizes that the plight of the Mayan people is an effect of war, neo-colonial global restructuring, and the collaboration of Mexico's *comprador* government. Readers who are familiar with Leslie Marmon Silko's *Almanac of the Dead*—a novel that relates to Armstrong's novel in numerous ways—recognize that Penny witnesses, according to a descendant of the Maya, a character in Silko's novel, "[t]he time called 'Death-Eye Dog'" or "'The Reign of Fire-Eye Macaw'" (257). Both phrases refer to the ecological and human catastrophes that followed in the wake of the European invasion of the Americas and mark the "radicalising of modernity" Anthony Giddens calls globalization (*Consequences* 52). As Emilio tells Penny, since the NAFTA, the "Mayan cooperatives" have been squeezed out of the "market" and suffered "severe economic hardships." In old colonial fashion, the NAFTA first makes sure that Mayan lands are no longer protected under Mexican law and then gradually "force[s coffee and textile co-ops] to sell their land cheap" (168). As a corollary, the local autonomy of indigenous populations is, in Roland Robertson's terms, "globally instituted" (172). The dialectical but unequal relationship between the global and the local has turned McLuhan's utopia of the "global village" into permanent "global pillage" (Giddens, *Runaway* 64).

Through structural adjustment programs, the former Mayan collective landowners become landless labourers for a ruthless "tributary system" that ensures, in Spivak's and Samir Amin's Marxist analysis, the feudalization of global social and economic relationships in the interest of the "financialization of the globe" (*Critique* 95). Similar to Amin and Spivak, Penny diagnoses the global expansion of capitalism as a systemic form of social and economic violence inherent in development. The "global system," she argues, "relies on the violence of poverty itself as a way to insure [*sic*] commerce continues and expands. It squashes people who are at the lowest of income levels" (189). For this reason, globalization erodes the classical division between economic centres and peripheries, a phenomenon Penny observes on her journey through the poverty-stricken areas of Los Angeles. Globalization no longer polarizes along the lines of colonially established geographies. Instead, as Amin, along with other critics of development, contends, "[u]nderdevelopment is . . . the effect of the logic of accumulation [of capital] on a world scale. The law of accumulation and pauperization operate on this scale and not in the centers treated artificially in isolation" (64). Polarization, then, depends on the flows and blockages of capital and the continuation of global dependency of the postcolonial nation-state. In a cogent article on the communal identity of the Okanagan people in the age of "world economic disorder," Armstrong shifts Amin's argument into an indigenous context. "Indigenous people," she writes, "do not survive well in this atmosphere of aggression and dispassion," where "[w]ar itself becomes continuous as dispossession, privatization of lands, and exploitation of resources and a cheap labor force become the mission of 'peacekeeping.' The goal of finding new markets is the justification for the westernization of 'undeveloped' cultures" ("Sharing" 467). The subtlety of Armstrong's argument lies in its refusal to reduce the forces of globalization to the intrinsic operations of capitalism. What she advocates is both a clearer understanding of media-generated global cultures of emotional poverty and a skepticism towards an easy formation of global citizenship. Thus, given the state's obligation to transnational agencies in the service of global market development, indigenous rights movements can neither rely on the nation-state as a political ally nor depend on dominant NGOs. On the contrary, as Menchú and Smith emphasize, in "a self-determining indigenous world," "nation states [may not] remain . . . effective political ways of organizing polities" (115). Instead, various alliances of "globally based" collaborative "interest groups suggest a possible space for indigenous peoples" (Smith 115).

The most devastating effect of the dispossession of indigenous land, however, is, according to Penny, the simultaneous destruction of "the only hope for protecting biodiversity" and "natural sustainability" (147). Without indigenous land control, transnational biotechnology and pharmaceutical industries can engage freely in bio-prospecting of indigenous genetic materials, cell lines, and resources of knowledge. Rather than going into the politics of bio-piracy, I am interested in the rhetoric of what is clearly a new global phase of older forms of ecological imperialism. In her provocative article "Indigenous Nations and the Human Genome Diversity Project," Sandra S. Awang outlines the stated goals of the project, one of which is to "preserve DNA cell lines of indigenous populations before these populations and/or their cell lines become extinct . . . through intercultural marriage" (123). In this example, the term "biodiversity" acts as a rhetorical cloak for a neo-colonial investment in old racial categories of genetic purity and racial degeneration through hybridization. The rhetoric of the architects of the Human Genome Diversity Project (HGDP), Professors Luigi Luca Cavalli-Sforza and Allan Wilson, conjures the image of the "vanishing" and disintegrating "Indian" that characterizes, to put it mildly, the assimilationist ideology of, for example, Duncan Campbell Scott's "Onondaga Madonna." In the HGDP debate, hybridity acts as a biological determinant and presents one of the two binary poles of the colonial debate over racial authenticity. As with earlier colonial discourses on authenticity, biodiversity is premised, as Patricia Monture-Angus argues, on "the existence of colonizers and those that are colonized. That is a relation of power" (28). Under the pretext of scientific progress, the HGDP has produced a "life industry" (Awang) that exploits indigenous bio-capital in ways reminiscent of the racial objectives of the eugenics movement of the Third Reich. This legacy, I think, demonstrates in the most radical form globalization's indebtedness to the project of modernity and its perversions.

Of course, proponents of the HGDP not only deny that the project "will benefit financially" from possible "commercial products" that result from their work (Cavalli-Sforza 4), but they also object to comparisons of their enterprise with any form of racist selection program that leads to genocide. Penny's comments on bio-piracy and her outrage about "collecting gene samples from unsuspecting Indigenous people . . . [or] from tribes going extinct . . . because there's big money to be made" (223) Cavalli-Sforza is likely to equate with the language of "science haters" who mix "ignorance" with their "personal political agenda" (7). Indeed, Cavalli-Sforza contends that a central goal of the project is to battle racism, for mapping the human genome shows that although "individual humans are genetically quite diverse . . . [,] the average differences among human groups are small" (6). For this reason, he proposes to "replace the common word 'race'" with the term "population" (6). The politically sanitizing effects of Cavalli-Sforza's proposal, not to mention its historical naïveté and its ignorance of the research undertaken by critical race theorists, I think, is self-evident. What is stunning, however, is Cavalli-Sforza's belief in the explanatory rather than potentially destructive power of genetics when confronted with cultural and anthropological questions.

It is precisely this blindness that defines what Donna Haraway calls "gene fetishism" (116). In her article "Deanimations: Maps and Portraits of Life Itself," Haraway discusses the ways in which scientists construct the gene as the new transcendental signifier of Western progress in the discourse of "contemporary technoscience," including the HGDP (112).[15] The gene, she forcefully argues, has been advanced to the Kantian "thing-in-itself where no trope can be admitted" (113). Similar to eighteenth-century empiricists, today's geneticists believe that science must and does occupy a space beyond metaphor and representation. Positioned outside the "economy of troping," the gene operates, as Haraway aptly argues, as the new, high-tech commodity fetish (113). In other words, in the context of the HGDP, biodiversity, and bio-prospecting, "genes are sources of 'value'" (113) and, through a considerable amount of ideological work, reified and prepared for the global market. But, as we have learned from Marx, reification is but an ideological ruse that conceals the labour, human interaction, and production that goes into the making of a commodity. According to Haraway, then, "gene fetishism rests on the denial of all the natural-social articulation and agentic relationships . . . that bring 'genes' into material-semiotic being" (116) and requires the "fetishist['s] [such as Cavalli-Sforza's] constitutional inability to recognize the trope that denies its own status as figure" (115). Thus, along with Armstrong's novel, we need to ask, what kind of knowledge does the symbolic language of the HGDP produce, and what does it deny? What is the project's cultural logic?

The dominant rhetoric of the HGDP draws from "new-world imagery" (Haraway 129) and metaphors of mapping that all promise the discovery of new frontiers of technological invention and exploration. Rather than acknowledging that maps produce the reality they purport to represent, the cartographers of the human genome insist that their maps objectively chart the reality of the genes themselves without being encumbered by metaphor. But like older colonial cartographic practices, mapping the human genome is primarily directed at claiming and controlling indigenous space and territory. In the present context, the space to be mapped is the indigenous body. In fact, mapping and sequencing the body "spatializ[es]" and "enclos[es]" the body for scientific purposes (Haraway 115, 120). The logic of colonial and genetic cartographies clearly intersect in that they both rely on a practice of consecutively surveying, naming, categorizing, claiming, and controlling the indigenous body/land as a quarry for precious DNA strings and the symbolic means to articulate the emergence of the "Global Native" (Haraway 130). In her ingenious discussion of a New England BioLabs advertisement for "Mapping the Human Genome," Haraway demystifies the epistemological violence through which the HGDP operates. The advertisement depicts an indigenous woman whose naked body is wrapped in a transparent facsimile of what looks like a nineteenth-century colonial map of the world. She "embodies," as Haraway points out, "the Global Gene, literally" (130). Thus the HGDP erases indigenous particularity in the name of a universally shared human genome. Under the guise of scientific objectivity and genetic authenticity, the HGDP simultaneously aestheticizes and sexualizes the indigenous body, while participating in what might be called genetic necrophilia, namely the mining of DNA from extinct indigenous peoples or from those who are on the verge of extinction (Armstrong, *Whispering* 238). The indigenous body once again serves as the object rather than subject of new Western master-narratives of technological development and the origin of life, regardless of how much these narratives violate indigenous integrity, autonomy, and belief systems. Subsequently, as David rightly contends, "breaking the illusion of western development and progress as a world order is critical to changing it" (189–90).

What is at stake in such programs as the HGDP is perhaps not the revival of Mengele-style eugenics. Instead, the HGDP perpetuates the logic of cultural authenticity as an ideology of marketable difference; encourages quick fixes for environmental disease; strives for complete cultural and genetic transparency; and increasingly depoliticizes the structures of indigenous exploitation and resistance. The shift of modern biotechnology from examining such external causes for diseases as chemical toxins, environmental pollution, and widespread poverty, towards internal, genetic explanations of old and new diseases puts the blame for such diseases on their victims and forestalls a debate over political accountability. Moreover, as Penny ceaselessly argues, in the discourse of biodiversity, indigenous peoples find themselves in a predicament because as the objects of bio-prospecting, they are its victims, but since they are all that stands between "the untouched land" left to them and its transformation into global real estate, they are also "the only hope for protecting biodiversity" (147). The protection of biodiversity involves both the development of "direct sustainable support" for "local Indigenous communities" (*Whispering* 223) and the ability to decipher the rhetorical logic of the HGDP and its commodification of the indigenous subject for the sake of gene fetishism. As should be clear by now, the HGDP is not interested in genuine diversity. Instead, it instrumentalizes the human body and tends to "mistak[e] heterogeneous relationality for a fixed, seemingly objective thing [the human genome]" (Haraway 116). Yet, against its own desire for purity, it cannot keep metaphor at bay and thus confirms that it is in part about "inhabiting" narratives of life and disavowal (117) that are always already hybrid, always contaminated by metaphor.

Narrative Plottings: Metaphors of Global Disease and Local Recovery

In Armstrong's novel, as everywhere else, metaphors have an ambiguous status. In a discussion of *Star Trek*, Julie ridicules Penny's interpretation of the show's organizing metaphors: "Metaphor, smetaphor! . . . There is always a boss in command." "But," answers Penny, "that's what a metaphor is!" (77). Here, metaphor functions as a master trope that imposes and homogenizes identities through operations of resemblance and substitution. At the same time, the overdetermined and self-deconstructive tendencies of metaphor force knowledge and truth claims into a productive crisis. But more importantly, in the context of Armstrong's writing and language, metaphor is a means of communication, memory, and cultural survival because, as she explains it, "[the Okanagan's] character, our world view, the relationship we have to each other as a people, our humanness towards the world and how we relate to the spiritual is wrapped up in the metaphors we use" ("Words" 26–27). The central metaphors of *Whispering in Shadows*, however, are not readily identifiable as culturally particular metaphors. Nor do they act in conventional ways through substitution. Instead, Armstrong's metaphors of cancer and "cell memory" enact different experiences of globalization while generating a critique and counter-narrative of neo-ecological imperialism. They literally reshape Penny's body and mediate her changing perception of her environment on a global, communal, and individual level.

When she is diagnosed with a rare form of cancer that "show[s] up in people exposed to strong pesticides and some gulf war veterans" (254), Penny locates its causes not in a genetic predisposition to cancer but in the environmental pollution and technological alterations wrought on the planet through the pressures of neo-colonial globalization. If, as Penny contemplates, the body is itself a "natural environment" (84) that symptomatically registers the violence done to it through ideologies of progress and development, then cancer becomes a direct inscription of this violence on the human body. Both drug addiction and cancer can be interpreted as diseases resulting from ecological imperialism. It is therefore not surprising and perhaps not at all metaphorical when the novel's implied narrator describes Penny's disease as "the shadows of the new world" she carries "inside her body" (276). Metaphorically, Penny's cancer embodies what Susan Sontag, in "Illness as Metaphor," defines as the disease's primary discursive characteristics. More precisely, according to Sontag, cancer signifies a "pathology of space" and a "disease of the body" (14, 18), insofar as the body constitutes an integral and living organism of the planet as a whole. As Armstrong explains in a number of essays and interviews, the relationship between land, place, body, earth, and healthy living provides the core element of the Okanagan worldview. In the Okanagan community, Armstrong elaborates, "the flesh that is our body is pieces of the land come to us through the things that the land is . . . We are our land/place. Not to know and to celebrate this is to be without language and without land. It is to be dis-placed" ("'Sharing'" 465–66). Penny's cancer, then, is not merely a symptom of the violated environment written on her body but a physical manifestation of the disintegration and dis-placement of indigenous life, both under the rules of global capital and in a cultural and emotional atmosphere of "destructive disquiet . . . [and] discontent" (*Whispering* 274).

Furthermore, Armstrong adopts the metaphorical language of cancer to expose the human effects of globalization. In a self-reflexive passage of the novel entitled "Prose Fragment From Her Note Book," Penny enters a string of sentence fragments that could be both part of the poem on globalization or non-fiction: "globalization and supremacy deceit and grudging paternalism sys/tematized racism colonial practice . . . I THINK IT'S PART OF THE STORY/ OR THE PLOT/ A piece here and a piece there" (185). The fragmented and boundless structure of this passage enacts the uncontrolled growth and erratic spread of cancer cells to foreground the disruptive, divisive, and chaotic effects of globalization. While Armstrong's metaphorical use of disease corresponds to Sontag's comparison of cancer with the operations of "advanced capitalism" (63), it also questions predominantly individualist and psychosomatic explanations of cancer. Instead, cancer features as a sickness that signals a lack of communal and "environmental consciousness" (*Whispering* 245), so that the humans themselves have become the cancer that invades and modifies the environment. As a result, the "natural order in this world . . . is out of balance" and is turning upon itself, generating transformations of which cancer is only one manifestation. However, instead of arguing that "corporations [and] money mongers . . . are responsible" for the mutation of the environment, Penny suggests that cancer may also be considered as the body's "way [of] transform[ing], cop[ing] with things confronting it," and, paradoxically, of mutating into a new state of balance.

What is needed to ensure indigenous survival is a recovery of what Penny calls "cell memory," for the multi-layered and ever-expanding constitution of "cell memory" unites different indigenous rather than national imaginaries and provides a counter-narrative to the commodification of biodiversity. In one of her prose poems, Penny writes that

> we are bound together by old blood mixed and remixed over time as we feel its memory stir . . . words pass between the North and the South . . . on their old movement through eons to warm lands which our blood together claims that which our cell memories celebrate each time we dance to this rhythm we all know so well. (289)

In this context, "cell memory" suggests a hybrid and globally connected form of memory and community, Penny's "rainbow" (272). It lives in the recognition of the sound of an unknown yet familiar language (181), and shapes the relationship between the land, the body, the community, and the individual. It also inhabits, produces, and cites metaphors of language, specifically those that are related to the poem "frogs singing" (111, 191), which I discussed at the beginning of this essay. Cell memories, Penny writes, are also strong in "Coyote stories about the . . . transformation of the world" (247), where they provide one version of indigenous globe plotting.

It seems to me that the presence of Coyote also indicates the ideological but necessary risks that reside in an at once culturally specific and biologically defined notion of memory and identity. Put differently, "cell memory" might be understood as a fundamentally hybrid form of memory. This is not to deny that hybridity, as I argued earlier, operates as a normalizing rhetoric of biologistic discourses of race. Rather, "cell memory" is organized around an understanding of hybridity that both refuses to move, in Robert Young's terms, from "biologism and scientism to the [deceptive] safety of culturalism" and "shows the connections between the racial categories of the past and contemporary cultural discourse" (27). It is this double inscription that also underpins Neal McLeod's recent indigenous reconceptualization of hybridity as a variation of Gerald Vizenor's "Trickster hermeneutics," which adopts "elements of the colonial presence and transform[s] them to subvert them" (25). In McLeod's trickster account and Armstrong's related narrative of cell memory, hybridity is intrinsic to an understanding of "culture [as] a living organism" and to the metaphorical and tropological configuration of "tribal narratives and paradigms" (McLeod 33, 31). As a corollary, Penny recovers her understanding of cell memory through the cancerous disintegration of her own cells that ultimately facilitates Penny's reconnection with her land and family after years of travelling and political activism across the Americas. In contrast to the metaphorical language of cancer and gene fetishism, the language of cell memory emphasizes the essential heterogeneity of human existence and co-operation, and the inseparability of language, body, and environment. In this way, Armstrong's novel teaches us that becoming transnationally literate involves outlining the limits of the theoretical models through which we—theorists, critics, students, and teachers—interpret texts and our global present. It requires rigorous analyses of occluded narratives and emerging tropes and metaphors of globalization. It is this commitment to a political and literary critique of the cultural, social, and eco-biological effects of globalization in a specifically but not exclusively indigenous context that Armstrong's novel invites its readers to make.

ACKNOWEDGEMENTS

I would like to thank the SSHRC for its generous support of my current research project of which the present essay is a substantial part.

NOTES

1. The original poem is published in Johnson's *Flint and Feather.*
2. "Frogs singing" was first published in *Durable Breath* (Smelcer and Birchfield). It is reprinted in Armstrong's essay "Land Speaking."
3. In "Land Speaking," Armstrong describes "frogs singing" as a poem that resulted from "a long discussion on our language and worldview with my sister Delphine, who . . . pointed out that the stars and the frogs in the Okanagan summer nights have the same rhythm." In recalling it, "the rhythm filled her soul and became hers" (189). Thus the poem creates a unity between land, body, and language that is also crucial to Penny's quest for social justice and communal and personal survival.
4. Lee Maracle, for example, praises Pauline Johnson's "translations of old stories [*Legends of Vancouver*]" for their faithfulness to the "voice of Capilano. . . . She was true to his voice, the beautiful language that he used in English. I also wanted to do it that way" (171).
5. I here refer to the Songhees of the Salish First Nation in BC and the Chippewas in London, ON.
6. The concept of commodity fetishism has of course been paramount to both Fredric Jameson's discussion of the "cultural logic of late capitalism" and postcolonial theories of colonial identity and desire. For example, see Ahmad, Bhabha, and Huggan. My reading of Smith's critique of hybridity is indebted to the work of all of these theorists.
7. Although I couldn't agree more with Findlay's warning that within a collaborative situation, outsider theorizing about indigenous concerns "must be respectfully strategic rather than presumptuously exotic" (313), I am worried that such collaborations still risk reproducing imperial patterns of behaviour and thinking. An example of a failed joint project that comes to mind is Maria Campbell's and Linda Griffiths's collaboration on *The Book of Jessica*. But more importantly, the research alliances Findlay envisions would still be based in academic institutions that, to my mind, are still concerned with reproducing Eurocentric discourses of knowledge and power production. Before it becomes possible to speak of the "Postcolonial Canadian University," we need to rethink what *postcolonial* means in transnational terms. On an institutional level, academic departments of the humanities must do more than pay lip service to interdisciplinary studies, be more successful in hiring First Nations faculty, and use the term *postcolonial* in more responsible ways than just as an umbrella term for an unspecified notion of cultural studies across the periods.
8. I use the term *pharmakon* in the way Derrida discusses it in his essay

"Plato's Pharmacy." In its Greek translation, "this *pharmakon*, this 'medicine,' this philter, which acts as both remedy and poison, already introduces itself into the body of the discourse with all its ambivalence" (*Dissemination* 70). The notion of the *pharmakon* also works as a concept-metaphor to describe the historical and political over-determination of hybridity. Rather than defining hybridity in one particular way, the notion of the *pharmakon* allows us to fold the multiple and contradicting dimensions of hybridity into such different contexts of critical analysis as scientific racism, colonial discourse analysis, and biotechnology.

9. "Critical localism" considers the local as a site through which "to work out the most fundamental contradictions" of globalization (Dirlik 23), while acknowledging the impossibility of de-linking the local from the global.

10. For an overview of the decade between 1980 and 1990 of Guatemala's civil war, the period that saw most of the 669 massacres committed against Mayan villages, see Diskin and Warren.

11. In this context Mayan anthropologist Victor D. Montejo's observations concerning "a group of testimonies collected in the Mayan language" are elucidating: "The Mayan survivors' descriptions of the torture that has taken place in military barracks are parallel to the cases of torture and dismemberment denounced by las Casas. The comparisons show that five centuries after the first contact, the same crimes continue to be committed against indigenous populations of the Americas" (211), including, one might add, those enacted against indigenous peoples living within Canada's national borders.

12. See chapter 13 in *I, Rigoberta Menchú*.

13. For a discussion of Menchú's multiple subject positions see Susan Sánchez-Casal.

14. In an interview with Hartwig Isernhagen, Armstrong elaborates upon this point:

> And we found the commonalities there to be surprising: . . . they were the same battles, principally, that we were fighting to bring ourselves, as writers and as people who are carriers of their own literatures, forward through colonialism. [We were] fighting for that space to identify what those literatures are and how those literatures emerged and not to try to emulate the literatures of the people who were the colonizers, and to try to find the difference between the two and to try to state that difference to each other. (137)

15. Cavalli-Sforza emphasizes that the HGDP is not a Western project but an "international anthropology project that seeks to study the genetic richness of the entire human species" that "make[s] the involvement of UNESCO and other international organizations particularly appropriate" (1). Yet, given that "some countries will not, in the foreseeable future, acquire the "'cutting edge' technol-

ogy" that is needed for the mapping and sequencing of the HGDP" (2), it is clear that those who possess this kind of technology (i.e., the US, Europe, and Japan) will be at the forefront of the project. Other countries may act as secretarial handmaidens, "collecting and typing . . . samples from their own region" (2). Ultimately, those poorer countries and indigenous nations that cannot afford Western "'cutting edge' technology" can be usefully enlisted "for spreading the new biotechnology knowledge and methods around the world" (5). In short, the HGDP is prone to serve future development programs regardless of the effects biotechnological knowledge may have on the targeted population.

WORKS CITED

Ahmad, Aijaz. *In Theory: Classes, Nations, Literatures*. London: Verso, 1992.

Amin, Samir. *Re-Reading the Postwar Period: An Intellectual Itinerary*. New York: Monthly Review, 1994.

Amnesty International. "News Release: International Criminal Court: Immunity for Peace-Keepers Is a Set Back for International Justice." 15 July 2002. Amnesty International. 18 July 2002. <http://www.amnesty-usa.org/news/2002/world07152002.html>.

Armstrong, Jeannette. Interview. *Momaday, Vizenor, Armstrong: Conversations on American Indian Writing*. Ed. Hartwig Isernhagen. Norman: U of Oklahoma P, 1999. 135–83.

———. "Land Speaking." *Speaking for the Generations: Native Writers on Writing*. Ed. Simon J. Ortiz. Tucson: U of Arizona P, 1998. 174–94.

———. "'Sharing One Skin': Okanagan Community." *The Case against the Global Economy: And for a Turn Toward the Local*. Ed. Jerry Mander and Edward Goldsmith. San Francisco: Sierra Club, 1996. 460–70.

———. *Whispering in Shadows*. Penticton: Theytus, 2000.

———. "Words." *Telling It: Women and Language across Cultures*. Ed. The Telling It Book Collective. Vancouver: Press Gang, 1990. 23–29.

Awang, Sandra S. "Indigenous Nations and the Human Genome Diversity Project." *Indigenous Knowledges in Global Contexts: Multiple Readings of Our World*. Ed. George J. Sefa Dei, et al. Toronto: U of Toronto P, 2000. 120–36.

Bauman, Zygmunt. *Globalization: The Human Consequences*. New York: Columbia UP, 1998.

Bhabha, Homi. *The Location of Culture*. London: Routledge, 1994.

Brydon, Diana. "Introduction: Reading Postcoloniality, Reading Canada." *Essays on Canadian Writing* 56 (1995): 1–19.

Cavalli-Sforza, Luigi Luca. "The Human Genome Diversity Project." Speech presented at UNESCO, International Bioethics Committee, Proceedings, Session 2, Report from Mrs Lenoir. 1995. UNESCO. 1 Aug. 2002. <http://mirror.eschina.bnu.edu.cn/Mirror2/unesco/www.unesco.org/ibc/en/actes/s2/cavalli.html>.

Cheah, Pheng. "Given Culture: Rethinking Cosmopolitical Freedom in Transnationalism." *Cosmopolitics: Thinking and Feeling Beyond the Nation.* Ed. Pheng Cheah and Bruce Robbins. Minneapolis: U of Minnesota P, 1998. 290–328.

Derrida, Jacques. *Dissemination.* Trans. Barbara Johnson. Chicago: U of Chicago P, 1981.

Dirlik, Arif. "The Global in the Local." *Global/Local: Cultural Production and the Transnational Imaginary.* Ed. Rob Wilson and Wimal Dissanayake. Durham: Duke UP, 1996. 21–45.

Diskin, Martin, ed. *Trouble in Our Backyard: Central America and the United States in the Eighties.* New York: Pantheon, 1983.

Findlay, Len. "Always Indigenize!: The Radical Humanities in the Postcolonial Canadian University." *ARIEL* 31.1 (2000): 307–26.

Giddens, Anthony. *The Consequences of Modernity.* Stanford: Stanford UP, 1990.

———. *Runaway World: How Globalization Is Reshaping Our Lives.* London: Routledge, 2000.

Goldie, Terry. *Fear and Temptation: The Image of the Indigene in Canadian, Australian, and New Zealand Literature.* Montreal: McGill-Queens UP, 1989.

Grewal, Inderpal, and Caren Kaplan, eds. "Introduction: Transnational Feminist Practices and Questions of Postmodernity." *Scattered Hegemonies: Postmodernity and Transnational Feminist Practices.* Minneapolis: U of Minnesota P, 1994. 1–33.

Griffiths, Linda, and Maria Campbell. *The Book of Jessica: A Theatrical Transformation.* Toronto: Playwrights Canada, 1989.

Haraway, Donna. "Deanimations: Maps and Portraits of Life Itself." *Hybridity and Its Discontents: Politics, Science, Culture.* Ed. Avtar Brah and Annie E. Coombes. London: Routledge, 2000. 111–36.

Haunted Land. Dir. Mary Ellen Davis. Productions B'Alba, Montreal, 2002.

Healy, Jack J. "Literature, Power and the Refusals of Big Bear: Reflections on the Treatment of the Indian and of the Aborigine." *Australian/Canadian Literatures in English: Comparative Perspectives.* Ed. Russell McDougall and Gillian Whitlock. Melbourne: Methuen, 1987. 68–93.

Huggan, Graham. *The Postcolonial Exotic: Marketing the Margins.* London: Routledge, 2001.

Johnson, Pauline. *Flint and Feather: Collected Verse*. Intro. by Theodore Watts-Dunton. Toronto: Musson Book Co, 1916.

King, Thomas. "Godzilla vs. Post-Colonial." *World Literature Written in English* 30.2 (1990): 10–16.

Knox, Paul. "On the Right to Remember: The Petanac Massacre." *Globe and Mail* 29 Mar. 2002: A13.

Mackey, Nathaniel. *Discrepant Engagement: Dissonance, Cross-Culturality, and Experimental Writing*. New York: Cambridge UP, 1993.

Maracle, Lee. "Lee Maracle." *Contemporary Challenges: Conversations with Canadian Native Authors*. Saskatoon: Fifth House, 1991. 169–79.

McLeod, Neal. "Coming Home through Stories." *(Ad)dressing Our Words: Aboriginal Perspectives on Aboriginal Literatures*. Ed. Armand Garnet Ruffo. Penticton: Theytus, 2001. 17–36.

Menchú, Rigoberta. *Crossing Borders*. Trans. Ann Wright. London: Verso, 1998.

———. *I, Rigoberta Menchú: An Indian Woman in Guatemala*. Ed. and intro. Elisabeth Burgos-Debray. Trans. Ann Wright. London: Verso, 1984.

Mohanty, Chandra T. "Under Western Eyes: Feminist Scholarship and Colonial Discourse." *Colonial Discourse and Postcolonial Theory: A Reader*. Ed. Laura Chrisman and Patrick Williams. New York: Harvester Wheatsheaf, 1993. 196–220.

Montejo, Victor. *Voices from Exile: Violence and Survival in Modern Maya History*. Norman: U of Oklahoma P, 1999.

Monture-Angus, Patricia. "Native America and the Literary Tradition." *Native North America: Critical and Cultural Perspectives*. Ed. Renée Hulan. Toronto: ECW, 1999. 20–46.

Projet Accompagnement Québec-Guatémala, Mateo Pablo, Henry Monroy, Lesvia Vela, and Mary Ellen Davis. "Public Statement: In Guatemala, the Perpetrators of Genocide Are Still in Power. They Must Be Brought to Justice!" *Rights & Democracy* Web site. n.d. International Centre for Human Rights and Democratic Development (ICHRDD). 15 Apr. 2002. <http://www.ichrdd.ca/english/urgentActions/statementGuatemala.html>.

Robertson, Roland. *Globalization: Social Theory and Global Culture*. London: Sage, 1992.

Said, Edward. *Culture and Imperialism*. New York: Vintage Books, 1993.

Sánchez-Casal, Susan. "I Am [Not] Like You: Ideologies of Selfhood in *I, Rigoberta Menchú*." *Haunting Violations: Feminist Criticism and the Crisis of the "Real."* Ed. Wendy S. Hesford and Wendy Kozol. Chicago: U of Illinois P, 2001. 76–110.

San Juan, Jr., E. *Beyond Postcolonial Theory*. New York: St. Martin's, 1998.

Scott, Duncan Campbell. "The Onondaga Madonna." *An Anthology of Canadian Literature in English*. Vol. 1. Ed. Russell Brown and Donna Bennett. Toronto: Oxford UP, 1982. 198.

Silko, Leslie Marmon. *Almanac of the Dead: A Novel.* New York: Penguin, 1991.

Smelcer, John E., and D.L. Birchfield, eds. *Durable Breath*. Anchorage: Salmon Run, 1994.

Smith, Linda Tuhiwai. *Decolonizing Methodologies: Research and Indigenous Peoples.* London: Zed, 1999.

Sontag, Susan. *Illness as Metaphor and AIDS and Its Metaphors*. New York: Anchor-Doubleday, 1990.

Spivak, Gayatri Chakravorty. *A Critique of Postcolonial Reason: Toward a History of the Vanishing Present*. Cambridge: Harvard UP, 1999.

———. "Diasporas Old and New: Women in the Transnational World." *Class Issues: Pedagogy, Cultural Studies, and the Public Sphere*. Ed. Amitava Kumar. New York: New York UP, 1997. 87–116.

———. *Outside in the Teaching Machine*. London: Routledge, 1993.

Strong-Boag, Veronica, and Carole Gerson. *Paddling Her Own Canoe: The Times and Texts of E. Pauline Johnson (Tekahionwake)*. Toronto: U of Toronto P, 2000.

Tennant, Paul. "Native Political Organization in British Columbia, 1900–1960: A Response to Internal Colonialism." *BC Studies* 55 (1982): 3–49.

Trinh, Minh-ha T. *Woman, Native, Other: Writing Postcoloniality and Feminism*. Bloomington: Indiana UP, 1989.

Warren, Kay B. "Interpreting *La Violencia* in Guatemala: Shapes of Mayan Silence and Resistance." *The Violence Within: Cultural and Political Opposition in Divided Nations*. Ed. Kay B. Warren. Boulder: Westview, 1993. 25–56.

Young, Robert. *Colonial Desire: Hybridity in Theory, Culture and Race*. London: Routledge, 1995.

Teaching the Talk That Walks on Paper: Oral Traditions and Textualized Orature in the Canadian Literature Classroom

SUSAN GINGELL

> Did [the grandmothers] know our memory and our talk would walk on paper?
>
> — Sky Dancer Louise Bernice Halfe, "The Tears That Wove Our Songs"

THE CALL TO INCLUDE Aboriginal oral traditions in post-secondary English department curricula was among the urgings of the Canadian Association of Commonwealth Literature and Language Studies' roundtable on Aboriginal Literatures in 2000, and this paper considers ways of beginning to answer that call. Roy Harris has suggested in his book *The Origin of Writing* that the West has "a scriptist bias," a bias based on the idea that writing is an "idealization which captures those essential features often blurred and distorted in the rough and tumble of everyday utterance" (46). However, even when spoken words are part of formal oral traditions, this scriptist bias entails the subordination of orature to literature in the hierarchy of cultural production. Thus the curriculum expansion proposed at the CACLALS roundtable has considerable potential as one means of decolonizing our teaching programs, but also carries with it a number of attendant difficulties.

I cannot address the difficulties that teachers wanting to include oral traditions in curricula might face in finding Aboriginal storytellers or oral poets to come into the classroom, mainly because I have limited experience in this area, and the situation and protocol will vary from context to context. However, I learned from Métis community worker, educator, and writer Maria Campbell to observe the Aboriginal protocol of offering tobacco to storytellers, poets, and singers when inviting them to share their words with members of the university community. This paper chiefly intends to suggest approaches to the teaching of textualized orature within a Canadian literature curriculum, both as a worthy activity in its own right and as groundwork for the integration of the teaching of truly oral traditions into the classroom. I use the term *textualized orature* to distinguish oral work that has been transcribed—whether from a live performance, tape recording, compact disk, film, or video tape—from two related terms: *orature* itself, which is work composed and recomposed in performance and passed on orally, and what I call *textualized orality*, which term I use to refer to a writer's representation of the non-standard speech habits and oral strategies of communication used by speakers of a variety of a language other than that of the dominant socio-cultural group. Textualized orality is usually not based on a text composed, or primarily circulated, orally.

My contention is that teachers need to prepare most post-secondary students, who have been reared principally on literary aesthetics, to hear orature respectfully and appreciatively, not just as quaint myths or colourful children's stories or songs. Respectful and appreciative reception requires learning about what Anishinaubee critic Kimberly Blaeser in her contribution to *Talking on the Page: Editing Aboriginal Oral Texts* identifies as an oral aesthetic. One further desirable part of pedagogical preparation includes making students from predominantly literate cultures aware that oral traditions are not something exotic and static, something that other cultures have but theirs does not.

Chanting to Canadian students a little rhyme like "Trick or treat, trick or treat, give us something good to eat" quickly establishes that oral traditions are alive and well even in our secular culture, and discussing local university rituals may be useful for communicating to students from deeply literate cultures the power that oral traditions can have. The "E-plant" at my own institution, the University of Saskatchewan, is a case in point. This neo-barbaric rite involves the abduction and mock-crucifixion of an Agriculture student on a rise outside the Arts building. Engineers body-painted and attired in the college colour, red, try to defend the large wooden E to which a kidnapped high-status Agriculture student is tied, while the blue-attired Agros besiege the hill to try to free their E-planted colleague. Professors who have had their noon-hour classes disrupted by the thundering footsteps and chant of the Engineers as they approach the rise and the many students who gather as spectators of this contemporary agon can attest to the compelling effects of the event, which is kicked off by the boisterous repeated chanting in unison of

> We are, we are, we are the engineers,
> We can, we can, demolish forty beers;
> Drink rum, drink rum,
> And come and be with us,
> For we don't give a damn
> For any damn man,
> Who don't give a damn for us, heh![1]

When prompted by questions, my students can easily identify in this ritual such things as the importance of chanting for group cohesion and identity, the mnemonic value of repetition and rhyme, and the contributions of the paralinguistic signals of vigorously pumping arms and breaking into a whooping run that are part of the display of power. The E-plant ritual, with its song, is an exemplary instance of the "high somatic component" that Walter J. Ong reports characterizes the operation of oral memory (67). He cites the following observations of Berkley Peabody as corroborating evidence: "From all over the world and from all periods of time . . . traditional composition has been associated with hand activity. The aborigines of Australia and other areas often make string figures together with their songs. Other peoples manipulate beads on strings. Most descriptions of bards include stringed instruments or drums" (qtd. in Ong 67).

Using an example like that of the E-plant engineers' song of course runs the risk of associating orature with barbarity, so a teacher needs to subvert such overdetermined interpretations by employing such means as pointing out that reciting the Lord's Prayer, singing "Happy Birthday," or performing dub poetry are all part of contemporary Canadian oral traditions. Moreover, a discussion of the Engineers' chant allows for acknowledgement of the often conservative and sometimes exclusive nature of oral traditions.

Performing at least part of Dennis Gruending's poem "chucker chatter" is an additionally effective means that I have found to demonstrate the vitality of oral traditions in many Canadian communities. The poem points back to the oral performances of baseball catchers across the nation encouraging their pitchers to throw the best possible pitch at any given moment of a game:

hudda buddy
hudda buddy
now you gonowyou go
fireball fireball
righthaner
shoot to me buddy
shoot to me buddy buddy
fireball now fireball
righthander

ohhh
now you smoke
now you smoke buddy now you smoke buddy
buddy
now you hot
now you hot shot ohhh
now you hot
buddy buddy

c'mon babe c'mon babe
c'mon shooter
c'mon shooter buddy buddy
you 'n me honey
all they is
honey
all they is honey honey
buddy buddy
way to mix
way to mix now righthander (70–71)

Reference to the un-textualized utterances of the catcher allows the teacher to establish the difference between the always changing phrasing of the chucker chatter at actual soft- and hard-ball games and the fixity of Gruending's written text, so that students are aware of one of the distortions that textualizing orature produces.

Gruending's poem can also help students understand the importance of knowing the original context of a work of orature that has been transcribed. Teachers can ask students to think for a moment how people encountering Dennis Gruending's poem on the page would likely respond to it if baseball were an altogether alien sport to them or even one known only through television broadcasts, so that the imagined readers had never heard a catcher's chatter to the pitcher. When I teach this poem in this way, I give a second deliberately inept performance of the opening 13 lines of "chucker chatter" in which I tentatively read rather than chant the poem, ignore what I know about proper intonation for this text, and deliver the lines

righthaner

shoot to me buddy
shoot to me buddy buddy

and "now you smoke buddy" in an increasingly puzzled way to indicate both the reader's growing fear that the text may be unreliable and her or his nascent recognition that if the text is accurate, a literal understanding of terms like *shoot* and *smoke* does not work to produce a meaningful text. Such a performance strategy is meant to establish that orature is intended to operate inside a closed community, in a context in which the story, poem, or chant is widely known, and that without an insider to provide the kind of detailed cultural information and the intonation and emphasis necessary to a competent performance of the work, distortions in the performance and devaluations in the reception are a very real possibility, if not a virtual certainty.

With this kind of groundwork in place, a teacher can then turn to textualized works of Aboriginal oral tradition. To suggest one way to teach textualized orature I am going to use texts attributed to the Iglulik *angákoq*, or shaman, Aua,[2] texts entitled "Magic Words" in Daniel David Moses and Terry Goldie's widely-used *Anthology of Canadian Native Literature in English*. Though I believe there are problems with the edition of Aua's words presented in this anthology, Moses and Goldie have done a valuable service in making these texts available in an eminently teachable anthology.

Students who are shown or encouraged to see the stunning Zacharias Kunuk film *Atanarjuat: The Fast Runner* can gain a strong sense of the central place of oral traditions among the Inuit, but further desirable background for understanding Aua's words is Ong's discussion of cultures in a state of primary orality, that is cultures untouched by any form of writing (9). Such cultures are verbomotor cultures (68) because sounded words, being dynamic, are conceived of as having great power. Language, then, is understood as a mode of action, not as an encoding of thought. Words can heal or produce good fortune, just as they can blast health or create misfortune. Thus, many transcriptions of orature record ritual words intended to produce specific effects or bring about a desired condition. Two short texts recording the *Erinaliu·tit*, or shamanic words,[3] of Aua, for which the Greenlandic anthropologist Knud Rasmussen bartered, are exemplars of such ritual words.[4] As Robin McGrath comments in *Canadian Inuit Literature*, "Because of Rasmussen's superior knowledge of Inuktitut, Danish, and English, and because of his exceptional sensitivity to poetry, Rasmussen's work is generally considered to be the best source of traditional Inuit poetry in English today" (40).[5]

The first *Erinaliu·tit*, the *angákoq* Aua explained to Rasmussen, was designed to lighten heavy loads on a sled or make a person light-footed and untiring on a long journey, and the second was meant to cure or possibly prevent sickness when one's neighbours had fallen ill. Because these are shamanic words, Rasmussen reports that they were to be jerkily whispered or muttered in order to preserve secrecy (165). The Moses and Goldie anthology presents Aua's words in the following way:

> Magic Words/Aua
>
> *To Lighten Heavy Loads*
>
> I speak with the mouth of Qeqertuanaq, and say:
>
> I will walk with leg muscles strong as the sinews on the shin of a little caribou calf.
>
> I will walk with leg muscles strong as the sinews on the shin of a little hare.

I will take care not to walk toward the dark.
I will walk toward the day.

To Cure Sickness among Neighbours
I arise from my couch with the grey gull's morning song.
I arise from my couch with the grey gull's morning song.
I will take care not to look toward the dark,
I will turn my glance toward the day. (3)

Two of the potential problems with the editorial practice in presenting the texts of what Moses and Goldie call Inuit "Traditional Songs" are, first, a question about whether all of them are truly songs—Aua's whispered words provoke such a question, though McGrath argues "there is no getting around the fact that traditional Inuit poetry is oral song" (40)—and, second, there is a possibility that many readers could mistake the names following the titles for namings of particular groups of people. The Inuit names, like Aua's, provided after a solidus following the titles in the first section of the anthology are treated quite differently from the names of authors that head the sample of their work anthologized in later parts of Moses and Goldie. A sample of Alexander Wolfe's work, for example, is presented as follows:

Alexander Wolfe b. 1927

SAULTEAUX

The Last Grass Dance

Told by Standing Through the Earth

The printing of Aua's name following the solidus reproduces the consistent practice in John Robert Colombo's *Poems of the Inuit*, which Moses and Goldie list as their source text, and that practice appears to have been followed without thought of the potential confusions thus produced. Moreover, in the case of works from the written tradition, the Oxford anthology gives an author's First Nation or Métis identification under the author's name. In the case of the Inuit "Songs," no further ethnic designation is given, though Rasmussen clearly differentiates between six dialect and cultural groups in the "General Plan and Methods" section that prefaces *Intellectual Culture of the Iglulik Eskimos* and devotes separate volumes to the intellectual cultures of Iglulik and Caribou Eskimos. Penny Petrone's *Northern Voices: Inuit Writing in English* distinguishes eight cultural groups. However, to find out that Aua was an Iglulik person, Moses and Goldie's enquiring readers would have to go to Colombo's *Poems of the Inuit* or to Rasmussen's *Across Arctic America*, which was Colombo's source.

A further issue with Aua's texts in Moses and Goldie relates to their titling and paucity of contextualizing. In this anthology, both the title "Magic Words" and italicized headings "To Lighten Heavy Loads" and "To Cure Sickness among Neighbours" are the additions of a literate culture. In *The Intellectual Culture of the Iglulik Eskimos,* Rasmussen presents the second text under the heading "*Words to be used in the morning on getting up*" and explains that they are to be uttered "If there is sickness in a village, but not in one's own household" (166). He thus provides grounds for speculating whether the words were preventative in addition to curative medicine, but in his later popularized summary of his findings, *Across Arctic America,* Rasmussen prefaces the untitled and unheaded words with statements that deny a preventative dimension to the medicine:

> A charm for curing sickness among neighbors may be uttered by one who is well. The speaker gets up early in the morning before anyone else is astir, takes the inner garment of a child, and drawing his own hood over his head, thrusts his arms into the sleeves of the child's garment as if to put it on. Then these words are uttered. (137–38)

Colombo and his followers Moses and Goldie subsequently use Rasmussen's first prefatory statement as the source of a title. An enriched understanding of Aua's *Erinaliu tit* proceeds from the fuller contextualizing material that Rasmussen provides for Aua's words, and those interested in more information about shamanism among the Inuit can be directed to chapter five of *The Intellectual Culture of the Iglulik Eskimos,* "The Angákut or Shamans."

Petrone also titles Aua's words in *Northern Voices,* but she uses Rasmussen's *Intellectual Culture* as her source for the first of Moses and Goldie's "songs" by Aua, taking the exact wording of Rasmussen's heading "Words which make heavy things light" for her title. She follows the title by a parenthetical, truncated statement of context "(to be uttered beside a heavily laden sledge)" (7), a practice which produces an improvement over the totally uncontextualized version in the Moses and Goldie text, but she does not provide all the contextualizing details Rasmussen offers in *Intellectual Culture*. Rasmussen indicates not only that "The speaker stands at the fore end of the sledge, speaking in the direction of the traces," but also that the words could be employed in more than one context: "Also used when setting out on a long journey, and wishing to be light-footed and untiring" (165). Knowledge of this alternate context of usage is particularly important for the argument I will make later about a politicized reading of this text. It is also worth noting that in his scholarly text Rasmussen does not make the reference to Qeqertuanaq part of his text of Aua's *Erinaliu·tit*, instead explaining in a prefatory statement that "Aua's method of referring to Qiqertáinaq when using her magic words was . . . as follows: . . . 'because I wish to utter an Erinaliu·tit . . . using as my mouth the mouth of Qiqertáinaq'" (165). Petrone's anthology does, however, have the added interest of publishing a picture of a man in shamanic apparel that she identifies as Aua, thus making apparent that the uttering of such a text is an embodied performance, one in which the shaman's clothing can contribute to the power of the performance.

The accuracy of Petrone's identification is, however, questionable. The anthropologist Bernard Saladin d'Anglure in "Ijiqqat: Voyage au pays de l'invisible Inuit" captions the same photograph in a way that links the image to Aua's father: "très vraisemblablement du chamane Qinqailisaq revêtu de son manteau à la mode Ijiqqat" (80). The photo, D'Anglure explains, was taken on board the whaling vessel *l'Era* in 1902 and is now in the Comer collection of the Mystic Seaport Museum, but it is Rasmussen who explains both the symbolism of the coat and its fate:

> My father, who was a great shaman, went home [after a triumphant encounter with mountain spirits known as i^{j}Erqät] and had a dress made like that of the i^{j}ErAq [singular of *i^{j}Erqät*], but with the picture of the hands in front on the chest to show how the i^{j}ErAq had attacked him. . . . There were a number of white patterns in the dress, and it became a famous dress, which was bought by him who was called: ahak'oq (the well known whaler and collector for the American Museum of Natural History, Capt. George Comer), and my father was paid a high price for the garment. (*Intellectual* 206)

A picture of Aua whose authenticity is more sure is a pencil sketch Rasmussen reprints in *The Intellectual Culture of the Iglulik Eskimos* of Aua and his wife Orulo inside a snow hut (49).

Moses and Goldie's source for Aua's *Erinaliu·tit,* Colombo, chose as copy text *Across Arctic America* (Danish original, *Grφnland til Stillehavet,* published 1933–34), Rasmussen's popularizing of his scholarly work *The Intellectual Culture of the Iglulik Eskimos* (Danish original published 1929). In the scholarly book, Rasmussen provides both the Inuktitut original and English translation of Aua's *Erinaliu·tit.* The English translation differs from the text in *Across Arctic America* in lineation and phrasing, and the words in the *Intellectual Culture* text also suggest the speaker *will* look towards the dark: "I arise from my couch / With the morning song to look towards the dark" (166). The *Across Arctic America* text says he will do the opposite: "I will take care *not* to look toward the dark" (138, emphasis added).

The ground for questioning the choice of copy text here relates to the greater concern for accuracy that one might expect Rasmussen to have in preparing a scholarly edition of a work, and the five years that elapsed between the scholarly report of the Fifth Thule Expedition of 1921–24 and the publication of the Danish book that was translated as *Across Arctic America.*[6] However, lest this uncertainty confirm a sense that the wisest thing is to avoid teaching these texts because of the translation problem, teachers might want to consider the observation Craig Womack makes in the context of arguing that Native literatures (his term certainly includes, if it is not here synonymous with, oratures) have "sufficient literary excellence that they retain something of their power in translation" (64). He notes, "What happens when Native literatures are rendered to the realm of problem (like the Indian problem, we have the translation problem) is that Native cultural production is then examined as ethnography rather than tribal national literatures" (64). Responsible teaching of Aua's texts at the moment, however, means calling students' attention to both the discrepant translations and the contextualizing that Rasmussen provides.

Having discussed the problems regarding the available texts of Aua's shamanic words, teachers can direct students to consider the multiple markers of the oral in these texts. The first text ascribed to Aua begins by acknowledging how the words came to him; no claim to originality is made in the way that writers warrant their originality by subscribing their names as authors of their work. Aua speaks with the mouth of Qeqertuanaq, the old woman from whom he had learnt the words, because only by uttering her name and repeating the words in the right order would they have any power (*Intellectual* 165). Parallelism patterns the syntactical structures, making them easier to remember, and the mnemonic anaphora "I will walk," which opens most statements in this work, is in the penultimate statement varied to "I will take care not to walk" before the return to the original formula in the final line.

The formulaic quality of the final two statements of the first work becomes clear when we hear or see a variant of them at the end of the second work, where the walking is now replaced by references to looking. What Ong identifies as the copiousness, or rhetorical fullness (39–41), of orature is evidenced in the iteration and immediate reiteration of the opening statement of the second work, "I arise from my couch with the grey gull's morning song," though the extent of the repetition varies depending on the edition of the text used. Robert Bringhurst observes in "Reading What Cannot Be Written," the prologue to his *A Story Sharp as a Knife*, that "Once it is transcribed, oral literature *looks* like writing" (15). His point is, of course, that looks are deceiving, and if one judges textualized orature on the basis of literary aesthetics, the reiterated phrases or lines are likely to seem dully repetitive when read, or, more likely, quickly read over. However, if the teacher has models like "trick or treat, trick or treat," "we are, we are, we are the engineers," and "hudda buddy hudda buddy" to refer back to, such depreciations may be at least somewhat subverted. Such attempted subversion is important because the general agreement that Robin McGrath affirms, namely that "repetitions in oral literature are the concern of native speakers and ethnographers" (13), arises from a form of ethnocentrism related to literary as opposed to oral aesthetics.

Because students need to be directed to consider how repetition in orature is functional, they might also be encouraged to think about the ramifications of Alfred B. Lord's classic statement in *The Singer of Tales* that "an oral poem is not composed *for* but *in* performance" (13). Whoever among Qeqertuanaq's ancestors[7] faced the original demands of spontaneous composition would in part have met those demands through the use of formulaic structures, but that person may also have relied on repetition to give her or himself the time to decide where the poem would go next. John Hollander in his verses from *Rhyme's Reason* that exemplify blues improvisation makes this point more memorably:

Now a blues has stanzas, stanzas of a funny kind—
Yes a blues has stanzas of a very funny kind;
(Do that again, singer, while you make up your mind) . . .

Make up your mind, while the next line gives you time,
Make up your mind, yes, while this line's giving you time,
Then your train of thought comes running after your rhyme.
(45, ellipsis in original)

If repetition is seen to be functional in the oral context, students are less likely to see it as a weakness or an aesthetic flaw, and reference to almost any contemporary popular song will show students that repetition of the sort found in Aua's *Erinaliu·tit* is a characteristic of the songs most of them find appealing.

In Aua's shamanic words, the oral culture's belief in the power of language to produce desired effects is evident not only in the assertions of what the speaker will do or is doing in order to lighten a heavy load or cure sickness, but also in the refraining from articulating obstacles to the desired state. No mention is made of weight or sickness, lest the articulation summon that which the angákoq is seeking to overcome or banish. Teachers seeking to combat the idea that these texts provide traces of at best quaint and at worst primitive practices can remind students that some contemporary psychotherapists claim an efficacy in having clients repeat affirmations in order to overcome doubts, insecurities, and negative convictions. Moreover, the still common practice of responding to negative news—like an announcement of snowfall in April—by saying something like "Don't even tell me about it" evidences an even more widespread persistence of the idea that putting something into words makes it real.

Creek author and critic Craig Womack offers a powerful suggestion that would validate interpreting Aua's words as vital for this moment when he expresses concern with the de-politicized readings critics have given to Native oral traditions and writing in an era when land settlements and other treaty entitlements are critical issues in Native communities. In *Red on Red: Native American Literary Separatism*, Womack discusses the question of whether it is "appropriate to look for political meaning when dealing with the sacred" (53). Having asserted that "Politics without spirituality is not only out of balance but potentially oppressive," he goes on to argue that "spirituality without politics appropriates belief systems without taking responsibility for human liberation." Womack thus opens the possibility of unfixing Aua's words from the specific context in which they were originally performed so that we may think about how they might act contemporaneously. In an era of snowmobiles and other forms of northern transport, the need to utter powerful words beside a heavily laden sledge has arguably been much diminished and the preventative or curative medicine needed to cure or ward off sickness afflicting Inuit neighbours is as likely to have to address despair at social and economic conditions as physical ailment. However, if the heavily laden sledge, the need for strong and determined walking, the rising with the grey gull's morning song, and the looking not toward the dark but to the day be understood as referring to the burdens contemporary Inuit must carry in securing land title and eagerly journeying towards a brighter, healthier future, then these texts might have new and powerful circulation as liberatory words in contemporary struggles. When the texts are read in this way, the reason for Aua's avoiding a focus on the obstacles to the desired state becomes even clearer, and the gift of the ancestors in articulating an empowering vision of capability for the Inuit even more obvious. The study of oral traditions and textualized orature could then be seen as the study of living wisdom rather than as anthropological artifact or outmoded form of cultural production. And if we as professors of Canadian literature would use such postcolonial Indigenous thought[8] as Womack's in teaching such texts, we could be putting our power in the service of people of Aboriginal ancestry even as we enrich all our students' appreciation for the range of verbal cultural production in this country.

NOTES

1. I checked my memory of this song and details of the ritual with a third-year civil engineering student at the University of Saskatchewan, Riley Jestin. He also told me that on other occasions the Engineers' chant is not chanted but sung to a tune I identified as that of "The Battle Hymn of the Republic." His testimony thus suggests the way in which orature is adapted to different occasions, originality in the context of orature being understood as the ability to fit a received text to specific occasions. Julie Cruickshank's account of the tellings of the Tlingit story

of *Kaax'achgook* by Angela Sidney, an account given in her article "The Social Life of Texts," provides another instance of this oral originality.

2. Aua's name is explained in Rasmussen's *Intellectual Culture of the Iglulik Eskimos* in a passage that reports Aua as saying that his "first helping spirit was [his] namesake, a little aua. . . . An aua is a little shore spirit, a woman, that [*sic*] lives down by the sea shore. . . . They are bright and cheerful when one calls them, and resemble most of all sweet little live dolls" (119). Despite being marked to be an angákoq before his birth, and despite evidence of his practising his people's form of shamanism up to and presumably beyond the time of his first meeting with Rasmussen, Aua reportedly told the explorer on their second meeting, "I am a Christian, and so I have sent away all my helping spirits" (*Across* 127). Rasmussen learnt that "the business of an angákoq [was] to heal the sick, to protect the souls of his fellows against the machinations of hostile wizards, to intercede with the Mother of the Sea when seal are scarce, and to see that traditional customs are properly observed."

3. Rasmussen uses the term *magic words*, but because of the negative connotation of *magic* as illusory, I prefer the term *shamanic words*.

4. Rasmussen notes,

> Obviously it is almost impossible to elicit any *Erinaliu·tit* from people who themselves believe in the miraculous power of the words. Those who possess the words will not part with them, or if they do, it is at a price which would soon ruin an expedition. A gun with an ample supply of ammunition was regarded, for instance, as a very natural price for a few meaningless words. One can, however, instead of buying, sometimes obtain *Erinaliu·tit* by barter, and I availed myself of this, giving magic words from Angmagssalik, in East Greenland, in exchange for others from Iglulik. In this manner I obtained the following magic words from Aua. (*Intellectual* 165)

5. Peter Freuchen, a member of Rasmussen's Fifth Thule Expedition of 1921–24, during which Rasmussen bartered for Aua's healing words, explains that Rasmussen was born in Greenland in June of 1879 to a Danish missionary father and a half-Eskimo mother (16). Freuchen reports Knud's father was a gifted linguist who became a recognized scholar of Greenlandic. In *Across Arctic America*, Rasmussen himself reports, "It was my privilege, as one born in Greenland, and speaking the Eskimo language as my native tongue, to know these people in an intimate way. . . . My playmates were native Greenlanders; from the earliest boyhood I played and worked with the hunters" (vi).

6. Though I have questions about the accuracy of some translations in *Across Arctic America*, that book's versions of Aua's words accord more closely with a

European literary aesthetic, and therefore might be expected to have a wider appeal.

7. Rasmussen reports of Qeqertuanaq, "She was very old, and her family had handed down the words from generation to generation, right from the time of the first human beings" (*Intellectual* 165).

8. I borrow this term from Marie Battiste's introduction to *Reclaiming Indigenous Voice and Vision*, where she explains:

> Postcolonial Indigenous thought should not be confused with postcolonial theory in literature. Although they are related endeavours, postcolonial Indigenous thought also emerges from the inability of Eurocentric theory to deal with the complexities of colonialism and its assumptions. Postcolonial Indigenous thought is based on our pain and our experiences, and it refuses to allow others to appropriate this pain and these experiences. It rejects the use of any Eurocentric theory or its categories. (xix)

WORKS CITED

Atanarjuat: The Fast Runner. Dir. Zacharias Kunuk. Igloolik Isuma Productions, 2001.

Aua. "Magic Words." Moses and Goldie 3.

———. "Words Which Make Heavy Things Light." Petrone 7.

Battiste, Marie, ed. *Reclaiming Indigenous Voice and Vision*. Vancouver: U of British Columbia P, 2000.

Blaeser, Kimberly. "Writing Voices Speaking: Native Authors and an Oral Aesthetic." *Talking on the Page: Editing Aboriginal Oral Texts*. Proceedings of Thirty-Second Annual University of Toronto Conference on Editorial Problems. Ed. Laura J. Murray and Keren Rice. Toronto: U of Toronto P, 1999. 53–68.

Bringhurst, Robert. *A Story as Sharp as a Knife: The Classical Haida Mythtellers and Their World*. Vancouver: Douglas and McIntyre; Lincoln: U of Nebraska P, 1999.

Colombo, John Robert. *Poems of the Inuit*. Ottawa: Oberon, 1981.

Cruickshank, Julie. "The Social Life of Texts: Editing on the Page and in Performance." *Talking on the Page: Editing Aboriginal Oral Texts*. Ed. Laura J. Murray and Keren Rice. 97–119.

Freuchen, Peter. *I Sailed with Rasmussen*. New York: Julian Messner, 1958.

Gruending, Dennis. "chucker chatter." *Draft: An Anthology of Prairie Poetry*. Ed. Dennis Cooley. Winnipeg: Turnstone; Downsview: ECW, 1981. 70–71.

Halfe, Sky Dancer Louise Bernice. "The Tears That Wove Our Songs: Reflections on Living in the Feminine Gender." *NeWest Review* 20.3 (April/May 1995): 12–13.

Harris, Roy. *The Origin of Writing*. London: Duckworth, 1986.

Hollander, John. *Rhyme's Reason: A Guide to English Verse*. New, enlarged ed. New Haven: Yale UP, 1989.

Jestin, Riley. Personal Interview. 12 Apr. 2002.

Lord, Alfred. *The Singer of Tales*. New York: Atheneum, 1974.

McGrath, Robin. *Canadian Inuit Literature: The Development of a Tradition*. National Museum of Man Mercury Series. Canadian Ethnology Service Paper No. 94. Ottawa: National Museum of Man, 1984.

Moses, Daniel David, and Terry Goldie, eds. *An Anthology of Canadian Native Literature in English*. 2nd ed. Toronto: Oxford UP, 1998.

Ong, Walter J. *Orality and Literacy: The Technologizing of the Word*. London: Routledge, 1982.

Petrone, Penny, ed. *Northern Voices: Inuit Writing in English*. Toronto: U of Toronto P, 1988.

Rasmussen, Knud. *Across Arctic America: Narrative of the Fifth Thule Expedition*. New York: Putnam's, 1927.

———. *Intellectual Culture of the Iglulik Eskimos*. Report of the Fifth Thule Expedition 1921–24. Vol. VII. No. 1. 1929. Rpt. New York: AMS, 1976.

Saladin d'Anglure, Bernard. "Ijiqqat: Voyage au pays de l'invisible Inuit." *Études Inuit Studies* 7.1 (1983): 67–83.

Womack, Craig. *Red on Red: Native American Literary Separatism*. Minneapolis: U of Minnesota P, 1999.

"Outsiders" and "Insiders": Teaching Native/Canadian Literature as Meeting Place

LAURIE KRUK

Is NATIVE LITERATURE ALSO Canadian literature? Or is that a "simple" question, posed at the "Postcolonialism and Pedagogy" symposium, May 2002?[1] In 1999, I, the resident Canadianist at my small undergraduate institution, was asked to put together a new course in Native Literature in English, to be cross-listed with our developing Native Studies program. I had incorporated Native-authored literature within my Canadian survey, by the addition of a token text—either Tomson Highway's *The Rez Sisters* or *Dry Lips Oughta Move to Kapuskasing*, perennial favourites—but this new program initiative meant putting the "insider" into the "outsider" position. My institution shares the Ojibway/Anishinaabe name of the region's dominant body of water and an avowed commitment, as a "university in a Northern Ontario community, . . . to reflect and respond to the region" ("Mission Statement"). However, there is a stronger Native presence and population at our sister institution, Canadore College, to which many Northern Cree travel, coming down "south" from James Bay in Northern Quebec, often for the first time. As part of the approval process, I consulted with our Native Studies program coordinator and also presented my course outline to the Aboriginal Council on Education, comprising representatives from the Native community as well as interested parties from the university.

My reading list was, I felt proudly, an ambitious one—the teacher as over-achiever dies hard—and included four novels, one play, one entire volume of poetry (a departure from the anthologized/marginalized experience of teaching poetry), plus numerous selections from a new standard in this emerging area, the Moses/Goldie *Anthology of Canadian Native Literature in English* (2nd edition), published by an institutional mainstay and "symbol of Empire" in itself, as Goldie points out (xxix), Oxford University Press. The novels were Thomas King's *Green Grass, Running Water*; Tomson Highway's controversial *Kiss of the Fur Queen*; Beatrice Culleton Mosionier's *In Search of April Raintree*; and Ian McCulloch's thoughtful exploration of Native identity via road trip/vision quest, *Childforever*. I hoped King's playful postmodernism would provide a counterbalance to three very serious, society-indicting narratives, which incorporate as central to the experiences of their Native or Métis protagonists, alcoholism, sexual abuse, rape, and suicide. And though utilizing very different writing styles and strategies, each invokes the life history/biography as framework, suggesting a documentary intent. Putting *The Book of Jessica* on the list meant students read more than a play, of course; they also immersed themselves in the fascinating record (edited by Linda Griffiths) of a painful and perilous collaboration that became a virtual war of words, and of world views.[2] And I took literally the encouragement from the Native Studies coordinator to question that border, which is so important to a Canadianist, yet so abstract or arbitrary to many Native (North) *Americans*, and included New Mexico Muscogee poet/saxophonist Joy Harjo's jazz-inflected poetry collection, *The Woman Who Fell from the Sky*, alongside the anthologized writing of poets Pauline Johnson, Lee Maracle, Armand Garnet Ruffo, and Lenore Keeshig-Tobias. My course outline was accepted, and I was approved to teach it—although the hope was expressed that a qualified instructor of Native background might be available in the future, as I was visibly a "paleface" of Anglo-European descent. Later, a member of the committee (self-identifying as Native) confided to me that he didn't feel an instructor had to be Native to teach Native literature, making the analogy of a professor offering a course in Greek literature.

Such a process may be familiar to many Canadianists: it is part of our newly self-conscious stance, in the late twentieth/early twenty-first century, as instructors who are also the inheritors of a political, intellectual, and cultural privilege won at the expense of other people and their perspectives. For Canadian literature to exist, there had to be an imperialist project called "Canada," which put down borders and boundaries—most notably the 49th parallel—in the interests of creating an alternative (better, many of us thought) to "the American dream." Yet these boundaries have always been permeable, not just politically, in letting alleged terrorists across them, in post–September 11th accounts, but also, intellectually, since they are redrawn daily as we rethink what Canada is and can be within a global economy that can be both liberating and alienating. Whose voices best represent Canada today? For instance, is the acclaimed darkly lyrical novel celebrating Newfoundland, *The Shipping News*, by American E. Annie Proulx (who also lives in Newfoundland), a good candidate for a "CanLit" reading list? Other books by Canadian citizens may now be as readily set in Bombay, Sri Lanka, or Poland, Greece, and Toronto in turn—are these also appropriate for a Canadian literature survey?[3] Where is the famous "Canadian" component—does it lie in textual origin or setting, or in the citizenship or residency of the author, or in something more nebulous, like the "garrison mentality," "survival," or even the "Wacousta Syndrome"?[4] A national vision that has frequently been suggested is the very multiplicity of voices or "community of communities"—exemplified by the virtual community created by CBC's *Morningside*, some might say, under its late host Peter Gzowski—that CanLit, we are often fond of saying, encompasses.[5] For example, many of us point out to our students that, relative to their American sisters, Canadian women writers have been prominent since the colonial period, and continue to be in the forefront of our best-selling, critically-acclaimed literature today.[6] Many of us agree with Linda Hutcheon that "Canada often speaks with a doubled voice, with the forked tongue of irony. . . . [w]hich allows speakers to address and at the same time slyly confront an 'official' discourse: that is, to work *within* a dominant tradition but also to challenge it—without being utterly co-opted by it" (1–2). So it is tempting to see Native literature as representing merely another "difference" we can easily encompass within our polyphonous, pluralistic national discourse.

However, anyone who has wrestled with the disturbing allure of the "Indian poems" of D.C. Scott, administrator of government policy "to take care of the Indians until, in Scott's words, they 'disappear as a separate and distinct people'" (Dragland 7), realizes that a bureaucratic burial of *this* particular difference has been the imperialist/nationalist aim of our

Canadian government and its institutional practices of cultural and linguistic extinction. We cannot so easily impose Canadian citizenship on works by those who identify as Native, *not* Canadian, thank you very much—at least, not before we spend some time questioning where we stand, as non-Native, especially White, teachers, critics, writers, and readers, in relation to these works and writers who have been so long held in the shadows by racism, poverty, and/or sexism. Maria Campbell trenchantly reveals the reality of many Native (including Métis) people's attitude towards the issue of citizenship: "[I] guess I'm a Canadian because that's who the conqueror happens to be today" (Griffiths and Campbell 98). So much for our community of communities. We can't simply see difference outside ourselves—as in a one-way reflecting mirror—and teaching Native literature involves more than raising the question, difficult as it is, of "Who is a Native writer?" Instead, we must pause and look around the "Native Lit" classroom and ask, "Who is reading it, and for what purposes?" Is the purpose to engage honestly and fully with its differences or difficulties? Or, to seek out a reflection of our own needs, questions, concerns? Both impulses are probably at work for students and teachers, and it is worth raising this tension at the start of our work, even if only to acknowledge that we routinely read seeking reflections of ourselves. Such a discussion of motives goes beyond merely the fashionable use of identity politics to monitor the staffing of Native literature courses. Yet too much social self-consciousness is not helpful either: overemphasizing the social and political context behind the texts may cause us, in a simplistic essentializing broadbrush, to overlook the genuine variety, tonal range, and explosive intensity of the individual works and writers themselves, and to betray their particular voices.

Nobody has more eloquently captured this complex dialogue of Self and Other than Helen Hoy, author of *How Should I Read These? Native Women Writers in Canada* (2001). This book articulates in passionate detail the pitfalls and paradoxes of teaching Native Canadian literature as an "outsider," using postcolonial theory to illuminate the power politics implicit in this enterprise. I won't replay her lengthy, considered introduction to teaching Native literature here. Hoy writes with admirable candour, weaving into her discussion anecdotes that are self-implicating, in order to illustrate even more dramatically, because personally, the dance of silence/silencing lived by a sensitive, committed instructor, approaching these texts as an "Other."[7] She is highly aware of the risk that we may simply "re-colonize" the work by eliding or ignoring its challenge to our ideas of what literature is. Beth Brant is a Native woman writer who argues for a different audience, intent, and objective, one that may conflict with the objectives of the academy and English programs in Canada: "I believe that the writing being created by First Nations women is writing done with a community consciousness. Individuality is a concept and philosophy that has little meaning for us" ("Good Red Road" 19). This declaration—by one writer, of course, bringing into imaginative being "First Nations women" as a community, as we ourselves are often called upon to speak for non-Native readers and critics—also forces us to reconsider our selection criteria in choosing texts, or our dismissive reactions ("It's bad writing") to Beatrice Culleton Mosionier's *In Search of April Raintree*, for instance. The critical edition of this much-taught novel, edited by Cheryl Suzack, was just being put together when I started planning my course (in fact, as proof of its rising status the publishers sought my input on a student-friendly cover price). It puts nine critical essays, including one by Hoy (plus a piece by the author), in dialogue with a novel that at first appears overwhelmed by such attention. Hoy candidly turns her critical eye back on her own initial position on the novel: "My concern about formulaic characterization and plotting, wooden dialogue, flat, recapitulative narration, sensationalizing, and stylistic blandness (in most of which I echo the reviewers I have critiqued) draws on the norms of high (bourgeois) realism, with its focus on the individualizing of experience, refinements of self-understanding, aptness of detail, originality of language" ("'Nothing'" 287). Standards of art that we protect as somehow sacred in an agnostic university may indeed have cultural roots which, if uncovered, leave we English instructors subsumed under the category of *White* feeling particularly exposed.

Hoy's self-critique makes me return to Brant's insistence on a "community consciousness" behind Native women's writing, although as Renée Hulan reminds us, the community/individual opposition is too simplistic, like all such starting positions, including, I hope to show, *insider* and *outsider*. For the challenge, if we are open to truly *learning from* teaching Native literature, Hulan reveals, is both to our aesthetic and our epistemological perspectives: not just, is this "good writing," but what makes writing "good," and why do we value it the way we do, in the form we do?

Are there other possible models of narrative presentation or creation? Hulan points out that "the continued influence of modernist aesthetics—even by those who espouse postmodernism—ensures that the focus remains on judging the quality of *writing* when most critics do not have sufficient knowledge of the hybridized forms that Native writers produce to judge" (223). If storytelling, the oral tradition that predates literacy, survives in Native culture because it is viewed still as a healing art, does that help explain the critical disagreement over *In Search of April Raintree?* Its appeal to our students is precisely its accessibility of language, storyline, character motivation, and the metonymic association of the sisters Cheryl and April with a suppressed, silenced Métis culture. Yet for those of us invested in "literariness," and the range of interpretations that we may draw from it, such a text, pointed and powerful in its most indelible conclusions, creates discomfort. Is this because it gives the students a sense of readerly authority over a text and its most persuasive interpretation, for a change? Their unexpectedly intense identification with the book and its characters threatens our own demonstrated mastery over the works we analyze and praise for their complexity, ambiguity, irony—and individuality. The objective that is implicit in Culleton Mosionier's text—healing the fractured Métis community—verges on the educational, if not the didactic, which immediately alarms and perturbs many of us, as we were taught to distrust such writing. If we accept this therapeutic thrust of the novel, the individual author and her vision are somehow made less prominent, less relevant to discussion, and we are thrown back into (re)inventing Native cultural community—which means inhabiting the learner position.

So, where does our authority in teaching Native literature come from? Who is best qualified to teach it? Is it a matter of having the identity of *Native,* however that is determined: By bloodline? Status card? Matrilineage? Self-declaration? Ian McCulloch comes from mixed European and Cree parentage, and claims "his Native heritage has always been a source of great pride. Many social factors in his life and in the lives of his ancestors, however, made his a *somewhat abstract inheritance*" (backcover, my italics). When the inheritance is "somewhat abstract," the temptation is to return to "noble savage" romanticizing, a hunger for millennial spiritual renewal replayed today through popular curiosity about powows, sweatlodge ceremonies, shamanism. Making too quick an identification with the powerful messages of psychic and spiritual healing embedded in these historic practices, we may turn away from the evidence of social, political, economic, and, yes, spiritual impoverishment in Native communities today, and their silencing in the very recent past. We may be silencing Native voices again in the name of achieving a monolithic (and illusory) Canadian, spiritual identity.

Should we instead put the emphasis on *literature,* and an appreciation of "literariness," as the defining criterion for teaching Native literature? Again, who fills the classroom? Is it Native students, or as is still more likely, non-Natives with the curiosity, and opportunity, of the privileged outsider, to take our courses, with varying degrees of both interest in and experience with Native culture, falsely totalized though it may be? Despite our institution's name, and our Mission Statement's commitment to reflecting our Northern Ontario region, Native students, especially Anishinaabe from the area, are still a rarity in my classes. Given the historical emphasis on orature, storytelling, and the fluidly defined community consciousness maintained by many Native writers, we may even pause to question our need for literariness as well as literacy, for texts with the self-evident (to us) merits that echo, reinforce, and justify our education. We want to study the Other, but we want to be able to recognize it, in our terms, in our language. bell hooks summarizes this ongoing problem for minority writers: "The over-riding fear is that cultural, ethnic, and racial differences will be continually commodified and offered up as new dishes to enhance the white palate—that the Other will be eaten, consumed, and forgotten" (qtd. in Hoy 3). In other words, there will be no real challenge made to our intellectual nourishment, only a diverting night out dining on "ethnic food."

Perhaps this is where we must return to the idea of identity, and authority, and how they are related, with finer discrimination. If we allow ourselves to play a dichotomous game of insider/outsider, whereby the authority swings completely to one side of the equation—the Native student has the authority in Native Lit class, the non-Native student has the authority outside—then we will struggle, exhausted and frustrated, to create a dialogue rather than a series of rants from either side, entrenching attitudes of resentment and resistance. Beth Brant provokes us, for instance, when she turns the tables, saying, "As a Mohawk, I am very much inside my own world-view, my own Nation, and I am looking at you—the descendants of the European fathers who colonized that world" ("From the Inside" 49). The provocation is proper, but we don't want to target an Other, at least, not one *outside* of ourselves. As critically-aware teachers, we need to encourage students (and ourselves) to question their insouciant, post-adolescent belief in "free will." We must challenge the illusion of a self-maintained, singular identity, such as "Native" or "non-Native" or even "Canadian." *Identity*, that fascinating word for our students, needs to be complicated inasmuch as our own self slides between what is given, what is (unconsciously) constructed, and what is self-created. So it is with approaching the issue of Native identity. Whether we are insiders or outsiders, we realize that we are tangled in a web of cultural stereotypes, positive *and* negative, and gaps in knowledge of the Other that we struggle to evade. Speaking from her own extensive experience as teacher and outsider in this area, Renée Hulan writes, "Distinguishing between 'knowing' and 'appropriating' requires understanding that there is always a close relationship between 'speaking for' and 'speaking about' others" (220). She reminds us of the sobering fact that there remains a link between appropriation and education, a fact made starkly evident when we consider the recent history, still being compiled, of a century of residential schools forced upon Native youth in Canada, and the abuse they fostered.[8] The different experiences of exploitation suffered by the Okimasis brothers at the hands of the monstrous Catholic priest, Father Lafleur, in *Kiss of the Fur Queen*, is a searing indictment of this self-righteously blind objectification of the Native outsider.

Teaching Native literature as a non-Native means wrestling fully with this historicized understanding of difference between insiders and outsiders. For if the course is to go beyond a superficial thematic survey that simply creates different categories from familiar oppositions, it is necessary to question the categories *Native* and *non-Native*, to revisit this historical interdependence and ask what makes them possible, and positive, terms today. We must acknowledge, first, that we are each subjects, occupying many different relational postures and attitudes during a single *class*, not just a single day. Yet as Paul Smith formulates it, "the human being, caught within the trammels of subjection or given over to the social formations which he/she inhabits, is never entirely a 'subject.'" He helpfully suggests the term *agent* as the "place from which resistance to the ideological is produced or played out" (xxxiv–xxxv). Therefore, identity encompasses all three potentials—*subject, individual,* and *agent*—and returns us to the struggle between what is given, what is constructed, what is self-created. I support this triangulation as a way out of the rhetoric of victimization, on the one hand, or the paralysis of liberal White guilt on the other, as we interrogate any overly-simple, absolute, and unchanging political identification. Daniel David Moses insightfully describes this guilt as a "wound you don't want to heal. . . . In romanticism, you're dancing around a wound" (xxiv). Hulan shares the opinion of Native elders that "instead of raiding the spiritual and cultural material of First Nations, in effect 'going Native,' Euro-Canadians should look to their own traditions before joining the circle to listen to and learn about First Nations" (215). This is advice Maria Campbell also gave Linda Griffiths, when she said, "I couldn't understand why you didn't know your own history. . . . the history of your pain and all the things that happened to your people [Scots] was exactly the same as our history" (Griffiths and Campbell 35). She puts her hope, she says, in a healing conversation based on a shared knowledge of historical common ground that would create a "meeting place" for Native and non-Native today (35).

The potential for such a meeting place, through individual and collective agency, despite multiple ideological pressures, is still there. Agency is possible in each reader's response, student or teacher, to texts that, simply by arousing the debate and disagreement that they do, prove that categories like *Native writer* or *Native woman writer* are inevitably reductive. We are never merely "White" or "Native," for obviously, we are also invested in other alliances and loyalties that may be in opposition to these categories of privilege, when we are the "in group," or impoverishment, when we are "out." As an instructor, I thus am prepared to question identity politics at its most simplistic—"You must be part of the *in group* to understand or identify with our view"—while never denying or rewriting the historical fact of cultural heritage and the loss of community values that many Native writers insist on. Thomas King, for instance, who is identified as Cherokee-Greek by Hoy, offers a definition that, while acknowledging community consciousness, suggests a certain amount of postmodernist free play: "For Native people, identity comes from community, and it varies from community to community. I wouldn't define myself as an Indian in the same way that someone living on a reserve would. That whole idea of 'Indian' becomes in part, a construct. It's fluid. . . . We identify ourselves . . . and that's what counts" ("Coyote

Lives" 90–91). I think we agree, as teachers, critics, writers, and academics, that identity is multi-faceted, but we need to acknowledge also that there are formative experiences that particularly shape our combination of voices, that provide a grounding for our impulses towards greater agency, and that these are largely cultural differences. Here, *culture* may be defined in ways both broad and visible (Euro-Canadian, Anishinaabe) and localized, invisible, or idiosyncratic (the culture of academia, the culture of the reserve, the culture of Stephen King fans, etc.).

So when I first put together my Native literature course, entitled Studies in the Native Literatures of North America, it was with an unusual degree of excitement and also a sense of responsibility—not just to the institution, but to my own Northern, read *Native,* community. I taught it to a very select group of six female students, including one identified as Anishinaabe. I am teaching this course again, fall 2002, to a full class (35 students), and from this vantage point, I would like to review where I was then, my subject position as instructor to my imagined audience, and consider my own continuing learning process. I begin with my original course description, taken from my outline:

> *Studies in the Native Literatures of North America*
>
> Fittingly, we end the 20th century by looking back and "*revisioning*" *our history as North Americans.* This *new* course is an historical and self-reflexive exploration of Native *North American Literature written in English* (with some early work *in translation*) and its *meaning* for us, whether Native or non-Native. Aside from grounding discussions of *Native mythology and its "orature" (mediated* through print), we will be focusing on works created in the *last two centuries*, with an emphasis on the *Modern and Contemporary* periods. We will attempt to break down a *"Eurocentric"* hierarchical model of learning by inviting *guest speakers* and active student participation in the form of presentations, research questions, "debatable discussions" or position papers, and journal reflections. A *field trip* to a *Native community centre* (i.e. Indian Friendship Centre) will be investigated in order to facilitate *cultural sharing.*

When I re-read this now, I am struck by my millennialist enthusiasm—the "revisioning" of North American history, before September 2001, seemed to be both much more possible and positive. I am also aware of my unabashed privileging of the literature aspect of the course, the de-emphasizing of the oral and the translated, treated in quick, preliminary gestures before the clean break with the past, in this attractively "new" course. I register the bias towards those (early) modern and contemporary writers, from Pauline Johnson to Daniel David Moses to Thomas King, who are "double agents" in their eloquent ability to use the language of the enemy (as some would see it) and invoke their declared subject position as Natives as the source of their carefully crafted reflections. Their work seems to depend upon deployment of the "*Irony Oppositional*" in Hutcheon's classification: "the subversive doubling within and against the dominant that can be seen especially in the work of those artists concerned with issues of class, race, gender, sexual orientation, and post-colonial identity" (8). The angry writers—the activists first, writers second (or the community-builders?)—were less likely to get on the course. I emphasized that the course was not just for Native students, but in fact, the composition of my first class was predominantly Euro/Anglo-Canadian. While I introduced the term *Eurocentric* to signal a decentering of cultural authority (if not mine as professor), it is questionable whether guest speakers and even a field trip to a pre-determined Native community centre are really enough to achieve this. I think now that these moments are more artificial than I realized, akin to the popular participation, mentioned earlier, in Native cultural ceremonies often marketed alongside, or even within, Canadian tourism. In fact, the gathering at the Indian Friendship Centre was an awkward, if earnest, evening where my non-Native students and I tried to "fit in," and became more concerned with how we "consumed" the event—who was dancing? was it the right way? did we choose the moose as well as the pickerel? "how should I eat these?" (Hoy 3)—than with connecting beyond the evening to the lives and issues of our hosts, most of whom lived and worked right around us in North Bay. The evening offered the possibility of a cross-cultural "meeting place," to borrow Campbell's hopeful paradigm, but we didn't seem to have a vocabulary or an understanding for sharing otherness, theirs *and* ours. Perhaps next time we should take our cue from Thomas King's astute point—also exemplified by Drew Hayden Taylor's essays in *Funny, You Don't Look Like One*—that comedy, if used thoughtfully, can work strategically to open otherwise closed minds, including our own (King, "Coyote Lives" 97), and reveal an important element of shared human experience. If we can take the initial social risk of admitting our own awkward unease as outsiders to the literature and cultural events we have committed ourselves to honestly engaging with, we may well find that the oppositional walls dividing *out* from *in* melt away. Sharing our own discomfort, honestly and without blame-placing, allows humour to creep back in—and humour, especially when self-directed, tends to keep us humble, putting our often clumsy feet, non-Natives and Natives alike, back on common ground.

The course material I presented was organized through a number of guiding topics, and the one we spent the most time on was what I dubbed "Identity Puzzles." This was designed both to disarm any perceived criticism of my authority to teach the course—my initial anxiety, which appeared unfounded—and to encourage the students to consider their own complex of subject positions in ways that made them open to the possibility of a Native identity as something more than another "special interest group," in the resentful language of the national climate (again, so much for the Canadian community of communities). The course was aimed at second-year students, and my impression of (typical, not so-called "mature") students at this stage is that they are still laying down their core markers of identity by means of frequent bursts of enthusiasm and disgust, and impatient with the idea of limits or checks channelling that energy, whether imposed by society, the economy, or me, as instructor. I think in a way I was protecting both the students *and* myself from the full exploration of these questions of identity. Allowing more time, and outlets, for this exploration might have led to franker discussions of the meaning of "Native identity" and, perhaps, its particular cultural difference, gleaned gradually from our reading, talking, and listening—and, perhaps, from the reflected-upon experience of Native students or guest speakers among us. That is, I may have given in to the temptation—as do so many of us as teachers—to emphasize *relevance* at the expense of *difference*. I was nervous about a rejection of the course's preliminary thesis—that there *is* a difference, growing up Native in Canada, that we, as sympathetic outsiders, may still not have access to—and so, probably politely downplayed it. Instructor discomfort with texts like *In Search of April Raintree* and its perceived aesthetic weaknesses may also stem from our resistance to content that frightens as it implicates us. The inevitable movement, in teaching Native literature, towards teaching cultural studies, which emphasizes "radical contextualism," as one proponent puts it, at the expense of artistic absolutes, also invites us to think about the challenge of shifting more consciously in the direction of what Henry Giroux has famously termed "critical pedagogy," where the teacher "simply" aspires to be a "model of thoughtfulness" (qtd. in Grossberg 19). We may see this shift as a loss of one kind of authority, the authority many of us once saw embodied in a reified professor-ideal. But we may also see it as a liberating embrace of our true "impurity," our genuine hybridity in language, culture, identity. Ultimately, I feel, this will allow for greater honesty as we begin to share, if not shed, our pretences as teachers and students—pretences to objectivity, to mastery, to complete honesty, for a start.

As an example of how I would like to embrace the "impurity" of teaching Native literature as a non-Native in an academic setting, I return to another cultural event I organized for the class that had unexpected effects. Eager to start the year off with "Native voices," I invited the White Tail Singers, a local group of Natives who performed traditional drumming and "singing" in their native tongue (more like crying or wailing to my untrained ears) and which has been revived as a healing art. The intent was to have them perform outside, on the hill beside our pond, where we could remind ourselves of the ecological emphasis of Native spirituality and commune with nature at the same time. However, rain put an end to that plan, and in the absence of an appropriate space—the classroom was too small they decided; the gym, even if appropriate, already booked—the Singers set up in the large, open foyer beside the cafeteria. This meant that we had a captive audience, around 9:50 a.m., of a lineup of bleary-eyed students, teachers, and employees, all craving their Tim Horton's coffee (franchised by our food services), and serenaded by the Singers. Some became intrigued, and we attracted a separate crowd for a little while, but I felt uncertain about the stares we got, and my discomfort grew as the singers continued with their program, creating a pounding rhythm that travelled through the halls, and the executive secretary to the Vice-President appeared to inform me that exams were being written nearby, and to please close as many doors between them and us as possible. We should, of course, also ask permission for such a performance, next time. I was vividly reminded of the scene at the conclusion of *Kiss of the Fur Queen* where the burning of sweetgrass by a medicine woman sets off smoke alarms in the hospital where Gabriel is dying and brings firefighters charging into the scene (304–05). We brought an "impure" effect into an otherwise routine, coffee-drinking day. The students and I discussed this mixed reaction afterwards, but probably with more embarrassment than we should have—and with less (self-directed, critical) humour than we could have brought to our interpretation of this collision of cultures.

I think when I teach Native literature again, I will look more frequently to other voices, in the classroom—and I hope, other Native voices there—and the Native community that I may discover by making my own forays into the possibilities around us. Native people may then be found to speak from their perspective, which would sit against our abstract, inquisitive, literary outsider perspective. Ideally, I would like the cultural sharing to occur more loosely and spontaneously, through student ideas, curiosity, and community contacts . . . within *and* without the classroom and the text discussion. I would like to invite students to take responsibility, as part of their course mark, for making this happen. Allowing for this possible input and energy may mean the literature I have selected for discussion will be—temporarily—decentred at times. This may mean I will more often occupy the listener position: not an easy one for many of us. My authority may come mostly as a facilitator, perhaps a mediator, and a resource person for literary studies. Naturally, I remain in the end the ajudicator of marks and assignments, and so my institutional authority is unchanged. But perhaps the different perspectives we invoke, in text and discussion but also in more careful sharing and listening, if taken seriously enough by all, may make it clear that, especially in this teaching/learning experience, gaining an *A*, *B*, or *C* is not the most important achievement of this course. Nor is my own need to cram as many texts into a year, and the students, as possible. Perhaps, instead, a better sense both of humour and of honesty will be our mutual gain.

To return to the literature, will I teach the same books again? Mostly, yes—and time permitting—partly for my greater learning the second time around, and partly for their own obvious educational challenges to me and the students. I have already intimated my own mixed feelings about *In Search of April Raintree*. This highly accessible novel was a powerful one—especially the controversial rape scene, with its explicit racist and misogynist overtones—and I found that my most reticent student was inspired to speak up, unprompted, to comment on its deeply-felt effect on her. Should such a scene, loaded with implications, be presented in a more subtle, understated manner? My own intellectual distance—jaded? or sophisticated?—felt inadequate in the face of stories of students being moved to tears in empathetic identification with the two sisters. *Kiss of the Fur Queen* was easily the most disturbing work, given its explicit detailing of sexual abuse of boys by priests in a residential school. This content was made more challenging for many of us as it was framed by the gay lifestyles of the two adult brothers, and the complex interplay between moments of sexual exploitation and moments of presumably willing initiation. For instance, the molesting priest's prominent crucifix, and the naked body of Christ, becomes an eroticized icon in memory, then fantasy. Highway's outrageous trickster-as-drag-queen fantasies jostle against horrific victimization scenes in a tragicomic manner, making *Green Grass, Running Water*'s biblical parodies seem mild by comparison. I felt that Highway's sudden shifts of tone, mood, and mode of writing—realism to fantasy to satire to black humour—violated cherished views about unity and structural integrity. Again, was this my own limitation, or the text's? McCulloch's novel appealed with its quest pattern, poetic "Coyote" passages, and attention to the unrecorded tragedies still occurring on reserves today. *The Book of Jessica,* play and dialogue, was a good way to get students to question their own attitudes coming into the course—do they identify more with Linda or Maria in their conflicted collaboration, and why? Discussing it, we were able to take a step back, and survey our own liberal White guilt, or the "wound" as Moses describes it, in the comfort of observing another's mistakes and misunderstandings on the way to the qualified triumph that is the play. Inspired by Maria, performed by Linda, created by both, it is truly a half-breed child.[9]

The poetry was received with mixed interest, as poetry often is, though the students responded well to the narrative, or storytelling, poems, and quickly identified the "irony oppositional" operating in many. The (First) Preface to the Moses/Goldie anthology, "Two Voices," written in the form of a conversation between the editors, was also a helpful way to introduce the material, and its many issues, modelling the dialogical mode I hoped to achieve in class on a regular basis. Of course, like many of our teaching goals, this was achieved partially and imperfectly . . . I need to inhabit the listener position more often. I hope, with my second attempt, and more voices to counterbalance mine, to revisit this discourse more frequently.

In her discussion of the problems of teaching Native literature, Hoy draws on postcolonial critics for their strategies for resolving insider/ outsider impasses. She observes the tendency towards a "retreat response," when differences are felt intensely and there is a retreat from anger's danger into a more passive, or apathetic, silence masked as politeness:

> In the classroom, Chandra Mohanty suggests, this can produce "a comfortable set of oppositions: people of color as the central voices and bearers of all knowledge in class, and white people as 'observers,' with no responsibility to contribute and/or with nothing valuable to contribute" (194).
>
> What this simple divide misses, Mohanty suggests, is the necessary acknowledgment of "co-implication," awareness of asymmetrical but mutually constitutive histories, relationships, and responsibilities. (qtd. in Hoy 17)

This reminder of "co-implication" in history, in time, and in space, whether the space of Canada or the space of the classroom, is a good corrective to either silencing or silence. Reading the classroom for such dynamics is key for a White instructor who needs to shift between listener/learner and resource person/discussion leader. Keeping the dialogue alive and in the present is our best strategy and guarantee of interpretive authority, Margery Fee feels, "Without a conversation with living First Nations people about what they think and feel about their writing, their culture and their lives, the likelihood that we will have produced bad interpretation arises, as we make ourselves the experts, and them into the mute subjects of monologic expertise" (7). Hence the need for the "meeting place," where the equal right to speak and to listen is assured, through the tactics of honest sharing and doses of critical humour.

"Silence is also / a two-edged sword," observes Joy Kogawa, acclaimed author of *Obasan,* which won redress for the Japanese Canadians affected by internment during World War Two ("Jericho Road" 71). Power, too, cuts both ways—sometimes deep cuts, sometimes minor nicks: the power of the teacher to grade students, the power of the students to shape the class positively or negatively, the power of educational privilege, the power of lived, embodied knowledge. Kogawa has also said, "Every certainty must be surrounded by doubt" ("Every Certainty" C1). Can a non-Native, White instructor teach Native literature, and teach it well? It is a continually negotiated tension, for me, between acknowledging the experiential authority of cultural otherness, and making my own contribution to the passionate curiosity about unique voices and artful narratives of all kinds, times, and peoples that provides the initial—and Canadian?—ground, I hope, for our meeting place. If we recognize that we are always both outsiders and insiders to each other, but joined by our human need to make meaning out of our experiences, then we may learn the "methodological humility" that careful critics like Hoy advocate. We may even realize the agency that may come with the "simple" wisdom found through humility and maintained through a (self)-critical sense of humour.

NOTES

1. The "Postcolonialism and Pedagogy: Canadian Literatures in the Classroom" symposium, was held 3–5 May 2002 at the University of Ottawa. This paper was presented in the session "Teaching *First Nations* Literature" (my italics), reminding me, by these initial differences in naming this emerging area of study—*Aboriginal, First Nations, Indigenous, Native* are its varying descriptors—how provisional and self-reflective our critical responses must be.

2. With reference to Andy Belyea and Lia Marie Talia's dramatic presentation at the "Postcolonialism and Pedagogy" symposium, "Classroom Encounters with *The Book of Jessica*."

3. I'm thinking of, for instance, Rohinton Mistry's *Such a Long Journey*, Michael Ondaatje's *Running in the Family*, and Anne Michaels's *Fugitive Pieces*, to name a few random examples.

4. See Frye, "Conclusion to *The Literary History of Canada*"; Atwood, *Survival*; and Gaile McGregor, *The Wacousta Syndrome*.

5. This spring, *Morningside*'s replacement, *This Morning* (host Shelagh Rogers), ran a panel of celebrities and writers on the "Battle of the Books," which aimed to discover the one book "all Canadians should read." Contenders were Atwood's *The Handmaid's Tale*, Mistry's *Such a Long Journey*, Clarke's *Whylah Falls*, Laurence's *The Stone Angel*, and Ondaatje's *In the Skin of a Lion* (the winner).

6. Perception may be at times stronger than reality; I acknowledge Carole Gerson's careful work on the actual numbers of women represented in Canadian literature anthologies, although I see evidence in the newer teaching anthologies (often highlighting the modern and contemporary periods, it's true) of more gender-sensitive editorial and selection principles. For instance, in the revised and

abridged edition of *An Anthology of Canadian Literature in English*, edited by Russell Brown, Donna Bennett, and Nathalie Cooke, there are 72 authors included, and 31—very close to half—are women.

7. Of course, part of her personal/professional disclosure, and likely a factor in Hoy's special interest in this area, is her well-known partnership with Cherokee-Greek writer Thomas King, and their family life together. It is only fair to note that I, too, have a "special interest" now, being married to Cree-Scottish writer Ian McCulloch, whose novel I have chosen to put on my course, for its teachability, excellence, and relevance.

8. See John Milloy, *"A National Crime": The Canadian Government and the Residential School System, 1879 to 1986*.

9. Maria Campbell is probably best known as the author of the disturbing memoir, *Halfbreed*.

WORKS CITED

Atwood, Margaret. *The Handmaid's Tale*. Toronto: Seal, 1985.

———. *Survival: A Thematic Guide to Canadian Literature*. Toronto: Anansi, 1972.

Belyea, Andy, and Lia Marie Talia. "Classroom Encounters with *The Book of Jessica*." Presented at the "Postcolonialism and Pedagogy: Canadian Literatures in the Classroom" symposium. University of Ottawa. 3–5 May 2002.

Brant, Beth. "From the Inside." *Writing as Witness: Essay and Talk*. Toronto: Women's Press, 1994. 49–54.

———. "The Good Red Road." *Writing as Witness* 5–21.

Brown, Russell, Donna Bennett, and Nathalie Cooke, eds. *An Anthology of Canadian Literature in English*. Rev. and abridged ed. Toronto: Oxford UP, 1990.

Campbell, Maria. *Halfbreed*. Toronto: McClelland, 1973.

Clarke, George Elliott. *Whylah Falls*. Vancouver: Polestar, 2000.

Culleton Mosionier, Beatrice. *In Search of April Raintree*. Critical edition. Ed. Cheryl Suzack. Winnipeg: Portage and Main, 1999.

Dragland, Stan. *Floating Voice: Duncan Campbell Scott and the Literature of Treaty 9*. Concord, ON: Anansi, 1994.

Fee, Margery. "Reading Aboriginal Lives." *Canadian Literature* 167 (Winter 2000): 5–7.

Frye, Northrop. "Conclusion to *A Literary History of Canada*." *The Bush Garden: Essays on the Canadian Imagination*. Toronto: Anansi, 1971. 213–51.

Gerson, Carole. "Anthologies and the Canon of Early Canadian Women Writers." *Re(dis)covering Our Foremothers: Nineteenth-Century Canadian Women Writ-*

ers. Ed. and introd. Lorraine McMullen. Ottawa: U of Ottawa P, 1990. 55–76.

Griffiths, Linda, and Maria Campbell. *The Book of Jessica: A Theatrical Transformation*. Toronto: Playwrights Canada, 1989.

Grossberg, Lawrence. "Bringin' It All Back Home—Pedagogy and Cultural Studies." *Between Borders: Pedagogy and the Politics of Cultural Studies*. Ed. Henry Giroux and Peter McLaren. New York: Routledge, 1994. 1–25.

Harjo, Joy. *The Woman Who Fell from the Sky: Poems*. New York: Norton, 1994.

Highway, Tomson. *Dry Lips Oughta Move to Kapuskasing*. Saskatoon: Fifth House, 1989.

———. *Kiss of the Fur Queen*. Toronto: Doubleday, 1998.

———. *The Rez Sisters*. Saskatoon: Fifth House, 1988.

Hoy, Helen. *How Should I Read These?: Native Women Writers in Canada*. Toronto: U of Toronto P, 2001.

———. "'Nothing But the Truth': Discursive Transparency in Beatrice Culleton." Culleton 273–93.

Hulan, Renée. "Some Thoughts on 'Integrity and Intent' and Teaching Native Literature." *Essays on Canadian Writing* 63 (1998): 210–30.

Hutcheon, Linda. *Splitting Images: Contemporary Canadian Ironies*. Toronto: Oxford UP, 1991.

King, Thomas. "Coyote Lives." Interview with Jeffrey Canton. *The Power to Bend Spoons: Interviews with Canadian Novelists*. Ed. Bev Daurio. Toronto: Mercury, 1998. 90–97.

———. *Green Grass, Running Water*. Toronto: HarperCollins, 1994.

Kogawa, Joy. "'Every Certainty Must Be Surrounded By Doubt.'" Interview with Val Ross. *Globe and Mail* 21 Mar. 1992: C1, C15.

———. "Jericho Road." *Jericho Road*. Toronto: McClelland, 1977. 71.

Kruk, Laurie. *Studies in the Native Literatures of North America*. English 2275 Course Outline. Nipissing University, 1999–2000.

Laurence, Margaret. *The Stone Angel*. Toronto: McClelland, 1988.

McCulloch, Ian. *Childforever*. Stratford: Mercury, 1996.

McGregor, Gaile. *The Wacousta Syndrome: Explorations in the Canadian Langscape*. Toronto: U of Toronto P, 1985.

Michaels, Anne. *Fugitive Pieces*. Toronto: McClelland, 1996.

Milloy, John. *"A National Crime": The Canadian Government and the Residential School System, 1879 to 1986*. Winnipeg: U of Manitoba P, 1999.

"Mission Statement." Nipissing University Calendar. 2002–03. 8.

Mistry, Rohinton. *Such a Long Journey*. Toronto: McClelland, 1991.

Moses, Daniel David, and Terry Goldie. "Preface to the First Edition: Two Voices." *An Anthology of Canadian Native Literature in English*. 2nd ed. Toronto: Oxford UP, 1998. xix–xxix.

Ondaatje, Michael. *In the Skin of a Lion*. Markham, ON: Penguin, 1987.
———. *Running in the Family*. Toronto: McClelland, 1982.
Proulx, E. Annie. *The Shipping News*. New York: Touchstone, 1993.
Smith, Paul. *Discerning the Subject*. Minneapolis: U of Minnesota P, 1988.
Taylor, Drew Hayden. *Funny, You Don't Look Like One: Observations from a Blue-Eyed Ojibway*. Penticton: Theytus, 1996.

Getting In and Out of the Dark Room: *In Search of April Raintree* as Neutral Ground for Conflict Resolution

DANIELLE SCHAUB

CLASSICAL BLACK-AND-WHITE photography and Polaroid photography share one major prerequisite with regard to their finished product, namely a negative exposed to light. In other words, for both systems, the positive print cannot come into being without the negative film. But unlike Polaroid photography whose negatives become useless once peeled off the positives, classical black-and-white photography features negatives of a different nature.[1] The film negative in classical black-and-white photography can be used with much greater flexibility. The making of a positive print involves the negative in a greater combination of variables subjected to manipulation and control, non-existent in the case of Polaroid photography. These images serve as a metaphor for ways of reading Canadian texts within heterogeneous groups experiencing strife and controversy.

Owing to its heterogeneity, Canadian literature can elicit expressions of empathy, repression, trauma, anger, and healing.[2] Such texts deal with what Diana Brydon defines in this volume as "issues that matter enough to get people angry" (57), and I would add, "or sad." For a foreign reader, Canadian texts of resistance enable the externalization of numbing alienation and traumatic experience in the safe literary distancing of other cultures, other times, other bodies. By analyzing the strategies used in such texts, students from different geopolitical contexts can examine how different cultural groups depict antagonism, self-discovery, and, at times, even healing and growth. Simultaneously and specifically, such approaches can help open empathetic communication between groups that are ambivalently delineated by prejudice, fear, longing, hate, and desire.

Examined in this way, Beatrice Culleton's *In Search of April Raintree* allows for a psycho-literary and psychodramatic interplay of self and group communication in heterogeneous Israeli classes with Beduin, Christian, Druze, Jewish, Muslim, and other self-identified students.[3] The negotiation of space and place for the Métis within the Canadian national framework allows Israeli students from diverse communities and foreign students to apprehend conflicts they face in their own lives. The analysis of their response shows how by reading texts about people involved in conflictual situations different from, yet similar to, their own, Middle-Eastern students look at their predicament with a less jaded eye. The pedagogical impact of the literary approach afforded by Canadian literature cannot be overlooked, for the introduction of Canadian texts empowers students, enabling self-expression and inspiring unfeigned respect for opposed views. As they find constructive language to express themselves and their concepts of one another, they become aware that they carry a heavy load of stereotypical thought.

In Search of April Raintree depicts the lives of two Métis sisters, almost identical twins except for their age difference and their skin colour. Assigned to foster homes on account of their parents' alcoholism, April, the paler of the two, idealizes White society. She perceives that her dream of extreme upward mobility remains contingent on divorcing herself from her Métis past, and especially on distancing herself from her younger sister. April's darker sister, Cheryl, romanticizes the Métis tradition, idealizing a return to a pure Aboriginal culture. Cheryl angrily criticizes April's estrangement from her people, but becomes dangerously embroiled in the very cycle of violence, drugs, drink, and prostitution that April seeks to escape. After a generous divorce settlement from her adulterous White husband, April lives well until the announcement of Cheryl's hospitalization. Having lost contact with her sister for an extended period, she discovers that Cheryl is lost to alcohol, drugs, anger, and apathy. She attempts to re-establish her maternal older-sister relationship with Cheryl. April's approach to life drastically changes when she is gang raped by men who mistake her for Cheryl in a racist and misogynist act of punitive violence. While Cheryl blames herself for April's traumatized post-rape condition, April is too focused on her pain to recognize Cheryl's terrible sense of guilt. Cheryl commits suicide and April finds herself the sad inheritor of her sister's diaries. Yet Cheryl's narratives help April realize that in order to overcome the trauma of her childhood and her experience of rape, she must accept her Métis heritage as integral to her configuration of a new self—even if that new self is highly motivated and shaped by values attributed to White Christian culture, values inherited from her good foster parents, the Dions. Through the diaries, April also discovers that Cheryl had a son. At the end of the novel, April determines to adopt her sister's child and to provide him with a better self-image. She also personalizes her involvement in the Métis community, joining in a struggle against alcoholism, which she sees as a primary destructive threat to her people.

When we read *In Search of April Raintree* in my literature classes,[4] I ask my students to keep a running journal of their reflections. At the end of the reading, each student writes a free-style essay. In it they identify the character with whom they most relate and discuss how their literary experience reflects their own perception of identity and conflict in Israel.[5] Typically, the participants have strong responses that reflect cultural clashes separating and joining them. One of the tasks I give them in class involves a sheet with anonymous reflections taken from their writings. I ask them to read the statements and match the probable identities of their authors. We discuss our findings and experiences at several levels, with some interesting results.

I have included the text of this exercise in an appendix to this essay. My handout to the class contains 14 journal excerpts and 14 identities to match. When I give my handout to the class, I give them the following instructions:

> You will have *10 minutes* for this task. Read the extracts and, without consulting anyone else, attempt to assign each statement a probable author. Work individually otherwise the next part of the activity becomes pointless. After ten minutes, I will ask you to turn to the person sitting next to you. Each one of you will be given two minutes to discuss how the texts and this task have affected you. Then we'll have a general discussion of your experience and matched entries/identities.[6]

Many of my students thought they knew one another well enough to predict which person would likely say one or another statement. They were often mistaken. The students' answers implied that at some level their expectations were unconsciously fraught with their own prejudices. When making decisions under pressure, they fell back on stereotypes. This exercise helps both to confirm and trouble the borders of cultural expectations. The answers we got show that nothing is purely black and white, that grey dots infest every area, even from within a minority position.

Returning to my metaphor of photography, even a field as binary as black and white photography produces borders that blur and merge. The photograph of a glass ceiling in Vienna (see Figure 1) shows clear demarcations between the black and the white. No doubt, the metal frame delimits the glass panes in a clear-cut manner. Yet when blowing up one section of the photograph (see Figure 2), the eye perceives how dots of white invade even the seemingly black areas and vice versa. Moreover, the dividing line, the border, becomes ever more complex when looked at in detail, affording an analogy to close-up visions of identities. Even when identities seem to be inscribed in black and white, the blackness and the whiteness are never pure, always discontinuous and temporary, threatening to bleed over and fade into the other. This in part helps explain why certain elements in our cultures often fear exposure to other cultures: they fear their purity will be lost and the borders of difference might break down.

In discussing Culleton's novel, some Muslim Arabs identify with Cheryl, saying that her story reflects their own or that of their brothers and sisters in the Occupied Territories. They find negative characters styled as White akin to some Israeli Jews. But not all Israeli Muslim Arabs feel this way; some identify with April, enjoying their life in Israel, and while sympathetic to those on the other side of the Green Line, they confess feeling somehow estranged from them. Some expressly speak against the Israeli-Palestinian conflict and have humanistic views, such as the young Muslim female student who wears the symbols of the three major monotheistic religions and conducts seminars about the Holocaust. Druze and Beduin students, both members of communities whose men serve in the Israel Defence Force, sometimes feel awkward about the conflict because they have sworn allegiance to the State of Israel while maintaining their cultural Arab identity. Christian Arabs are also divided in their perspectives. While some have assimilated into Israeli society and find themselves

FIGURE 1. Glass Ceiling of the Haass-Haus Shopping Mall, Vienna. Photo: D. Schaub.

FIGURE 2. Detail from Figure 1. Photo: D. Schaub.

much like April, others claim that Cheryl represents the position of Christians in the Palestinian Territories amongst the Muslims who outnumber them and with whom they sometimes struggle for space and place. Amongst Jewish students, opinions vary widely. Different immigrants and minority groupings identify with Cheryl as the unwanted other. Moroccan, Russian, Ethiopian, Yemenite Jews, and others sometimes see the dominant culture as less accepting of them than of long-term residents of Polish and German descent. Yet even the privileged old-timers oppose one another in matters of politics, religious practice, choices of secular lifestyle, and views about what the State of Israel should strive to be.

Needless to say, because of the variety of views expressed, mediating the discussion involves strenuous attention not to let relations degenerate to a point of no return.[7] Heated discussions, however, demonstrate that voicing anger and frustration—about being othered, about not having equal rights—helps everyone feel better, more so than becoming violent. Sometimes when class discussions reach a peak in tension, I ask the students to enact, as in psychodrama, the role of the character in Culleton's novel that they least identify with. I ask them to put in words and body language what the other side fails to see about this estranged position. Dramatic action, following the model proposed by the American Society of Group Psychotherapy and Psychodrama, forces the students "to examine problems and issues raised" by that character while "facilitat[ing] insight, personal growth, and integration on cognitive, affective, and behavioral levels" (American Society). At other times, I ask the students to engage in sociodrama and enact a passage from the book, giving each student the part of a character with views diverging from his/her own. At times, the students choose to represent a character with whose views they agree, making the most of the "natural and automatic process" involved in psychodrama, "*externalising* their internal world onto a theatrical stage" so as to solve a conflict they themselves experience (Yablonsky 3–4).[8] While enacting a part, the students are given "the opportunity to practice new and more appropriate behaviors, and evaluate its effectiveness within the supportive atmosphere of the group" (National Coalition). By dramatizing some positions and "mov[ing] very fully into [others'] subjective world without judgement" (Brodie), the students understand the problematic nature of dividing lines. Because of the discussion after each dramatic improvisation, these exercises help students develop empathy with people and positions other than their own. In this way the students engaged in reading *In Search of April Raintree* succeed in at least recognizing the falsity and dangers of belief systems based on binary oppositions. After going through this process, my students usually reach the conclusion that everyone feels trapped by stereotypical definitions of belonging.[9]

Then they feel ready to move on and work together against prejudice. At this point I mention B.Z. Goldberg's project of bringing together Palestinian and Jewish children as part of his film *Promises* (*Haftachot*). The film shows superbly that when brought together children forget dividing lines, enjoy one another's presence, and play together regardless of identity. Notions of belonging to one community or another no longer matter when children engage in fun activities. At this point the students come up with projects promoting multicultural education that challenge binary modes of thinking.

Binary thinking may well be deeply embedded in our cultures, if only to control chaos,[10] but we can become aware of its existence in ourselves. We can challenge ourselves to think more creatively, communicate more openly, struggle to create new identities that complicate divisions between "us" and "them." In this respect, I would like to mention that a number of my students have pointed out that characters like the Dions (April's first foster family), the Steindalls (Cheryl's second foster family), Roger (April's friend), and other White characters in the novel display warm, unquestioning acceptance that provides April with valuable lessons in faith, understanding, and forgiveness. A number of students have also noted that April does not get any support from the Métis elders, that in a state of cultural deprivation her parents have failed to pass on any values from a Métis perspective. Some students have pointed out that even Cheryl's immersion in Native culture does not strengthen her sufficiently to survive.

These recognitions open up discussions about our abilities to draw strength from diverse cultural sources, at whatever opportunity may arise. Such awareness alerts us that we can enrich one another with our own developed skills in negotiating reality—including how to struggle, together and peaceably, to change reality if necessary. Through April's final acceptance of her people, the students realize that one can sometimes get the strength to accept and draw upon one's native culture thanks to the enrichment provided by a culture different from one's own. Important messages come across: April may be in a sorry position as a child, losing her family, but the book shows how even the "real" Whites go through difficult experiences too, such as the Dions who lose their maternal figure. April learns another positive lesson, namely that it is good to cry and share one's loss. She realizes that her presence helps the Dions overcome the loss of Mrs. Dion to cancer. Even when April faces abuse in her second foster family, the deRosiers, which initially causes her to abandon faith, she returns to religious principles to forgive herself and others as an adult. Both April and Cheryl invent a past. April invents a White past, obliterating the story of her parents. Cheryl claims a romantic Aboriginal past. But both prove problematic. Both attempts at identity formation rely on a binary black-and-white approach that is analogous to trying to obtain a positive print while destroying the original film negative. Both April and Cheryl try to be purely one identity or the other, and attempt to destroy elements of the other culture that invade these identities.

To return to my consideration of the photography metaphor, I am reminded again that the line of demarcation between the white and the black is anything but clear. Opposites blur into one another. When my students first encounter *In Search of April Raintree*, they have no idea that it will shape their concepts of self and other. This text and the process of reading we undergo help the students understand that we are kept in check by narratives that ignore the many common issues we have with divergent groups, and the many differences we have with people defined by those narratives of our own culture. When they become conscious that the poor in the Beduin, Christian, Druze, Jewish, and Muslim quarters all live in more difficult conditions than their rich rulers; that sometimes religious people of different cultures have more values in common than they have with their own secular groupings; that secular people in one group share more interests with secular people of different cultures than they do with their religious peers—all of this teaches students that imagining pure black and white does not help facilitate progress.

When I opened my essay with an allusion to photography, I deliberately left the reader hanging as to why the negative can stand alone as a thing for-itself and in-itself while the positive cannot exist without the negative. The approach to reading *In Search of April Raintree* that I have outlined shows that individuals produced by culture are in many ways like a negative: a product of culture and biology. But in the process of making the print, individuals can consciously choose to empathize with other cultures while maintaining what they feel is most important about their source culture. In photography, the positive can undergo a series of deliberate and controllable changes. It can be colour washed, lightened, darkened, blurred, have elements added or erased, be printed on grainy paper, and so on.

When April attempts to erase her Métis origins completely and invents a pure White past, her situation is analogous to trying to make a positive print without having a film negative to start with. Only after Cheryl's death does she realize that she cannot formulate herself without her film negative, that is, without accepting her past. At the end of the novel, she realizes that by accepting her past, she has the ability to shape and foster her identity. In order to do so, she must accept her past and embrace all or any aspects of other cultures that will help her to build a more viable sense of self. Like April, the students who read the text as I have outlined discover that they must become self-conscious print-makers of both themselves and the reality that their children and they themselves will face.

APPENDIX

Responses from Students to Beatrice Culleton's *In Search of April Raintree*

Handout – Page 1

IDENTITIES AND CHARACTERISTICS OF THE CORPUS

a. 19-year-old Muslim female active in Holocaust programmes

b. 21-year-old female Yemenite Jew

c. 22-year-old female Muslim Arab with family in Jenin

d. 23-year-old female Ethiopian Jew

e. 25-year-old female Sabra (5th generation in Israel)

f. 26-year-old male Druze (has served in the Israeli army)

g. 27-year-old male Ashkenazy leftist

h. 27-year-old male English volunteer on a kibbutz

i. 29-year-old female right-wing Israeli

j. 30-year-old male Beduin (reserve officer/Israeli army)

k. 30-year-old female Orthodox (mother)

l. 30-year-old female Russian immigrant

m. 32-year-old female Christian Arab living in Haifa

n. 42-year-old female Moroccan Jew (mother)

Handout – Page 2

1. I identify with April when she feels torn between her roots and her desire to belong to white society. I also see how by not sticking to my people, I could progress more, have better living conditions, struggle less.

2. Like April, I find myself criticizing two cultures; when she says, "I became quite good at it, seeing all the negative sides and criticizing them [the whites] to high heaven to myself. It came to me that I had criticized the native people and here I was doing the same thing to white people. Maybe that's what a half-breed was all about, being a critic-at-large" (125) I feel like that too. They are just trying to wipe us out. But then we also get extremely violent at times. Where is this fight taking us?

3. I feel like Cheryl. We have been betrayed and let down. Why should life be so hard for us when they have everything? We're not given a chance to get out of our difficult life conditions. We're going to remain stuck in our hole.

4. While I was reading the novel, I kept thinking of unpleasant aspects about my people. I also don't like how my people live. They've lost their self-respect, don't fight for their rights and have lost all hope. They have no jobs, or jobs that don't pay well and there is a lot of family violence and even drinking or taking drugs out of despair.

5. I like Cheryl a lot. I like the way she wants to fight for the rights of her

people and what she writes. She is right when she criticizes the whites; they have robbed them of everything. We too should fight and get what's ours.

6. I think Cheryl exaggerates. If her people really wanted to live differently, they could do something about their lives. And April's attitude is wrong too. Why should she envy what others have? Perhaps she could find it within herself to improve things. Nothing comes free of charge. You have to earn what you get in this life.

7. I feel like Cheryl. We've also lost a lot. We've lost our traditions, our habits, our homes. And we also don't have an easy life. Maybe if we put up a tougher fight things will change and we'll regain our pride. And I hope that we won't be defeated the way Cheryl is in the end.

8. I'm not sure either April or Cheryl are right. Why should there be tension? Cheryl is aggressive against the whites but doesn't try hard enough to improve things for her people. And April only wants what the whites have. It's like here. Why fight and not try to make things better? Sometimes there are better solutions than fighting.

9. April and Cheryl stand at opposite ends. But couldn't they have a better time if they weren't engaged in a pointless struggle? It's like things over here. Isn't there enough space for everybody? Can't both people live side by side without hating each other? I don't understand what the whole fuss is about.

10. I feel upset about the tension between Cheryl and April. They come from the same family and yet they can't agree. It's like the tension between Israelis and Palestinians. We too come from the same family and have a lot in common. When we struggle against each other, we struggle against ourselves.

11. I can't accept Cheryl's position. She makes claims to land that make no sense whatsoever. Once the whites negotiated the land it became theirs. Why should they give it back? They've developed towns, cultivated the land. They shouldn't give in. Besides where would they go? Back to Europe or wherever they originally came from? That's unlikely.

12. I feel like April but I'm disgusted with her at the same time. I want to assimilate and get all the benefits of the majority but I feel guilty that I might be abandoning my people.

13. Cheryl is right when she wants to discover her roots and keep her people's traditions. But she's wrong because she thinks that celebrating her culture means she has to fight against the whites. This is what burns her out and causes her to die. She's too angry and can't forgive.

14. It's good that Cheryl gets the opportunity to live with people who give her books about her cultural background and history. They help her develop pride and a sense of identity that her parents irresponsibly failed to do. But she makes a great mistake by mixing her wonderful spiritual revelation with politics and anger. The wisdom of the elders is lost on her.

NOTES

1. The laws of light exposure are virtually the same with a difference: once a black-and-white negative has been exposed, the markings of light cannot be erased from it, but, technically, the film could be double exposed or overexposed to admit more light markings. Admittedly, this is not common practice.

2. I have used the approach discussed here with texts such as Neil Bissoondath's *Digging Up the Mountains,* Dionne Brand's *In Another Place, Not Here*, Maria Campbell's *Halfbreed*, Cheryl Foggo's *Pourin' Down Rain*, Thomas King's *Medicine River*, Lee Maracle's *Ravensong*, and Shani Mootoo's *Cereus Blooms at Night*.

3. For more information on psychodrama, see Blatner, and Blatner and Blatner. Shorter explicative texts about psychodrama can be found on the Robert Brodie Home Page, the Web site of the American Society of Group Psychotherapy and Psychodrama, and the Web site of the National Coalition of Creative Arts Therapies Associations. The use of the term *psychodrama* here includes sociometry (a technique that highlights acceptance and rejection while seeking group cohesion), and sociodrama (a technique that involves group drama on social issues). A related technique that involves both text and enacting, dramatherapy also allows one to slide in and out of text and reality, and those involved in the therapy have to find ways of empowering themselves through their interaction with the text whether written or imagined (see Jones). For an exploration of plays in the context of bibliotherapy and enacting, see Jenkins.

4. The students participating in the course are in their second, third, or fourth year, and will eventually graduate with a BA in English Language and Literature as well as a Certificate of Education.

5. I entirely agree that keeping a journal, as Arun Mukherjee notes in her essay in this volume, helps students "negotiate their identities" through the text (191).

6. The key to the quiz is as follows: 1=n, 2=g, 3=b, 4=l, 5=c, 6=m, 7=d, 8=e, 9=h, 10=a, 11=i, 12=f, 13=j, 14=k.
7. For instance, in a community course at Oranim, the Academic College of Education, a BA-granting institution in the north of Israel, the educator divided the students along Jewish/Arab lines after a workshop where opposing views were voiced along those lines, thereby causing a rift in a class that had until then handled the contraries with much ease and tolerance. It took quite some time to rectify the situation as a delicate balance had been upset.
8. The dividing line between psychotherapy, sociodrama, and dramatherapy in this case proves rather thin.
9. Alienation resulting from restrictive definitions of belonging particularly affects people who have moved from country to country. Theirs is a fragmented vision of the self, where all the terms of the complex equation must be present for the sum to be correct. In referring to their approach as a nomadic experience, Rosi Braidotti rightly alludes to the cross-fertilization from one vision to another, akin to the experiential enrichment afforded by the multiple adjustments nomads have to make to different surroundings.
10. In particular, spatial polarities organize our thinking around binaries such as up/down, in/out, etc., binaries that have social and political implications with regard to notions of belonging.

WORKS CITED

American Society of Group Psychotherapy and Psychodrama (ASGPP). "General Information about Psychodrama." ASGPP Home Page. 3 Sept. 2003. 16 Jan. 2004. <http://www.asgpp.org/pdrama1.htm>.

Bissoondath, Neil. *Digging Up the Mountains: Selected Stories*. Toronto: Macmillan, 1985.

Blatner, Adam. *Acting-In: Practical Applications of Psychodramatic Methods*. 3rd ed. New York: Springer, 1996.

Blatner, Adam, and Allee Blatner. *Foundations of Psychodrama: History, Theory, and Practice*. New York: Springer, 1988.

Braidotti, Rosi. *Nomadic Subjects: Embodiment and Sexual Difference in Contemporary Feminist Theory*. New York: Columbia UP, 1994.

Brand, Dionne. *In Another Place, Not Here*. Toronto: Knopf, 1996.

Brodie, Robert. "What Is Psychodrama?" Robert Brodie Home Page. 19 Dec. 2003. 14 Jan. 2004. <http://www.users.on.net/iam/Pdis.html>.

Campbell, Maria. *Halfbreed*. 1973. Toronto: McClelland-Bantam, 1978.

Culleton, Beatrice. *In Search of April Raintree*. 1983. Winnipeg: Peguis, 1992.

Foggo, Cheryl. *Pourin' Down Rain*. Calgary: Detselig, 1990.
Jenkins, Marina. *The Play's the Thing: Exploring Text in Drama and Therapy.* London: Routledge, 1996.
Jones, Phil. *Drama as Therapy: Theatre as Living*. London: Routledge, 1996.
King, Thomas. *Medicine River*. 1989. Toronto: Penguin, 1991.
Maracle, Lee. *Ravensong: A Novel*. Vancouver: Press Gang, 1993.
Mootoo, Shani. *Cereus Blooms at Night*. 1996. Toronto: McClelland, 1998.
National Coalition of Creative Arts Therapies Associations (NCCATA). "Psychodrama." NCCATA Home Page. 11 Feb. 2002. 13 July 2002. <http://www.nccata.org/psychodrama.html>.
Promises (*Haftachot*). Dir. B.Z Goldberg, Justine Shapiro, and Carlos Bolado. United States/Israel/Palestine, 2001.
Yablonsky, Lewis. *Psychodrama: Resolving Emotional Problems through Role-Playing*. New York: Basic Books, 1976.

Thinking about Things in the Postcolonial Classroom

MISAO DEAN

My father died two years ago, after a year-long illness with colon cancer. The doctors performed some palliative surgery at the time of his diagnosis, but as the cancer grew he could digest less and less of what he ate. So the year was spent, essentially, waiting for him to starve to death. It was a long time to wait. He was a person of great gifts, creative, intellectual, and personal; he played jazz trumpet, and is lauded in histories of Canadian jazz as one of the pioneers of the genre in Canada; he was a corporate lawyer who was committed to giving his clients good service for their money; he was a father who inspired his children to successful careers in the arts and professions, and a person with great capacity for enjoyment as well as for despair. In retirement he had taken up playing the bass guitar, and rode his bike down the Don Valley to the beach several times a week. His illness made him demanding and reflective and distraught in turns, and caused him to rethink many of these pursuits; one of our main comforts, as his children, is our sense that despite the problems of his last few months he at least came to understand that we felt he had no small role in our successes.

His illness affected all his children profoundly, and made me, like him, demanding and reflective and distraught in turns. But it also caused me to rethink who I am as an academic, as well as a daughter, a mother, and a person. I certainly feel, profoundly, that I am his daughter; my drive to achieve and my intellectual curiosity are a product of his influence, no less than my awkward social sense, my blasted sense of humour, and my crooked baby fingers. Like Morag Gunn, I often hear my father's words emerge from my mouth, and hear them in the mouths of my daughters. I rarely thought of these things extending back more than one generation, but now I know they must; I feel an incredible sense of loss that I don't know more about my own family history, and I want to use my skills as an academic to think about that. In a way, I now realize, I have always been exploring that heritage in my academic work: my work on Brantford-born novelist Sara Jeannette Duncan was partly an exploration of the ideas and sly ironies I recognized as typical of my mother's family, who are descended from pioneer farmers in Flesherton, Ontario; I associate my interest in the left-nationalist politics of the 70s with the historical marker for Montgomery's Tavern, which my Dad introduced me to on a shopping trip when I was about eight. White, anglophone Canadians, especially those of us who are committed to a progressive politics, do not often celebrate familial and cultural continuity; instead we emphasize diversity, mobility, hybridity, the breaking down of the systems of power that continue to sustain violence and inequality both in our own country and in the world, the family among them. But at some moments, it becomes not only appropriate but necessary to think about what we have inherited from previous generations, and how that inheritance both enables and limits who we can be.

Most of my inheritance is intangible; my memories, my mannerisms, my interests, my vocabulary, are all part of it. It might be misleading to attribute those to my parents; maybe they came from their parents, or even further back—maybe there is no source, but only a retreating path through genealogy, an unsatisfactory path of repeated bereavement. But after my father's death, when I resumed my life in Victoria, a life that has no connection to my childhood family, I realized how much inheritance has come to mean tangible things: the rugs and bookshelves I inherited when my Mom moved into an apartment, my Dad's canoe paddle, which hangs on the wall in my office, and his old fleece jacket that I wear curling. These things survive through time, and their materiality comes to compensate for the way that people disappear, leaving no trace.

Inherited objects are a visible sign of loss; as Ethel Wilson wrote in *Swamp Angel*, the symbol comes to substitute for the reality. The material objects I have inherited have become signifiers of my father, and their histories of manufacture, exchange, and use allow them to serve as reminders of the meanings and histories lost with his death. Their function as mnemonics is a stark illustration of the relationship between signs and their referents: the sign is a substitute for the referent, an admission of its absence, an attempt to recall to presence that which we can never recover. Even an accumulation of objects owned by my father can never be more than a Derridean supplement, a fruitless attempt to fill in the gap between their materiality and his. Their very constitution as signifiers of my father is an admission of his material absence: as Peter Schwenger has written, "The death of the thing, then, is the price we pay for the word" (100). The objects themselves, constituted as signs of a reality that can never be recovered, are what remains to be interrogated.

The inherited object with most meaning for me is my father's canoe paddle. It's not an old paddle—he received it as a retirement gift from a colleague when he left his law firm, about ten years before his death. This paddle is made from a single piece of hardwood—cherry—not laminated: this makes it more flexible and responsive to the pressure of water. Some people don't like paddles made this way, because the slight give in the blade leads to a loss of power in the stroke. But I'm not much of a power paddler—I don't have the upper body strength, for one thing—and I'd rather go someplace at a leisurely pace than wear myself out half a mile from home. I like it, and my Dad liked it, because it's a beautiful piece of wood, an example of craftsmanship, and its possession marks us as particular kinds of people, who can afford to own and appreciate beautiful things, and particular kinds of paddlers, who stick to the flat water and think of ourselves as sensitive to the natural world. Though it's a little bit too big for me, I like to use it when I take my kids canoeing.

The last time I saw my Dad use this paddle, I was six months pregnant with my second daughter, and we were going to canoe around the lake a bit, as we often did on vacation. I wasn't much help getting the canoe into the water, but I could paddle, and the landscape always made much more sense from the water side. This paddle also reminds me of the cottage we had in Haliburton when we were children, and the time we spent there. The first canoe I remember was a canvas and cedar fifteen foot, which we discarded after my brother and my Dad tried chopping down a few trees to improve the view from the deck. They assured my mother that they knew how to make the tree fall where they wanted; luckily, only the canoe ribs were broken. In that canoe, I learned that I was strong enough to propel myself where I wanted to go; I learned to be still, and to watch for the blue heron that sometimes came to our lake. So besides the memories of my father and my family, this paddle reminds me of important things about myself.

One of the places we used to go in Muskoka was a cottage near Kilworthy, a place where members of my Dad's family used to have a hunting camp in the first decades of the twentieth century. I never knew any of these people: I struggle to make a connection with the picture of my grandfather as a young man with a thin mustache, holding up a lake trout by the gills, and with his mother in a white middy blouse in the background of a photo featuring rifles and a dead deer. My father's interest in canoeing must derive from this history, and so my paddle is inextricably related to these images. This paddle means that members of my family have been vacationing in Muskoka for a hundred years and reminds me that my grandmother and great grandmother probably had their own paddles.

Thus far this paddle appears to have meaning transparently and naturally, because it is associated with my childhood, my love of canoeing, my father, and his family. But I know that these meanings are an illusion, a product of a process that resulted in what Marx called the fetishism of commodities. Marx argued that the social relations that produce value in objects are obscured in the process of exchange, and value taken to inhere objectively in objects rather than in the social relations that produced them. Thus "productions of the human brain appear as independent beings endowed with life, and entering into relation both with one another and the human race" (321). My paddle seems to brim with meaning, connecting me to my father, my mother and siblings, and my father's family, but I know that this life, these meanings, are socially constituted. Things can only be constituted as objects in the social process of identity formation, for when a thing is named "it is also changed. It is assimilated into the terms of the human subject at the same time that it is opposed to it as object, an opposition that is indeed necessary for the subject's separation and definition" (Schwenger 101). Thus "all of our knowledge of the object is only knowledge of its modes of representation—or rather of *our* modes of representation, the ways in which we set forth the object to the understanding" (Schwenger 101). While objects come into being through social processes, and their meanings are culturally created, this process is obscured as the meanings projected onto the object are attributed to the object itself. The paddle does not really have any of these meanings in and of itself; it has these meanings because I have externalized the aspects of my identity that I associate with my father and his family, and certain memories of my childhood, and projected them onto the paddle. According to Daniel Miller, in *Material Culture and Mass Consumption*, my coming to own the paddle is part of a process whereby I will recognize that these meanings are self-created, and re-incorporate them into my own identity.

An analysis of this kind affords different sorts of satisfaction. By thinking about my father's paddle, I express my longing for his presence; I also construct characteristics of my own identity, my self-reliance, my love of the natural world, my occasional stillness, by attributing those associations to the paddle. The paddle acts as a souvenir, literally, reminding me of who I am as a daughter, as a scholar, a person. I have a whole collection of these souvenirs of myself: the brooch my mother gave me when I graduated from high school, the desk I bought when I moved to Victoria, first editions of Sara Jeannette Duncan's novels. Each one is a souvenir of some aspect of myself, a reminder of episodes in my personal history. But these personal histories are not the only meanings I associate with my father's canoe paddle. Even as a child, I knew that the canoe was the means whereby Canada "became a nation": it facilitated exploration and the fur trade, those two east-west movements which eventually united the nation "*a mari usque ad mare.*" The canoe occupies a unique place in the nationalist discourse I study: as Pierre Trudeau wrote in his famous essay, "Exhaustion and Fulfillment," it was the means whereby Canadians could learn a patriotism that was "felt in the bones." The canoe is still an important means by which urban Canadians like myself claim a first-hand experience of the landscape, and a sense of themselves in relation to it. My canoe paddle is also the means by which I identify myself with the larger political community and with the aims of the Canadian state, an identification that seems fully compatible with my family, who as third-generation Ontarians have always been disparaging of anything "American," and suspicious of anything Brit. Because my paddle is a material object that I have used and inherited, that identification seems "natural."

*

Roland Barthes gives an account of the way that material objects can operate as *myth*, making historically contingent concepts like nationality seem to have the validity of objective science. In Barthes' account, myths offer an artificial resolution to cultural contradictions by referencing two levels of signification that he calls first and second orders. Similarly, Susan Pearce in *Museums, Objects and Collections* suggests that objects function like myth to naturalize cultural hegemony by resolving metonymic[1] and symbolic values. Both theorists suggest that the materiality of objects allows them to function as evidence or "proof" of the cultural values they seem to symbolize. Taking my canoe paddle as an example: I invest the paddle as signifier with the signifieds of my family history of paddling, and thereby objectify the paddle as a signifier of me-in-relation-to-my-family. The relationship between the paddle and its signification is not arbitrary—because it was my father's, and now is mine, because both he and I have used it to paddle, it is metonymically a *part* of the family activity of paddling, and to that extent seems to be a *natural* or intrinsic sign of this activity; in addition, because the paddle endures in time, and has indeed outlived my father, it carries into the present the memories associated with him in a material form. But the paddle-as-sign of me-in-relation-to-my-family also operates as signifier in a secondary system, in which it mythically or symbolically represents a second signified—the metanarrative of Canadian nationality constructed around exploration, the fur trade, and, more recently, wilderness camping and environmental protection. In this system, the paddle is emptied of its metonymic significance—that is, its status as a real part of my family history—and is available to be filled up with symbolic meaning as a signifier of a particular version of the history of Canada. Because the paddle can function alternately as sign (paddle as natural sign of me) and as signifier (paddle as historically constructed symbol of the nation) it works to insert me into the narrative of nationality.

The materiality of the paddle is an important aspect of the way it functions in this system. Material objects are perceived first through what theorists of material culture call their presentational qualities; that is, their weight, solidity, colour, texture, dimensions, aesthetic, and sensual appeal. My paddle is demonstrably *real*; it's also beautiful and valuable, and for that reason I will keep it, allowing it to "carry forward" its history of manufacture, use, and exchange. Because the paddle has weight and solidity, it can serve as material evidence to prove the validity of the narratives within which it is an important signifier. Beyond this, the paddle is materially in my possession: because it is materially a part of my relationship to my father and my canoeing memories, and because it is old enough to have survived my father, it can serve as "proof" of my narrative of self, and of the interrelationship between my personal narrative and the larger cultural narrative, as "proof" of my Canadianness. As Daniel Miller writes, "The artefact . . . tends to imply a certain innocence of facticity; it seems to offer the clarity of realism, an assertion of certainty against the buffeting of debate, an end or resting point which resolves the disorder of uncertain perspectives" (Miller 106). Its materiality is instrumental to the stability of the larger cultural myth it comes to represent.

That cultural myth of Canadian nationality became the subject of much of my work as a scholar. I was trained at graduate school in the 70s, when the focus of Canadian literary studies was the definition and elaboration of the nation in literary works. I never doubted that a *Canadian identity* existed, as the question was posed in those days: I knew what it was, and it was mine. I knew what it was because I had a personal, and multi-generational, attachment to a particular place that was in Canada; I knew it because I connected my personal history and my family history to the history of Canada that extended beyond my lifetime; I knew it because I had paddled. The "ideology of the canoe," as Daniel Francis calls it, allows Canadians like me to construct an identity in which subjectivity and nationality form a seamless whole, and each seems to both confirm and contribute a satisfying depth to the other.

But because my paddle is material, and because material objects can "bear perpetual symbolic reinterpretation" (Pearce 27), it can also represent radically different and even contradictory identities and values. The interpretation of my paddle-as-sign-of-me elides many alternative interpretations which challenge the stable integrated "Canadian" identity I've constructed for myself, and of which I've become increasingly aware, especially since I've moved to the other end of the country. At least one of these must be the paddle as an *intrinsic* or natural sign of the technologies and material possessions our culture appropriated from First Nations. Birch-bark canoes are unique to northern North America; while other cultures built frames and covered them with skins or bark, Cree people and Mi'kmaq and Anishnabe built frames inside pieces of birch-bark, and propelled them with paddles carved by hand out of single pieces of wood, rather like my paddle. Europeans adopted this technology, "improved it" with the techniques of mass production, and used it to try to make money out of the land inhabited by the canoe-makers. Out here in British Columbia, this happened without even the treaties imposed in some other parts of the country. My paddle has come to be a reminder that my "Canadianness" also implicates me in the theft of the land that comprises Canada. In this system of signification, the paddle-as-sign-of-me, and of my most intimate memories of a happy and materially comfortable childhood, is tied directly to my status as a beneficiary of White privilege, and the complicity of my forebears in cultural genocide and theft.

From this point of view, my paddle no longer resolves the issues raised by my longing for my father; instead, the personal identity objectified in my paddle, which I experienced as a vital, natural, and self-defining connection between me and the geographical spaces of my childhood and my family history, is undermined and destabilized. Indeed, any reading of my paddle must acknowledge that it signifies at least two incompatible systems of meanings, meanings that work to contradict each other and that cannot be reconciled into a single system. The feeling of *being at home*, of "topophilia" (Tuan) or love of place that is the effect of its physicality, and of the link that I construct between it and my family, is contaminated. Minnie Bruce Pratt, a lesbian from a Southern US White family, recounts a similar recognition in her essay "Identity: Skin Blood Heart," when she concludes that her childhood home was built on "the grave of the people [her] kin had killed, and [her] foundation, [her] birth culture, was mortared with blood" (35). Pratt's nostalgia is undone by her recognition of the racism that underpins it, her understanding that "home was an illusion of coherence and safety based on the exclusion of specific histories of oppression and resistance, the repression of differences even in oneself" (Martin and Mohanty 196). Rather than resolving differences like these into a comfortable sentimentalism, my paddle becomes their repository, and the means of constructing a link between my personal identity and the history of colonialism that shapes it.

Newly constructed as a sign of contradiction and instability, my paddle begins to suggest the way that objects can function in the postcolonial classroom. For the meanings I create when I take things as objects are elements in a discourse in which subjectivity overlaps with metanarratives of nationality and imperial power. The meanings that my paddle seems to signify emerge from a discourse of colonialism, and the introduction of my paddle into the classroom provides an opportunity to analyze this discourse. This sort of analysis can be extended to the objects taken as self-defining by communities and nations, that is, museum objects, heritage sites, and buildings. Just as I take my paddle as object to represent aspects of my constructed self, so cultural collectivities, institutions, and states take museum objects to represent aspects of their constructed histories, identities, and unities. As those histories and identities shift and change through public discourse, collections are augmented and objects discarded, heritage sites acquired and displays modified and rebuilt, with the articulated goal of *reflecting* identity through material objects. Such objects often figure in public discourse as an inheritance held in common by all members of the group, and a trust for future generations; taken together, they *represent* a cultural collectivity supposedly comprised of all persons of Canadian nationality. Their *realness*, their incontestable physicality and their aesthetic appeal, function to stabilize and reproduce the cultural identities they supposedly represent, to "naturalize the rhetoric of national affiliation and its forms of collective expression" (Bhabha 143).

Like my paddle, objects in museums are often held to be repositories of meaning in themselves, of *stories*: these stories conventionally include the histories of their use and manufacture, ownership, exchange, and preservation. Such stories, like the history of my father's paddle and my memories of him using it, have a metonymic relationship to objects: the object is literally a part of these stories, and therefore seems to be a natural or intrinsic sign of its own history. Individual objects, however, often appear in museum displays as signifiers of a larger metanarrative—of nationality, progress, scientific mastery. As in the case of the canoe paddle, the materiality of the object, its metonymic signification as a true part of real history, acts to elide the contradictory meanings that might challenge the metanarrative. The object as sign of its own use and manufacture becomes a signifier in a secondary system, which is much more open to contestatory readings. Thus a classroom practice that would engage with objects should have two goals: to show the way that the materiality of objects is mobilized to legitimize larger metanarratives; and to demonstrate the way that research into their metonymic significance, their particular and individual histories of use, manufacture, ownership, and exchange, might suggest other, and contradictory, meanings. These two practices might be formulated as two kinds of reading, one which reveals the way the object works within the systems of signification that the museum display constructs for it, and one which reads against those systems to reveal their elisions and omissions.

*

There is a fragment of brick on display in the British Columbia Maritime Museum. It's about three inches by five, the longer side broken off irregularly: brick-coloured, mottled with lighter, sandy tones, obviously old. It's mounted on the wall in a Plexiglas box, at about eye level. The label provides the information that suggests its metonymic meanings: it came from an oven built at the Spanish Fort San Miguel in Nootka Sound, circa 1789. Not a building, an oven: an oven for baking loaves of yeast-leavened bread, a sign of European culture if there ever was one. This brick is positioned at the physical beginning of a narrative display representing the history of navigation in the waters off the coast of "British Columbia" as physical evidence in the diplomatic dispute between Britain and Spain, known as the "Nootka controversy," which resulted in the British government's military assertion of sovereignty over the Nu-Chaa-Nulth territory. This is the moment, in most conventional histories, that created the territory of the Nu-Chaa-Nulth people as British Columbia; as part of a dispute between Britain and Spain, the land mass of the west coast of North America is re-conceived as an imperial possession, and the claims of the First Nations elided. Thus the brick inaugurates a narrative retold sequentially in the Maritime Museum as the history of European people on the central and northern coasts of North America. Positioned as it is in the display, its first order signification as part of a historical event is appropriated to legitimize a larger metanarrative, as evidence of the historical reality of British Columbia.

My second-year cultural studies students practise this sort of reading in the Modern History Gallery of the Royal BC Museum. The display consists of a two-storey hall filled with life-size reproductions of the exteriors of buildings representing a late nineteenth-century British Columbia town, which serve as a context for historical artifacts displayed "realistically" in cases representing shop windows. Rather than consuming this display in a prescribed order, visitors simply "step into the past," experiencing sound effects such as horses' hooves and even smells. However, the elements included in "Old Town" suggest an implicit narrative structuring. "Old Town" includes a railway station and a hotel, as well as the various services that a regional "metropolis" might offer its surrounding "hinterland." The visitor exits "Old Town" into displays that focus on resource industries, including logging, mining, farming, and fishing. As this account suggests, the display is structured by the "Frontier and Metropolis" thesis articulated by historian J.M.S. Careless, who asserted that although "Canada took shape through the successive occupation of frontiers" (8), the development of frontiers was vitally dependent upon regional metropolitan centres. The organization of the Modern History Gallery, which requires the visitor to pass through "Old Town" and then into the hinterland of resource industries, thus represents Careless's idea that "the very people who took up the forward margins often came there through outside direction and provision" (19); they were essentially "metropolitan outrunners in the primeval forest" (15).

While the visitor's experience of "Old Town" is non-linear and the representation is synchronous, the display works to reify the ideological categories that govern it by suggesting its completeness and its adequacy *as* a representation. Indeed, the structure of the "Old Town" itself, with its sound effects and scents, suggests that evocation of cultural context in its materiality and completeness was a major goal of the exhibit. However, this sense of completeness, or closure, is itself dictated by the way that visitors and curators prefigure the historical field; as Pearce points out, this process involves the acceptance that the ideological categories that organize the display "have an external reality" and that they are part of the physical world. These categories are reproduced in the display through the concept of completion: one must have already decided what a "complete" representation of the past would be, in order to judge whether it has been achieved, and this decision is based upon the "fiction" (Pearce 85) that categories of classification are "real." The exhibit reproduces the very ideological categories which it is supposed to merely *display*. The organization of the Modern History Gallery assumes that the operations of capital are the determining element in the settlement of British Columbia; that these kinds of work, work done by men, and especially by White men, are appropriate organizing categories for historical representation; that gender and race are "special interests," which are appropriately represented as additions to the main display; that First Nations are not part of "Modern History."

A similar kind of reading might be performed on a slightly larger "object," that is, the heritage site at Hell's Gate, a rock formation in the Fraser River Canyon just south of Lytton. At Hell's Gate the perpendicular stone cliffs that rise from the waters of the Fraser River create an opening barely 100 feet wide. The narrow channel is filled with whirlpools, barely visible from above, that circle ceaselessly from the bottom to the surface of the water, from rock faces to the boulders. Such rapids upset Simon Fraser's canoes and almost killed several of the voyageurs travelling with him—they lost paddles, lots of them, over the course of their journey to the Pacific. Fraser determined to travel around the rapids by scaling the sheer rock walls, an experience described in his "Journal": "we had to pass where no human being should venture" (Fraser 327). This quotation is the theme of interpretation at the current heritage site, which includes a restaurant, gift shop, and "fudge factory," as well as a heritage marker. Access to the site is provided by the Hell's Gate Airtram, a commercially operated cable car suspended over the river.

Fraser's statement emphasizes the danger faced by humans trying to navigate the waters of Hell's Gate; this theme also governs the interpretation of the more recent history of the site as "an obstacle to transportation" on the heritage marker. The CPR and Highway One both cling to the sides of the canyon in what is surely an engineering marvel; the famous "fishways" completed in the 1960s help the salmon to overcome the force of the turbulent waters on the way up the Fraser to spawn. The Airtram offers a close-up look at the turbulent waters, and is itself a topic for historical interpretation in a display dedicated to its construction. Thus the meaning of the site, from the heritage marker to the federal fisheries display to the commercial businesses, is constructed as part of a single narrative, that of Western technology overcoming nature. The site elicits this already formed cultural narrative within the context of the metanarrative of nation-building, by which state-sponsored enterprise built the nation by overcoming the obstacles posed by its geography, and private enterprise keeps it going.

However, historical research on Hell's Gate can reveal the possibility of various counter-narratives that situate the site quite differently. While current interpretation focuses on the building of the fishways as an engineering marvel, a different metanarrative might focus on the reason why they were necessary in the first place: blasting for the building of the CPR in 1913 caused the channel at Hell's Gate to narrow even further, and eliminated the eddies that provided a haven for the salmon as they travelled up the Fraser. The ladders were necessary to restore the salmon run that the engineers had destroyed. The "engineering marvel" is diminished when it is repositioned as part of a different metanarrative, an account of the environmental consequences of the North American will to technique. Similarly, a counter-narrative to the construction of the canyon as a geographical barrier overcome by Canadian technology is revealed by revisiting the famous quotation, "where no human being should venture." When placed in its context in Fraser's journal, this fragment of text points in quite another direction. Fraser persisted in attempting to travel down the river despite repeated warnings from the local people that the river was dangerous and could not be navigated. The Nlaka'pamux people were obliged to offer to guide him along the existing trail they had established for themselves. Fraser's commentary continues:

> We had to pass where no human being should venture. Yet in those places there is a regular footpath impressed, or rather indented, by frequent travelling upon the very rocks. And besides this, steps which are formed like a ladder, or the shrouds of a ship, by poles hanging to one another and crossed at certain distances with twigs and withes, suspended from the top to the foot of precipices, and fastened at both ends to stones and trees, furnished a safe and convenient passage to the natives. (327)

Clearly, there is a counter-narrative here, of the history of the Nlaka'pamux people and the materialization of their relationship with the land, which completely undermines the interpretation of the site as evidence of the successful expansion of the nation by way of superior Canadian technology.

I'm not suggesting that these counter-narratives should supplant the previous ones; I am suggesting that the meanings of objects are constructed in discourse, and are therefore open to the same kinds of readings we perform on other kinds of cultural texts. A classroom practice that problematizes the seemingly "natural" meaning of objects and heritage sites can be a useful way to introduce basic concepts like the structure of signs and the function of signifiers as well as more advanced ideas like the narrativization of the historical past and the interpellation of subjects by ideology. More importantly, it can demonstrate the way that the fetishizing of objects and places compensates for the absence and uncertainty of the referent, whether that referent be the nation, the self, or even the father.

*

Thinking about my canoe paddle has helped me to understand how inherited objects can work to stabilize and reproduce subjectivity. As the sign of my absent parent and the repository of projected aspects of my self, my canoe paddle is a signifier of myself, a reminder of who I think I am. Museum objects perform the same kinds of functions in a more collective context, by stabilizing the shifting and changing self-representations of cultural collectivities, states, communities, and classes. Objects can do this because they are material: the seeming transparency and obviousness of their metonymic meanings is mobilized to provide "proof" of the larger metanarratives of cultural history and therefore a seeming resolution to the cultural contradictions they pose. And because this resolution is only seeming, investigation of the ways that objects function in personal and cultural narratives can open up possibilities and provide for the rethinking of cultural categories like *subjectivity, nationality, race*, and *community*.

Deborah Root has written that White North American culture often "seems so bankrupt and uninteresting" as to be "emptied of meaning," composed of nothing but strip malls and television. She argues that the inability of White anglophone Canadians to rethink our own tradition, to oppose the "destructive soulless ethos" of capitalism, prevents us from being able to act in solidarity with First Nations or truly understand what a racially diverse and equal society would be like. "Rather than seeking authenticity elsewhere, we need to transform how we look at our histories and traditions and find ways to unravel these from all the racist versions to which we have been subjected" (232). I would suggest that thinking about things in the postcolonial classroom is a good way to rediscover the continuity between the personal and the cultural, and to tease out our personal investments in the cultural discourses of colonialism. But it might also be a way to oppose the paralysis that a burgeoning postcolonial awareness can provoke in people, and to investigate what might have been inherited from within Western culture that can help to address the inequities that have resulted from those discourses. In this way my canoe paddle can still represent the familial and cultural continuity I want to preserve. I can use my inheritance of self-reliance, and stillness, and good memories, and commitment to place, to change the way I think of Canada and my place in it.

NOTE

1. My use of the word *metonymic* will have several resonances for readers. One of these will be Roman Jakobsen's use of the word in contradistinction to *metaphoric* in "Two Aspects of Language and Two Types of Aphasic Disturbances." Jakobsen distinguishes between metaphoric language, which relates words on the basis of similarity and substitutability, and metonymic language, which relates words together by contiguity and contextuality. My paddle (like Jakobsen's word) is metonymically related to a group of objects defined by their status as constituting the material context of my childhood. For Jakobsen, synecdoche is a kind of metonymy, because in both cases part is related to whole by contiguity. Pearce discusses Jakobsen's terms metonymy and metaphor, Barthes's first and second order signification, and her own terms intrinsic sign and metaphoric symbol (38) as slightly different but parallel concepts.

WORKS CITED

Barthes, Roland. *Mythologies*. Trans. Annette Lavers. London: Granada, 1972.

Bhabha, Homi. *The Location of Culture*. London: Routledge, 1994.

Careless, J.M.S. *Frontier and Metropolis*. Toronto: U of Toronto P, 1989.

Francis, Daniel. *National Dreams*. Vancouver: Arsenal Pulp, 1997.

Fraser, Simon. "Journal of a Voyage from the Rocky Mountains to the Pacific Ocean, 1808." *Canadian Exploration Literature: An Anthology*. Ed. Germaine Warkentin. Toronto: Oxford UP, 1993. 317–35.

Jakobsen, Roman. "Two Aspects of Language and Two Types of Aphasic Disturbances." *On Language*. Ed. Linda Waugh and Monique Monville-Bursten. Cambridge: Harvard UP, 1990. 115–33.

Martin, Biddy, and Chandra Mohanty. "Feminist Politics: What's Home Got To Do with It." *Feminist Studies/Critical Studies*. Ed. Teresa de Lauretis. Bloomington: Indiana UP, 1986. 191–212.

Marx, Karl. "*Capital* Vol. 1 Part One: Chapter One: 'Commodities.'" *The Marx-Engels Reader*. Ed. Robert Tucker. New York: Norton, 1978. 302–29.

Miller, Daniel. *Material Culture and Mass Consumption*. Oxford: Blackwell, 1987.

Pearce, Susan. *Museums, Objects, and Collections*. Washington: Smithsonian, 1992.

Pratt, Minnie Bruce. "Identity: Skin Blood Heart." *Yours in Struggle: Three Feminist Perspectives on Anti-Semitism and Racism*. By Elly Bulkin, Minnie Bruce Pratt, and Barbara Smith. Ithaca: Firebrand, 1984. 11–63.

Root, Deborah. "'White Indians': Appropriation and the Politics of Display." *Borrowed Power: Essays on Cultural Appropriation*. Ed. Bruce Ziff and Pratima V. Rao. New Brunswick, NJ: Rutgers UP, 1997. 225–33.

Schwenger, Peter. "Words and the Murder of the Thing." *Critical Inquiry* 28 (2001): 99–113.

Trudeau, Pierre. "Exhaustion and Fulfillment: Ascetic in a Canoe." 1944. Rpt. *Che-mun* 102 (2002). <http://www.canoe.ca/che-mun/102trudeau.html>.

Tuan, Yi-Fu. *Topophilia: A Study of Environmental Perception, Attitudes and Values*. Englewood, NJ: Prentice-Hall, 1974.

Wilson, Ethel. *Swamp Angel*. 1954. Rpt. Toronto: McClelland and Stewart, 1990.

Postcolonial Collisions of Language: Teaching and Using Tensions in the Text

MARGARET STEFFLER

> The moment in the heart
> where I roam restless, searching
> for the thin border of the fence
> to break through or leap.
>
> — Michael Ondaatje, "Last Ink"

WHILE TEACHING AS a CUSO co-operant in Nigeria in the early 1980s, I was asked by my Form Two students to speak "Canadian." I replied, rather erroneously I realized, that I *was* speaking Canadian, but they continued to press me to speak the language of my own country rather than that of England, or at least to speak the English language as I spoke it at home—as my mother spoke it—as opposed to the way I spoke it in the classroom. My response raised confusion in my students, who understandably found it difficult to believe that the English I spoke and taught in the classroom was the only language in which I was truly fluent. At the time, my students' questions raised in me feelings of linguistic inadequacy and guilt; over the years those same questions have played an important role not only in how I read and teach literature, but also in how I approach and understand language, culture, postcolonialism, and pedagogy.

My Nigerian students' enthusiasm for, interest in, and love of language, in both a vernacular and a literary context, moved me to look at language, and particularly the English language, in new and different ways. The English language spoken and written by my students in Nigeria was the language described by Chinua Achebe, who maintains that "the English language will be able to carry the weight of my African experience. But it will have to be a new English, still in full communion with its ancestral home but altered to suit its new African surroundings" ("African Writer" 84). The "altered" language I both heard and read in Nigeria, a dynamic hybridization, emerged in a violent and political manner out of the collision of cultures, and cannot and should not be considered simply an evolution or adaptation of English. Achebe stresses the submission of the language itself to those who consciously use and change it, claiming that "the price a world language must be prepared to pay is submission to many different kinds of use" ("African Writer" 82). Achebe demonstrates the power of forcing the English language to be submissive, telling stories and relating history in a language that exists precisely *because* those stories and that history have taken place.

Coming back from Nigeria to study and eventually teach English Canadian literature, I found that along with a longing for the extreme ways in which my senses were stretched and challenged in Nigeria, there was also a longing for the dynamic and political use of language. While reading Ken Saro-Wiwa's 1994 novel, *Sozaboy,* I recalled those probing questions posed by my students. Lomber One of Saro-Wiwa's *Sozaboy*, subtitled "A Novel in Rotten English," begins as follows:

> Although, everybody in Dukana was happy at first.
>
> All the nine villages were dancing and we were eating plenty maize with pear and knacking tory under the moon. Because the work on the farm have finished and the yams were growing well well. And because the old, bad government have dead, and the new government of soza and police have come. (1)

The Canadian equivalent of the altered or new English described by Achebe and so prominently displayed in the work of Saro-Wiwa would obviously be found in the way in which Canadian Aboriginal communities and writers, Canadians colonized by English politics and language, use the English language, forcing it to submit and become altered as it is used.[1] As I taught English Canadian literature, I was struck, however, by the way in which the literary language in the postcolonial context in Canada, at least in the works I was teaching, seemed to be stuck in a stage of collision, pointing out the collisions, but not allowing the emergence of an altered language or the provision of a submission or resolution to the collision. The "other" language in the texts—the non-English—and the attention drawn to its presence constitute a hybridization in process, but not achieved, and apparently not moving or working towards completion. The state of tension remains, is at the centre of the text, and seems to be what holds our attention.

In the second-year English Canadian prose course I have taught for the past ten years, these colliding languages are central to our tutorial discussions about the texts in the "Crossing Cultures" unit of the course. The "other" languages vary as we change the books and the course from year to year, but the presence of the other language is always of great interest and importance in our discussions and often seems to open up the books in valuable and startling ways. This year, for example, we were drawn to the Gaelic in Alistair MacLeod and Jane Urquhart, the Latin in Urquhart and Sheila Watson, the Parsi in Rohinton Mistry, the Japanese in Joy Kogawa, the Sinhalese in Michael Ondaatje, the Cherokee in Thomas King, the Low German in Rudy Wiebe, and references to Yiddish and Hebrew in Adele Wiseman. The presence of other languages raises in the reader questions about semiotics, focusing particularly, as do Achebe and Saro-Wiwa, on breaking down assumptions about the ownership of language. Saussure's insistence on difference and opposition within language itself (88) can provide a basis for an understanding of the refusal of these other languages to coalesce or integrate with the dominant language of English in these Canadian works.

Colliding Languages

Although Thomas King does give his readers glimpses into the ways in which Aboriginal communities have altered and used the English imposed upon them, more often than not he draws attention to the collisions of languages rather than the alterations. The seamless integration of Ibo proverbs and the English language into something entirely new in Achebe's work does not have an equivalent in King's work, which is not the place to look for this equivalent, as King, in a spirit of duality, stresses the separations and collisions of languages, drawing attention both orally and visually to the coexistence of two types of language—that of the colonizer and that of the colonized. The abrupt dismissals of the English language attempts of "'*Once upon a time . . .*'" (11), "'*A long time ago in a faraway land . . .*'" (12), and "'*In the beginning, God created the heaven and the earth*'" (14) to begin stories in *Green Grass, Running Water* are further undercut by the application of the dismal and listless attempt of the English language to articulate native experience and culture: "'*Many moons comechucka . . . hahahahahahahahahahaha*'" (13). The Cherokee and English in *Green Grass, Running Water* are forced to share the same page and the same line, albeit separated for the most part—the English on the left side of the page or sentence and the Cherokee on the right—and thus have no choice but to take one another into consideration even while maintaining a distinct distance. Using and drawing attention to translation, the text visually places the two languages in diametric opposition, separated by the identification of the speaker, who acts as both a barrier and a connector between the two languages:

> "That's better," said Hawkeye. "Tsane:hlanv́:hi."
> "Listen," said Robinson Crusoe. "Hade:lohó:sgi."
> "It is beginning," said Ishmael. "Dagvyá:dhv:dv:hní." (15)

The emphasis on the distinction, separation, and translation contrasts with Achebe's emphasis on the submission of one language to another and the emergence of an altered language. According to Achebe, the political and deliberate *use* of an instrument, whether that instrument be a trumpet, a language, or a literary genre, will result in a new sound: "did not the black people in America, deprived of their own musical instruments, take the trumpet and the trombone and blow them as they had never been blown before, as indeed they were not designed to be blown? And the result, was it not jazz?" ("Colonialist Criticism" 23). King stresses the collision and difference of sound rather than the use, submission, and emergence of sound.

The placement of Cherokee syllabary at the beginning of each of the four parts of *Green Grass, Running Water* further increases the exclusion of the English-only reader. Once students accept the inaccessibility of the words on the page, however, realizing that King is deliberately marginalizing them, they appreciate experiencing the position of the "other" language and culture—a position which necessarily begins as one of exclusion. It is often a powerful moment when students suddenly feel the exclusion through their position as reader and extend that feeling beyond the text to the culture and society in which they live, a natural step in an English literature course that is cross-listed as a Canadian studies course.

This feeling of exclusion and difference extends to other works included in this "Crossing Cultures" section of the course. Each of the authors studied, like King, draws attention to collisions of language, often emphasizing difference in a highly visual manner. Rohinton Mistry, for example, in "Auspicious Occasion," the first story in *Tales from Firozsha Baag,* uses Parsi and English words together in a single sentence, without any translation, italicizing the Parsi words, rendering them foreign and visually setting them apart from the English text. The character, Rustomji, for example, explains his dilemma to his wife Mehroo: "*Saala chootia* spat *paan* on my *dugli* and you think that is fun?" (17). The hard sounds of the "ch," "sp," "d," and "g," emphasized through their contrast with the lingering double vowels, mimic the actual spitting of the bus passenger from the upper deck and reflect Rustomji's tone of anger and frustration as he spits out his questioning complaint. Similarly, in *Running in the Family,* Michael Ondaatje actually provides the Sinhalese script on the typed page, its very presence drawing the reader's attention not only to the different language but to the shapes and structure of an unfamiliar alphabet. The narrator describes his emotional and aesthetic response to this written language, in which "the insect of ink curves into a shape that is almost sickle, spoon, eyelid. The letters are washed blunt glass which betray no jaggedness" (69). The texture of the brittle Ola leaf of Ceylon on which language was written was responsible, Ondaatje tells us, for the transformation of the verticals of Sanskrit into the "curling alphabet" or "moon coconut" of Sinhalese, resembling "the bones of a lover's spine" (69). Both Mistry and Ondaatje work with the senses in order to bring the other language off the page, giving it a texture and depth of difference both in itself and through its contrast with English.

In *Running in the Family* and *Tales from Firozsha Baag*, the colliding languages work to establish other tensions and oppositions in the text. The thematic mixture of the sacred and profane in "Auspicious Occasion," for example, grows out of and is consonant with the dislocations aroused by the paradoxical separation and mixture of the two languages; the yoking of the two languages and the two attitudes is startling. "*Ashem Vahoo,* / See the tits on that chickie-boo," repeats Rustomji, maintaining that it takes "a trained ear to sift through their mumbles and separate the prayers from the obscenities" in the language used and heard in the temple (Mistry 14). Similarly, the disparity between the beauty of the Sinhalese alphabet and the incongruous message it conveys—"We must not urinate again on Father Barnabus' tires" (Ondaatje 69–70)—extends the linguistic tension into a thematic tension, focusing on the opposition between what is said and how it is conveyed.

In Mistry's "The Ghost of Firozsha Baag," Jaakaylee responds to the Tamil and Keralite languages, "with their funny *illay illay poe poe*" sounds (46). For her, such difference increases the numbers of those who belong to the group who do not speak like the Parsis, relieving some of her own difference as a "Goan Catholic" of "very dark skin colour" (46). The introduction of more languages means that there are more collisions and tensions to deal with, but a less obvious position of power for the majority group within Firozsha Baag. This refusal of the languages to submit or coalesce illustrates Homi Bhabha's contention that "the nation is no longer the sign of modernity under which cultural differences are homogenized in the 'horizontal' view of society," but instead "reveals, in its ambivalent and vacillating representation, the ethnography of its own historicity and opens up the possibility of other narratives of the people and their difference" ("DissemiNation" 300). For Ondaatje, the different surfaces on which language is written—Ola leaves, paper, classroom boards, walls, desks, rock faces, notebooks, ceilings, and hidden corners of the university campus (69–70)—are the battlegrounds where these linguistic collisions take place and where potential victories, based on which language is wiped out and which is preserved, are taken back to the state of the collision as Ondaatje focuses on the surfaces of the battlegrounds themselves.

In Joy Kogawa's *Obasan,* the Japanese language is visually prominent, unbalancing the English-only reader as do the Cherokee, Parsi, and Sinhalese in the texts already discussed. In *Obasan,* however, the Japanese language is often accompanied by a translation in an apparent attempt to bring the two cultures together and provide clarification rather than accentuate difference. But as Aunt Emily "works the translation" of a Japanese haiku into English (217), the loss of form and meaning is apparent. The merging or connection of the two languages through translation or understanding essentially fails, leaving them in a state of tension. Even the way in which the attempts at translation are explained points out the difference, this linguistic incompatibility of structure, that defies a literal word-by-word translation: "'Yoku ki ga tsuku ne,' Grandma responds. It is a statement in appreciation of sensitivity and appropriate gestures" (56). The separation of these two languages in this translation statement is very similar to the structure of King's single-line treatment and translation of Cherokee and English. In Kogawa's work, however, the second part of the statement, following the identification of the speaker, is a holistic description of the meaning and tone of all the spoken words together rather than an attempt at a literal translation. Again, the linguistic difference introduces and is expanded into a thematic and cultural tension, in this case the Canadian government's political oppression of Canadians of Japanese descent. The difference between the Japanese and English language, most obvious during these discussions of translation, provides insight into the cultural and political positions of the oppressor and oppressed: "'It was not good, was it,' Mother says. 'Yoku nakatta ne.' Three words. Good, negation of good in the past tense, agreement with statement. It is not a language that promotes hysteria" (60). Conversely, of course, the rhetoric used by the Canadian government *does* cause and promote hysteria. In this discussion of language and hysteria there is an attempt at a type of word-by-word translation of the Japanese, but again the attempt manages to reveal the difficulty of translation and emphasizes difference in the way the other language is constructed, each word building on the word that comes before. The reader's attention is drawn to the concise, economical, and yet emphatic manner in which this language works, the actual meaning of the statement becoming secondary to the explanation of how the three words relate to one another.

In Rudy Wiebe's *The Blue Mountains of China* we can hear the "other" language of Low German even in the background of the English. Frieda Friesen's voice is a translation in process as the syntax of the English language makes clear: "I was healthy and worked in the barn and the field though it wasn't with me what it would have been with a boy" (9). The migrant experience of the Mennonites explains to some extent the linguistic tension, according to Bhabha, who argues that the "liminality of migrant experience is no less a transitional phenomenon than a translational one; there is no resolution to it because the two conditions are ambivalently enjoined in the 'survival' of migrant life" (*Location* 224). The awareness of the other language as the source of the translated English draws attention to its difference from English. The translation is both awkward and poetic at the same time, an appropriate vehicle to convey the tone of Freida's immense faith as reflected in her refrain—"it does come all from God, strength and sickness, want and plenty" (10). Elizabeth Driediger comments on Jakob Friesen's "strange, foregone-conclusion kind of talk" (187). Like Freida's tone and style, Jakob's words set him apart from the modern and "progressive" world. The retention of the other language of Low German guarantees his position as other in the new world, the language being the means and the sign of his remaining apart from the dominant culture. The calm and polite tones of Freida's and Jakob's carefully translated English contrast with Irene's modern voice, which shocks and assaults in its brazenness: "'Hey o poppo,' her eyes flashed up, 'can we stay the weekend and drive to Jasper and swim in the hotsprings and take one of the big motor boats along and go up a mountain, just a little, poppo mine, huh?'" (200). The contemporary crassness of Irene's English contrasts with the polite and formal Low German that translates into a polite and formal English. The German is more attractive than the dominant language of English, as are the culture and tone embodied by that Low German in translation. The difference is unmistakable. The more extreme contrast of language in Wiebe's novel is found in the chapter, "The Vietnam Call of Samuel U. Reimer," in which the religious and prophetic voice heard by Sam Reimer is neither heard nor believed by anybody else. The Old Testament flavour—"'I am the God of your fathers, the Lord your God. Go and proclaim peace in Vietnam'" (158)—is far removed from the television world in which Sam's children live. As in Mistry's stories, the religious and the secular collide, stressing the conservative nature of the former and the consumerism of the latter. There is no openness in the Canada of 1967 to spiritual and biblical voices that command and proclaim as does the voice in "The Vietnam Call of Samuel U. Reimer." The state of diaspora and exile for the Mennonite community is thus reflected in the collision of languages in their Canadian experience.

Jane Urquhart, also dealing with migrant characters, uses two "other" languages in *Away*—Latin and Irish Gaelic—both archaic and out of vernacular use. There is an incongruity in the barefoot Irish children of the hedgerow school droning "in the voice of Caesar" "'*Insula natura triquetra, cuius unum latus est contra Galliam*'" (30). The disparities and ironies between the language, its content, the speaker, and the hedgerow institution are many. An ancestor of the current Sedgewick landlords even places Latin in the mouth of a puffin, who intones, "'*Ego sum Fratercula arctica . . . Habito in ora Hibernica*'" (40). Other fragments of Latin are those of the church, "'*Pater noster . . . In Deo speramus, Te Deum laudamus*'" (48), and taxonomy: "*Solanum tuberosum*," pronounces Osbert Sedgewick, referring to the potato (66). With no translations provided, readers are at the mercy of their own knowledge and memories of Latin, but even with "small Latin and less Greek" (69),[2] the fragmentary and irrelevant nature of the classical language for those using it is obvious to the reader.

As in *Running in the Family*, new and unfamiliar languages are examined from many perspectives in Urquhart's novel. Liam responds to Latin's "soft sounds, the *Ulli, arum, alla, orae*, which tumbled near the fire" (147). Mary notes "the shape of the English words . . . their silence on the slate after the deliberate noise of putting them there," likening them to "a collection of sticks and stones tossed up on a beach" (60). The English language is associated with the outer world, with a political and global context within which Mary attempts to position herself and her country. She has to work hard, however, to tear herself away from the "traces of songs and poems" associated with "another" world (60), a mystical realm far removed from the English language and the concrete countries of the globe revealed in geography books.

Although *Away* is steeped in references to Gaelic, the actual Irish language is only offered in the small fragment, "*Rian fir ar mhnaoi*" (205). These words, spoken by Brian to Eileen just before he dies, sound "unfamiliar, untranslatable in their ears" (205). The break between the old language/old world and new language/new world has widened to a large void, approaching in its extremity the incomprehensible chasm that lies between the watery world of Mary's mystical sailor and the inhospitable earth and rocky terrain of Ireland and the Canadian Shield. It is Liam who recalls the meaning of that Irish phrase—"the trace of a man on a woman" (206)—providing the translation for the reader, and taking the reader to the novel's Irish triad epigraph, interestingly offered in the translated English rather than the original Irish. In Brian's school, the Gaelic and English remain apart, separated into two vertical lists on the slate board. Liam sees "a list of Gaelic nouns written in his father's hand, and beside them their English equivalents written in the hand of a child: 'famine,' 'sorrow,' 'homeland' . . ." (206). The separation of the languages accentuated by the listing formation of two columns is wrenched into violence and oppression for Liam by the imagined interruption of the school trustees, who put a stop to the child's completion of the word *castle*, and an end to the slate-board map "filled with violent arrows and forbidden words" (207).

As in *Away*, the Latin in Sheila Watson's *The Double Hook* is fragmentary, ritualistic, and incomplete. The mixture of phrases from which Felix can draw is definitely classified and separated by the two different languages: "You're welcome. Put your horse in. Pull up. *Ave Maria. Benedictus fructus ventris. Introibo*" (41). Felix's provision of a translation of "Pax vobiscum" for Lenchen provides no relevance or relief as she has no place to "go in peace." Felix's possession of words to dismiss Lenchen —"keep moving, scatter, get-the-hell-out"—is very limited, leaving him with nothing to do but "put a stick on the fire" (41). The consumable nature of the combination of the elements of wood and fire (particularly a single stick of wood) is associated with the insubstantiality of Felix's words and contrasts with the words of Coyote, which come out of the much more substantial rock and ground, issuing from the crevasses and creases, from the very bowels of the earth. Coyote's song, which "fret[s] the gap between the red boulders" near the beginning of the novel, includes the pervasive element of air in the form of the east wind and affects "those who cling to the rocks" (16). At the conclusion of the novel, the voice of Coyote, coming "from a cleft of the rock . . . crying down through the boulders" (118), brings words that control the position of humanity on earth—"on [the] soft ground," "on the sloping shoulders / of the world" (118). Coyote's words are the source of stability, a foundational rock, in a way that Felix's fragmented words never can be. Felix's and Coyote's words contrast and collide in their sources, textures, powers, and effects—the one set gathered haphazardly and randomly from the surface of the human mind and the other set emanating from the core of the earth as it opens up to meet the soil of the surface.

In Alistair MacLeod's *As Birds Bring Forth the Sun* it is again the collision of two different languages that provides the foundation for the thematic tensions at the heart of the stories. In the first story, "The Closing Down of Summer," the narrator, along with the other miners, speaks and sings Gaelic, which provides a familiar comfort, particularly the "Gaelic songs because they are so constant and unchanging and speak to us as the privately familiar" (19). The young soldiers in "Vision" turn to Gaelic for similar reasons. The Gaelic songs and words used by the miners clash with contemporary pop lyrics, as out of place as the narrator's hands and body in a kitchen filled with the latest avocado-coloured appliances. The Gaelic is a sign of the isolation of the miners as they live apart from their families and communities, pushed into the position of "other," regressing to a language that is of the old world and perhaps more suited to articulating and mining the depths of that ancient earth. The Gaelic of the miners collides with the technical language and jargon of law and dentistry that will be the world of the children. In "Vision," the final story in the collection, MacLeod sets up the two languages in the familiar translation statement, the Gaelic and English separated by the identity of the speaker:

> "Cò a th'ann?" she called. "Who's there?"
> "'Se mi-fhìn," he answered quietly. "It's myself!" (151)

Here the Gaelic beckons toward that other world of passion and sexuality that has been reined in and controlled in the story's action in much the same way as the English reins in and controls the Gaelic in the sentence itself.

In "The Tuning of Perfection" we are confronted with songs written in Gaelic, which the unknowing eye must more or less skim over, not knowing how to read or pronounce the words. The non-Gaelic reader stumbles, visually and orally, over the line, "Is tric mi 'sealltainn o 'n chnoc a 's airde" (96). MacLeod not only shows us the disparity on the page, but also explains the difference in a later story, suggesting that the people favour Gaelic as the original and thus the purer language: "The story was told in Gaelic, and as the people say, 'It is not the same in English,' although the images are true" (160). The Gaelic song lyrics are juxtaposed with slogans on bumper stickers and T-shirts that assault us, forcing us to read them even if we would prefer not to. The slogan on the bumper sticker reads, "If you're horny, honk your horn" (97), and on the T-shirt, "if you've got it, flaunt it" (106). The jolting dislocation of the traditional and poetic Gaelic beside the crass and succinct English slang reflects in an exaggerated manner the thematic struggle proposed and embodied by the two main characters in this short story, Carver and Archibald. Carver wants to popularize the past culture by modifying and updating it, whereas Archibald stands firm, determined to preserve a pure culture by refusing to compromise or alter it. In a way, Carver is forcing the Gaelic culture and language to submit to a use that will empower it by making it relevant, just as Achebe's and Saro-Wiwa's use of the English language empowers through its relevance, which demands the submission of the original language itself. A language or culture that does not touch the heart of the people obviously fails to move or affect those for whom it is intended.

Moving from Excluded to Other

When reading these texts, students slip into the position of the excluded, lightly pushed by the language that not only lies outside their knowledge and experience, but also defies attempts to be recognized, read, or pronounced. The transition from the position of the excluded to the position of "other" is a step that becomes familiar. This othering of the reader extends to areas of the text in which language is not a central issue. For example, the moment in Adele Wiseman's *Crackpot* when Hoda suddenly jumps into Mrs Limprig's body, when she is "jerked through her own skin" (271), is one for which we have been well prepared through our position as excluded and other. These positions have been initiated by the tensions and collisions of language, in this case English, Yiddish, and Hebrew, which lead us to an ability to empathize with the other as Hoda does: "[Hoda] cried out against expanding suddenly into another's world, experiencing another's flesh, another's senses, comprehending another's anguish" (272). Here we have Wiseman's sharply accurate definition and description of the essence of human compassion. As Hoda resists it, so do we as readers resist a position that necessarily and often painfully moves us to experience and view life from the other perspective and point of view, but eventually, like Hoda, we find that we crave it: "It was gone almost immediately, her revelation, and Hoda, who had cried out against it, wanted it back, the sudden enlargement, the unbidden, anguished thrill, the knowing that was not just trimmed to your head but flowed through your whole being" (272). As readers, we come to feel for Hoda the compassion that she herself is experiencing for others and, to use Edward Said's words, we sense that "it is more rewarding—and more difficult—to think concretely and sympathetically, contrapuntually, about others than only about 'us'" (336).

Our feeling of exclusion has been translated into the ability to "be jerked through our own skin" in most of these books. The realization is sudden and uncontrollable, as Hoda describes it. It is not something that we have planned or orchestrated. The reader who is excluded from the other language in these books experiences the knowledge and insight into the other, albeit very limited, as a progression from initial feelings of resentment and confusion based on exclusion. The collisions and tensions of language remain, making the leap into the other all the more startling and effective for the reader. When we confront these colliding languages, so consciously emphasized and highlighted by these writers, the initial moment of apparent textual fission (the act or process of breaking apart) is translated by the reader's response into a moment and experience of fusion. The two disparate elements create a third, the collision itself, which forces the reader to re-evaluate the familiar signifiers and signs in terms of the other language and within the context of the collision. This re-evaluation requires a singularly demanding resolution each time, repeatedly and relentlessly drawing on the cultural and personal responses of individual readers. The demands of this re-evaluation are the result of what Bhabha identifies as the "borderline work of culture [that] demands an encounter with 'newness' that is not part of the continuum of past and present," but "creates a sense of the new as an insurgent act of cultural translation" (*Location* 7).

We are very aware that the letter read to Naomi and Stephen at the end of *Obasan* is written and read in Japanese, that the letters and words exchanged between Kersi and his parents in "Swimming Lessons," the final story in *Tales from Firozsha Baag*, are full of Parsi terms and vocabulary, that the stories told to the narrator in the final section of *Running in the Family*, "The Ceylon Cactus and Succulent Society," are told in a language and a way that reflect the sensuous nature of Sri Lanka itself, that parts of "Vision," the final story in MacLeod's collection, were once told aloud and in Gaelic. As the characters, often in the position of narrator or storyteller, gain levels of understanding and compassion, so do we as readers extend our boundaries, surprising ourselves because, used to being on the inside, we are now on the outside and feel the tremendous space as we leap across in Hoda-like fashion.

Students become accustomed to shifting into the other position, so that the acceptance of the tension of the colliding languages in the more contemporary texts invites comparisons with earlier texts also containing tensions closely allied with language. Anna Jameson's *Winter Studies and Summer Rambles in Canada*, for example, includes German accompanied by English translations in the first half of the book. By the latter part of her journey, Jameson is translating a far different language, shifting from a literary interest in the written European language to a fascination with the pronunciation of the North American Native language: "Wigwam, a house, they pronounce *wee-ga-waum*; moccasin, a shoe, *muck-a-zeen*; manitou, spirit, *mo-nee-do*,—lengthening the vowels, and softening the aspirates" (389). Jameson attempts to capture and control this Chippewa language and voice,[3] maintaining that she is "bent on bringing you [in England] an Indian song, if I can catch one" (389). She does manage to capture and package several Chippewa songs, in translation at first (473–75), but eventually "in the original" as she attempts to reproduce on the page the sounds of the Chippewa language. The reader of Anna Jameson is faced with the unfamiliar language of the new world, as inaccessible as the Cherokee, Sinhalese, and Parsi in later Canadian texts: "We ah, bem, ah dè / We mah jah need dè" (476). The lyrics are even accompanied by a musical score as Jameson attempts to carry back this language and sound to her English readers in the terms and systems of England. Jameson can only do this after summarizing the meaning of the song "without the perpetual repetitions and transpositions" (475) and spending a fair amount of time describing the structure and sound of the language:

> The language of the Chippewas, however figurative and significant, is not copious. In their speeches and songs they are emphatic and impressive by the continual repetition of the same phrase or idea; and it seems to affect them like the perpetual recurrence of a few simple notes in music, by which I have been myself wound up to painful excitement, or melted to tears. (472–73)

The use of the other languages in Jameson's text measures her change from the old world to the new world, from a European outlook to a North American perspective. She moves from positioning herself with German intellectuals to positioning herself with Aboriginal women. The collisions are between her own English and the other languages available to her: the literary language of her reading and education, and the Aboriginal language of the land through which she is travelling, which moves her beyond the conventions of her upbringing and the relationship of her marriage. For the reader, the languages reflect Jameson's collisions—the conventional and limited relationships from which she is seeking to break away and the unknown and unfamiliar to which she is attracted, but cannot become attached. The collisions and tensions remain in the text as Jameson is never completely able to forego the European or embrace the Canadian. Through an understanding of Jameson's use of the other languages as a writer, the reader gains insight into the collisions and tensions within Anna Jameson the woman.

The split in Susanna Moodie as English gentlewoman and Canadian pioneer is another tension that is not resolved, and it is precisely the lack of resolution that makes her story interesting. Margaret Atwood's poem, "The Double Voice," in *The Journals of Susanna Moodie* effectively illustrates the two English "languages" that collide in *Roughing It in the Bush*—the one politely mannered or Romantic and the other realistically practical. The formal and mannered voice can be seen as old-world English and the more practical voice as Canadian English. In addition, Moodie exposes her readers to English as it is spoken by Irish immigrants and by Yankees.

Students use the postcolonial refusal to resolve colliding languages to highlight and explain other refusals to move towards resolution. This conscious and unyielding juxtaposition of English and the other language can be a powerful and effective way to position readers to experience other collisions and tensions. Within the classroom, the transition from literature to culture and society can be a tricky one, but it is a transition that students are eager to make and one that must be made in a course that includes both English literature and Canadian studies students. After a close reading of the language in *Green Grass, Running Water,* students see that the master narratives of Christopher Columbus and John Wayne are intimately connected with the British and American influences that caused so much tension for Susanna Moodie, whose position and contradictions are perhaps not as far removed from our own as we might think. From there we can move into Susanna Moodie's colonialist perspective and discourse. These are the connections that excite students when studying Canadian literature and result in animated and perceptive discussions in the classroom—discussions that address political issues of power, race, gender, and class. The examination of the postcolonial collisions of language is an extremely rich starting point for initiating and establishing the leaps and connections that provide insight not only into Canadian literature, history, society, and culture, but also into these "Canadianisms" as they are situated in a global context. The fuller explanation or response to the questions posed by my Form Two students in Nigeria lies, I believe, in these collisions of language, which lead us to leap, like Wiseman's Hoda, into the difference, into the other, taking into account the collisions and tensions that invite us and allow us to leap.

ACKNOWLEDGEMENTS

The ideas in this paper have come about as the result of teaching a specific course for a number of years. I am indebted to the lectures and ideas of my colleagues at Trent University, where this course is truly team-taught. I have been inspired by and have benefited from the teaching of Gordon Johnston, Orm Mitchell, James Neufeld, Michael Peterman, Zailig Pollock, and Beth Popham in this course. I am also greatly indebted to my students in Canadian literature courses at Trent University, who, like my students in Nigeria, have taught me so much.

NOTES

1. Louise Halfe's poetry provides one example of how Canadian Aboriginal writers have used and forced the English language into submission: "In da name of da fadder, poop / I dought da geezuz kind but / I is no good. I can't read hen write" ("In Da Name of Da Fadder").

2. Urquhart is quoting this phrase from Ben Jonson's poem, "To the Memory of My Beloved, The Author, Mr. William Shakespeare, and What He Hath Left Us."

3. Kehoe explains that Ojibway "is often spelled Chippewa in the United States" (Kehoe 217). Jameson clarifies the spelling and the pronunciation: "*Chippewa* is properly *O-jîb-wày*" (389).

WORKS CITED

Achebe, Chinua. "The African Writer and the English Language." *Morning Yet on Creation Day*. New York: Anchor, 1976. 74–84.

———. "Colonialist Criticism." *Morning Yet on Creation Day*. New York: Anchor, 1976. 3–24.

Atwood, Margaret. *The Journals of Susanna Moodie*. Toronto: Oxford UP, 1970.

Bhabha, Homi K. "DissemiNation: Time, Narrative and the Margins of the Modern Nation." *Nation and Narration*. Ed. Homi K. Bhabha. London: Routledge, 1990. 291–322.

———. *The Location of Culture*. London: Routledge, 1994.

Halfe, Louise. "In Da Name of Da Fadder." *Native Poetry in Canada: A Contemporary Anthology*. Ed. Jeannette C. Armstrong and Lally Grauer. Peterborough: Broadview, 2001. 247–48.

Jameson, Anna. *Winter Studies and Summer Rambles in Canada*. 1838. Toronto: McClelland, 1990.

Kehoe, Alice B. *North American Indians: A Comprehensive Account*. Englewood Cliffs: Prentice-Hall, 1981.

King, Thomas. *Green Grass, Running Water*. Toronto: HarperCollins, 1993.

Kogawa, Joy. *Obasan*. 1981. Toronto: Penguin, 1983.

MacLeod, Alistair. *As Birds Bring Forth the Sun*. 1986. Toronto: McClelland, 1992.

Mistry, Rohinton. *Tales from Firozsha Baag*. Toronto: McClelland, 1992.

Moodie, Susanna. *Roughing It in the Bush; or, Life in Canada*. 1852. Toronto: McClelland, 1989.

Ondaatje, Michael. "Last Ink." *Handwriting*. Toronto: Vintage, 2000. 72–75.

———. *Running in the Family*. 1982. Toronto: McClelland, 1993.

Said, Edward W. *Culture and Imperialism*. New York: Knopf, 1993.

Saro-Wiwa, Ken. *Sozaboy*. New York: Longman, 1994.

Saussure, Ferdinand de. "Course in General Linguistics." *Literary Theory: An Anthology*. Ed. Julie Rivkin and Michael Ryan. Oxford: Blackwell, 1998. 76–90.

Urquhart, Jane. *Away*. Toronto: McClelland, 1993.

Watson, Sheila. *The Double Hook*. 1959. Toronto: McClelland, 1989.

Wiebe, Rudy. *The Blue Mountains of China*. 1970. Toronto: McClelland, 1975.

Wiseman, Adele. *Crackpot*. 1974. Toronto: McClelland, 1978.

Re-Placing Ethnicity: New Approaches to Ukrainian Canadian Literature

LISA GREKUL

OVER THE PAST 50 YEARS, Canadian writers of Ukrainian descent have produced a substantial body of literature written in English that makes a rich contribution to Canadian literature. Sadly, however, Ukrainian Canadian writing is under-represented in Canadian literary studies, even though this literature has much to offer current debates going on within the Canadian literary institution. Why is Ukrainian Canadian literature rarely studied by literary scholars? Why are Ukrainian Canadian literary texts largely absent from classroom syllabi? In this paper, I suggest some possible answers to these questions. More importantly, I will outline several strategies through which Ukrainian Canadian literature can become part of the scholarship on and teaching of Canadian literature.

Admittedly, as a third-generation Ukrainian Canadian and a writer, I have a two-pronged personal investment in the production and reception of Ukrainian Canadian literature. I started thinking about Ukrainian Canadian literature near the end of my undergraduate degree, when I first noticed that I'd never been assigned any Ukrainian Canadian texts in my English courses. I assumed that I'd never studied these texts because they didn't exist. Why wasn't my ethnic group represented in my national literature? In order to fill the gap I perceived, I set out to write a Ukrainian Canadian novel. In the process of writing my book, which ultimately doubled as my MA thesis, I discovered that more than a few Ukrainians before me had in fact published novels—novels, plays, poetry, short stories, and non-fiction. Indeed, I came to understand that the writing and publishing of literary works doesn't necessarily fill gaps in literary canons and literary studies. My novel, *Kalyna's Song*, a comic *bildungsroman* about a young Ukrainian Canadian woman, was published by Coteau Books in 2003. As I made the final revisions to my manuscript, I found myself wondering what would become of my book once it was published: would it be reviewed, studied, taught? If so, how? Where? And by whom?

Over the past decade, scholars of Canadian literature have been debating the relation between so-called ethnic minority literatures and mainstream literary studies. Few would disagree that Canada's colonial legacies are British and French but that the nation has always also comprised a vast array of cultural groups. From its beginnings until the present day, Canadian literature has been shaped by writers from many different cultural backgrounds. Certainly since the early 1970s—as a result, in part, of Lester B. Pearson's Royal Commission on Bilingualism and Biculturalism (1963), Pierre Trudeau's announcement of a "Policy of Multiculturalism within a Bilingual Framework" (1971), and the passing of the Multiculturalism Act (1988) by Brian Mulroney's government—myriad changes in the publishing, reviewing, teaching, and critiquing of Canadian literary texts increasingly reflect the relevance of so-called racial and ethnic minority writing to mainstream Canadian literary studies.[1]

Scholars are divided, however, in their evaluation of the inclusiveness of the Canadian literary institution. In the introduction to their controversial anthology *Other Solitudes: Canadian Multicultural Fictions* (1990), Linda Hutcheon and Marion Richmond, for example, suggest that the Canadian literary canon has always been, by definition, multicultural, and that Canadian literary studies have always embraced ethnic minority writers. After all, some of the earliest Canadian writers to achieve canonical recognition—Laura Salverson, Frederick Philip Grove, and A.M. Klein—came from ethnic minority backgrounds. The recent popularity, moreover, of minority writers such as Joy Kogawa, Rohinton Mistry, Wayson Choy, Michael Ondaatje, and many others indicates that the boundaries between "minority" and "mainstream" literatures are becoming increasingly blurred. But as Smaro Kamboureli argues, the token inclusion of a few ethnic minority writers in the canon fails to challenge traditional, Anglo-Canadian definitions of Canadian literature: "[r]epresenting Canada's multiculturalism," she writes, "with a spattering of only one or two authors, making such writers visible only by viewing them as representative of their cultural groups, does virtually nothing to dispel the 'marginality' attributed to those authors" (*Making a Difference* 3). And, as Enoch Padolsky observes—correctly, I think—many minority texts are still published by small, minority-oriented presses; these texts are less likely to be reviewed, and they are usually studied or taught by minority critics (375).

The fundamental concern in all debates about the relation between ethnic minority writing and mainstream Canadian literary studies is the extent to which multiculturalism actually promotes diversity. Ideally, the ideologies and practices of multiculturalism preserve and promote the cultural heritages of Canada's ethnic groups. Realistically, however—and this is the argument advanced by such literary critics and theorists as Kamboureli, Himani Bannerji, and Roy Miki—multiculturalism manages difference while maintaining the Anglo-Canadian status quo.[2] Multiculturalism evokes difference in order to neutralize it (Bannerji 109).

What effect has multicultural policy had on Ukrainian Canadians, their literature, and the study of this literature? Prior to the 1970s, most Ukrainian Canadian writers published Ukrainian-language poetry and short fiction in North American Ukrainian newspapers. Aside from novelists Vera Lysenko (whose novels *Yellow Boots* and *Westerly Wild* were published in 1954 and 1956, respectively) and Illia Kiriak (whose trilogy *Sons of the Soil* was published in Ukrainian between 1939 and 1945, and translated into English in 1959), few Ukrainian Canadians wrote in English about their experiences as members of an ethnic minority group because of the intense pressure they experienced to assimilate to Anglo-Canadian society. Ukrainian Canadians did not begin writing about their experiences of ethnicity until the 1970s, when ideologies and practices of assimilation gave way to the *mosaic* model of Canadian nationhood. As Anglo-Canadian society began to recognize the value of ethnic minority groups to the multicultural nation, Ukrainian Canadians began to take pride in Ukrainian folk music, dance, and art. Ukrainian Canadian writers, though sometimes critical of this ethnic revival, benefited both directly and indirectly from Anglo-Canadian society's increasing openness to cultural diversity. They benefited, too, from the general development of the Canadian literary establishment. Multiculturalism created audiences and funding for Ukrainian Canadian literary works, so Ukrainian Canadian writers were ostensibly able to acknowledge and explore their Ukrainian backgrounds for the first time with neither embarrassment nor shame.

Beginning in the 1970s, and influenced by more inclusive definitions of Canadian nationhood and by the burgeoning of Canadian literature, a number of second- and third-generation Ukrainian Canadians started to write. Ironically, however, what they wrote, and how they wrote it, often revealed their ambivalent feelings toward the language, institutions, and values of both their ethnic and national communities. Although these writers were ostensibly empowered to explore and even celebrate their ethnic subjectivity, the experience of assimilation had profoundly affected them: most, if not all, had adopted English as their mother tongue, and the vast majority had accepted that the immigrant generations' way of life must necessarily give way to the modernity of Anglo-Canadian society. Yet almost without exception, Ukrainian Canadian writers felt an urgent responsibility to document the personal or private (hi)stories of their people, previously unrecorded in official or public narratives of Canadian history. Many writers, when faced with the self-appointed task of authentically articulating the histories of Ukrainian Canadians, questioned the appropriateness of standard English in communicating the lived experiences of Ukrainian Canadians, and they rejected established literary styles and genres that seemed inadequate for exploring the complex, hybrid identities of individuals who straddle two worlds. Both thematically and formally, these writers foregrounded the uneasy relation between ethnic and national identity, as well as the gap they perceived between language and reality.

Hyphenated identity, however, was—and is—not the only issue addressed by Ukrainian Canadian writers. For example, writers such as Helen Potrebenko, Maara Haas, and Marusya Bociurkiw critically examine the political allegiances, patriarchal social structures, and heterosexism of their Ukrainian Canadian communities.[3] Other writers of poetry, drama, and short fiction, including Andrew Suknaski, Ray Serwylo, Maara Haas, George Ryga, and George Morrissette, address the commonalities and conflicts between Ukrainian Canadians and other ethnic minority groups (especially First Nations people).[4] All of these writers question their sense of belonging, or their right to belong, in a prairie space that they share with other communities. Writers such as Myrna Kostash and Janice Kulyk Keefer question their sense of belonging to the Old Country from which their parents or grandparents emigrated.[5] In other words, for numerous Ukrainian Canadian writers, the specific matter of Ukrainian Canadian ethnicity (what it means to be Ukrainian Canadian) intersects with broader issues of politics, gender, and race, as well as history, language, and place.

That Ukrainian Canadian literature in English developed alongside discourses of multiculturalism is no coincidence. Nor is it coincidental that Ukrainian Canadian cultural studies programs (and scholarship related to Ukrainian Canadian cultural production) emerged alongside the introduction and institutionalization of multiculturalism. Although Professor Kost Andrusyshen established the Chair of Ukrainian Language Studies at the University of Saskatchewan in 1945 (Marunchak 732), and although some scholarly texts related to Ukrainians in Canada were published prior to the 1960s—for example, Charles Young's *The Ukrainian Canadians: A Study in Assimilation* (1931), William Paluk's *Canadian Cossacks: Essays, Articles and Stories on Ukrainian Canadian Life* (1943), Vera Lysenko's *Men in Sheepskin Coats: A Study in Assimilation* (1947), and Paul Yuzyk's *The Ukrainians in Manitoba: A Social History* (1953)—no concentrated unfolding of Ukrainian Canadian scholarship occurred until discussions around multiculturalism began to take place. Not surprisingly, given their long history of social organization and political activism, Ukrainian Canadians—and, in particular, Ukrainian Canadian scholars—played an active, if not central, role in lobbying for the institutionalization of multiculturalism.

In 1963, when Prime Minister Lester B. Pearson launched the Royal Commission on Bilingualism and Biculturalism, Ukrainian Canadians, many of whom had experienced political oppression in the Old Country, balked at institutionalized anglophone and francophone cultural hegemony: according to Bohdan Bociurkiw, they "undoubtedly played the leading role in the development and dissemination of the ideas and policy demands that eventually crystallized into the policy of multiculturalism" (Bociurkiw 100). Between 1963 and 1971, groups such as the Ukrainian Canadian Congress (UCC), the Association of United Ukrainian Canadians (AUUC), the Ukrainian Canadian University Students' Union (SUSK), and the Ukrainian Professional and Business Federation, as well as prominent individuals and representatives from the Ukrainian Canadian press, voiced their staunch disapproval of a bipartite model of nationhood. At public forums and conferences, in newspaper articles and scholarly papers, Ukrainian Canadians reiterated the argument that bilingualism and biculturalism would "[condemn] . . . other ethnic groups to an inferior, 'non-founding' status and their cultures to eventual submersion in one of two 'official cultures'" (Bociurkiw 105). As an alternative to the proposed "B&B" framework, Ukrainian Canadians called for the federal government to "support the efforts of all ethnocultural groups to maintain and develop their cultural-linguistic heritage"; they suggested that a federal ministry of culture be established to "recognize and give unlimited support to all the cultures of the Canadian multicultural society" (Bociurkiw 105). Interestingly, when Prime Minister Pierre Trudeau eventually announced his new policy of multiculturalism within a bilingual framework, in October 1971, he did so at a meeting of the Ukrainian Canadian Congress (Hryniuk and Luciuk 3).

Discussions among Ukrainian Canadians about multiculturalism, however, did not wane following Trudeau's announcement: now the work of consolidating multicultural policy—and Ukrainian Canadians' status within a multicultural state—began. Between 1971 and 1988, Ukrainian Canadian scholars convened on numerous occasions to formulate strategies for preserving and promoting the Ukrainian way of life in Canada. In 1974, for example, the "All-Canadian Conference on Ukrainian Studies Courses," held in Winnipeg, brought together university professors from across the country (and across disciplines) to discuss the development and coordination of Ukrainian studies in Canadian universities (Marunchak 732). In 1977, at the University of Alberta, Ukrainian Canadian historians and political scientists gathered for a conference on "Ukrainian Canadians, Multiculturalism, and Separatism," where they evaluated the current political situation of Ukrainians vis-à-vis Quebec. "Identifications: Ethnicity and the Writer in Canada," a conference held at the University of Alberta in 1979, brought debates about multiculturalism into the literary arena, giving both writers and literary scholars the opportunity to discuss unique concerns surrounding ethnic minority writing. (In fact, while the conference title suggests cross-cultural perspectives, the primary focus of the conference was Ukrainian literature in Canada. As Winfried Siemerling points out, this is hardly surprising given that the conference was organized by the Canadian Institute of Canadian Studies on the occasion of the seventy-fifth anniversary of Ukrainian publishing in Canada [26].)

Interestingly, however, in the *Identifications* conference proceedings, statements made by writers such as Maara Haas and George Ryga illustrate their refusal to identify themselves as "Ukrainian" Canadian writers: because they feel that ethnic labels segregate them from the Canadian writerly community, they prefer to be seen as "Canadian" writers or simply "writers." In Maara Haas's words,

> [i]t takes great discipline on my part not to vomit when I hear the word ethnic. My reflex action is to spit on the word that was spat on me in my formative years of the middle thirties. Dirty ethnic, rotten Slavic ethnic, ghetto freak ethnic. I was hyphenated, set apart by the English, Scottish, Irish factors outside the ghetto. Each time the word ethnic rears its hyphenated head, the odour of a clogged sewer smelling of racism poisons the air. (Balan 136)

For Haas, the ethnic label is "alienating, segregating, hyphenating": it "hyphenates the writer off the scene" (136). Similarly, Ryga suggests that

> [w]e're discussing Canadian literature in a Canadian context and everything that implies. As a contributor to that literature, I find it difficult to see myself as a so-called hyphenated Canadian. . . .When I wake up in the morning, I check myself out to see if I am still a man. Having determined that I am, I then face the world on its merits. . . . I do not live in the past. I do not live in my father's frame of reference. (qtd. in Balan 140–42)

Ironically, while multiculturalism—the ideology so vigorously advocated by many Ukrainian Canadians—had given Ukrainian Canadian writers opportunities to write about their experiences as hyphenated Canadians, some of these writers were simultaneously critical of the ways in which multiculturalism relegated them and their work to the margins of Canadian literary discourse.

But despite some Ukrainian Canadian writers' uneasiness with identifying themselves, or being identified, as ethnically distinct from other Canadian writers, Ukrainian Canadian scholars, often capitalizing on multicultural funding opportunities, continued to work toward establishing distinct Ukrainian Canadian studies programs within Canadian universities. In 1976, the Canadian Institute of Ukrainian Studies (CIUS) was established at the University of Alberta and the University of Toronto:

broadly focused on Ukrainian studies in Canada and internationally (especially in Ukraine), the CIUS Press publishes the *Journal of Ukrainian Studies* as well as scholarly books. In addition to running the Stasiuk Program for the Study of Contemporary Ukraine, the Ukrainian Canadian Program, the Ukrainian Church Studies Program, and the Kowalsky Program for the Study of Eastern Ukraine, the CIUS also undertakes several large scholarly projects including the Encyclopedia of Ukraine, and the Canada Ukraine Legislative and Intergovernmental Project. In 1979, the Chair of Ukrainian Studies was founded at the University of Toronto and, in 1981, the Centre for Ukrainian Canadian Studies (which publishes the *Canadian Ethnic Studies* journal) was established at the University of Manitoba, providing courses in Ukrainian (and Ukrainian Canadian) literature, folklore, history, and arts. More recently, in 1989, the University of Alberta introduced its Ukrainian Folklore Program. Headed by the Huculak Chair of Ukrainian Culture and Ethnography, the Ukrainian Folklore Program offers students at the undergraduate and graduate level courses in folk song, dance, art, rites of passage, and calendar customs. The University of Saskatchewan, too, in 1999, reorganized its Ukrainian studies program: the Prairie Centre for the Study of Ukrainian Heritage and the newly founded Heritage Press are directed by the Lesya Ukrainka Chair of Ukrainian Studies.

Over the years, out of these centres, institutes, and programs, an impressive body of scholarly work on Ukrainians in Canada has emerged.[6] Aside from works by Frances Swyripa and John-Paul Himka (*Loyalties in Conflict: Ukrainians During the Great War*, 1983), Vladimir Kaye (*Ukrainian Canadians in Canada's Wars*, 1983), and Lubomyr Luciuk (*Searching for Place: Ukrainian Displaced Persons, Canada, and the Migration of Memory*, 2000), the pioneer period of immigration has received more scholarly attention than the interwar or post–World War II periods.[7] Some studies of Ukrainian Canadian demographics have been assembled, including William Darcovich and Paul Yuzyk's *A Statistical Compendium on the Ukrainians in Canada, 1891–1976* (1981) and Lubomyr Luciuk and Bohdan Kordan's *Creating a Landscape: A Geography of Ukrainians in Canada* (1989). With Martha Bohachevsky's *Feminists Despite Themselves: Women in Ukrainian Community Life 1884–1939* (1988) and Frances Swyripa's *Wedded to the Cause: Ukrainian Canadian Women and Ethnic Identity 1891–1991* (1993), feminist scholarship on Ukrainian Canadian women has begun to emerge.

In comparison to the significant body of existing scholarly work on Ukrainian Canadian (and, importantly, Ukrainian) history and ethnography, however, much less work on Ukrainian Canadian literature (in Ukrainian or in English) has been undertaken by Ukrainian Canadian scholars. Although most historical overviews of Ukrainian Canadians include discussions of Ukrainian Canadian literature, these discussions are often brief and primarily comprise biographical sketches of Ukrainian Canadian (predominantly Ukrainian-language) writers. M.I. Mandryka's *History of Ukrainian Literature in Canada* (1968), then, stands out as the only book-length study of Ukrainian Canadian literature by a Ukrainian Canadian scholar.[8] But Mandryka's book focuses exclusively on Ukrainian-language writers: it is a compilation of biographical information accompanied by some summary of selected texts but virtually no textual analysis. Generally speaking, when Ukrainian Canadian scholars turn their attention to literature, they study or translate the works of Ukrainian-language authors from Ukraine (such as Tara Shevchenko and Ivan Franko). Considerably less work is done on Ukrainian-language authors in Canada, and still less on English-language Ukrainian Canadian writers.[9]

In the 1990s, scholars began to publish papers on English-language Ukrainian Canadian texts, primarily in academic periodicals focused on the study of ethnic minorities (the *Journal of Ukrainian Studies*, for example, and *Canadian Ethnic Studies*). As with all literary studies, works of fiction—especially novels—seem to receive more attention than poetry, drama, or non-fiction (there exists a disproportionate body of work related to Lysenko's novel *Yellow Boots*[10]). Just as many Ukrainian Canadian historians concentrate on the first wave of Ukrainian immigration, so too do Ukrainian Canadian literary scholars show particular interest in literature related thematically to early Ukrainian settlement. And, not unlike current trends in Ukrainian Canadian historical scholarship, feminist studies of Ukrainian Canadian pioneer literature are becoming increasingly common (see Mycak, "A Different Story"; and Palmer Seiler, "Including"). At the same time, in other scholarly essays, Ukrainian Canadian texts are included in broader discussions of multicultural themes in Canadian writing (see Redl and Kirtz). In "Multi-vocality and National Literature," Palmer Seiler discusses the ways in which multicultural texts (including Ukrainian Canadian texts) can be approached through post-colonial theoretical frameworks. Occasionally, Ukrainian Canadian scholars touch upon the formal aspects of Ukrainian Canadian texts: Robert

Klymasz, for example, examines the use of Ukrainian words in English-language texts, and Tatiana Nazarenko explores the distinctly Ukrainian features of Ukrainian Canadian visual poetry. Others seek to establish and articulate the thematically unique aspects of Ukrainian Canadian texts: in "Simple Sentimentality or Specific Narrative Strategy?," Mycak examines the role of nostalgia for the ethnic homeland in Ukrainian Canadian literature and film, and Maxim Tarnawsky addresses the treatment of Ukrainian history and language in Ukrainian Canadian fiction.

After reading through the relatively small corpus of scholarly work on English-language Ukrainian Canadian literature, however, my feeling is that the gaps in Ukrainian Canadian literary criticism are more telling than the existing body of scholarship. Ukrainian Canadian writers frequently criticize multicultural ideology and its repercussions for hyphenated Canadians; in their works, they often probe the relation between ethnic and national identity, ethnic and racial identity, ethnic and gendered identity; and, perhaps most importantly, many Ukrainian Canadian writers experiment with narrative style and genre in their attempts to articulate the complex, uneasy realities of hyphenated subjectivity. But with few exceptions, Ukrainian Canadian scholars concentrate on texts that follow traditional generic conventions (realist fiction, most commonly), overlooking texts that challenge generic boundaries. So, for example, Andrew Suknaski's long poems and experimental visual poetry have received little critical attention from Ukrainian Canadian scholars; nor have these scholars studied the works of creative non-fiction by Myrna Kostash or Janice Kulyk Keefer.[11] Similarly, Ukrainian Canadian scholars tend to focus on texts (such as Lysenko's *Yellow Boots*) that portray Ukrainian characters actively preserving Ukrainian traditions and customs rather than texts that explore Ukrainians' difficulties in maintaining their ethnic identity within Canadian society. Hence, few scholars have written about numerous works by Ted Galay, Maara Haas, and George Morrissette. Although feminist scholars appear to foreground the role of women within Ukrainian Canadian texts, they approach select texts (again, like *Yellow Boots*) that fail to challenge pervasive patriarchal social structures within Ukrainian Canadian communities and that implicitly affirm the cohesive nature of Ukrainian Canadian communities. Texts by Helen Potrebenko and Marusya Bociurkiw that explicitly criticize patriarchal and heterosexist discourses within Ukrainian Canadian communities remain unexamined.

Why, when Ukrainian Canadian scholars undertake critical work on Ukrainian Canadian literature, do they tend to engage with Ukrainian Canadian texts that affirm (rather than challenge) the cohesive nature of Ukrainian Canadian communities? Why do they do so almost exclusively within the structures of Ukrainian Canadian studies programs?

In a sense, Ukrainian Canadian literary scholars' hands are tied. Since the 1970s (initially in response to the threat of assimilation to dominant anglophone and francophone cultures), the Ukrainian Canadian academic community as a whole has focused its scholarly energy on promoting and preserving particular notions of "the" Ukrainian Canadian community. "The" Ukrainian Canadian community's history is a narrative of progress in which, out of hardship and strife, despite pressures to assimilate to Anglo-Canadian society, Ukrainian Canadians retained a distinct, unified cultural heritage (a cultural heritage that often relies on folkloric expressions of ethnicity). To voice dissent openly—to advance arguments related to the fissures and fractures within Ukrainian Canadian communities, as articulated by Ukrainian Canadian writers—is perceived as a disloyal challenge to the established institutionalized structures and discourses of the Ukrainian Canadian scholarly community.[12] Literary texts that explore the complex and uneasy realities of Ukrainian Canadian experience—literary texts that question existing notions of Ukrainian Canadian ethnicity—receive little or no critical attention from Ukrainian Canadian scholars precisely because they challenge the celebratory rhetoric of multiculturalism espoused by the Ukrainian Canadian academic institution.

Ukrainian Canadian scholars are in the unique position to teach others about the existence and value of Ukrainian Canadian literature, but to do so, they need to look closely at both how and where they do such teaching; how and where they critically engage non-Ukrainian Canadians in this literature. Instead of reading Ukrainian Canadian literature as *Ukrainian* (and as relevant only to Ukrainian Canadian scholars), scholars need to read it as Ukrainian Canadian *literature* by exploring its relevance to literary debates about colonialism, race, gender, and sexuality, as well as ethnicity. Rather than guarding Ukrainian Canadian literature against non–Ukrainian Canadian critical audiences, Ukrainian Canadians need to open this literature to the lively exchange of wide-ranging ideas and arguments within Canadian literary studies. Insofar as Ukrainian Canadian texts can contribute to ongoing debates about ethnicity, nationality, and multiculturalism, and insofar as the Ukrainian Canadian academic institution is resistant to such debates, Canadian literary studies represent a promising alternative—a space where the relation between ethnic minority literatures, multicultural ideology, and mainstream literary culture is already hotly debated, and where more scholarly work on Ukrainian Canadian literary texts can take place.

NOTES

1. I distinguish between "racial" and "ethnic" minority writing because, as Winfried Siemerling suggests, "[e]thnicity has . . . been rejected sometimes as a serviceable category by those who feel that it might depoliticize issues by conflating them, for instance those [issues] concerning minorities in general with those concerning visible minorities" (11). While I use the terms *ethnic minority* and *mainstream* literatures, I use them cautiously and provisionally, conscious of the possibility that such terms, by perpetuating a rigid division between centre and margin (Anglo-Canadian versus non-Anglo-Canadian cultural practices and institutions), fail to account for the heterogeneity and fluidity of both.
2. See Kamboureli, *Scandalous Bodies*; Bannerji; and Miki.
3. Potrebenko's works include a novel, *Sometimes They Sang* (1986), and *Hey Waitress* (1989), a collection of short fiction. Haas has published *The Street Where I Live* (1976), a novel, and *On Stage With Maara Haas* (1986), a collection of poetry and short fiction. Marusya Bociurkiw has published a collection of short fiction, *The Woman Who Loved Airports* (1994), and a collection of poetry, *Halfway to the East* (1999).
4. See, for example, Suknaski's *Wood Mountain Poems* (1976), *the ghosts call you poor* (1978), *In the Name of Narid* (1981), and *The Land They Gave Away: New and Selected Poems* (1982); Serwylo's novel *Accordion Lessons* (1982); Ryga's play *A Letter to My Son* (1981); and Morrissette's long poem *Finding Mom at Eaton's* (1981).
5. Kostash writes about her travels to Ukraine in *Bloodlines: A Journey into Eastern Europe* (1993) and *The Doomed Bridegroom: A Memoir* (1998), and Kulyk Keefer documents her return to Ukraine in *Honey and Ashes: A Story of Family* (1998).
6. Numerous historians and ethnographers have produced or edited broad studies of Ukrainian Canadians that touch upon various aspects of Ukrainian life in Canada, beginning with the arrival of the first pioneers: see Paul Yuzyk's

Ukrainian Canadians: Their Place and Role in Canadian Life (1967); Ol'ha Woycenko's *The Ukrainians in Canada* (1968); Michael Marunchak's *The Ukrainian Canadians: A History* (first published in 1970); Manoly Lupul's *A Heritage in Transition: Essays in the History of Ukrainians in Canada* (1982); Jaroslav Rozumnyj's *New Soil—Old Roots: The Ukrainian Experience in Canada* (1983); Jars Balan's *Salt and Braided Bread: Ukrainian Life in Canada* (1984); O.W. Gerus and J.E. Rea's *The Ukrainians in Canada* (1985); Lybomyr Luciuk and Stella Hryniuk's *Canada's Ukrainians: Negotiating an Identity* (1991); Ramon Hnatyshyn and Robert Klymasz's *Art and Ethnicity: The Ukrainian Tradition in Canada* (1991); and Orest Subtelny's *Ukrainians in North America: An Illustrated History* (1991).

Some historians have focused on more specific aspects of the Ukrainian experience—settlement patterns and social trends, for example, in particular provinces and/or during specific time periods: see Vladimir Kaye's *Early Ukrainian Settlement in Canada 1895–1900* (1964); J.G. MacGregor's *Vilni Zemli [Free Lands]: The Ukrainian Settlement of Alberta* (1969); Helen Potrebenko's *No Streets of Gold: A Social History of Ukrainians in Alberta* (1977); Zonia Keywan's *Greater Than Kings: Ukrainian Pioneer Settlement in Canada* (1977); and Manoly Lupul's *Continuity and Change: The Cultural Life of Alberta's First Ukrainians* (1988).

Other scholars have recorded first-person accounts of settlement: see Harry Piniuta's *Land of Pain, Land of Promise: First Person Accounts by Ukrainian Pioneers 1891–1914* (1978); and William Czumer's *Recollections About the Life of the First Ukrainian Settlers in Canada* (1981).

7. Ukrainians immigrated to Canada in three distinct waves. From the 1870s until 1914, approximately 170 000 Ukrainians came to Canada; between the wars, some 68 000 immigrated; and between 1947 and 1950, a further 32 000 arrived.

8. Watson Kirkconnell, a "scholar, university administrator and prodigious translator of verse from dozens of languages" (Woodsworth 13), is often cited as one of the first scholars, translators, and promoters of Ukrainian Canadian literature. His *Twilight of Liberty* (1946) examines Ukrainian pioneer literature (in Ukrainian). Kirkconnell's other work on Ukrainian Canadians include: *The Ukrainian Canadians and the War* (1940), *Our Ukrainian Loyalists* (1943), *The Ukrainian Agony* (1943), and *Seven Pillars of Freedom* (1944).

9. Marta Tarnawsky's bibliographies *Ukrainian Literature in English: Books and Pamphlets, 1840–1965* (1988) and *Ukrainian Literature in English: Articles in Journals and Collections, 1840–1965* (1991) offer comprehensive (though not up-to-date) information on Ukrainian Canadian literary scholarship. The vast majority of works assembled by Tarnawsky relate to English studies of Ukrainian (as opposed to Ukrainian Canadian) authors and their texts.

10. See Rasporich; Glynn; Redl; Palmer Seiler, "Including"; and Mycak, "Simple."

11. Tarnawsky's "What Is Told in the Green Library" discusses Kulyk Keefer's novel *The Green Library* (1996).

12. Ukrainian Canadian writer and critic Janice Kulyk Keefer makes this point in "'Coming Across Bones': Historiographic Ethnofiction": "I know that in the eyes of the Ukrainian Canadian community, my emphasis on a history that cuts both ways, showing Ukrainians as both oppressed and oppressors, may be perceived as the attitude of someone so alienated from her ancestry that she has taken to fouling her own nest" (99).

WORKS CITED

Balan, Jars, ed. *Identifications: Ethnicity and the Writer in Canada*. Edmonton: Canadian Institute of Ukrainian Studies, 1982.

Bannerji, Himani. "On the Dark Side of the Nation: Politics of Multiculturalism and the State of Canada." *Journal of Canadian Studies* 31.3 (1996): 103–28.

Bociurkiw, Bohdan. "The Federal Policy of Multiculturalism and the Ukrainian-Canadian Community." *Ukrainian Canadians, Multiculturalism, and Separatism: An Assessment*. Ed. Manoly Lupul. Edmonton: U of Alberta P; Canadian Institute of Ukrainian Studies, 1978. 98–128.

Glynn, Alexandra Kruchka. "Reintroducing Vera Lysenko—Ukrainian Canadian Author." *Journal of Ukrainian Studies* 15.1 (1990): 53–70.

Grekul, Lisa. *Kalyna's Song*. Regina: Coteau Books, 2003.

Hryniuk, Stella, and Lubomyr Luciuk, eds. *Multiculturalism and Ukrainian Canadians: Identity, Homeland Ties, and the Community's Future*. Toronto: Multicultural Society of Ontario, 1993.

Hutcheon, Linda, and Marion Richmond, eds. *Other Solitudes: Canadian Multicultural Fictions*. Toronto: Oxford UP, 1990.

Kamboureli, Smaro, ed. *Making a Difference: Canadian Multicultural Literature*. Toronto: Oxford UP, 1996.

———. *Scandalous Bodies: Diasporic Literature in English Canada*. Don Mills: Oxford UP, 2000.

Kirtz, Mary K. "Old World Traditions, New World Inventions: Bilingualism, Multiculturalism, and the Transformation of Ethnicity." *Canadian Ethnic Studies* 28.1 (1996): 8–21.

Klymasz, Robert B. "Art of Intrusion: Macaronicism in Ukrainian-Canadian Literature." *Canadian Review of Comparative Literature* 16.3–4 (1989): 763–69.

Kulyk Keefer, Janice. "'Coming Across Bones': Historiographic Ethnofiction." *Essays on Canadian Writing* 57 (1995): 84–104.

Marunchak, Michael H. *The Ukrainian Canadians: A History*. Winnipeg: Ukrainian Free Academy of Sciences, 1970.

Miki, Roy. *Broken Entries: Race Writing Subjectivity*. Toronto: Mercury, 1998.

Mycak, Sonia. "A Different Story by Helen Potrebenko: The Pioneer Myth Re-Visited." *Canadian Ethnic Studies* 28.1 (1996): 67–88.

———. "Simple Sentimentality or Specific Narrative Strategy? The Functions and Use of Nostalgia in the Ukrainian-Canadian Text." *Canadian Ethnic Studies* 30.1 (1998): 50–63.

Nazarenko, Tatiana. "Ukrainian-Canadian Visual Poetry: Traditions and Innovations." *Canadian Ethnic Studies* 28.1 (1996): 89–126.

Padolsky, Enoch. "Canadian Ethnic Minority Literature in English." *Ethnicity and Culture in Canada: The Research Landscape*. Ed. J.W. Berry and J.A. Laponce. Toronto: U of Toronto P, 1994. 361–86.

Palmer Seiler, Tamara. "Including the Female Immigrant Story: A Comparative Look at Narrative Strategies." *Canadian Ethnic Studies* 28.1 (1996): 51–66.

———. "Multi-Vocality and National Literature: Toward a Post-Colonial and Multicultural Aesthetic." *Journal of Canadian Studies* 31.3 (1996): 148–65.

Rasporich, Beverly. "Retelling Vera Lysenko: A Feminist and Ethnic Writer." *Canadian Ethnic Studies* 21.2 (1989): 38–52.

———. "Vera Lysenko's Fictions: Engendering Prairie Spaces." *Prairie Forum* 16.2 (1991): 249–63.

Redl, Carolyn. "Neither Here nor There: Canadian Fiction by the Multicultural Generation." *Canadian Ethnic Studies* 28.1 (1996): 22–36.

Siemerling, Winfried. Introduction. *Writing Ethnicity*. Spec. issue of *Essays on Canadian Writing* 57 (1995): 1–32.

Tarnawsky, Maxim. "What Is Told in the Green Library: History, Institutions, Language." *Canadian Ethnic Studies* 31.3 (1999): 104–13.

Woodsworth, Judy. "Watson Kirkconnell and the 'Undoing of Babel': A Little-Known Case in Canadian Translation History." *Meta* 45.1 (2000): 13–28.

To Canada from "My Many Selves": Addressing the Theoretical Implications of South Asian Diasporic Literature in English as a Pedagogical Paradigm

MARIAM PIRBHAI

i breathe harder
with my many selves,
        turning back

— Cyril Dabydeen, "I Am Not"

By race I am Indian
Not Carib Indian.
East Indian-born North
Of the Amazon Basin.

By religion I'm Buddhist
By history British
By culture Caribbean
And by ambition American.
. . . .
And if perchance you want a pen pal
Write to me at my native address.
P.D. Sharma P.O. Box 472 Georgetown Guyana
WEST INDIES.

— P.D. Sharma, "Diaspora"

As the above excerpts indicate, writers of the South Asian diaspora self-consciously foreground their multiply positioned identities. In evoking their "many selves," South Asian diasporic writers call upon a diverse range of literary fields, at least as they are defined in cultural and national terms. For instance, Cyril Dabydeen, Ottawa's former poet laureate (1984–87) of Indo-Guyanese origin, can just as readily fall under the rubric of Canadian literature as that of English, Guyanese, Caribbean, Indo-Caribbean, South American, and South Asian literature. To this end, the Toronto-based diasporic writer M.G. Vassanji suggests: "The term *South Asian* . . . does not represent a single stand, a single outlook or concern in political, cultural or literary matters. . . . *South Asian* is then perhaps a term best used as one of *contrast*" (4).[1]

South Asian diasporic literature thus poses a particularly poignant challenge to the Canadian curriculum, for, in their cross-cultural habitations, South Asian diasporic writers bring to the fore what James Clifford refers to as "a processual configuration of historically given elements—including race, culture, class, gender, and sexuality—different combinations of which may be featured in different conjunctures" (116). Subsequently, South Asian diasporic writers challenge the reader, teacher, and critic alike to re-evaluate the narrowly defined literary and cultural paradigms through which diasporic texts are commonly apprehended.

In addressing the theoretical implications of the South Asian diasporic writer's multiply positioned identity, I find myself asking a two-fold question: a) how is South Asian diasporic literature presently approached in the Canadian literary curriculum and by Canadian scholars?; and b) how should South Asian diasporic literature ideally be approached, given the culturally and historically diverse backgrounds of South Asian diasporic writers and their ever-growing literary output, the bulk of which is written in English?

The answer to the first question is relatively straightforward. Despite their multiple positionings, South Asian diasporic writers continue to be taken as wholesale representatives of a qualitative *South Asianness* on the one hand and of a quantitative *minority* status on the other—at least as they are studied, theorized, and perceived in the academic arena. For the most part, these writers continue to be viewed as a homogeneous entity regardless of their complex networks of identification. They are, in turn, examined in terms of their status as immigrants, which is quite often synonymous with their position as visible minorities (a misnomer in such metropolises as Toronto where South Asians have earned the arguably absurd label as an "ethnic majority-minority").

Though labels such as *minority, immigrant*, and, more recently, *diaspora* itself are avowedly meant to foster constructive discussions of identity and identity politics, each of the above categories is defined by a yardstick of comparison that is strictly posited in relation to North American constructions of difference, which are themselves the lingering vestiges of Eurocentric cultural and racial norms. Such seemingly inclusive gestures ironically tend to efface the cultural dynamics at play within each author's work. Indeed, like the ideological trappings of a discretely hierarchized multicultural mosaic, the South Asian writer is both homogenized and kept at arm's length from the dominant culture and its literary canons.

There are two interrelated casualties in such fields of containment: namely, the cross-continental diversity of South Asian peoples themselves and their equally extensive literary output. In fact, the vast majority of South Asian diasporic writers are all too often eclipsed by a negligible number of international celebrities who have come to comprise a modest canon.[2] Moreover, even the canonized few are taken to represent a shared South Asian perspective regardless of each writer's very different cultural, national, or ideological points of view. In other words, such figures as V.S. Naipaul, Salman Rushdie, Michael Ondaatje, and Rohinton Mistry are often examined under the rubric of "Post-Colonial Literature," or for their positions as "minorities" or "immigrants" in Western countries. The canonization of this small coterie of writers seems to have precluded a more dialogic, cross-cultural, and contextualized approach to a burgeoning number of writers from the numerous regions of the South Asian diaspora.

This brings me to my second question: if present conceptual literary and cultural models and existing canons are not up to the task of apprehending a body of literature that can stem as easily from India or Pakistan as from South Africa, Canada, or Fiji, where do we go from here? My second question is best addressed with a concomitant consideration of the sociocultural implications of diasporic experience more generally and a brief historical overview of the South Asian diaspora in particular. This is because diasporic peoples make explicit Stuart Hall's notion of cultural identity as "a 'production' which is never complete" (392).

In his seminal article, "Cultural Identity and Diaspora," Hall writes against essentialist and decontextualized notions of identity:

> Cultural identity . . . is a matter of "becoming" as well as of "being." It belongs to the future as much as to the past. . . . Cultural identities come from somewhere, have histories. But, like everything which is historical, they undergo constant transformation. Far from being eternally fixed in some essentialized past, they are subject to the continuous "play" of history, culture and power. Far from being grounded in mere "recovery" of the past . . . identities are the names we give to the different ways we are *positioned by, and position ourselves within*, the narratives of the past. (394; emphasis added)

Since the past is not so much lost as it is re-imagined and reconstructed through time, cultural identity can be seen as processual and transformative. As Hall notes, cultural identity signals a positioning between "the narratives of the past" (which are themselves multiple and hybrid) and the realities or exigencies of the present.

Through their own multiple positionings, then, diasporic writers further James Clifford's call for "a better comparative awareness of . . . 'diaspora cultures'" as a means of inviting "a reconception—both theoretical and political—of familiar notions of ethnicity and identity" (108).[3] By bringing to view the contextual, processual, and transformative networks of identity formation, diasporic writers consciously or implicitly challenge static and totalizing definitions of cultural identity. In other words, diasporic writing, like diasporic cultures, signals inherently cross-cultural networks of production, which in turn give rise to a comparative cultural, literary, and theoretical framework. Indeed, a comparative view of a diasporic body of writing best illustrates the reductive nature of categories of literary study, which insist on positing Manichean dichotomies and simplistic cultural binaries at the expense of the heterogeneous contours and widely dispersed landscapes of the diasporic imagination.

As I have suggested, however, South Asian writers are often examined for their articulations of migrancy, wherein significant distinctions between such varying phenomena as diaspora, immigration, exile, expatriatism, and refugeeism are rarely made. For example, Salman Rushdie's cosmopolitan world view, which upholds that modern-day émigrés "straddle two cultures . . . [or] fall between two stools" (15), is commonly applied to other kinds of migrant South Asian writers. When we examine diasporic authors, however, Rushdie's paradigm of migrancy as a split perspective or a paradoxically permanent state of "in-betweenness" is greatly nuanced, if not problematized. Unlike their immigrant, exilic, or transnational counterparts, diasporic writers often make it clear that, at least for second and subsequent generations, this state of "in-betweenness" is not always applicable to people whose links to the "homeland" have long been severed but who nonetheless retain their cultural roots; in other words, for those who do not necessarily feel physically or psychologically torn between their diasporic location and the site of their genealogical origins.

This is not the "diaspora" (co-opted by postmodern and postcolonial theory alike), therefore, that typecasts all manner of migrants, regardless of their historical or cultural trajectories, as free-floating, homeless entities.[4] In fact, the dispersal of South Asian peoples has rarely led to a detribalized, decentred, or de-territorialized consciousness. On the contrary, diasporic South Asians generally form tight-knit cultural, ethnic and, most intrinsically, religious enclaves with strong social structures, traditional practices, and endogamous relations which help preserve a deeply rooted sense of community. These communities should not be mistaken, in turn, as unitary or homogeneous, but are dynamic, highly stratified, and often contentious alliances, internally divided by such factors as language, religion, caste, political ideology, nationalist feeling, generational differences, and the orientation to the host society itself.

I employ the term *diaspora*, then, to connote a history of migration arising out of common historical conjunctures, which has resulted in the multiple signifiers of a cross-cultural identity. The South Asian diaspora can thus be seen as the most literal symbol of the Indian Subcontinent as a crossroads of intercultural exchange and an often daunting diversity. In fact, South Asian diasporic writers give voice to multiple generations of migratory subjects who interpret their surroundings anywhere from the perspective of a first-generation immigrant to that of a fifth-generation descendant of earlier waves of diasporic peoples.

Though the total number of diasporic South Asians seems modest in relation to the one billion plus population of the Indian Subcontinent, these peoples nonetheless constitute very substantial portions of local populations around the world and, in some cases, have come to dominate the ethnic, political, and cultural scene therein:

> As of 1981, the number of people born in India and living outside of India was estimated at more than 13 million—more than 400 000 in the United States, 440 000 in Trinidad, 500 000 in Britain, 800 000 in South Africa, more than a million each in Burma and Malaysia. . . . As of about 1960, South Asians were more than one-third of the population of Trinidad and Suriname, and nearly half the population of Guyana and Fiji, and two-thirds of the population of Mauritius. (Sowell 310, 313)

It is also important to note that the movements and migrations of South Asian peoples predate European colonial history, tracing back to several millennia of intercultural contact that is most tellingly manifested in the imprint of Hindu, Buddhist and, later, Islamic civilisations in other parts of the world.[5] However, the largest physical exodus of South Asian peoples occurred under the colonial infrastructure between the 1830s and the turn of the twentieth century in the demand for labour in a post-emancipation economy. Many writers of South Asian origin are thus descendants of early migrants who braved life in the numerous colonies of the British Empire as contractual workers on such projects as the East Africa Railway, as indentured labourers on colonial plantations, as clerics, administrators and servicemen, or as fortune-seeking merchants and traders.[6]

The British colonies were not the only recipients of South Asian migrants; indeed, the Western hemisphere's history of South Asian immigration is as old as the British Raj itself. As K. Laxmi Narayan states, South Asians have populated Britain for almost three hundred years as "seamen, domestic servants, politicians, barristers [and] doctors" (16). In addition, as early as the 1820s, a group of Punjabi-Sikhs migrated to the south-western United States, where they eventually established their own relatively prosperous farm-owning communities. At the turn of the twentieth century, Punjabi-Sikhs also formed the first major South Asian community in Canada, settling in British Columbia where they worked mainly as agricultural labourers.

Shortly after the earliest influx of Chinese and South Asian peoples to Britain, the United States, and Canada, each of these countries prohibited or severely curtailed "Asian" immigration up until the post-war era. In the United States, for example, the implementation of "the Oriental Exclusion Act in 1924 virtually banned all immigration from Asia" (Narayan 18); similarly, in Canada, South Asian immigration was banned in 1908 and remained strictly controlled as late as the 1970s.[7] Since the post–World War II era, South Asian diasporic peoples have comprised more recent streams of migration to both the Middle East and the Western hemisphere. The period between the 1960s and 1980s witnessed a phenomenal increase in emigration as a response to either the mid-east oil boom, or to Europe and North America's shortage of industrial, skilled, and professional labour and the subsequent lifting of its racially-based immigration policies.

Generally, the South Asian diaspora does not conjure images of ethnically or religiously allied groups fleeing political or other forms of persecution. There are striking and significant exceptions, however. A large proportion of those recruited for indentured labour during the colonial era, for instance, were Hindus hoping to flee the rigid hierarchy of the caste system. The en masse expulsion of South Asians from Uganda under the notorious edict of Idi Amin is a more recent exception.[8] When we speak of diasporic South Asians today, therefore, we are referring to a people—be they descendants of the earliest diasporic communities or part of more recent migrations—who now occupy a common position away from the Indian Subcontinent, a distance that is experienced, to differing degrees, in geographic, national, linguistic, political, socioeconomic, ethnocultural, religious, and gendered terms.

On the one hand, these differences can be traced to the Indian Subcontinent itself, a densely populated region whose cultural fabric is as ancient as it is changing, and as cohesive as it is fragmented. On the other hand, South Asian identity continues to be shaped by geopolitical and cultural contexts which stretch from East to South Africa, West to South East Asia, the Caribbean Region, North America, Europe, Australia, as well as the islands of the Indian Ocean and the Pacific Rim. South Asian peoples thus bring to the fore the complex permutations of diasporic identity in what Hall aptly refers to as a transformative process that is paradoxically grounded in history.

In *Displacement, Diaspora, and Geographies of Identity*, Smadar Lavie and Ted Swedenburg correctly describe the "already hybridized" nature of both the diasporic subject's "mother country" (i.e., his/her originary culture) and "country of settlement" (i.e., his/her diasporic location):

> "Diaspora" refers to the doubled relationship or dual loyalty that migrants, exiles, and refugees have to places—their connection to the space they currently occupy and their own continuing involvement with "back home." Diasporic populations frequently occupy no singular cultural space but are enmeshed in circuits of social, economic, and cultural ties encompassing both the mother country and the country of settlement. . . . Yet many studies of borders and diasporas tend to focus on the processual shuttling of peoples and capital between two distinct territorial entities, as if these cultures were not both already hybridized. (14, 15)

However, Lavie and Swedenburg's discussion of a "dual loyalty" disregards the multiple migrations in which diasporic peoples are often engaged. As many diasporic writers reveal (particularly those living in the Western hemisphere), diasporic experience has often resulted in subsequent migrations from the country of settlement to other destinations. Indeed, South Asian diasporic peoples might migrate from and to any number of locations worldwide; moreover, they often do so not as Sri Lankans or Bangladeshis but as Trinidadians or Tanzanians (to name only a few examples). Ironically, then, for the second- or third-generation diasporic subject, the mother country may come to signify the historic country of settlement rather than the originary culture. Thus, diasporic peoples might occupy multiple hybridized spaces in which "origins" and "home/homeland" become highly individuated and mutable concepts.

Novelist and critic Peter Nazareth, for instance, is a second-generation Ugandan who writes from his location in the United States, although his novels are set in Uganda where they flip between not only an East African and South Asian but also a specifically Goan perspective. Similarly, author Farida Karodia is a second-generation South African, for whom the process of migration signals her own personal journey from South Africa to Canada and her father's historical journey from the Indian Subcontinent to South Africa, a generation earlier. Like many diasporic writers, then, Karodia shifts between multiple points of reference; in Karodia's case, these include her Gujerati-Muslim heritage, her South African place of birth, and her immigrant status in Canada. To this end,

South Asian diasporic writers often juxtapose the mythic proportions of the ancestral journey from the Subcontinent with the actual, contemporary experience of a subsequent move away from the diasporic location to a third destination (rather than a return journey "back home").

Sociologist Mohammed A. Rauf rightly suggests that change itself, for the diasporic community, operates at the generational level as well as in terms of contact with other groups: "Cultural continuities usually become the first victims of fragmentation as a result of increasing contact with other cultural segments at the descending generational levels. . . ." (106). However, even Rauf's conclusion must be further nuanced in a globalized, technologically driven economy wherein cultural contact occurs not only locally but also transnationally. In this sense, the descendants, or more recent waves, of diasporic peoples are often less acutely disconnected from the "homeland" than their ancestors, given both the facilitation of frequent travel and the dissemination of information, news, and cultural products without the requisite "return home." Having said this, however, it is important to clarify that such channels of communication are further dependent on numerous other factors, such as urban or rural settings, financial resources, levels of education, class privileges, the preservation of the mother tongue, gender biases, etc.

Even in their more commonly positioned roles as postcolonial authors, therefore, South Asian diasporic writers problematize key postcolonial paradigms such as *hybridity*, the *subaltern*, *resistance literature*, the *national allegory*, etc.[9] As Arun Mukherjee attests in her convincing critiques of postcolonial theory's tendency to eclipse historical specificity in its totalizing view of postcolonial societies, "Too often, one finds an unproblematic conflation of 'postcolonial writers' with 'postcolonial people.' The 'postcolonial writer' supposedly speaks for all 'postcolonial people' through the 'postcolonial text'" (*Postcolonialism* 12). Indeed, South Asian diasporic writers consciously or implicitly deconstruct theoretical and cultural labels when they are used as strategies of containment, which rarely correspond to the diverse, if not often fractious, reality of human relations. For example, Peter Nazareth's fictionalized account of the former Ugandan President Idi Amin's decision to drive "South Asians" out of their "African" homeland ironizes both the postcolonial moment as one of national "unity," as well as Amin's rejection of a population whose own political and ethnic allegiances were as varied as they were internally split.

As Nazareth's omniscient narrator wryly observes of the South Asian population in East Africa:

> Even more ridiculous, Goans were at such pains to point out that they were not Indians and most of them were still angry over the Indian takeover of Goa from the Portuguese, instead of being pleased that they were freed at long last from one of the most vicious of Imperialists!
>
> On the other hand, George had to admit that Goans *were* different from Indians. (*General* 22)

Nazareth's satirical portrait of the divisive internal politics of post-independence Uganda warrants a careful consideration of the South Asian diasporic population's long-established history in the East African context. Indeed, an examination of Nazareth's *In a Brown Mantle* and *The General Is Up* as South Asian diasporic texts, rather than simply as postcolonial texts, would bring into view the author's scathing critique not only of neo-colonial structures, but also of the antagonisms between and, more importantly, among East Africa's African and South Asian communities. In this regard, a contextualized reading of Nazareth's novel disturbs the standard foci of postcolonial theory, such that his multiracial characters are not seen to be restricted to their experiences as an unproblematically aligned group of colonial subjects.

To this end, diasporic writers such as Nazareth emphasize their pre-colonial histories as insistently as they foreground the complicity of hegemonic forms of discourse across the colonial and postcolonial era. Subsequently, they also bring to view a more nuanced apprehension of minority experience and group dynamics as they are determined by class and caste hierarchies, gendered, racial and sexual discriminations, and inter-ethnic and inter-religious tensions. A comparative view of South Asian diasporic writing illustrates, therefore, that in their own investigations of difference, these texts first raise the question, in relation to *what* or to *whom*?

Thus, even the most cursory comparative glance of a few diasporic writers from radically different contexts such as Malaysia, Trinidad, Guyana, and South Africa, complicates issues of postcoloniality. For instance, Malaysian writer K.S. Maniam's majority Tamil position among the South Asian diasporic community of the Malay Peninsula is paradoxically overshadowed by his minority Hindu position in an Islamic Republic. Moreover, in choosing to write in English in post-independence Malaysia, Maniam has quite consciously situated his oeuvre against the grain of the dominant Malay culture, thereby affording himself greater international recognition as a member of an elite circle of English-language writers.[10] Guyanese writers such as Narmala Shewcharan further nuance postcolonial paradigms in ironizing the albeit modest majority status that South Asian peoples maintain in contemporary Guyana under what was, until recently, an Afro-Guyanese political stronghold.[11] In *A Butterfly in the Wind*, the Trinidadian writer Lakshmi Persaud offers a feminist revisioning of Indo-Trinidadian experience in juxtaposing Hindu and colonial patriarchal structures, while betraying her own caste and class privileges.

In her first novel, *Daughters of the Twilight*, South African writer Farida Karodia's portrait of the disenfranchisement of both African and South Asian peoples under apartheid policies such as the Group Areas Act[12] renders the postcolonial paradigm particularly inoperative. Karodia's *bildungsroman* focuses on the offspring of a Muslim–South Asian father and a "coloured" mother—that is, a family that brings together the many persecuted ethnic and racial communities of South Africa. That is to say, Karodia provides an alternative and more complex vision of South African society in giving voice to a community that is rarely discussed in the context of apartheid. Moreover, she offers a unique consideration of the political and cultural dynamic between South Asian and African peoples in their shared struggle for emancipation. But Karodia is careful not to idealize her fictitious family's interracial hybridity as the sole impetus for overturning a racially delineated system. Postcolonial critic Homi Bhabha's theorization of *hybridity* as a subversive strategy of resistance collapses in Karodia's vision of South Africa—a context in which even the hybrid or "coloured" subject is officially classified and contained in the insurance of a purist racial ideology.[13]

Karodia and other writers of the diaspora thus do not so much expose the inapplicability of current conceptual models as highlight the limitations of relying on a handful of pre-existing paradigms or, indeed, a handful of writers, to apprehend a heterogeneous and cross-continental body of work. A categorical and static approach to South Asian writing not only reigns in the ongoing creative output of the South Asian diaspora, but it also denies diasporic writers and critics a wider forum of cross-cultural engagement. The formidable reputation of the recent Nobel Prize recipient, V.S. Naipaul, offers perhaps the most recognizable case in point.

At least in terms of Indo-Caribbean literature, little to no attention has been accorded Naipaul's successors, who now comprise two subsequent generations of writers. Such glaring oversights leave considerable gaps in our appreciation of the cultural and literary developments and ideological shifts that have taken place since Naipaul's canonization as a "Caribbean" or "postcolonial" writer. Ironically, then, many non-Western critics quite consistently contest Naipaul's often racially-motivated diatribe against Caribbean, African, South Asian, and Islamic societies, while most Western critics pay homage to Naipaul on the basis of his "honest" assessment of the "Third World."[14] Despite the fact that non-Western critics often take issue with Naipaul's ideological position, I predict that such criticism will continue to carry little weight so long as the latter's work is divorced from the cultural dialogues to be found across the body of Caribbean and/or South Asian writing.[15]

Without a comparative look at South Asian diasporic writing, then, the historically specific and simultaneously intertextual landscapes of the diasporic imagination are systematically levelled or, at the very least, glossed over. This is as true of writers such as Rooplall Monar, Gopal Baratham, or Deepchand Beeharry who write from their respective locations in Guyana, Singapore, and Mauritius, as is it of writers situated in Canada. Indeed, in the Canadian context, Yasmin Ladha, Lakshmi Gill, and Shani Mootoo provide a basis for comparison which reveals the insights to be gained from a more specialized approach to an otherwise seemingly unitary group of "South Asian immigrant" writers.

Yasmin Ladha was born in Tanzania; Lakshmi Gill is a mestiza of Punjabi and Filipina origins; Shani Mootoo was born in Ireland and grew up in her parents' native Trinidad. They are each of Muslim, Sikh/Christian, and Hindu backgrounds, respectively. Ladha's "Circum the Gesture" is quite literally set "between" locations on a "flight from Delhi to Cochin" (155); Gill's "Altered Dreams" is set in "any town," New Brunswick, and Mootoo's "The Upside-Downness of the World as It Unfolds" flips between Trinidad and Vancouver. Both in their shared and divergent South Asianness, as well as in their unique styles and subject matter, writers such as Ladha, Gill, and Mootoo evoke a South Asian diasporic identity that defies any singularly identifiable characteristic.

Ladha, Gill, and Mootoo offer feminist readings of South Asian and Canadian identity from their narrators' contrasting immigrant perspectives and respective Canadian settings. In juxtaposition, their stories bring to view the diverse and relative terms upon which even their feminist positions are constructed—terms which nuance, if not challenge, their status as "immigrant" or "minority" writers or, indeed, their positions as "subaltern" women. To this end, Ladha's "Circum the Gesture" exposes the extent to which chauvinistic attitudes are re-inscribed in both secular and religious domains. Gill's "Altered Dreams" ironically reverses cultural stereotypes from the perspective of a Sikh woman who finds herself trapped in a provincial atmosphere and her professional goals compromised not by Sikh orthodoxy but by her conservative English-Canadian husband. Thus, her narrator ironically remarks, "Just as he was free to do what he wished, so she was free to do what she wished, if it didn't inconvenience him—this was called the democratic way, another virtue" (174). Shani Mootoo's "The Upside-Downness of the World as It Unfolds" deconstructs, from a lesbian perspective, a hetero-normative ethos that pervades religious, political, and cultural credos, alongside a Western feminist discourse, which falls prey to its own brand of Orientalism in the exoticization of South Asian women or the reductive perception of a shared victimhood.

In his study, "The Literature of Canadians of South Asian Origin," Suwanda Sugunasiri commendably offers the first comparative study of its kind to be funded in Canada. However, when applied to the ongoing production of South Asian diasporic writing in Canada, Sugunasiri's overview is quickly dated by its uncritical use of an essentialist cultural discourse. Thus, many of Sugunasiri's assertions are informed by an oppositional cultural aesthetic that traps the South Asian writer within a binary discourse of otherness. Sugunasiri's study also betrays a distinctly multicultural ethos in which the "ethnic writer" is examined in terms of two monolithic cultural paradigms: namely, his or her assimilation to or cultural distinction from what appears to be an unchanging, opaque, and dominant "Canadian mainstream." To this end, Sugunasiri makes a sweeping generalization about the "significant development in the area of the English-language short story . . . [given] the entry on the scene of second-generation Canadians." According to Sugunasiri, stories by first-generation writers reveal a continued attachment to and thematization of the "homeland"; in contrast, stories by second-generation writers "bear *no trace of South Asianness*. Thus we see Canadian rural life and very *ordinary Canadian mainstream* situations depicted" (21; emphasis added).

Though Sugunasiri offers a helpful preliminary overview, the rhizomatic, hybrid, and unfolding networks of cultural identity and, by extension, cultural production are rarely factored into his observations. Where, for instance, would one place a first-generation writer like Gill whose story could well be construed as "ordinary Canadian mainstream," considering the fact that it deals with a bourgeois New Brunswick household, and raises such ostensibly Canadian concerns as a woman's struggle to live up to her competing roles as a mother, wife, and professional? To carry Sugunasiri's argument to its logical conclusion is thus sadly to concede that Gill's story is somehow less Canadian in its inclusion of a Sikh character and an interracial marriage.

Sugunasiri also tends to impose a singular literary framework over writers of South Asian origin in the following assertion: "If there is a predominant feature that characterizes the South Asian Canadian short story, it is realism" ("Reality" 33). Again, in their strikingly different styles, Ladha's, Gill's, and Mootoo's stories topple such monolithic frameworks. Though Gill's "Altered Dreams" may be described as a realist narrative, the same cannot be said of Mootoo's "The Upside-Downness of the World as It Unfolds" nor of Ladha's "Circum the Gesture." In a narrative ploy that is echoed in her novel, *Cereus Blooms at Night*, Mootoo juxtaposes autobiography and fiction so as to foreground the constructability of identity and to mirror the inner workings of a selective memory. Finally, Ladha's story is the most experimental in form. In its narrative slippages between quotations, poetry, dialogue, and prose; in its iconoclastic juxtaposition of Islamic, Christian, and Hindu beliefs alongside everyday pop cultural references; in its linguistic and syntactical fragmentation and inter-lingual punning, Ladha's story constitutes a dizzying narrative gesture that quite self-consciously circumvents generic codification altogether:

> In Urdu, to conjure up mirrors is to lose one's senses. Who has gone potty, *Baba*? . . . In Arabic, she is *fitna*, one name for chaos and beauty. In Urdu, she is *rundi*, whore. She is *rundi*, widow. . . .
> But I cannot discard like male, instead I, Muslim woman, follow my own cadence. It is true, so true
>
> When Rushdie Babu comes home
> I will knead flour with flying fingers.
> ("Circum the Gesture" 158)

Ladha, Gill, and Mootoo thus challenge what Mukherjee accurately refers to as the "homogenizing tendencies of much Western scholarship which speaks of 'the third world woman' or the 'South Asian woman' as though these terms denoted actual, existing entities whose characteristics could be quantified . . ." (Introduction 10). As their stories illustrate, a reductive view of a variously positioned identity holds South Asian diasporic writers hostage to a contained univocality that stifles the dialogic relationship between each writer's "sense of unique experience and sense of collective history" (Espinet 100). Mukherjee's argument can thus be extended to include any such totalizing impulse which does not take into account the relative, transformative, and ongoing processes of identity formation and cultural production.

It seems that little has changed since Smaro Kamboureli's assertion that the "ethnic subject" has been "contaminated by the disciplinary practices of the social and cultural systems containing it" (14). To date, South Asian diasporic writers are included as part of the literary curriculum only in their representative capacity as "immigrants," "minorities," or, more generally, "postcolonial" subjects. As I have illustrated, a rigid reliance on such paradigms—even when used as a basis for comparison—precludes a more complex view of South Asian identity and experience as it is articulated both in Canada and abroad. Indeed, the continued decontextualization of ethnic writing within a handful of often ill-suited paradigms hems in the unfolding fabric of South Asian cultural and literary production. Moreover, when greater room is accorded ethnic writing, it is still hierarchically assessed against what we are to take as seemingly monolithic and impermeable Western literary traditions.

In "New Contexts of Canadian Criticism," Ajay Heble points to an alternative way of apprehending cultural diversity: "cultural listening is predicated on our ability to recognize and understand the role that multiple voices ('speaking simultaneously') have played [and continue to play] in the construction of Canada" (186). As Heble argues, the "multiple voices" of Canada produce a cultural discourse in which all members of Canadian society participate. Unfortunately, the theoretical containment of South Asian diasporic writers in such fields as "postcolonial literature" at the expense of a more cross-cultural view of Canadian and, by extension, English literature arrests the literary curriculum within a seemingly essentialist cultural and national discourse. Current conceptual models thus continue to drown out cross-cultural and transcultural channels of influence, which often reveal compelling patterns of development across the body of English literature as a whole, such as its increasingly heteroglossic texture or the growing proliferation of symbolic and mythic allusions to other, non-European cultural, religious, and philosophical traditions.

Perhaps what is called for is a two-pronged pedagogical approach that is simultaneously as specialized as it is comparative. In other words, a specialized treatment of South Asian diasporic literature is an essential step in apprehending the cultural developments, literary movements, critical dialogues, and ideological discourses in which South Asian diasporic writers are engaged. In turn, South Asian diasporic literature necessitates a comparative consideration—a cultural listening—of the multiple other cultural and national contexts which the diasporic writer's "many selves" inevitably occupy and address.

NOTES

1. Vassanji is a wonderful example of the multiply positioned diasporic writer. He was born in Kenya, grew up in Tanzania, and migrated to Canada where he launched his literary career.
2. Peepal Tree Press owner and Caribbean scholar Jeremy Poynting points to this depressing trend in terms of Caribbean literature specifically. See Poynting's article, "Anglophone Caribbean Literature: Towards the Millennium."
3. Note that James Clifford draws on Stuart Hall's theorization of diaspora in his own conclusions. My own definition of *diaspora* is greatly indebted to Hall's and Clifford's insightful discussions of cultural identity and diasporic experience.
4. Indeed, most literary scholars and critics use the term *diaspora* quite loosely as either a postmodern or postcolonial condition of migration. Even studies dedicated to diasporic writing seem to use the term quite freely, often restricting their studies to a few first-generation immigrant writers in the West or even a few writers who have never left the Indian Subcontinent, thereby entirely overlooking its sociohistorical implications. See, for instance, Crane and Mohanran, *Shifting Continents/Colliding Cultures.*
5. See Milton W. Meyer's *Asia: A Concise History.*
6. See K. Laxmi Narayan's demographic overview of the South Asian diaspora.
7. Narayan associates the change with the passage of the 1976 Immigration Act which institutionalized less racially selective admission practices.
8. On 5 November 1972, Uganda's most notorious President, Idi Amin,

called for the explusion of all South Asians from Uganda. Idi Amin's edict was an extreme manifestation of prevalent African–South Asian tensions in post-colonial East African nations.

9. See Arun Mukherjee's seminal study, *Postcolonialism: My Living*, for a comprehensive consideration of the theoretical limitations, cultural constraints, and ideological implications of the postcolonial paradigm in the North American academy.

10. See K.S. Maniam's autobiographical novel *The Return*.

11. See Narmala Shewcharan's *Tomorrow is Another Day* and Rooplall Monar's *Janjhat* for portrayals of post-independence Guyanese society.

12. The Group Areas Act was implemented by the apartheid regime in 1950. The policy designated the most uninhabitable stretches of land for occupation by people of a particular racial group, and the simultaneous seizure of businesses and properties from those classified as *coloureds* and *Indians*.

13. See Farida Karodia's *Daughters of the Twilight* and Peter Nazareth's *In a Brown Mantle*.

14. See Dolly Zulakha Hassan's study, *V.S. Naipaul and the West Indies,* for a comparative overview of Western and non-Western responses to Naipaul's oeuvre.

15. Naipaul's nephew, Neil Bissoondath, is one of the few members of a new generation of Indo-Caribbean writers to be heard in the Canadian classroom. Ironically, Bissoondath rejects being labelled as a Caribbean writer, insisting instead on his acceptance as a Canadian writer. Bissoondath's position is itself a hotly contested one among South Asian and other critics in Canada. For Bissoondath's own identity politics, see specifically *Selling Illusions*.

WORKS CITED

Aziz, Nurjehan, ed. *Her Mother's Ashes and Other Stories by South Asian Women in Canada and the United States*. Toronto: TSAR, 1994.

Bissoondath, Neil. *Selling Illusions: The Cult of Multiculturalism in Canada*. Toronto: Penguin, 1994.

Clifford, James. "Travelling Cultures." *Cultural Studies*. Ed. Lawrence Grossberg, Cary Nelson, and Paula Treichler. New York: Routledge, 1992. 96–116.

Crane Ralph J., and Radhika Mohanran, eds. *Shifting Continents/Colliding Cultures: Diaspora Writing of the Indian Subcontinent*. Atlanta: Rodopi, 2000.

Dabydeen, Cyril. "I Am Not." *Making a Difference: Canadian Multicultural Literature*. Ed. Smaro Kamboureli. Toronto: Oxford UP, 1996. 250–51.

Espinet, Ramabai. Interview. "A Sense of Constant Dialogue: Writing, Woman and Indo-Caribbean Culture." *The Other Woman: Women of Colour in*

Contemporary Canadian Literature. Ed. Makeda Silvera. Toronto: Sister Vision, 1995. 94–115.

Gill, Lakshmi. "Altered Dreams." Aziz 169–76.

Hall, Stuart. "Cultural Identity and Diaspora." *Colonial Discourse and Post-Colonial Theory: A Reader*. Ed. Patrick Williams and Laura Chrisman. New York: Columbia UP, 1994. 392–403.

Hassan, Dolly Zulakha. *V.S. Naipaul and the West Indies*. New York: Peter Lang, 1989.

Heble, Ajay. "New Contexts of Canadian Criticism: Democracy, Counterpoint, Responsibility." *New Contexts of Canadian Criticism*. Ed. Ajay Heble, Donna Palmateer Pennee, and J.R. Struthers. Peterborough, ON: Broadview, 1997. 78–97.

Kamboureli, Smaro. "Canadian Ethnic Anthologies: Representations of Ethnicity." *ARIEL* 25.4 (1994): 11–51.

Karodia, Farida. *Daughters of the Twilight*. London: Women's Press, 1986.

Ladha, Yasmin. "Circum the Gesture." Aziz 155–62.

Lavie, Smadar, and Ted Swedenburg. "Displacement, Diaspora, and Geographies of Identity." Introduction. *Displacement, Diaspora, and Geographies of Identity*. Ed. Lavie and Swedenburg. Durham: Duke UP, 1996. 1–25.

Maniam, K.S. *The Return*. 1981. London: Skoob Books, 1993.

Meyer, Milton W. *Asia: A Concise History*. Lanham, Maryland: Rowman and Littlefield, 1997.

Monar, Rooplall. *Janjhat*. Leeds: Peepal Tree, 1989.

Mootoo, Shani. "The Upside-Downness of the World as It Unfolds." *Out on Main Street*. Vancouver: Press Gang, 1993.

Mukherjee, Arun. Introduction. Aziz 1–15.

———. *Postcolonialism: My Living*. Toronto: TSAR, 1998.

Narayan, K. Laxmi. "Indian Diaspora: A Demographic Overview." Occasional Paper 3. n.d. Centre for the Study of Indian Diaspora, University of Hyderabad, Hyderabad, India. 8 Jan. 2002. <http://www.uohyd.ernet.in/sss/cinddiaspora/occ3.html>.

Nazareth, Peter. *The General Is Up*. Toronto: TSAR, 1991.

———. *In a Brown Mantle*. Nairobi: East Africa Literary Bureau, 1971.

Poynting, Jeremy. "Anglophone Caribbean Literature: Towards the Millennium." *Courier* 174 (Mar.–Apr. 1999): 70–72.

Rauf, Mohammed A. *Indian Village in Guyana*. Leiden, Netherlands: E.J. Brill, 1974.

Rushdie, Salman. *Imaginary Homelands*. London: Granta, 1991.

Sharma, P.D. "Diaspora." *They Came in Ships: An Anthology of Indo-Guyanese Prose and Verse*. Ed. Joel Benjamin et al. Leeds: Peepal Tree, 1998. 233–32.

Shewcharan, Narmala. *Tomorrow is Another Day*. Leeds: Peepal Tree, 1994.

Sowell, Thomas. *Migrations and Cultures: A World View*. New York: Harper Collins, 1996.

Sugunasiri, Suwanda. "The Literature of Canadians of South Asian Origin: An Overview." *The Search for Meaning: The Literature of Canadians of South Asian Origin*. Ed. Suwanda Sugunasiri. Ottawa: Department of the Secretary of State of Canada, 1988. 5–25.

———. "Reality and Symbolism in the Short Story." Vassanji 33–48.

Vassanji, M.G. Introduction. *A Meeting of Streams: South Asian Canadian Literature*. Ed. M.G. Vassanji. Toronto: TSAR, 1985. 1–6.

Literary History as Microhistory

HEATHER MURRAY

Now that the "linguistic turn" has been replaced by an "historical turn," it may seem unnecessary to argue for literary history as a mode of work. In recent years, English-Canadian literary criticism has been both deepened and enhanced by the wealth of writing (often by innovative junior scholars) on lesser-known authors and texts. (As a graduate student, I would have dated early Canadian literature as predating the Confederation poets; a student of today may well find Renaissance Canadian literature, or early Native discourses, a familiar terrain.) Literary work for English Canada is, by now, and by and large, historical in its orientation: in a wider time frame, and increasingly contextual. But the development has not been accompanied by a parallel dialogue on historical method. In this respect the situation of the 1990s and the new millennium differs markedly from the 1980s, when the importation of new literary theories to the Canadian critical scene occasioned energetic and extended debate over their suitability and applicability. To begin to generate a corresponding discourse on historical methods is part of my purpose here.

This essay presents a programmatic and somewhat polemical offering, which considers two related models for undertaking literary-historical work in English Canada. I am using the term *microhistory* to refer to both of these models, although this involves deploying the term in two different ways, one theoretical and technical and the other vernacular or commonsensical. The first microhistory refers to a specific historiographic practice or methodology. The second refers to restrictions of the scope or size of examination. While the methodology called microhistory is rooted in the attempt to incorporate peripheral or marginal events, figures, and communities into the historical picture (thus the prefix *micro*, which has continued to adhere), microhistory as a method need not necessarily be confined to micro phenomena (or indeed, as I hope to show, need not be restricted solely to past phenomena at all).

While microhistory as a method and microhistory as a focus have a shared origin and a continuing compatibility (in fact the two senses are often conflated), there is some profit at least initially in prying apart the two microhistories as much as possible and arguing their merits separately. Indeed, this division has a precedent in the position taken by microhistorian Giovanni Levi, who argues that "microhistory cannot be defined in relation to the micro-dimensions of its subject-matter" (94). To effect this distinction, and to avoid confusion, where necessary I will refer to Microhistory 1 (method) and Microhistory 2 (dimension). But this essay will go on to consider the special affinity of Microhistory 1 to Microhistory 2, and will suggest that both together can provide new direction for the writing of literary history in English Canada.

Since microhistory has generally not been used for purposes of literary historiography, but rather has remained within the precincts of social history, the transferability of this method needs to be considered. This essay will begin by surveying some of the pros and cons of both microhistories for historical work generally and literary-historical work in particular. In the absence of readily available models of literary microhistory, presentation of what we might call (like a 1960s hem length) a *mini-microhistory* is intended to be suggestive. The conclusion will try to draw out more explicitly some of the implications of a conjoined literary microhistory for both literary analysis and pedagogy. This method may offer ways to undertake multicultural yet national literary-historical work on premises more congenial to a postcolonial perspective, and hold pedagogic possibilities for teachers and students to think about the narratives and counter-narratives of English-Canadian literary history.

What is microhistory? (We are beginning here with a consideration of Microhistory 1, or microhistory-as-method.) This is a term not always readily familiar since microhistory has yet to develop as a separate current of historiography in North America, although its European legacy extends for a quarter of a century. Nonetheless, like Molière's prose speaker, a historian may well be a microhistorian without knowing it. Even surveys devoted to historical methods—such as Georg Iggers' *Historiography in the Twentieth Century*—define microhistory more easily by example than by its internal characteristics, referring invariably to the founding instance of Carlo Ginzburg's 1976 work *The Cheese and the Worms: The Cosmos of a Sixteenth-Century Miller*, a study of the heresy trial of Menocchio, a Friulian miller, whose strange cosmography evolved from an amalgam of eclectic reading, wayward religious contemplation, and ingrained peasant belief. (This example allows us to mark immediately two significant points: the rise of microhistory within the context of early Italian historiography, for dealing with communities within a non-national identity; and the initial interweaving of microhistory with questions of reading, writing, and textual access.) While Italy remains the centre of microhistorical studies, with other practitioners encountered principally in France and Spain, a North American readership may well be familiar with the other famous example of this mode, Natalie Zemon Davis' tour de force of 1983, *The Return of Martin Guerre*.

Surveys of historical methodology define microhistory not only by example but by negative definition, by what it is not and what it opposes. It stands, as the name would signify, against the grand *macro* methods, whether that macro is great personages and grand episodes (thus microhistory counters the exempla and *événements* school of European historiography), or the macro of overarching historical metanarratives. Microhistory aims to work in opposition to the teleological narratives of both social science (liberal-progressive) and Marxist (dialectical) historiographies, while continuing to share some of the techniques of the first and much of the politics of the latter. Initially conceived as a development in the functionalist-structuralist school of history (as epitomized by Fernand Braudel and the *Annales* school), microhistory eventually developed in opposition to it, stressing qualitative (documentary or discursive) analysis over the quantitative work of the *Annales* historians, and denying the structuralist's postulate of a networked unity of social systems. In addition, in its concern with the historical event or moment, microhistory differs markedly from the Annalistes' interest in large historical or geopolitical arcs, the *long durée*.

Let me continue this series of negative definitions by comparing microhistory to two other analytic modes with which it would seem to have strong resemblances. First, what is the difference between microhistory (often focused on the lives and times, or more properly, life in times, of an individual) and biography? The distinction, one could say, is that while microhistory does *not* see the subject as purely symptomatic (indeed, as with the Friulian miller, it may be strikingly eccentric), the goal is to understand an historically situated mentality; while biography, on the other hand, traditionally postulates the subject as more free-standing or differentiated and (in the case of literary biography) as the prime mover behind the texts he or she produces.[1]

New historicism would also seem to have significant similarities, and indeed originated as an attempt to graft onto literary studies various branches of European new historiography. As they have both developed, however, new historicism seems to have diverged from microhistory in several important respects. It retains an oddly optimistic faith in the evidentiary nature of texts, insofar as analyses tend to be "grounded" in them; and, following from this, the textual instances are read as representative. New historicism is more concerned with the dominant episteme, even if it is tracking the contradictions and complexities within it, and is as a result both more text-centric, and less eccentric, than its microhistorical cousin.

Even when the microhistorical method is described by one of its practitioners, the principles may be laid out somewhat elliptically. In his much-translated essay "Microhistory: Two or Three Things That I Know about It," Ginzburg provides a sort of microhistory of microhistory, from which methodological mimesis the following principles may be drawn:

- microhistory works on the "margin" and not in the centre
- it deals with the anomalous and not the representative
- it takes a single personage (usually), or event or circumstance (less usually), and relates this to networks of community, commodity, knowledge, and force, in ways that show both connection and exception
- it is narrative rather than reconstructive
- it stresses both ruptures and connections, narrating (in Ginzburg's words) while resisting the temptation to "fill[ ] the gaps in the

documentation to form a polished surface" ("Microhistory" 23). Or, as Davis informs her readers in the opening to *The Return of Martin Guerre*: "This book grew out of a historian's adventure with a different way of telling about the past" (vii).

That historiographers have approached microhistory by exempla, negative definition, and demonstration is not surprising. "It is no accident," states Levi in his essay "On Microhistory,"

> that the debate over microhistory has not been based on theoretical texts or manifestos. Microhistory is essentially a historiographical practice whereas its theoretical references are varied and, in a sense, eclectic. The method is in fact concerned first and foremost with the actual detailed procedures which constitute the historian's work, so microhistory cannot be defined in relation to the micro-dimensions of its subject-matter. (93)

While "experimental" and lacking a "mode of established orthodoxy," microhistory does have a set of "crucial" common elements or principles, which Levi traces to the microhistorians' effort to develop new forms of Marxist historiography. In the resulting formulation,

> all social action is seen to be the result of an individual's constant negotiation, manipulation, choices and decisions in the face of a normative reality which, though pervasive, nevertheless offers many possibilities for personal interpretations and freedoms. . . . In this type of enquiry the historian is not simply concerned with the interpretation of meanings but rather with defining the ambiguities of the symbolic world, the plurality of possible interpretations of it, and the struggle which takes place over symbolic as much as over material resources. (94–95)

This "struggle" over the symbolic, far from being the object of the historian's retrospective gaze alone, occurs in the practice of contemporary historiography itself: it is a question of developing methods of interpretation and description in keeping with the microhistorians' world-view, of "both acknowledging the limits of knowledge and reason whilst at the same time constructing a historiography capable of organizing and explaining the world of the past" (95).

While the method outlined by Ginzburg and Levi appears to involve a cautious treatment of texts, a strong evidentiary base, and a healthy dose of critical self-consciousness, microhistory has had voluble critics, whose principal objections have been summarized by Iggers:

> (1) that their methods, with their concentration on small-scale history, have reduced history to anecdotal antiquarianism; (2) that they have romanticized past cultures; (3) that because . . . they purportedly work with relatively stable cultures, they are incapable of working with the modern and contemporary worlds marked by rapid change; and (4) in this connection that they are incapable of dealing with politics. (113)

Of course, microhistory does have its own politics, and these may generate some internal contradictions, at least according to Dominick La Capra in his critique of *The Cheese and the Worms* (subtitled "The Cosmos of a Twentieth-Century Historian"). For La Capra, Ginzburg's insistence on the primacy of an oral and oppositional peasant culture to Menocchio's thought reinforces exactly the distinction between "low" and "high" cultures to which microhistorians are supposedly opposed. (And La Capra's subtitle further implies that Ginzburg may share with Menocchio an inventive, even wilful, rendition of texts in the interests of a particular world-view.) A critique may also be made of microhistory's lack of theoretical transparency: as historian Peter Burke has suggested, in common with other new histories, microhistory has failed to elaborate the premises upon which its own forms of textual interpretation take place, the methods used for reading texts and reading between the lines (9–12). This is in part what Levi alludes to when he refers to a lack of theoretical centralism, in other words, that microhistory is defined by its practices rather than its principles.

To the critiques noted by Iggers, La Capra, and Burke, one might add some other reservations: that microhistory appears to have abandoned diachronic analyses in favour of the deeply synchronic; that the history remains oddly, perhaps even contradictorily, individualizing in its focus on the particularities of discrete subjects; and that the narrativizing bent may lead the microhistorian to make connections on the basis of adjacency or speculation, as much as it permits her or him to self-critically or self-consciously foreground the *modus operandi*.

However, the advantages of the microhistoric method are apparent to anyone who has read *The Cheese and the Worms* or *The Return of Martin Guerre*. This is, as it is often termed, history with a human face: and that face is the face of the daily, the ordinary, the subaltern. Microhistory tells a story, often structured as the attempt to solve an interpretational puzzle or epistemic mystery of some kind. As fellow historians, document readers, and textual explicators, we appreciate being let in on the tradecraft, through the foregrounding of the procedures of research and interpretation. These are the charms of microhistory: there are more serious merits. Most fundamentally, this is a method suited to the writing of history on the margins, where documentation may be scant. It assumes that the lives and activities of the subaltern classes need not be told in the aggregate, but can be seen (at least some of them) in the particular; and that these features can emerge even through dominant documentation. Microhistorians see this particular focus—the individual, event, or text—as a uniquely situated nodal point of social, political, economic, and ideational forces. In this way, and perhaps most radically, microhistory undermines the model of historical "centres" and "margins" in the first place.

The potential of microhistory becomes further evident if we take the initial term, *micro*, under advisement. This prefix should not be seen as demanding a necessary limitation of analyses to individuals or to small-scale phenomena. (One could have a microhistory of an institution, or a city, or a war, for example.) Rather, the subject or event (of whatever magnitude) is seen as micro in the sense of being situated at a particular point or conjuncture, and as located within larger webs or networks. Just as microhistory need not be confined to the small-scale, nor need it deal necessarily with the marginal: figures at the (so-called) centre could be successfully treated with a microhistorical approach, which would have a sort of reverse effect of de-authorizing events seen to have been set in motion by unique individuals, and of discharging the charismatic accumulation of those personalities and their motivations. So, too, we may expand the base term *history*. Since it permits an analysis of figures and phenomena within contexts contemporary to it—and draws meaning from that analysis rather than from retrospective evaluation based on the knowledge of later results or consequences—there is no need for microhistory to be confined to the events of the past, although that has in fact been the tendency so far.

Micro, then, is a question not of size but of scale or of proportionality. And yet it appears to me that local phenomena, events, and formations are in fact the most promising foci for a new literary-historical analysis. I have arrived at this assessment primarily through my own work in the areas of literary and cultural history, although it must be admitted at the outset that this has been restricted to the nineteenth century primarily and Ontario almost solely. But from this necessarily limited perspective, I would like to turn to consideration of Microhistory 2, the question of the dimension or scope of examination.

What is the most promising focus (we might call it the centre of gravity) for renewed literary-historical work in English Canada? Would it be the author, especially if we saw the project of such microhistory as bringing to light lesser-known authors, or those from under-examined constituencies? Or should it be the reader? In the bush, on the farm, even in the new cities, we must have had our own Menocchios, idiosyncratic autodidacts in a print-hungry culture. Or should the focus be texts themselves? A microhistorical examination would place the text, as both message and artifact, in its web of historical, literary, and productive relations. There is merit to all of these: but my own sense is that the answer lies in none of the above—none of the author, reader, or text conceived in isolation—but rather the community, circle, or cultural formation. Four reasons may be offered in support of this choice.

The first reason is a simple one: other methods of organization have proven to be limited in their utility. Construction of a national literary history is rendered impossible by the simple fact that "state" and "nation" are in such a complex correspondence here. Other more general critiques may be made, which have been ably argued in the context of postcolonial studies: that "national" cultural histories are frequently the history of the urban centres and even more often of the dominant social groups; and that such macro structures seem inevitably accompanied by macro narratives of national progress and individuation. But histories organized along regional, provincial, sub-regional, and even bioregional grounds are unsatisfactory because (arguably) these do not mark corresponding cultural boundaries. At any rate, in the period with which I am most familiar—prior to 1900—the primary unit of cultural organization was the town, the small city, or the community defined on ethnic (and sometimes political or religious) principles. It may well be that the construction of a "national" literary history for pre-twentieth century Canada is an anachronism, not only because the time period is largely pre-national but, more significantly, because this does not represent the primary point of influence or identification for the figures and texts we might wish to study.

A second reason comes from a somewhat different consideration. While literary-historical work has often attempted a national narrative arc, literary-critical analysis, on the other hand, to date tends to be focused on single authors (in the form of biographical or bio-bibliographical studies) and single texts (in critical work that is largely elucidative or explicative). It is almost impossible to link this in any coherent way to a literary history constructed "nationally"; or, conversely, to use that national scale as a meaningful context for author and text studies. A more inflected sense of cultural formations is needed for work on authors and texts that is not solipsistic.

A third reason for choosing the community as a focus for examination—whether we define community as a geographic or demographic unit—is that this permits examination of literary institutions while keeping in view the participating individuals as distinctive agents. Unlike higher-level examinations, this focus allows audiences, amateurs, and intermittent cultural workers a place in the picture; unlike more specialized author or critical studies, it provides a ground for integrated studies of textual production, distribution, and reception. It permits micro examination that is not atomized.

A fourth reason for choosing this level of examination is that (as far as I can determine) it is the one most suited to the available resources. That point applies whether we are talking about communities defined as geographic areas or as elective networks. Small-town Canada is rich in print, archival, material, and oral resources dealing with cultural life past and present: diaries, letters, collections of memorabilia, association minute books, library records, newspaper accounts, local histories, personal memories, and family recollections. It must be admitted, however, that such material is sometimes hard to locate and identify, often dispersed, and usually uneven in its depth and quality. While the level of documentation may be insufficient to form a sharply focused portrait of an individual, and may be too particular or ephemeral to contribute substantially to the understanding of a national scene, it does allow exactly the sort of documentary *bricolage* suited to assembling collective or composite portraits.

When materials are varied or scattered, the historian's hand is forced: the discernment of patterns and connections, the accounting for documentary largesse and lacunae, are fundamental to the task and require inscription into it.

While it may seem that this argument has been converging toward a natural affinity or marriage between Microhistory 2 and Microhistory 1, more work needs to be done before the confetti starts to fly. The above has in some respects begged the question of how well microhistory can function in the interests of a specifically literary history; the previous points might be equally applicable to work in the areas of education history, religious history, and so on. Do we have already-available models of literary microhistoriography? I would argue not, and will take the quickest route through this issue by considering whether the work of book historian Robert Darnton is microhistorical or not. Or, more specifically, while it may be microhistorical in the sense of analyzing discrete events and practices, does it evidence microhistory-as-method?

Darnton is definitely a "new historian," often mentioned in the same context as Davis, Ginzburg, and Levi. His work has evident similarities to theirs, frequently focusing on a social curiosity or on displays of a dramatically different mentality: why would apprentices kill cats? what underlies the particular taxonomies of the Diderot encyclopedia? His work operates on the margins insofar as it traces the "street life" of texts, narratives, and—more recently—gossip. In his much-debated diagram of the production-distribution-consumption circuit, in the field-forming essay "What Is the History of Books?," he schematizes the place of economic and legal factors in the print communication circuit. But this model is somewhat at odds with the interests of microhistorians in several ways. It is intensely bibliocentric, rather than focused on human agents; and it shows a cause-and-effect wheel of ideational generation (from author to publisher/distributor to reader, with other forces relegated to an exteriorized contextual space) rather than the more complex (and multidirectional) system of determinations evidenced by a Carlo Ginzburg, for example.

In the absence of models ready to hand, I would like to offer, not an example (for this does not claim to be a fully achieved microhistorical reading) but a prospectus, which is nonetheless intended to be illustrative of how an event (and a circle of participants) *could* be approached from the point of view of a literary microhistorian. I call this episode "Murder in the

Debating Society," and it comes from work I've done elsewhere on the literary societies of mid-nineteenth-century African Canadians.[2] Researching this literary culture is challenging, given the paucity of records and the extremely complex webs of ideas, influences, mandates, and allegiances to be found in any text produced by or about the Fugitive community. It is difficult to study this particular cultural community without employing two of the primary techniques of the microhistorian: the thrifty habits of the *bricoleur*, and an attention to gaps and absences. In this instance, the metaphor of reading between the lines can be literalized: to read the cultural history of the African Canadians can sometimes involve reading, quite literally, in the "white" spaces.

I was not the first person to note this episode (it is mentioned in Rosemary Sadlier's book on Mary Ann Shadd, for example, and discussed in the more recent biography of Shadd by Jane Rhodes); but it still demanded elucidation. In Sandwich, Ontario (now Windsor), in 1853, there was a meeting of a debating society for young men of the Fugitive community, under the sponsorship of teacher and newspaperwoman Mary Ann Shadd, and the abolitionist and orator Samuel Ringgold Ward. At one meeting, a young man was murdered. What happened? And why, even more puzzlingly, did the Black community newspaper *The Voice of the Fugitive* accuse both Shadd and Ward of being "accessories to a murder"? (This charge, one should add, was never formally made.) This was the only literary society murder I had encountered in the course of my research, so my interest was doubly piqued.

Why take this episode as a focus for examination? It is to all appearances exceptional and therefore could not be presumed to be representative. We may pause here to highlight a fundamental and sometimes misunderstood aspect of the microhistorical method: its focus on the anomalous rather than the typical. It is counter-intuitive that such choices should have a scholarly validity. But one could explain the seeming contradiction in the microhistorical method in this way: what is exceptional to a modern viewer may not have been particularly so in its own day, and the seeming exceptionality may lie in a later lack of understanding of the frame within which a phenomenon (like sacrificed cats) may have been normalized. Thus what we would learn from examination of such an event would be its fittedness. On the other hand, if we are working on an incident which was considered exceptional or strange in its own day, we may very well find that the anomaly, the burst into prominence, was a sign that the episode was deeply ordinary in the sense of having been symptomatically revealing of its own time, at least to its contemporaries.

In the case of the murder in the debating society, there is little evidence of how this episode was viewed by the European-descent settlers (in part because area newspapers from the time period have not survived), but one can assume that this was judged by many to be normative rather than exceptional, taken as further evidence of the perceived lawlessness of the Fugitive community. (That this perception buttressed the mid-century backlash against the Fugitives is attested to by informants to Benjamin Drew's *The Refugee*, who complained that thefts in the district were invariably laid to their account.) In narrating and assessing this event and the response, a microhistorian would begin by wanting to know more about the incident and its consequences, including the primary personages involved: the society's sexton or order keeper, and the interloping heckler who felled him with a blow. How was the trial conducted, and what was the fate of the murderer? (Court records, as any reader of Davis, Ginzburg, or Levi will know, are an important source for microhistorians, not only for the density of the transcriptions but also because they are rare records of voices.) Did the society continue to meet, and what other responses were evidenced by the local communities, both Fugitive and European-descent? What forms of defence were required on the part of the Black inhabitants of Sandwich; and were the opponents of assisted settlement, or the groups advocating resettlement of this "surplus" population to the Caribbean, able to add this event to their arsenal? How can this episode, its consequences, and its coverage, open for us the complex politics of Black settlement in the Western District and indeed in Canada West more generally?

As a literary microhistorian, these considerations would not be irrelevant. But one would wish to situate this episode more specifically in the context of literary societies; in the practice and teaching of public rhetoric; in the history of newspaper publication in the Canadas; and in African-Canadian literary and cultural history: in other words, as a particular intersection of literary, rhetorical, educational, political, and racialized forces and factors. The incident was immediately framed in the African-Canadian press, not as exceptional but as expected, indeed predictable: what was being mobilized was a long-running set of cautions about the dangers of unfettered public discourse and its ability to inflame the passions beyond control. These arguments, I had found, surfaced whenever debating societies operated in contentious times (in Upper Canada prior to the Rebellion of 1837 for example), and easily could be dusted off 15 years later. In the hastily launched *Provincial Freeman*, rushed prematurely into print in order to mount the defence of both Shadd and Ringgold Ward (indeed, it is possible that one of the debating society's mandates was to generate support for this alternative to *The Voice of the Fugitive*), Shadd would draw on equally time-tested counter-propositions, about the role of such organizations in training and tempering public discourse. Evidenced here, as well, may be differing attitudes within the African-Canadian community as to what model of literary society should best be implemented: whether a society focused on self and mutual intellectual improvement, or whether (taking the powerful model of the literary-abolitionist societies established in the freed Black community of Philadelphia) such literary and rhetorical study should inevitably be accompanied by forms of community uplift and material assistance. But which way did the suspicion work: was the debating society suspect because it was devoted to words alone? or because it was operating in tandem with a political agenda which the (more separatist) editors viewed as assimilationist?

We can go some way to understanding the discrepancies between *The Voice of the Fugitive* editors, Henry Bibb and Mary Bibb, on the one hand, and Shadd and Ringgold Ward, on the other, from following out other chains of available information. Henry Bibb had escaped from slavery while Mary Bibb was modestly schooled; Shadd was well educated and Ringgold Ward attended Knox College at Toronto after fleeing the United States. To what degree did their different backgrounds account for their respective attitudes to rhetorical training? How much is this attitude in turn embedded in contemporary debates within the Black community as to whether their own schools should be constructed along American or British curricular lines? (That Mary Bibb and Mary Ann Shadd had been competing for the franchise of the same community school would not be extraneous here.)[3] We can follow, in addition, some of the more specifically rhetorical implications, most profitably (I would imagine) by examining the rhetorical theories and practices of Ringgold Ward (considered by some, in his day, an orator second only to the great Frederick Douglass) but also the rhetorical modes of Shadd, Mary Bibb, and Henry Bibb, in their newspaper and monographic publications. Lest we regress too far along this battle of words, about a battle of words, we may bring ourselves back to the realities of newspaper publishing in the perilous economic conditions of the 1850s: the attack on Shadd and Ringgold Ward may have been, as much as anything, a pre-emptive strike in a subscription war. Considering this can lead us into questions of serial and journalistic publication, distribution, and readership in the mid-nineteenth century.

While this is more a prospectus than an example, it is intended to illustrate how the two forms of microhistory are operating together: a small-scale phenomenon viewed as a node for the intersection of discourses, of institutions, and of economic, social, and cultural relations, many of which extended beyond the borders of Canada West. From this may be drawn six points in favour of a conjoined microhistorical approach in Canadian literary historiography.

First—and alluding to a distinction that has become increasingly common in recent years—a microhistorical approach allows us to look at literature *in* Canada rather than Canadian literature. (This distinction is already employed in the title of the History of the Book in Canada project, for example.) We need to understand how a variety of oral and written forms, from many nations and cultures, have been imported, circulated, understood, and used in Canadian contexts.

Second, this approach allows us to deal with different ethnic, racial, and elective communities both discretely and in their connections to other Canadian social units and to their home or country-of-origin communities: in other words, to develop a multicultural national literary history in an international frame.

Third, and this is an important contribution, it allows us to escape from the problem of "representation" and "representativeness," which seems invariably to vex examinations of (so-called) minority communities. The subject of microhistorical examination, whether an individual, a cultural formation, or a community, is not placed in a synecdochic or "standing for" figural relationship, but rather in a network of material and ideational conditions.

A fourth point is that microhistory allows the development of literary histories that are less bibliocentric than those developed under other models, and it considers the placement of print publication in relation to scribal and oral formulations.

Fifth, and perhaps most significantly, while providing the context for authors and texts known to us today, this approach will also "decentre" the literary system by bringing to light amateurs and autodidacts, revealing the reliance of seemingly more major authors on these local and social contacts.

To these theoretical benefits may be added a sixth, practical, consideration: the narrative (rather than reconstructive) tendency of the microhistorical method not only encourages self-reflexive work but allows for historical *bricolage* in areas where records are scattered or scanty. The working outwards from the texts to greater economic, political, and ideational systems means that the researcher is not confined solely by the state of the available archive.

I conclude with two questions about undertaking literary-historical work in this way. Most of us would not be willing to give over entirely the idea of history constructed on a diachronic model, no matter how suspicious we may be of triumphalist national sagas or crude models of causation and effect. But the microhistorical method appears to have a limited capacity for diachronic analysis. At the completion of a series of such examinations, would we really have a history of literature in Canada, or the materials on which a history could be based? The answer to that question would depend in part, I imagine, on our evolving sense of what we expect from literary histories in the first place. We may never again have over-arching national narratives within which all figures and texts are consonant—and we may never wish to. The question of how to interrelate microhistorical examinations still remains: historians Florike Egmond and Peter Mason use a morphological metaphor, suggesting that what is to be detected are points of similarity or "family resemblances" (in Wittgenstein's term) between features revealed by microhistorical examinations for different points in time and varying cultures. While this—as illustrated by Egmond and Mason's own analyses—does not yield a diachronic progression, it does allow microhistory to take on some of the mandates of traditional historiography and particularly the delineation of processes and patterns. The extension of microhistory into morphology is an attempt to answer the question of whether microhistorical research projects need always be discrete rather than comparative, and whether "there is any way to connect microhistory and the *long durée*" (3). Another avenue would be to pursue the assertion that microhistory need not be *micro* in scope in its most radical dimension: how *macro* in scale can the microhistorical method be?

There is a second point regarding the overall applicability of this method for English-Canadian literary history. The pairing of the microhistorical method with the micro level of the rural region, town, or community may be better suited to the period prior to the First World War, and less appropriate to the literary culture of the mid- or late-twentieth century. Or perhaps not, for where the cultural significance of the geographic community (and especially the small town) may have declined in the twentieth and twenty-first centuries, urban subcultures or the elective communities based on nation, race, gender, politics, or aesthetics may have assumed a proportionately greater importance. As mentioned before, one of the strengths of the microhistorical method is that it need not be confined to historical phenomena strictly speaking. It is best left to people who work more intensely in the writing cultures of modern and contemporary Canada to determine how useful this method might be for their purposes.

We may conclude on a somewhat speculative note, with some consideration of the pedagogic application of microhistory. In my own teaching I have come to focus more and more on literary works taught in relationship to their social and political formations (the literature of nineteenth-century African Canadians, for example, as in the example given above, or the rhetoric of reform writers in the Rebellion years). Students seem to enjoy the opportunity to work on literary cultures on a small scale, especially when this involves learning about an author from their home town, their neighbourhood, or their cultural background. Such geographic or community connections help to give immediacy to writing that is otherwise temporally or experientially very remote to these students. It appears that many other Canadian literature teachers are also deploying the more restricted focus of Microhistory 2 in the classroom or lecture hall. But Microhistory 1, the microhistorical method, also has pedagogic potential, insofar as it will move students away from textual explications to cultural implications, and will encourage them to reflect on the procedures and paradigms through which the story of Canadian literature has normally been told.

Indeed, while microhistory offers well-elaborated models for specific and sophisticated literary-historical studies, its main benefit may lie, paradoxically, in what it cannot provide. It asks—even as it does not answer—for a fundamental redefinition of the possibilities and purposes, methods and frameworks, of literary macro history.

ACKNOWLEDGEMENTS

I would like to acknowledge the helpful suggestions of historian Thomas McIntire, as well as beneficial comments and criticisms from participants at the "Postcolonialism and Pedagogy" symposium, especially Terry Goldie, Stephen Slemon, and Michael Vance.

NOTES

1. One extended attempt to compare biography to microhistory is made by United States historian Jill Lepore. However, I believe that Lepore misreads the intended figurative relationship of the microhistorical subject when she compares the biographer's "belief in the singularity and significance of an individual's life" to the microhistorian's interest in that life's "exemplariness, in how the individual's life serves as an allegory for broader issues effecting the culture as a whole" (133). The subjects examined by Davis or Ginzburg, for example, could not be said to be standing in a synecdochic or even allegorical relationship to their culture, although their lives are deeply revelatory of it.
2. For a more extensive account of the episode, see Murray 64–70.
3. These curricular debates have been traced by Afua Cooper, particularly in "Black Teachers in Canada West, 1850–1870: A History."

WORKS CITED

Burke, Peter. "Overture: The New History, Its Past, and Its Future." *New Perspectives on Historical Writing*. Ed. Peter Burke. University Park, PA: Pennsylvania State UP, 1991. 1–23.

Cooper, Afua. "Black Teachers in Canada West, 1850–1870: A History." PhD diss. U of Toronto, 1991.

Darnton, Robert. "What Is the History of Books?" *Daedalus* 111. 3 (1982): 65–83. Rpt. in *Reading in America: Literature and Social History*. Ed. Cathy N. Davidson. Baltimore: Johns Hopkins UP, 1989. 27–52.

Davis, Natalie Z. *The Return of Martin Guerre*. Cambridge: Harvard UP, 1983.

Drew, Benjamin. *The Refugee; or, The Narratives of Fugitive Slaves in Canada. Related by Themselves*. Boston: J.P. Jewett, 1856.

Egmond, Florike, and Peter Mason. *The Mammoth and the Mouse: Microhistory and Morphology*. Baltimore: Johns Hopkins UP, 1997.

Ginzburg, Carlo. *The Cheese and the Worms: The Cosmos of a Sixteenth-Century Miller*. Baltimore: Johns Hopkins UP, 1978.

———. "Microhistory: Two or Three Things That I Know about It." *Critical Inquiry* 20.1 (1993): 10–35.

Iggers, Georg G. *Historiography in the Twentieth Century: From Scientific Objectivity to the Postmodern Challenge*. Hanover: Wesleyan UP, 1997.

La Capra, Dominick. "The Cheese and the Worms: The Cosmos of a Twentieth-Century Historian." *History & Criticism*. Ithaca: Cornell UP, 1992. 45–69.

Lepore, Jill. "Historians Who Love Too Much: Reflections on Microhistory and Biography." *Journal of American History* 88.1 (2001): 129–44.

Levi, Giovanni. "On Microhistory." *New Perspectives on Historical Writing*. Ed. Peter Burke. University Park, PA: Pennsylvania State UP, 1991. 93–113.

Murray, Heather. *Come, Bright Improvement!: The Literary Societies of Nineteenth-Century Ontario*. Toronto: U of Toronto P, 2002.

Rhodes, Jane. *Mary Ann Shadd Cary: The Black Press and Protest in the Nineteenth Century*. Bloomington: Indiana UP, 1998.

Sadlier, Rosemary. *Mary Ann Shadd: Publisher, Editor, Teacher, Lawyer, Suffragette*. Toronto: Umbrella P, 1995.

Postcolonialism Meets Book History: Pauline Johnson and Imperial London

CAROLE GERSON

PAULINE JOHNSON OFFERS a rich opportunity to engage students with various intersecting features of turn-of-the-century society and culture in the larger British Empire. As a mixed-race woman, she personally embodied the sexual interaction between English conquerors and Aboriginal subjects that has recently received extensive attention from postcolonial critics. As an unmarried woman with a successful career, this implicit New Woman challenged patriarchal values. As a public performer and a published author, she wrote poetry for both the stage and the page. Simultaneously a Canadian nationalist and a staunch imperialist, she demonstrates the pull of the imperial centre even to those who celebrated the independent identity of a former settler colony. This tapestry of complex issues provides the context of Johnson's two major trips to London, in 1894 and 1906, which proved to be significant moments in her career. Moreover, an examination of her reception and publication in London offers an occasion to demonstrate the complementarity of book history and postcolonialism as critical methodologies, and to enrich classroom discussion with hands-on examples of textual representation in periodicals and books.

In a recent speech, historian Jonathan Rose nicely accounted for the current expansion of book history from the realm of bibliographers to the larger fields of literary, historical, and cultural studies, as well as the attraction of print culture as both a method and subject of pedagogy:

> Once upon a time, professors studied literary works. Then, for the past 25 years or so, they studied texts. Now, we should redirect our attention to books. The problem with focusing on texts is that no one can read a text—not until it is incarnated in the material form of a book. It is perfectly legitimate to ask how literature has shaped history and made revolutions, how it has socially constructed race, class, and gender [and so on]. But we cannot begin to answer any of these questions until we know how books (not texts) have been created and reproduced, how books have been disseminated and read, how books have been preserved and destroyed.

Bringing various early editions of books into the classroom raises students' awareness of the role of textual objects in shaping the reception of authors, and makes book history an integral component of their understanding of the relations between print and power, an idea they often first encounter in Benedict Anderson's discussion of the historical significance of print in creating national consciousness, in the second and third chapters of *Imagined Communities.* While not all instructors can show actual copies of rare Canadiana, it is now possible to access electronically the texts that have been digitized at Early Canadiana Online (www.canadiana.org). This collection, available without charge to anyone sitting at a sufficiently powerful terminal, includes one of the major texts under discussion in this essay—Johnson's first book, *The White Wampum* (1895)—as well as W.D. Lighthall's 1889 anthology, *Songs of the Great Dominion.* Johnson's second book, *Canadian Born,* is available on fiche as CIHM no. 73199. Also pertinent for students is the Pauline Johnson Web site at McMaster University, holder of the largest collection of Johnson papers, at www.humanities.mcmaster.ca/~pjohnson/home.html. Constructed in 1996, its major weakness is the absence of subsequent publications in its bibliography.

In his contribution to a recent collection of articles entitled *Women and British Aestheticism,* Edward Marx calls attention to two overlooked women from India who brought a touch of the exotic to late nineteenth-century English literary decadence. Young Sarojini Naidu, who arrived in London in 1895, and Adela Nicolson, who sent her work to London from remote military stations in central India, were welcomed for the oriental flavour of their sensuous, erotic verse. Both made strong impressions on leading literary figures of the day, including Arthur Symons and Thomas Hardy. However, they were not the first representatives of a remote, alluring region of the Empire to entice imperial London with nuances of cultural alterity. In the spring of 1894, Londoners were treated to the spectacle of a youngish woman from a different corner of the realm who not only wrote intriguing verse, but also recited it on stage, and in costume. She was Emily Pauline Johnson, of mixed Mohawk and English lineage, who sailed from Canada to London in order to enhance her growing reputation as a performer, and to issue her first book of poetry. While the 1895 publication of *The White Wampum* by John Lane at the Bodley Head situates Johnson in the field of London's aesthetes and decadents, her reputation in Canada long outlasted her profile in Britain.

Images and text on McMaster University's Johnson Web site can be used to enhance the story of Johnson's biographical connection with England, which begins with her 1861 birth into a family that identified with international Euro-American culture. Her father, George Henry Martin Johnson, was a mostly Mohawk hereditary chief and professional interpreter whose fascination with Napoleon inspired him to name his youngest child Pauline, after the sister of his hero. Her mother, Emily Susanna Howells, born in Bristol, was a cousin of the eminent American author, William Dean Howells. In the family home of Chiefswood, an elegant Georgian mansion on the Six Nations reserve at Ohsweken, Ontario, that has recently been restored as a national historic site, the four Johnson children were raised on English classic authors along with some Mohawk traditions. Imperial affection always lay close to their hearts: a treasured family memory was the 1869 induction of the young Prince Arthur, Duke of Connaught, as a "Chief of the Six Nations Indians" (*Legends* 170). Pauline's grandfather, Chief John Smoke Johnson, presided over the ceremony, whose rituals required the third and favourite son of Queen Victoria to stand on the chief's scarlet blanket "consisting of the identical broadcloth from which the British army tunics [were] made" (*Legends* 170–72). This blanket later became part of Pauline's costume, gracefully cloaking her shoulder and trailing onto the floor, according to her publicity photographs. (Students in British Columbia's Lower Mainland can see the blanket and her buckskin dress at the Vancouver Museum.) The Duke of Connaught himself was to serve as Governor General of Canada from 1911 to 1916, during which time he visited Johnson, now dying in

Vancouver, where he once again occupied the famous red blanket, this time draped over a hospital chair.

Johnson's literary reception in England predated her crossing of the Atlantic, when the influential English critic, Theodore Watts-Dunton, reviewed W.D. Lighthall's 1889 anthology, *Songs of the Great Dominion*, in *The Athenaeum,* one of Britain's most important cultural periodicals. Johnson contributed just two poems to Lighthall's nationalist project, but Watts-Dunton, reading the biographical notes as well as the verse, picked her out as "the most interesting English poetess now living" because she struck "a new note—the note of the Red Man's Canada" (412). Students looking at Lighthall's volume—in codex or electronic format—can see why Johnson's biography, with its stress on the abilities and loyalties of the Mohawks, captured the attention of a Londoner like Watts-Dunton. In the last years of the nineteenth century, the imperial centre was known for its qualified hospitality to interesting aboriginals and half-castes from its distant margins.[1] Those of elevated status in their homelands were especially appealing. For example, one analogue to Pauline Johnson was Princess Victoria Kaiulani, heir through her mother to the throne of Hawaii, despite having a Scottish father. Educated in England in the early 1890s, she was reputedly a protégé of Queen Victoria.[2]

Various factors seem to underlie Johnson's unusual decision to have her first book published in London. In the 1880s and 1890s, literary publication in Canada was notoriously precarious. Subscription publishing and authors' subsidies were the norm, as the buying public was too thinly distributed and unstable for most publishers to take risks with poetry or fiction. Most threatening to Canadian presses was the burgeoning American publishing industry, whose products inundated Canadian homes, schools, shops, and libraries. Hence the majority of ambitious literary Canadians flocked southward; as Sara Jeannette Duncan shrewdly commented in 1887, "The market for Canadian literary wares of all sorts is self-evidently New York" (518). However, none of the Canadian writers who published in Boston and New York were First Nations, and, as some of the clippings in Johnson's papers attest, Americans sometimes received her ungraciously. For example, in 1897 a journalist for the *Chicago Tribune* opined that "she does pretty much everything that a real Indian would not be expected to do, and leaves undone everything that one would expect from a child of the Iroquois" ("Poetess"). The racism of the day, along with long-standing imperial connections, were among the factors that led Johnson to John Lane (although precisely who facilitated this connection remains a mystery).[3]

Nearly all the poems that Johnson brought to London in 1894 had previously appeared in newspapers or magazines, mostly in Canada, with a few in the United States. Her writing career had commenced in earnest after her father's 1884 death had left his wife and daughters in straitened circumstances. Pauline wrote prose as well as poetry, and became well known for her sketches of recreation activities, especially canoeing, which was her own particular skill. In January 1892 she combined her talents for writing and performance in stage appearances that led to the *Magnet Magazine's* later pronouncement that she was "the most unique fixture in the literary world of today." That autumn, she enhanced the Indian content of her program by creating a costume that was a collage of various aspects of Native culture, inspired by an image of Longfellow's Minnehaha (according to her sister Evelyn Johnson's memoir in the Archives of Ontario) rather than a representation of any particular tribe. Johnson's usual practice of reciting her "Indian" poems in costume for the first half of the evening, and then reappearing in evening dress for the remainder of the program, gave audiences the thrill of a performance of savagery, which was subsequently contained within a model of decorum. Once on-stage appearances became Johnson's major medium, the dramatic monologue became her most effective genre. (Students can best get a sense of the orality of her verse by reading her monologues out loud.) When she arrived in London with elite letters of introduction, Johnson's reputation was well established and she was enthusiastically received as both a novel performer and a distinguished foreigner.

In the competitive arena of late nineteenth-century English publishing, John Lane created his niche by bringing out *The Yellow Book* and the works of the English *fin de siècle* avant-garde. Johnson fit his list quite nicely: she had penned a number of erotic love poems from a female perspective which qualify her as Canada's own "daughter of decadence," in line with Elaine Showalter's analysis of the New Woman counterparts of Beardsley and Wilde (Strong-Boag and Gerson 144–45). The on-line version of *The White Wampum* enables students to see that Lane's 1895 Catalogue, titled "List of Books in Belles Lettres," is bound in with Johnson's text. Here, by virtue of its alphabetical arrangement, Johnson's book is listed on the same page as Lane's sexually adventurous Keynote series, "each volume with specially designed title-page by Aubrey Beardsley" (Lane 9).

However, Lane and his designers constructed Johnson quite differently, foregoing the erotic to focus instead on the exotic. In so doing, they took their direction from Johnson's reception in the British press. Articles about her tended to open with sensational statements such as "To think of a red Indian is to shudder" ("Miss E. Pauline Johnson") and "Do not be alarmed, gentle reader" (P.A.H.). These attention-grabbing lines were quickly modified with adjectives like "cultured" and "charming" as their authors expanded upon both words in the term "noble savage." While commending Johnson's poetic gifts, reporters also noted how she had decorated her London studio at 25 Portland Road with "reminders of her Indian home and associations":

> On the mantelpiece rested the most hideous of masks, the bearded goggle-eyed mask of the mystical Medicine Man; on a screen were hung wampums which, it may be, have checked many a butchery in the past; while a fringed tunic of buckskin, ermine tails, and bracelets and necklaces of bear claws and panther teeth, all told of one who was proud of her Indian lineage and associations. (P.A.H.)

In Canada, Johnson did not travel with these artifacts. Their display in London was a dramatic ploy that generated substantial interest in her as a person, and in her cause of justice for Canada's First Nations. However, the effects of "playing Indian" (to cite Philip Deloria's title) to receptive English spectators would reach farther than she may have predicted in June of 1894. The arrangement and design of her first book, with its highlighted Native imagery, suggest that this little volume bears significant responsibility for the subsequent construction of the poet by her audiences and indeed inflected Johnson's self-construction as a public figure. When *The White Wampum* appeared, the distinguished American anthropologist Horatio Hale, himself a good friend of the Johnson family, shrewdly observed that "The first inclination of the reader will be to look in her poems for some distinctive Indian traits, and to be disappointed if these are not strikingly apparent. Her compositions will be judged as those of a 'wild Indian girl,' and not those of a well-bred and accomplished young Canadian lady with a dash of Indian blood, such as she really is" (Hale 4).

The White Wampum provides a valuable opportunity to demonstrate to students how the selection and arrangement of a volume of poems shapes their reading of the poet. Of the approximately 100 poems that Johnson had written before the end of 1894 and that were therefore available for inclusion in *The White Wampum*, only a dozen directly refer to First Nations topics. Eight of these are among the 36 selected for the book. More importantly, seven "Indian" poems are placed at the beginning of *The White Wampum*, thus casting a Native aura over the subsequent verses. The first poem, "Ojistoh," had not appeared in print before. While it proclaims female agency in a thrilling performance piece, it can also be read as a heightened account of pre-contact tribal warfare, much like the second poem, "As Red Men Die."

This arrangement of Johnson's verse to accentuate her few poems about primal Native conflict is complemented by the material book, whose design can be effectively deconstructed in the classroom. This volume marks her first significant use of the name "Tekahionwake," the only word to appear on the front cover. Here, a sense of the primitive is visually enhanced by both colour and image: the dark red-brown cloth (the colour of dried blood[4]) is decorated with a black linear design dominated by a tomahawk draped with a wampum belt, and enclosed in a broad border whose oblique geometric lines and angles suggest traditional Iroquois art (see Figure 1). In contrast, the spine shows the title "The White Wampum" stamped in gold, above the name E. Pauline Johnson.

While the exterior of the book thus separates Johnson's two identities, the title page unites them, surrounded with an elegant art nouveau frame illustration, as artificial as Johnson's buckskin costume. Teepees of Plains Indians are improbably pitched in a dense coniferous forest, against a background of lofty western mountains, behind which extend the rays of the setting sun (see Figure 2). Both designed by artist E.H. New, the illustrations on the cover and the title page are complementary, a significant feature of Bodley Head publications. While no details have survived concerning Lane's co-publishing arrangements with Copp Clark in Toronto and the literary house of Lamson, Wolffe in Boston, we can infer that the small crossed tomahawks placed above the names of the three firms on the title page—reiterating the large single tomahawk on the cover—were

FIGURE 1. Cover of *The White Wampum* (1895)

FIGURE 2. Title Page of *The White Wampum* (1895)

chosen as a potent image that promised readers on both sides of the Atlantic the thrill of encountering savagery within the comfort of a familiar aesthetic format. In this sense, the material book reproduces the impact of Johnson's stage appearances, with her disarming costume change from buckskin to evening gown, and loose hair to dressed hair.

This little book, which transformed Pauline Johnson from a woman writer into a First Nations writer, had three significant effects on her subsequent career. The most obvious result was the consistent addition of "Tekahionwake" to her signature, a name that had belonged to her grandfather. All available evidence indicates that she did not possess a Mohawk name (nor, apparently, any Native garments before the creation of her costume). After *The White Wampum*, Tekahionwake became a common addition to "E. Pauline Johnson," especially in foreign periodicals, and sometimes even a substitute. At home in the Vancouver *Province Magazine* she was usually Pauline Johnson, with or without the "E." But during her 1906 visit to London, she was further exoticized as "Tekahionwake, the Iroquois Poetess," the signature given to her articles in the London *Daily Express*.

The second effect of *The White Wampum*, as Hale had predicted, was that this book initiated a pattern of overdetermination that affected reading of her poetry for more than a century. Although the erotic verse that preceded *The White Wampum* identifies Johnson as Canada's own "daughter of decadence" and her nature poetry aligns her with the major male Canadian poets of her generation, her identity as Iroquois excluded her from these other categories, and thus from the mainstream of Canadian literary history as it was constructed in the middle of the twentieth century. One way to make this point in the classroom is to show students some of her non-Indian poems without identifying her as the author. Today, Johnson has been restored to the canon of Canada's national authors; in the canon of New Woman writers she is visible in Canada, but not yet known abroad.

The third outcome was the most profound. By constructing Johnson as distinctively Native, *The White Wampum* enabled her increasing politicization and fostered her image as an advocate of Native rights. This development is signalled by her revision of the ending of "A Cry of an Indian Wife" specifically for this volume. First published in 1885 during the course of the Northwest Rebellion, the poem originally concluded with lines that accept the outcome of history: "O! heart o'erfraught—O! nation lying low—/ God, and fair Canada have willed it so" (Gerson and Strong-Boag 292). We don't know how Johnson enacted this ending on the stage, but on the page, the word "fair," which carries at least three meanings ("just," "light-skinned," "favourable"), invites an ironic reading that could be missed by the casual reader. For her book, Johnson altered this connotative ending to denote a more political position by inserting three penultimate lines that assert Native rights by reiterating original ownership of the land by "our nation." The last line issues a challenge to "the white man's God" that locates the speaker outside European Christianity. Note the fabulous control of iambic metre and its variations to accentuate key words:

> Go forth, nor bend to greed of white man's hands,
> By right, by birth we Indians own these lands,
> Though starved, crushed, plundered, lies our nation low . . .
> Perhaps the white man's God has willed it so. (Gerson and Strong-Boag 14–15)

It is always illuminating to show students how a writer revised a text, but because Johnson's life on the road was not conducive to saving papers, there are few similar examples of her process of composition.

One focus of print culture is to investigate how the design of a book can be regarded as a form of instruction to its readers; in Megan Benton's concise formulation, "We cannot read a text without also, simultaneously and inevitably, reading its form" (5). Because Johnson subscribed to an English clipping service, her papers contain ample evidence of the extent to which British reviewers perceived her poetry as the work of an exotic "red Indian from Canada" ("Poet") whose verse was the swan song of an "ancient dying race" (unidentified clipping, 5 July 1895). Taking their cue from the book's illustrations and arrangement, reviewers who read Johnson's words through their visual presentation stated that "the subjects are mostly Indian" (Review, *The Sketch*). Unlike Canadian reviewers, who were already quite familiar with Johnson and her work, British reviewers strove to situate her within their previous literary acquaintance with Native North America by invoking such American writers as James Fenimore Cooper, Longfellow, and Whittier.

While all of Johnson's British reviews comment on her distinctive identity, many also contain a curious thread of resistance. Evincing discomfort with the "dash" and "melodrama and fustian" of Johnson's Native poems, they prefer her lyrics that "sing of those themes common to the world at large" (*Star*). In the words of one commentator, "When she is restful she charms" (unidentified clipping, 27 July 1895). The opinion that "her talent is better suited to reflective poetry" (Review, *The Academy*) or to "Nature poetry" (Review, *The Sketch*) seems to derive from a definition of poetry that excludes polemics. The review in *Black and White* best elucidated the situation. On the one hand, this journal found Johnson intriguing for voicing "the wrongs of the Indian" and giving "expression to the mind and the moods of a strange, interesting race, of which we have heard nothing hitherto save what was reported by observers from the outside." On the other hand, it describes her dramatic monologues like "The Cattle Thief" as "hardly poetry at all" ("Poet"). Although British reporters were interested in quoting at length her analysis of injustice to the Iroquois ("Fate of the Red Man"), British reviewers of her book were generally alienated by the published texts of the poems that excited her stage audiences. Within the current Canadian classroom, Johnson offers an opportunity for students to investigate definitions of poetry, as well as to consider the role of reviews in constructing a writer's immediate reception and long-term reputation.

The complex state of affairs surrounding the British publication and reception of Johnson's first book may help to explain her subsequent disconnection from London. After she returned to Canada, where her book was universally acclaimed, she placed a few poems and articles in London periodicals such as *Black and White* and the *Ludgate Magazine*, but her primary foreign market was to be American magazines. Yet her ideological allegiance to the Empire remained unshaken. In an era when Canadian authors like Charles G.D. Roberts found themselves "bidden to Manhattan Island" because "Your poet's eyes must recognize / The side on which your bread is buttered" (196–97), Johnson repudiated American values. Her title poem, "Canadian Born," written in 1897, not only celebrates the superiority of those "born in Canada beneath the British flag," but also proclaims "The Yankee to the south of us must south of us remain" (Gerson and Strong-Boag 125–26). A decade later, her acrostic

"Canada" celebrates the ship of state flying "her Empire's pennant" while avoiding the southern "rival's stealth" (Gerson and Strong-Boag 154).

Johnson's second book, *Canadian Born*, published in Toronto in 1903, seems to have gone unnoticed in the British press, perhaps because of its title. It is interesting to speculate whether its design was intended to reclaim her for Canada. In contrast to the dramatic artwork of *The White Wampum*, the visual appearance of *Canadian Born* seems decidedly demure. Issued by Morang without international co-publishers, *Canadian Born* was available in two different covers—pale blue or white—the latter probably higher priced. The front cover bears the title and the author's full name—E. Pauline Johnson (Tekahionwake)—stamped in graceful gold letters, discretely enhanced with one small maple leaf. Unlike the dark colours and strong images of *The White Wampum*, the delicate colours and lettering of *Canadian Born* convey restraint, and perhaps femininity. Inside, the undecorated title page in itself contains no overt instructions to the reader. However, it is accompanied by a frontispiece photograph of the author dramatically posed in her Native costume, the first of many such photos to grace subsequent editions of her work (see Figure 3). Like E.H. New's design of *The White Wampum*, these photographs shaped the reception of Johnson's poetry and prose by establishing the lens of race and gender through which all her work would be read. *The White Wampum* and *Canadian Born* were never reprinted after these original editions because their contents were later incorporated into *Flint and Feather* (1912).

It may have been a desire to pursue British publication that inspired Johnson to return to London for an extended visit in 1906. In typical fashion, she received newspaper publicity titled "From Wigwam to Concert Platform. Red Indian Chief's Daughter to Appear in London. Gruesome Ornaments." Her recital in Steinway Hall was attended by Lord Strathcona, the Canadian High Commissioner, as well as the knighted Canadian author Sir Gilbert Parker, and her old admirer, Theodore Watts-Dunton. The most important literary outcome of this visit was her publication of four articles in the London *Daily Express*, under the byline of "Tekahionwake, The Iroquois Poetess." The first in this series, "A Pagan in St. Paul's Cathedral," which she later described as her favourite piece of writing, became one of her best-known prose works. In this bravura performance she assumes the persona of an innocent moccasin-shod native

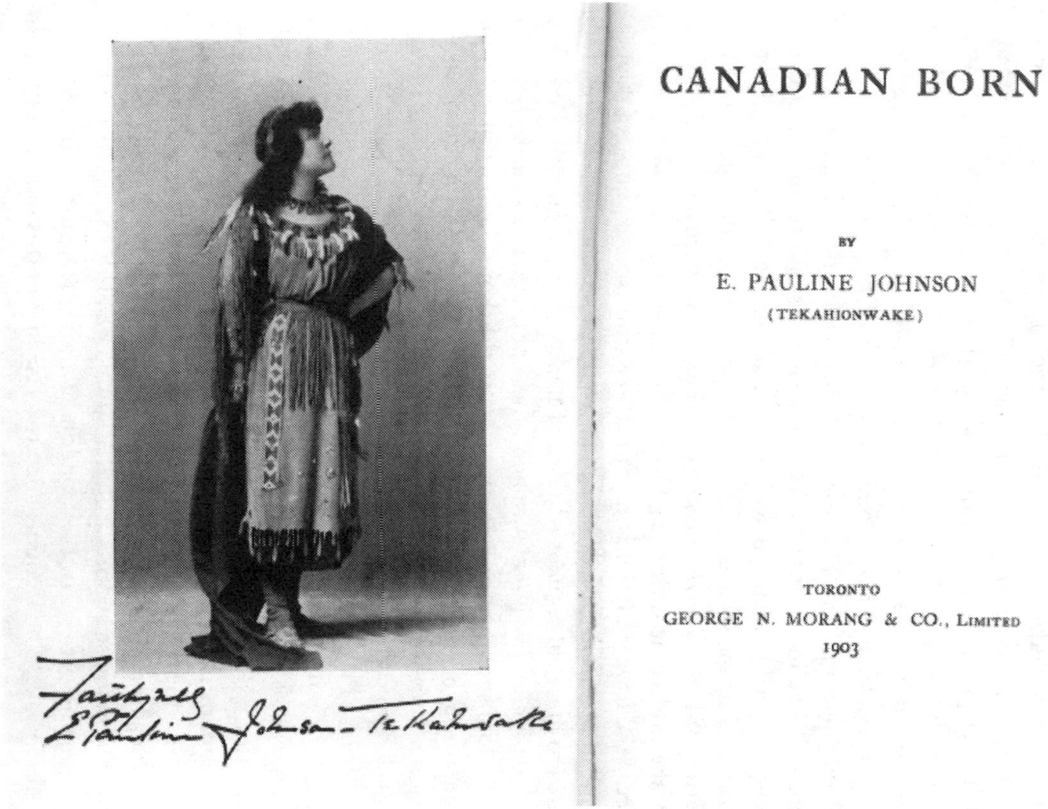

CANADIAN BORN

BY

E. PAULINE JOHNSON

(TEKAHIONWAKE)

TORONTO

GEORGE N. MORANG & CO., LIMITED

1903

FIGURE 3. Title Page of *Canadian Born* (1903)

of "far Saskatchewan" (Gerson and Strong-Boag 213), and concludes by equating Native spirituality with the practices of the Church of England. A subsequent visit to London in 1907 yielded no known publications.

During Johnson's last years, before her death from cancer in Vancouver in 1913, imperial values continued to sustain her. Although her connections with the capital of the Empire had been sporadic, her visits had occasioned the publication of her first book, and of some of her prose sketches. After her death, an unsigned obituary in the *Times Literary Supplement* opined that "her poems are but faint adumbrations of her dark and exotic grandeur" and were overrated by Watts-Dunton: "Certainly she never attained that technical mastery which characterizes the best work of Sarojini Naidu and . . . others who have come from afar" ("A Mohawk Poetess"). While this author believed that it was the "reinforcement of her stately presence" that created interest in her writings, Canadian opinion differed. Despite her exclusion from the canon of elite authors, Pauline Johnson's popularity with common readers endured, as evidenced in the many editions and re-editions of her work. Looking at these volumes through perspectives from book history and postcolonialism enables us to see how she was constructed by her appearances in print, and how, in turn, print constructed her.

NOTES

1. Antoinette Burton and Judith Walkowitz have documented how London welcomed natives of the Indian Subcontinent who presented polished displays of the exotic insider.
2. This detail does not appear in Kristin Zambucka's *Princess Kaiulani of Hawaii,* but was reported by a tour guide at Hulihe'e Palace in Kailua-Kona, Hawaii, in October 2000.
3. In "Pauline Johnson: Tekahionwake," Bertha Jean Thompson cites at length an account of the intervention of Clement Scott and "Professor Clark, of Trinity University." However, according to Hector Charlesworth's *Candid Chronicles,* the introduction was made by John Davidson, while Walter McRaye, in *Pauline Johnson and Her Friends,* cites Richard LeGallienne. An 1897 interview in the *Chicago Tribune* ("Poetess") claims that Andrew Lang and Sir Frederick Leighton were Johnson's advisors.

4. In 1895, Hector Charlesworth described the book as "an austere looking little tome, with its plum-colored cover and its bold device of tomahawk and wampum" (478), but all the volumes I have seen have the same dark red-brown cover.

WORKS CITED

Anderson, Benedict. *Imagined Communities*. 1983. London: Verso, 1991.

Benton, Megan. *Beauty and the Book: Fine Editions and Cultural Distinction in America*. New Haven: Yale UP, 2000.

Burton, Antoinette. *At the Heart of the Empire*. Berkeley: U of California P, 1995.

Charlesworth, Hector. *Candid Chronicles*. Toronto: Macmillan, 1925.

———. "Miss Pauline Johnson's Poems." *Canadian Magazine* 5 (Sept. 1895): 478–80.

Daily Express [London] 20 Nov. 1906: 4.

Deloria, Philip J. *Playing Indian*. New Haven: Yale UP, 1998.

Duncan, Sara Jeannette. "American Influence on Canadian Thought." *The Week* 7 July 1887: 518.

Early Canadiana Online. Canadian Institute for Historical Microreproductions. 7 Nov. 2003. <http://www.canadiana.org>.

E. Pauline Johnson fonds. William Ready Division of Archives and Research Collections. McMaster University, Hamilton, ON.

"Fate of the Red Man." *Ottawa Daily Free Press* 21 June 1894: 3.

"From Wigwam to Concert Platform. Red Indian Chief's Daughter to Appear in London. Gruesome Ornaments." *Daily Mirror* and *Dundee Evening Telegraph* 4 July 1906. Johnson fonds, McMaster.

Gerson, Carole, and Veronica Strong-Boag. *E. Pauline Johnson Tekahionwake: Collected Poems and Selected Prose*. Toronto: U of Toronto P, 2002.

Hale, Horatio. "The White Wampum." *The Critic* 4 Jan. 1896: 4–5.

Johnson, E. Pauline. *Canadian Born*. Toronto: Morang, 1903.

———. "A Pagan in St. Paul's Cathedral." *London Daily Express* 3 Aug. 1906: 4.

———. "A Royal Mohawk Chief." *Legends of Vancouver*. Toronto: McClelland, 1961.

———. *The White Wampum*. London: John Lane, 1895.

Johnson, Evelyn. "Chiefswood," ts. Accession 15601, MU 5462. Archives of Ontario, Toronto.

Lane, John. "List of Books in Belles Lettres." [1895 catalogue, bound in with E. Pauline Johnson's *The White Wampum*.] London: John Lane, 1895.

Lighthall, W.D. *Songs of the Great Dominion: Voices from the Forests and Waters, the Settlements and Cities of Canada*. London: W. Scott, 1889.

Magnet Magazine 6 Jan. 1897. Johnson fonds, McMaster.

Marx, Edward. "Decadent Exoticism and the Woman Poet." *Women and British Aestheticism*. Ed. Talia Schaffer and Kathy Alexis Psomdiades. Charlottesville: U of Virginia P, 1999. 139–57.

McRaye, Walter. *Pauline Johnson and Her Friends*. Toronto: Ryerson, 1947.

"Miss E. Pauline Johnson." *Canadian Gazette*. Rpt in unidentified newspaper, 20 July 1894. Johnson fonds, McMaster.

"A Mohawk Poetess." *Times Literary Supplement* 4 Dec. 1913: 590.

P.A.H. "Tekahionwake." *The Sketch* 13 June 1894: 358.

"The Pauline Johnson Archive." Online. E. Pauline Johnson Project, McMaster University. Oct. 1996. <http://www.humanities.mcmaster.ca/~pjohnson/home.html>.

"Poetess of the Iroquois." *Chicago Tribune* 28 Jan. 1897. Johnson fonds, McMaster.

"A Poet of the Prairie. Miss E. Pauline Johnson: 'Tekahionwake.'" *Black and White* 28 Dec. 1895: 839.

Rev. of *The White Wampum*. *The Academy* 17 Aug. 1895. Johnson fonds, McMaster.

Rev. of *The White Wampum*. *The Sketch* 24 July 1895. Johnson fonds, McMaster.

Roberts, Charles G.D. "The Poet is Bidden to Manhattan Island." *Canadian Poetry: From the Beginnings through the First World War*. Ed. Carole Gerson and Gwendolyn Davies. Toronto: McClelland, 1994. 196–97.

Rose, Jonathan. "From Book History to Book Studies." Acceptance speech. APHA Institutional Award for the Society for the History of Authorship, Reading & Publishing (SHARP). New York Public Library. 27 Jan. 2001. 14 Jan. 2004. <http://www.printinghistory.org>.

Star 11 July 1895. Johnson fonds, McMaster.

Strong-Boag, Veronica, and Carole Gerson. *Paddling Her Own Canoe: The Times and Texts of E. Pauline Johnson, Tekahionwake*. Toronto: U of Toronto P, 2000.

Thompson, Bertha Jean. "Pauline Johnson: Tekahionwake." *McMaster University Monthly* (Dec. 1904): 104–07.

Unidentified clipping. 5 July 1895. Johnson fonds, McMaster.

Unidentified clipping [London]. 27 July 1895. Johnson fonds, McMaster.

Walkowitz, Judith. "The Indian Woman, the Flower Girl and the Jew: Photojournalism in Edwardian London," *Victorian Studies* 42.1 (1998/99): 3–46.

Watts-Dunton, Theodore. Rev. of *The White Wampum*, by E. Pauline Johnson. *The Athenaeum* 28 Sept. 1889: 412.

Zambucka, Kristin. *Princess Kaiulani of Hawaii*. Honolulu: Green Glass, 1998.

Margaret Atwood's Historical Lives in Context: Notes on a Postcolonial Pedagogy for Historical Fiction

RENÉE HULAN

IN NOVEMBER 1996, Margaret Atwood delivered the Bronfman lecture at the University of Ottawa, a lecture that was later published as *In Search of Alias Grace* by the University of Ottawa Press and then reprinted in the *American Historical Review* in December 1998 as part of the AHR Forum on "Histories and Historical Fiction." The introduction to the AHR Forum avows, more than 25 years after the publication of Hayden White's *Metahistory*, that "[s]torytelling has returned to claim a prominent place in history" (1502). While this announcement is late arriving, its striking similarity to the statements of anthropologists like James Clifford a decade earlier locates the discussion within the "linguistic turn" in the social sciences. The AHR Forum presents this turn, or return, as a historical moment; in Michel de Certeau's terms, it is one of the ruptures that announces the present. For literary critics, this moment has placed literary analysis, especially literary revisionism, at the centre of historical interpretation. For professional historians, however, the return to narrative has served a number of different purposes, including arguments for resisting the use of social scientific methodology (see Stone; Burke).

Nevertheless, in both disciplines, scholars debate ideas advanced by postmodernists, particularly the need to undermine master narratives of history by narrative means. The theoretical discussion of master narratives shapes the criticism of contemporary Canadian historical fiction, with literary studies by Dennis Duffy, Bernd Engler and Kurt Muller, Martin Kuester, and Herb Wyile building on Linda Hutcheon's work in *The Canadian Postmodern*. This critical work provides a theoretical context for a proliferation of self-reflexive historical fiction in the latter half of the twentieth century based on the premise that, as Wyile phrases it succinctly, contemporary Canadian historical novels "highlight the codes and discursive conventions that govern historical writing and reflect the sense that the politics and technologies of representation of traditional history and historical fiction need to be questioned" (33).[1]

As literary critics grapple with literature that reconstructs marginalized historical lives, calls for a return to the master narratives of a national history follow on the backlash brought by Jack Granatstein's *Who Killed Canadian History?* While some literary critics attempt to reduce what professional historians do to a set of writing strategies, extreme nationalists attack professional historians for failing to produce a coherent narrative. Citing their own surveys based on testing facts, these nationalists bemoan the failure of citizens to respond correctly to their arbitrary questions, warning that this means the future of the nation is at stake. In this way, they attempt to manufacture a crisis in the teaching of Canadian history whereby "Canadians" generally, but often "young people" specifically, are said to not know what they ought to know about Canadian history.[2] These discussions leave the impression that "history" is a set of names, dates, and other details, a warehouse of data to which historians hold the key; that is, precisely the idea of history that academic historians spend their time trying to dispel from the minds of undergraduates.

Attacks led by Granatstein and his followers are often, not surprisingly, directed at politically committed revisionists, including feminist, multiculturalist, and social historians, some of whom have answered with excellent rebuttals, such as Timothy J. Stanley's "Why I Killed Canadian History: Towards an Anti-Racist History in Canada." For Stanley, anti-racist history "kills" nationalist history, in part, because it is *better* history. Stanley embraces postcolonial critique as a mode of inquiry dedicated to understanding the way imperial and national narratives shape the lives of colonizer and colonized. In his work on the history of the Chinese in British Columbia, he dispels the notion that historical meaning derives solely from the rhetorical strategies the historian chooses, by emphasizing the sources that have been ignored or discounted, including Chinese language books and newspapers. From the historian's point of view, and it is a view I share, a history that takes these sources into account is by definition *better* than a history that does not. Using this example, Stanley counters Granatstein's naive nationalism by demonstrating that there cannot be a disinterested historical interpretation since there can be no world of "facts" without interpretation, and therefore, interest. The anti-racist historian, then, is *interested in* both studying and eliminating racism.

For postcolonial scholars who are actively engaged in decolonization, such as committed anti-racists like Stanley, consciousness is a first step towards making visible the discourses shaping any society. In literary studies, it is also a powerful counterweight to the appreciation model still gripping many English departments. Teaching how to evaluate literature by cultivating literary taste and value through appreciation only prepares students to be discriminating consumers in the exchange of cultural capital. Rather than merely preparing students to fulfill their roles as individual consumers of cultural products, postcolonial pedagogy is meant to enable and to transform in a collective way. Yet, postcolonial critique can have its own exchange value if it is treated only as a standpoint and not as both a methodology and a form of knowledge. In such a case, meaningful social transformation may be confounded by a purely instrumental use of postcolonial literature and theory.

The manufacturers of the crisis in Canadian history education, with their trivia quizzes and sets of facts, imply a model of education that has been thoroughly discredited. In this model, students are empty vessels who, once filled up with the appropriate contents, become good citizens, and professors are the keepers of heritage, passing it on to the next generation. The ideological foundations of the pedagogy advocated by nationalists were critiqued in Paulo Freire's *Pedagogy of the Oppressed* three decades ago. As Freire shows, the model that treats students as receptacles filled up with the stories the professor tells them, or as the *tabula rasa* on which academics trace their ideas, plays a "domesticating" function. Freire calls for a pedagogy based on materialist analysis that would emphasize cultivating critical consciousness and that would reject the paternalism inherent in the education system. Consciousness means developing the awareness necessary to generate a critique and propose a course of action, not learning the prescribed vocabulary or merely reciting theories.

Postcolonial pedagogy works for decolonization through advocacy and engagement while maintaining an open-ended learning process. How to achieve this is an ongoing challenge for politically engaged teaching and research, but the consensus of those who embrace advocacy, like the essayists collected in *Advocacy in the Classroom* (Spacks), seems to be that professors can balance advocacy and openness if they use an inclusive approach. In English departments, this striving for balance is often framed in response to Gerald Graff's call to "teach the conflicts" (see Cain). While Graff's *Professing Literature* provides a much needed historical analysis of English as a discipline, *Beyond the Culture Wars* presents a model for curricular reform, not pedagogy. In it, Graff argues that a curriculum built around debates over the subject, rather than isolating competing positions by adding courses, will offer students a more complete understanding of the discipline and give them greater access to the academic community. This essentially pluralist approach is based on the conviction that "the meaning of any text is determined within a conversation of readers" (85). As in *Professing Literature*, Graff demonstrates the shortcomings of a curriculum organized to minimize conflict. Not only does the "insularity" of the classroom and the absence of peer review protect professors from criticism and from potential conflict, it prevents them from preparing students to join the debate (107–14). What Graff also calls the "course fetish" or "cult of the great teacher" further undermines the intellectual community by eliminating opportunities for discussion and debate: "Our very use of the term 'the classroom' to stand for the entire educational process is a symptom of this constricted way of thinking . . ." (114). But, if there really is no intellectual community, no "conversation of readers," the question becomes what is there for students to access? Graff proposes to bring such a community into being by reforming programs, not individual courses, according to his teaching the conflicts model.

Whereas Graff's criticism of the way we use the term *the classroom*, with its emphasis on the individual professor and course, indicates why it is not possible for a professor to constitute a community by merely representing difference in the classroom, an analysis of power relations in the classroom further demonstrates the serious constraints on the professor's ability to represent conflicting positions. As the adjudicator of balance, the professor retains power over the subject. Even if it is assumed that all professors are ethical individuals who work hard to treat subjects (in all senses of the word) fairly, there are still serious problems with a model that relies on the professor's ability to both advocate a position and articulate opposing, even incommensurable, positions. Inclusion tends to highlight the oppositional stance of the advocate, but it can also be counterproductive. What anti-racist would want to give equal time to racist views, for example? Not me.

In contrast, Spivak calls on postcolonial critics and professors to "suspend the mood of self-congratulation as saviors of marginality" (*Outside* 61) and to adopt a strategy based on an awareness of their own capacities. In an interview with Ellen Rooney, she describes this approach: "I will share with you what I have learned about knowing, that these are the limitations of what I undertake, looking to others to teach me. I think that's what one should do rather than invoke multiplicity" (19). As Spivak's answer indicates, the professor's authority is the most serious limitation on the teaching the conflicts model. Given the professor's responsibility to evaluate the student's work in the course, professor and students are not on the same footing in the classroom, no matter how hard one might try to modify the imbalance. Even if a conflict is covered, opposing views aired, and counter-arguments included, the professor's standpoint may still be regarded as authoritative if she is the one who determines how students do in the course. Peer evaluation can modify this effect, but creates other pitfalls. In any case, professors are ultimately responsible for evaluation and thus have institutional power regardless of their intentions and methods. If a proposed pedagogy relies only on the professor and the professor's methods, and not on envisaging students as fully committed participants, it cannot produce transformation. The challenge is to create opportunities for positive transformation without overdetermining the learning process or avoiding responsibility.

For these reasons, any pedagogy that makes the university "classroom" the agent of meaningful social transformation invites scepticism. Moreover, each time a well-planned syllabus, assignment, or lesson plan meets with the real students in a real classroom, we encounter the unruliness of experience and the uncertain but exciting possibilities that education holds for both professor and student. For Freire's pedagogy to be achieved, the professor has to embrace unruliness and give up control, not necessarily of the classroom, but of the knowledge generated by those in it. Yet, classroom experience may set up conditions for a radical pedagogy, even if such a pedagogy cannot be achieved within it. Radical pedagogy depends on the teacher's engagement in the same process—not a narrative of "when I was a student before I was a professor," but working with the class *as* a student and struggling to find ways to alter and to eliminate the subject-object relation of the classroom. Bearing this in mind, I have been working with two objectives: first, to promote a postcolonial view of Canadian history by placing historical events in the imperial context described in the historiography; and second, to develop critical thinking and to create the conditions necessary for a radical critique by concentrating on the methods used by historians and asking students to learn these methods.

When I started teaching at Saint Mary's University in 1998, I was surprised to hear from students that some did not know that slavery had existed in Nova Scotia, the province in which they had lived all their lives and been educated, before taking the survey of Canadian literature with me. Having grown up on the myth of Scottish Nova Scotia, they were shocked to learn that slavery was still practised as free Black Loyalists were settling and being settled in the most inhospitable places. Although this experience indicates that the concerns about historical awareness are not completely unfounded, neither is the social history I wish to emphasize of any concern to the nationalists clamouring for more Canadian history in schools. Teaching Canadian literary history and Canadian history, including some of what nationalists would call basic facts, and a great deal that they would not, quickly became a priority in my feminist and anti-racist agenda. Over the years, students have prepared seminars and critical essays comparing novels such as *Away* and *The Englishman's Boy* to their acknowledged sources; they have held roundtable discussions comparing *Roughing It in the Bush* and *The Journals of Susanna Moodie,* read literary history and criticism by Misao Dean, Carole Gerson, and others, and debated the uses of history in a number of short stories, plays, and novels. I began to revise the Canadian literature courses I had inherited accordingly and included classes on how to approach the past, how to distinguish evidence from argument, and how historical method can contribute to the study of literature. At the same time, I found the literary analysis of history too narrowly focused on rhetoric—as indicated by critics' appeals to Hayden White to the virtual exclusion of other historians—to provide students with an understanding of historical research and historiography. Indeed, the analysis of the writing of history has its own history, one which links it to similar discussions in social sciences but which does not adequately represent what goes on in historiography. If I was going to think about historical research and writing, it seemed important to find out what historians had to say and to treat it seriously. Instead of teaching a "conflict" between literary theory and history, I decided to structure the discussion of history around works by historians and to introduce some of the research on primary sources that I was doing myself. Rather than recount those earlier experiences in this discussion, I have chosen to explore these pedagogical issues by using the example of *Alias Grace*, a novel that I have yet to teach. By doing so, I will avoid the ethical pitfalls associated with writing about one's classes, while sharing some of my more recent research.

The AHR Forum on *Alias Grace* presents an excellent opportunity to teach about literature, historiography, and their interdisciplinary contact. The forum is comprised of Atwood's Bronfman lecture and brief responses by three American historians who, according to the preface, "share an interest in experimenting with the forms of historical presentation" (1502). These historians were: Lynn Hunt, a professor at the University of Pennsylvania who studies the French Revolution and has also published on cultural history; Jonathan D. Spence, a specialist in Chinese history who teaches at Yale; and John Demos, also from Yale, a social historian specializing in American colonial history. Given their expertise, it is not surprising that the discussion is *metahistorical* and sometimes has little to do with the novel.

Reading the preface to the discussion, which introduces Atwood as "one of our era's master storytellers," a reader could easily mistake Atwood for an American novelist (1502). The American scholars situate the novel within the present American hegemony, virtually ignoring the Canadian content; indeed, only Lynn Hunt makes passing reference to Canadian history, even though Atwood's lecture insists on it. In fact, it is Atwood's insistence on the period in question as part of "Canadian history" that complicates the interpretation of the novel.[3] When she describes the "climate" of the day and argues its importance in the lecture, she presents it as a Canadian, not a colonial or an imperial climate. Atwood's lecture describes a particular narrative of Canadian historical development with her send-up of the brazen little "burps" in the peaceable kingdom, the historical compromise of rational participants. In her account of why

Canadian writers have turned to historical fiction, Atwood again stresses the "Canadian" in what she calls the "real Canadian past" (1515). Yet, none of the participants comment on the particular history that Atwood is dealing with. Indeed, when Jonathan Spence likens Atwood's comments on the cultural relevance of "geology" and "weather" to his own attempts to link personal experience to "cosmic forces," it is clear that he has missed her point (1522). But all three recognize Atwood's method in the attention paid to daily life—as Demos calls them: the "how-to-store-parsnips" details of history (1529). Since *Alias Grace* represents a moment in Atwood's lifelong conversation with Susanna Moodie, Canadian literary historians, and perhaps readers more generally, recognize where some of the detail comes from (see Hamill). Like the tricks of Jerome DuPont's trade, the lamp and the veil, the writer uses detail to establish the credibility of what she calls fiction's "plausible whoppers." Interestingly enough, when Atwood uses this phrase, a phrase that captures the panel's attention, she is comparing writers not to historians but to politicians. Unlike politicians, Atwood claims, writers "do not come with the usual props and backups" or "the graphs, the studies, the statistics, the blue and red books, the Royal Commissions and omissions, and so forth" to sell an "otherwise bald and unconvincing tale" (1503).

As Burkhard Niederhoff argues, such comments indicate that Atwood's approach to history is generally pragmatic. "Any plot is a *this* followed by a *that*;" writes Atwood, "there must be change in a novel, and change can only take place over time, and this change can only have significance if either the character in the book—or, at the very least, the reader—can remember what came before" (1506). Describing her method, Atwood writes, "when there was a solid fact, I could not alter it" (1515) no matter how enticing the fictional prospects; "but," she goes on, "in the parts left unexplained—the gaps left unfilled—I was free to invent" (1515). Yet, as Hunt points out, Atwood does not espouse, as Hunt describes it, "an explicit postmodernist stance that claims the culture has exhausted the potential of modernism and with it scientific standards of truth, the conviction that history can capture an objective reality, the belief that individual identity displays continuity over time, and so on" (1519). Rather, while maintaining an awareness of the structural similarities between historical and fictional forms, her refusal to clearly separate history and fiction may be seen as an indication not of a generic distinction but an epistemological one, although Niederhoff does not think so. He argues that because Atwood is "less interested in the truth (or falsehood) value of historical and biographical reconstruction," her interest is "pragmatic, not epistemological" (81–82). As evidence of a pragmatic approach, Niederhoff quotes the final section of the lecture in which Atwood states: "The past belongs to us, because we are the ones who need it" (1516; qtd. in Niederhoff 82).

Novelists do take a pragmatic approach to historical writing, mining it for those "how-to-store-parsnips" details, but their work also engages with how we know the past. Asking students to apply "the 5 Ws" of historical method to the AHR forum on *Alias Grace* presents the opportunity to teach historical methods of research and to consider the writer's pragmatic choices while addressing epistemological questions. Once the students have determined *what* the debate is about and *who* is participating in it, they may be asked to imagine how the forum might have been constructed differently. What if certain Canadian historians had been on the panel? What if each of the participants represented a branch of relevant historiography? The debates in the historiography of the period are represented in a number of studies, including: Constance Backhouse's *Petticoats and Prejudice: Women and the Law in Nineteenth-Century Canada* (1991), Elizabeth Jane Errington's *Wives and Mothers, School Mistresses and Scullery Maids: Working Women in Upper Canada, 1790–1840* (1995), Cecilia Morgan's *Public Men and Virtuous Women: The Gendered Languages of Religion and Politics in Upper Canada, 1791–1850* (1996), and Peter Oliver's *"Terror to Evil-Doers": Prisons and Punishments in Nineteenth-Century Ontario* (1998), to name a few. Learning about historiography informs the students' reading of the novel. As an assignment, students might hold a round table or panel discussion mimicking the AHR panel. Presentations might include arguments concerning which historians would be invited to participate in such a panel and why, or analyses of the novel's relationship to the historiography. Panel discussions combine the individual contribution of the seminar format and group work, thus modelling intellectual community. Ultimately, discussion of the historiography leads to interpretive questions about the novel: What is the representation of women in the novel? How is it constructed? When read in the contemporary context, what does it suggest about "women" by representing a nineteenth-century woman?

Rather than evaluate the historical accuracy of the historical fiction, the class would be encouraged to bring their knowledge to bear on the interpretation and to produce multiple readings of the text. As an example of such a reading, I demonstrate my own learning process with an interpretation of the novel's domestication of Grace Marks.[4] As Stephanie Lovelady argues of the "public/private distinction so fundamental to the novel, both in narrative and thematic terms" (36), "Grace gains a measure of freedom by conforming, both in terms of assimilation and by creating a conventional, domestically bound life for herself—in other words, by retreating as far as possible in both ethnic and gender terms into the private sphere" (58–59). As Lovelady argues, "it is an improvement, but not a triumph" (58).

A number of critics note that Atwood draws on Moodie's account of her encounter with Grace Marks in the Toronto Asylum; indeed, Moodie's depiction of Grace is one of the images the novel contests strongly. However, Atwood's decision to locate the narrative present several years after her supposed meeting with Moodie is also "pragmatic," offering a range of possibilities for characterization and plot development. At this point, Grace spends an increasing amount of time in the home of the governor performing the domestic function she had before the murders of Thomas Kinnear and Nancy Montgomery. This setting allows Grace to observe the ladies of the town and to be observed by them. It is through this relationship that Atwood is able to develop a characterization of Grace as an alluring figure in the public mind and to develop a critique of the distinction between respectability and depravity that Moodie's account of Grace draws.

In the novel, Grace represents the labour sustaining the domestic sphere, but her domestication also serves to characterize her as an unlikely murderess—what intrigues the ladies also confounds the reader. Who is she? Is she an innocent, exploited servant, or a coolly calculating accomplice? Grace is characterized through her analysis of the standards of respectability the ladies represent when her voice parodies the women she overhears:

> Oh imagine, I feel quite faint, they say, and You let that woman walk around loose in your house, you must have nerves of iron, my own would never stand it. (24)

These reform-minded ladies, like the Reverend Verringer, represent the stuffy, repressed Victorian sensibility everyone knows. The contrast between the apparently guileless but apparently guilty Grace and the other women is strong. The governor's wife, who "likes to horrify her acquaintances" with her scrapbook (27), is also compared to a cast of "other women": Simon's domineering mother, the suspicious Mrs. Quennell, the frivolous Lydia, the stolid Dora,[5] and the ruined Rachel Humphreys. But, it is ultimately their attitude towards sex that Grace knows accounts for her own allure:

> That is what really interests them—the gentlemen and the ladies both. They don't care if I killed anyone, I could have cut dozens of throats, it's only what they admire in a soldier, they'd scarcely blink. No: was I really a paramour, is their chief concern, and they don't even know themselves whether they want the answer to be no or yes. (28)

This domestic detail does more than accentuate the historical realism that allows the reader to suspend disbelief. It contributes to a view of Victorian women that has implications for contemporary women, a view based on dominant patterns in popular representation of the period. The reconstruction of Upper Canadian society here is based on the evidence presented in newspapers, but how closely sensational accounts matched the public's attitudes and tastes is hard to tell. Judith Knelman argues convincingly that the account in the *Toronto Star* that Atwood relied on for what she calls "a solid fact" was a "formulaic description derived from English newspaper accounts of women, especially young women, who were not intimidated by rituals of justice" (679). Knelman's point is not to criticize the novel for inaccuracy; rather, it is to demonstrate the literary conventions at work in reports of Grace's behaviour and thus highlight the necessity of interpretation in identifying and representing historical "facts." Similarly, those portions of the narrative set in the Kingston penitentiary tend to emphasize discipline and punishments, revealing the brutality of nineteenth-century penal institutions, but without the complexity provided by the historiography of crime and punishment in Upper Canada discussed below. Atwood reproduces a standard interpretation of women's lives in the past, one which is contested in studies by social historians, such as Cecilia Morgan, who study women in the period.

In *Public Men and Virtuous Women*, Morgan shows that the division of public and private spheres is not "simply a projection of feminist historians eager to find a paradigmatic framework for their research" (10) but that "separate spheres" was a metaphor, or more precisely a "trope," in nineteenth-century society. After studying what she calls the "stuff of public discourses"—newspapers, printed sermons, travel literature, pamphlets, biographies, and published reports—Morgan surveyed the historiography on Ontario, which she considers both "locality" and "part of a larger, transatlantic society" (6). In presenting her examination of the research, she shows how "tropes were not just intriguing literary devices but were instead strategies whereby relations of power were produced, organized, and maintained" (10) in order to settle and to facilitate the colonization of Native peoples. Acknowledging that the separate spheres paradigm has allowed women's historians to discover much that was unknown about women, Morgan nevertheless demonstrates that "Upper Canadian society was more complex than these binary opposites might lead us to believe" (8). Morgan cautions the reader that we must attend to "the elements of struggle over language and discourse and that we must avoid the trap of seeing them as totalizing and all-powerful *in themselves,* impervious to counterclaims" (16, emphasis added).

The interpretation of separate spheres as a "totalizing discourse," rather than as a "trope," leads to a view of nineteenth-century womanhood that does not allow for the counter-discursive and resistant acts of women that Morgan discovers. Atwood carefully constructs images of the Victorian period, including attitudes towards domestic service, religion, and respectability, in order to maintain Grace's alias and to facilitate her fictional empowerment. Indeed, Herb Wyile argues that while Grace is presented with the choice of ignorance or insanity, "[t]he structure of *Alias Grace*, however, allows for the consideration (and subversive dissection) of these alternatives and for the restoration to Grace—through her skillful, compelling, and ultimately ambiguous narrative—of a sense of agency and power" (80). Grace *serves* as a figure whose lack of power depends on a historical location where her class and gender make her highly vulnerable to exploitation and mistreatment. The representation of a historical figure such as Grace Marks based on this trope would seem to support the view of women fabricated through it; moreover, it inscribes, if not naturalizes through temporal distance, the powerlessness of women like her. Thus,

Alias Grace also enacts the "progressive narrative of liberation from oppressive gender norms" that Misao Dean observes in literary criticism of nineteenth-century women's writing in *Practising Femininity*. In her study, Dean demonstrates that "[t]he assumption underlying these readings is that while women were oppressed in the past, they have been and are struggling as active agents to free themselves, and that representations of women thus become progressively more free and accurate as literature progresses from the nineteenth to the twentieth century" (5). With the help of Dean's argument and the historiography discussed, I would argue that Atwood's historical realism does not merely "fill in the gaps"; rather, it presents an interpretation of women's history by reproducing separate spheres in fictional form. Placing the novel, and the historical research on which it is based, in the context of historiography illustrates the way writers construct fictional worlds that offer interpretations of the past that conform with their views on the present.

This is the sort of critique that studying literature and historiography together can draw from a class, one of many readings that might be produced when the work of historians is considered alongside historical fiction. To read *Alias Grace* through a postcolonial view of Canadian history then means treating the period as a colonial period and the society as one defined by imperial interests rather than as a nascent nation preparing the way to Confederation. Postcolonial studies comparing histories and historical figures across the empire further help to understand nineteenth-century Canada as part of the British empire either by examining the historiography that contextualizes and takes such a comparative approach, like Cecilia Morgan's, or by incorporating historical research on primary sources. In my own research, I am bringing together two subjects in Atwood's writing which have yet to be explicitly related to each other: the historical lectures in *Strange Things: The Malevolent North in Canadian Literature* and the historical fiction in *Alias Grace*. In both, Atwood reconstructs historical lives. While Grace Marks emerges from the shadows of historical representation to become the heroine of a novel, Sir John Franklin, the ill-fated explorer whose story is well-known, serves as a target in *Strange Things*. These two figures, the failed hero and the condemned woman, share a historical context. Indeed, Grace was imprisoned only two years before Franklin set out on his last expedition. But it is more than the coincidence of their lives that bears reflection. Franklin's term as governor of Van Diemen's Land and his writing on the subject of convict women indicates dominant ways of seeing and dealing with women like Grace Marks in colonial settings. Franklin's report on the state of convict women in Van Diemen's Land, his correspondence, and some of the newspaper reports of the time support the historical detail in the novel. As part of the imperial context, these two people lived in societies structured around similar systems, ideas, and values, especially with regard to social reform.

In the period of Grace Marks's incarceration, according to Peter Oliver, the punishments Atwood's Grace describes, particularly whipping and the silent system, were regularly practised and the liberties taken by both matrons and keepers are well documented. However, the Reverend Verringer's speech concerning the "notoriously corrupt" Warden Smith takes on a different significance when considered in the political context provided in Oliver's study *"Terror to Evil-Doers."* In 1849, Smith was removed as warden after being found guilty of a number of charges from mismanagement to cruelty by a commission led by George Brown. Oliver states that "[t]he commission's verdict on the Smith administration stands today as the conventional wisdom about early Canadian penal administration" (139). In a detailed study of the published reports, minute books, and other documents relating to the Kingston Penitentiary, including the Brown Commission of 1849, and without attempting to exonerate Smith, Oliver reconstructs the political and bureaucratic structures and hypocrisy that led to the administration's demise: "They provide a portrait of a warden whose reformist recommendations were rebuffed year after year by an indifferent government that had only two ideas about the provincial penitentiary, the need for harsh punishments and economical administration" (171). To ensure the latter, the prisoners' labour was contracted out to provide revenue or used to sustain the prison and expand it. As the foundation of industrial prisons in the late nineteenth century would seem to attest, labour was considered beneficial in the reformation of criminals; however, this seems to have been far from the minds of the governing elite, and, Oliver argues, in their eagerness to blame the warden personally, the commission failed to address the structural problems that would continue to grow until exposed in the Archambault Commission in 1938 (185, 193). When Reverend Verringer pronounces sentence on the warden, not only does he confirm "conventional wisdom" about the penitentiary but he also aligns himself with an established elite, one that would hang Warden Smith out to dry.

The Franklins were part of a very similar colonial society in Van Diemen's Land. Throughout his brief period as governor, Franklin proposed policies that were deeply influenced by the Christian Social Reform movement with its emphasis on promoting moral and spiritual health; for example, he advocated employment and education for men as well as women convicts. References to vice and depravity were more than Victorian moral panic, as several documents of the period suggest precautions to prevent attacks on the women both in the factories and on board ship. In his *A Confidential Despatch from Sir John Franklin on Female Convicts* (1843), Franklin describes the use of watch-houses to lodge convicts as an improvement by which "the great evils to which women were exposed formerly in travelling under the escort of constables to or from the factories are in some degrees remedied" (24). Throughout his report, Franklin refers to the various forms of corruption among the local officials and the dangers they presented to the future of the colony. It would be easy to dismiss Franklin's final report on women convicts as an apology for his own failures and a parting salvo against his political enemies were it not for the recurrence of the problems and issues he raises in the correspondence of the officials who were to follow him. Three years later, his successor would voice similar concerns. Records suggest that the description of the allegedly false pregnancy of Grace Marks might be read, not as a sign of mental instability or duplicity, as it often has been, but as evidence that rape was a common danger for women in detention.

In her discussion of quilting in *Alias Grace*, Margaret Rogerson refers to another aspect of the context shared by these historical figures when she notes that, "[i]n the nineteenth century, the activity of piecing together tiny scraps of fabric to make aesthetically harmonious and useful products was recognized in the areas of medical and social rehabilitation" (6) and cites Fry's introduction of needlework and knitting to Newgate's female prisoners as an application of this theory. As a devoted follower of the Social Reform movement, Lady Franklin corresponded with Elizabeth Fry and shared many of her views. As she worked to implement these ideas in Van Diemen's Land, the popular press accused her of meddling and chided Franklin for being governed by a woman. Like the respectable ladies who gather in the parlour in *Alias Grace,* Jane Franklin's social conscience was shaped by gender and class essentialism and Christian paternalism, but she and other women like her were also susceptible to gender discrimination.

In her lecture "Concerning Franklin and his Gallant Crew," Atwood abridges Franklin's life story by describing only his most famous and final mission, the failed attempt to navigate the Northwest Passage. After introducing the subject by telling her Oxford audience that, in Canada, the word "Franklin" *means* disaster and referring to the "Franklin fiasco," she minces no words: "the truth was—according to Native sources anyway—that the man was always somewhat of a fool, and had on previous occasions ignored local advice and gone places he'd been told not to" (14).[6] As in the reconstructed life of Grace Marks, the fiction implies a narrative of development from a time when Europeans foolishly discounted the advice of indigenous people—as if no one would dream of doing that today—to the present. Of course, Atwood's purpose is to entertain her audience while demonstrating the longevity and tenacity of the Franklin myth, which is quite different from writing a biography of the man or a history of Arctic navigation. However, what she presents as the "bare bones" of the story, in which, for example, Jane Franklin is only mentioned for offering a reward to the person who found her lost husband, is already a normative account derived from literary representation and presented as myth. Such representations are questioned when students are encouraged to engage with the documentary records regarding the Franklins as well as the historiography on convict women. This questioning opens the novel to complex readings while undermining the implied narrative of progress and presenting the colonial period as imperial rather than proto-national.[7] It asks them to "think postcolonial."

The postcolonial view of Canadian historical fiction takes into account the imperial context, including historiography, and raises questions about implied narratives of progress in the history. For the nationalist historian, "revisionism" means forgetting "our" shared past, our cultural inheritance, the story of our nation. In a review of Patrick J. Geary's *The Myth of Nations,* R.I. Moore argues that the "legacy of historiography no more passes as an unopened parcel from generation to generation than that of 'national inheritance' itself" (5), and consequently, the particular combination of pride and prejudice that constitutes the myth of national origin "need not have been selected for survival, or combined together so noxiously" (5). The failure of modern historiography, according to Moore, is not that historians have believed in the history of nations as originary narrative "but that they failed to prevent others from doing so" (5). To this end, it is the social historians, including Timothy J. Stanley, Cecilia Morgan, and Peter Oliver, not the self-styled nationalists, who have much to teach us about the historical contexts for historical fiction written today, including how to develop postcolonial pedagogy.

ACKNOWLEDGEMENTS

For access to the Franklin papers, the author gratefully acknowledges the Mitchell Library, Sydney, Australia. Research for this paper was conducted with support of the SSHRC.

NOTES

1. Appropriately, much of the criticism on *Alias Grace* also draws on Linda Hutcheon's work on the postmodern. For example, categorizing *Alias Grace* as historiographic metafiction, Hilde Staels argues that Atwood subverts both the historical novel and detective story. Burkhard Niederhoff qualifies the use of the term ***postmodern*** with the statement that the "[self-reflexive] aspect does not take the form of narratorial comment or digression. Instead, it is contained in a separate plot line. . . . Reflexion is bound up in action" (72).
2. In a similar vein, Lynn Hunt ponders her students' tendency to call any book a "novel," and muses: "Has the distinction between history and fiction . . . vanished among the young?" (1517). It is not that students are unaware of their place in history, even if they may not have explanatory narratives for specific periods. In my experience, students are aware that they are living in and subject to an era of globalization. Many are resistant to it; some are anti-globalization activists.
3. As Cynthia Sugars reminded me after the presentation of the conference paper on which this article is based, the Bronfman lecture was created, in part, to celebrate national culture, and the intended audience may have influenced the lecture's emphasis. Indeed, Atwood's Clarendon lectures were similarly nationalistic.
4. Some critical discussions of *Alias Grace* have focused on Atwood's use of the domestic as a device. For instance, Margaret Rogerson expertly deconstructs the use of quilt-making as a private female discourse and "metaphor for the

literary artefact." Cristie March explores the signifying use of clothing and other objects.

5. Hilde Staels ventures that this obvious allusion to Freud's Dora, a patient who resisted analysis as Grace resists Simon's investigations, provides an anachronistic psychoanalytic context for the narrative.

6. The truth claim here is authorized by "Native sources" even though Rae and McClintock consulted Inuit, and Franklin travelled with Chipewyan on his 1819–22 and 1825–26 expeditions.

7. In the discussion following my conference presentation, Wendy Roy rightly noted that, in the novel, Grace refers to the Empire when she mentions the riots in Cawnpore (25). Such references help to establish the reality effect in the novel.

WORKS CITED

Atwood, Margaret. *Alias Grace*. Toronto: McClelland, 1996.

———. "Concerning Franklin and His Gallant Crew." *Strange Things: The Malevolent North in Canadian Literature*. Oxford: Clarendon, 1995. 7–34.

———. "In Search of *Alias Grace*: On Writing Canadian Historical Fiction." *American Historical Review* 103 (1998): 1503–16.

Backhouse, Constance. *Petticoats and Prejudice: Women and Law in Nineteenth-Century Canada*. Toronto: Osgoode Society/Women's Press, 1991.

Burke, Peter. "History of Events and the Revival of Narrative." *New Perspectives on Historical Writing*. Cambridge: Cambridge UP, 1991. 231–48.

Cain, William E., ed. *Teaching the Conflicts: Gerald Graff, Curricular Reform, and the Culture Wars*. New York: Garland, 1994.

de Certeau, Michel. *The Writing of History*. Trans. Tom Conley. New York: Columbia UP, 1988.

Dean, Misao. *Practising Femininity: Domestic Realism and the Performance of Gender in Early Canadian Fiction*. Toronto: U of Toronto P, 1998.

Demos, John. "In Search of Reasons for Historians to Read Novels . . ." *American Historical Review* 103 (1998): 1526–29.

Duffy, Dennis. *Sounding the Iceberg: An Essay on Canadian Historical Fiction*. Toronto: ECW, 1986.

Engler, Bernd, and Kurt Muller, eds. *Historiographic Metafiction in Modern American and Canadian Literature*. Paderborn: Ferdinand Schoningh, 1994.

Errington, Elizabeth Jane. *Wives and Mothers, Schoolmistresses and Scullery Maids: Working Women in Upper Canada, 1790–1840*. Montreal: McGill-Queen's UP, 1995.

Franklin, Sir John. *A Confidential Despatch from Sir John Franklin on Female Convicts, Van Diemen's Land, 1843*. Adelaide, Australia: Sullivan's Cove, 1996.

Freire, Paulo. *The Pedagogy of the Oppressed.* New York: Seabury, 1973.

Graff, Gerald. *Beyond the Culture Wars: How Teaching the Conflicts Can Revitalize American Education*. New York: W.W. Norton, 1992.

———. *Professing Literature: An Institutional History*. Chicago: U of Chicago P, 1987.

Granatstein, J.L. *Who Killed Canadian History?* Toronto: HarperCollins, 1998.

Hammill, Faye. "Margaret Atwood, Carol Shields, and 'That Moodie Bitch.'" *American Review of Canadian Studies* 29.1 (1999): 67–91.

Hunt, Lynn. "'No Longer an Evenly Flowing River': Time, History, and the Novel." *American Historical Review* 103 (1998): 1517–21.

Hutcheon, Linda. "Historiographic Metafiction." *The Canadian Postmodern: A Study of Contemporary English-Canadian Fiction*. Toronto: Oxford UP, 1988. 61–77.

———. *A Poetics of Postmodernism: History, Theory, Fiction*. New York: Routledge, 1988.

Knelman, Judith. "Can We Believe What the Newspapers Tell Us? Missing Links in *Alias Grace*." *University of Toronto Quarterly* 68.2 (1999): 677–86.

Kuester, Martin. *Framing Truths: Parodic Structures in Contemporary English-Canadian Historical Novels*. Toronto: U of Toronto P, 1992.

Lovelady, Stephanie. "I Am Telling This to No One But You: Private Voice, Passing, and the Private Sphere in Margaret Atwood's *Alias Grace*." *Studies in Canadian Literature* 24.2 (1999): 35–63.

March, Cristie. "Crimson Silks and New Potatoes: The Heteroglossic Power of the Object in Atwood's *Alias Grace*." *Studies in Canadian Literature* 22.2 (1997): 66–82.

Moore, R.I. "A Toxic Waste Dump? Inventing the Goths and Other Ancestors." Rev. of *The Myth of Nations*, by Patrick J. Geary. *TLS* 15 Mar. 2002: 4–5.

Morgan, Cecilia. *Public Men and Virtuous Women: The Gendered Languages of Religion and Politics in Upper Canada, 1791–1850*. Toronto: U of Toronto P, 1996.

Niederhoff, Burkhard. "How To Do Things with History: Researching Lives in Carol Shields' *Swann* and Margaret Atwood's *Alias Grace*." *Journal of Commonwealth Literature* 35.2 (2000): 71–85.

Oliver, Peter. *"Terror to Evil-Doers": Prisons and Punishments in Nineteenth-Century Ontario*. Toronto: U of Toronto P, 1998.

Oxley, Deborah. *Convict Maids: The Forced Migration of Women to Australia*. Cambridge UP, 1996.

Rogerson, Margaret. "Reading the Patchworks in *Alias Grace*." *Journal of Commonwealth Literature* 33.1 (1998): 5–22.

Spacks, Patricia Meyer, ed. *Advocacy in the Classroom: Problems and Possibilities.* New York: St. Martin's, 1996.

Spence, Jonathan D. "Margaret Atwood and the Edges of History." *American Historical Review* 103 (1998): 1522–25.

Spivak, Gayatri Chakravorty. "In a Word: Interview." With Ellen Rooney. *Outside* 1–23.

———. *Outside in the Teaching Machine*. New York: Routledge, 1993.

Staels, Hilde. "Intertexts of Margaret Atwood's *Alias Grace*." *Modern Fiction Studies* 46.2 (2000): 427–50.

Stanley, Timothy J. "Why I Killed Canadian History: Towards an Anti-Racist History in Canada." *Histoire sociale/Social History* 33.65 (2000): 79–103.

Stone, Lawrence. "The Revival of the Narrative: Reflections on Old and New History." *Past and Present* 85 (1979): 3–24.

White, Hayden. *Metahistory: The Historical Imagination in Nineteenth-Century Europe*. Baltimore: Johns Hopkins UP, 1973.

Wyile, Herb. *Speculative Fictions: Contemporary Canadian Novelists and the Writing of History*. Montreal: McGill-Queen's UP, 2002.

At Normal School: Seton, Montgomery, and the New Education

JENNIFER HENDERSON

IN THE FIRST DECADE of the twentieth century, two texts that were to become classics of Canadian children's literature were published just five years apart: Ernest Thompson Seton's *Two Little Savages: Being the Adventures of Two Boys and What They Learned*, in 1903, and L.M. Montgomery's *Anne of Green Gables,* in 1908. The story of the education of Anne, the imaginative orphan, is better known today than the story of Seton's Yan, a pale and sickly boy who achieves courage and self-respect through independent play in the woods. But in their historical moment, both of these narratives resonated with a new, emancipatory view of the child as a creature with independent desires, interests, and imagination. This was the moment when, in the discourse of European and North American philanthropists and progressive educators, the child was being liberated from the repressions and constraints of nineteenth-century models of discipline. The institutionalization of orphaned and dependent children was condemned as an unnatural and disabling form of care;[1] the Humane Society campaigns of the nineteenth century—at first organized to combat cruelty to animals—were consolidated in the powers of newly formed provincial departments of neglected and dependent children and their local children's aid societies;[2] the mastery of traditional school subjects was rejected as the primary pedagogical goal by progressive educators, in favour of a more holistic, moral, and practical education of the "whole child."

Two Little Savages and *Anne of Green Gables* register this emerging view of the child as an independent being, in narratives about children who are fostered out under terms that their own passions and interests overturn. In *Two Little Savages*, a boy is sent away to be toughened up through farm work but instead he winds up playing; in *Anne of Green Gables*, the brother and sister, Matthew and Marilla, place an order for a farm worker but what they receive is a family member. These protagonists embody an irrepressible curiosity and a resistance to rote learning that make them the model objects of the new pedagogy as well as vehicles for criticism of the old. Perhaps nothing so effectively condenses the status and function of these liberated and liberating turn-of-the-century literary cousins as Marilla's observation that her own "secret, unuttered critical thoughts had suddenly taken visible and accusing shape and form in the person of this outspoken morsel of neglected humanity" (*Anne* 106).

But while the theme of the emancipated child found wide circulation at the turn of the century, many Canadians were more preoccupied with the pragmatic question of how to cultivate a healthy and productive national "stock" in a context of rapidly growing population, urbanization, and industrial production. They critiqued what they called the old "forcing system" of education for its emphasis on rote learning and instead promoted a pedagogy centred on "living practice." It was not through the memorization of tables or the parsing of poems that the child would develop the lifelong disposition, tastes, habits, and skills that would fit him or her for a law-abiding, self-sufficient, active, and useful existence, they argued. Indeed, these outdated pedagogical techniques produced deleterious "nerve influences" in the very human material that would soon be sent out into the world to find useful occupations and make healthy homes. From the inaugural volume of the *Canada Educational Monthly and School Chronicle*—a journal established in 1879 to disseminate the latest currents of contemporary educational thought—teachers and school inspectors had been worrying about a truant "Arab population springing up in our midst," destined to become the "jail-birds" of the future, and a school regimen that subjected girls to severe mental strains that violated the "laws of nature and inheritance" (McAllister, "Aims" 97; Allen 417). Contributors criticized rigidly classical curricula that, by "neglecting the education of the hand[,] . . . weakened the power of the State" and threatened to produce a nation of "clerkly people" ("Education" 629).

Such warnings established the frame of reference in which the imperialist vision of Canada as the great hope of the British Empire was staked on policies and programs for the socialization of the child. Although these projects were divergent and contested, reformers generally agreed that the roots of social problems lay in the home, but were best addressed through the school, the "agent that shaped 'the homes of the next generation'" (Sutherland 173).

At the turn of the century, these projects of socialization often took the form of compromises between romantic educational philosophy and more utilitarian educational schemes to prepare pupils for work in rural and urban Canada. Of particular concern was the dwindling attractiveness of rural life or, as the Ontario Agricultural College Professor, James Wilson Robertson, put it, that "our vast areas of good lands could and should carry happy homes for millions more" and that Canada should not allow its population to be "huddled into big towns where the children cannot play" (qtd. in Sutherland 188). The most wide-ranging project in the early years of the century was the MacDonald-Robertson campaign to redesign public education around the goal of raising a generation of competent and contented rural workers, with an enduring taste for agricultural life.[3] While *Anne of Green Gables* and *Two Little Savages* endorse the turn of the century's emancipatory view of the child, they also expose the complex intersection of this view with such utilitarian projects, centred on the child as the malleable material of the future. The emancipated childhoods of Anne and Yan are "nation-tinged": they tell stories about the development of the nation's human resources, and the development of national culture.[4] Anne makes a home in a settler community into which she ventures as an outsider; Yan achieves courage and self-respect by moving into the bush and becoming an amateur naturalist and make-believe Indian. The narratives are driven by their protagonists' respective desires for family feeling and plant and animal life, the two sides of a natural order of nationhood apparently untouched by history and social conflict. Anne and Yan can thus be read as the passionate pursuers of proper places in the agrarian life of an expanding settler society.

Their drives to belong to the spheres of family and nature—their drives to, in effect, indigenize themselves—are laden with the value of the turn of the century's reconceptualization of the child. The indigenizing subject is not just a child in these narratives, but a child who has only recently been revalorized as an autonomous being with a rich interior life and an undeniable need for freedom. Just as we are now witnessing calls for educational reforms to prepare children to serve as valuable human capital in a globalized world, the turn-of-the-century reconceptualization of childhood was an earlier moment of educational renovation that sought to remake the child for a particular imagined future. As Harry Hendrick and others have argued, the history of childhood is the history of such "reconstructions" of the child; it is the history of the intimate relationships between successive "scientific" or "expert" knowledges of childhood—always grounded in authoritative claims to know the needs of the child—the dynamics of capital, and national and imperial projects to foster the development of certain kinds of social actors. The "expert" truths pronounced about children's needs and natures—truths that are inseparable from configurations of power—at least partly shape the space of possibility within which children live at any given moment.[5] Needless to say, children do not represent themselves in these "expert" knowledges; indeed, for over 200 years they have occupied "the receiving end of a project of knowledge-production in which the positions of subject and object of knowledge are painstakingly distinguished" (Benzaquen 34).

The maintenance of this painstaking distinction in the knowledges of childhood makes it especially interesting to consider the function of literature that claims to enter into the child's own perspective. As Jacqueline Rose has argued, the desire to collapse the distance between adult and child, to speak directly to or for the child as if the child as such already existed either for or "in" the book, is the foundational impossibility of children's fiction. If children's fiction construes an image of the child, it does so in an attempt to grasp and fix the child who remains outside of and beyond the book; to claim otherwise "is to confuse the adult's intention *to get at* the child with the child [the book] portrays" (2; emphasis added). It is just such a confusion that drives the narratives of *Two Little Savages* and *Anne of Green Gables,* in which independent young protagonists are celebrated as representatives of the radical distance and alterity of childhood, even as they voice the very adult imperatives of turn-of-the-century schemes of progressive education.

*

The theme of the emancipated child was one that would not have escaped the notice of Montgomery and Seton, given their respective connections to formal and informal education. Before writing *Anne of Green Gables*, Montgomery attended one of Canada's more innovative Normal Schools—just as these teacher training institutions were beginning to specialize as professional schools for the dissemination of current pedagogical methods and theories, rather than places for the continuation of high-school subjects.[6] By the turn of the century, Seton's animal stories formed almost the entirety of the nature study curriculum in the schools of Manitoba, where he held the position of the province's officially appointed naturalist (Sutherland 187). In 1902, Seton founded the Woodcraft youth recreation movement—"a man-making scheme with a blue sky background," as he called it (Seton, *Birch Bark* xiii); later on, he was recruited to serve as the Chief Scout of the Boy Scouts of North America, an organization from which he would eventually resign out of a distaste for its militarist ethos (MacDonald 142).

One impetus for the specialization of the Normal School that was under way while Montgomery was being trained as a teacher was the emerging conception of education as a science in its own right, requiring some knowledge of developmental and educational psychology on the part of its practitioners. Subtler methods of "unconscious tuition" were also coming into vogue as techniques of moral training in the school, and these were seen to rely upon "an educating power issuing from the teacher"—a "certain internal character or quality . . . acting as a positive, formative and mighty force" (Huntington 265, 267–68). The emphasis on the force of example as a pedagogical device meant that Normal Schools now carried responsibility for ridding teachers-in-training of any "ill-regulated power" and "eccentric habits" (McAllister, "Teacher" 530, 532). Exemplary character was not just a pedagogical technique, but a criterion for graduation from Normal School with a first-class teacher's licence.[7] A Normal School textbook published in Toronto in 1912 thus advises its readers that after 20 years of school reforms, "[m]uch more is now demanded of teachers": "the growing tendency to devolve upon the school responsibilities which were once recognized as duties of the home has greatly changed the relationship of the teacher to his charge. . . . He has, in fact, become an official of the state" (Salisbury 3). The textbook does not stop at recommending that this state representative "ought to have a wholesome, engaging personality"; it goes on to argue that "[i]rritability, 'nervousness,' hypochondria and all the brood of morbid moods which follow in the train of physical abnormality and weakness have no right to cast their shadow over the lives of school children, even though they may be often encountered in the home" (67).

As Irene Gammel and Ann Dutton have observed, the teacher figures in Montgomery's fiction illustrate an entire "spectrum of pedagogues," from the "demonic" and tyrannical to the charismatic (106). Already in *Anne of Green Gables,* there is a sharp contrast between two teachers, which permits Anne's progress as a student in the Avonlea schoolhouse to be charted as the effect of particular educational reforms. Mr Phillips is Anne's first teacher, an uninterested pedagogue who has been able to secure his position in the Avonlea schoolhouse only through the nepotism of a well-placed uncle. The certainty of Mr Phillips' demise and replacement by Miss Stacy, the more respectable and progressive "lady teacher," is assured not just by his recourse to the outmoded techniques of whipping and humiliation, but also by his habit of "making eyes at Prissy Andrews" (*Anne* 137).[8] The feminized sanitization of classroom morality that is implied in Mr Phillips' replacement with Miss Stacy is echoed in the novel's explicit gendering of the "lady teacher's" penchant for positive motivation as opposed to punishment and humiliation. Miss Stacy's feminized pedagogy in fact reflects a wider connection between the reform of the school and the reform of the family at the end of the nineteenth century. The "unconscious personal influence" (Salisbury 125) recommended by the Normal School textbook as a means of moral training drew on an ethic of "mother-love" that was articulated across the literature of the child in the second half of the nineteenth century. The literature of "disciplinary intimacy"—to borrow Richard Brodhead's term—sentimentalized the disciplinary relation in the context of the family by advocating an intensification of the emotional bond between authority and its charges (Brodhead 71). This newly intensified bond worked its discipline through the "implantation of moral motivation," that is to say, by instilling in the child an autonomous compulsion to make the beloved parent's imperatives his or her own (82).

The reformed school that arose as the tutelary adjunct of middle-class domesticity carried this psychological transaction between mother and child into the classroom. The principle that "[w]hom we love we would therefore please" was applied not just to the "right-minded child [who] will put forth effort in a direction which he knows to be pleasing to his parents," but also to the school pupil whose "[a]ffection towards a teacher will go far towards inducing the effort to please" (Salisbury 111). In *Anne of Green Gables*, this historical movement of "mother-love" from the home to the school is reversed, however, as "mother-love" is situated as a form of expertise that must be disseminated starting *from* the school. Miss Stacy's influence thus extends beyond the walls of the classroom, to reach Anne's adoptive mother through the agency of Anne herself, once she has come under the teacher's influence. Montgomery's novel marks the point at which the "lady teacher" comes to embody the moral authority and preventative outlook of the state in relation to the home, where "all the brood of morbid moods" might "cast their shadow," though they have been purged from the school.

It is something of a truism in the criticism of children's literature that the child who has "never belonged to anybody," or has been separated from his or her birth parents, makes for a more independent protagonist with greater "scope for the imagination," to use Anne's signature expression (*Anne* 16, 17). But in the separation of the child from the parents in both *Anne of Green Gables* and *Two Little Savages* it is also possible to read the intrusion of the turn of the century's new professionals of childhood, or at least their specialized knowledges of children's natures and development. In these two texts, the narrative of the self-inventing child without ties to a birth family allows expertise to replace blood as the legitimate form of adult-child relation. Anne, we are told, is the orphaned daughter of a "lady teacher" and this biographical fact colours her lifelong desire "to say 'mother'" as the yearning of a pupil for the "mother-love" of a progressive teacher (51). When, after passing through homes of drunkenness, immoderate breeding, violence, and exploitation, Anne finally finds adoptive parents in the aging brother-and-sister couple, Matthew and Marilla, it is not simply the narrative of Anne's education at the Avonlea schoolhouse that then ensues, but also the narrative of the education of Marilla as a mother. Marilla, in short, must be taught to exercise the kind of "mother-love" that the teacher has already turned into a pedagogical technique in the public school.

Marilla mistakenly "conceive[s] it to be her duty to drill Anne into a tranquil uniformity of disposition as impossible and alien to her as to a dancing sunbeam on one of the brook shallows" (228). It is her brother, Matthew, in fact, who voices the alternative logic of disciplinary intimacy, suggesting that Anne is "one of the sort you can do anything with if you only get her to love you" (62). But this logic works both ways, and Anne, as it turns out, can do almost anything with Marilla once she has gotten Marilla to love her. Anne must "earn her keep" in Marilla's household, but she must do so by deploying the strategy that will eventually "mellow" a fairy-tale cruel stepmother into a sentimental mother (394). Anne thus offers Marilla a transformative flow of affection, the power of which is condensed in her kiss, which thrills Marilla with a "sudden sensation of startling sweetness" (117).

At school, Anne is the object rather than the subject of disciplinary intimacy, and her moral and intellectual development begins with her affection for Miss Stacy. This affection inaugurates an effort to please that the text describes as an almost botanical event. In Miss Stacy, Montgomery's narrator explains, Anne finds a "true and helpful friend. Miss Stacy was a bright, sympathetic young woman with the happy gift of winning the affections of her pupils and bringing out the best that was in them mentally and morally. Anne expanded like a flower under this wholesome influence" (243). Anne expands *like* a flower, but she also expands *in the midst* of plant life, as Miss Stacy takes her pupils to the nearby woods for field days during which "they study ferns and flowers and birds" (241). Montgomery's ironic strategy reserves commentary on these unorthodox lessons for the village gossip, Rachel Lynde, but it is Anne who reports Rachel's sceptical commentary and transforms it into an argument on behalf of women teachers: "Mrs. Lynde says she never heard of such goings-on and it all comes of having a lady teacher. But I think it must be splendid and I believe I shall find that Miss Stacy is a kindred spirit" (241).

Anne's resemblance to and contiguity with nature under Miss Stacy's care describes the status of the child within an educational scheme that was as closely associated with the special talents of the "lady teacher" as the technique of disciplinary intimacy. The kindergarten scheme of the eighteenth-century educational philosopher, Friedrick Froebel, was based on the child's capacity for independent discovery of the natural laws of the universe through direct sense-perception and voluntary "self-activity." As one of Froebel's turn-of-the-century interpreters wrote, it was by playing "among living things, near to Nature's heart," that the child would "learn his first baby lessons without any meddlesome middleman" (Wiggin 13–14). Revived by progressive educators, the kindergarten was hailed as a plan that should be "carried out through our educational fabric to the end of the university career" (Mills 18). Montgomery's text stages the argument for extending kindergarten pedagogy beyond the elementary grades by tracing Anne's plant-like flourishing under Miss Stacy's innovative care. The "lady teacher" introduces a holistic curriculum that includes the new subjects of nature study, physical culture, English composition, and dramatic recitation, but more importantly, she presides over the Avonlea schoolhouse with what the narrator describes as a "tactful, careful, broad-minded guidance. She led her class to think and explore and discover for themselves" (232).

As much as the Froebelian kindergarten seemed to provide the ideal setting for the emancipation of the overworked pupil who had been victimized by the "forcing methods" of a classical education (Mills 18), it also provided a perfect complement to the new intellectual prestige of natural science within liberal culture and to the connections between education and evolution that were being drawn by figures such as the second-generation Darwinist, Herbert Spencer. What the subject of free "self-activity" learned in the kindergarten, ideally, was an elementary form of natural science that doubled as a form of moral training: the "scientific truths [of] correct living" as evidenced by the order of nature, the "inevitable consequence, the reaction of organic law upon its transgressor" (Gundry 25, 81). Thus, it is not just in the name of propriety that Miss Stacy, as Anne reports, "took all us girls who are in our teens down to the brook" to talk to them about "it"—that is to say, about the importance of forming habits of self-regulation early on in relation to young men (306). Nature, in Montgomery's text, is the ideal setting for the inculcation of a sense of the natural order of things.

Anne's expansion "like a flower" under Miss Stacy's wholesome influence connects her education to the ideas of progressive educators for whom the kindergarten was the starting point for a natural evolutionary order in education, beginning with the cultivation of the "active instincts of childhood" that were also the instincts of the human race in its stage of infancy (Wiggin 196). For these educators, a normal childhood recapitulated the evolutionary stages of human or "racial" history. The kindergarten's function was to serve, precisely, as a garden of children—a setting for the undisturbed evolution of the "nature of childhood" (Hespera 29). By allowing the child to observe and explore through tactile play, the non-interfering teacher or "child gardener" permitted the "harmonious development" of the child's nature "according to the laws of its being," without "hurrying forward to another stage before its present stage is completed" (Hespera 29).[9] This was the point at which Froebel's romantic educational philosophy connected up with an emerging science of normal child development, for what was gently inculcated through child's play in the kindergarten was nothing other than the newly discovered "nature" of childhood itself. In the kindergarten, the "healthy child" was supposed to discover for him- or herself, and manifest to the observant eye of the teacher, what were now conceived to be the normal developmental stages of "infant-nature" (Von Marenholtz-Burlow 62).[10]

The emphasis on the child's spontaneity and autonomy in this space for learning how to be a child "without any meddlesome middleman" suggests that the kindergarten was being conceived as another kind of Normal School, in which a process of standardization would be achieved, and the abnormal separated out from the normal, through the subtly directive and constraining effects of the norm.[11] As François Ewald explains, "[r]ather than being willed by anyone in particular" or "imposed from the outside," the norm is an essentially self-referential value; its apparent neutrality stems from the fact that it is "derived from those for whom it will serve as a standard" (154–55). A norm does not have to be imposed; its power as a form of regulation and stabilization requires only that it be exhibited and identified as an attribute that is characteristic of the given population. Thus, norms appear to derive spontaneously from those who, having internalized them as typical of their group, voluntarily re-enact them as part of their self-expression. For Ian Hunter, this is precisely the point of connection between the kindergarten playground and the English lesson in the history of liberal modes of governance in education. In the normalizing milieux of the playground and the literature lesson (once the latter was freed from the rote activities of memorization and parsing, and focused on the pupil's individual communion with the work), the unleashing of the pupil's originality and imagination became the very basis for the exhibition, assimilation, and subtle correction of behavioural norms. This pedagogy worked through a "double structure" in which, on the one hand, freedom and play were *necessary* if the child's self was to find expression in the school; on the other hand, it was the function of the school to "mould and shape this self in accordance with developmental norms that [were] supposedly those of life or, more scientifically, the psyche" (116).

Anne's famous need for what she calls "scope for the imagination" thus should be read in the context of a pedagogical strategy that combined freedom and self-expression with correction. This strategy was at the heart of a new approach to the teaching of English literature that was being promoted by progressive educators during the time that Montgomery attended Normal School and followed a course of literary studies at Dalhousie College in Halifax. The new approach was cast as a rejection of parsing and other exercises performed on the text as object, in favour of the student's far less closely directed, more open-ended engagement with the text as a conduit of feeling, spirit, or the "mental atmosphere which [the author] breathed" (qtd. in Robinson 510). If it was now the teacher's role to "watch and wait for the flashing eye and the glowing cheek that mark the electric contact of soul and soul," this new method only made English a more practical school subject—like physical culture, nature study, and manual training, directed toward the cultivation of a "vigorous, independent race of scholars" (Robinson 514, 510). In the consensus between idealistic kindergarten enthusiasts and more utilitarian advocates of prevocational education, there was no perceived contest between this kind of "applied English" and resolutely practical forms of hand-and-eye training. Reformers were agreed that if the goal of education was to fit children for the work of life through the harmonious development of hand, head, and heart, the "school day [should] be arranged less and less on subjects" and "more and more on occupations, projects and interests" (qtd. in Sutherland 200).[12]

Seton's *Two Little Savages* is a text that endeavours to manage those "occupations, projects and interests" in detail. While *Anne of Green Gables* provides the narrative representation of an adolescent girl's maturation as the effect of a practical education, Seton's *Two Little Savages* is not content to represent. The text does not simply narrativize its protagonist's immersion in nature, it also endeavours to engage the reader as a subject of forest games. Thus, whereas *Anne of Green Gables* relies for its effects on the reader's alternating identifications with the wildly imaginative Anne and a narrator who intervenes to put things into perspective, *Two Little Savages* uses a more direct form of address to urge the reader to imitate Yan and his forms of play. Indeed, for long stretches, narrative movement is almost minimal in Seton's voluminous, 552-page text, as forward momentum is subordinated to painstakingly detailed description and the provision of charts, diagrams, game pieces, owl-stuffing instructions, and teepee-cutting patterns. Doubling as a narrative and a do-it-yourself manual for outdoor play, the text strives to enlist the reader's participation in its protagonist's activities. If it was the role of literature within the new education to extend the "free self-activity" of kindergarten play into adolescence and even adulthood, *Two Little Savages* takes this utilitarian understanding of the connection between literature and play to the limit, proposing itself as a practical record of the tactile experiments and experiences of its young protagonist—a record so practical that it can guide the reader through the practice of these same activities.

Yan, as we are told at the beginning of the text, "never got over" the usual "keen interest in Indians and in wild life"; indeed, "as he grew older, he found a yet keener pleasure in storing up the little bits of woodcraft and Indian lore that pleased him as a boy" (19, 20). In town, Yan's attachment to these boyhood pleasures is punished by parents and teachers, but once he is unleashed from their disciplinary regime, he becomes the protagonist of a narrative that is about the forestalling of a certain kind of maturation and the making of a "natural" boy. As Gillian Brown has observed, the boys' play represented in children's fiction of the period tends to affirm Charles Dudley Warner's assertion that "[e]very boy who is good for something is a natural savage" (qtd. in Brown 91). Narratives of boyhood primitivism were informed by the same psychological theories of human development that encouraged turn-of-the-century educators to revive the Froebelian kindergarten as a scene of instinctual play. But they also drew on a more particular elaboration of normal male adolescent development as a recapitulation of the stages of human evolution that situated the adolescent boy at the stage of the "natural savage," driven by hunting, initiation, hero-worship, and gang instincts.[13] Although this was the natural condition of adolescent boyhood, some coaching through its various aspects was required: careful "habit-making was the method, the outdoors was the scene of operations" (MacDonald 133). Other youth movements, for which outdoor, fresh-air life was essential preparation for the defence of the Empire or the vanquishing of the frontier, drew upon the purported virtues of the Zulu warrior or the Indian brave, but did not establish these figures as adequate models of manhood (MacDonald 137). Seton's Woodcraft League was much more insistent in its appointment of the Indian as an ideal figure of "*all round development*," but the habits and aptitudes that the League endeavoured to cultivate in its members were modelled on received fantasies of Indianness (*Birch Bark* xxi).[14]

The Woodcraft League was a North American recreation movement that was designed to cultivate in youth a passionate curiosity about plant and animal life, as well as the practical skills necessary to survive in nature. "In the beginning," Seton writes in *The Birch Bark Roll of Woodcraft*, the handbook of the Woodcraft League of America, "Woodcraft was the only science known to man, because he lived in the woods, and there had to master the things of his everyday life" (3). In the modern world—where the practical knowledge and skills that this first scientist of the woods mastered are increasingly transferred to the factory—peoples and nations are losing the essential "power to do," which has been the key to national greatness and prosperity (115). *Two Little Savages* narrativizes Yan's equipment with this "power to do" once he is sent away to a farm and liberated to play Indian in the woods with his new companion, Sam Raften. But while their practical doings are very often activities such as deer hunting and moccasin-making, what *Two Little Savages* really stages is an Indianness without Indians. The boys' desire to be authentic Indians is often a source of ironic humour as the narrator underlines the performative element of their camp play and the constant improvisation with makeshift substitutes that is necessary to carry off their games. Even when the text lays out explicit and detailed instructions for sacred fire-making or "Injun medicine men" owl-stuffing, Native people do not figure as teachers or authority figures (401). It is chiefly the old trapper, Caleb, married to a "squaw" in earlier days, who mediates Native knowledge and practices for the boys (371). The feminized Asian, Sin Lee (who would, as one of the boys comments, "make a better squaw than both of them" [372]), also helps them to stitch their wigwam and instructs them in the art of owl-stuffing. It might be possible to argue that the Woodcraft expertise that the boys accumulate is a makeshift product of cross-cultural *bricolage*, but it is rather more tempting to read the owl-stuffing episode as a metaphor for the process of Indian re-enactment that the text as a whole promotes, one that seems, in the end, to amount to an ethno-cultural taxidermy. Native people appear only very briefly in the narrative—for the space of a single page—and even this appearance seems to be strikingly inconsequential: on a long trek, Yan happens upon a camp, has no trouble communicating with its inhabitants, and is soon on his way again after receiving a gift of deer tongue from the chief. Following this transaction, the narrator comments, the Indians "did not take further interest" in Yan, but it would seem to be Yan, rather, who takes no further interest in them (520).

Native characters are thus relegated to the distant background of *Two Little Savages,* as Seton's narrativization of his "man-making scheme with a blue sky background" self-consciously calls upon a much more familiar store of highly mediated representations of Indianness. But it is not enough to observe the marginalization of historical Native people in Seton's narrative of boys playing Indian, for there is a further irony to this picture. The program for practical education and "*all round development*" that Yan and Sam enact in the process of their play actually owes much to the ambitious project of Indian education that was implemented in Canada 20 years earlier, when industrial boarding schools were established with the goal of effecting a radical transformation of Indian character that would equip youths to compete with Euro-Canadians as farmers or skilled workers. The historian J.R. Miller suggests that this project to provide Native youths with a practical education can be viewed as relatively optimistic, in contrast to later schemes. However self-serving the project may seem to us today, policy-makers of the 1880s believed in the possibility of a thorough economic and cultural assimilation of Native people in schools that would be devoted to moral development and vocational training. In contrast, by the time that Seton was writing *Two Little Savages,* the federal minister responsible for Indian Affairs expressed a widely held view when he insisted on the impracticability of ambitious industrial schooling for Native children, as "the Indian cannot go out from school, making his own way and compete with the white man," because he is without the "physical, mental or moral get-up" (Clifford Sifton, qtd. in Miller 135).

Thus, just when schemes for the practical education of the whole child were being introduced to provincial education systems and the principles of agricultural and industrial education were moving into the mainstream of public education—as they were being discussed in educational journals and promoted in the demonstration schools of the MacDonald-Robertson reform movement in the first decade of the twentieth century—they were being discredited and dismantled at the level of federally administered Indian education. The education of the Native child was being downgraded, at this moment, to unpaid labour in a custodial institution. What practical education was to mean for the Native child separated from his or her parents and enclosed in a residential school was simply the half of every day spent outside of the classroom, performing the routine chores necessary to the upkeep of the institution. Seton's *Two Little Savages* thus demonstrates the healthful effects of forest games on a Euro-Canadian boy at the very historical moment when, in a movement in the opposite direction, Native children were being gathered up into residential schools that no longer even had the old mandate to develop the potential of the Indian through assimilation. As politically suspect as the "progressivism" of the earlier campaign had been, it was now seen as impractical: the Indian child was beyond the pale of enculturation and, in any case, was not worth the expense.

The migration into the educational mainstream of the practical education that was at first reserved for society's marginal elements was explicitly recommended by Canadian educators like Thomas Bengough, whose 1902 text, *Learning How to Do and Learning by Doing,* reports on his visits to two American institutions for the "betterment of deficient human material" through industrial and agricultural training (Bengough 61, 4). Virginia's Hampton Normal and Agricultural Institute (for the education of Black and Native children and the training of the successful graduate "to work with and for his people" [64]) inspires Bengough to cite the pronouncement that "the finest, soundest and most effective educational methods in use in the United States are to be found in certain schools for negroes and Indians, and in others for young criminals in reformatory prisons" (qtd. in Bengough 61). By generalizing the educational model designed for the purposes of moral rehabilitation and enforced enculturation, public schools might provide pupils with a "practical capacity in common things" that would provide a sounder basis for their entry into the "social and industrial commonwealth" (qtd. in Bengough 61). Seton's account of his inspiration for the Woodcraft League suggests a similar beginning in ideas about correctional programs for marginal elements and, more specifically, the preventative function of regulated recreational activity. The idea of inculcating a taste for nature and all things "Indian" in youths as a basis for wholesome recreational activity is reported to have occurred to him when he encountered a gang of young vandals on his property and was prompted to wonder how they might be steered away from lives of criminality (MacDonald 139). It is not surprising, then, that Seton's prefatory comments in *The Birch Bark Roll of Woodcraft* advertise the benefits of Woodcraft in terms of a source of pleasure and recreation that pre-empts the degeneration of the "play instinct" into "wrong methods of amusement" (xvi–xvii).

In *Two Little Savages,* it is only when Yan is allowed to escape into nature to pursue the "tastes which incline him to wildlife" and act on his "inborn impulse to up and away," that his apparently troublesome independence is turned into a capacity for object lessons and practical experiments in the woods (26). In the text's narrative trajectory of progressive liberation, Yan moves from the corporal punishments of his own family, to the warmth and lenience of the Raften farm family, to, finally, independent play in the woods. Although there are no parents in sight at the end of this trajectory, its terminal point is the Froebelian program of pedagogical play in which the rules and protocols are established by adults from a distance. Indeed, Yan's notion of play is at times suspiciously close to school work—especially in the eyes of his companions, who are less interested in the mathematical and geometrical problems that Yan calls "White-man's Woodcraft" because they can see that "it looked 'too much like school'" (507). Yan tries to get Sam to help him build a dam by suggesting that they pretend to be beavers ("'Now, wasn't it worth it?' asked Yan, who had had much difficulty in keeping Sam steadily at play that looked so very much like work" [192]). Together, the boys also spontaneously design their own motivational exercises—a set of competitive games and an accompanying reward system, which together operate as an inducement to "play Injun properly" (304).

There may be no parents in sight in Seton's picture of pedagogical play, but the play cannot seem to proceed after a certain point without the frequent visits and assistance of a surrogate-parent, the old trapper Caleb, whom the boys adopt as their make-believe Medicine Man, a consultant on the details of camping and Indian habits (461). Another boyish adult who wants to participate in the make-believe Indian camp but comes close to supervising it instead is the Irishman William Raften, the "warm-hearted happy-looking" foil to Yan's own father, and a man who is "a good deal of a boy at heart" (108, 254). Through Raften, Seton's text depicts a form of fatherhood to match the new pedagogy's emphasis on the importance of respecting children's pleasures and investments and building on these as a means of socialization. It is thus Raften who urges the two boys to extend their daytime excursions into the woods to setting up a camp: "That's what I'd do if I was a boy playin' Injun; I'd go right in an' play," he counsels (251). Raften furthermore establishes the rules of the boys' camp ("no snakin' home nights to sleep. Ye can't hev no matches an' no gun"), rules that the boys subsequently enforce among themselves (252). Thus, the boys' play in *Two Little Savages* cannot help but reveal that it is being stage-managed, that play's games and objects are those with which adults wish children to be preoccupied, for their own good and for the good of a nation that requires citizens equipped with the "power to do."[15]

*

For Seton, play was the most potent of instincts or "inherited habits of the race, a weapon and a force of invincible power" that dominated the child in his/her formative years and, when properly cultivated in youth, assured the adult a capacity to recreate wholesomely through pleasure "in the things of the imagination and the beauties of nature" (*Birch Bark* xv, xiv). In his prefatory comments to *The Birch Bark Roll of Woodcraft*, Seton carefully distinguishes his model for outdoor recreation from that of other youth organizations (notably the Boy Scouts) by insisting that Woodcraft lays the groundwork for "avocation," not vocation, that is to say, for the worker's happily independent pursuit of regenerative, health-sustaining recreational activities in his/her free time. Whereas other organizations attempt to steer children toward particular forms of work or merely aim to be "feeders for the army, . . . adding the color of adventure to reconcile the rank and file to irksome duties," Woodcraft concerns itself with the harmonious and fully rounded development of the whole person, especially in his/her capacity to find meaning and contentment in "the daily life" (xiii, 115).

This problematization of free time, recreational capacity, and everyday contentment as arenas of life that require some form of government connects Seton's educational program to an important shift in normative conceptions of subjectivity and citizenship in early twentieth-century Britain and North America. This shift saw the nineteenth-century ideal of moral character, with its emphasis on work, discipline, self-mastery, and conformity, being displaced by the emergent ideal of personality, organized around the development of individuality and the quest for a unique self (White and Hunt 95). In *Two Little Savages*, the results of character-building are figured in the person of Yan's older brother, who is described as "plucky and persevering, but . . . cold and hard"; although "religious, and strictly proper in his life and speech," he is Yan's inferior at school, and is capable of bragging that he has "no enthusiasms" (28). In contrast, Yan himself is "full of warmth, enthusiasm, earnestness and energy, but [possesses] a most passionate and ungovernable temper," which leads him to have "strange, uncertain outbreaks of disrespect for his teachers" (31, 82).

It is partly in the imaginative and independent child's "outbreaks of disrespect" for the teacher inclined to brutal forms of punishment that *Two Little Savages* enunciates its critique of character-building, but the text also denounces character-building in the context of the family. Thus, beating, "stern, religious training," the father's "unwise command [to Yan] to give up what was his nature," the mother's mere affectation of an interest in his pursuits—all of these techniques are shown to produce at best "cold and hard" individuals bereft of enthusiasms and at worst the pale, sickly, and "heart-hungry" version of Yan at 14 that his family sends away to labour on a farm (535, 20). But even the childhood of "personality" into which Yan is liberated from that point on turns out to be governed by adults—not just in the narrow sense that Yan and Sam's make-believe Indian camp is supervised from a distance, but also in the more general sense that Yan's trajectory of liberation follows the double structure of the new pedagogy. This pedagogy freed the child to engage in uninhibited play and self-expression in a regulated space, but by this very means, exposed the child's "infant-nature" to observation and gentle direction. At the end of the summer of wholesome forest games, therefore, Yan comes around to acknowledging his "binding duty" to obey his parents all on his own, as he realizes that he "could not rebel if he would." Resolving to compromise with his father's expectation that he "go as errand boy at the first opening," Yan decides that after another year in farm country he will "go back—be errand boy or anything to make a living, but in his hours of freedom . . . keep a little kingdom of his own," the "kingdom of the Birds and Beasts and the power to comprehend them" (535).

In fact, the rebellion and the embrace of duty become one and the same thing, because Yan's revenge against his father will consist in his secret knowledge that his father had unwittingly provided him with the "largest opportunity of his life," by sending him to the country as a punishment (534, 535). Yan's determination to preserve the memory of his woodland life in the future and to refuse to flinch as he pursues his dream of becoming a naturalist—though the "road to it might lie through the cellar of a grocer's shop"—thus nicely coordinates a rebellious independence with obedience to a father's wishes (536). Even the narrator's assurance that Yan is not giving up his determination to become a naturalist is not enough to quell our sense that the ultimate place for woodcraft games is *memory*, and that freedom—shrunken in future to the hours allotted for recreation—will consist in the nostalgic recollection of these years of play in the "kingdom of the Birds and Beasts."

At the end of *Two Little Savages*, therefore, Yan voluntarily assumes an adult perspective on the childhood pleasures of discovery, observation, and adventure in nature: he assumes the nostalgic investment in these pleasures that has in fact pervaded the narration of the text as a whole. Earlier on, the narrative has already demonstrated the function of the memory of childhood pleasures as an instrument of homo-social national bonding, when a forest adventure culminates in the boys assisting in bringing about the reconciliation of two old-time woodcrafters. "Oh, the magic of the campfire!" Seton's narrator exclaims at the end of this reconciliation: "No unkind feeling long withstands its glow. For men to meet at the same campfire is to come closer, to have a better understanding of each other, and to lay the foundations of a lasting friendship. 'He and I camped together once!' is enough to explain all cordiality between the men most wide apart, and Woodcraft days are days of memories happy, bright and lifelong" (489). The narrator's rapturous comments at the end of this episode build on the text's construction of enthusiastic masculine citizenship as a lasting fascination with the nation's natural order. What they do not acknowledge is the fact that the reconciliation of these "men most wide apart" has been achieved through their vanquishing (with the help of Yan and Sam) of common enemies—the capture of a criminal tramp and the ejection from the community of a set of "dirty paupers" (494). Thus, the circle of campfire affect that binds these lovers of nature also maps a division between the normal and the abnormal, the vigorous citizen and the unsavoury vagrant.

In *Anne of Green Gables*, as in *Two Little Savages*, the child quarantined from the influence of her birth family is a figure of normativity rather than marginality. The double structure of the new pedagogy is enacted in a narrative in which the protagonist's seemingly irrepressible originality and imagination become the very basis for her training as a particular kind of social agent. In the end, the education that allows for the unrepressed flourishing of Anne's "natural" disposition leads her to make the decision to remain at Green Gables as Marilla's faithful caregiver, and to embrace the properly feminine "joys of sincere work[,] worthy aspiration and congenial friendship" in lieu of taking up a scholarship and going away to college (396). In order to allow Anne to become the sort of womanly girl who would make such a sacrificial choice, Montgomery has had to close down the story's extra-generic excursions into the genre of the boy's adventure story, and to orchestrate a scene of heterosexualization in which only a near death-by-drowning in the midst of the performance of a Victorian poem of feminine tragedy is enough to bring Anne around to the "odd, newly awakened" idea that the "half-shy, half-eager expression in Gilbert's hazel eyes was something that was very good to see" (288).[16]

Prior to this point, Anne's imaginative play has consisted of a number of "queer enterprises," to borrow a term from Gillian Brown, in which Anne is allowed to be free like a boy—that is to say, "free to act without [her] actions having predictable consequences," free like the boy whose pleasures are supposed to represent the "radical distance and difference of childhood" (Brown 98). Anne insists on walking the ridge-pole of a roof in order to defend her honour against a dare; later on, she stops "in ecstasy" while reciting Scott's "Marmion," picturing herself as a heroic soldier (292). Some of her other pastimes might seem closer to Brown's description of girl's play as a rehearsal for a pre-programmed domestic future, but Anne's failures at feminine household practices are quite spectacular, and even her construction of a playhouse with her friend Diana at Idlewild, the girls' romantically named hill-grove retreat, is too coloured by their rapturous intimacy to count as the prefiguration of normal housekeeping.

Hence the extremity of the narrative curve—or, as the chapter is entitled, "The Bend in the Road"—that brings Anne to the place of a dutiful daughter at the end of the story. Anne insists on her free choice of this narrowed horizon—"you can't prevent me," she tells Marilla, "I'm sixteen and a half [and] obstinate as a mule" (391)—in a way that only underlines the success of an education that has equipped her to internalize norms of conduct as the expressions of her own free will. The ambivalence of this ending is registered in Marilla's "queer sorrowful sense of loss" upon discovering that the "child she had learned to love had vanished somehow and here was this tall, serious-eyed girl of fifteen, with the thoughtful brows and the proudly posed little head, in her place" (324).[17] In Marilla's sense of loss, the novel seems to acknowledge that spontaneous child's play has, after all and in retrospect, been something quite different: a training for normal adulthood.

ACKNOWLEDGEMENTS

This essay was written with the support of a postdoctoral fellowship from the Social Sciences and Humanities Research Council of Canada.

NOTES

1. It was in the 1890s that the critique of congregate, institutionalized childcare was first put forward by an emerging cadre of child welfare professionals in Canada. Reflecting developments in educational theory and child psychology, they argued that institutionalization only produced unhealthily submissive and dependent children—"precise, well disciplined inmates," fit only for early exploitation (Rooke and Schnell 202).

2. The Prince Edward Island Children's Aid Society, it is worth noting, was founded in 1901—one year after the publication of *Anne of Green Gables*. For a novel that mounts its critique of orphan asylums in the rhetoric of the campaign against cruelty to animals, see Marshall Saunders' popular 1901 orphan narrative, *'Tilda Jane*. The most damning evidence that the novel can offer against the asylum is (in Tilda Jane's words) that it "ain't a place for children what likes animiles" (138).

3. On the history of the MacDonald-Robertson movement (1900–1913) and its establishment of a series of demonstration schools to promote the introduction of nature study, manual training, and domestic science, see Sutherland.

4. I am borrowing the term "nation-tinged childhood" from Berlant 45.
5. A nation's politics, as Robert Coles has astutely observed, constitute the parameters of a child's everyday psychology (qtd. in Stephens 3).
6. For a brief history of teacher training in Canada, see Phillips 571–92. Prince Edward Island had been at the forefront of educational reforms in Canada from the mid-nineteenth century (Gammel and Dutton 108). By 1913, it was one of the provinces that had institutionalized the goals of practical, agricultural education: it had implemented bonuses for teachers who developed school gardens and provided agricultural instruction, and introduced a summer school in agricultural education at Prince of Wales College in Charlottetown—where Montgomery earned her first-class teacher's licence in 1894 (Sutherland 188). During her year of teacher training at Prince of Wales College and what was then its affiliated Normal School, Francis Bolger reports, Montgomery "led her year in English drama, English literature, Agriculture and School Management" (139).
7. Even in 1879, in order to obtain a first-class teaching licence, one required a certificate from the Normal School principal testifying that one had paid attention to one's duties and was morally fit to proceed to the qualifying examinations. See "Contributors' Department," *Canada Educational Monthly and School Chronicle.*
8. As one historian of moral regulation in nineteenth-century schooling has argued, the alliance that was forged between women teachers and the state called upon a melodrama of sexual danger, which allowed both the publicly funded school and the new female teacher to purchase respectability through claims to an essential womanly instinct for drawing lines of decorum in the classroom. See Theobald.
9. Toronto was in fact the second city in the world to make the kindergarten a part of its regular school system (Phillips 422). The chief exponent of the educational doctrines of Froebel in Canada was James L. Hughes, inspector of public schools in Toronto from 1874 to 1914.
10. In the last decade of the nineteenth century, the details of these stages were articulated by the Child Study movement, which set out to identify the "periods and aspects of child life" against a backdrop of anxieties about national efficiency and race degeneration (qtd. in Hendrick 48). Composed of teachers, middle-class parents, and "scientific" experts such as doctors and psychologists, the Child Study movement applied the techniques of natural history to the study of children and succeeded in diffusing a view of the child as a creature that passed through distinct stages of mental development (Hendrick 48–49).
11. The kindergarten is regularly described in the educational literature by means of circular constructions: "The free activity of childhood is . . . the natural means for developing a child"; "What is our first index to a child's nature?—Evidently, its manifestations . . . we must seek in the child's play" (Von Marenholtz-

Burlow 62). This circularity is not so much a logical fallacy as the badge of a "scientific" reasoning that claims that the norms of healthy childhood, rather than being imposed arbitrarily from the outside, are exhibited by the children themselves.

12. Sutherland is citing the report of the 1910 Royal Commission on Industrial Training and Technical Education in Canada.

13. The "expert" statement of the theory of recapitulation was provided by the American psychologist, G. Stanley Hall, in his late nineteenth-century essays on child development and especially in his book, *Adolescence* (1904). Hall's theory was disseminated in a more popular form in William B. Forbush's *The Boy Problem* (1901), which sounded the race degeneration alarm in relation to the urban working-class boy who was held back from instinctual re-enactment of the "Race Life" (qtd. in MacDonald 133). Forbush praised Seton's Woodcraft movement as an "orderly endeavour to systematize and direct that fever for 'playing Indian'" so widespread among adolescent boys who "are nearly primitive man [*sic*]" (qtd. in MacDonald 141).

14. In the "Health" section of *The Birch Bark Roll of Woodcraft*, the reader is counselled "Don't Turn Out Your Toes Too Much" and enticed with the heading, "The Keen Eyes of the Indian. Do You Wish to Have Them?" (124).

15. The other interfering adult is of course Seton's narrator, who intervenes to correct the boys' exaggerations and miscalculations, and to point the reader to the sketches and diagrams that accompany the narrative.

16. Anne and her friends are "playing Elaine" (288)—staging a dramatization of the plot of Tennyson's poem, "Lancelot and Elaine" from *Idylls of the King*, with Anne as Elaine, floating down the river on her gloriously maudlin death-barge—when she finds herself forced to accept the chivalrous assistance of her nemesis, Gilbert Blyth.

17. Montgomery's use of the word "queer" to mean something like "not of the family" underlines her sense of the imaginative, unconventional aspect of the orphan, a special apartness that her narrators seem to cherish, even as the stories they tell move inexorably toward the rectification of this difference in formulaic conclusions, which turn on surprise discoveries of relatives and unlikely conversions of decidedly un-maternal, "gaunt and grey haired" women into sentimental figures of "mother-love" (*Akin to Anne* 40).

WORKS CITED

Allen, N. "The Education of Girls, as Connected with Their Growth and Physical Development." *Canada Educational Monthly and School Chronicle* 1.9 (Sept. 1879): 413–20.

Bengough, Thomas. *Learning How to Do and Learning by Doing.* Toronto: L.K. Cameron, 1902.

Benzaquen, Adriana. "On Childhood, Wildness, and Freedom." *Childhood.* Ed. Christina Ritchie and Jacob Wren. Spec. issue of *Public* 21 (2001): 33–41.

Berlant, Lauren. *The Queen of America Goes to Washington City: Essays on Race, Sex, and Citizenship*. Durham: Duke UP, 1997.

Bolger, Francis. *The Years Before "Anne."* Charlottetown: Prince Edward Island Heritage Foundation, 1974.

Brodhead, Richard. "Sparing the Rod: Discipline and Fiction in Antebellum America." *Representations* 21 (1988): 67–96.

Brown, Gillian. "Child's Play." *differences* 11.3 (1999/2000): 76–105.

"Contributors' Department." *Canada Educational Monthly and School Chronicle* 1.3 (Mar. 1879): 167.

"Education." *Canada Educational Monthly and School Chronicle* 2.12 (Dec. 1879): 629.

Ewald, François. "Norms, Discipline, and the Law." *Representations* 30 (1990): 138–61.

Gammel, Irene, and Ann Dutton. "Disciplining Development: L.M. Montgomery and Early Schooling." *L.M. Montgomery and Canadian Culture.* Eds. Irene Gammel and Elizabeth Epperly. Toronto: U of Toronto P, 1999. 106–19.

Gundry, A.W. "First Principles of Education." *Canada Educational Monthly and School Chronicle* 1.1 (Jan. 1879): 24–30; 1.2 (Feb. 1879): 77–82.

Hendrick, Harry. "Constructions and Reconstructions of British Childhood: An Interpretative Survey, 1800 to the Present." *Constructing and Reconstructing Childhood: Contemporary Issues in the Sociological Study of Childhood.* Ed. Allison James and Alan Prout. London: Falmer, 1997. 34–62.

Hespera. "The Kindergarten." *Educational Weekly* [Toronto] 1.1 (Jan. 1885): 13; 1.2 (Jan. 1885): 29.

Hunter, Ian. *Culture and Government: The Emergence of Literary Education.* Houndmills, UK: MacMillan, 1988.

Huntington, Rev. H.D. "Unconscious Tuition." *Canada Educational Monthly and School Chronicle* 2.11 (May–June 1879): 265–68.

MacDonald, Robert H. *Sons of the Empire: The Frontier and the Boy Scout Movement.* Toronto: U of Toronto P, 1993.

McAllister, Samuel. "The Aims of Our Public School System." *Canada Educational Monthly and School Chronicle* 1.2 (Feb. 1879): 90–97.

———. "The Teacher's Deportment in the School-Room." *Canada Educational Monthly and School Chronicle* 1.10 (Oct. 1879): 530–32.

Miller, J.R. *Shingwauk's Vision: A History of Native Residential Schools*. Toronto: U of Toronto P, 1996.

Mills, T.M. "Some Thoughts on School Hygiene." *Canada Educational Monthly and School Chronicle* 1.1 (Jan. 1879): 14–19.

Montgomery, L.M. *Akin to Anne: Tales of Other Orphans*. Ed. Rea Wilmshurst. Toronto: McClelland, 1988.

———. *Anne of Green Gables*. 1908. Toronto: Ryerson, 1942.

Phillips, Charles E. *The Development of Education in Canada*. Toronto: Gage, 1957.

Robinson, Geo. "English Literature in Canadian Schools." *Canada Educational Monthly and School Chronicle* 1.10 (Oct. 1879): 507–14.

Rooke, Patricia T., and R.L. Schnell. *Discarding the Asylum: From Child Rescue to the Welfare State in English-Canada, 1800–1950*. Lanham, NY: UP of America, 1983.

Rose, Jacqueline. *The Case of Peter Pan, or The Impossibility of Children's Fiction*. Philadelphia: U of Pennsylvania P, 1992.

Salisbury, Albert. *School Management: A Text-Book for County Training Schools and Normal Schools*. Toronto: Educational Book Company, 1912.

Saunders, Marshall. *'Tilda Jane: An Orphan in Search of a Home*. Boston: Page, 1901.

Seath, John. "The Training of First-Class Teachers." *Canada Educational Monthly and School Chronicle* 1.1 (Jan. 1879): 19–24.

Seton, Ernest Thompson. *The Birch Bark Roll of Woodcraft*. 1902. New York: Brieger, 1925.

———. *Two Little Savages: Being the Adventures of Two Boys Who Lived as Indians and What They Learned*. New York: Grosset & Dunlap, 1903.

Stephens, Sharon. "Children and the Politics of Culture in 'Late Capitalism.'" *Children and the Politics of Culture*. Ed. Sharon Stephens. Princeton: Princeton UP, 1995. 3–48.

Sutherland, Neil. *Children in English-Canadian Society: Framing the Twentieth-Century Consensus*. Toronto: U of Toronto P, 1976.

Theobald, Marjorie. "Moral Regulation and the Nineteenth-Century 'Lady Teacher.'" *Discipline, Moral Regulation, and Schooling: A Social History*. Ed. Kate Rousmaniere, et al. New York: Garland, 1997. 161–82.

Von Marenholtz-Burlow, Baroness. "The Importance of Children's Play." *Educational Weekly* [Toronto] 1.4 (1885): 61–62; 1.5 (1885): 77; 1.8 (1885): 125; 1.9 (1885): 141.

White, Melanie, and Alan Hunt. "Citizenship: Care of the Self, Character, and Personality." *Citizenship Studies* 4.2 (2000): 93–116.

Wiggin, Kate Douglas. *Children's Rights: A Book of Nursery Logic*. Cambridge, MA: Riverside, 1892.

Cornering the Triangle: Understanding the "Dominion-itive" Role of the Realistic Animal Tale in Early Twentieth-Century Canadian Children's Literature

KATHLEEN MARIE CONNOR

Introduction

Postcolonial concerns are important to understanding the place of children's literature in pedagogical and extracurricular pursuits. Peter Hulme has described "the classic colonial triangle . . . [as] the relationship between European, native and land" (qtd. in Bradford 196). In his view, territories, culture, and world-views are appropriated once certain tropes of superiority and dominion over "others" have been established by colonizers. It would be naive not to recognize that realistic animal tales for children were part of the discursive practice of colonialism in Canada's history. These tales cohere around colonial constructs of dominion, had a significant role in the civilizing or taming of European and British settler children, and can be studied as both literary and cultural artifacts.

The popular early twentieth-century children's stories of Ernest Thompson Seton, who produced many acclaimed realistic animal tales that received wide circulation in the early 1900s (Waterson 97–98), were avidly consumed by several generations, and continue to this day to be enjoyed by readers. My project in examining these realistic animal tales in children's literature is to discover the colonialist and postcolonial themes embedded in narratives that are ostensibly delightful and enthralling tales of the animal kingdom A case may be made that Seton, as part of an early nationalist experiment in writing for children, employed the arts of the storyteller with the insights of the pedagogue in the employ of the Dominion of Canada. Whether justifying historical events by showing the "natural law" of dominion in the wild, or plotting to gain mastery within and over the landscape, this genre of writing was not mere innocent pleasure, nor was it vacant of colonialist intent.

Deconstructing Worlds: Children's Literature and Postcolonial Pedagogy

What is lacking in the contemporary public-school classroom is a means to use extant literature in working toward anti-colonialist understandings. An effective pedagogical intervention would encourage a discourse that recognizes situatedness on the ground—that is, where we've been, where we are, and where we're going—and would present children with a means to assess the history of colonialism and its continuation in processes of neo-colonialism and global transnational capitalism. Peter McLaren states that "Post-colonial pedagogy . . . is a pedagogy for anti-imperialism which challenges the very categories through which the history of the colonized has been written" (228). Although young readers in the classroom are exposed to the narrative act and questioned about the sequence of events and literal meaning, they are rarely asked to explore the "actual functioning of the language" in the "fictive worlds" constructed by writers (Hutcheon 30)—nor do they consider these worlds as co-constructed by the writer and the reader.

Young readers are perfectly capable of being guided toward understanding colonialist mindsets through analysis of the "internalized grammar or code" of genres (Hutcheon 30)—in Seton's case, realistic nature/animal stories. In my observations of student-teacher projects in a course teaching approaches to reading for elementary-school students, the main interests of the teachers-in-training were the aesthetics of picture books, how stories helped children in their daily personal relationships, and narrative progression. Only poetry was analyzed for how it worked, not merely what it said. It seems a rather chauvinistic oversight to keep children from deeper literary understandings of the novels and stories they invest time in. Stories—written, spoken, and cinematic—are the primary means by which children learn of their world and their place in it. An early acquisition of the tools to read between the lines can aid in producing critical thinkers for the postmodern and globalized world.

> The absence of children's literature from an understanding of the degree to which power is played out in the socially constructed interactions with language devalues and silences children as readers, divorcing their experience of text from the awareness of the nature of fiction from which notions of literary pleasure derive. Excluding children's literature from the map of a theory of literature constructed in the academic mainstream enforces these silences, by attempting to redefine a literary discourse without acknowledging the relevance of these formative experiences. (Thacker, "Feminine" 4)

Children's literature and its reception have been marginalized in mainstream academic discourse, a fact which has been examined by several scholars in the field of children's literature and childhood studies. Mary Galbraith examines this problem in her article "Hear My Cry: A Manifesto for an Emancipatory Childhood Studies Approach to Literature." Part of her argument is that the link between adult and childhood experiences and relations must be explored despite the supposed gap:

> In fact, controversy has been raised over whether there can be any adult experiential access to this subject position. At the same time, it is fairly uncontroversial to say that our own undergoing, from the child position, of the meeting between childhood and adulthood determines how each of us experiences existence, freedom, belonging, and possibility throughout life. Therefore, childhood studies is in some sense a conceptual trunk linking all other critical and emancipatory human studies, but a trunk not easily perceived through its surrounding branches. (188)

Deborah Thacker also observes how children are marginalized within mainstream literary studies, and broadly asserts that children's literature is ignored by theoreticians who either reluctantly or never refer to children's literature ("Disdain").

Seton and the Realistic Animal Tale Genre

Ernest Thompson Seton was born into a Scots-English settler family that immigrated to Ontario, Canada, after his father lost his fortune as a ship-owner. From a young age, Seton was attracted to art, and he attended the Royal Academy of Art in London. Upon his return to Canada, he moved to Manitoba where he was able to immerse himself in natural history. In 1883 he began to visit and correspond with various naturalists, ornithologists, and writers in the United States, and became an established wildlife artist. His first animal story, "Lobo, Rag, and Vixen," was published in *Scribner's School Book* in 1899. Later stories appeared in the 1899 and 1900 *Wild Animals I Have Known* books with Seton's illustrations.

Wild Animals I Have Known is probably Seton's best-known and most widely disseminated collection of nature stories for children, and it has been republished into the latter half of the twentieth century. He is also known in Canadian children's literature for his *Two Little Savages: Being the Adventures of Two Boys Who Lived as Indians and What They Learned*, first published in 1903. Seton gained wide acclaim as a naturalist and educator for youth, and his ideas were adopted by the Boy Scouts of America movement. Seton was also responsible for the inception of The Woodcraft League of America. A brief article in *National Wildlife* entitled "A Man ahead of His Time" portrays him as supremely absorbed by and dedicated to his craft, for "He prided himself on the biological accuracy of his writing and drew on his own experiences. He had observed wolves in New Mexico and had even buried himself in a Yellowstone National Park garbage dump to get a close look at bears" (Darland 1).

Why did Seton choose animals as the main actors in his stories for children? One obvious answer is that he wrote, as he drew, what he knew. On a broader level, why were animals, the "four-footed friends" and the denizens of air and water, of such compelling interest in children's tales, and considered to be appropriate characters to appear in stories for youth of the recently established nation?

Settler colonies are part of the historical, political, and social phenomena of colonization, and involve "the displacement of native populations and the inculcation of a European worldview on them" (Yew 1). As well, settler colonies have the self-appointed task of defining and maintaining suitable enculturation devices to continue the colonial order. Enlisting the native animals of the new territory provided lessons on how to know and master the lands constituting the Canadian dominion. In creating an imaginative world for children of the normative educated, bourgeois upper and middle classes of turn-of-the-century Canada, and likely intended to be transmitted to all sub-colonies within the nation, stories such as those written by Seton constructed a means to simultaneously order and civilize notions of the land, while laying claim to and establishing dominion from coast to coast.

The stories in *Wild Animals I Have Known* are a living colonial artifact in the sense that they were read by readers from 1898, the time of initial publication, and continue to be read today. They are compiled in an easily accessible Dover Publications paperback (2000), and are on library and children's bookshelves throughout North America in various other printings. This accessibility and the instant accessibility on-line of the text of "The Snow Shoe Rabbit," another Seton story, are manifestations of the continuing status of classic children's stories, often available in updated formats. Understanding the popularity of books and stories read in the past and which continue to be read today has often been "explained" under the rubric of studies of classic children's works. However, a postcolonialist framework, in conjunction with a cultural studies approach, particularly as articulated by Richard Johnson and others (Storey 1–13), also holds promise for new insights and new opportunities in the classroom. In the case of Seton's *Wild Animals I Have Known*, tales of nature can be explored in terms of their message to both young colonial lords and ladies and present-day readers.[1]

Two Cases of Seton's Tales: "Raggylug, the Story of a Cottontail Rabbit" and "Redruff, the Story of the Don Valley Partridge"

To read Seton's "true" stories, for his animal characters were all "real" (see his "Note to the Reader" in *Wild Animals*), is to enter the world of an artist-observer who chronicled the changing and disappearing natural habitats of Canada. "Raggylug, the Story of a Cottontail Rabbit" is a story of the training and survival of a young cottontail rabbit. The perils of the young rabbit's life are documented and a theme of mother-love, the love and protection of Raggylug's mother, Molly, runs throughout the tale. In the end, Raggylug's survival is effected by Molly's sacrifice of her own life to save her son. Thus, the story ends tragically, but realistically, as the balance of nature pivots upon life and death. Redruff, the Don Valley Partridge, "really lived in the Don Valley north of Toronto, and many of my companions will remember him. He was killed in 1889, between the Sugar Loaf and Castle Frank" ("Note to Reader" 11), by a man Seton called "Cuddy" who was intent on killing all the game in his vicinity. Redruff was symbolic of the disappearance of a race once extant in the Don Valley, and Seton chronicled every event of his hard-won survival and eventual demise at the hands of a ruthless colonial power. Clearly, Seton's sympathies were with the noble animals who were once the original denizens of Canada's wild.

If Seton's two stories, "Raggylug" and "Redruff," are examined in terms of the theory of narrative exchange discussed by Jack Zipes (136–40), it can be proposed that Seton's gifts to readers were the insights of his years of observation and drawing animals in the wild. Readers were to reciprocate with unequivocal sympathy for, and identification with, the noble animals he brought to life in the pages of *Wild Animals I Have Known*. The animals were to be appreciated and mourned as corporeal evidence of the vanished paradises that once were "Oliphant's Swamp" (in "Raggylug") and the Don Valley (in "Redruff"). Thus, lessons were drawn up for the youth of the Dominion of Canada that, although a way of life must disappear, as the cost of progress, one may still feel emotions of regret and nostalgia. Lessons of moral indebtedness and justification of conquest were thus embedded within the stories.

In "Raggylug, the Story of a Cottontail Rabbit," the narrator poses as the guide leading the way through nature. The story begins with a declaration of realism: "Those who do not know the animals well may think I have humanized them, but those who have lived so near them as to know somewhat of their ways and their minds will not think so." He further validates his observation, making of himself a broker of animal customs, an anthropologist of the rabbit realm: "Truly rabbits have no speech as we understand it, but they have a way of conveying ideas by a system of sounds, signs, scents, whisker touches, movements, and example that answers the purpose of speech; and it must be remembered that though in telling this story I freely translate from rabbit into English, *I repeat nothing that they did not say*" (72–73). The reader cannot help but be intrigued and thus drawn into the narrative of what life was really like in the real natural realm of Raggylug and other animal denizens of the swamp.

The world recreated by Seton is at once familiar to those who have gone out to natural sites, and simultaneously unfamiliar, for Seton's observations take the reader-initiate on a guided tour below the surface of observations to the emotions and tensions of the animal realm: "After a while he [Raggylug] heard a strange rustling of the leaves in the near thicket. It was an odd, continuous sound, and though it went this way and that way and came ever nearer, there was no patter of feet with it" (73). This is a description of the baby bunny Raggylug's first experience with a snake, an almost fatal encounter mediated by the bunny's vigilant mother Molly: "No longer a shy, helpless little Molly Cottontail, ready to fly from a shadow: the mother's love was strong in her. The cry of her baby had filled her with the courage of a hero, and—hop, she went over that horrible reptile" (74–75). No matter that the feckless Raggylug had gotten into trouble with the snake due to curiosity to investigate the unknown sound of the snake's slithering, his maternal saviour was there to bail him out. Thus was the young colonialist reader aware that sovereign (parental) power was present to fall back on while exploring and taking command of the new lands.

The drama of the ever-present struggle of animal parents to secure the safety of their young is a theme also in "Redruff, the Story of the Don Valley Partridge." The partridge family that Redruff originates from is aptly tutored by wise old Mother Partridge who is able to lead them through many natural obstacles but whose tutelage falters when faced by the obstacle Man, in the persona of a hunter. In his turn, through an unusual twist of fate not always seen in nature, Redruff himself becomes the protective parent, his mate having been killed by the hunter. Lessons of parental bonding with young would be of great interest to juvenile readers learning who can be trusted and who must be feared. A common enemy of the hunted animal and the young colonialist is the wanton hunter, who does not conserve and kills only to feed his own ego, a hunter characterized by the ignorance of "Cuddy," the Don Valley squatter who exemplifies a coarse and immoral attitude toward nature. Thus, the naturalist-educator Seton strove to teach lessons of conservation and responsibility to young colonial children through empathy with the noble animals striving to survive and, more importantly, to altruistically save their families from foes.

Seton's discursive strategies are based upon his own experiences as a naturalist, illustrator, and note-taker. His narrative is narcissistic, but with a larger purpose to support and promote his philosophy that mankind has been exceedingly unfair to their animal kin ("Note to the Reader" 12). Seton managed to create a hybrid form of literature, combining British traditions and history with an indigenous worldview. Although he attempts to portray the reality of the frontier environment, its representation is mediated through the sensibilities of the author and presented to readers as a simultaneous placement and displacement.

Just as a "process of displacement and estrangement" serves to disarm a dominating discourse (Allen 3), so the tensions created by illustrating how one does not belong but could if certain rules were followed are present in Seton's stories. Tales such as "Raggylug" and "Redruff" are crafted to instill in the reader a desire for knowledge of the land (love and compassion for animals and the changing Canadian landscape) while seemingly distancing the reader from the colonial depredations enacted upon the land. Although the way of life that Seton knew disappeared even as the tale was told, it was now in the possession of the (child-)reader as he or she sat at the knee of the storyteller. As Hulme has argued, cornering the triangle of land, colonizer, and colonized resulted in clearly drawn cultural and social templates and served to initiate future young leaders of the realm into a literature calculated to make them feel one with nature and the land, while preserving the vigilance required for mastery of new lands. Seton's animal stories served to make the strange familiar and the familiar strange (after educational anthropologist George Spindler), thus establishing eminent domain over the symbolic and the real Canada.

In order for present-day educators and school children to read the postcolonial message in Seton's *Wild Animals I Have Known*, they must be shown that a subtext resides within the nature tales. Furthermore, they would have to understand the "institutional literacy" of colonialism (Collins 204). Increasingly, in today's schools, students are made aware that history is currently being revised and expanded to include space for the stories of the minority cultures of Canada, stories that were silenced by a dominant discourse of the colonizing powers. Thus, an awareness of the subtext of colonialism within Seton's tales can be cross-curricular, drawing from social studies and other relevant subject areas. However, a reading of Seton's tales *becomes* social studies in demonstrating how his dedication to illuminating a vanishing world was inspired by colonialism. Seton is a chronicler *and*, just as importantly, a commentator on change brought to the natural realm by the civilizing forces of the European settlers.

Interpretation of the Realistic Animal Stories: Sentient Animals—Metaphors or Agents?

Seton's strategic placement of thinking, feeling, and talking animals within stories for children promoted notions that civilized British culture was superior to others by imposing colonial terms of reference upon nature. The values Seton developed and promoted, that mankind was kin to animals, and that humans have a responsibility to their animal brethren, were not opposed to colonial dominion. The internalized grammar or code of the stories in *Wild Animals I Have Known* is a product of Seton's own colonial upbringing. It was his mission to educate, while simultaneously enchanting, his reader-audience. The metaphorical fantasy of sentient animals who could commune with them, think like them, and instruct them in the all-important lessons of survival was, no doubt, seductive and appealing.

Perhaps the continuing status of *Wild Animals I Have Known* as a children's classic can be attributed to its mode of narration that sets up a relationship between animals and people. Many writers have recognized and used the childhood fascination with and trust of animals in their stories. The ideology that there rightly is, and should be, a connection between humans and (wild) animals is part of a colonial domesticating policy that naturalist authors from Jack London (*Call of the Wild*) to Sterling North (*Rascal*) to E.B. White (*Charlotte's Web*) have drawn upon. Thus, the appeal of Seton's tales, now and in the past, was/is to fulfill an immediate desire of children: to find allies to confide in and trust. Through Seton's tales, children can walk with and "talk with" the animals.

Guided by Perry Nodelman in *Pleasure and Genre: Speculations on the Characteristics of Children's Fiction*, Thomas Travisano explores the intersections of childhood literature with childhood studies. He examines how certain works of literature contribute to forming a "divided consciousness" within adult and child reading audiences. According to Travisano, one of the most fascinating and important effects of literature intended for children is that, in the process of reading, the child crosses over at times into dangerous or adult social worlds while safely residing within the realm of childhood. The ability to be aware of and recognize this state of reading permits the child a knowledge of socially constructed relationships and processes while safely residing in childhood. The ritual re-enactment of the move from childhood to maturity, innocence to knowledge, is a recurrent theme in coming-of-age stories, with the added feature that, for settler colonies, knowledge of new terrain and flora and fauna means survival and mastery, and failure to learn the lessons means extinction and surrender of territory. Sentient animals are thought of as a "safe" third party and a simple subject suitable for consumption by the child. The delightful intimate dialogue interpreted by the child as a direct message from the animals takes children to the threshold or "boundary between nature and culture" (Kristeva, qtd. in Morgenstern 115). According to Julia Kristeva, rhythmic lessons set up between desire and duty are tied to the early language of childhood, which is made both palatable and compelling for the child to attend to. However, tension is created when the child realizes that he/she must return to civilization. Thus, "The symbolic is firmly in command" (Morgenstern 115), and the placement of children into the colonial order is complete.

As Canadian children were led to believe in the ability to commune with sentient animals of the colonial landscape, they could be further led to an implacable belief in their personal and collective powers, and thus be convinced that mastery of the lands was their "domin*ion*-itive" right. In addition, the colonial order of adult hierarchy over children was preserved by the dimin*u*tive positioning of children in a hierarchy of being more or less equal in status to the sentient animals, while holding out the promise that they would be in a position to advance over the animals some day. That is, it was understood from the structure of the stories that once children mastered the lessons taught by the animal characters, they would become second in the hierarchy of Euro-British adult humans at the top, children in the middle, and animals at the bottom as the willing teachers/servants of the settlers.

Engagement with the natural world was part of the means to position as subjects the future Euro-British lords of the realm. As they learned about the landscape, they would gain familiarity and ease with the habits of the natural denizens, the wild animals portrayed in the tales, and also appropriate Native rhetoric to the hegemonic colonial-imperial order. With the natural denizens of the earth, sky, and water as allies and sponsors, children would be positioned to see themselves as possessing a right to the new territories, as having the agency to exercise dominion from sea to sea. Although Native Peoples did not always appear in the animal tales, part of the lessons of colonialism would be to learn that the human predecessors, the indigenous peoples, should be treated benignly, under the rules of a patriarchal colony, particularly as embodied in The Indian Acts. This lesson is apparent in how Native Canadian or American voice was used, or appropriated, in adaptations such as Seton's "The Snow Shoe Rabbit." Although only animal characters appear in the tale, the voices of unseen Native deities serve as the teachers/servants, with the hapless Snow Shoe Rabbit the device for learning about natural adaptation to the North American landscape, and the presumed audience and beneficiary of the information the Euro-British settler child who needed to know these things.

As a naturalist and hunter of wildlife at the end of the nineteenth and beginning of the twentieth century, Seton was quite cognizant of the "disappearing wilderness" and biological populations in danger of extinction. Was Seton perhaps also cognizant that the old colonial order was, in its truest sense, at an end, and a postcolonial order was being negotiated and formulated in Canada? Part of the project of settler colonies is to retain a nostalgic sense of the past, and this nostalgia is often the material informing tales passed on to children. Seton, as a naturalist-author, had decided to enlist animals, part of Canada's natural landscape, during a period of emergent nationalism in the early twentieth century, as a signifying device to construct a unique Canadian children's literature drawing upon first-person observations and transliterations of Native lore and legend, presenting it in a Europeanized package.

The archival preservation of vanishing ways is part of the colonial mindset, for even if progress must erode populations and cultures, they can at least be documented for the sake of nostalgia and to ease any qualms of settler guilt. Several years ago when I visited Head-Smashed-In-Buffalo Jump, a World Heritage Site in Southern Alberta, part of the tour featured the guide reconstructing, through a scripted narrative, the panorama of the multitude of buffalo that roamed the plains below the cliff. There are no buffalo now, but phantom buffalo are symbolically summoned to an archaeological interpretative site that seeks to atone for years of colonial usurping of Blackfoot lands and the lands and resources of other First Nations across Canada. The popularity of Seton's realistic animal tales then and now reflects their rootedness in the nostalgia for a vanished time and place written even as the time and place were vanishing into the order of colonizing "progress."

My examination of the survival of Seton's stories in contemporary contexts is guided by the idea that they can be viewed as colonialist writing with appeal to a postcolonial audience. Clare Bradford writes of Australian children's texts of the early 1900s that "omit Aborigines from accounts of Australian history or reconfigure historical events to produce stories of white heroism and black savagery, thus positioning child readers to see themselves as citizens of a white Australia and the inheritors of a tradition of pioneer endeavor" (197). This use of children's literature is only one means to promote new national identity, via re-inscribing the past. A postcolonial archaeology would excavate the colonial past as well as the childhood past to come to terms with present realities of neo-colonialisms in what is generally considered to be a grown-up world. Healing processes for colonized populations are part of this archaeological project. For example, in "Writing the Childhood Self: Australian Aboriginal Autobiographies, Memoirs and Testimonies," Australian children's literature scholar Heather Scutter elucidates Australian Aboriginal attempts to deal with "two centuries of cultural loss by calling sharply on childhood memories in order to restore, to use the poet Errol West's words, a sense of reality, significance, wholeness" (226).

When I think of pedagogical implications, I think of the classroom and also the learning space outside the classroom, particularly that which is accessible to children through literature and other experiential resources, such as museums or field trips. I think of the pedagogical opportunities forged by educators who are able to teach on multiple levels, that is, seeing a Seton animal tale as natural history, as an example of social history, and as literature. Many educators who espouse anti-racism as part of an anti-colonial practice teach in this manner, and they are remarkably successful. These critical educators are employing border pedagogy to "make visible the historically and socially constructed strengths and limitations of those places and borders we inherit and that frame our discourses and social relations" (Giroux 32). According to Henry Giroux, "border pedagogy" seeks to assist postcolonial discourse in rewriting "the relationship between the margin and the center by deconstructing the colonialist and imperialist ideologies that structure Western knowledge, texts, and social practices" (27). The themes presented in Seton's realistic animal tales are a perfect site for the practice of border pedagogy.

Conclusion

> The colonial past is variously rehearsed, reinscribed, and contested in postcolonial children's texts, and it is increasingly a site of tension, producing different and conflicting significances. (Bradford 198)

In the contemporary Canadian classroom of multicultural and gendered realities, one can be blissfully unaware, ignorant, or complacent about the historical contexts of colonization. Knowledge of this history can promote paradigm shifts and lead to mediated social constructions to be articulated in literature, in pedagogy, at conferences, and in other contexts. The examination of historical literary case conditions may serve as a postcolonial interrogation by making people aware of what specifically influences their formation as members of a former colony. In the case of classic Canadian children's literature, teaching children to be aware of how to read the intertwined stories of colonialism and postcolonialism will prepare them for the neo-colonialisms they will encounter. The teachable moments reside in the actual stories and in the equally fascinating stories within the stories.

If a study of postcolonialism in education is to be something more than an autopsy of worlds that collided, a decision needs to be made about how to extend theory into pedagogical practice. Children are capable of understanding and benefiting by having the ripple effects of colonization pointed out to them, in turn leading to an ability to analyze the contemporary effects they live with, such as racism, sexual discrimination, economic exploitation, silencing, and other injustices. In order to focus on constructions that may deliberately cohere around issues of postcolonialism and pedagogy, I have found it useful to "corner the triangle." For this paper, a concluding triangle of *critical reading, awareness,* and *theorizing* offers a template situated within cultural studies to present the lessons and delights of those tales socially and culturally constructed for young people who will grow into their future worlds.

NOTE

1. When I use the terms *colonial* and *colonialist* to describe the readership of Seton's stories, I am of course referring to the colonial character of the culture at the time and not to the actual political status post-Confederation.

WORKS CITED

Allen, Chadwick. "Postcolonial Theory and the Discourse of Treaties." *American Quarterly* 52.1 (2000): 59–89.

Bradford, Clare. "The End of Empire? Colonial and Postcolonial Journeys in Children's Books." *Annual of the Modern Language Association Division in Children's Literature and the Children's Literature Association* 29 (2001): 196–218.

Collins, James. "Socialization to Text: Structure and Contradiction in Schooled Literacy." *Natural Histories of Discourse.* Ed. M. Silverstein and G. Urban. Chicago: U of Chicago P, 1996. 203–28.

Darland, Robert. "A Man ahead of His Time." *National Wildlife* Feb./Mar. 2000: 43.

Galbraith, Mary. "Hear My Cry: A Manifesto for an Emanicipatory Childhood Studies Approach to Literature." *Lion and the Unicorn* 25.2 (2001): 187–205.

Giroux, Henry. *Border Crossings: Cultural Workers and the Politics of Education.* New York: Routledge, 1992.

Hutcheon, Linda. *Narcissistic Narrative: The Metafictional Paradox.* Waterloo: Wilfrid Laurier UP, 1980.

Kristeva, Julia. *Tales of Love.* Trans. Leon S. Roudiez. New York: Columbia UP, 1987.

McLaren, Peter. "Post-Colonial Pedagogy: Post-Colonial Desire and Decolonized Community." *Postmodernism, Postcolonialism and Pedagogy.* Ed. Peter McLaren. Somerville, Australia: James Nicholas, 1995. 227–68.

Morgenstern, John. "Children and Other Talking Animals." *Lion and the Unicorn* 24.1 (2000): 110–27.

Scutter, Heather. "Writing the Childhood Self: Australian Aboriginal Autobiographies, Memoirs and Testimonies." *Lion and the Unicorn* 25.2 (2001): 226–41.

Seton, Ernest Thompson. *Wild Animals I Have Known.* New York: Scribner's, 1898; 1926.

Spindler, George D. "Roger Harker and Schoenhausen: From Familiar to Strange and Back Again." *Doing the Ethnography of Schooling.* Toronto: Holt, Rinehart, 1982. 20–47.

Storey, John. "Cultural Studies: An Introduction." *What Is Cultural Studies?: A Reader.* Ed. J. Storey. New York: St. Martin's, 1996. 1–30.

Thacker, Deborah. "Disdain or Ignorance?: Literary Theory and the Absence of Children's Literature." *Lion and the Unicorn* 24.1 (2000): 1–17.

———. "Feminine Language and the Politics of Children's Literature." *Lion and the Unicorn* 25.1 (2001): 3–16.

Travisano, Thomas. "Of Dialectic and Divided Consciousness: Intersections between Children's Literature and Childhood Studies." *Children's Literature* 28 (2000): 22–29.

Waterson, Elizabeth. *Children's Literature in Canada.* New York: Twayne, 1992.

Yew, Leong. "Notes on Colonialism." The Postcolonial Web, University Scholars Programme, National University of Singapore. 5 Apr. 2002. 24 Apr. 2002. <http://www.scholars.nus.edu.sg/landow/post/poldiscourse/colonialismnotes.html>.

Zipes, Jack. *Happily Ever After: Fairy Tales, Children, and the Culture Industry.* New York: Routledge, 1997.

The Teacher Reader: Canadian Historical Fiction, Adolescent Learning, and Teacher Education

LINDA RADFORD

KARLEEN BRADFORD'S *There Will Be Wolves*, written in 1992, won the Canadian Library Association Best Young Adult Book Award and was nominated for several others. As one of my students in the Bachelor of Education program at the University of Ottawa pointed out, "students will enjoy this historical novel because it is similar to the popular TV program *Survivor*, except there is far more bloodshed and no bikinis." Bradford's book transports you back to medieval times and demythologizes our romantic notions of the period. This medieval board of chess is a time when streets stank, people did not bathe, and seeing yet another execution was just another day at the market. There is none of the typical pageantry of the knights and ladies in waiting that still holds the fascination of our culture as evidenced in what is popularly read and watched by children. In this juvenile historical fiction, Bradford presents a story in which the religious and political belief systems of European medieval life around the time of the Crusades affect human existence and thinking in deeply profound ways.

Bradford insightfully plays with the archives of colonialism, as *There Will Be Wolves* is set in Cologne, Germany, the city that was built over the ruins of one of the most powerful cities of the Roman Empire—Colonia Agripa. According to the *Oxford English Dictionary*, by the middle of the fourteenth century the word *colonye* was used to describe the Roman colonia. Colonia, *colonye*, or colonialism describes the Roman experience of "settling, creating outposts, or occupying lands outside of the Roman city-state" (Yew 1). As Leong Yew points out, "the term colonialism emerged around the nineteenth century to reify European practice that followed the same pattern of the distant Roman Empire" (1). Such practice and patterns are intimately connected with imperialism. Bradford provides an entry point into this concept that begins with the colonial subject or the sovereign subject of religious authoritarianism—the Crusader. In its treatment of the Eurocentric associations underpinning the Crusades, the novel moves the pieces around the board and recreates the movements of the colonialist psyche.

There Will Be Wolves is one of the texts I am using to carry out a cultural study of teachers' reading practices (the other is Karen Cushman's 1995 *The Midwife's Apprentice*). A study of textual reading practices provides partial access to the hidden histories and possible implications of identificatory processes. My doctoral research investigates reading practices of pre-service teachers through historical fiction. My inquiry is grounded in the rationale that teachers' reading practices have important implications for their actions and behaviours with children in classroom learning situations. Juvenile historical fiction presents challenges and difficulties to classroom literature teachers. These affective and epistemological obstacles exist because stories about historical occurrences frequently engage readers with difficult knowledge, as exemplified in *There Will Be Wolves*. In this study, it is not only the psychic dimensions of such representations that interest me, but also how they function epistemologically. For example, when teachers read juvenile narratives about medieval life, to what extent do they think about being in history and the possibility of history, the historicity of human existence, and the historicity of narratives? Because teachers decide how and if a historical fiction will be formally studied in a classroom, their reading practices are culturally productive sites deeply implicated in identity, community formation, ongoing social memory, and collective historical understanding.

Postcolonial and feminist excursions into literature by researchers such as Roberta Seelinger Trites, Carolyn Steedman, Valerie Walkerdine, and Gayatri Chakravorty Spivak reveal that dynamics exist in learning/reading situations that result in the repetition or repression of social and psychic histories, including colonial pasts, racism, misogyny, and heteronormativity. Psychoanalytic educational researchers demonstrate how meanings that readers construct from literary texts rely in part on unconscious realities that grow out of readers' histories as they engage dynamically with the aesthetic qualities of the narrative (Robertson, "Art" 39–42; Britzman and Pitt 121–23). In this paper, my purpose is to explore how teachers' reading engagements with such juvenile historical texts as Bradford's *There Will Be Wolves* may be used as a site for postcolonial education. A postcolonial pedagogy calls for the same opening of space that Bradford allows in her feminist rewriting of the medieval colony.

There Will Be Wolves deals with the first Crusade called the People's Crusade that set out in the spring of 1096 CE to liberate the Holy Land and Jerusalem from the heretic Moslems. As experienced by Ursula, the 15-year-old protagonist of this historical fiction, the Crusades are a murderous spree rather than a glorious mission. The Crusades are a fanatic drive against non-Christian "Killers of Christ," particularly the Jews (Bradford 32). Early on in the story, we learn that Germanic law marginalized the Jews. Jews were not allowed to own land, including the land their own houses stood upon. While many of them depended on trade and usury as a form of economic survival, Christians equated usury with sin and despised the Jews for it; their disdain turned to hatred when they became deeply indebted to them (Bradford 14–15). Undermining all traces of the romance, heroism, and spirituality conventionally associated with the Crusades, Bradford's narrative takes us through chapters of intense drama. Before leaving Cologne, Germany, where the story begins, Christian Crusaders kill Jews. During their march for God, where they invade towns and people's homes for food and goods, the Crusaders kill Christians and Moslems. Avenging the Crusaders' crimes against their people, the Turks go after the Crusaders and slaughter almost everyone on the Crusade. Bradford shows the devastating conclusion of a crusade spurred by the rhetoric of absolution, cleansing, eternal salvation, and land.

In "Books and Reading in Young Adult Literature Set in the Middle Ages," Rebecca Barnhouse critiques the representation of medieval life in *There Will Be Wolves* as being inaccurate. Barnhouse suggests that Bradford is perpetuating "anachronistic fallacies, allowing [her] didactic tendencies to overshadow historical accuracy . . . [which] unintentionally reinforce misconceptions about books and literacy in the Middle Ages" (364). Barnhouse charges Bradford with creating in Ursula an accomplished female reader in an historical period when few individuals outside of the clergy could read. Ursula uses her literacy to do what others cannot. Through reading what is deemed a holy book that a sick priest, labelled as insane by his peers, gave to Ursula on his death bed, this young girl knows how to use more than just herbs to treat common ailments, as, for instance, when she sets the broken bones of a dog, saving its life. Distrusted because she can read, and disliked by her neighbours because of her sharp wit and impatience with the ignorance of others, she is accused of being a witch. Following this accusation, Ursula is condemned as a witch by an ecclesiastical court and, subsequently, when she denies this verdict, is charged for having opposed religious authority. In exchange for her life, Ursula's father, Master William, one of the city's apothecaries, strikes an easy bargain with local authorities (church and state). He will go on the Crusade and provide the herbal remedies they require and Ursula will accompany him to atone for her sins.

This historical narrative provides possible avenues for learning that are much greater than Bradford's simple goal—presumably to inspire literacy. Margaret Atwood argues that "Fiction is where individual memory and experience and collective memory and experience come together, in greater or lesser proportions. The closer the fiction is to us as readers, the more we recognize and claim it as individual rather than collective" (3). Ursula's reading practices propel the plot. The possibility of a young girl being able to read during this time period is a strange twist of circumstances, but it is through such a twist that the young reader may identify with the character's desire and struggle. Barnhouse works from the premise that historical fiction's usefulness for learning depends singularly and straightforwardly on the accuracy or inaccuracy of the representations. What this premise forgets is that meaning is made for learners in a dynamic encounter with representations where some form of identification takes place (Brooks, *Discourse* 9–11).

As teachers struggle to understand how to develop children's understanding of historical events through the use of narrative forms, it would be alarming if literature teachers avoided texts that present profound knowledge about a particular time and place because they contain elements of fiction. Ursula's ability to read may not be historically accurate. Yet the Church and local community's reaction to her reading practice underscores how colonial discourse is an "apparatus of power" (Bhabha 70).

In *There Will Be Wolves*, the invasiveness of colonial discourse is enacted through the major disagreement and intellectual debate about the Crusades between Master William, Ursula's father, a respected member of the community, and Bruno, Ursula's friend, a character who questions the prevailing attitudes. For Bruno, the "holy venture" is "an insanity" (31), while in response to the killing of the Jews, Master William can only whisper: "The Crusade is to be a glorious endeavour. How can it be born out of such things? Out of such evil?" (50). For a moment and only in a whisper, Master William challenges the party line, but quickly declares his allegiance to the Church when he exclaims to Bruno that the Crusades have been authorized by the Pope himself. To understand this surveillance of self, Homi Bhabha stresses the need to explore the colonial subject in psychoanalytic and historical terms (66–84). Master William pays homage to the Church's authority, illustrating Bhabha's point that "Like voyeurism, surveillance must depend for its effectivity on 'the active consent'" of the colonial subject (76). Bradford uses the Crusades as a representation to point out how the vicissitudes of ethnic hatred are connected to what Bhabha calls the "conflictual economy of colonial discourse" (85). This portal to the past may be useful in moving to the kind of "communicative action" that Cameron McCarthy suggests will get us beyond the "implacable categories of Eurocentrism and the reductive forms of multiculturalism" (21).

Considering the enabling and distinctive educative value of the aesthetic experience of literature (see Nussbaum 343–65; Ricoeur in Valdes 5; Bruner 64–66), it is interesting that in Ontario many teachers are turning to historical fiction as a convenient means of addressing the many expectations of a new interdisciplinary curriculum. Yet this goal of fulfilling curriculum expectations is fraught with complexities. For instance, in teacher education at the University of Ottawa, *There Will Be Wolves* is taught under the heading of "risky story" because the story presents "graphic" scenes of "degradation, pain, and death" (Simon and Armitage Simon 264). The concept of "risky stories" is developed by Roger Simon and Wendy Armitage Simon and refers to stories that require a pedagogical response because the story represents painful issues or events that may be emotionally invasive for young readers (Robertson, "Teaching" 278). For teachers, a pedagogical response means using classroom practices that provide adequate space and time for students to work through the difficult knowledge by developing historical literacy and actively reflecting on their own reading of the text through oral and written expression. What students struggle with in their learning can become constructive in the way it forges insight for the individual. As Robertson argues, in teaching risky stories the key element is to assist readers in recognizing the connection that exists between the impossible past and one's own ongoing implication in it (Robertson, "Teaching" 283). Later in this paper I will return to the implications of this argument. Now, I would like to point to a study that documents the riskiness of Bradford's story because of its contradictory treatment of the "glorious crusades."

Explaining the phenomenon of dealing with the risky story, Shoshana Felman argues that one's desire to ignore is "less cognitive than performative . . . it is not the simple lack of information but the incapacity—or the refusal—to acknowledge one's own implication in the information" (79). Robertson presents her experience of how teachers will resist memory and protect their own subjectivity by blocking pedagogical interference in relation to difficult knowledge. Asking students to read *There Will Be Wolves*, Robertson suggests that her students "imagine how the novel might be used to instigate thinking in an elementary classroom" ("Art" 27). In response, some students adamantly assert that they cannot imagine using this text with children. While the first reactions of the teacher candidates focus on the obstacle of the text being "too sensitive" or "parents would find the portrayals offensive" (29), they eventually respond by writing, "Bradford's portrayal of the atrocities perpetrated by Crusaders against European Jews in 1096 represents 'a demotion of Catholicism.' And with disquieting anxiety, they concluded: *We don't talk about these things*" (30).

The subjects in Robertson's study perform like Bradford's Master William when they are destabilized by what challenges their system of beliefs. Master William responds with outrage to Bruno's equation of Church rhetoric with violence, just as Robertson's students respond with hostility to this exercise of reading. As Deborah Britzman and Alice Pitt assert, "the stakes are most obvious when the teacher's self becomes destabilized in her encounter with others who refuse the role of self-reflecting mirror to the teacher's desire" (122). The outpouring of anger projected onto Robertson in her classroom and onto the book itself is understandable if reading encounters are related to identity formation in teacher education. By avoiding a text because of its supposed sensitive issues, a teacher can hope to protect the fantasy of self and the power he/she obtains through collective avoidance. A denial of the struggle with unconscious realities emerging from the readers' histories as they engage dynamically with texts sanctions, as Robertson asserts, "new practices of authority: the Jew outside of representability, outside of culture, outside of education, and outside of human values" (42). This example is a devastating sign of the dynamics in reading and learning situations that result in the repetition and repression of social and psychic histories.

From Robertson's study, it is obvious that what should be read and what should not be read is not divorced from a world where power continues to play out in particular ways. Part of the process of teacher education is to provide a space where the students can do the work of learning so they can attach what they have learned and who they are to their new identity as "teachers." In Ontario, there is a visible authority structure that still defines teacher education. Robertson's research reveals that:

> Faculties of Education in Ontario are juristically bound by virtue of a Constitution Act in 1867 and the Education Act of Ontario to provide programmatic support for the doctrinal education of aspiring Roman Catholic teachers. Despite a United Nations bias ruling that Canada permits religious discrimination because Ontario funds Roman Catholic schools and not the schools of other faiths, the government has not rectified this relationship between religion and schooling in Ontario, nor addressed the injurious effects on non-Catholic groups who are denied privileged access to a similar sanctioned canonical education. ("Art" 33)

History is not a hidden factor here; practices and patterns of conquest and settlement are visible and contemporary. Yet teacher education programs appear to provide little space for teachers to understand the "psychological self" by placing themselves in a cultural context. In "Cultural Myths in the Making of a Teacher," Britzman summarizes the predominant model of teacher education. It is organized on the implicit theory of immediate integration of the student into the classroom: "the university provides the theories, methods, and skills; schools provide the classroom, curriculum, and students; and the student teacher provides the individual effort; all of which combine to produce the finished product of a professional teacher" (442). Drawing on her own experience as a teacher educator, Britzman argues that this training model "ignores the role of the social and political context of teacher education while emphasizing the individual's effort" (442). Further research in teacher education supports how the anxiety of student teachers over mastery is provoked by "the structure of teacher education and the epistemology of education itself, with its push toward remedy, control and expertise" (Britzman and Pitt 119).

The teacher willing to support the construction of knowledge through the story worlds of historical narrative will be open to strategies that help learners to work through difficult knowledge (Simon and Armitage Simon 267; Robertson, "Teaching" 289–90). Providing spaces within the classroom for students to express how they feel is essential to helping them understand why a text evokes emotions that may be difficult. The emotionally charged reconstruction of history allows students to connect more fully to human experience of the past and avoids the popular hegemonizing of the experience where a "false empathy" results from the belief that one's suffering is the same as another's (Morris 12). What educators must consider is what happens to the possibilities of children's learning if the historical representation is treated as a cultural artifact about which teachers say, "This is what was," rather than dealing with how the text affects the students. In my recent experience as a teacher educator, the pre-service student teachers rushed to collect lesson plans and master the practical methods of delivering them. This rush to have and apply knowledge while not fully understanding the implications of it struck me as problematic. It is this pressure for mastery that hinders the teacher from forming a crucial link with other learners. A focus on mastery separates the individual from the "dynamics of locations" such as race, gender, class, and sex, requiring him or her to imagine the past as "discontinuous with the present" and leaving little space for any new conditions of learning (Britzman and Pitt 123). Between the teachers' own refusal to discuss a text and the teacher education program's limitations, the "I am teacher" (all knowing) and "you are student" (empty vessel) model remains entrenched despite all of the well-intended talk about student-centred learning and critical thinking skills.

According to Marla Morris, who assesses issues of curriculum, memory, and history, historical fiction reflects much more than just a writer's success at reproducing the authenticity of the context. Discussing the recent surge of attention to historical fiction, Atwood explains that now "part of the interest for writers and readers of historical fiction, . . . [is that] by taking a long hard look backwards, we place ourselves" (27). Yet Atwood insists that historical fiction is more than just a representation of the time; it also reminds us that history is about individuals because it is at such points that "memory, history, and story all intersect" (7). Atwood goes as far as to say that historical fictions are about human nature: "pride, envy, avarice, lust, sloth, gluttony, and anger. They are about truth and lies, and disguises and revelations; they are about crime and punishment; they are about love and forgiveness and long-suffering and charity, they are about sin and retribution and sometimes even redemption" (38–39). If we identify with this human quandary of being part of a world where love and hate and truth and lies operate at the same time, Atwood reminds us that we are not on an easy reading field. The convenient tendency of forgetting and the hard work of remembering is central to the dynamics of the mind when it comes to difficult knowledge, but there always exists "the lure of the unmentionable—the mysterious, the buried, the forgotten, the discarded, the taboo" (19). Throughout her discussion, Atwood plays with the idea that some historical fiction can move us towards the cliff of remembering. On this cliff, we may come close enough to the edge that we make a life-saving grab at a relation of the self to an essential moment of human loss or suffering. But there is also an impulse to repress certain knowledge of this nature, and, thus, as Atwood says, the "unsavoury repressed memories [are] stored in our heads like rotten apples in a barrel, festering away but essentially unknowable, except for the suspicious smell" (11–12). This is the knowledge that Lacan qualifies as "'knowledge that can't tolerate one's knowing that one knows'" (qtd. in Felman 77).

Self-reflexive reading practices have much to contend with when it comes to the dynamics of the mind. Being aware of the "suspicious smells" and appreciating that learning is a psychic event is essential to understanding the self before teaching others. In *There Will Be Wolves*, Bradford represents some of the psychological effects of colonial authority. Historical novels offer a portal, a frame of observation, and, here, one cannot help but think that Bradford's opus actually provides a space through which the colony may look back upon itself. This is a perilous venture. Following

Lacan's theorizing of ambivalence, Bhabha asserts that the gaze of colonial authority never rests easy, for it is well known that colonial identity owes part of its constitution to that colonized other and that revolt is potentially immanent (86). Therefore, in Bhabha's formulation, teachers are positioned hegemonically to mimic the forms and values of dominant culture because this is whom they represent (85–86).

The relationship between reading, narrative experience, and learning is not well understood, especially in relation to its interdisciplinary significance. Deborah Thacker sees the study of children's literature, its readers (adults and children), and the psychic and social uses of these texts as an area that has been "astonishingly" understudied considering the impact these texts have upon the social construction of readers (2). She also suggests that the historicity of readers must be considered. Such observations clearly connect to my own research where I am presently studying the connection between the emergent classroom practices of pre-service teachers and their reading practices; what these implications say about identity formation and reading practices; and how specific pedagogies of reading may support the conditions of learning about identity and our reading practices in the study of education.

Studying the interpretive process and contextual factors of reading, I rely on cultural reception theories (Staiger 8–48) stemming from the interdisciplinary field of cultural studies that displaces the focus from the literary work to the reader. Psychoanalytic theories of narrative are also important to this study of how narrative functions in teachers' reading practices. Peter Brooks' theory of how the aesthetic form of narrative acts as a place where we may understand the affective and epistemological implications of identification complements Richard Johnson's idea of how cultural forms enter into the subjective realities and life-worlds of readers. Brooks argues that "students need in their work on literature to encounter a moment of poetics—a moment in which they are forced to ask not only *what* the text means but also *how* it means, what its grounds as a meaning making sign system are and how we as readers . . . activate and deploy systems that allow us to detect or create meaning" ("Aesthetics" 517). Johnson calls for a "structuralist ethnography" to look at the social or cultural forms of knowledge that are made available in a discursive field (13, 58). The following research questions, developed from Johnson's "Cultural Circuit" model (11–15), inform this study:

1. What are the conditions of production of the works of historical fiction written for children and adolescents?
2. How does the textual form work to influence the literary forcefulness of the historical narratives?
3. How does the development of the teachers' identity within the institutional conditions of their formation influence the conditions of readership?
4. How does the reading of historical fiction reflect the lived struggles within communities that have an influence on social memory, pedagogy, and collective historical understanding?

Specific questions about the form of narrative are the means for investigating some of the larger questions above. Johnson says that formal elements of a text "realize and make available subjective forms" (58). Brooks suggests that to "slow up the work of interpretation, the attempt to turn the text into *some other* discourse or system, and to consider it as a manifestation of the conventions, constraints, and possibilities of literature" (517), the aesthetic as a constituted domain must be reasserted.

Observing the vicarious relationship between narrative and reader so that the interpretive processes and contextual factors are revealed, I am asking the participants to take a formalist approach to analyzing the texts and then asking how they would employ this analysis in their teaching methods. A formalist approach also coincides with what teacher candidates are required to undertake in relation to the Ontario Curricula Grades 1–10 English. Participants' responses to the literary aspects (plot, setting, narrative point of view, characterization, author's context, theme, style, and so forth) of the historical fictions will create a medium through which I can study the meanings and uses of historical fiction by beginning teachers.

To study the relationship between literary forms produced for juveniles and teachers' uses of these texts in developing their own conditional selfhood within the institutional forces of their formation, I need to understand the dynamics between the texts and the readers. The term *rhetorical analysis* refers specifically to the relationship between readers and texts because it relates to "how humans are constantly engaged in the productive deployment of texts, a cultural practice that involves meaningful but complex negotiations of power and desire through language"

(Robertson, "Cinema" 14). Employing specific strategies that will be useful in addressing this phenomenon with pre-service teachers, I utilize the rhetorical methodology of Felman. I am collecting data on the participants by examining and analyzing their oral and written responses to the two adolescent narratives for the repetition of ideas, themes, and memories in response to the formal structures of the historical narrative, their biographical background, and their pedagogical perspectives. The participants' level of engagement with the representations of medieval life offered in the text, as well as their consciousness of how their own responses to these representations may affect classroom life, will be examined.

Teacher education and practices of pedagogy intersect with ongoing problems of domination and oppression. The promise of using historical fiction in the classroom *to place ourselves* may provide a means to interrupt the colonialist cycle. Without the opportunity to think about learning in relation to difficult knowledge, beginning teachers may not understand the value of and need for self-reflexive reading practices. From my very preliminary observations of the participants in my study, beginning teachers who are trying to understand how to develop children's understanding of historical events through the use of the narrative form benefit from thinking about their reading subjectivity. As I see Bradford's project, the feminist and "othered" character of Ursula offers a departure point for thinking about reading practices. While beginning teachers are understandably anxious about their first teaching experiences and preoccupied with having the perfect lesson plans, thinking about reading practices in relation to teaching practices is essential to an anti-colonial project. For those willing to go there, and the participants in my study have volunteered on this basis, the aesthetic form of narrative can act as a place where we can explore and discuss the affective and epistemological implications of identifications within the framework of learning how to teach others to learn.

WORKS CITED

Atwood, Margaret. *In Search of Alias Grace*. Charles R. Bronfman Lecture in Canadian Studies. Ottawa: U of Ottawa P, 1996.

Barnhouse, Rebecca. "Books and Reading in Young Adult Literature Set in the Middle Ages." *The Lion and the Unicorn* 22.3 (1998): 364–75.

Bhabha, Homi K. "The Other Question: The Stereotype and Colonial Discourse." *Screen* 24.4 (1983): 18–36.

Bradford, Karleen. *There Will Be Wolves*. Toronto: HarperCollins, 1992.

Britzman, Deborah. "Cultural Myths in the Making of a Teacher: Biography and Social Structure in Teacher Education." *Harvard Educational Review* 56 (1994): 442–72.

Britzman, Deborah P., and Alice J. Pitt. "Pedagogy and Transference: Casting the Past of Learning into the Presence of Teaching." *Theory Into Practice* 35.2 (1996): 117–23.

Brooks, Peter. "Aesthetics and Ideology: What Happened to Poetics?" *Critical Inquiry* 20 (1994): 509–24.

———. *Discourse in Psychoanalysis and Literature*. New York: Methuen, 1987.

Bruner, Jerome. Introduction. *Thought and Language*. By L.S. Vygotsky. Cambridge: MIT Press, 1962. 1–8.

Cushman, Karen. *The Midwife's Apprentice*. New York: HarperCollins, 1995.

Felman, Shoshana. *Jacques Lacan and the Adventure of Insight: Psychoanalysis in Contemporary Culture*. Cambridge: Harvard UP, 1997.

Johnson, Richard. "What Is Cultural Studies Anyway?" *What Is Cultural Studies?: A Reader*. Ed. John Storey. New York: St Martin's, 1996. 75–114.

McCarthy, Cameron. *The Uses of Culture: Education and the Limits of Ethnic Affiliation*. New York: Routledge, 1998.

Ministry of Education and Training. *The Ontario Curriculum, Grades 1–8: Language*. Toronto: Queen's Printer for Ontario, 1997.

———. *The Ontario Curriculum, English Grades 9–10*. Toronto: Queen's Printer for Ontario, 1999.

Morris, Marla. *Curriculum and the Holocaust: Competing Sites of Memory*. New Jersey: Lawrence Erlbaum, 2001.

Nussbaum, Martha C. "Exactly and Responsibly: A Defense of Ethical Criticism." *Philosophy and Literature* 22 (1998): 343–65.

Robertson, Judith P. "'Art Made Tongue-Tied by Authority': A Literary Psychoanalysis of Obstacles in Teacher Learning." *Journal of Curriculum Theorizing* 17.1 (2001): 27–44.

———. "Cinema and the Politics of Desire in Teacher Education." PhD diss. U of Toronto, 1994.

———. "Teaching about Worlds of Hurt through Encounters with Literature: Reflections on Pedagogy." *Teaching for a Tolerant World, Grades K–6: Essays and Resources*. Ed. Judith Robertson. Urbana: National Council of Teachers of English, 1999. 275–93.

Simon, Roger, and Wendy Armitage Simon. "Teaching Risky Stories: Remembering Mass Destruction through Children's Literature." *Teaching for a Toler-*

ant World, Grades K–6: Essays and Resources. Ed. Judith Robertson. Urbana: National Council of Teachers of English, 1999. 263–74.

Spivak, Gayatri Chakravorty. "The Making of Americans, the Teaching of English, and the Future of Culture Studies." *New Literary History* 21 (1990): 781–98.

Staiger, Janet. *Interpreting Films.* Princeton: Princeton UP, 1992.

Steedman, Carolyn. *The Tidy House: Little Girls Writing.* London: Virago, 1982.

Thacker, Deborah. "Disdain or Innocence?: Literary Theory and the Absence of Children's Literature." *The Lion and the Unicorn* 24.1 (2000): 1–17.

Trites, Roberta Seelinger, ed. "Psychoanalytic Approaches to Children's Literature." Spec. issue of *Children's Literature Quarterly* 25 (2000): 1–3.

Valdes, Mario, ed. *A Ricoeur Reader: Reflections and Imagination.* Toronto: U of Toronto P, 1991.

Walkerdine, Valerie. *Schoolgirl Fictions.* London: Verso, 1990.

Yew, Leong. "Notes on Colonialism." Contemporary Postcolonial and Post Imperial Literature in English, University Scholars Program. National University of Singapore, 6 June 2002. 15 Nov. 2002. <http://www.scholars.nus.edu.sg/landow/post/poldiscourse/colonialism notes.html>.

Afterword

STEPHEN SLEMON

I FOUND MYSELF UNSTEADY on a number of this volume's conceptual superordinates —postcolonialism, pedagogy, Canadian literature, and "the classroom"—and so, in a desperate bid to remind myself of the scholarly debate around at least one of our organizing problematics, I dug into the bottom drawer of my documents cabinet and came up with a file I'd begun in my first year of classroom teaching as a university-level postcolonial pedagogue. The file was called, simply, "Pedagogy," and it contained articles on a topic that I had pursued with zeal in the late 80s and early 90s—until the moment my sabbatical leave came around in 1994, at which point I seemed to have stopped storing critical articles in that Pedagogy file, and after which my teaching evaluations took a sharp step upwards. Chronologically, the first article in the Pedagogy file was Gerald Graff's "Taking Cover in Coverage," from 1986; the last was Henry Giroux's "Living Dangerously: Identity Politics and the New Cultural Racism: Towards a Critical Pedagogy of Representation," from 1993; and in the middle of the file I found articles like Don Bialostosky's "The English Professor in the Age of Theory," Chandra Mohanty's "On Race and Voice: Challenges for Liberal Education in the 1990s," Peter McLaren's "Multiculturalism and the Postmodern Critique: Towards a Pedagogy of Resistance and Transformation," and—still my favourite for giving a sense of that academic period of a decade ago, and how much things have changed—Gregory Ulmer's "Textshop for Psychoanalysis: On De-programming Freshmen Platonists."

I reread these articles recently in a spirit of dissonant fascination. On the one hand, I was struck by their acuteness in describing the general tenets of an emancipatory pedagogy in the humanities, and at this general level I agreed with just about everything they proposed: that the struggle over meaning is foundationally a struggle over power relations; that the classroom is a political site, and its accommodations and contestations pertain to the construction of social knowledges and the reification of social group; that merely acknowledging racial or other differences gets you nowhere in postcolonial pedagogy—for human social differences are asymmetrical and incommensurate, and they cannot be reduced to a liberal discourse of multicultural harmony. But on the other hand, at the specific level of what it was that these articles seemed to imagine as the most immediate, the most material, of obstacles to the achievement of an emancipatory, politically alert pedagogy of engagement, I found myself silently accusing these extraordinary and committed critical theorists of a certain innocence in analysis—perhaps a better term would be a certain optimism. Seen now, from the palindromic optics of 2002, the articles I had collected in the Pedagogy file struck me as curiously enthusiastic about what political work actually *would* be accomplished by a thorough curriculum review, for example, or by a shift from teaching the "content" to "teaching the conflicts," or by the classroom foregrounding of the politics of culture, or by strategic teacherly self-positioning, or by celebrating resistances, and extolling agency, and practising cross-cultural respect. "Theory," Gregory Ulmer wrote, has to be "assimilated into the humanities . . . . by critical interpretation *and* by artistic practices" (760). "The political side of culture," claimed Henry Giroux, "*must* be given primacy as an act of resistance and transformation" (2; emphasis mine). But a decade of pedagogic reformations enacted along these lines has *not* secured postcolonial or literary or cultural studies in the university to the project of genuine social change. The powerful departmental traditionalist, the hostile department chair, the exasperated Dean of Arts who likes a little less noise in the house—these figures have not everywhere faded, but for some postcolonial pedagogues at least, these immediate, human obstacles to pedagogical innovation have at least waned in effectiveness. Or perhaps these obstructionist deans, and chairs, and departmental traditionalists are simply cunning, and find nothing in our actual practice that constitutes a hazard to that which they hold dear. We are now in the aftershock of a decade of indifferent achievement in the practice of postcolonial literary pedagogy, and one of the great projects of this scholarly collection is to attempt to confront the fact that the most persistent obstacles to a postcolonial pedagogy for the literatures in Canada do not simply reside in those human figures who will vote us down in the department meeting; they are not simply our disciplinary bosses who mean us harm; they do not forbid us to practise the art of "living dangerously" in the classroom, although the ramifications of danger are everywhere in vigilant postcolonial pedagogies, as scholars such as Arun Mukherjee tells us in her essay here. It is part of the work of this collection to attempt a more radical critique of why it is that "postcolonialism *and* pedagogy"—that is, the two together, in productive dissonance—do *not* easily come together in the study and teaching of the Canadian literatures in Canadian universities. I want now to address just one of the several arguments being made in this volume—in different voices and in different applications—about why it is that the institutional study of the literatures in Canada does not sit easily beside the general project of postcolonial pedagogical critique.

There is a structural incommensurability between postcoloniality and the lexical and historical force of pedagogy itself in the apparatus of English and Englishness. The *Oxford English Dictionary* locates the first use of the word *pedagogy* in the practice of submission to a discipline: "this should be as a rule, or a pedagogie, unto us," reads the 1583 quotation. Contained within the original concept of pedagogy, in English, is the implication of a determinate relation to God: Milton wrote that "the law of Moses was ordained to last untill the time of the Pedagogie of God's people, or introduction to Christ, should be expired." The concept of pedagogy is also associated with the concept of pedagog*ism*, which means the condition in which exegesis overwhelms common sense (one quotation, from 1838, notes that "literature and pedagogism are in Germany identic in spirit"). And the concept of pedagogy has never been free from a dual identification with both slavery and childhood—this is carried in its association with the concept of *tutelage*. Indeed, the oldest of all references to the lexical massive of pedagogic understanding in the *OED* is to the word *tuition* itself: *tuition* means "looking after or taking care of"; it means "safe-keeping, protection, custody, care, tutelage"; and in medieval usage the word *tuition* is synonymous with the concept of military defence. No wonder that a number of scholars equate pedagogy itself as a *mise en scène* for both children at their lessons *and* for the figure of the colonized subject: in the language of pedagogy, they are both recalcitrant objects who must be constrained. No wonder that, in designating the paradigmatic site of learning in the West, the adjective in the term *ivory tower* resonates with the long history of colonialist pillage. This residual imperative to pedagogy is everywhere in evidence in the cardinal documents that define the work of literary study within liberal education. Jean-Jacques Rousseau's *Émile* grounds pedagogy to the principle of guardianship guided by the great text of "nature." John Locke's 1693 essay *Some Thoughts Concerning Education* grounds pedagogy to the construction of "young Gentlemen," not *Daughters*, whose work as students is to appropriate the experiences of others—for example, the poor and their wet feet—as a preliminary step towards self-consolidation in a ruling class. Thomas Macaulay's "Minute" of 1835 grounds pedagogy in the Bengal Presidency to a coherent strategy for inculcating, through the study of English literature, an affect of cultural self-loathing, which will inform "a class who may be interpreters between us and the millions whom we govern; a class of persons, Indian in blood and colour, but English in taste, in opinions, in morals, and in intellect" (61). And the Newbolt Report on Education of 1921 grounds literary pedagogy to the marshalling of nationalism against the contradictions of class: the study of English Literature, the Report claims, will produce "a new element of national unity, linking together the mental life of all classes." These documents are breadcrumbs along the path of literary pedagogy's work as an exercise in social engineering: that path runs through generations of imperial and colonial subjects taught our discipline through *The Queen's Primers* and the Nelson *Royal Readers*, and at the sick heart of everything we do in English class, K to 12 to PhD, you can hear the inalienable murmur of John Milton's exhortation "To the Parlament of England with the Assembly": "Let not England forget her precedence of teaching nations how to live" (232).

This incommensurability between the place in our university teaching for the literatures in Canada and the idea of something genuinely emancipatory in our pedagogy is at the core of this collection. Diana Brydon calls postcolonial pedagogy an "'impossible' to fix" activity (61). Donna Pennee argues that the nation is at once anathema to, and the bedrock of, a postcolonial pedagogy for Canadian writing. This incommensurability resounds, too, in the many essays in this volume—Lisa Grekul's is one of them—that register an asymmetry between, on the one hand, minority and diasporic peoples and their literatures, or Native peoples and their literatures, or underclass constituencies and their literatures, and, on the other hand, the corporate university itself, whose mission it is to manufacture normative national subjects and to secure the profit-taking motive. Gary Boire concludes: "radical pedagogy cannot exist within the precincts of the university—and even if it tries to come into being, it does so within a state of siege" (230). There is a performative oxymoron—perhaps it is a performative catachresis—in Boire's claim: such a trope is one way of representing the kind of incommensurability that is foundational to a structure. Foundational incommensurability—not something simply "fixable"—is the focal point of this volume. Its elaboration is one of the steps in the general project of a postcolonial pedagogical critique.

Let me sum up this single argument of this volume through a reductive formulation. The corporate university in late modernity has a social mission whose religion is capital, and there is a foundational incommensurability between that social mission and the project that Paulo Freire once called a "pedagogy of hope."

One of the most troubling implications of this argument, which so many contributors to this volume voice so well, is that it easily knocks on to a politics of despair. I have seen this despair at work in *some* modalities of that general turn in academia away from postcolonial commitments to the rising phoenix of globalization studies—as though a conceptual shift out of the colonial/postcolonial dyad could finesse the structural incommensurability between political emancipation and the relations of production in the corporate university. I have seen this despair, too, in the growing suspicion of the work of "theory"—whose promise really did outshine its achievement throughout the 90s, but whose partial failings provided too many of us with an alibi for too much pedagogical comfort. But one of the things I will take away from these essays is Terry Goldie's clarifying analysis of the question "Is there a subaltern in this class(room)?"—in my view, Goldie's clarification has implications for what it means to aspire to the postcolonial in pedagogical engagement. Let me restate this clarification as a polemic proposition. The constituency of a classroom for

Canadian literature in a Canadian university, whatever its local specifics, inescapably comprises a conceptual syllogism. That syllogism reads as follows. Thesis: there is genuine difference within this classroom; its modes are uncountable; we cannot live up to our postcolonial commitments if we fail to inhabit the implications of that difference. Antithesis: the difference that resides within this classroom is not in itself a just representation of all human differences. There are others beyond our framework for inclusivity; those others are at the centre of the postcolonial imagination but they live beyond the horizon of our gaze; most of them labour in ways that university workers find unimaginable; their predictive and possibly inevitable futures are ones that everything in postcolonial commitment seeks most passionately to forestall. Against this thesis and antithesis—and this is my thesis for this paper—against this recalcitrance, there can be no synthesizing, third term. The impossibility of fulfilling this syllogism means that a postcolonial pedagogy for the literatures in Canada *can only* take place within the materiality of dialectics. This postcolonial pedagogy cannot function meaningfully either as top-down instruction *or* as bottom-up enablement; this pedagogy can neither disperse itself into pure cultural relativism nor rise to the propositional level of a unified and coherent postcolonial*ism*; a postcolonial pedagogy for the literatures in Canada *can only* walk the line, dialectically, *between* identification and disidentification, between recognition and unfathomability, between accommodation and opposition, between speaking from authority and speaking truth to power. That dialectics of engagement is our insuperable situation in postcolonial pedagogy. Whatever else it will be, that dialectics must also be our strength.

And so: beyond an innocence about the obstacles to a postcolonial pedagogy, but still in that spirit of hope which, despite all, informed generations of colonizing and colonized school children and university students, at home and away, who came to the scene of literary learning in search of something emancipatory; in that spirit that weaves its way from Paulo Freire's pedagogy of hope through a pedagogy of theoretical relocation in Bialostosky, Giroux, Graff, McLaren, Mohanty, and Ulmer; in that spirit that presides over the work of this volume's scholarly contributors, whose collectivity Cynthia Sugars has so hopefully organized; in *that* spirit, I want to propose this small tenet—necessary but not sufficient—towards, if not quite for, a future-oriented, postcolonial pedagogy for

Canadian literary practice. A postcolonial pedagogy, whatever its constituency, wherever it obtains, cannot do other than seek out the genuine difficulty inherent in the material it finds before itself. That difficulty is the inalienable ground zero of a postcolonial political commitment. It is a professional postcolonial pedagogue's best hope for contributing towards a future of progressive social change.

WORKS CITED

Bialostosky, Don. "The English Professor in the Age of Theory." *Novel* 19 (1986): 164–70.

Freire, Paulo. *Pedagogy of Hope: Reliving Pedagogy of the Oppressed.* Trans. Ana Maria Araújo Freire. New York: Continuum, 1997.

Giroux, Henry. "Living Dangerously: Identity Politics and the New Cultural Racism: Towards a Critical Pedagogy of Representation." *Cultural Studies* 7.1 (1993): 1–27.

Graff, Gerald. "Taking Cover in Coverage." *Profession* (1986): 41–45.

Locke, John. *Some Thoughts Concerning Education.* 1693. Ed. R.H. Quick. London: Cambridge UP, 1934.

Macaulay, Thomas Babington. "Minute on Indian Education (February 2, 1835)." *Imperialism & Orientalism: A Documentary Sourcebook.* Ed. Barbara Harlow and Mia Carter. Oxford: Blackwell, 1999. 56–62.

McLaren, Peter. "Multiculturalism and the Postmodern Critique: Towards a Pedagogy of Resistance and Transformation." *Cultural Studies* 7.1 (1993): 118–46.

Milton, John. "To the Parlament of England, with the Assembly" [Preface to *The Doctrine and Discipline of Divorce*]. *Complete Prose Works of John Milton.* Vol. II: 1643–1648. New Haven: Yale UP, 1959. 222–33.

Mohanty, Chandra Talpade. "On Race and Voice: Challenges for Liberal Education in the 1990s." *Cultural Critique* (1989–90): 179–208.

Newbolt, Henry John. *The Teaching of English in England, Being the Report of the Departmental Committee Appointed by the President of the Board of Education to Inquire into the Position of English in the Educational System of England.* London: HMSO, 1921.

Rousseau, Jean Jacques. *Émile.* 1762. Trans. Barbara Foxley. London: Dent, 1974.

Ulmer, Gregory. "Textshop for Psychoanalysis: On De-programming Freshmen Platonists." *College English* 49.7 (1983): 756–69.

Contributors

GARY BOIRE is Dean of Graduate and International Studies at Lakehead University. His interests include law and literature, postcolonial literary theory, contemporary British film, and Keith Richards and the Stones.

DIANA BRYDON, Robert and Ruth Lumsden Professor of English, teaches Canadian and postcolonial literatures and theory at the University of Western Ontario. She conducts her current research on fictions of home, diaspora, and the postcolonial within the interdisciplinary context of a SSHRC-funded Major Collaborative Research Initiative examining "Globalization and Autonomy" and within the disciplinary contexts of a SSHRC grant investigating "The Ends of Postcolonialism." She is currently writing a book entitled *Dwelling Places of the Imagination*.

ROB BUDDE teaches creative writing at the University of Northern British Columbia. He has published four books: two poetry collections (*Catch as Catch* and *traffick*) and two novels (*Misshapen* and *The Dying Poem*).

BRENDA CARR VELLINO is an Associate Professor of Canadian literature and twentieth-century poetry in the Department of English at Carleton University. "'A Network of Relations': Ethical Interdependence in Bronwen

Wallace's Talking Lyric" is forthcoming in *Postmodernism and the Ethical Subject*, ed. Barbara Gabriel (McGill-Queen's, 2004). She is currently working on two studies: one on Margaret Atwood's human rights witness poems and the other on poetic citizenship in Adrienne Rich's later poetry. These will be part of a larger work in progress: "Lyric Citizenship, Lyric Consequence."

KATHLEEN MARIE CONNOR is a doctoral candidate in Education at the University of Ottawa, and has taught Anthropology, Education Foundations, and ESL in universities and colleges in Canada and the United States. She presented a paper on Seton's *Rolf in the Woods* at the 2003 Researching New York State History conference at SUNY Albany.

MISAO DEAN is a Professor in the English Department at the University of Victoria. She is the author of books and articles on early Canadian fiction, and the editor of *Early Canadian Short Stories* (Tecumseh Press, 2000).

CAROLE GERSON is a Professor in the English Department at Simon Fraser University, where she teaches Canadian literature. She has published extensively on Canadian literary history, and, with Veronica Strong-Boag, has co-authored a study of Pauline Johnson and a scholarly edition of Johnson's work. She is a member of the editorial team of the *History of the Book in Canada/Histoire du livre et de l'imprimé au Canada*, for which she is co-editor of volume 3 (1918–80).

SUSAN GINGELL teaches and researches Canadian and other decolonizing anglophone literatures at the University of Saskatchewan. Her current research project is on textualizing orature and orality in Canadian/Turtle Island and Afro-Caribbean contexts; and in the 2002–03 academic year, she team-taught an honours seminar on oral traditions, orality, and literature with Maria Campbell and organized a double session on textualizing orality at the ACCUTE conference. She is also editing a forthcoming special number of *Essays on Canadian Writing* (#83) on this subject.

TERRY GOLDIE teaches English and social and political thought at York University. He is the author of *Pink Snow: Homotextual Possibilities in*

Canadian Fiction (Broadview, 2003) and *Fear and Temptation: The Image of the Indigene in Canadian, Australian and New Zealand Literatures* (McGill-Queen's, 1989), editor of *In a Queer Country: Gay and Lesbian Studies in the Canadian Context* (Arsenal Pulp, 2001), and co-editor, with Daniel David Moses, of *An Anthology of Canadian Native Literature in English* (Oxford, 1998).

LISA GREKUL holds a PhD from the University of British Columbia, where she now teaches Canadian literature. Her thesis is a critical study of literature written in English by Canadians of Ukrainian descent. Her novel, *Kalyna's Song*, was published by Coteau Press in 2003.

HEIKE HÄRTING is an Assistant Professor in the Department of English at the Université de Montréal. She is also a SSHRC co-investigator for the Globalization and Autonomy Major Collaborative Research Initiative project at McMaster University. She is currently completing a book, *Unruly Metaphor: Body, Nation, and Performativity in Canadian Diaspora Writing*.

BEVERLEY HAUN is a PhD candidate at OISE/University of Toronto. Her research explores the possibilities of opening up spaces in the curriculum of Ontario for the engagement of postcolonial pedagogical issues.

JENNIFER HENDERSON is the author of *Settler Feminism and Race Making in Canada* (University of Toronto Press, 2003). She teaches in the Department of English at the University of Toronto.

PAUL HJARTARSON, Professor of English at the University of Alberta, writes and teaches primarily in the area of Canadian literature and culture. His books include: *A Stranger to My Time: Essays by and about Frederick Philip Grove* (1986); *Da Capo: The Selected Poetry of E.D. Blodgett* (1990); (with D.O. Spettigue) *Baroness Elsa: The Autobiography of the Baroness Elsa von Freytag-Loringhoven* (1992); and (with Tracy Kulba) *The Politics of Cultural Mediation: Baroness Elsa von Freytag-Loringhoven and Felix Paul Greve* (2003).

RENÉE HULAN is Associate Professor of English at Saint Mary's University, Halifax. She is the author of *Northern Experience and the Myths of*

Canadian Culture (McGill-Queen's, 2002), and the editor of *Native North America: Critical and Cultural Perspectives* (ECW, 1999).

SMARO KAMBOURELI is professor of Canadian literature and post-colonial theory at the University of Victoria. Her most recent publication is *Scandalous Bodies: Diasporic Literature in English Canada* (Oxford, 2000).

LAURIE KRUK is an Assistant Professor in English Studies at Nipissing University, where she specializes in Canadian literature. She is the author of *The Voice Is the Story: Conversations with Canadian Writers of Short Fiction* (Mosaic, 2003). A new interview with Neil Bissoondath is coming out in *Canadian Literature* (2004).

ZUBIN MEER is a second-year doctoral candidate in the Department of English at York University, Toronto. Broadly speaking, he works in the areas of postcolonial studies, South Asian studies, and Marxist literary criticism.

ROY MIKI is a writer, poet, and editor who teaches contemporary literature in the English Department at Simon Fraser University. His third book of poems, *Surrender* (Mercury Press, 2001), received the 2002 Governor General's Award for Poetry. Most recently, he has edited *Meanwhile: The Critical Writings of bpNichol* (Talonbooks, 2002) and is the author of *Broken Entries: Race, Subjectivity, Writing* (Mercury Press, 1998).

LESLIE MONKMAN is the J.R. Strathy Professor of English Language and Literature at Queen's University. His research and teaching have focused on Canadian and other post-colonial literatures in English. He is currently serving as Special Advisor to the Principal at Queen's.

ARUN MUKHERJEE did her graduate work in English at the University of Saugar, India, and came to Canada as a Commonwealth Scholar in 1971 to do a PhD at the University of Toronto. She is currently an Associate Professor of English at York University. She is the author of *Towards an Aesthetic of Opposition: Essays on Literature, Criticism and Cultural Imperialism* (Williams-Wallace, 1988), *Oppositional Aesthetics: Readings from a Hyphenated Space* (TSAR, 1995), and *Postcolonialsim: My*

Living (TSAR, 1998). Most recently, she has translated, from Hindi, *Joothan: A Dalit's Life*, by Omprakash Valmiki (published simultaneously in 2003 by Columbia UP and Samya, Kolkata).

HEATHER MURRAY teaches in the Department of English at the University of Toronto. She is the author of *Working in English* (1996) and *Come, Bright Improvement! The Literary Societies of Nineteenth-Century Ontario* (2002).

DONNA PALMATEER PENNEE is an Associate Professor in the School of English and Theatre Studies, and Associate Dean of Arts and Social Sciences at the University of Guelph. She is the author of two monographs on Timothy Findley, articles and reviews in *Essays on Canadian Writing, Studies in Canadian Literature, International Journal of Canadian Studies,* and *Canadian Literature,* and co-editor of *New Contexts of Canadian Criticism* (Broadview, 1997).

MARIAM PIRBHAI recently received her PhD in English literature from the Université de Montréal. Her dissertation examines the role of indenture history in the creation of a "South Asian diasporic imaginary" in East Africa, South Africa, the Mascarene Archipelago, the Caribbean and South-East Asia. Her publications include articles on Salman Rushdie (*International Fiction Review*), Indo-Guyanese writing (*World Literature Written in English*), and creative writing (*When Your Voice Tastes Like Home: Immigrant Women Write*). She teaches full-time in the English Department of Vanier College in Montreal.

LINDA RADFORD teaches part-time in the Teacher Education Program at the University of Ottawa. She is also a doctoral candidate studying teachers' reading practices of juvenile historical fiction, and the relationship between teachers' reading engagements with children's literature and pedagogy in language arts classrooms.

DANIELLE SCHAUB teaches at Oranim, the Academic College of Education in Israel. Her research focuses on Canadian fiction and autobiographical writing by women, multiculturalism, the interaction between text and image, and spatial representations of female subjectivities.

STEPHEN SLEMON teaches postcolonial literatures and theory at the University of Alberta. His current research comprises two book projects: a cultural history of "thugs," and an analysis of mountaineering writing in the context of globalization.

MARGARET STEFFLER is an Assistant Professor in the Department of English Literature at Trent University. She has published in the areas of children's literature and women's life-writing. She is currently studying the figure of the female child in recent Canadian fiction.

CYNTHIA SUGARS is an Associate Professor in the Department of English at the University of Ottawa. She has published numerous articles on Canadian literature and postcolonial theory, and is the editor of a collection of the foundational essays of Canadian postcolonialism entitled *Unhomely States: Theorizing English-Canadian Postcolonialism* (Broadview, 2004).

GERRY TURCOTTE is Head of the School of English Literatures, Philosophy and Languages at the University of Wollongong, Australia. He is Founding Director of the Centre for Canadian-Australian Studies. His most recent publications are *Compr(om)ising Post/colonialisms: Challenging Narratives & Practices* (Dangaroo, 2001), co-edited with Greg Ratcliffe, and *Winterlude* (Brandl & Schlesinger, 2002).

REAPPRAISALS: CANADIAN WRITERS

Reappraisals: Canadian Writers was begun in 1973 in response to a need for single volumes of essays on Canadian authors who had not received the critical attention they deserved or who warranted extensive and intensive reconsideration. It is the longest running series dedicated to the study of Canadian literary subjects. The annual symposium hosted by the Department of English at the University of Ottawa began in 1972 and the following year University of Ottawa Press published the first title in the series, *The Grove Symposium.* Since then our editorial policy has remained straightforward: each year to make permanently available in a single volume the best of the criticism and evaluation presented at our symposia on Canadian literature, thereby creating a body of work on, and a critical base for the study of, Canadian writers and literary subjects.

Gerald Lynch
General Editor

Titles in the series:

THE GROVE SYMPOSIUM, edited and with an introduction by John Nause

THE A. M. KLEIN SYMPOSIUM, edited and with an introduction by Seymour Mayne

THE LAMPMAN SYMPOSIUM, edited and with an introduction by Lorraine McMullen

THE E. J. PRATT SYMPOSIUM, edited and with an introduction by Glenn Clever

THE ISABELLA VALANCY CRAWFORD SYMPOSIUM, edited and with an introduction by Frank M. Tierney

THE DUNCAN CAMPBELL SCOTT SYMPOSIUM, edited and with an introduction by K. P. Stich

THE CALLAGHAN SYMPOSIUM, edited and with an introduction by David Staines

THE ETHEL WILSON SYMPOSIUM, edited and with an introduction by Lorraine McMullen

TRANSLATION IN CANADIAN LITERATURE, edited and with an introduction by Camille R. La Bossière

THE SIR CHARLES G. D. ROBERTS SYMPOSIUM, edited and with an introduction by Glenn Clever

THE THOMAS CHANDLER HALIBURTON SYMPOSIUM, edited and with an introduction by Frank M. Tierney

STEPHEN LEACOCK: A REAPPRAISAL, edited and with an introduction by David Staines

FUTURE INDICATIVE: LITERARY THEORY AND CANADIAN LITERATURE, edited and with an introduction by John Moss

REFLECTIONS: AUTOBIOGRAPHY AND CANADIAN LITERATURE, edited and with an introduction by K.P. Stich

RE(DIS)COVERING OUR FOREMOTHERS: NINETEENTH-CENTURY CANADIAN WOMEN WRITERS, edited and with an introduction by Lorraine McMullen

BLISS CARMAN: A REAPPRAISAL, edited and with an introduction by Gerald Lynch

FROM THE HEART OF THE HEARTLAND: THE FICTION OF SINCLAIR ROSS, edited by John Moss

CONTEXT NORTH AMERICA: CANADIAN/U.S. LITERARY RELATIONS, edited by Camille R. La Bossière

HUGH MACLENNAN, edited by Frank M. Tierney

ECHOING SILENCE: ESSAYS ON ARCTIC NARRATIVE, edited and with a preface by John Moss

BOLDER FLIGHTS: ESSAYS ON THE CANADIAN LONG POEM, edited and with a preface by Frank M. Tierney and Angela Robbeson

DOMINANT IMPRESSIONS: ESSAYS ON THE CANADIAN SHORT STORY, edited by Gerald Lynch and Angela Arnold Robbeson

MARGARET LAURENCE: CRITICAL REFLECTIONS, edited and with an introduction by David Staines

ROBERTSON DAVIES: A MINGLING OF CONTRARIETIES, edited by Camille R. La Bossière and Linda M. Morra

WINDOWS AND WORDS: A LOOK AT CANADIAN CHILDREN'S LITERATURE IN ENGLISH, edited by Aïda Hudson and Susan-Ann Cooper

WORLDS OF WONDER: READINGS IN CANADIAN SCIENCE FICTION AND FANTASY LITERATURE, edited by Jean-François Leroux and Camille R. La Bossière

AT THE SPEED OF LIGHT THERE IS ONLY ILLUMINATION: A REAPPRAISAL OF MARSHALL MCLUHAN, edited by John Moss and Linda M. Morra

HOME-WORK: POSTCOLONIALISM, PEDAGOGY, AND CANADIAN LITERATURE, edited and with an introduction by Cynthia Sugars